THE
AMERICAN
ALMANAC
OF
JOBS AND
SALARIES

THE AMERICAN ALMANAC OF JOBS AND SALARIES

2000–2001 EDITION

JOHN W. WRIGHT

AVON BOOKS ◆ NEW YORK

AVON BOOKS, INC.
An Imprint of HarperCollins *Publishers*
10 East 53rd Street
New York, New York 10022-5299

Copyright © 2000 by John W. Wright
Published by arrangement with the author
ISBN: 0-380-80303-8
www.harpercollins.com

Seventh Avon Books Trade Paperback Edition, First Printing: February 2000

AVON TRADEMARK REG. U.S. PAT. OFF. AND IN OTHER COUNTRIES, MARCA REGISTRADA, HECHO EN U.S.A.

Printed in the U.S.A.

QM   10   9   8   7   6   5   4   3

This book is gratefully dedicated to my mother,
Elizabeth Wright,
who taught me about the dignity of work.

Acknowledgments

The two people most responsible for putting this edition together are Laura Wallis and Susan McMichaels. Their never-say-die researching techniques (both on the phone and the Internet) and their accomplished writing skills are abundantly clear throughout this edition. (See especially Laura's work on "The Airlines" and "New Media," and Susan's on "Doctors" and "Women's Wages.")

Doug Dietrich, founder of Dietrich Associates in Phoenixville, Pennsylvania, once again provided us with excellent salary surveys in several important areas.

A few writers brought specialized knowledge to several sections: Jim Benagh and Grant Flowers (Sports); Mary Quigley (Journalism); and Robert L. Spring (Science).

The following people served as writers and editors on various parts of the book, most notably Alan Joyce, Kate Hallgren, Justin Martin, Roseann Marulli, Cynthia McElroy, Steven McElroy, Carolyn Michelman, and Brendan Quigley. Most of the data entry was handled by Arlene Jacks.

Finally, at Avon Books, Jennifer Brehl and Bret Witter greatly facilitated the passage of this edition from idea to printed book.

Contents

Preface to the Seventh Edition

When the last edition of this book appeared in 1996, unemployment stood at 5.5 percent and inflation at 3 percent, a remarkable comeback from the early years of the decade. Although every economist and TV pundit knew the economy was strong and that future prospects looked positive, only a very few predicted that strong growth would continue at the rate of 3 to 4 percent a year, or that by early 1999 inflation would tumble to less than 2 percent and unemployment to 4.2 percent, numbers not seen in 40 years or more.

As a result the job market in 1998–99 was one of the strongest on record. Anyone who lost their job—and many thousands did in our era of downsizing—usually found a new one within six weeks. For new college graduates, new MBAs, computer professionals, and graduates of professional schools, the job market suddenly burst open as businesses across the country made long-term plans for greater and greater expansion. As most of the entries for those jobs in this edition make clear, this was the best of times.

Of course much of this job expansion has been due to the totally incredible growth of the Internet and the World Wide Web over the past three years. While everyone knows that all retail businesses have gone on-line to increase consumer sales, the greatest impact of the new digital world has been to increase the efficiency of many businesses, freeing up capital for investment in both new equipment and new employees. Throughout this edition readers (and job-seekers) will find information about the Internet and its impact on the everyday world of work.

Unfortunately there are unpleasant aspects to this new great economy and some may not be easy to eradicate. The gap between rich and poor continues to widen, as it almost certainly must under a capitalist system where those with great wealth and power set the wage rates of those who have little of either. One obvious result is that the pay of CEOs is now almost 300 times higher than the average salary at the companies they run. Executive pay continues to rise at 10 percent or more while most workers must be content with 2 to 3 percent.

But the globalization of the work force has arrived, quickly, almost unnoticed, and with it the fear of American workers that if they complain or go on strike they'll lose the good life they have and drive jobs to low-wage countries. This may happen despite their current acquiescence, of course, as corporations seek profits relentlessly.

As this book goes to press the economy looks very strong, and unemployment a distant memory. Then again "Dilbert" remains enormously popular, too, so perhaps it's best to guard against unbridled enthusiasm.

J. W. W.

New York City, June 1999

Labor is prior to, and independent of, capital. Capital is only the fruit of labor, and could never have existed if labor had not first existed. Labor is the superior of capital, and deserves much the higher consideration.

Abraham Lincoln,

First Annual Message to Congress, 1861

Introduction

This book is about work and its rewards in contemporary America. As the success of the previous editions has demonstrated, such a book is bound to be of interest to students of American life, and to students just beginning life in the world of work. It is also a book for career changers seeking guidelines and for women seeking equal pay for equal work.

With such audiences in mind, the *Almanac* has deliberately been given a white-collar service sector orientation. The largest entries are all aimed at the career-minded. They will find detailed information on accountants, doctors, engineers, lawyers, scientists, and health-care workers as well as the most up-to-date information on jobs in computer technology. Whether readers are interested in a specialized field such as human resources, public relations, or purchasing, or in a particular kind of business such as advertising, banking, or insurance, they will find complete job descriptions and an evaluation of future job opportunities as well as a full range of salaries for most levels and positions. Special entries on the starting salaries of new college graduates and newly minted M.B.A.s will prove invaluable to younger members of the workforce. This emphasis on white-collar careers is, however, not based simply on some biased point of view, nor is it a cynical attempt to boost sales. In fact, it reflects the very real and extraordinary changes in the character and shape of the American workforce that have occurred over the last four decades.

Between 1950 and 1990, for example, while the population was growing by just over 60 percent, the labor force doubled in size. The single most dramatic change was the growth in the number of women workers, from 18 million to 56 million. In 1950, about 30 percent of the total workforce were women, but by 1990, women made up nearly half of all working people. Other important changes, such as the growth in the white-collar workforce from less than 40 percent to more than half, and the rise in education levels of all workers—close to 80 percent have finished high school, compared with less than half in the 1950s—are indications of a society significantly rearranging its daily worklife.

The kind of work being done by Americans changed just as drastically. For example, the number of workers employed in the production of goods (including manufacturing, mining, and construction, but not agriculture) grew from 20 million to 31 million between 1960 and 1997. But as a percentage of the workforce, these workers declined from 37 percent to 16 percent. Moreover, the number of production workers in relation to non-production workers declined from five to one in 1950 to less than two to one today, while the percentage of blue-collar workers declined from 40 percent of the workforce in 1950 to under 25 percent in 1997. These trends have continued through the decade.

In many industries, the number of production workers has been declining steadily for many reasons, including, but not limited to, automation, increased competition from abroad, and the aging of particular segments of American industries. Between 1960 and 1985, the steel and auto industries each lost half a million jobs; textiles lost 600,000; and manufacturing lost over 1.1 million. Although manufacturing rallied in the late 1980s, jobs in this industry resumed their decline in the 1990s, and 1991 levels were lower than they were at any point in the 1980s. Meanwhile, agriculture, which accounted for 11 percent of the workforce in 1950, employed less than 2 percent in 1991.

While America's production industries were waning, the service industries were booming. Over the past four decades the service sector has grown from 27 million employees to over 90 million, and from 55 percent of the workforce to over 78 percent. Today more than 75 percent of working Americans are employed in areas such as accounting, banking, engineering, consumer services, education, health care, legal work, transportation, and wholesale and retail trade. Moreover, there are millions employed in the public sector. In 1950, just over 6 million civilian employees—about 10 percent of all workers—were employed by federal, state, and local governments; by 1997, over 20 million civilians—17 percent of the labor force—were on public payrolls.

This last point should help to explain why so much space in the *Almanac* is given to the section "On the Public Payroll." This is the first book to present an in-depth look at the jobs and salary levels of the enormous federal bureaucracy, from typists and secretaries to members of the Senior Executive Service. Of course, the salaries and perks of the president, his cabinet, and his advisers are all included, along with those of federal judges and members of Congress. But the large entry on the highest paying jobs in almost every federal agency is what reveals more about levels of pay in Washington than a mere cataloging of the top officials.

On the state and local government levels, the *Almanac* contains information on high-ranking officials in every state and in many major cities. Public employees ranging from city managers and police chiefs to bus drivers, sanitation workers, and social workers are all included. Wherever possible, examples of salary scales in the states, selected cities, and in institutions are provided. Under "University and College Professors," for example, the salaries of full professors, associate professors, assistant professors, and instructors are listed for almost one hundred public and private institutions nationwide.

Despite the *Almanac*'s obvious emphases, it is designed to provide data for a wide variety of occupations. So, in addition to professional careers, high-paying white-collar occupations, and bureaucratic sinecures, the *Almanac* also gives all kinds of information on ordinary jobs in the workaday world. Office workers, construction workers, and maintenance workers are all included.

Finally, a word about the section called "In the Public Eye and Behind the Scenes." Although some of the entries contain valuable career information for people interested in modeling or working in film or television, the major attraction here is bound to be the high-salaried public personalities so familiar to millions of Americans. Included, among others, are movie stars, musicians, singers, and professional athletes. Readers will discover that in the world of television, movies, and sports, many stars and personalities surpass the magical sum of $10 million a year. (They will also discover elsewhere in the book that many corporate executives, Wall Street financiers, and Hollywood producers, among other executives, also have reached that exalted plateau.)

The point of this section goes beyond a mere inventory of highly compensated celebrities. When people can be paid so much money for their acting skills or their athletic ability, or for simply reading the news on television, the effects can be as interesting as they are various. First, this practice drives up the salaries of the highest paid people in other industries. Why should the heads of major corporations, large law firms, or accounting firms make less than Mariah Carey, Mo Vaughn, Oprah Winfrey, or David Letterman? Second, such high payments help to point out just how inequitable the distribution of income is: Since only 5 percent of all workers earn over $75,000 while total family income was about $44,000 for half of America's families in 1996, these celebrities have attained extraordinary wealth.

Most Americans have only hazy notions about how wages are distributed in this country. Only 20 percent of the 70 million families earned more than $75,000 in the 1996, while almost 60 percent made less than $50,000 (the median was $42,300). If this trend continues—and there's no indication it can be stopped—the number of families earning $75,000 or more will increase but they will be an increasingly smaller percentage. People's responses to these figures usually vary on the basis of their own economic status. Those individuals making about $75,000 are almost always incredulous when told that they are among the top 5 percent of all wage earners; and people earning $50,000 find it hard to believe they make more than most families.

One could argue that by its very nature this *Almanac* also raises serious questions about the kinds of work America values most. Just about everyone who did research on this book was struck at some time by the glaring in-consistencies and obvious inequities that exist in our pay structure. Here are a few random examples:

- Why do most "creative" directors in advertising agencies earn more than most doctors?
- Why do successful traders and brokers on Wall Street earn more than the most highly regarded scientists?
- Why do senior engineers always earn less than their companies' con-trollers?
- Why do architects almost always earn significantly less than account-ants?
- Why do directors of nursing make less than hospital administrators?
- Why do most laborers earn less than most truck drivers?
- Why do most college football coaches earn more than most full pro-fessors?
- Why do librarians and flight attendants earn about the same amount?

The notion of comparing job worth is not new, but only in recent years has it become a way of fighting for higher pay. Women, particularly, have used this argument in their struggle to establish economic equality. The surge of women into the workforce over the last twenty years is one of the most important developments in American labor history. The insistence of many women that pay levels are influenced more by gender by the marketplace is bringing about a radical shift in women's wage rates, especially in the public employment sector.

By providing a wide range of information—as well as opinion—we hope we won't be accused of playing the careerist's game, in which good job possibilities and large compensation potential are seen as the only vital factors in a career path. It is not unusual today to hear young people entering college say they intend to study computer science even though their math grades are below average, or others express an interest in signing on for a six-year program leading to a law degree when they have no idea about the everyday demands of the profession or the potential future difficulties caused by the sudden surge in the number of lawyers all around the country. Such premature or unrealistic career choices often make for very disgruntled thirty-year-olds.

We know we can't stop the trend toward that kind of thinking, but we believe it's important to take a stand against it. Our goal remains as the presentation of an overview of the American workforce that will help people understand its present character and its future shape. We can only hope that readers will use this information wisely and that they will find it valuable in planning their future forays into the world of work.

THE AMERICAN WORKFORCE TODAY

In 1998 about 130 million people were employed in the United States. Almost 30 percent of the workforce (38 million) occupied executive, managerial, and administrative positions. The largest single grouping in this category was the 4 million elementary and secondary school teachers. About 3.2 million worked in health-related occupations, and just over 3 million were employed in engineering and science-related jobs. In a society that is growing increasingly litigious, the number of lawyers and judges topped 900,000 in 1998. About 25 million Americans were engaged in trade, mainly retail selling, while another 20 million worked in service-providing industries. The standard manufacturing and construction sectors employed just over 28 million people, or 22 percent of the total workforce.

THE GROWTH INDUSTRIES OF THE 1990s

Industry	Number Employed (in thousands)		Change in Number 1989–95	Percentage Change 1989–95
	1989	1995		
Agriculture	2,934	3,440	506	17.2%
Mining	679	627	−52	−7.7
Construction	7,232	7,666	434	6.0
Manufacturing	21,569	20,493	−1,076	−5.0
Transportation, communications, and other utilities	8,049	8,709	660	8.2
Wholesale trade	4,492	4,986	494	11.0
Retail trade	19,138	21,086	1,948	10.2
Finance, insurance, and real estate	7,968	7,983	15	0.2
Services	38,329	43,953	5,624	14.7
Public administration	5,456	5,957	501	9.2
TOTAL EMPLOYED	115,846	124,900	9,054	7.8

SOURCE: Bureau of Labor Statistics, *Employment and Earnings,* January 1996 monthly.

During the 1980s, three sectors of the American economy experienced an overall decline in the number of jobs, even though the total number of jobs in the economy grew by 16.7 percent overall. Mining (−30.6 percent), agriculture (−12.8 percent), and manufacturing (-1.7 percent) were the losers. Public administration jobs grew by only 2.1 percent during the same time period. Finance and services were the biggest growth sectors, with each gaining 33 percent in the number of jobs. Other sectors experiencing above-average growth were transportation, communication, and utilities (+23.4 percent), and retail trade (+17.6 percent). Construction (+16.4 percent) and wholesale trade (+14.6 percent) grew at a slightly less than average pace. In times of recession, of course, construction jobs decline significantly except in those rapidly developing areas of the country, most notably Florida. In 1992, construction employed 4 percent of all workers down from 5 percent in 1990. By 1998, however, the booming economy raised it to about 6 precent.

One significant result of this changing character of the workforce is the continuous decline of labor unions over the last twenty years. And clearly they will continue to decline. Today the American labor movement stands at its lowest point in decades. In 1955, 35 percent of the workforce belonged to unions, but in 1997, only 14 percent held membership cards. Moreover, union membership declined by over 6 million members. This decrease has been fed not only by the declining fortunes of traditional manufacturing industries and the unions' failures to realize widespread penetration into the white-collar ranks, but also by a concerted effort on management's part to weaken the role of unions. Outside of some traditional bastions of union solidarity like the Teamsters, labor unions appear to be a weak shell of their former power. Since the 1980s, labor unions have by and large been willing to grant concessions on wages in return for staving off cuts in benefits and gaining improved job security protections.

During the 1990s, the labor movement has seized some opportunities to halt its decline. In the health-care area, for instance, where pay and working conditions have declined relatively in the past decade, opportunities to organize workers have been successfully pursued. Also, the unions have shown a new sophistication in the use of public relations and they have learned to spend a good deal of money supporting political candidates who favor labor's goals.

U.S. MEMBERSHIP IN AFL-CIO AFFILIATED UNIONS, BY SELECTED UNION, 1979–95

Labor organization	(Numbers in thousands)		
	1979	1985	1995
Total[1]			
Actors and Artists	75	100	80
Automobile, Aerospace, and Agriculture (UAW)	NA	974	751
Bakery, Confectionery, and Tobacco	131	115	96
Boilermakers, Iron Shipbuilders[2,3]	129	110	NA
Bricklayers	106	95	84
Carpenters[2]	626	609	378
Clothing and Textile Workers (ACTWU)[2]	308	228	129
Communications Workers (CWA)	485	524	478
Electrical Workers (IBEW)	825	791	579
Electronic, Electrical, and Salaried[2,4]	243	198	135
Operating Engineers	313	330	298
Firefighters	150	142	151
Food and Commercial Workers (UFCW)[2]	1,123	989	983
Garment Workers (ILGWU)	314	210	123
Glass, Molders, Pottery, and Plastics[2]	50	72	69
Government, American Federation (AFGE)	236	199	153
Graphics Communications[2]	171	141	94
Hotel Employees and Restaurant Employees	373	327	241
Ironworkers	146	140	82
Laborers	475	383	352
Letter Carriers (NALC)	151	186	210
Longshoremen's Association	63	65	61
Machinists and Aerospace (IAM)[2]	688	520	448
Mine Workers	NA	NA	75
Office and Professional Employees	83	90	86
Oil, Chemical, Atomic Workers (OCAW)	146	108	83
Painters	160	133	95
Paperworkers International	262	232	233
Plumbing and Pipe Fitting	228	226	220
Postal Workers	245	232	261
Retail, Wholesale, Department Store	122	106	76
Rubber, Cork, Linoleum, Plastic	158	106	79
Seafarers	84	80	80
Service Employees (SEIU)[2,5]	537	688	1,027
Sheet Metal Workers	120	108	106
Stage Employees, Moving Picture Machine Operators	50	50	51
State, County, Municipal (AFSCME)[5]	899	997	1,183
Steelworkers	964	572	403

U.S. MEMBERSHIP IN AFL-CIO AFFILIATED UNIONS, BY SELECTED UNION, 1979–95

Labor organization	(Numbers in thousands)		
	1979	1985	1995
Teachers (AFT)	423	470	613
Teamsters[6]	NA	NA	1,285
Transit Union	94	94	95
Transport Workers	85	85	75
Transportation Union, United	121	52	58

NOTE: NA = Not applicable.
Figures represent the labor organizations as constituted in 1989 and reflect past merger activity. Membership figures based on average per capita paid membership to the AFL-CIO for the two-year period ending in June of the year shown and reflect only actively employed members. Labor unions shown had a membership of 70,000 or more in 1989.
[1]Includes other AFL-CIO affiliated unions, not shown separately.
[2]Figures reflect mergers with one or more unions since 1979.
[3]Includes Blacksmiths, Forgers, and Helpers.
[4]Includes Machine and Furniture Workers.
[5]Excludes Hospital and Health Care Employees which merged into both unions on June 1, 1989 (membership of 23,000 in 1985, and 58,000 in 1989).
[6]Includes Chauffeurs, Warehousemen, and Helpers.
SOURCE: American Federation of Labor and Congress of Industrial Organizations, *Report of the AFL-CIO Executive Council* (annual).

JOB GROWTH IN THE NEAR FUTURE

As the new century begins, the U.S. economy is at its apex with low inflation, unprecedented job growth, and unemployment rates declining to almost 4 percent. The reasons are still not entirely clear, but surely not all of them are purely economic.

One of the chief factors in the declining unemployment rate, for example, are the results of the rapid and sudden decline in the birth rates and fertility rates of the late 1960s and 1970s. There are simply far fewer people entering the labor force than during the periods when the baby boom generation was coming of age. In addition, more and more people are retiring at age sixty-five or earlier, so many jobs have opened up by simple attrition. Over the next five years the U.S. Department of Labor projects a noticeable slowing down in the growth of the labor force.

The most recent projections done by the Department's Bureau of Labor Statistics (BLS) were done for the period 1996–2006, and here are the results:

● The Bureau of Labor Statistics projects that the labor force will grow by 14.9 million between 1996 and 2006, rising from 133.9 million to 148.8 million. This is 1.2 million less than the previous ten years reflecting a slower growth in the civilian noninstitutional population of sixteen years of age and older. Growth was much faster from 1976 to 1986, when the baby boomers were entering the labor force.

● The labor force will grow 11 percent between 1996 and 2006, slightly slower than during the 1986–96 period but only half the rate of growth during the 1976–86 period.

● As a result of an increase in the percentage of the population working or looking for work, the labor force will continue to grow faster than the population rate.

● Between 1996 and 2006, employment will increase by 18.6 million or 14 percent. This is slower than during the 1986–96 period, when the economy added 21 million jobs.

● Wage and salary worker employment will account for 94 percent of this increase. In addition, the number of self-employed workers is expected to increase to 11.6 million in 2006, while the number of unpaid family workers will decline.

Barring any sudden change in government policies, the trends in the kinds of jobs available to U.S. workers will remain the same as they have for three decades: White-collar, service-oriented jobs, especially in health care and business services, will be the strongest areas. The fastest growing jobs, and the jobs with the largest increases, will be almost exclusively in these areas, as the tables that follow make clear.

OCCUPATIONS WITH THE LARGEST NUMBER OF NEW JOBS, 1996–2005
(Numbers in thousands)

	Employment		Change in Employment	
Occupation	1996	2006	Number	Percent
Cashiers	3,146	3,677	530	17%
System analysts	506	1,025	520	103
General managers and top executives	3,210	3,677	467	15
Registered nurses	1,971	2,382	411	21
Salespersons, retail	4,072	4,481	408	10
Truck drivers, light and heavy	2,719	3,123	404	15
Home health aides	495	873	378	76
Teacher aides and educational assistants	981	1,352	370	38
Nursing aides, orderlies, and attendants	1,312	1,645	333	25

OCCUPATIONS WITH THE LARGEST NUMBER OF NEW JOBS, 1996–2005
(Numbers in thousands)

Occupation	Employment		Change in Employment	
	1996	2006	Number	Percent
Receptionists and information clerks	1,074	1,392	318	30%
Teachers, secondary school	1,406	1,718	312	22
Child care workers	830	1,129	299	36
Clerical supervisors and managers	1,369	1,630	262	19
Database administrators, computer support specialists	212	461	249	118
Marketing and sales worker supervisors	2,316	2,562	246	11
Maintenance repairers, general utility	1,362	1,608	246	18
Food counter, fountain and related workers	1,720	1,963	243	14
Teachers, special education	407	648	241	59
Computer engineers	216	451	235	109
Food preparation workers	1,253	1,487	234	19
Hand packers and packagers	986	1,208	222	23
Guards	955	1,175	221	23
General office clerks	3,111	3,326	215	7
Waiters and waitresses	1,957	2,163	206	11
Social workers	585	772	188	32
Adjustment clerks	401	584	183	46
Cooks, short-order and fast-food	804	978	174	22
Personal and home-care aides	202	374	171	85
Food service and lodging managers	589	757	168	28
Medical assistants	225	391	166	74

SOURCE: Bureau of Labor Statistics

FASTEST GROWING OCCUPATIONS, 1996–2005
(Numbers in thousands)

Occupation	Employment		Change in Employment	
	1996	2006	Number	Percent
Database administrators, computer support specialists	212	461	249	118%
Computer engineers	216	451	235	109
Systems analysts	506	1,025	520	103
Personal and home-care aides	202	374	171	85
Home health aides	495	873	378	76
Medical assistants	225	391	166	74
Desktop publishing specialists	30	53	22	74
Physical therapists	115	196	81	71
Occupational therapy assistants and aides	16	26	11	69
Paralegals	113	189	76	68
Occupational therapists	57	95	38	66
Teachers, special education	407	648	241	59
Human services workers	178	276	98	55
Data processing equipment repairers	80	121	42	52
Medical records technicians	87	132	44	51
Speech-language pathologists and audiologists	87	131	44	51
Dental hygienists	133	197	64	48
Amusement and recreation attendants	288	426	138	48
Physician assistants	64	93	30	47
Respiratory therapists	82	119	37	46
Adjustment clerks	401	584	183	46
Engineering, science, and computer systems managers	343	498	155	45
Emergency room technicians	150	217	67	45
Manicurists	43	62	19	45
Bill and account collectors	269	381	112	42
Residential counselors	180	254	74	41
Instructors and coaches, sports and physical training	303	427	123	41
Dental assistants	202	278	77	38
Securities and financial sales workers	263	363	100	38

SOURCE: Bureau of Labor Statistics

OCCUPATIONS WITH THE LARGEST JOB DECLINE, 1996–2006
(Numbers in thousands of jobs)

Occupation	Employment 1996	Employment 2006	Change in Employment Number	Change in Employment Percent
Sewing machine operators, garment	453	334	−118	−26%
Farmers	1,109	997	−112	−10
Bookkeeping, accounting, and auditing clerks	2,250	2,147	−102	−5
Typists and word processors	653	552	−100	−15
Secretaries, except legal and medical	2,881	2,794	−87	−3
Cleaners and servants, private household	505	421	−84	−17
Computer operators, except peripheral equipment	258	181	−77	−30
Farm workers	873	798	−75	−9
Duplicating, mail, and other office machine operators	196	149	−47	−24
Welfare eligibility workers and interviewers	109	76	−34	−31
Textile draw-out and winding machine operators and tenders	183	155	−28	−15
Station installers and repairers, telephone	37	10	−27	−74
Child care workers, private household	275	250	−25	−9
Inspectors, testers, and graders, precision	634	610	−24	−4
Central office operators	48	26	−23	−47
Machine tool cutting operators and tenders, metal and plastic	127	105	−22	−17
Film strippers, printing	26	7	−20	−75
Peripheral computer equipment operators	33	17	−17	−50
Directory assistance operators	33	18	−16	−47
Custom tailors and sewers	87	73	−15	−17
Textile machine setters and setup operators	41	27	−14	−34
Highway maintenance workers	171	158	−14	−8
Statistical clerks	78	65	−13	−17
Butchers and meat cutters	217	205	−12	−6
Pasteup workers	15	4	−11	−75
Typesetting and composing machine operators and tenders	14	3	−10	−75
Drilling and boring machine tool setters	46	36	−10	−22
Proofreaders and copy markers	26	16	−10	−38
Lathe and turning machine tool setters	71	61	−10	−14
Payroll and timekeeping clerks	161	151	−10	−6

SOURCE: Bureau of Labor Statistics.

JOB GROWTH BY INDUSTRY

During the ten-year span from 1996 to 2006, the Bureau of Labor Statistics predicts that employment in the service industries will grow by 30 percent. Business, health, and education services will account for 70 percent of the growth with the services sector:

- Health-care services will increase 30 percent and account for 3.1 million new jobs, the largest numerical increase of any industry from 1996 to 2006. Factors contributing to continued growth in this industry include the aging population, which will continue to require more services, and the increased use of innovative medical technology for intensive diagnoses and treatment. Patients increasingly will be shifted out of hospitals and into outpatient facilities, nursing homes, and home health care in an attempt to contain costs.
- Educational services are projected to increase by 1.8 million jobs between 1996 and 2006. Most jobs will be for teachers, who are projected to account for 1.3 million jobs.
- Computer and data processing services will add over 1.3 million jobs from 1996 to 2006. The 108 percent increase is due to technological advancements and the need for higher skilled workers. The high percent increase makes this the fastest growing industry over the projection period.

In the other sectors, manufacturing is projected to continue its decline with only 13 percent of all wage and salary workers in 2006 compared with 16 percent in 1996. Construction employment will continue to grow but will be about 25 percent slower than in the previous ten-year period. Mining jobs will continue to decline dramatically, perhaps by 20 percent, just slightly less than in the previous ten-year period.

JOB GROWTH BY REGION

In a country as vast and economically diverse as the United States, regional employment levels can be as different as winters in Maine and Arizona, and as volatile as the value of pork bellies. In 1995, for example, the unemployment rates in many parts of New England topped 10 percent while the rates in almost all of the western states and many upper midwestern states were below 6 percent.

Employment in the United States is expected to grow by more than 58 million new jobs by the year 2025, according to the National Planning Association, a Washington economic research organization. Almost half of that growth is projected for thirty metropolitan statistical areas, primarily in the southern and western United States. Each of the top thirty metropolitan areas are projected to grow by a minimum of 470,000 jobs. Twelve areas will have growth of a million or more; eleven more will have growth of 600,000 or more. Eight of the top thirty areas are in California, and five are in Texas. Atlanta and Phoenix top the list of expanding areas, while Florida as a whole will start to reach capacity over the next few decades.

Charting regional and metropolitan area job growth is chancy at best, and all the projections included in the accompanying tables are based on population growth and the age of the area's workforce. But this gives an incomplete picture of the job market. For although many large cities have little if any new job growth, they often have many more jobs available because of the large number of retirements, firings, job changes, deaths, and other so-called separations. They also offer higher pay rates, as the tables on "Average Annual Pay" make clear.

30 METROPOLITAN AREAS WITH HIGHEST JOB GROWTH, 1997–2025

| Rank | Metropolitan Statistical Area | Number of Jobs | | Jobs Added |
		1997	2025	1997–2025
1.	Atlanta	2,401,900	4,326,900	1,925,000
2.	Phoenix	1,703,500	3,291,000	1,587,500
3.	Houston	233,200	3,907,000	1,573,900
4.	Los Angeles-Long Beach	5,205,100	6,704,900	1,499,900
5.	Dallas	2,177,900	3,589,400	1,411,400
6.	Washington, D.C.-MD-VA-WV	3,159,800	4,568,500	1,408,700
7.	San Diego	1,537,300	2,773,300	1,235,900
8.	Orange County, CA	1,691,600	2,903,500	1,212,000
9.	Seattle	1,618,000	2,782,700	1,164,700
10.	Tampa-St. Petersburg-Clearwater	1,264,800	2,299,200	1,034,400
11.	Denver	1,320,300	2,331,400	1,011,100
12.	Orlando	922,000	1,931,600	1,009,600
13.	Minneapolis-St. Paul	1,996,700	2,940,600	943,900
14.	Chicago	4,824,700	5,718,200	893,500
15.	Boston[1]	3,771,800	4,655,200	883,400
16.	Riverside-San Bernardino, CA	1,184,300	1,953,100	768,800
18.	Las Vegas, NV-AZ	770,600	1,508,400	737,800
18.	Sacramento	852,700	1,576,400	723,700
19.	Salt Lake City-Ogden, UT	849,300	1,549,000	699,700
20.	Austin-San Marcos, TX	722,600	1,411,700	689,100
21.	Portland-Vancouver, OR-WA	1,165,200	1,837,600	672,400
22.	Fort Worth-Arlington, TX	895,200	1,528,300	633,100
23.	San Jose, CA	1,167,700	1,778,700	611,000

30 METROPOLITAN AREAS WITH HIGHEST JOB GROWTH, 1997–2025

		Number of Jobs		Jobs Added
Rank	Metropolitan Statistical Area	1997	2025	1997–2025
24.	Fort Lauderdale	798,500	1,378,500	580,000
25.	Oakland, CA	1,247,000	1,775,700	527,800
26.	Raleigh-Durham-Chapel Hill, NC	734,500	1,256,300	521,800
27.	San Antonio	848,900	1,367,200	518,200
28.	Miami	1,162,200	1,680,100	517,900
29.	San Francisco	1,324,700	1,801,000	476,200
30.	Nashville	801,800	1,274,700	472,900
	TOTAL 30 MSAs	**50,454,600**	**78,399,800**	**27,945,200**

[1]Includes Worcester, Lawrence, Lowell, Brockton, and portions of New Hampshire.
SOURCE: NPA Data Services, Inc., *Regional Economic Growth in the U.S. Projections for 1997–2025.*

15 METROPOLITAN AREAS WITH FASTEST JOB GROWTH, 1997–2025

		Number of Jobs		Annual Percent Increase
Rank	Metropolitan Statistical Area	1997	2025	1997–2025
1.	Punta Gorda, FL	48,600	110,500	3.0%
2.	Orlando, FL	922,000	1,931,600	2.7
3.	Naples, FL	117,500	243,000	2.6
4.	Las Vegas, NV	770,600	1,508,400	2.4
5.	Austin-San Marcos, TX	722,600	1,411,700	2.4
6.	Phoenix-Mesa	1,703,500	3,291,000	2.4
7.	Sarasota-Bradenton, FL	348,900	674,000	2.4
8.	Bryan-College Station, TX	84,700	163,100	2.4
9.	Provo-Orem, UT	173,800	334,700	2.4
10.	Myrtle Beach, SC	111,100	213,600	2.4
11.	Fort Pierce-Port St. Lucie, FL	128,500	245,900	2.3
12.	Laredo, TX	72,000	137,700	2.3
13.	Fort Meyers-Cape Coral, FL	199,100	379,700	2.3
14.	Olympia, WA	104,300	198,300	2.3
15.	Fort Collins-Loveland, CO	145,200	274,500	2.3

SOURCE: NPA Data Services, Inc., *Regional Economic Growth in the U.S. Projections for 1997–2025* (1998).

METROPOLITAN AREAS WITH HIGHEST AVERAGE ANNUAL PAY, 1995–96

| | Average Annual Pay | | Percent |
| | 1995 | 1996 | Change |
All Metropolitan Areas	$29,099	$30,250	4.0%
New York	$42,272	$45,028	6.5%
San Jose, (CA)	42,409	44,819	5.7
San Francisco	37,975	40,016	5.4
Middlesex-Somerset-Hunterdon (NJ)	37,925	39,631	4.5
New Haven-Bridgeport-Danbury (CT)	37,546	39,488	5.2
Newark (NJ)	37,224	38,886	4.5
Trenton (NJ)	36,614	37,598	2.7
Bergen-Passaic (NJ)	35,746	36,840	3.1
Jersey City (NJ)	34,621	36,833	6.4
Washington, DC-MD-VA-WV	34,910	36,383	4.2
Detroit	34,710	35,748	3.0
Kokomo (IN)	33,967	34,779	2.4
Oakland (CA)	33,180	34,402	3.7
Boston-Worcester-Brockton (MA-NH)	32,798	34,383	4.8
Chicago	32,523	33,907	4.3
Seattle-Bellevue-Everett (WA)	31,550	33,588	6.5
Anchorage	33,650	33,501	−0.4
Los Angeles-Long Beach	32,445	33,478	3.2
Flint (MI)	33,389	33,294	−0.3
Wilmington-Newark (DE-MD)	31,439	33,223	5.7
Philadelphia-NJ	31,695	33,080	4.4
Dallas	31,500	32,996	4.7
Nassau-Suffolk (NY)	31,635	32,993	4.3
Houston	31,390	32,895	4.8

SOURCE: Bureau of Labor Statistics.

METROPOLITAN AREAS WITH LOWEST AVERAGE ANNUAL PAY, 1995–96

| | Average Annual Pay | | Percent Change |
All Metropolitan Areas	1995	1996	1995–96
Goldsboro (NC)	$20,343	$21,417	5.3%
Yuba City (CA)	21,237	21,374	0.6
Lawrence (KS)	20,860	21,198	1.6
Daytona Beach (FL)	20,497	21,121	3.0
Panama City (FL)	20,491	21,121	3.1
Great Falls (MT)	20,213	21,073	4.3
Abilene (TX)	20,365	21,035	3.3
Chico-Paradise (CA)	20,573	21,021	2.2

METROPOLITAN AREAS WITH LOWEST AVERAGE ANNUAL PAY, 1995–96

All Metropolitan Areas	Average Annual Pay		Percent Change 1995–96
	1995	1996	
Lawton (OK)	$20,780	$20,916	0.7%
Merced (CA)	20,256	20,909	3.2
Rapid City (SD)	20,107	20,719	3.0
Sumter (SC)	19,880	20,708	4.2
Bryan-College Station (TX)	19,788	20,683	4.5
Fort Walton Beach (FL)	19,788	20,653	4.4
Enid (OK)	19,934	20,629	3.5
Grand Forks (ND-MN)	19,904	20,476	2.9
Laredo (TX)	19,174	20,388	6.3
Las Cruces (NM)	20,186	20,371	0.9
Yakima (WA)	19,271	19,780	2.6
Visalia-Tulare-Porterville (CA)	19,439	19,768	1.7
Brownsville-Harlingen-San Benito (TX)	18,566	19,056	2.6
McAllen-Edinburg-Mission (TX)	18,031	18,928	5.0
Myrtle Beach (SC)	17,910	18,551	3.6
Yuma (AZ)	18,286	18,213	-0.4
Jacksonville (NC)	16,951	17,534	3.4

SOURCE: Bureau of Labor Statistics.

SALARIES AND WAGES IN THE NEAR FUTURE

Since 1994, the U.S. economy has soared into a kind of overdrive that has created new jobs at such an astonishing clip that by 1998, unemployment rates had sunk below 5 percent for the first time in thirty years. At the same time, inflation dipped to less than 2 percent, a level not seen since the 1950s. While politicians and pundits flood the airwaves with boastful claims of the nation's great economic achievements, a disturbing trend has developed in the wage levels offered to average American workers. The harsh reality is that in the midst of unprecedented wealth, real wages for many continue to decline while for the rest only a slight increase can be seen.

In the 1950s, average hourly earnings of nonfarm workers increased by 2.5 percent (with inflation factored in), then increased again by 1.7 percent in the 1960s. In the 1970s, there was a small increase of 0.2 percent, but in the 1980s, they declined 0.3 percent. Average weekly earnings in manufacturing have in fact declined by over 14 percent since 1973; median household income for manufacturing workers has dropped over 6 percent.

This trend has continued throughout the 1990s as shown in the accompanying table "Average Weekly Earnings by Private Industry Group, 1980–97"; calculated in what economists call "constant dollars," these figures factor inflation into the results.

What is not clear from these statistics is that the earnings of white-collar workers with college educations have actually witnessed an increase of over 5 percent in recent years. Education will continue to play a major role in what workers earn. For young people who do not attend college, there is a high likelihood that they will encounter periodic unemployment or a work-life of jobs with poverty-level incomes and little chance of advancement. Low-paying service jobs are one of the fastest growing sectors of the labor force and should be responsible for a large percentage of the job growth for noncollege graduates. Unemployment rates for high school graduates are almost double that of college graduates, and median monthly incomes are half of what a college graduate earns. (See, in Part IX, "The New College Graduate.")

There is no reason to believe that these economic trends will not continue. The political challenge will be how to justify the ever-growing income inequality between the top 5 percent of all households and the bottom 20 percent. In 1994 the top income group had $109,821 in income, over 8 *times* that of the $13,426 averaged by those at the 20 percent level of household income. Between 1968 and 1994 the top household experienced a 30 percent growth in average income but the average income at the bottom 20 percent grew by only 8 percent.

The next decade will be a time of great challenges for business and political leaders since the chances of a recession must be seen as a real possibility. How the American people will respond to stagnant wages in a time of trouble might be quite different from today's period of prosperity.

AVERAGE WEEKLY EARNINGS BY PRIVATE INDUSTRY GROUP 1980–97
(in constant 1982 dollars)

Industry Group	1980	1985	1990	1997
Mining	$ 464	$ 471	$ 453	$ 451
Construction	430	421	395	384
Manufacturing	337	350	332	340
Transportation, public utilities	410	408	373	365
Wholesale trade	312	319	309	317
Retail trade	172	158	146	148
Finance, insurance, real estate	245	262	268	296
Services	223	233	240	246
TOTAL	$ 275	$ 271	$ 259	$ 261

SOURCE: Bureau of Labor Statistics.

1

On the Public Payroll

In 1995, the latest year for which data is available, more than 20 million men and women, or one in six working Americans, were on the public payroll:

2.9 million civilians worked for the federal government
1.5 million were in the military
4.7 million worked for state governments
2.6 million worked for municipalities
2.3 million worked for counties
5.2 million worked for school districts
1.5 million worked for towns, villages, and special districts

Despite the attempts by politicians everywhere to create a smaller, leaner government, the number of people on the public payroll continues to grow steadily. As the accompanying table shows, public sector employment has more than doubled since 1957. The biggest culprit has not been the federal government—federal employment has remained fairly constant since the end of World War II, and actually declined by 9 percent recently—but rather state and local governments, which have nearly tripled in size since 1957.

Such statistics have made the subject of public employment—its uses and abuses, accomplishments and wastefulness—a political issue of central importance. By presenting as much information about salaries of public employees as is possible within the limits of this book, we hope to add something of value to the ongoing debate. That discussion is bound to include such items as: wide regional discrepancies for people doing the same job;

1

the issue of "work comparability" (who decides what a job is worth and how that decision is made); and the paradoxical situation of governors, mayors, and legislators voting large increases for themselves while opposing the wage demands of public employees.

This section is the largest in the book. It is divided into three chapters. First is the federal government, including leading government officials and an analysis of the salary scales in the infamous federal bureaucracy. Next come the salaries of state and local government officials—the most important management jobs in government. And, finally, are some examples of salaries and wages for common, everyday jobs on the state and local levels.

Jobs and Salaries
in the Federal Government

At the end of the eighteenth century the influential French philosopher and statesman Saint-Simon noted with considerable dismay that before the Revolution the royal bureaucracy had grown so pervasive that eighty thousand men were needed just to administer the salt tax. In our own day, Jack Anderson, a somewhat less than philosophical observer of the political scene, has calculated that America's 3 million civilian employees and 1.8 million military personnel drain the taxpayers of over $100 billion a year. Unlike the case in monarchies or dictatorships, the cost of ruling is always a major element in the administration of democracies and republics. In contemporary times, the salaries and perquisites of politicians and bureaucrats have taken on a new importance in representative forms of government.

Every republic such as ours eventually faces the dilemma of just how much money its citizens should pay government officials, especially those in the highest ranks. Giving too much may raise the specter of elitism, but paying too little makes officials vulnerable to bribery and corruption, a vulnerability all too frequently proven in American history. In any event, no systematic method for determining equitable pay scales in government service has ever been established. Instead, every few years Congress and the president seem to take a rather casual look at the economy and at salary ranges in the private sector and arrive at a set of figures somewhere in the upper-middle range. For the top levels today, that's over $100,000.

Over the last thirty years or so the inflationary spiral has added a new dimension to the question of how much government officials should be paid. Since 1965 the salary for just about every important federal job (except the president and the vice president) has at least doubled. These increases took place despite the fact that in 1987, President Carter froze the salaries of many upper-level bureaucrats at $51,000, in 1982, President Reagan raised the limit to $57,500. Today, those freezes seem a long way in the past, as most senior level bureaucrats earn over $100,000.

The vast size of the federal government and the complex nature of its operations preclude any simple responses to the issues involved in pay cuts for politicians and federal employees. It is our hope that the long list of facts and figures that follow will help our readers to make informed judgments in the future.

3

UNDERSTANDING THE FEDERAL PAY SYSTEM

As of March 31, 1997, there were 1,740,631 full-time nonpostal federal civilian employees. Nearly 97 percent of the federal civilian workforce was employed in the United States; 12,424 (0.7 percent) worked in U.S. territories; and 41,437 (2.4 percent) worked in foreign countries. The majority of government employees worked in metropolitan statistical areas (MSAs), led by the Washington, DC, MSA, with 271,793, or 15.6 percent of the total.

Four executive departments accounted for nearly 70 percent of the federal civilian workforce. The Department of Defense employed 727,907 civilians (41.8 percent of the total); Veterans Affairs, 198,417 (or 11.4 percent); the Treasury, 151,556 (or 8.7 percent), and Justice, 109,552 (or 6.3 percent).

Federal government civilian employees are paid according to a number of different systems: the General Schedule (GS), Federal Wage Systems, and other acts and administratively determined systems. Overall, the average salary for full-time civilian government employees was $43,873. Employees under the General Schedule on average earned more than those on Federal Wage Systems ($42,326 to $33,834), but not as much as employees covered by other acts and administrative determinations, who averaged $58,782. Average General Schedule salaries by major geographic areas were: United States, $43,429; Washington, DC, area, $54,456; foreign countries, $35,846; and U.S. territories, $33,776.

If you browse through only the listings in this section, you'll get the impression that this is an unwieldy, amorphous mass of information, reflecting perhaps what we all believe to be the chaotic state of the federal bureaucracy itself. But, in fact, the federal salary system has, relatively speaking, a logical structure that can be easily understood, keeping two things in mind. First, *never* divide the nearly 5 million federal employees according to branch of government, since just about everybody works for the Executive Branch (the Legislative Branch employs only 38,000 people; the Judicial, only 22,000). Included in the Executive Branch are the military, the independent agencies, and the executive departments (State, Defense, etc.).

Second, always think in terms of four basic categories: civilian employees, military employees, blue-collar workers, and white-collar workers. All federal employees are paid under salary schedules formulated on these rather obvious distinctions. Since most people know that the military has a separate pay scale, let's look at civilian workers first.

White-Collar Workers

More than 75 percent of the more than 3 million federal civilian employees are classified as white-collar workers. Most work under the so-called General

U.S. FEDERAL EMPLOYMENT, 1992–97

Description	1992	1996	1997
Executive Branch civilian employment[1]	2,226,778	1,933,931	1,871,791
U.S. Postal Service[2]	792,049	852,333	853,350
Military personnel on active duty[3]	1,847,600	1,506,965	1,473,699
Department of Defense	1,808,131	1,471,722	1,438,562
Department of Transportation (Coast Guard)	39,469	35,243	35,137
Total Executive Branch employment	4,866,427	4,293,229	4,198,840
Legislative Branch	38,509	31,547	31,355
Judicial Branch	27,987	29,581	30,641
TOTAL federal employment	4,932,923	4,354,357	4,260,836

[1] Excludes Postal Service employees.
[2] Includes Postal Rate Commission.
[3] Excludes reserve components.
SOURCE: Office of Management and Budget, Budget of the United States Government, FY 1999 (1998).

Schedule or the Executive Schedule, while some top officials are under the New Senior Executive Service. In 1997, the mean annual salary of white-collar workers in the federal government was $43,239.

THE GENERAL SCHEDULE

Because almost 1.3 million people work under this salary scale, it is by far the most important in the federal government. It consists of fifteen grades (GS-1 to GS-15), each with a salary range of ten steps, and each defined according to level of responsibility, type of work, and required qualifications. Theoretically, employees are promoted through steps 1, 2, and 3 on a yearly basis—i.e., they move one step each year; in steps 4, 5, and 6, they move one step every two years; and in steps 7, 8, and 9, they move one step every three years. How this works in practice is another matter. Frequently, when people are promoted to a higher GS level, they begin at a step higher than step 1 so that their salaries will surpass what they were making at the lower GS level but at an advanced step. For example, someone at GS-5, step 7 ($23,965) who was promoted to GS-6 would have to start at least at step 6 or else suffer a cut in pay.

In 1993, the Clinton administration set out to trim the size of the federal bureaucracy and, unlike its Republican ("we hate big government") predecessors, it actually cut the white-collar workforce by 9 percent within four years.

Foreign Service Personnel and Veterans Affairs
There were 4,439 Foreign Service Officers in 1997, with an average salary of $72,214. Nonofficers in the Foreign Service numbered 6,255 and averaged $51,038 in salary. The pay system of the Department of Veterans Affairs covered 7,460 physicians and dentists, with an average salary of $91,391; 190 podiatrists and optometrists ($81,609); 32,199 nurses ($48,028); and 1,028 physician assistants ($57,758).

GENERAL SCHEDULE EMPLOYEES AND MEAN SALARY BY GRADE

Grade	Employees	Mean Salary
GS-1	272	$14,046
GS-2	1,491	16,338
GS-3	19,383	18,432
GS-4	67,303	21,496
GS-5	137,145	24,229
GS-6	96,115	27,196
GS-7	132,243	29,969
GS-8	41,251	33,959
GS-9	127,489	36,178
GS-10	16,106	40,764
GS-11	180,851	43,943
GS-12	213,465	52,759
GS-13	154,152	63,583
GS-14	67,014	76,240
GS-15	35,529	91,411
TOTAL/Mean	1,289,809	43,239

SOURCE: Office of Personnel Management, *Pay Structure of the Federal Civil Service* (1997).

GENERAL SCHEDULE: ANNUAL SALARIES BY GRADE AND STEP

Level	1	2	3	4	5	6	7	8	9	10
GS-1	$12,960	$13,392	$13,823	$14,252	$14,685	$14,938	$15,362	$15,791	$15,809	$16,214
2	14,571	14,918	15,401	15,809	15,985	16,445	16,925	17,395	17,865	18,335
3	15,899	16,429	16,959	17,489	18,019	18,549	19,079	19,609	20,139	20,669
4	17,848	18,443	19,038	19,633	20,228	20,823	21,418	22,013	22,608	23,203
5	19,969	20,635	21,301	21,967	22,633	23,299	23,965	24,631	25,297	25,963
6	22,258	23,000	23,742	24,484	25,226	25,968	26,710	27,452	28,194	28,936
7	24,734	25,558	26,382	27,206	28,030	28,854	29,678	30,502	31,326	32,150
8	27,393	28,306	29,219	30,132	31,045	31,958	32,871	33,784	34,697	35,610
9	30,257	31,266	32,275	33,284	34,293	35,302	36,311	37,320	38,329	39,338
10	33,320	34,431	35,542	36,653	37,764	38,875	39,986	41,097	42,208	43,319
11	36,609	37,829	39,049	40,269	41,489	42,709	43,929	45,149	46,369	47,589
12	43,876	45,339	46,802	48,265	49,728	51,191	52,654	54,117	55,580	57,043
13	52,176	53,915	55,654	57,393	59,132	60,871	62,610	64,349	66,088	67,827
14	61,656	63,711	65,766	67,821	69,876	71,931	73,986	76,041	78,096	80,151
15	72,525	74,943	77,361	79,779	82,197	84,615	87,033	89,451	91,869	94,287

SOURCE: Office of Personnel Management, *Pay Structure of the Federal Civil Service*, 1997.

FOREIGN SERVICE STAFF AND OFFICERS SCHEDULE

Step	Class 1	Class 2	Class 3	Class 4	Class 5	Class 6	Class 7	Class 8	Class 9
1	$70,894	$57,466	$46,548	$37,718	$30,563	$27,322	$24,425	$21,835	$19,520
2	73,021	59,169	47,994	38,850	31,480	28,142	25,158	22,490	20,106
3	75,211	60,944	49,383	40,015	32,424	28,986	25,912	23,165	20,709
4	77,468	62,773	50,864	41,215	33,397	29,855	26,690	23,860	21,330
5	79,792	64,656	52,390	42,452	34,399	30,751	27,491	24,575	21,970
6	82,186	66,596	53,962	43,725	35,431	31,674	28,315	25,313	22,629
7	84,651	68,594	55,581	45,037	36,494	32,624	29,165	26,072	23,308
8	87,191	70,651	57,248	46,388	37,589	33,603	30,040	26,854	24,007
9	89,806	72,771	58,966	47,780	38,716	34,611	30,941	27,660	24,727
10	92,161	74,954	60,735	49,213	39,878	35,649	31,869	28,490	25,469
11	92,161	77,203	62,557	50,690	41,074	36,718	32,825	29,344	26,233
12	92,161	79,519	64,433	52,211	42,306	37,820	33,810	30,225	27,020
13	92,161	81,904	66,366	53,777	43,576	38,955	34,824	31,131	27,831
14	92,161	84,361	68,357	55,390	44,883	40,123	35,869	32,065	28,666

SOURCE: U.S. Department of State. As of January 1, 1997.

50 WHITE-COLLAR FEDERAL GOVERNMENT OCCUPATIONS:
NUMBER EMPLOYED AND AVERAGE ANNUAL SALARIES

Occupation	Total Number Employed	Average Annual Salary
Air Traffic Controller	23,781	$65,252
Architect	1,867	57,289
Border Patrol	6,819	37,253
Cartographer	1,097	53,238
Chaplain	605	53,627
Chemist	6,348	61,253
Clerk-Typist	2,962	23,789
Computer Operator	3,893	32,229
Computer Specialist	55,301	53,806
Criminal Investigator	34,576	58,907
Dentist	801	84,455
Doctor	10,760	87,947
Economist	5,252	67,343
Engineer, Aerospace	7,996	67,251
Engineer, Chemical	1,100	62,814
Engineer, Civil	12,390	58,605
Engineer, Electrical	4,542	59,315
Engineer, General	18,997	71,522
Engineer, Mechanical	10,243	59,324
Engineer, Nuclear	2,248	69,080
Engineer, Petroleum	334	61,432
Engineering Technician	18,797	43,009
Hospital Administrator	501	41,355
Inspector, Aviation Safety	3,574	64,842
Inspector, Customs	7,299	39,668
Inspector, Food	6,696	32,939
Internal Revenue Agent	14,609	56,299
Lawyer, General	25,385	79,867
Librarian	2,747	53,985
Library Technician	2,787	27,786
Management and Program Analyst	39,492	55,882
Mathematician	1,575	64,565
Medical Technologist	5,470	40,878
Messenger	88	24,682
Museum Curator	368	57,507
Nurse	40,165	47,488
Nurse's Assistant	11,439	23,425
Paralegal	5,701	44,228
Pharmacist	4,494	54,489
Photographer	1,190	38,783

50 WHITE-COLLAR FEDERAL GOVERNMENT OCCUPATIONS: NUMBER EMPLOYED AND AVERAGE ANNUAL SALARIES

Occupation	Total Number Employed	Average Annual Salary
Physicist	2,944	$73,985
Psychologist	3,563	62,784
Secretary	64,484	28,376
Security Guard	4,095	25,444
Social Insurance Claims Examiner	254	44,227
Social Worker	4,817	46,966
Statistician	2,599	60,558
Telephone Operator	1,436	21,883
Veterinarian	1,840	57,986
Writer and Editor	1,533	47,115

SOURCE: Office of Personnel Management, *Occupations of Federal White-Collar and Blue-Collar Workers,* September 1997.

THE EXECUTIVE SCHEDULE

The Executive Schedule covers only senior-level employees in the Executive Branch. It was established in 1964 as a way of attracting first-rate managers to Washington by paying salaries that went beyond the maximums of the General Schedule. It also enabled a newly elected president to handpick top officials across the whole spectrum of government, theoretically freeing the administration from the stranglehold of a bureaucracy not politically committed to the executive's programs. On the other hand, it greatly increased the power of presidential patronage.

Most of the jobs that fall under the Executive Schedule can be found in the listings of executive departments and independent agencies. But, first, here's a quick look at how the system is structured.

Level I—All cabinet members.

Level II—Some special presidential assistants; deputy secretaries of major departments (e.g., State: Defense); secretaries of Army, Navy, and Air Force; a few chief administrators, including the heads of the Agency for International Development and the Federal Aviation Administration; the U.S. representatives to the United Nations and to NATO.

Level III—Most presidential advisers; chief administrators of large, independent agencies; most undersecretaries in executive departments.

Level IV—Most assistant secretaries, deputy undersecretaries, and gen-

THE EXECUTIVE SCHEDULE

Level	Employees	1997 Salary
I	13	$148,400
II	31	133,600
III	81	123,100
IV	265	115,700
V	19	108,200
TOTAL/Average	409	$119,561

SOURCE: Office of Personnel Management, *Pay Structure of the Federal Civil Service, 1997.*

eral counsels in executive departments; many directors such as those at Civil Defense, National Cancer Institute, and National Institutes of Health.

Level V—Many deputy assistant secretaries; most administrators, commissioners, and directors.

THE SENIOR EXECUTIVE SERVICE

In 1979, fifteen years after the establishment of the Executive Schedule, Congress approved yet another form of compensation for top-level government bureaucrats. This time, however, double-digit inflation and pervasive public skepticism about the size and efficiency of the federal bureaucracy required that strong justification be made for any increase in government salaries. According to the director of the Office of Personnel Management, the purpose of this new system was "to create a cadre of extraordinarily competent

THE SENIOR EXECUTIVE SCHEDULE

Level	Employees	1997 Salary
ES-1	667	$97,000
ES-2	764	101,600
ES-3	1,021	106,200
ES-4	2,738	111,900
ES-5	1,195	115,700
ES-6	595	115,700
TOTAL/Average	6,980	$110,668

SOURCE: Office of Personnel Management, *Pay Structure of the Federal Civil Service, 1997.*

and dedicated people who will be accountable for the execution of government programs. Its members will be eligible for additional compensation and benefits based on their performance."

Linking compensation to performance in a government job struck most observers as such a novel idea that few took notice of the relevant details. The Senior Executive Service (SES) is limited temporarily to 8,500 members, almost all drawn from Senior Level management and from the Executive Levels IV and V. By law, 90 percent of Senior Executive Service members must be on career assignment and not subject to removal by a change in presidential administrations, and not in jobs requiring Senate confirmation. Moreover, the law stipulates that 70 percent of all SES members must have held not less that five current, continuous years of federal civilian service. In other words, the upper echelon of the existing structure would remain protected from any presidential promise to revamp the bureaucracy or threat to introduce modern management techniques into government. In addition, they would be better paid.

The Senior Executive Service currently has six salary rates, the lowest equaling the first step of GS-16, the highest not to exceed the rate for Level IV of the Executive Schedule. There are no grades for the SES, and each member negotiates his or her salary individually with the particular agency. Unlike in the General Schedule and the Executive Schedule, pay rates in the Senior Executive Service are not subject to automatic annual cost-of-living increases.

The true financial rewards of the SES, however, are to be found in its bonus system. So-called "Performance Awards" are given to the best managers within an agency as judged by a Performance Review Board and approved by an agency head or an agency Executive Review Board. Lump-sum payments of up to 20 percent of the recipient's base salary will be made every year. According to the government's official booklet, "If you are a top performer, you may receive a bonus every year."

"Presidential Ranks" are another way of rewarding exceptional SES employees with cash bonuses. The first of these, "Meritorious Executive," carries with it a lump-sum payment of $10,000, while "Distinguished Executive" adds $20,000 to the recipient's income. These awards, given for exceptional performance over an extended period of time, are limited each year to 5 percent (about 425) of SES membership for the Meritorious, and 1 percent (about 85) for the Distinguished.

The designers of this system realized that a few executives would stand out immediately and might receive several different awards. For this reason, total compensation for members of the Senior Executive Service is not to exceed the salary of cabinet-level appointees at Level I of the Executive Schedule, which in 1997 was $148,400.

Blue-Collar Workers

THE FEDERAL WAGE SYSTEM

About 325,000 blue-collar workers throughout the country are paid under this system, which is based on locally prevailing wage rates for trade, craft, and labor occupations. The Defense Department employs three quarters of these workers (179,679) at installations in the United States and abroad. In 1997, the average annual salary for federal blue-collar workers in the United States was $33,968, and $26,982 in foreign countries. Below are average salary figures for the most common blue-collar jobs. Although these salaries appear to be in line with private-sector wages, critics of federal pay policies claim that given the extremely good benefits all federal employees receive, these basic salary rates are much too high. Of course, most of these critics earn two to three times what blue-collar workers make.

**SELECTED BLUE-COLLAR OCCUPATIONS IN THE FEDERAL GOVERNMENT:
EMPLOYEES AND AVERAGE ANNUAL SALARIES, 1997**

Title	Total Number Employed	Average Salary
Air Conditioning Mechanic	3,404	$34,566
Aircraft Mechanic	12,604	35,671
Automotive Mechanic	6,139	33,664
Banknote Engraver	18	78,293
Boiler Plant Operator	2,616	35,648
Boilermaker	806	38,151
Bowling Equipment Repairer	16	27,581
Carpenter	3,360	33,548
Cook	4,184	30,822
Crane Operator	1,173	36,124
Custodian	14,045	21,913
Electric Power Controller	2,335	35,830
Electronics Mechanic	9,545	35,742
Elevator Operator	33	20,274
Engineering Equipment Operator	3,498	34,081
Explosives Operator	1,074	29,206
Food Service Worker	8,373	21,948
Forklift Operator	897	28,022
Gardener	1,199	28,894
Industrial Equipment Mechanic	1,625	38,412
Instrument Mechanic	1,649	36,613
Insulator	968	35,941
Laborer	6,652	21,530
Laundry Worker	1,386	21,411

SELECTED BLUE-COLLAR OCCUPATIONS IN THE FEDERAL GOVERNMENT:
EMPLOYEES AND AVERAGE ANNUAL SALARIES, 1997

Title	Total Number Employed	Average Salary
Lock and Dam Operator	1,420	$32,640
Machinist	5,730	37,243
Maintenance Mechanic	11,938	33,225
Maintenance, Miscellaneous	3,059	43,681
Marine Machinery Mechanic	2,650	38,681
Materials Handler	18,429	28,476
Meat Cutter	1,709	29,769
Motor Vehicle Operator	8,213	29,414
Offset Press Operator	903	37,129
Packer	2,425	28,188
Painter	5,072	32,341
Pipe fitter	5,630	37,169
Plasterer	100	32,496
Plumber	1,539	32,726
Rigger	207	31,601
Sewing Machine Operator	263	24,904
Sheet Metal Mechanic	8,556	34,023
Shipfitter	1,598	38,178
Telephone Mechanic	663	35,863
Toolmaker	634	39,392
Tractor Operator	1,208	27,728
Warehouse Worker	788	30,395
Welder	3,586	35,649
Woodworker	1,016	30,966

SOURCE: Office of Personnel Management, *Occupations of Federal White-Collar and Blue-Collar Workers* (1998).

The Postal Service

If the Watergate scandal exposed Richard Nixon's profound contempt for our laws and political traditions, his reorganization of the federal postal structure revealed his passionate, if somewhat naive, belief in the old American system of free enterprise. According to one aspect of this theory, any operation can be made efficient if it is run for profit. So the Post Office was made an independent agency—not part of the Executive Branch, not subject to the whims of presidential patronage. Next, high-powered executives were brought in to administer this enormous operation. In order to attract the right personnel, the U.S. Postal Service was given a separate salary schedule which, at least at the upper echelon and in middle-management positions, was competitive with the outside world.

During the late 1980s and early 1990s, automation allowed the Postal Service to reduce its workforce from close to 800,000 employees in 1989 to 682,000 in 1992. Since then, however, the number of employees has crept back up to 856,000. In 1996, the Postal Service employed 297,000 clerks and mail handlers and 332,000 mail carriers. They all belong to unions that try to enforce strict work rules and keep their members happy despite relatively low pay. Postal workers have excellent benefits and can retire with a pension after only twenty years' service.

The American Postal Workers' Union (APWU) represents 366,000 union members; the National Association of Letter Carriers (NALC) has 315,000 members; and the other two major bargaining units, the National Postal Mail Handlers' Union (NPMHU) and the National Rural Letter Carriers' Association (NRLCA), represent close to 500,000 employees between them.

According to a Census Bureau survey, Postal Service workers are better paid than comparably skilled employees in the private sector. Base pay for full-time postal clerks who operate scanning and sorting machines ranges from $24,599 for beginners to a maximum of $35,683 after fourteen years of service. Experienced, full-time mail carriers earn an average of $34,135 a year.

Pay Rates in the Military

For the majority of positions in the armed forces, the educational requirements are low—and with the end of the cold war, so is the likelihood of ever seeing combat duty, making a career in the military an attractive option for poor people. Average pay rates in the military nearly doubled during Ronald Reagan's years as president. Soldiers also receive free room and board, albeit a barracks bunk and military mess hall, so their paychecks go a lot farther than those of people who pay monthly rent and grocery bills. The lowliest private earns over $13,000 per year in what amounts to spending money, while a Navy lieutenant with ten years of service brings in more than $37,000 annually. Salaries for enlisted personnel average more than $25,000, while the average officer's total compensation package tops $50,000.

In 1998 Congress and President Clinton approved a 2.8 percent increase for all military personnel and in 1999 another increase of just over 4 percent was put through as a way of keeping military personnel from leaving the services, a trend that was causing high-ranking officials great concern. This is not reflected in the accompanying table.

MONTHLY BASE PAY OF MILITARY PERSONNEL

Pay Grade	Army Rank	Navy Rank	2 years of service	10 years of service	26 years of service
Commissioned Officers					
O-10	General	Admiral	$7,832.40	$8,133.00	$10,424.70
O-9	Lt. General	Vice-Admiral	6,881.40	7,206.60	9,197.70
O-8	Maj. General	Rear Admiral	6,255.90	6,881.40	8,333.70
O-7	Brig. General	Commodore	5,389.80	5,958.00	7,354.80
O-6	Colonel	Captain	4,109.40	4,379.10	6,461.70
O-5	Lt. Colonel	Commander	3,512.70	3,868.80	5,272.50
O-4	Major	Lt. Commander	3,070.80	3,721.20	4,407.90
O-3	Captain	Lieutenant	2,619.90	3,546.00	3,812.40
O-2	1st Lieutenant	Lieutenant (J.G.)	2,231.70	2,828.70	2,828.70
O-1	2nd Lieutenant	Ensign	1,846.50	2,231.70	2,231.70
Warrant Officers					
W-5	Chief Warrant Officer	Chief Warrant Officer	NA	NA	$ 4,534.50
W-4	Chief Warrant Officer	Chief Warrant Officer	2,561.70	2,979.90	4,077.60
W-3	Chief Warrant Officer	Chief Warrant Officer	2,353.80	2,739.30	3,453.60
W-2	Chief Warrant Officer	Chief Warrant Officer	2,056.20	2,443.20	3,005.70
W-1	Warrant Officer	Warrant Officer	1,815.30	2,231.70	2,681.10
Enlisted Personnel					
E-9	Sgt. Major	Master C.P.O.	NA	$2,777.40	$ 3,576.00
E-8	Master Sgt.	Senior C.P.O.	NA	2,396.10	3,193.50
E-7	Sgt. First Class	Chief Petty Officer	1,755.60	2,074.80	2,873.10
E-6	Staff Sergeant	Petty Officer, 1st Class	1,524.90	1,845.30	2,097.00
E-5	Sergeant	Petty Officer, 2nd Class	1,336.20	1,685.70	1,779.90
E-4	Corporal	Petty Officer, 3rd Class	1,209.30	1,433.70	1,433.70
E-3	Pvt. 1st Class	Seaman	1,137.90	1,230.30	1,230.30
E-2	Private	Seaman Apprentice	1,038.30	1,038.30	1,103.30
E-1	Recruit	Seaman Recruit	926.10	926.10	926.10

Note: Effective November, 1997.   SOURCE: U.S. Department of Defense.

BASIC ALLOWANCES

In addition to their salaries, military personnel not living on a base receive supplementary allowances for quarters and subsistence.

MONTHLY BASIC ALLOWANCE FOR QUARTERS, 1997

Pay Grade	Single Rate	Married Rate
Officers		
O-7 through O-10	$847.80	$1,043.70
O-6	779.90	939.60
O-5	749.10	905.70
O-4	694.20	798.30
O-3	556.50	660.60
O-2	441.30	564.90
O-1	371.70	504.30
Warrant Officers		
W-5	$705.30	$ 770.70
W-4	626.40	706.50
W-3	526.50	647.40
W-2	467.40	595.50
W-1	391.50	515.10
Enlisted Personnel		
E-9	$514.50	$ 678.30
E-8	472.20	625.20
E-7	403.50	580.50
E-6	365.10	482.40
E-5	336.90	482.40
E-4	293.10	419.40
E-3	287.40	390.30
E-2	233.40	371.70
E-1	208.20	371.70

SOURCE: U.S. Department of Defense.

BASIC ALLOWANCE FOR SUBSISTENCE

Officers	$155.70 per month ($1,868.40 per year)	

Enlisted Members	E-1, LESS THAN FOUR MONTHS	ALL OTHER ENLISTED
When on leave, or authorized to mess separately:	$ 6.86/day	$ 7.43/day
When rations in-kind are not available:	7.73/day	8.38/day
When assigned to duty under emergency conditions where no messing facilities of the United States are available:	10.26/day	11.10/day

PLUM JOBS: HIGH-PAYING POSITIONS IN THE FEDERAL GOVERNMENT

In recent years, every time a new president is elected, Congress issues a large book called *U.S. Government Policy and Supporting Positions*. Known popularly as *The Plum Book*, it lists several thousand key jobs in all the executive departments and independent agencies.

In the pages that follow, the upper echelon of the federal bureaucracy can be found. Keep in mind that many of these jobs are presidential appointments, so they represent the heart of the executive's power of patronage. The data reflects plum jobs (and salaries) in the Clinton administration in 1997.

Executive Departments

DEPARTMENT OF AGRICULTURE

Secretary	Level I
Deputy Secretary	Level II
4 Undersecretaries	Levels III–IV
General Counsel	Level IV
Deputy General Counsel	Senior Executive Service
Inspector General	Level IV
Chief of Staff	Senior Executive Service
Counsel to the Secretary	Senior Executive Service

Executive Assistant to the Secretary	Senior Executive Service
9 Administrators	Level V and Senior Executive Service
3 Assistant Secretaries	Level IV
13 Associate and Assistant General Counsels (career incumbents included)	Senior Executive Service
9 Associate Administrators (including career incumbents)	Senior Executive Service
22 Deputy Administrators (including career incumbents)	Senior Executive Service
16 Special Assistants	GS 14–15
71 Confidential Assistants	GS 11–15
8 Executive Assistants	Senior Executive Service and GS–15
48 State Executive Directors	GS-15
46 State Directors	GS-15
9 Deputy Undersecretaries	Senior Executive Service

DEPARTMENT OF COMMERCE

Secretary	Level I
Deputy Secretary	Level II
5 Undersecretaries	Level III
10 Assistant Secretaries	Level IV
General Counsel	Level IV
Inspector General	Level IV
2 Directors	Level IV
Deputy Assistant Secretary	Level V
2 Assistant Commissioners	Level V
40 Executive Assistants and Special Assistants	GS 13–15
24 Directors	GS 14–15 and Senior Executive Service
3 Deputy Directors	GS–15

DEPARTMENT OF DEFENSE

Office of the Secretary

Secretary	Level I
Deputy Secretary	Level II

5 Undersecretaries	Levels II and III
2 Principal Deputy Undersecretaries	Levels II and III
2 Directors	Level IV
9 Assistant Secretaries	Level IV
General Counsel	Level IV
Inspector General	Level IV
12 Special Assistants	Senior Executive Service
20 Directors	Senior Executive Service

Department of the Air Force

Secretary	Level II
Undersecretary	Level IV
3 Assistant Secretaries	Level IV
General Counsel	Level IV
Principal Deputy Assistant Secretary	Senior Executive Service
3 Deputy Assistant Secretaries	Senior Executive Service
Director	Senior Executive Service

Department of the Army

Secretary	Level II
Undersecretary	Level IV
5 Assistant Secretaries	Level IV
General Counsel	Level IV
3 Principal Deputies	Senior Executive Service
4 Directors	Senior Executive Service

Department of the Navy

Secretary	Level II
Undersecretary	Level IV
4 Assistant Secretaries	Level IV
General Counsel	Level IV
4 Deputy Assistant Secretaries	Senior Executive Service

DEPARTMENT OF EDUCATION

Secretary	Level I
Undersecretary	Level IV
8 Assistant Secretaries	Level IV
Inspector General	Level IV
General Counsel	Level IV
27 Special Assistants and Executive Assistants	GS–15

HEALTH AND HUMAN SERVICES

Secretary	Level I
Deputy Secretary	Level II
3 Assistant Secretaries	Level IV
3 Commissioners	Levels IV and V
Inspector General	Level IV
General Counsel	Level IV
2 Administrators	Level IV
2 Directors	Levels IV and V
8 Regional Directors	Senior Executive Service
9 Deputy Assistant Secretaries	Senior Executive Service

DEPARTMENT OF HOUSING AND URBAN DEVELOPMENT

Secretary	Level I
Deputy Secretary	Level II
Director	Level II
6 Assistant Secretaries	Level IV
Chief Financial Officer	Level IV
General Counsel	Level IV
Inspector General	Level IV

DEPARTMENT OF THE INTERIOR

Secretary	Level I
Deputy Secretary	Level II
Inspector General	Level IV
Special Trustee (American Indians)	Level II
Solicitor	Level IV
5 Assistant Secretaries	Level IV
3 Directors	Level V
Commissioner (Bureau of Reclamation)	Level V
Chairman, National Indian Gaming Commission	Level IV
2 Associate Members of that Commission	Level V
6 Special Assistants	Senior Executive Service

DEPARTMENT OF JUSTICE

Attorney General	Level I
Director FBI	Level II
Deputy Attorney General	Level II
Associate Attorney General	Level III
Inspector General	Level IV
10 Assistant Attorney Generals	Level IV
83 U.S. Attorneys	
88 U.S. Marshals	
5 U.S. Parole Commission Members	Levels IV and V
6 Directors and Administrators	Level IV
Commissioner	Level IV

DEPARTMENT OF LABOR

Secretary	Level I
Deputy Secretary	Level II
3 Assistant Secretaries	Level IV
Inspector General	Level IV
Administrator	Level V
Commissioner, Labor Statistics	Level V
Chief Finanacial Officer	Level IV
11 Deputy Assistant Secretaries	Senior Executive Service
2 Special Assistants	Senior Executive Service

DEPARTMENT OF STATE

Secretary	Level I
Deputy Secretary	Level II
Ambassador-at-Large	Level IV
Chief of Protocol	Level IV
19 Assistant Secretaries	Level IV
Inspector General	Level IV
5 Undersecretaries	Level III
Chief Financial Officer	Level IV

DEPARTMENT OF TRANSPORTATION

Secretary	Level I
Deputy Secretary	Level II
Assistant Deputy Secretary	Level V
4 Assistant Secretaries	Level IV
General Counsel	Level IV
Inspector General	Level IV
2 Administrators	Level II
6 Administrators	Levels III and IV
Deputy Administrator	Level IV
Director	Level V

DEPARTMENT OF TREASURY

Secretary	Level I
Deputy Secretary	Level II
Inspector General	Level IV
General Counsel	Level IV
3 Undersecretaries	Level III
8 Assistant Secretaries	Level IV
Commissioner of Customs	Level IV
Comptroller of the Currency	Level III
Commissioner of the IRS	Level III
Chief Counsel, IRS	Level V
15 Deputy Assistant Secretaries	Senior Executive Service

DEPARTMENT OF VETERANS' AFFAIRS

Secretary	Level I
Deputy Secretary	Level II
Inspector General	Level IV
Chairman, Board of Veterans' Appeals	Level IV
General Counsel	Level IV
5 Assistant Secretaries	Level IV
2 Undersecretaries	Level III
Deputy Undersecretary	Level IV

Independent Agencies—Selected

APPALACHIAN REGIONAL COMMISSION

Federal Chairman	Level III
Alternate Chairman	Level V

CENTRAL INTELLIGENCE AGENCY

Director	Level II
Deputy Director	Level III
Statutory Inspector General	Level IV

COMMODITY FUTURES TRADING COMMISSION

Chairman	Level III
4 Commissioners	Level IV

CONSUMER PRODUCT SAFETY COMMISSION

Chairman	Level III
2 Commissioners	Level IV

DEFENSE NUCLEAR FACILITIES SAFETY BOARD

Chairman	Level III
Vice-Chairman	Level III
3 Members	Level III

ENVIRONMENTAL PROTECTION AGENCY

Administrator	Level II
Deputy Administrator	Level III
8 Assistant Administrators	Level IV
General Counsel	Level IV
Inspector General	Level I
3 Associate Administrators	Senior Executive Service
8 Regional Administrators	Senior Executive Service

EQUAL EMPLOYMENT OPPORTUNITY COMMISSION

Chairman	Level III
Vice-Chairman	Level IV
2 Members	Level IV

EXPORT-IMPORT BANK OF THE UNITED STATES

President	Level III
First Vice-President	Level IV
3 Board Members	Level IV

FARM CREDIT ADMINISTRATION

Chairman	Level III
2 Members	Level IV
Federal Communications Commission	
Chairman	Level III
3 Commissioners	Level IV

FEDERAL DEPOSIT INSURANCE CORPORATION

Chairman	Level III
Deputy to the Chairman for Policy	Level IV
Director, Office of Corporate Communication	Level III
Director	Level IV
Inspector General	Level IV
General Counsel	Level IV

FEDERAL ELECTION COMMISSION

Chairman	Level IV
Vice-Chairman	Level IV
3 Members	Level IV

FEDERAL EMERGENCY MANAGEMENT AGENCY

Director	Level II
Deputy Director	Level IV
Associate Director	Level IV
Administrator	Level IV
Inspector General	Level IV
General Counsel	Senior Executive Service
2 Directors	Senior Executive Service
2 Deputy Assistant Associate Directors	Senior Executive Service
10 Regional Directors	Senior Executive Service

FEDERAL ENERGY REGULATORY COMMISSION

Chairman	Level III
4 Members	Level IV
General Counsel	Senior Executive Service

FEDERAL LABOR RELATIONS AUTHORITY

Chairman	Level IV
2 Members	Level V
General Counsel	Level V

FEDERAL MARITIME COMMISSION

Chairman	Level III
4 Members	Level IV

FEDERAL MEDIATION AND CONCILIATION SERVICE

Director	Level III

FEDERAL MINE SAFETY AND HEALTH REVIEW COMMISSION

Chairman	Level III
2 Member	Level IV
3 Attorney-Advisors	GS-15

FEDERAL TRADE COMMISSION

Chairman	Level III
4 Members	Level IV
4 Directors	Senior Executive Service
3 Assistant Directors	Senior Executive Service
Associate Director	Senior Executive Service
General Counsel	Senior Executive Service

GENERAL SERVICES ADMINISTRATION

Administrator	Level III
Inspector General	Level IV
6 Associate Administrators	Senior Executive Service
7 Regional Administrators	Senior Executive Service

INTER-AMERICAN FOUNDATION

President	Level IV

MERIT SYSTEMS PROTECTION BOARD

Chairman	Level III
Vice-Chairman	Level IV
Member	Level IV
Chief Counsel to the Chairman	Senior Executive Service
Director, Office of Appeals	Senior Executive Service
Chief of Staff	Senior Executive Service

NATIONAL AERONAUTICS AND SPACE ADMINISTRATION

Administrator	Level II
Inspector General	Level IV
2 Associate Administrators	Senior Executive Service
Chief Financial Officer	Senior Executive Service

NATIONAL ARCHIVES AND RECORDS ADMINISTRATION

Archivist of United States	Level III
Presidential Diarist	Senior Executive Service
3 Presidential Library Directors	Senior Executive Service

NATIONAL CREDIT UNION ADMINISTRATION

2 Chairmen	Level III
Vice-Chairman	Level IV
Member	Level IV

NATIONAL FOUNDATION ON THE ARTS AND HUMANITIES

Chairman, Humanities	Level III
Director, Museum Services	Level IV
2 Deputy Chairmen	Senior Executive Service

NATIONAL LABOR RELATIONS BOARD

Chairman	Level III
3 Members	Level IV
General Counsel	Level IV

NATIONAL MEDIATION BOARD

Chairman	Level III
2 Members	Level IV

NATIONAL SCIENCE FOUNDATION

Director	Level II
Deputy Director	Level III

NATIONAL TRANSPORTATION SAFETY BOARD

Chairman	Level III
Vice-Chairman	Level IV
3 Members	Level IV

NUCLEAR REGULATORY COMMISSION

Chairman	Level II
4 Commissioners	Level III
Inspector General	Level IV
Chief of Staff	Senior Executive Service

OCCUPATIONAL SAFETY AND HEALTH REVIEW COMMISSION

Chairman	Level III
2 Commissioners	Level IV

OFFICE OF GOVERNMENT ETHICS

Director	Level III

OFFICE OF NAVAJO AND HOPI RELOCATION

Commissioner	Level IV

OFFICE OF PERSONNEL MANAGEMENT

Director	Level II
Deputy Director	Level III
Inspector General	Level IV
Counselor to the Director	Senior Executive Service
Chief of Staff	Senior Executive Service
General Counsel	Senior Executive Service
Director	Senior Executive Service

OFFICE OF SPECIAL COUNSEL

Special Counsel	Level IV

PANAMA CANAL COMMISSION

Administrator	Level IV
Deputy Administrator	Level IV
8 Board of Directors Members	Level V

PEACE CORPS

Director   Level III
Deputy Director   Level IV

POSTAL RATE COMMISSION

Chairman   Level III
3 Commissioners   Level IV

SECURITIES AND EXCHANGE COMMISSION

Chairman   Level III
3 Commissioners   Level IV

SELECTIVE SERVICE SYSTEM

Director   Level IV

SMALL BUSINESS ADMINISTRATION

Administrator   Level III
Deputy Administrator   Level IV
Chief Counsel for Advocacy   Level IV
Inspector General   Level IV

SOCIAL SECURITY ADMINISTRATION

Commissioner   Level I
Deputy Commissioner   Level II
Inspector General   Level IV

TENNESSEE VALLEY AUTHORITY

Chairman   Level III
2 Board Members   Level IV

U.S. ARMS CONTROL AND DISARMAMENT AGENCY

Director	Level II
Deputy Director	Level III
Chief Science Advisor	Level IV
2 Assistant Directors	Level IV

U.S. INFORMATION AGENCY

Director	Level II
Deputy Director	Level III
3 Associate Directors	Level IV
General Counsel	Senior Executive Service

U.S. INSTITUTE OF PEACE

President	$141,000
Executive Vice-President	$133,600
Vice President, Finance and Management	$133,600
Director, Research and Studies	$110,000
Director, Office of Administration	$ 95,531
Director, Grants Program	$ 95,517
Director, Fellowship Program	$ 90,632
Director, Education and Training Program	$ 90,232
Director, Religion and Human Rights	$ 85,801
Director, Communications	$ 83,284
Director, Publications	$ 79,134
Director, Library	$ 77,052
Senior Scholar	$ 73,486

U.S. INTERNATIONAL DEVELOPMENT COOPERATION AGENCY

Director (Administrator)	Level II
Deputy Director	Level III
Inspector General	Level IV
7 Assistant Administrators	Level IV

OVERSEAS PRIVATE INVESTMENT CORPORATION

President	Level III
8 Board Members	Level IV

U.S. INTERNATIONAL TRADE COMMISSION

Chairman	Level III
Vice-Chairman	Level IV
4 Commissioners	Level IV
4 Staff Assistants (Legal)	GS-15

Executive Office of the President

OFFICE OF MANAGEMENT AND BUDGET

Director	Level I
2 Deputy Directors	Level II
Comptroller	Level III
2 Administrators	Level III

COUNCIL OF ECONOMIC ADVISORS

Chairman	Level II
Council Member	Level IV

COUNCIL OF ENVIRONMENTAL QUALITY

Chairman	Level II
2 Members	Level IV

OFFICE OF THE U.S. TRADE REPRESENTATIVE

U.S. Trade Representative	Level I
3 Deputy Trade Representatives	Level III

OFFICE OF SCIENCE AND TECHNOLOGY POLICY

Director	Level II
4 Associate Directors	Level III
2 Deputy Directors	GS-15
Special Assistant	GS-15

OFFICE OF NATIONAL DRUG CONTROL POLICY

Director	Level I
Chief of Press Relations	GS-15

EXECUTIVE OFFICE OF THE PRESIDENT

The growth in the power of the presidency can be seen very clearly in both the size and the nature of the executive staff. There are about four hundred full-time civilian employees in the White House. This includes everyone from gardeners, domestics, and telephone operators to press secretaries, deputy secretaries, and special assistants. All of the lower-level jobs are paid under the General Schedule. By law, the president's staff may not have more than twenty-five people at Level II; twenty-five people at Level III; and fifty people at the GS-18 level. (See previous section, "Plum Jobs," for some specific jobs.)

Perks of the Presidency

The president receives an annual salary of $200,000, from which all private living costs must be paid. But the perks of office insure that the president rarely has to open his wallet. Indeed, George Bush occasionally forgot to carry cash during his tenure and had to have aides pay for his personal purchases, reimbursing them later. A staff of about one hundred attends to the first family's every need. In addition to the usual assortment of butlers, maids, painters, carpenters, electricians, and plumbers, the president's staff includes five chefs, a phalanx of secret service agents, and a military nurse to give him a rubdown each night. The president receives free health care at Bethesda Naval Hospital, while members of his staff may utilize the free clinic at the White House for emergencies and minor ailments. When the president travels, he has at his disposal a total of twenty-three aircraft, including Marine helicopters and two Boeing 747s; local transportation is provided by two armored limousines costing $600,000 each. And of course the nation's highest office comes with two palatial residences: the White House in Washington (which has an annual operating budget of $7.2 million), and the Camp David retreat in Maryland's Catoctin Mountains (just a free helicopter ride away).

In recent years, the most enriching aspect of the presidency has become the memoirs that are nearly de rigueur. Ronald Reagan, for example, negotiated a deal for an estimated $6 million for two books on his presidency. Reagan earned an additional $2 million simply by delivering two twenty-minute speeches to a Japanese media company after his presidency.

The office of the vice-president, though much derided, is not without its own set of perks. The second-in-command receives $171,500 annually and is allowed to reside rent-free at the sixteen-room Admiral's House on grounds adjacent to the Naval Observatory. The budget for the house is $285,000, including $75,000 for entertainment. In addition, the vice-president has a staff of seventy, with an annual budget of $2.1 million.

NATIONAL SPACE COUNCIL

Executive Secretary	Level II

OFFICE OF NATIONAL DRUG CONTROL POLICY

Director	Level I
2 Deputy Directors	Level III
1 Associate Director	Level IV

MEMBERS OF CONGRESS AND THEIR STAFFS

Senate

President pro tempore, majority and minority leaders	$148,400
Expense allowance	10,000
Senators	133,600
Expense allowance for majority and minority whips	5,000
Expense allowance for chairmen of majority and minority conference committees	3,000

House of Representatives

Speaker of the House	$171,500
Expense allowance	25,000
Majority and minority leaders	148,400

Expense allowance $ 10,000
435 Representatives   133,600
Expense allowance for majority and minority whips   5,000

In addition to these direct salaries, members of Congress for years earned many times their salaries in honoraria for speaking engagements, often before political action committees (PACs) seeking to influence national policy. But faced with mounting opposition to these honoraria, the House in 1991 voted to ban its members from accepting speaking fees (in exchange for a substantial pay raise); the Senate followed suit a year later. In addition, since 1976, members of Congress have been subject to a 15 percent limit on earnings over and above their salaries. This limit does not, however, apply to unearned income from stocks and bonds.

The 1991–92 check-floating scandal at the House bank attracted unprecedented media and public attention on the perks of elected office. Some perks, such as the sergeant-at-arms who routinely fixed parking tickets for members of Congress, were abolished in the wake of the check scandal, as were the House bank and post office. But many others—like $5 haircuts, taxpayer-subsidized meals, and free airport parking—remain. An abbreviated list of the job-related and not-so-related benefits includes the following:

Pension: 401-K plan, optional civil service retirement.
Medical: Staff of doctors available for members at the Capitol.
Franking: Free mailing to constituents (this privilege is especially abused around reelection time, when incumbents flood their constituents' mailboxes with information to fend off political challengers).
Parking: Special tags allow parking at any curb space in Washington except fire hydrants, fire stations, and loading docks.
Decorations: Plants supplied by the U.S. Botanical Garden; two framed reproductions available from the National Gallery of Art on request.
Phone: Free long-distance calls via two WATS lines per member.
Exercise: Gym in Rayburn House Office Building; exercise rooms in Russell and Dirksen Senate office buildings.

Members of Congress also receive free office space with furnishings in Washington and at home, free printing service, and generous stationery allowances. Large amounts of money are allocated for keeping members in touch with their constituents. Members of the House make an average of twenty-six trips to their home areas; senators make an average of forty. House members receive an average expense allowance of $176,000 for maintaining contact with their home districts (the actual amount depends on each member's travel distance to and from Washington and the price of office space in the member's home district). Senators' expense allowances range from

$44,000 to $200,000. Special allowances also exist for traveling abroad on government business, a chore some lame-duck members have found especially necessary in the months after they were defeated for reelection.

The most important benefit of all, finally, is the allowance every member of Congress receives to hire and maintain a personal staff to assist with everything from filing, typing, and speechwriting to hosting parties, dealing with the media, and shaping legislation. Each member of the House of Representatives may employ a maximum of twenty-two people at a total cost not to exceed $515,760. Senators may employ as many people as they wish, but also under strictly controlled limitations based on state populations. For example, senators representing California receive $1,764,000, while senators from the least populous states receive $814,000. Senators also receive an allowance of $280,000 for three employees to work on committees.

Despite this impressive array of pay and perquisites, congressional salaries and benefits have been long regarded as short-term rewards. Many of the rewards of Congressional service are realized, as they are with the presidency, after the congressman or senator leaves office. The power and prestige of national office almost always enables members to build lucrative law practices, to serve as officers of corporations, and to earn large fees for speaking engagements.

THE FEDERAL JUDICIARY

Judges

	Salary 1992	Salary 1998
Chief Justice of the United States	$166,200	$171,500
Associate Justices of the Supreme Court	159,000	164,100
United States Circuit Judges	137,300	141,700
United States District Judges	129,500	133,600
Judges, Court of International Trade	129,500	133,600
Judges, United States Claims Court	129,500	133,600
United States Bankruptcy Judges	119,140	123,000
United States Magistrates (full-time)	119,140	123,000

All federal judges are also allowed a personal staff consisting of secretaries and law clerks. These people are paid under the Judicial Salary Plan, which is roughly equivalent to the General Schedule. The salary range for career law clerks is $26,798 to $70,987. Most one-year law clerks are hired at a grade of GS 11-1, or $33,623 in 1994. All twenty-four law clerks working for Supreme Court justices earn $31,619.

Judicial Offices: Administrative Office of U.S. Courts

Director	$129,500	$133,600
Deputy Director	119,140	123,000

Federal Judicial Center

Director	$129,500	$133,600
Deputy Director	119,140	123,000

How to Find a Job
in the Federal Government

The government of the United States employs slightly less than 3 million civilians, so it should not be surprising that there are literally thousands of job openings all the time and in many parts of the country as well as overseas. In 1996 more than 500,000 people found jobs in the federal government, jobs spanning the entire employment spectrum from professional (the government employs over 25,000 lawyers, and more than 40,000 accountants), technical (there are over 100,000 engineers and 49,000 computer specialists), and clerical (there are over 100,000 secretaries) to almost every kind of blue-collar occupation (over 15,000 aircraft mechanics, 10,000 pipefitters, and 23,000 warehouse workers are among those employed as of 1992).

So, yes, federal jobs are plentiful, but finding one can require arduous searching so it's important to overcome some common prejudices. The prospect of a "government job" has rather negative connotations for some people who conjure up images of an insurmountable bureaucracy and employees lost under stacks of paper. Opportunities in the federal government can, however, far exceed these expectations. Salaries are not quite commensurate with similar positions in private corporations, but job security and excellent benefits are also strong incentives. The government continues to be an important employer of minorities, offering and enforcing equal opportunity programs that are often sidestepped in the private sector.

A trip to one of the forty-four Offices of Personnel Management Federal Job Information Centers (FJIC) can be daunting for any prospective federal employee. Posted in these offices are the semimonthly Federal Job Opportunities Listings. Published on the first and sixteenth of every month, these are long lists of current federal job vacancies, although they are by no means complete.

The first list, *GPA 001*, contains the jobs in the region where the Federal Job Information Center is located; the second list, *Nationwide*, gives federal job opportunities anywhere in the nation or the world. These lists can also be requested through the mail by writing to the FJIC in a particular location. The positions available can range from unskilled worker to nuclear physicist and run the gamut on the General Salary Schedule.

As a guide through the application procedure, the code and control numbers for each position are included on the Opportunities Listings. Each position also has a Qualifications Information Statement (QIS), which gives the required skills, education, and experience necessary for each opening. Applications and QIS statements can be obtained at the FJIC window or by written request. These job centers may also have federal personnel manuals and other reference books on hand.

As incongruous as it may seem, the federal government does not keep a list of *all* federal jobs currently available. Many agencies of the federal government have direct-hire authority and will fill positions rapidly instead of going through the FJIC. To be aware of agency openings you must keep in contact with those agencies that are of interest to you. In recent years, for example, the Central Intelligence Agency (CIA) has been actively recruiting economists, among other specialists, on many college campuses.

There are two privately run publications that can be very helpful. *Federal Jobs Digest,* a biweekly newspaper, tracks federal job vacancies, lists U.S. Postal Exams, and has articles about job fairs, a "College Corner," and veterans' information. Each issue contains an average of approximately 3,000 jobs (Phone: 1-800-824-5000). *Federal Career Opportunities* is a similar publication concentrating on the G-5 level and above. It also catalogs federal job openings in a systematic manner (Phone: 1-800-822-5627). Both publications are also available at most major libraries.

JOBS FOR COLLEGE GRADUATES

In November 1990, the federal government began a new program to attract college graduates into civil service jobs. The Administrative Careers, with America (ACWA) program encompasses 100 types of entry-level jobs that are on the GS-5 to GS-7 levels of the General Schedule (salaries range from $19,969 to $32,150 per annum). The positions are divided into six occupational groups:

1. Benefits Review, Tax, and Legal
2. Business, Finance, and Management
3. Law Enforcement and Investigation
4. Personnel, Administration, and Computers
5. Health, Safety, and Environmental Occupations
6. Writing and Public Information

To be eligible for this program, the applicant must have a bachelor's degree (or expect to receive one within eight months) or a minimum of three years of work experience. A combination of education and experience is also acceptable. There is a written test for each of the six occupational groups. Each test is administered periodically across the nation. After passing the test, the candidate's name is placed on a list from which agencies with vacancies select. A series of interviews are then conducted by the specific agency.

To apply for Administrative Careers with America, first obtain a copy of the Qualifications Information Statement (QIS) for one of the six occupational groups. These can be obtained from any Federal Job Information Center located across the country and can be requested by mail.

Jobs and Salaries
in State and Local Government

In the first part of this section will be found the salaries for thousands of leading state and local government leaders—the management team, so to speak, of the political system. Included are governors, mayors, district attorneys, state judges, police and fire chiefs, and commissioners of everything from aviation and sanitation to budgets and zoos. There is a listing for every state and for an array of major cities and counties, and even a sprinkling of data from small towns and villages.

Whether the reader peruses this information or merely skims over each part, he or she will be struck by the incredible diversity of salary levels throughout the country. Some patterns can be seen. For instance, large states and cities usually pay their officials better than small ones do, and the salaries of officials in large cities are usually comparable to those in their state government. But to explain why salaries of officials in Texas are so high when their public employees are paid so low, or why Tennessee and South Carolina have such well-paid officials when they rank near the bottom among all states in per capita income is beyond the scope of this book.

Readers should keep in mind, however, that just as the pressure for higher executive salaries in the private sector comes from within, so it is with politicians. If the voters express concern, the reason most often cited for a pay raise is that other officials in the same job elsewhere are getting more money. Another tactic is for the governor or mayor to take the lead in a propaganda campaign aimed at convincing the voters that pay raises are needed at the executive level in order to attract highly talented people into government. Sometimes the question never becomes an issue. On the state level, for example, pay raises for executives are frequently tied to increases for legislators, so bipartisan support is easily achieved.

None of the above is meant to imply that most government officials are currently overpaid, nor does it mean they shouldn't receive salary adjustments for inflation. There is, of course, the age-old argument that government service should be just that, service—not a means to a substantial income. After all, anyone in government getting paid $100,000 a year or more is earning double the median family income for the entire nation. And, finally, it is imperative for the people to remember that most elected officials are only politicians, not experts in finance, technology, or administration, and their earnings should reflect this.

THE FIFTY STATES

In the following pages can be found the 1997–98 salaries for almost every elected and many appointed officials in every state of the union, including all judges who fall under state jurisdiction. Expense allowances are noted whenever they are a significant part of the remuneration, but not every perquisite has been included. All governors, for example, have cars, most have private planes, and about half have private helicopters. In addition, governors of all but five states (Arkansas, Idaho, Massachusetts, Rhode Island, and Vermont) have fully staffed private residences. (The governor of California's residence is paid for by a private nonprofit foundation). The reader should assume that all government officials receive some kind of travel and food benefits.

Most browsers in this section will notice right away that the highest salaries are, quite predictably, paid in the largest, wealthiest states (California, New York, Texas) or heavily industrialized ones (Michigan, Ohio), while small states (Delaware, Rhode Island), or sparsely settled ones (the Dakotas) and impoverished areas (Maine, Mississippi) pay substantially less. Of course Alaska has special requirements, so just about everyone there earns at least $70,000.

Note that the salaries of some important state administrators (Education, Personnel, etc.) also appear in other sections of the book. Check the Index for references. The major source of all state figures is *The Book of the States, 1997/98,* published by the Council of State Governments.

ALABAMA

Governor	$87,643	*Judges*	
Lieutenant Governor	90,720	Supreme Court	$115,695
Secretary of State	61,780	Court of Criminal	
Attorney General	115,695	Appeals	114,615
Treasurer	61,780	Court of Civil Appeals	114,615
		Circuit Courts	80,615

Legislature: 140 members each receive $10 a day, $2,280 a month, plus $50 three times a week for committee meetings. The Speaker of the House receives an additional $2 a day.

Selected Administrative Officials

Administration	$ 65,958	Budget	$65,958
Agriculture	61,350	Commerce	96,592
Banking	135,000	Community Affairs	65,958

Consumer Affairs	$ 50,076	Insurance	$ 65,958
Corrections	79,000	Labor	65,958
Education	130,000	Natural Resources	65,958
Elections	31,048	Parks and Recreation	50,076
Employment Services	50,076	Personnel	106,407
Energy	65,016	Public Utility Regulation	75,000
Environmental Protection	104,500	Purchasing	53,976
General Services	46,436	Solid Waste Management	50,076
Health	160,745	Tourism	65,958
Highways	65,958	Transportation	65,958
Historic Preservation	69,660		

ALASKA

Governor	$81,648	*Judges*	
Lieutenant Governor	76,176	Supreme Court	$111,552
Attorney General	83,292	Court of Appeals	105,384
		Superior Court	103,152

Legislature: 60 members receive $24,012 each, plus $168 for expenses. The president of the Senate and the Speaker of the House each receive an additional $500 a year.

Selected Administrative Officials

Administration	$86,292	Highways	$83,124
Banking	92,844	Historic Preservation	67,488
Budget	86,292	Insurance	83,124
Civil Rights	86,244	Labor	86,292
Community Affairs	86,292	Licensing	74,592
Consumer Affairs	62,784	Natural Resources	86,292
Corrections	86,292	Parks and Recreation	74,592
Education	86,292	Personnel	80,244
Elections	83,124	Public Utility Regulation	83,124
Employment Services	80,244	Purchasing	89,484
Energy	74,592	Social Services	86,292
Environmental Protection	86,292	Solid Waste Management	67,488
General Services	89,484	Tourism	74,592
Health	92,448	Transportation	86,292

ARIZONA

Governor	$75,000	*Judges*	
Secretary of State	54,600	Supreme Court	$114,257
Attorney General	76,440	Court of Appeals	111,536
Treasurer	54,600	Superior Courts	108,816

Legislature: 90 members receive $15,000 each, plus expenses of $35 a day for the first 120 days of regular session and $10 a day thereafter. (Members outside Maricopa County receive an additional $25 and $10, respectively.)

Selected Administrative Officials

Administration	$114,130	Highways	$96,574
Agriculture	87,125	Historic Preservation	52,826
Banking	87,000	Insurance	105,530
Budget	93,500	Labor	101,345
Civil Rights	98,061	Natural Resources	62,803
Commerce	104,520	Parks and Recreation	90,476
Consumer Affairs	90,000	Personnel	62,400
Corrections	117,875	Public Utility Regulation	77,250
Education	54,600	Purchasing	77,576
Employment Services	83,659	Social Services	113,302
Energy	104,520	Solid Waste Management	80,771
Environmental Protection	112,600	Tourism	87,849
General Services	85,000	Transportation	110,301
Health	117,500		

ARKANSAS

Governor	$65,182	*Judges*	
Lieutenant Governor	31,505	Supreme Court	$108,883
Secretary of State	40,739	Court of Appeals	105,440
Attorney General	54,318	Chancery Courts	101,990
Treasurer	40,739	Circuit Courts	93,702

Legislature: 135 members receive $12,500 each, plus $95 a day for expenses. The president pro tem of the Senate and the Speaker of the House each receive an additional $14,000 a year.

Selected Administrative Officials

Administration	$101,665	Historic Preservation	$54,872
Agriculture	68,438	Insurance	85,000
Banking	90,602	Labor	83,676
Budget	76,790	Natural Resources	65,453
Corrections	97,225	Parks and Recreation	77,538
Education	100,213	Personnel	76,790
Employment Services	95,995	Public Utility Regulation	82,263
Energy	77,621	Purchasing	71,640
Environmental Protection	84,615	Social Services	105,301
General Services	83,485	Solid Waste Management	66,234
Health	144,909	Tourism	56,521
Highways	109,824	Transportation	109,824

CALIFORNIA

Governor	$114,286	*Judges*	
Lieutenant Governor	94,500	Supreme Court	$131,085
Secretary of State	94,500	Courts of Appeals	122,893
Attorney General	107,100	Superior Court	107,390
Treasurer	94,500		

Legislature: 120 members receive $75,600 each, plus $110 a day for expenses. The president pro tem of the Senate and the Speaker of the House each receive $90,720; the Senate majority leader and House majority and minority leaders each receive $83,160.

Selected Administrative Officials

Agriculture	$115,083	Health	$107,939
Banking	107,939	Highways	80,820
Budget	115,083	Historic Preservation	71,340
Civil Rights	95,239	Insurance	95,052
Commerce	115,083	Natural Resources	115,083
Community Affairs	82,164	Parks and Recreation	107,939
Consumer Affairs	107,939	Personnel	107,939
Corrections	115,083	Public Utility Regulation	103,178
Education	107,100	Purchasing	107,939
Employment Services	98,652	Social Services	107,939
Energy	103,178	Solid Waste Management	103,178
Environmental Protection	115,083	Tourism	93,096
General Services	107,939	Transportation	107,951

COLORADO

		Judges	
Governor	$70,000		
Lieutenant Governor	48,500	Supreme Court	$94,000
Secretary of State	48,500	Court of Appeals	89,500
Attorney General	60,000	District Courts	85,000
Treasurer	48,500		

Legislature: 100 members receive $17,500 each, plus $45 for expenses ($99 for members outside Denver metro area).

Selected Administrative Officials

Administration	$96,640	Highways	$95,640
Agriculture	115,083	Historic Preservation	70,008
Banking	107,939	Insurance	91,500
Budget	115,083	Labor	95,640
Civil Rights	82,260	Licensing	95,640
Community Affairs	81,160	Natural Resources	98,000
Consumer Affairs	76,296	Parks and Recreation	91,020
Corrections	95,640	Personnel	95,640
Education	120,000	Public Utility Regulation	76,992
Elections	55,680	Purchasing	84,660
Energy	75,000	Social Services	93,300
Environmental Protection	84,060	Solid Waste Management	82,260
Health	95,640	Transportation	95,640

CONNECTICUT

		Judges	
Governor	$78,000		
Lieutenant Governor	55,000	Supreme Court	$117,610
Secretary of State	50,000	Appellate Court	109,359
Attorney General	60,000	Superior Courts	104,469
Treasurer	50,000		

Legislature: 187 members receive $16,760 each. The president pro tem of the Senate and the Speaker of the House each receive an additional $6,400 a year; majority and minority leaders in both houses receive an additional $5,290. The Speaker pro tem receives an additional $3,860, and assistant leaders in both houses receive additional amounts ranging from $2,540 to $3,860 per year.

Selected Administrative Officials

Administration	$84,000	Highways	$83,500
Agriculture	64,000	Historic Preservation	63,087
Banking	64,000	Insurance	87,000
Budget	94,763	Labor	83,500
Civil Rights	64,000	Licensing	75,500
Community Affairs	72,000	Natural Resources	96,317
Consumer Affairs	64,000	Parks and Recreation	96,583
Corrections	89,000	Personnel	90,420
Education	84,000	Public Utility Regulation	103,360
Elections	61,642	Purchasing	60,000
Employment Services	64,000	Social Services	95,000
Energy	64,000	Solid Waste Management	95,954
Environmental Protection	72,000	Tourism	92,505
General Services	95,000	Transportation	107,586
Health	95,000		

DELAWARE

Governor	$107,000	*Judges*	
Lieutenant Governor	44,600	Supreme Court	$121,200
Secretary of State	89,900	Superior Courts	115,300
Attorney General	99,100		
Treasurer	79,700		

Legislature: 62 members receive $27,500 each, plus $6,500 per annum for expenses. The president pro tem of the Senate and the Speaker of the House each receive an additional $11,254 per year; majority and minority leaders in both houses earn an additional $8,765 per year.

Selected Administrative Officials

Administration	$ 83,800	Health	$124,100
Agriculture	83,800	Highways	89,900
Banking	83,400	Historic Preservation	68,800
Budget	96,300	Insurance	76,200
Civil Rights	54,500	Labor	83,800
Consumer Affairs	66,700	Natural Resources	89,900
Corrections	89,900	Parks and Recreation	73,900
Education	113,700	Personnel	89,900
Elections	50,500	Public Utility Regulation	67,600
Energy	38,646	Purchasing	62,200

Social Services	96,300	Tourism	58,734
Solid Waste Management	113,600	Transportation	89,900

FLORIDA

Governor	$107,961	*Judges*	
Lieutenant Governor	103,415	Supreme Court	$137,314
Secretary of State	106,870	District Court of Appeals	123,583
Attorney General	106,461	Circuit Courts	110,754
Treasurer	106,870		

Legislature: 160 members receive $24,912 each, plus $102 a day for expenses (not to exceed $3,000 for 1997). The president pro tem of the Senate and Speaker of the House each receive an additional $9,672 per year.

Selected Administrative Officials

Administration	$101,143	Health	$130,000
Agriculture	106,460	Highways	104,500
Budget	105,029	Historic Preservation	75,732
Civil Rights	50,933	Labor	108,223
Community Affairs	101,143	Parks and Recreation	84,496
Consumer Affairs	66,837	Personnel	84,549
Corrections	108,004	Public Utility Regulation	105,987
Education	106,870	Purchasing	85,951
Elections	70,448	Social Services	101,143
Employment Services	88,580	Solid Waste Management	74,244
Energy	82,782	Tourism	74,160
Environmental Protection	101,143	Transportation	101,485
General Services	101,143		

GEORGIA

Governor	$111,480	*Judges*	
Lieutenant Governor	72,812	Supreme Court	$120,000
Secretary of State	89,538	Court of Appeals	119,246
Attorney General	102,211	Superior Courts	86,125
Treasurer	96,804		

Legislature: 236 members receive $11,347.80 each, plus $59 for expenses ($3,000 per diem differential account with a maximum of 50 days). The Speaker of the House receives $52,260.80 per year, total salary. The Senate president pro tem and Speaker pro tem each receive an additional $4,800 per year; majority and minority leaders in both houses receive an additional $2,400 per year.

Selected Administrative Officials

Administration	$86,814	Historic Preservation	$ 79,404
Agriculture	89,545	Insurance	89,508
Banking	86,835	Labor	89,537
Budget	109,020	Licensing	81,798
Civil Rights	73,183	Natural Resources	98,256
Commerce	103,764	Parks and Recreation	79,014
Community Affairs	103,764	Personnel	100,242
Consumer Affairs	87,768	Public Utility Regulation	86,184
Corrections	86,832	Purchasing	67,782
Education	91,578	Social Services	89,424
Elections	75,204	Solid Waste Management	74,832
Employment Services	77,850	Tourism	95,376
Environmental Protection	99,234	Transportation	150,000
Health	135,570		

HAWAII

Governor	$94,780	*Judges*	
Lieutenant Governor	90,041	Supreme Court	$93,780
Attorney General	85,302	Intermediate Court	89,780
		Circuit Courts	86,780

Legislature: 76 members receive $32,000 each, plus expenses of $80 for members living outside Oahu; $10 a day for members on Oahu. The president of the Senate and the Speaker of the House each receive an additional $5,000 per year.

Selected Administrative Officials

Agriculture	$85,302	Elections	$77,966
Banking	74,655	Employment Services	72,444
Budget	85,302	Energy	90,624
Civil Rights	75,000	Environmental Protection	76,404
Commerce	85,302	Health	85,302
Community Affairs	74,800	Highways	82,932
Consumer Affairs	65,700	Insurance	72,886
Corrections	85,302	Labor	85,302
Education	90,041	Natural Resources	85,302

Parks and Recreation	$71,352	Social Services	$85,302
Personnel	85,302	Solid Waste Management	71,160
Public Utility Regulation	77,964	Transportation	85,302
Purchasing	77,964		

IDAHO

Governor	$85,000	*Judges*	
Lieutenant Governor	22,500	Supreme Court	$86,468
Secretary of State	67,500	Court of Appeals	85,468
Attorney General	75,000	District Courts	81,043
Treasurer	67,500		

Legislature: 105 members receive $12,360 each, plus $75 for expenses ($40 for legislators with no second residence in Boise). The president pro tem of the Senate and the Speaker of the House each receive an additional $3,000 per year.

Selected Administrative Officials

Administration	$68,203	Highways	$101,566
Agriculture	72,009	Historic Preservation	55,993
Banking	73,008	Insurance	63,253
Civil Rights	50,565	Labor	69,992
Community Affairs	46,654	Licensing	44,491
Corrections	79,040	Parks and Recreation	78,728
Education	67,500	Personnel	73,528
Elections	68,390	Public Utility Regulation	69,992
Employment Services	69,992	Social Services	69,888
Energy	61,048	Solid Waste Management	54,143
Environmental Protection	76,502	Tourism	52,540
General Services	53,560	Transportation	101,566
Health	87,401		

ILLINOIS

Governor	$126,590	*Judges*	
Lieutenant Governor	89,357	Supreme Court	$126,579
Secretary of State	111,697	Appellate Court	119,133
Attorney General	111,697	Circuit Courts	101,876
Treasurer	96,804		

Legislature: 177 members receive $47,039 each, plus $82 for expenses. The president of the Senate, the Speaker of the House, and minority leaders in both houses each receive an additional $19,093 per year; the majority leader in the House receives an additional $16,109 per year. Assistant leaders receive additional amounts between $12,529 and $14,319 per year.

Selected Administrative Officials

Administration	$ 93,080	Highways	$96,346
Agriculture	89,357	Historic Preservation	79,780
Banking	92,636	Insurance	81,911
Budget	92,563	Labor	81,911
Civil Rights	77,444	Licensing	81,911
Commerce	89,357	Natural Resources	89,357
Corrections	104,369	Personnel	71,796
Education	149,203	Public Utility Regulation	95,629
Elections	86,760	Purchasing	64,932
Employment Service	96,804	Social Services	94,535
Environmental Protection	89,357	Solid Waste Management	85,224
Health	96,804	Transportation	96,804

INDIANA

Governor	$77,199	*Judges*	
Lieutenant Governor	64,000	Supreme Court	$115,000
Secretary of State	45,999	Court of Appeals	110,000
Attorney General	59,202	Circuit Courts	90,000
Treasurer	45,994	Superior Courts	90,000

Legislature: 150 members receive $11,600 each, plus $109 for expenses. The president pro tem of the Senate and the Speaker of the House each receive an additional $6,500 per year; majority and minority leaders receive an additional $5,000 per year. Supplements for assistant leaders range from $1,000 to $5,000 per year.

Selected Administrative Officials

Administration	$77,000	Budget	$73,673
Agriculture	63,617	Civil Rights	59,094
Banking	77,461	Community Affairs	46,752

Consumer Affairs	$ 69,545	Natural Resources	$77,000
Corrections	82,212	Parks and Recreation	57,872
Education	63,099	Personnel	73,467
Employment Services	78,522	Public Utility Regulation	75,309
Energy	48,249	Purchasing	53,362
Environmental Protection	77,000	Social Services	83,417
Health	100,103	Solid Waste Management	63,862
Insurance	64,490	Tourism	68,350
Labor	62,675	Transportation	80,080

IOWA

Governor	$101,313	*Judges*	
Lieutenant Governor	70,919	Supreme Court	$103,600
Secretary of State	80,524	Court of Appeals	99,600
Attorney General	94,485	District Courts	94,800
Treasurer	80,524		

Legislature: 150 members receive $20,120 each, plus $86 for expenses (Polk County members receive $65). The president of the Senate, Speaker of the House, and all majority and minority leaders receive an additional $10,910 per year. The Senate president pro tem and the Speaker pro tem each receive an additional $1,290 per year.

Selected Administrative Officials

Administration	$82,620	Highways	$86,949
Agriculture	80,524	Historic Preservation	73,510
Banking	64,400	Insurance	89,381
Budget	98,664	Labor	77,598
Civil Rights	71,400	Licensing	53,500
Commerce	89,381	Natural Resources	86,938
Community Affairs	79,165	Parks and Recreation	79,165
Consumer Affairs	82,950	Personnel	82,620
Corrections	85,000	Public Utility Regulation	94,000
Education	102,560	Purchasing	68,744
Employment Services	91,993	Social Services	86,944
Energy	79,165	Solid Waste Management	68,744
Environmental Protection	79,165	Tourism	68,169
Health	82,596	Transportation	98,579

KANSAS

Governor	$85,225	*Judges*	
Lieutenant Governor	96,661	Supreme Court	$96,489
Secretary of State	66,206	Court of Appeals	93,044
Attorney General	76,144		
Treasurer	66,206		

Legislature: 165 members each receive $63 a day, plus $80 for expenses. The president of the Senate and the Speaker of the House each receive an additional $815.34 per month; majority and minority leaders receive $735.56. The Speaker pro tem, Senate vice-president, and assistant leaders in both houses receive an additional $416.16 per month.

Selected Administrative Officials

Administration	$ 83,835	Health	$ 81,000
Agriculture	82,363	Historic Preservation	65,990
Banking	63,036	Insurance	66,206
Budget	83,257	Labor	69,547
Civil Rights	58,879	Licensing	53,500
Commerce	96,661	Parks and Recreation	82,354
Community Affairs	59,704	Personnel	73,984
Consumer Affairs	61,036	Public Utility Regulation	95,581
Corrections	86,069	Purchasing	65,680
Education	112,000	Social Services	85,638
Elections	66,206	Solid Waste Management	61,036
Employment Services	82,354	Tourism	56,872
Energy	41,423	Transportation	87,169
Environmental Protection	74,997		

KENTUCKY

Governor	$93,905	*Judges*	
Lieutenant Governor	79,832	Supreme Court	$98,800
Secretary of State	79,832	Court of Appeals	94,767
Attorney General	79,832	Circuit Courts	90,734
Treasurer	79,832		

Legislature: 138 members each receive $102.70 a day, plus $88 a day for expenses. The president of the Senate and the Speaker of the House each receive an additional $25.68 per day; majority and minority leader in both houses receive an additional $20.54 per day; and the Senate president pro tem and the Speaker pro tem, each receive an additional $15.14 per day.

Selected Administrative Officials

Administration	$ 69,417	Historic Preservation	$ 57,595
Agriculture	79,832	Insurance	71,663
Civil Rights	75,870	Labor	82,688
Community Affairs	77,343	Licensing	55,292
Corrections	82,273	Parks and Recreation	73,500
Education	151,938	Personnel	82,688
Elections	71,691	Public Utility Regulation	66,661
Energy	61,169	Social Services	76,950
Environmental Protection	73,660	Solid Waste Management	57,100
Health	136,138	Tourism	82,688
Highways	85,946	Transportation	82,688

LOUISIANA

Governor	$95,000	*Judges*	
Lieutenant Governor	85,000	Supreme Court	$103,336
Secretary of State	85,000	Court of Appeals	97,928
Attorney General	85,000	District Courts	92,520
Treasurer	85,000		

Legislature: 144 members receive $16,800 each, plus $75 for expenses. The president of the Senate and the Speaker of the House each receive $32,000 per year.

Selected Administrative Officials

Administration	$119,600	Historic Preservation	$47,028
Agriculture	85,000	Insurance	85,000
Banking	75,920	Labor	80,000
Budget	81,192	Licensing	63,000
Civil Rights	20,800	Natural Resources	85,400
Consumer Affairs	65,000	Parks and Recreation	61,200
Corrections	75,000	Personnel	88,920
Education	115,008	Public Utility Regulation	75,000
Elections	85,000	Purchasing	57,564
Employment Services	57,372	Social Services	80,000
Energy	73,800	Solid Waste Management	73,800
Environmental Protection	77,700	Tourism	61,200
Health	99,804	Transportation	80,000

MAINE

Governor	$70,000	*Judges*	
Secretary of State	60,154	Supreme Judicial Court	$90,909
Attorney General	69,347	Superior Courts	85,975
Treasurer	66,144		

Legislature: 186 members receive $7,500 each, plus $38 for lodgings or mileage and $32 for meals. The president of the Senate and the Speaker of the House both earn base salary, plus 50 percent; majority and minority leaders, 25 percent; and assistant leaders, 12.5 percent.

Selected Administrative Officials

Administration	$74,110	Historic Preservation	$60,154
Agriculture	74,110	Insurance	77,896
Banking	73,258	Labor	74,110
Budget	68,557	Licensing	58,406
Civil Rights	52,666	Parks and Recreation	61,256
Consumer Affairs	61,256	Personnel	68,557
Corrections	77,896	Public Utility Regulation	76,336
Education	74,110	Purchasing	59,218
Elections	43,035	Social Services	77,896
Energy	68,557	Solid Waste Management	64,209
Environmental Protection	77,896	Tourism	54,226
General Services	68,557	Transportation	77,896
Health	77,896		

MARYLAND

Governor	$120,000	*Judges*	
Lieutenant Governor	100,000	Court of Appeals	$107,300
Secretary of State	70,000	Court of Special Appeals	100,300
Attorney General	100,000	Circuit Courts	96,500
Treasurer	100,000		

Legislature: 188 members receive $29,700 each, plus expenses up to $86 for lodging, $30 for meals. The president of the Senate and the Speaker of the House each earn an additional $10,000 per year.

Selected Administrative Officials

Administration	$89,330	Banking	$ 65,660
Agriculture	89,330	Budget	104,195

Civil Rights	$ 70,912	Insurance	$ 95,000
Commerce	104,195	Labor	70,912
Community Affairs	65,660	Licensing	89,330
Consumer Affairs	65,660	Natural Resources	96,475
Corrections	76,585	Parks and Recreation	65,660
Education	119,000	Personnel	70,912
Elections	65,600	Public Utility Regulation	94,191
Employment Services	60,798	Purchasing	65,660
Energy	65,660	Social Services	70,912
Environmental Protection	89,330	Solid Waste Management	65,660
Health	104,195	Tourism	70,912
Historic Preservation	65,660	Transportation	104,195

MASSACHUSETTS

Governor	$75,000	*Judges*	
Lieutenant Governor	60,000	Supreme Judicial Court	$107,730
Secretary of State	85,000	Appeals Court	99,690
Attorney General	62,500	Trial Court	95,710
Treasurer	60,000		

Legislature: 200 members receive $46,410 each, plus $15–50 for expenses, depending on distance from the State House. The president of the Senate and the Speaker of the House earn $81,410 per year; majority and minority leaders, $68,910; and assistant leaders, $61,410 per year.

Selected Administrative Officials

Administration	$73,156	Historic Preservation	$63,273
Agriculture	53,570	Insurance	66,000
Banking	69,015	Labor	55,648
Budget	77,547	Licensing	63,273
Civil Rights	50,117	Natural Resources	77,547
Consumer Affairs	64,482	Personnel	73,156
Corrections	58,912	Public Utility Regulation	69,015
Education	77,547	Purchasing	73,156
Elections	69,015	Social Services	77,547
Energy	63,272	Solid Waste Management	68,048
Environmental Protection	66,606	Tourism	50,117
Health	77,547	Transportation	70,666
Highways	73,156		

MICHIGAN

		Judges	
Governor	$124,195		
Lieutenant Governor	91,686	Supreme Court	$124,770
Secretary of State	112,439	Court of Appeals	114,788
Attorney General	112,439	Circuit Courts	104,807
Treasurer	99,994		

Legislature: 148 members receive $51,895 each, plus $8,925 in yearly expense allowances for session and interim. The Speaker of the House earns an additional $23,000 per year; the Senate majority leader, an additional $21,000. Minority leaders in both houses receive an additional $17,000 per year, and the Senate president pro tem and the Speaker pro tem each receive an additional $5,000 per year. Assistant majority floor leaders in both houses earn an additional $10,000 per year, while assistant minority leaders earn an extra $8,000.

Selected Administrative Officials

Agriculture	$96,027	Insurance	$81,369
Banking	81,369	Labor	93,000
Budget	99,994	Licensing	95,777
Civil Rights	95,985	Natural Resources	96,006
Commerce	95,777	Parks and Recreation	66,190
Consumer Affairs	101,560	Personnel	97,405
Corrections	99,994	Public Utility Regulation	81,369
Education	97,363	Purchasing	60,761
Employment Services	77,569	Social Services	99,994
Environmental Protection	96,027	Solid Waste Management	66,190
General Services	66,190	Tourism	71,994
Health	99,994	Transportation	95,985
Historic Preservation	66,190		

MINNESOTA

		Judges	
Governor	$114,506		
Lieutenant Governor	62,980	Supreme Court	$94,395
Secretary of State	62,980	Court of Appeals	88,945
Attorney General	89,454	District Courts	83,494
Treasurer	62,980		

Legislature: 201 members receive $29,675 each, plus up to $56 a day for expenses; members sign an affidavit for how much they want at the beginning of session. The Senate housing allowance is up to $750; the House, up to $735 during session. In the Senate, the president and majority and minority leaders earn an additional $11,878.80 per year; in the House, the Speaker and majority and minority leaders earn an additional $988.59 per year.

Selected Administrative Officials

Administration	$67,505	Highways	$90,202
Agriculture	67,505	Labor	67,505
Banking	67,505	Licensing	67,505
Civil Rights	60,009	Natural Resources	67,505
Commerce	67,505	Parks and Recreation	67,505
Community Affairs	65,505	Personnel	67,505
Consumer Affairs	78,509	Public Utility Regulation	60,009
Corrections	67,505	Purchasing	67,505
Education	78,509	Social Services	67,504
Employment Services	67,505	Solid Waste Management	75,210
Energy	60,009	Tourism	67,505
Environmental Protection	61,909	Transportation	78,509
Health	67,505		

MISSISSIPPI

Governor	$83,160	*Judges*	
Lieutenant Governor	40,800	Supreme Court	$98,300
Secretary of State	75,000	Court of Appeals	91,500
Attorney General	90,800	Chancery Courts	88,700
Treasurer	75,000	Circuit Courts	88,700

Legislature: 174 members receive $10,000 each, plus $94 a day for expenses, paid only if the member is present for the days in session. The president pro tem of the Senate earns an additional $5,000 per year.

Selected Administrative Officials

Administration	$67,623	Elections	$63,690
Agriculture	75,000	Employment Services	70,000
Banking	85,000	Energy	76,164
Budget	65,685	Environmental Protection	85,000
Commerce	85,000	General Services	67,623
Community Affairs	82,985	Health	126,292
Consumer Affairs	60,611	Highways	85,000
Corrections	85,000	Historic Preservation	70,000
Education	107,243	Insurance	75,000

Licensing	$37,172	Purchasing	$51,406
Parks and Recreation	80,000	Solid Waste Management	52,972
Personnel	75,000	Tourism	72,153
Public Utility Regulation	65,000	Transportation	85,000

MISSOURI

Governor	$107,268	*Judges*	
Lieutenant Governor	64,823	Supreme Court	$108,783
Secretary of State	86,046	Court of Appeals	101,591
Attorney General	93,120	Circuit Courts	82,961
Treasurer	86,046	Municipal division of	82,961
		Circuit Courts	

Legislature: 197 members receive $26,802.96 each, plus $35 for expenses. The Speaker of the House earns an additional $2,500 per year; the president pro tem of the Senate and majority and minority leaders in both houses earn an additional $1,500 per year.

Selected Administrative Officials

Administration	$93,211	Highways	$101,064
Agriculture	84,193	Historic Preservation	44,076
Banking	70,536	Insurance	84,324
Budget	79,680	Labor	75,645
Civil Rights	51,360	Licensing	67,548
Community Affairs	64,608	Natural Resources	84,192
Corrections	84,192	Parks and Recreation	71,904
Education	101,748	Personnel	67,548
Elections	38,880	Public Utility Regulation	82,590
Employment Services	69,660	Purchasing	67,548
Energy	67,596	Social Services	87,804
Environmental Protection	76,248	Solid Waste Management	56,748
General Services	67,548	Tourism	70,536
Health	92,268		

MONTANA

Governor	$78,246	*Judges*	
Lieutenant Governor	53,407	Supreme Court	$77,092
Secretary of State	62,848	District Courts	72,042
Attorney General	66,756		
Treasurer	70,420		

Legislature: 150 members each receive $58.49 per legislative day, plus $70 for expenses. The president of the Senate and the Speaker of the House receive an additional $5 per day.

Selected Administrative Officials

Administration	$70,420	Health	$70,420
Agriculture	40,420	Highways	70,420
Banking	70,420	Historic Preservation	46,702
Budget	70,420	Insurance	58,658
Civil Rights	51,230	Labor	70,420
Commerce	70,420	Licensing	48,197
Community Affairs	48,197	Natural Resources	70,420
Consumer Affairs	51,904	Parks and Recreation	48.197
Corrections	70,420	Personnel	50,425
Education	62,848	Public Utility Regulation	57,819
Elections	35,256	Purchasing	43,095
Employment Services	52,732	Social Services	70,420
Energy	58,477	Solid Waste Management	48,478
Environmental Protection	70,420	Tourism	57,162
General Services	42,999	Transportation	70,420

NEBRASKA

Governor	$65,000	*Judges*	
Lieutenant Governor	47,000	Supreme Court	$101,648
Secretary of State	52,000	Court of Appeals	96,566
Attorney General	64,500	District Courts	94,025
Treasurer	49,500		

Legislature: 49 members receive $12,000 each, plus $83 for expenses, $30 for members within 50 miles of the capital.

Selected Administrative Officials

Administration	$78,000	Corrections	$79,970
Agriculture	74,405	Education	100,237
Banking	82,984	Employment Services	56,460
Budget	77,689	Energy	58,305
Civil Rights	67,301	Environmental Protection	86,720
Community Affairs	49,823	General Services	65,284
Consumer Affairs	51,979	Health	91,961

Highways	$89,034	Parks and Recreation	$82,000
Historic Preservation	78,175	Personnel	65,616
Insurance	65,934	Public Utility Regulation	51,046
Labor	63,461	Social Services	91,961
Licensing	79,500	Solid Waste Management	60,830
Natural Resources	64,391	Tourism	44,083

NEVADA

Governor	$90,000	*Judges*	
Lieutenant Governor	20,000	Supreme Court	$85,000
Secretary of State	62,500	District Courts	79,000
Attorney General	85,000		
Treasurer	62,500		

Legislature: 63 members each receive $130 a day. The president pro tem of the Senate, Speaker of the House, and majority and minority leaders all receive an additional $900 per session. The Speaker earns an extra $2 per day in session.

Selected Administrative Officials

Administration	$87,581	Health	$72,109
Agriculture	64,915	Historic Preservation	38,546
Banking	65,623	Insurance	75,731
Civil Rights	57,655	Labor	87,581
Commerce	87,581	Natural Resources	87,581
Community Affairs	36,165	Parks and Recreation	65,847
Consumer Affairs	52,384	Personnel	73,570
Corrections	87,581	Public Utility Regulation	81,143
Education	87,581	Purchasing	44,073
Elections	41,350	Social Services	87,953
Employment Services	72,110	Tourism	77,357
Energy	36,962	Transportation	87,581
Environmental Protection	81,143		

NEW HAMPSHIRE

Governor	$86,235	*Judges*	
Secretary of State	53,375	Supreme Court	$95,623
Attorney General	76,983	Superior Courts	89,646
Treasurer	53,375		

Legislature: 424 members receive $200 each. The president of the Senate receives an additional $50 per year, plus $200; the Speaker of the House receives an additional $25 per year, plus $200.

Selected Administrative Officials

Administration	$76,983	Historic Preservation	$47,230
Agriculture	45,167	Insurance	57,490
Banking	57,490	Labor	45,176
Budget	76,983	Natural Resources	76,983
Civil Rights	41,340	Parks and Recreation	57,487
Commerce	76,983	Personnel	53,375
Community Affairs	62,232	Public Utility Regulation	76,983
Corrections	59,542	Purchasing	37,850
Education	76,983	Social Services	74,939
Employment Services	53,375	Solid Waste Management	53,375
Energy	48,787	Tourism	37,850
Environmental Protection	59,542	Transportation	76,983

NEW JERSEY

Governor	$ 85,000	*Judges*	
Secretary of State	100,225	Supreme Court	$132,250
Attorney General	100,225	Appellate Division of	124,200
Treasurer	100,225	Superior Court	
		Superior Courts	115,000

Legislature: 120 members receive $35,000 each. The president of the Senate and the Speaker of the House each earn an additional one-third above the base salary.

Selected Administrative Officials

Agriculture	$100,225	Energy	$100,225
Banking	$100,225	Environmental Protection	100,225
Budget	95,000	General Services	85,000
Civil Rights	83,483	Health	100,225
Commerce	100,225	Highways	100,225
Community Affairs	100,225	Historic Preservation	84,349
Consumer Affairs	91,639	Insurance	100,225
Education	100,225	Labor	100,225
Elections	63,000	Licensing	91,639
Employment Services	79,507	Natural Resources	100,225

Parks and Recreation	$ 76,688	Social Services	$100,225
Personnel	100,225	Solid Waste Management	71,802
Public Utility Regulation	100,225	Tourism	84,500
Purchasing	86,100	Transportation	100,225

NEW MEXICO

Governor	$90,000	*Judges*	
Lieutenant Governor	65,000	Superior Court	$83,593
Secretary of State	65,000	Court of Appeals	79,413
Attorney General	72,500	District Courts	75,443
Treasurer	65,000		

Legislature: 112 members receive $163 each for expenses.

Selected Administrative Officials

Administration	$75,352	Highways	$75,532
Banking	61,895	Historic Preservation	60,100
Budget	71,148	Insurance	68,166
Civil Rights	48,810	Labor	75,532
Community Affairs	56,516	Licensing	75,532
Consumer Affairs	$69,832	Natural Resources	75,532
Corrections	75,532	Parks and Recreation	66,608
Education	85,001	Personnel	70,695
Elections	49,991	Public Utility Regulation	69,713
Employment Services	75,532	Purchasing	62,795
Energy	75,532	Social Services	75,532
Environmental Protection	75,532	Solid Waste Management	56,851
General Services	75,532	Tourism	75,532
Health	75,532		

NEW YORK

Governor	$130,000	*Judges*	
Lieutenant Governor	110,000	Court of Appeals	$125,000
Secretary of State	90,832	Appellate Divisions of	119,000
Attorney General	110,000	Supreme Court	
Treasurer	80,000	Supreme Courts	113,000

Legislature: 211 members receive $57,500 each, plus $89 for expenses ($130 for the New York City metro area and out-of-state travel), or $45 for partial legislative days. The president pro tem of the Senate and the Speaker of the House each earn an additional $30,000 per year; the House majority leader and minority leaders in both houses earn an extra $25,000 per year. Assistant positions receive supplements ranging from $9,500 to $24,500 per year.

Selected Administrative Officials

Agriculture	$90,832	General Services	$95,635
Banking	90,832	Health	102,335
Budget	105,805	Insurance	90,832
Civil Rights	82,614	Labor	95,635
Commerce	90,832	Licensing	71,588
Consumer Affairs	76,421	Parks and Recreation	90,832
Corrections	102,335	Personnel	90,832
Education	136,500	Public Utility Regulation	95,635
Elections	82,614	Social Services	102,335
Environmental Protection	95,635	Transportation	102,335

NORTH CAROLINA

Governor	$107,132	*Judges*	
Lieutenant Governor	94,552	Supreme Court	$100,320
Secretary of State	94,552	Court of Appeals	96,140
Attorney General	94,552	Superior Courts	90,915
Treasurer	94,552		

Legislature: 170 members receive $13,951 each, plus $104 for expenses. The Speaker of the House receives $38,151 per year; Speaker pro tem, $21,739; all majority and minority leaders, $17,048; and the president pro tem of the Senate, $16,956. The deputy president pro tem of the Senate receives $21,739 per year.

Selected Administrative Officials

Administration	$92,378	Budget	$113,875
Agriculture	94,552	Civil Rights	52,354
Banking	94,552	Commerce	92,378

Community Affairs	$ 76,632	Labor	$94,552
Corrections	92,378	Natural Resources	92,378
Education	94,552	Parks and Recreation	69,742
Elections	76,089	Personnel	92,378
Employment Services	117,520	Public Utility Regulation	95,592
Energy	59,293	Purchasing	81,120
Environmental Protection	72,056	Social Services	89,411
Health	115,632	Solid Waste Management	50,921
Highways	110,676	Tourism	78,352
Historic Preservation	61,917	Transportation	92,378
Insurance	94,552		

NORTH DAKOTA

Governor	$73,176	*Judges*	
Lieutenant Governor	60,132	Supreme Court	$82,164
Secretary of State	55,464	District Courts	75,824
Attorney General	62,592		
Treasurer	55,464		

Legislature: 147 members each receive $111 a day, plus $650 a month for housing and $250 a month additional compensation. The Speaker of the House and all majority and minority leaders receive an additional $10 per day; assistant Senate leaders receive an additional $5 per day, and assistant House leaders receive an additional $15 per day.

Selected Administrative Officials

Agriculture	$55,464	Insurance	$55,488
Banking	55,488	Labor	54,948
Consumer Affairs	41,040	Natural Resources	48,396
Corrections	54,540	Parks and Recreation	56,472
Education	56,568	Personnel	58,560
Elections	26,640	Public Utility Regulation	55,464
Employment Services	63,864	Purchasing	42,024
Energy	47,904	Social Services	93,732
Environmental Protection	67,200	Solid Waste Management	47,400
Health	86,760	Tourism	52,000
Historic Preservation	42,228	Transportation	72,552

OHIO

Governor	$111,467	*Judges*	
Lieutenant Governor	57,637	Supreme Court	$107,350
Secretary of State	82,347	Court of Appeals	99,950
Attorney General	85,509	Courts of Common Pleas	91,950
Treasurer	82,347		

Legislature: 132 members receive $42,426.90 each. The president of the Senate and the Speaker of the House receive $66,133 per year; the Senate president pro tem, Speaker pro tem, and both minority leaders, $60,340 per year. The House majority leader receives $56,838 per year. Assistant leaders receive salaries ranging from $44,385 to $56,838 per year.

Selected Administrative Officials

Administration	$95,326	General Services	$95,326
Agriculture	90,376	Health	94,120
Banking	62,005	Insurance	90,376
Budget	106,683	Labor	75,130
Civil Rights	82,950	Licensing	92,123
Commerce	92,132	Natural Resources	96,616
Community Affairs	91,270	Parks and Recreation	75,154
Consumer Affairs	103,376	Personnel	82,888
Corrections	101,650	Public Utility Regulation	99,507
Education	135,845	Purchasing	82,867
Elections	74,547	Social Services	106,683
Employment Services	95,202	Solid Waste Management	70,699
Energy	72,571	Tourism	65,811
Environmental Protection	96,408	Transportation	105,560

OKLAHOMA

Governor	$70,000	*Judges*	
Lieutenant Governor	62,500	Supreme Court	$97,807
Secretary of State	42,500	Court of Appeals	93,530
Attorney General	75,500	District Courts	88,511
Treasurer	70,000		

Legislature: 149 members receive $32,000 each, plus expenses of $35 for those unable to reside at home. The president pro tem of the Senate and the Speaker of the House each receive an additional $14,944 per year; the

Speaker pro tem, majority and minority leaders, and assistant Senate majority leader all receive an additional $10,304 per year.

Selected Administrative Officials

Administration	$70,520	Highways	$111,200
Agriculture	68,000	Historic Preservation	58,611
Banking	78,318	Insurance	70,000
Civil Rights	50,200	Labor	58,000
Commerce	101,660	Personnel	61,661
Consumer Affairs	52,316	Public Utility Regulation	78,000
Corrections	74,180	Purchasing	70,520
Education	75,000	Social Services	108,651
Elections	67,961	Solid Waste Management	50,594
Energy	66,493	Tourism	65,442
Environmental Protection	72,000	Transportation	111,200
Health	97,620		

OREGON

Governor	$88,300	*Judges*	
Secretary of State	67,900	Supreme Court	$93,600
Attorney General	72,800	Court of Appeals	91,500
Treasurer	67,900	Circuit Courts	85,300
		Tax Court	88,000

Legislature: 90 members receive $13,104 each plus $87 for expenses. The president of the Senate and the Speaker of the House each receive an additional $1,092 per month.

Selected Administrative Officials

Administration	$95,544	Health	$78,624
Agriculture	78,624	Historic Preservation	85,000
Banking	71,256	Labor	67,900
Civil Rights	64,668	Parks and Recreation	78,624
Community Affairs	78,600	Personnel	78,624
Corrections	86,616	Public Utility Regulation	78,624
Education	67,900	Purchasing	71,256
Elections	78,624	Social Services	95,544
Employment Services	78,624	Solid Waste Management	53,160
Energy	71,256	Tourism	64,668
Environmental Protection	78,624	Transportation	95,544

PENNSYLVANIA

		Judges	
Governor	$105,035		
Lieutenant Governor	83,027	Supreme Court	$122,864
Secretary of State	72,024	Superior Court	119,016
Attorney General	107,016	Commonwealth Court	119,016
Treasurer	107,016	Courts of Common Pleas	106,704

Legislature: 253 members receive $57,367 each plus $108 for expenses. The president pro tem of the Senate and the Speaker of the House each receive an additional $32,186.92 per year. Majority and minority leaders in both houses earn an additional $25,750.52 per year. Other leadership positions earn supplements ranging from $8,047 to $19,542.

Selected Administrative Officials

Administration	$96,400	Historic Preservation	$78,749
Agriculture	92,640	Insurance	92,640
Banking	72,024	Labor	80,026
Budget	99,300	Licensing	92,300
Civil Rights	87,942	Natural Resources	80,026
Commerce	97,787	Parks and Recreation	82,038
Corrections	80,026	Personnel	95,100
Education	80,026	Public Utility Regulation	100,361
Elections	54,142	Purchasing	54,142
Employment Services	88,600	Social Services	89,500
Environmental Protection	90,900	Solid Waste Management	78,749
General Services	76,025	Tourism	49,585
Health	102,934	Transportation	80,026

RHODE ISLAND

		Judges	
Governor	$69,900		
Lieutenant Governor	52,000	Supreme Court	$110,761
Secretary of State	52,000	Superior Courts	99,722
Attorney General	55,000		
Treasurer	52,000		

Legislature: 150 members receive $10,250 each.

Selected Administrative Officials

Administration	$83,763	Insurance	$63,676
Agriculture	51,139	Labor	70,922
Banking	58,294	Licensing	53,516
Budget	82,557	Parks and Recreation	59,343
Civil Rights	41,073	Personnel	72,283
Community Affairs	69,079	Public Utility Regulation	77,165
Corrections	83,763	Purchasing	78,191
Education	105,000	Social Services	105,383
Elections	38,057	Solid Waste Management	42,724
Employment Services	80,954	Tourism	52,189
Environmental Protection	78,626	Transportation	99,159
Health	112,593		

SOUTH CAROLINA

Governor	$106,078	*Judges*	
Lieutenant Governor	46,545	Supreme Court	$106,713
Secretary of State	92,007	Court of Appeals	104,045
Attorney General	92,007	Circuit Courts	101,377
Treasurer	92,007		

Legislature: 170 members receive $10,400 each, plus $1,000 a month and $88 a legislative day for expenses. The president pro tem of the Senate and the Speaker of the House each earn an additional $11,000 per year. The Speaker pro tem earns an additional $3,600 per year.

Selected Administrative Officials

Administration	$111,296	Health	$104,328
Agriculture	92,007	Historic Preservation	33,552
Budget	72,154	Insurance	74,378
Civil Rights	65,755	Labor	72,850
Commerce	100,661	Natural Resources	79,268
Consumer Affairs	74,378	Parks and Recreation	72,850
Corrections	104,328	Personnel	72,154
Education	92,007	Public Utility Regulation	61,631
Elections	54,820	Purchasing	44,157
Employment Services	107,014	Social Services	104,328
Energy	44,157	Solid Waste Management	45,922
Environmental Protection	74,097	Tourism	72,850
General Services	74,097	Transportation	94,549

SOUTH DAKOTA

		Judges	
Governor	$84,740		
Lieutenant Governor	30,766	Supreme Court	$78,762
Secretary of State	57,576	Circuit Courts	73,556
Attorney General	71,973		
Treasurer	57,576		

Legislature: 105 members receive $4,267 each in odd years; $3,733 in even years.

Selected Administrative Officials

Administration	$70,745	Historic Preservation	$44,678
Agriculture	70,745	Labor	70,745
Banking	74,900	Licensing	28,691
Civil Rights	70,745	Natural Resources	70,745
Commerce	70,745	Parks and Recreation	57,853
Consumer Affairs	47,382	Personnel	70,795
Corrections	72,513	Public Utility Regulation	55,995
Education	70,745	Purchasing	40,456
Elections	42,083	Social Services	84,444
Employment Services	57,123	Solid Waste Management	55,648
Energy	77,250	Tourism	65,000
Health	70,745	Transportation	77,250
Highways	68,661		

TENNESSEE

		Judges	
Governor	$85,000		
Secretary of State	86,484	Supreme Court	$107,820
Attorney General	107,820	Court of Criminal	102,804
Treasurer	86,484	Appeals	
		Chancery Courts	98,364
		Circuit Courts	98,364
		Criminal Courts	98,364

Legislature: 132 members receive $16,500 each, plus $120 for expenses. The president of the Senate and the Speaker of the House each earn three times the legislative base salary.

Selected Administrative Officials

Agriculture	$81,264	Historic Preservation	$45,194
Banking	81,264	Insurance	81,264
Budget	75,804	Labor	81,264
Civil Rights	65,100	Natural Resources	81,264
Consumer Affairs	40,488	Parks and Recreation	62,460
Corrections	81,264	Personnel	81,264
Education	86,484	Public Utility Regulation	81,264
Elections	68,748	Purchasing	68,016
Employment Services	72,000	Social Services	67,236
Energy	49,272	Solid Waste Management	47,376
General Services	81,264	Tourism	81,264
Health	120,000	Transportation	81,264

TEXAS

Governor	$99,122	*Judges*	
Lieutenant Governor	99,122	Supreme Court	$113,000
Secretary of State	79,966	Court of Appeals	107,350
Attorney General	79,247	District Courts	101,700
Treasurer	79,247		

Legislature: 181 members receive $7,200 each, plus $95 for expenses.

Selected Administrative Officials

Agriculture	$79,247	Historic Preservation	$63,362
Banking	97,056	Insurance	150,000
Budget	99,000	Labor	99,999
Civil Rights	54,768	Licensing	62,494
Commerce	79,536	Natural Resources	105,000
Community Affairs	79,536	Parks and Recreation	105,000
Corrections	120,000	Personnel	55,834
Education	156,014	Public Utility Regulation	74,263
Elections	79,966	Purchasing	74,965
Employment Services	99,999	Social Services	156,014
Energy	67,500	Solid Waste Management	65,526
Environmental Protection	105,000	Tourism	54,000
General Services	78,000	Transportation	105,000
Health	148,681		

UTAH

		Judges	
Governor	$87,600		
Lieutenant Governor	68,100	Supreme Court	$99,500
Attorney General	73,700	Court of Appeals	94,950
Treasurer	68,100	District Court	90,450

Legislature: 104 members each receive $100 a day, plus $35 for expenses. The president of the Senate and the Speaker of the House each earn an additional $1,000 per year; majority and minority leaders in both houses earn an additional $500 per year.

Selected Administrative Officials

Administration	$82,497	Health	$97,489
Agriculture	76,191	Historic Preservation	60,782
Banking	76,191	Insurance	76,191
Budget	82,495	Labor	76,191
Civil Rights	59,133	Licensing	64,185
Commerce	73,080	Natural Resources	88,197
Community Affairs	82,184	Parks and Recreation	81,912
Consumer Affairs	57,587	Personnel	84,000
Corrections	88,197	Public Utility Regulation	65,939
Education	65,939	Purchasing	73,498
Elections	35,350	Social Services	97,489
Employment Services	81,912	Solid Waste Management	79,720
Energy	50,279	Tourism	66,002
Environmental Protection	89,199	Transportation	97,489
General Services	82,497		

VERMONT

		Judges	
Governor	$80,725		
Lieutenant Governor	40,289	Supreme Court	$90,584
Secretary of State	60,825	Superior Courts	80,486
Attorney General	61,027	District Courts	80,486
Treasurer	60,825		

Legislature: 180 members each receive $510 a week, plus $50 for rent and $37.50 for meals (commuters receive $32 for meals). The president of the Senate and the Speaker of the House receive an additional $565 per week during session. The Speaker also receives an additional $8,735 per year.

Selected Administrative Officials

Administration	$73,008	Historic Preservation	$55,265
Agriculture	60,528	Insurance	63,128
Banking	63,128	Labor	61,006
Commerce	69,638	Licensing	43,908
Community Affairs	69,638	Natural Resources	69,638
Consumer Affairs	56,222	Parks and Recreation	62,774
Corrections	67,828	Personnel	60,008
Education	67,350	Public Utility Regulation	78,894
Employment Services	61,360	Purchasing	53,144
Energy	69,047	Social Services	73,944
Environmental Protection	72,737	Solid Waste Management	62,108
General Services	65,852	Tourism	55,993
Health	79,996	Transportation	67,537

VIRGINIA

Governor	$110,000	*Judges*	
Lieutenant Governor	32,000	Supreme Court	$116,526
Secretary of State	76,346	Court of Appeals	110,700
Attorney General	97,500	Circuit Courts	108,175
Treasurer	93,573		

Legislature: 140 members receive $18,000 (Senate) or $17,640 (House) each, plus $102 for expenses. The Speaker of the House earns an additional $14,360 per year.

Selected Administrative Officials

Administration	$82,417	Health	$113,558
Agriculture	73,185	Highways	96,187
Banking	103,136	Historic Preservation	71,666
Budget	94,778	Insurance	103,136
Civil Rights	62,318	Licensing	48,290
Commerce	104,097	Natural Resources	104,097
Community Affairs	104,097	Parks and Recreation	71,666
Corrections	100,369	Personnel	82,417
Education	116,113	Public Utility Regulation	103,136
Elections	62,318	Purchasing	82,417
Employment Services	82,417	Social Services	94,778
Energy	95,036	Tourism	116,113
Environmental Protection	96,911	Transportation	96,187
General Services	82,417		

WASHINGTON

Governor	$121,000	*Judges*	
Lieutenant Governor	62,700	Supreme Court	$112,078
Secretary of State	64,300	Court of Appeals	106,537
Attorney General	92,000	Superior Courts	100,995
Treasurer	84,100		

Legislature: 147 members receive $28,800 each, plus $79 for expenses. The Speaker of the House receives a salary of $36,300 per year. The Senate majority leader and minority leaders in both houses earn a salary of $32,300 per year, and the House majority leader earns $28,300 per year.

Selected Administrative Officials

Administration	$93,659	Historic Preservation	$63,084
Agriculture	93,659	Insurance	77,200
Banking	93,659	Labor	93,660
Civil Rights	72,351	Licensing	93,660
Commerce	93,660	Natural Resources	86,600
Consumer Affairs	98,400	Parks and Recreation	86,976
Corrections	93,660	Personnel	93,659
Education	86,600	Public Utility Regulation	86,974
Elections	64,656	Purchasing	67,956
Employment Services	66,288	Social Services	115,823
Energy	72,120	Solid Waste Management	66,288
Environmental Protection	93,659	Tourism	66,288
General Services	93,659	Transportation	105,065
Health	93,659		

WEST VIRGINIA

Governor	$99,000	*Judges*	
Secretary of State	65,000	Supreme Court of	$85,000
Attorney General	75,000	Appeals	
Treasurer	65,000	Circuit Courts	80,000

Legislature: 134 members receive $15,000 each, plus $85 for expenses ($45 for noncommuters). The president of the Senate and the Speaker of the House each earn an additional $50 a day during session, plus $100 a day for 80 days per calendar year. Majority and minority leaders in both houses receive an additional $25 a day during session.

Selected Administrative Officials

Administration	$70,000	General Services	$34,032
Agriculture	70,000	Historic Preservation	50,000
Banking	55,000	Insurance	55,000
Budget	36,420	Labor	45,000
Civil Rights	40,000	Natural Resources	65,000
Commerce	105,000	Personnel	50,000
Community Affairs	105,000	Public Utility Regulation	70,000
Consumer Affairs	54,504	Social Services	70,000
Corrections	55,000	Solid Waste Management	52,056
Employment Services	65,000	Transportation	70,000
Environmental Protection	65,000		

WISCONSIN

Governor	$101,861	*Judges*	
Lieutenant Governor	54,795	Supreme Court	$100,690
Secretary of State	49,719	Court of Appeals	94,804
Attorney General	97,756	Circuit Courts	90,661
Treasurer	49,719		

Legislature: 132 members receive $39,211 each, plus $75 for expenses. The Speaker of the House receives an additional $25 per month.

Selected Administrative Officials

Administration	$101,859	Health	$89,183
Agriculture	89,500	Historic Preservation	45,827
Banking	74,500	Insurance	83,831
Budget	86,161	Labor	90,552
Civil Rights	71,762	Licensing	76,339
Commerce	87,784	Natural Resources	99,591
Community Affairs	63,001	Parks and Recreation	67,923
Consumer Affairs	89,880	Personnel	90,124
Corrections	94,238	Public Utility Regulation	78,001
Education	88,089	Purchasing	70,572
Elections	64,074	Social Services	94,290
Employment Services	88,011	Solid Waste Management	83,606
Energy	69,336	Tourism	85,662
Environmental Protection	90,669	Transportation	100,228

WYOMING

		Judges	
Governor	$95,000	Judges	
Secretary of State	77,000	Supreme Court	$85,000
Attorney General	80,000	District Courts	77,000
Treasurer	77,000		

Legislature: 90 members receive $125 a day, plus $80 for expenses. The president of the Senate and the Speaker of the House each earn an additional $3 per day.

Selected Administrative Officials

Administration	$68,000	Health	$72,000
Agriculture	65,662	Historic Preservation	41,148
Banking	55,008	Insurance	59,000
Budget	60,000	Labor	71,000
Civil Rights	41,941	Licensing	57,965
Commerce	66,647	Natural Resources	60,000
Community Affairs	52,962	Parks and Recreation	52,693
Consumer Affairs	44,040	Personnel	57,120
Corrections	71,000	Public Utility Regulation	61,333
Education	77,000	Purchasing	44,676
Elections	28,038	Social Services	68,000
Employment Services	62,652	Solid Waste Management	60,012
Energy	40,320	Tourism	63,022
Environmental Protection	69,000	Transportation	72,000
General Services	68,000		

Large Cities

In this section we provide annual salaries of the leading officials in a range of major American cities. The data is primarily taken from publications of the International City/County Management Association. The section includes a table that shows the average annual salaries for municipal officials across the United States, and a table listing the salaries of individual officials in the largest cities.

AVERAGE SALARIES OF MUNICIPAL OFFICIALS, 1987–1997

Title	Salary 1987	Salary 1991	Salary 1993	Salary 1994	Salary 1997
Mayor	$ 7,595	$ 9,209	$ 9,963	$10,191	$12,870
City Manager	49,241	60,803	65,221	67,274	70,541
Chief Appointed Administrator	38,756	49,467	53,999	56,074	56,207
Assistant City Manager/Assistant CAO	40,879	51,945	56,285	58,216	56,485
City Clerk	26,511	32,799	35,305	36,366	37,743
Chief Financial Officer	39,521	50,136	54,050	55,946	55,139
Treasurer	32,371	34,851	38,122	38,236	38,081
Director of Public Works	36,521	45,919	49,689	51,274	52,306
Engineer	42,755	51,278	55,006	56,798	58,188
Police Chief	36,342	44,563	48,412	50,104	54,169
Fire Chief	37,470	45,406	49,263	50,820	53,805
Planning Director	38,872	48,948	52,476	54,501	55,489
Personnel Director	36,934	46,310	50,276	52,183	51,543
Director of Parks/Recreation	39,088	45,948	49,650	51,453	47,531
Superintendent of Parks	28,756	37,743	40,707	42,042	40,455
Director of Recreation	29,400	36,627	39,432	40,975	41,124
Librarian	28,704	36,297	39,376	40,889	41,043
Director of Data Processing	37,679	48,495	52,262	54,088	56,426
Purchasing Director	30,816	37,562	40,760	42,367	43,667

NOTE: Average salaries are for cities that have consistently reported data over the past six years.
SOURCE: International City/County Management Association, *Municipal Yearbook, 1998.*

20 BEST-PAID U.S. MAYORS, 1997

Rank, Mayor	City	Salary
1. Richard M. Daley	Chicago, IL	$170,000
2. Rudolph Giuliani	New York, NY	165,000
3. Sharpe James	Newark, NJ	147,000
4. Dennis Archer	Detroit, MI	143,000
5. Willie Brown	San Francisco, CA	142,610
6. Bob Lanier	Houston, TX	133,000
7. S. J. Schulman	White Plains, NY	121,000
8. Richard Riordan[1]	Los Angeles, CA	117,876
9. John Spencer	Yonkers, NY	115,000
10. John A. Delaney	Jacksonville, MI	113,140
11. Norman Rice	Seattle, WA	112,731
12. John O. Norquist	Milwaukee, WI	112,362
13. Thomas Menino	Boston, MA	110,000

20 BEST-PAID U.S. MAYORS, 1997

Rank, Mayor	City	Salary
14. Willie W. Herenton	Memphis, TN	$110,000
15. Edward Rendell	Philadelphia, PA	110,000
16. Dick A. Greco	Tampa, FL	110,000
17. Joseph P. Riley Jr.	Charleston, SC	108,815
18. Gregory Lashutka	Columbus, OH	103,968
19. Wellington E. Webb	Denver, CO	101,364
20. Michael R. White	Cleveland, OH	101,286

[1]Official salary. Riordan accepts only $1 of the mayoral salary.
SOURCE: U.S. Conference of Mayors.

MUNICIPAL OFFICERS' SALARIES IN 65 LARGE CITIES, 1995

City	Mayor	City Council President	City Council Member
Albuquerque, NM	$ 70,283	$ 14,056	$ 7,028
Anaheim, CA	12,000	NA	12,000
Arlington, TX	3,000	NA	2,400
Atlanta, GA	100,000	0	18,400
Austin, TX	35,000	NA	30,000
Baltimore, MD	60,000	53,000	29,000
Baton Rouge, LA	85,516	0	3,600
Birmingham, AL	68,000	17,400	15,000
Boston, MA	100,000	45,000	45,000
Buffalo, NY	79,380	52,920	41,895
Charlotte, NC	20,000	NA	12,000
Chicago, IL	80,000	0	27,600
Cincinnati, OH	50,686	NA	46,879
Cleveland, OH	82,500	46,287	35,683
Colorado Springs, CO	0	NA	0
Columbus, OH	95,000	30,000	25,000
Corpus Christi, TX	9,000	0	6,000
Dallas, TX	$50 per meeting	NA	$50 per meeting
Denver, CO	93,000	38,402	38,402
Detroit, MI	125,300	65,000	63,000
El Paso, TX	$ 27,562	NA	$16,537
Fort Worth, TX	$75 per meeting	0	$75 per meeting
Fresno, CA	57,270	NA	33,120
Houston, TX	133,975	NA	34,900
Indianapolis, IN	83,211	9,985	9,985
Jacksonville, FL	100,745	34,127	25,595
Kansas City, MO	47,000	NA	19,500
Las Vegas, NV	43,984	NA	33,480

MUNICIPAL OFFICERS' SALARIES IN 65 LARGE CITIES, 1995

City	Mayor	City Council President	City Council Member
Long Beach, CA	$ 86,659	$ NA	$ 21,664
Los Angeles, CA	117,876	90,680	90,680
Louisville, KY	71,464	27,995	27,995
Memphis, TN	100,000	0	6,000
Mesa, AZ	19,200	NA	96,000
Miami, FL	5,000	NA	5,000
Milwaukee, WI	102,544	50,563	45,146
Minneapolis, MN	71,500	52,500	52,500
Nashville, TN	75,000	8,652	5,562
New Orleans, LA	85,880	42,500	42,500
New York, NY	130,000	105,000	55,000
Newark, NJ	0	NA	0
Norfolk, VA	17,000	NA	15,000
Oakland, CA	89,000	NA	33,000
Oklahoma City, OK	2,000	NA	$20 per meeting
Omaha, NE	71,930	23,402	19,502
Philadelphia, PA	0	0	0
Phoenix, AZ	37,500	NA	18,000
Pittsburgh, PA	69,007	39,287	39,347
Portland, OR	75,254	0	65,644
Sacramento, CA	$925 per month	NA	$925 per month
St. Louis, MO	90,246	50,310	22,765
St. Paul, MN	75,216	3,000	30,000
San Antonio, TX	$50 per meeting	NA	$20 per meeting
San Diego, CA	65,000	NA	49,000
San Francisco, CA	130,083	23,924	23,924
San Jose, CA	80,000	NA	52,800
San Juan, Puerto Rico	0	NA	NA
Santa Ana, CA	2,400	NA	1,500
Seattle, WA	95,398	63,892	63,892
Tampa, FL	110,000	19,928	19,928
Toledo, OH	75,000	4,500	18,500
Tucson, AZ	24,000	NA	12,000
Tulsa, OK	70,000	12,000	12,000
Virginia Beach, VA	20,000	NA	18,000
Washington, DC	90,705	81,885	71,885
Wichita, KS	12,500	NA	7,500

NOTE: All salaries are annual unless otherwise noted. NA=Not available
SOURCE: National League of Cities, Database Report, March 14, 1995.

Average Salaries of County Officials, 1987–97

Many functions of county government vary dramatically from one area of the country to another, and so, therefore, do the salaries of county officials. Following are some averages for key positions in county government by region as compiled by the International City/County Management Association and *City and State* Government Manager.

AVERAGE SALARIES OF COUNTY OFFICIALS, 1987–94

Title	1987	1991	1993	1994	1997
Governing Board Chair/ President	$15,834	$18,016	$19,741	$19,947	$26,240
County Manager	54,598	68,742	73,712	76,183	88,929
County Administrator	43,339	51,804	55,890	58,539	59,124
Clerk to the Governing Board	24,373	29,956	32,027	32,976	38,033
Chief Financial Officer	29,549	40,269	44,357	45,815	51,189
County Health Officer	43,926	50,514	55,100	58,037	56,550
Planning Director	34,962	44,229	47,140	49,064	50,328
County Engineer	46,968	54,182	57,764	59,581	55,163
Director of Welfare/Human Services	38,650	48,700	51,271	52,931	54,909
Chief Law Enforcement Officer	31,948	41,257	44,179	45,722	47,969
Purchasing Director	32,083	42,226	44,870	46,365	43,053
Personnel Director	37,710	47,976	51,932	53,888	49,913

NOTE: Average salaries are for counties that have consistently reported data over the past six years.
SOURCE: International City/County Management Association, *Municipal Yearbook, 1998.*

AVERAGE SALARIES OF COUNTY OFFICIALS BY GEOGRAPHIC REGION, 1997

	Average Salaries				
Position	All Counties	Northeast	North Central	South	West
Chief Elected Offical	$26,420	$34,854	$19,422	$28,217	$31,810
County Manager	88,929	62,851	81,920	86,736	105,162
County Administrator	59,124	63,153	57,268	57,957	62,292
Clerk to the Governing Board	38,033	44,283	33,770	38,783	42,282
Chief Financial Officer	51,189	58,464	45,397	50,847	59,563
County Health Officer	56,550	68,950	44,647	66,554	70,964
Public Works Director	56,333	64,774	55,355	51,411	66,261

AVERAGE SALARIES OF COUNTY OFFICIALS BY GEOGRAPHIC REGION, 1997

Position	All Counties	Northeast	North Central	South	West
		Average Salaries			
County Engineer	$55,163	$63,308	$53,110	$55,953	$57,929
Director of Welfare/Human Services	54,909	58,766	51,884	54,041	59,846
Chief Law Enforcement Officer	47,969	53,257	43,139	49,966	52,287
Purchasing Director	43,053	44,041	44,428	40,011	52,043
Personnel Director	49,913	51,573	49,269	46,992	55,847

NOTE: Average salaries are for counties that have consistently reported data over the past six years.
SOURCE: International City/County Management Association, *Municipal Yearbook, 1995.*

The salaries of county officials usually rise and fall relative to the population of the area they serve in.

AVERAGE SALARIES OF COUNTY OFFICIALS BY POPULATION SIZE, 1997

	Over 1 million	500,000 to 1 million	100,000 to 250,000	50,000 to 100,000
County Manager	$142,792	$131,186	$94,706	$80,189
Clerk	79,311	68,359	48,581	41,122
Chief Financial Officer	99,224	87,917	63,615	52,050
Health Officer	120,868	102,827	70,191	57,163
Public Works Director	103,768	89,861	71,762	57,633
Engineer	89,211	76,382	60,957	56,189
Human Services Director	101,427	87,876	66,022	56,355
Chief Law Enforcement Officer	103,808	90,708	66,064	54,440
Personnel Director	91,821	77,010	55,304	45,598

SOURCE: International City/County Management Association, *The Municipal Year Book, 1998* (1998).

Salaries and Wages
of Public Employees

The jobs represented in this section are for state and local government employees only. Over the last two decades, these workers have become a potent force in the American economy. The importance of their work in maintaining the smooth and orderly functioning of society has increased steadily, especially in the key areas of education, public safety, transportation, and, most notably, health care.

Ironically, it is precisely their increased power and influence that have made public employees the targets of politicians and of citizens' groups who seek to blame them for high taxes, budget deficits, and the frequently mediocre quality of public service. This has led in turn to government resistance to increases for its employees and, predictably, to strikes and slowdowns by workers. Finally, to complete the circle, when higher taxes are sought, the government can point to the necessity of giving higher salaries to its employees.

The combination of relatively low wages with continual governmental and public disapproval has helped to increase markedly the unionization of government employees. The American Federation of State, Municipal and County Workers (AFSCME), for example, has achieved a membership of over 1 million in just the last few years. Millions of other workers belong to trade unions or other AFL-CIO–related organizations. How this will affect the relationship of employer and employee in the future is difficult to predict exactly, but the possibility of more strikes by public employees would seem to be a fairly safe bet, state or city laws to the contrary notwithstanding.

One note of caution to the researcher and the careful reader: The figures given below are base salaries *only;* they do not include overtime, pension, or health benefits, items that in the past have made public service attractive to many people.

JOBS AND SALARIES OF KEY PUBLIC EMPLOYEES

Corrections Officers

The approximately 320,000 people who stand guard in our prison facilities are among the most underpaid members of the working community. The image of the prison guard, "the screw," planted in the minds of the American public by the gangster films of the 1930s and 1940s, has given the job a distasteful aura, which the new euphemism "corrections officer" cannot conceal. In fact, these men and women perform a vital function. This is especially true in maximum-security prisons where, unarmed, they must deal with the constant threat of violence while at the same time being restrained by rules no policeman need obey.

Although they are frequently the victims of prisoner outbursts against the mythological "system," the guards are always cited as the real cause of prisoner upheavals. Policemen usually argue that because they constantly deal with life-and-death situations, they are entitled to higher pay than other public employees, and most people accept that premise. But why, then, do prison guards almost always earn significantly less than police in the same geographic area?

ANNUAL SALARIES OF CORRECTIONAL PERSONNEL

State	Director of Corrections	Entry-Level Officer	State	Director of Corrections	Entry-Level Officer
Alabama	$79,000	$17,823	Montana	$70,420	$16,465
Alaska	86,292	32,016	Nebraska	79,970	20,010
Arizona	117,875	19,407	Nevada	87,581	26,386
Arkansas	97,225	17,777	New Hampshire	59,542	21,143
California	115,083	24,012	New Jersey	NA	31,805
Colorado	95,640	24,300	New Mexico	73,352	16,180
Connecticut	89,000	22,958	New York	102,335	24,300
Delaware	89,000	20,694	North Carolina	92,378	20,136
District of Columbia	NA	21,707	North Dakota	54,540	14,988
Florida	108,004	17,361	Ohio	101,650	24,586
Georgia	86,832	19,242	Oklahoma	74,180	15,965
Hawaii	85,302	23,676	Oregon	86,616	24,444
Idaho	79,040	22,360	Pennsylvania	80,026	21,031
Illinois	104,369	24,300	Rhode Island	83,763	25,808
Indiana	82,212	19,302	South Carolina	104,328	17,805
Iowa	85,000	25,605	South Dakota	72,513	16,016
Kansas	86,069	17,868	Tennessee	81,264	15,432
Kentucky	82,273	16,260	Texas	120,000	16,524
Louisiana	75,000	14,736	Utah	88,197	20,546
Maine	77,896	17,721	Vermont	67,828	17,000
Maryland	76,585	22,004	Virginia	100,369	19,582
Massachusetts	58,912	30,870	Washington	93,660	23,280
Michigan	99,994	23,887	West Virginia	55,000	18,610
Minnesota	67,505	23,699	Wisconsin	94,238	19,000
Mississippi	85,000	16,238	Wyoming	71,000	16,692
Missouri	84,192	17,436	U.S. Virgin Islands	65,000	NA

SOURCE: Council of State Governments, *The Book of States, 1998-99; The Corrections Yearbook, 1997.* Criminal Justice Institute.

Jobs for corrections officers should be plentiful into the next century, as legislation requiring mandatory minimum sentencing for convicted felons will mean more and longer prison terms and a correspondingly greater need for prison guards. The table on page 83 lists salary ranges for various correction department workers.

Firefighters

More than 90 percent of America's approximately 295,000 paid firefighters work for municipalities. Some county governments, especially in the south and west, provide fire protection through paid personnel. No matter what the jurisdiction, however, salaries of firefighters are always discussed in relation to police pay. The struggle is always for parity, something the police usually resist on the familiar grounds that their work is more dangerous. The injury and death statistics, however, reveal at the very least that firefighting is frequently a hazardous occupation and, given various circumstances, at times more dangerous than police work. The whole question of compensation based on danger becomes even more complicated when we realize that taxpayers are forced to pay the same salaries to police officers who perform office work or to firefighters who rarely have to leave the firehouse as to those in obviously high-risk situations.

Resolving the issue of hazardous-duty pay will not be easy, but surely some kind of bonus or merit system could be established. As the salaries of public employees continue to lag farther and farther behind the Consumer Price Index, some way of rewarding excellence must be found or the grim prospect of continual strikes and sick-outs will become a reality.

The Department of Labor projects slower than average growth in the number of firefighters, as low educational requirements and high job security insure that the supply of qualified firefighters almost always exceeds the demand, keeping competition for jobs high. In addition, turnover is very low within the firefighting profession, despite its high-risk status. Some growth is occurring as a result of paid firefighters gradually supplanting volunteers as smaller communities see their populations expand.

Median weekly earnings for firefighters were $658 in 1996. Lieutenants and fire captains earned considerably more. Benefits paid to firefighters include liberal pension plans (which allow retirement at half pay at age fifty after twenty-five years of service), as well as medical and liability insurance, vacation, sick leave, and several paid holidays.

SALARY RANGES OF FIREFIGHTERS IN SELECTED CITIES[1], 1997

City	Total Personnel	Starting Salary	Maximum Salary
Albuquerque, NM	536	$29,615	$36,807
Anaheim, CA	264	31,740	46,912
Arlington, TX	282	28,176	37,752
Buffalo, NY	889	36,860	41,723
Charlotte, NC	837	22,863	30,638
Cincinnati, OH	766	35,553	39,563
Columbus, OH	1,350	24,960	38,189
Corpus Christi, TX	341	28,980	33,792
Dallas, TX	1,836	28,495	38,185
El Paso, TX	645	24,235	35,808
Fort Worth, TX	714	29,952	36,420
Honolulu, HI	1,065	42,132	47,388
Kansas City, MO	838	24,948	47,136
Long Beach, CA	498	37,121	45,965
Los Angeles, CA	3,310	41,259	51,365
Louisville, KY	647	19,510	22,385
Mesa, AZ	331	29,666	43,958
Milwaukee, WI	1,065	25,227	42,934
Minneapolis, MN	445	29,989	45,675
New Orleans, LA	865	19,872	21,948
Oklahoma City, OK	1,032	26,686	39,416
Omaha, NE	559	30,943	42,779
Sacramento, CA	513	30,360	40,680
San Antonio, TX	1,340	31,776	35,940
San Diego, CA	945	37,320	45,036
San Jose, CA	N/A	41,880	56,148
Santa Ana, CA	N/A	31,200	49,092
Seattle, WA	1,033	39,000	48,228
St. Louis, MO	732	27,963	40,050
St. Paul, MN	482	34,407	42,055
Tucson, AZ	495	28,008	37,536
Tulsa, OK	719	25,968	38,460
Virginia Beach, VA	375	27,085	39,274
Wichita, KS	377	25,143	36,117

[1] Populations over 250,000

SOURCE: International City/County Management Association, *Municipal Yearbook 1998*.

Librarians

The vast majority of the nation's 154,000 librarians work for federal, state, or municipal institutions or systems. In a field where just over 80 percent are women, men continue to start at higher salaries in all areas except the northeast, where women's salaries start, on average, 74 dollars higher than those of their male counterparts. The salaries are rather low for a profession that is highly valued by society, requires at least one advanced degree and a thorough understanding of the ever-changing and expanding world of electronic information resources. In academic settings, multiple advanced degrees, and even multiple languages, can be fairly standard requirements. Almost all librarians have to learn and keep up with the explosion in the use of technology and technology-based information systems. The standard tools of a librarian (card catalogs, paper indexes, and books) are being supplemented and, in many cases, replaced by OPACS (on-line public access computers), LANs (local area networks), CD-ROMs, on-line information services and the Internet. More and more, librarians are being hired for nontraditional library roles such as systems administrators, Web designers, Internet reference librarians, and World Wide Web specialists. This new emphasis on technology is having a positive effect on salaries.

Job prospects for new librarians have been mixed at best for over twenty-five years. Public libraries are often one of the first government institutions to have their budgets cut during financial hard times. Indeed, cutbacks for libraries have been a regular part of state and local budgeting politics ever since Richard Nixon was president. As a result, the prospect of fewer jobs dissuaded many people from entering the field. So after more than doubling in the 1960s, the number of librarians has remained constant ever since. According to the Department of Labor, this trend will most likely continue with job growth projected to increase only 4.8 percent by the year 2006. But as many of the older librarians begin to retire, there are openings in many areas of the country for well-trained librarians, especially for children's and academic librarians. Librarians with a specialization in mathematics, the sciences, and computers are also in high demand. Increasingly, librarians are being hired in nontraditional settings such as the information industry, corporations, and consulting firms, often for their research, organizational, and technological skills. They may hold titles such as database specialists, Web developers, and LAN coordinators.

In numerical terms, the number of 1996 library school graduates finding professional positions was up compared with their 1995 counterparts, although there were slightly fewer graduates. About 10 percent of graduates were able to find only part-time professional employment, down dramatically from the 16.5 percent reported for 1995 library school graduates. In addition, about 28 percent of the 1996 graduates found employment in non-traditional settings as opposed to only about 22 percent of 1995 graduates.

The following tables give a representative sample of librarians' salaries throughout the country and point out the gender-based differences in librarians' salaries on all levels and geographic regions. It should be noted that the Bureau of Labor Statistics estimates that over 78,000 people are employed in various capacities under the job title Library Technician. Pay rates vary widely by employer, geographical region, number of hours, education, and the type of work performed. The average salary for a library technical assistant ranges from $27,200 to $33,000.

AVERAGE STARTING SALARIES OF LIBRARIANS

Year	Average Starting Salary
1986	$20,874
1987	22,247
1988	23,491
1989	24,581
1990	25,306
1991	25,583
1992	26,666
1993	27,116
1994	28,086
1995	28,997
1996	29,480

SOURCE: *Library Journal,* October 15, 1997. Reprinted by permission.

SALARIES OF LIBRARIANS BY REGION AND TYPE OF LIBRARY, 1996

Library Type/Region	Low Salary		Median Salary		High Salary	
	Women	Men	Women	Men	Women	Men
Public Libraries						
Northeast	$13,832	$21,000	$28,000	$28,156	$38,500	$36,000
Southeast	17,388	22,500	24,700	26,750	53,500	35,000
Midwest	17,000	22,000	26,000	27,000	106,000	30,000
Southwest	22,464	20,000	25,900	27,500	36,000	32,000
West	17,500	32,000	32,500	33,500	55,000	35,000
All public libraries	13,832	20,000	26,000	27,900	106,000	36,000

SALARIES OF LIBRARIANS BY REGION AND TYPE OF LIBRARY, 1996

Library Type/Region	Low Salary		Median Salary		High Salary	
	Women	Men	Women	Men	Women	Men
School Libraries						
Northeast	$16,000	$23,000	$32,000	$30,000	$66,000	$42,000
Southeast	17,000	26,000	28,000	32,750	52,000	40,000
Midwest	15,000	11,700	30,000	27,500	55,000	41,000
Southwest	10,000	25,000	28,000	28,000	42,000	34,000
West	24,000	41,000	32,000	41,000	55,000	41,000
All school libraries	10,000	11,700	29,700	30,500	66,000	42,000
College/University						
Northeast	$23,000	$23,000	$31,250	$29,000	$85,000	$42,000
Southeast	17,085	21,000	27,000	27,198	47,000	70,000
Midwest	16,000	13,200	27,500	28,000	45,000	50,000
Southwest	15,000	19,000	26,500	28,000	33,000	35,000
West	23,000	21,500	30,600	25,250	35,916	29,000
All college libraries	15,000	13,200	28,000	28,000	85,000	70,000
Special Libraries						
Northeast	$21,000	$22,000	$30,000	$32,000	$50,000	$70,000
Southeast	19,000	22,000	30,000	30,000	37,000	37,000
Midwest	21,000	25,000	30,000	29,000	45,000	43,000
Southwest	18,000	32,000	25,000	32,000	36,000	32,000
West	23,000	31,000	32,000	33,500	45,000	38,000
All special libraries	18,000	22,000	30,000	32,000	50,000	70,000

SOURCE: *Library Journal,* October 15, 1997. Reprinted by permission.

JOB PLACEMENTS AND AVERAGE SALARIES OF LIBRARY SCHOOL GRADUATES, 1995–1996

	Class of 1995	Class of 1996
Total number of graduates	4,222	4,136
Total finding full-time work	1,766	1,549
Total finding temporary or nonprofessional work	437	324

JOB PLACEMENTS AND AVERAGE SALARIES OF LIBRARY SCHOOL GRADUATES, 1995–1996

	Class of 1995	Class of 1996
Total finding library work	2,203	1,924
Average salary	$28,997	$29,480
Total number in traditional library settings	1,721	1,342
Average salary	$28,627	$29,588
Total number in nontraditional library settings	482	562
Average salary	$30,595	$30,721

SOURCE: *Library Journal,* October 15, 1996 and October 15, 1997. Reprinted by permission.

Police

In 1997, local police, sheriffs' offices, and state police agencies employed about 1.2 million people, including 108,000 in supervisory positions. The general perception that these organizations are predominantly white and male is still accurate, but there has been meaningful change in recent years. In 1987, for example, women made up 7.6 percent of all local police officers, but by 1997 that figure had grown to 16.4 percent; the percentage of blacks also increased during that period, from 9.3 percent to 18.1 percent.

SALARY RANGES OF POLICE OFFICERS IN SELECTED CITIES,[1] 1997

City	Total Personnel	Starting Salary	Maximum Salary
Albuquerque, NM	891	$30,181	$39,645
Anaheim, CA	562	38,813	52,021
Arlington, TX	594	30,372	39,708
Buffalo, NY	1,115	31,792	42,984
Charlotte, NC	1,591	24,006	39,126
Cincinnati, OH	986	34,305	41,519
Columbus, OH	NA	28,434	43,534
Corpus Christi, TX	580	29,892	36,492
Dallas, TX	3,529	28,495	38,185
El Paso, TX	1,252	25,682	41,890
Fort Worth, TX	1,529	28,944	44,928
Honolulu, HI	2,236	29,772	44,364
Kansas City, MO	1,820	27,852	48,480
Los Angeles, CA	12,191	41,572	54,497
Long Beach, CA	1,225	38,976	48,252
Louisville, KY	885	21,611	27,706

SALARY RANGES OF POLICE OFFICERS IN SELECTED CITIES,[1] 1997

City	Total Personnel	Starting Salary	Maximum Salary
Mesa, AZ	915	$32,734	$44,187
Milwaukee, WI	2,877	31,705	42,934
Minneapolis, MN	1,167	29,989	45,675
New Orleans, LA	1,930	25,164	29,720
Oklahoma City, OK	1,257	28,814	34,703
Omaha, NE	868	29,159	44,482
Sacramento, CA	953	30,872	41,371
San Antonio, TX	2,341	29,184	37,140
San Diego, CA	2,646	31,244	47,215
San Jose, CA	NA	42,276	56,640
Santa Ana, CA	NA	45,180	54,948
St. Louis, MO	2,255	29,030	40,050
St. Paul, MN	760	34,407	42,055
Tucson, AZ	1,093	19,400	39,420
Tulsa, OK	936	26,662	41,362
Virginia Beach, VA	910	27,085	39,274
Wichita, KS	785	26,138	37,546

[1]Populations over 250,000
SOURCE: International City/County Management Association, *Municipal Yearbook, 1998.*

AVERAGE BASE STARTING SALARY FOR SELECTED POSITIONS IN LOCAL POLICE DEPARTMENTS

By size of population served, United Sates, 1993

| | Average Base Starting Salary | | |
	Entry-Level Officer	Sergeant	Chief of Police
Population Served			
All Sizes	$21,300	$28,500	$34,600
1,000,000 or more	$28,200	$44,600	$91,700
500,000 to 999,999	28,000	39,100	78,400
250,000 to 499,999	27,000	37,600	68,900
100,000 to 249,999	27,800	37,800	64,900
50,000 to 99,999	28,000	39,500	62,300
25,000 to 49,999	26,900	37,300	54,900
10,000 to 24,999	24,600	33,400	47,100

**AVERAGE BASE STARTING SALARY FOR SELECTED POSITIONS IN
LOCAL POLICE DEPARTMENTS, 1990**

By size of population served, United Sates, 1993

	Average Base Starting Salary		
Population Served	Entry-Level Officer	Sergeant	Chief of Police
2,500 to 9,999	$21,200	$27,500	$34,700
Less than 2,500	17,400	20,800	22,900

NOTE: Salary figures have been rounded to the nearest $100. Computations of average salary exclude agencies with no full-time employees in that position.
SOURCE: U.S. Department of Justice, *Sourcebook of Criminal Justice Statistics, 1996* (1997).

**AVERAGE BASE STARTING SALARY FOR SELECTED POSITIONS IN
SHERIFF'S DEPARTMENTS**

By size of population served, United States, 1993

	Average Base Starting Salary		
Population Served	Entry-Level Deputy	Sergeant	Sheriff
All Sizes	$19,300	$24,400	$37,700
1,000,000 or more	$28,300	$40,200	$89,800
500,000 to 999,999	23,900	33,300	67,200
250,000 to 499,999	23,400	31,900	63,800
100,000 to 249,999	22,200	28,600	53,500
50,000 to 99,999	20,600	26,200	42,400
25,000 to 49,999	19,200	23,900	37,900
10,000 to 24,999	18,500	22,900	33,800
Under 10,000	17,400	20,600	26,700

NOTE: Salary figures have been rounded to the nearest $100. Computation of average salary exclude agencies with no full-time employee in that position.
SOURCE: U.S. Department of Justice, *Sourcebook of Criminal Justice Statistics, 1996* (1997).

Social Workers

About 40 percent of the nearly 585,000 social workers in the United States are employed by a government agency, usually a city, county, or state welfare agency or hospital facility. Government agencies are increasingly opting to contract out social services—something that was all but unheard of just a few years ago—to the private sector. As a result, major employers of social workers include private hospitals and home health services. Many government-employed social workers are engaged as caseworkers in public assistance functions, particularly in the determination of whether or not a person or a family is eligible for welfare funds. Other social workers deal with orphaned or abandoned children, pregnant teenagers, battered wives, and, more frequently today, with lonely and poor old people who are without care.

An important branch of this occupation is psychiatric social work, which usually requires graduate school training. Acting as a liaison between the psychiatrist, the patient, and his family, as well as between the family and the hospital, the psychiatric social worker prepares family histories, conducts interviews with all parties, and explains treatments and their purpose.

AVERAGE ANNUAL SALARIES OF STATE DIRECTORS OF SOCIAL SERVICES, 1997

State	Salary	State	Salary
Alabama	NA	Montana	$ 70,420
Alaska	$ 86,292	Nebraska	91,961
Arizona	113,302	Nevada	87,953
Arkansas	105,301	New Hampshire	74,939
California	107,939	New Jersey	100,225
Colorado	93,300	New Mexico	75,352
Connecticut	95,000	New York	102,335
Delaware	96,300	North Carolina	89,411
Florida	101,143	North Dakota	93,732
Georgia	89,424	Ohio	106,683
Hawaii	85,302	Oklahoma	108,651
Idaho	69,888	Oregon	95,544
Illinois	94,535	Pennsylvania	89,500
Indiana	83,417	Rhode Island	105,383
Iowa	86,944	South Carolina	104,328
Kansas	85,638	South Dakota	84,444
Kentucky	76,950	Tennessee	67,236
Louisiana	80,000	Texas	156,014
Maine	77,896	Utah	97,489
Maryland	70,912	Vermont	73,944
Massachusetts	77,547	Virginia	94,778
Michigan	99,994	Washington	115,823
Minnesota	67,504	West Virginia	70,000
Mississippi	NA	Wisconsin	94,290
Missouri	87,804	Wyoming	68,000
		U.S. Virgin Islands	65,000

SOURCE: Council of State Governments, *The Book of the States, 1998–99.*

Since all social workers must possess a college diploma, and many supervisory personnel often have master's degrees, this must be regarded as a low-paying position. Compared to teachers, whose certification requirements are similar but who work many fewer hours, social workers are paid significantly less.

Limited information is available about specific salaries in the field of social work, but the Bureau of Labor Statistics estimated the median earnings of those holding an MSW (master's of social work) to be about $35,000 in 1997; for those with a bachelor's degree, $25,000. The average annual salary for all social workers in the federal government in nonsupervisory, supervisory, and managerial positions was $46,900 in 1997.

Teachers and Administrators, Grades K–12

By far, the largest number of public employees work in the educational system. Over 50 percent of all state and local government workers are paid under education budgets, and about 20 percent of all municipal employees work in schools or universities.

More than 1.7 million persons are employed as kindergarten and elementary school teachers. Another 1.4 million-plus serve as secondary school teachers, and an additional 407,000 work in special education. Over 80 percent of primary school teachers and 90 percent of secondary school teachers work in public schools.

In general, the number of teachers tends to parallel the number of school-age children. Thus, in the 1960s and 1970s, when children of the postwar baby boom generation filled schools, teaching positions were at their all-time highest. By the 1980s, however, as the number of school-age children declined, so did the number of teachers. According to the American Federation of Teachers, a total of 100,000 teachers were laid off between 1981 and 1982 alone. The decline in the growth rate of teachers also flattened out wage rates, causing teacher salaries to grow at less than the rate of inflation.

Throughout the 1990s, however, with baby boomers' children beginning their educational experiences, the number of teachers has expanded again, and promises to continue to grow dramatically. The Department of Education is predicting a need for 2.1 million new teachers in the nation's public schools over the next decade. This prediction is based on a number of factors, including an unusually large number of retirees—fully half of the teachers working today are expected to retire by the year 2007. Additionally, the school-age population is rising, particularly on the secondary school level. Another factor is the increased need for math and science teachers—

there is already a shortage in this area—and politicians and corporations alike are calling for increased emphasis on education in these fields to create the kind of skilled graduates needed for the future job market.

Accomplishing the monumental task of recruiting over 2 million teachers over ten years will not be easy. Many school systems are beginning to turn to alternative programs to find qualified teachers. Military retirees, mid-career changers, and other nontraditional applicants are joining these programs and entering the teaching world, mostly in inner cities and poor rural areas, which have difficulty attracting traditional teaching graduates. Support groups and mentoring programs are also being organized to help new teachers deal with the stressful adjustment period—in hopes to relieve the high "dropout rate" among first- and second-year teachers. While these programs begin to address the teacher shortage, there is no question that many jobs will be available to those qualified individuals who wish to teach—the caveat is that the greatest need will be in areas that many find less than desirable.

Because teachers are paid with taxpayer funds, their salaries are unlikely to equal those in private sector jobs with similar educational and training requirements. On the other hand, teachers usually enjoy good job benefits and work only nine to ten months out of the year. The average teacher salary was $38,509 in 1996–97, a 2.5 percent increase over the previous year. Taking inflation into account, the average salary has increased only 1.6 percent in the past decade. Of course, when taxpayers are footing the bill, it's not inappropriate to ask why teachers' salaries should increase at a faster rate than those of the rest of the economy.

The national average also reflects a wide disparity in salary by state. Teachers in Alaska, Connecticut, New York, and New Jersey, for example, all averaged over $49,000, while the average teacher salary in Mississippi, North Dakota, and South Dakota was less than $28,000. The state averages themselves also fail to reflect vast differences in salaries from one end of the state to the other—school payrolls are under local control—as well as cost-of-living indexes that make some salaries worth more than others. Salaries are higher for public school teachers than for private school teachers.

The principal reason why teachers (not to mention nurses, librarians, and social workers) earn less than other white-collar workers has to do mostly with gender discrimination. These occupations have traditionally been occupied by women, who earn considerably less than men for the same or similar work. To this day, 73.5 percent of public school teachers are women, with the percentages even more pronounced on the elementary level than on the secondary level. So while teachers' unions may be standardizing pay rates within the profession, the monetary rewards of the job remain a severe handicap to attracting and retaining the most talented people. So, too, do

AVERAGE ANNUAL SALARIES OF PUBLIC SCHOOL TEACHERS, 1996–97

State	Average Teacher Salary	Rank	State	Average Teacher Salary	Rank
Alabama	$32,549	37	Montana	$29,950[1]	44
Alaska	50,647[1]	1	Nebraska	31,768	39
Arizona	33,350[1]	32	Nevada	37,340	19
Arkansas	29,975[1]	43	New Hampshire	36,867[1]	21
California	43,474[1]	8	New Jersey	49,349[1]	4
Colorado	36,175[1]	22	New Mexico	29,715	45
Connecticut	50,426	2	New York	49,560	3
Delaware	41,436	11	North Carolina	31,225[1]	42
District of Columbia	45,012[1]	NA	North Dakota	27,711	49
Florida	33,881	29	Ohio	38,831	15
Georgia	36,042	23	Oklahoma	29,270	46
Hawaii	35,842	25	Oregon	40,900	13
Idaho	31,818	38	Pennsylvania	47,429	5
Illinois	42,679	10	Rhode Island	43,019[1]	9
Indiana	38,575	16	South Carolina	32,659	35
Iowa	33,275	33	South Dakota	26,764	50
Kansas	35,873	24	Tennessee	33,789	31
Kentucky	33,950[1]	28	Texas	32,644	36
Louisiana	28,347	47	Utah	31,750	40
Maine	33,800[1]	30	Vermont	37,200[1]	20
Maryland	41,148	12	Virginia	35,837[1]	26
Massachusetts	43,806	7	Washington	37,860	18
Michigan	44,251[1]	6	West Virginia	33,159	34
Minnesota	37,975[1]	17	Wisconsin	38,950[1]	14
Mississippi	27,720	48	Wyoming	31,721	41
Missouri	34,342[1]	27	**U.S. average**	**$38,509**	

[1]Estimate.
SOURCE: National Education Association.

the often rigid teacher licensing requirements that force prospective teachers to take courses that most deem irrelevant and boring.

In an attempt to make it easier for teachers to move from state to state without having to be recertified, the National Board for Professional Teaching Standards in 1993 created a national teacher certification program. Many states have already agreed to drop state licensing requirements for nationally certified teachers who relocate there; North Carolina has promised to repay the $975 exam fee and grant a 4 percent raise to any teacher who completes the program. The Board graduated its first eighty-one teachers in January 1995.

The greatest demand for teachers in the 1990s should be in those states with the fastest-expanding populations and where school enrollment rates will be increasing: Florida, Arizona, Georgia, California, Tennessee, and Texas, among others. For information about job opportunities in teaching, a group called Recruiting New Teachers Inc., provides a toll-free number (1-800-45-TEACH) that offers guidance on how to become a teacher and sends the names of prospective teachers to a network of school districts and teachers' colleges.

State Directors of Education

Most states have two entirely separate administrative offices for education: One sets policy for elementary, secondary, and special education; the other for the university, college, and community college systems.

SALARIES OF STATE DIRECTORS OF EDUCATION

State	Education	Higher Education	State	Education	Higher Education
Alabama	$130,000	$130,000	Montana	$ 62,848	$113,368
Alaska	86,292	NA	Nebraska	100,237	105,070
Arizona	54,600	66,975	Nevada	87,581	182,000
Arkansas	100,213	95,570	New Hampshire	76,983	36,961
California	107,100	131,004	New Jersey	100,225	95,000
Colorado	120,000	110,000	New Mexico	85,001	79,102
Connecticut	84,000	114,000	New York	136,500	NA
Delaware	113,700	61,200	North Carolina	94,552	240,000
Florida	106,870	206,515	North Dakota	56,568	139,909
Georgia	91,578	215,384	Ohio	135,845	157,394
Hawaii	90,041	156,060	Oklahoma	75,000	171,150
Idaho	67,500	N/A	Oregon	67,900	133,668
Illinois	149,203	150,000	Pennsylvania	80,026	77,900
Indiana	63,099	105,000	Rhode Island	105,000	112,289
Iowa	102,560	N/A	South Carolina	92,007	86,603
Kansas	112,000	115,955	South Dakota	70,745	126,000
Kentucky	151,938	NA	Tennessee	86,484	125,000
Louisiana	115,008	155,000	Texas	156,014	125,106
Maine	74,110	N/A	Utah	65,939	NA
Maryland	119,000	96,475	Vermont	67,350	NA
Massachusetts	77,547	80,067	Virginia	116,113	113,800

SALARIES OF STATE DIRECTORS OF EDUCATION

State	Education	Higher Education	State	Education	Higher Education
Michigan	$ 97,363	$ 65,605	Washington	$86,600	$100,008
Minnesota	78,509	108,360	West Virginia	NA	NA
Mississippi	107,243	138,530	Wisconsin	88,089	NA
Missouri	101,748	132,564	Wyoming	77,000	75,000
			U.S. Virgin Islands	65,000	61,600

SOURCE: Council of State Governments, *The Book of the States, 1998–99.*

School Superintendents

According to the American Association of School Administrators, the average salary of school superintendents was $94,000 in 1997. Superintendents in high-profile cities make much more (New York City, $245,000; Seattle, $186,000; Los Angeles, $178,973; and Chicago, $150,000). The school superintendent's job is a very difficult one to assess. How do you determine whether he or she is doing a good job? Test scores? Diminishing violence? Teachers' approval? Politicians' approval? In response to complaints about the state of primary education in our nation's cities, many communities are beginning to hold school superintendents responsible. Houston, Philadelphia, Minneapolis, and Cincinnati are just a few of the cities that indexed school superintendents' salaries to the test scores of their students. The Philadelphia superintendents' contracts are structured so that they get a bonus of up to 16 percent if student achievement improves over their five-year term, but take a 5 percent pay cut if it doesn't. In Houston, a superintendent can be fired if his or her students' scores on a statewide test don't increase.

AVERAGE SALARIES OF SCHOOL SUPERINTENDENTS BY DISTRICT ENROLLMENT SIZE, 1997–98

Position	300–2,499	2,500–9,999	10,000–24,999	25,000 or more
Superintendent	$84,563	$97,842	$106,457	$126,631
Deputy/Associate Superintendents	NA	84,199	91,883	100,443
Assistent Superintendents	74,197	83,273	86,315	91,711

SOURCE: Educational Research Service, *National Survey of Salaries and Wages in Public Schools, 1997–98,* (1998). Reprinted by permission.

Of course, such innovations were not without pitfalls. Educators experimented with similar pay for performance agreements during the 1970s, but abandoned them after learning that many superintendents were raising test scores by simply giving students the answers to the standardized tests in advance.

Teacher Aides and School Bus Drivers

Most of the nation's 981,000 teacher aides work in elementary schools in large cities; an increasing number are being hired to help in bilingual programs. Most school districts pay aides by the hour, but in areas where aides are considered essential, salaries are calculated on a monthly basis, and a distinction is drawn between teaching and nonteaching personnel. The average hourly rate for teacher aides involved in teaching activities was $9.04 an hour in 1995–96; for those involved in nonteaching activities, it was $8.52.

According to the Educational Research Service, school bus drivers employed by public schools averaged $10.69 per hour during the 1993–94 school year. Since driving a school bus is a part-time job, most school bus drivers probably earn less than $20,000 per year. As school enrollments continue to grow, however, the number of jobs for school bus drivers is expected to increase. And because of high turnover, these jobs should be easy to get.

School Counselors

Counselors use a variety of methods to enable students to understand their abilities better. They advise them on personal, special, educational, and career problems and concerns. High school counselors advise on college admissions requirements and financial aid, noncollege career options, and social, behavioral, and other problems. About 175,000 people are employed as counselors, mostly in secondary schools. Jobs as counselors are expected to grow about as fast as the overall rate of job growth between now and the year 2006. New jobs will be created by recent legislation requiring counselors in elementary schools, as well as by the ever-increasing role that counselors are expected to play. However, budget restraints within school districts could have a limiting effect on hiring, as schools generally choose to hire teachers over counselors when limited funds are an issue. The average salary of school counselors in 1995–96 was about $44,100.

AVERAGE SALARIES OF SCHOOL PRINCIPALS BY DISTRICT ENROLLMENT SIZE, 1997–98

Principals	300–2,499	2,500–9,999	10,000–24,999	25,000 or more
Elementary schools	$67,596	$72,530	$69,847	$71,439
Jr. high/middle school	68,810	75,985	73,047	74,343
Sr. high school	74,251	81,633	78,966	80,718
Assistant Principals				
Elementary schools	$61,770	$61,525	$59,112	$59,286
Jr. high/middle school	63,700	66,740	62,860	62,232
Sr. high school	65,833	69,456	66,711	65,772

SOURCE: Educational Research Service, *National Survey of Salaries and Wages in Public Schools, 1997–98* (1998). Reprinted by permission.

School Principals and Assistant Principals

As of 1996 there were 87,125 public schools, including 61,000 elementary schools and 21,000 high schools. All of these buildings are supervised by a management team, headed by the principal, that deals with the issues of curriculum, safety, student counseling, etc. Virtually all of the people in these jobs have extensive teaching experience, but they are also required to take courses in administration and policy making. Their salaries reflect this extra effort, with assistant principals usually earning $10,000 more than experienced faculty members, and principals $20,000 more.

University and College Professors

The number of students enrolled as undergraduates and graduate students in America's 3,600 accredited colleges and universities continues to increase each year. Although the growth has not been as high as the 41 percent recorded between 1970 and 1980, enrollment at institutions of higher education jumped about 20 percent between 1980 and 1996. It stands to reason, therefore, that the number of teachers required to instruct this army of would-be scholars is also increasing. In fact, the number of instructors is growing even faster than the number of students. According to the U.S. Department of Education, in 1980 there were 686,000 teachers at public, private, and religious institutions of higher education charged with instructing 10.5 million undergraduates and 1.5 million graduate students. That's 17.49 students per instructor. By 1992, the number of undergraduates had jumped to 12.5 million, while graduate students skyrocketed to 2.1 million. Instructors, meanwhile, increased to 880,000, for a ratio of 16.54 students per instructor. This figure has remained stable ever since. Wages for professors are ordinarily determined by the salary scale at each institution. There are usually four levels in each scale, with promotions coming from recommendations by senior faculty members:

Instructor—An entry-level position for persons who have not quite completed the requirements for the Ph.D. degree (they are usually in the midst of writing a dissertation). For the most part, instructors teach nine to twelve hours a week, in all the basic courses: English composition, surveys of history, general chemistry, etc. Salaries for the 56,000 instructors in the United States averaged $29,680 in 1994–95. Average total compensation (including health insurance, disability protection, retirement contributions, and, in some cases, room and board) was $37,870.

Assistant Professor—This is also an entry-level job, but usually the Ph.D. is required. These people also teach nine to twelve hours a week, and frequently supervise the running of the large undergraduate courses. At the same time, they must write scholarly articles or books if they wish to become permanent, tenured members of the faculty. To be granted tenure by the department means that you have been accepted as an able scholar and teacher, that you are eligible for promotion, and that you can be dismissed from your job only for the gravest of reasons (ineptitude or failure to live up to your potential are not included). Salaries for the 111,000 assistant professors averaged $39,050 in 1994–95; total compensation averaged $49,350.

Associate Professor—Almost always a tenured position, this rank has become increasingly difficult to obtain. These people teach an average of six to nine hours a week, usually most of the upper-division courses, a few graduate courses, and occasionally they supervise doctoral dissertations. The 116,000 associate professors in the United States averaged $47,040 in salary; their total compensation averaged $59,350.

Full Professor—Promotion to the highest level is based exclusively on one's publications and intellectual standing within the academic community; only rarely does teaching ability enter into the decision. At most universities, full professors teach three to six hours a week and supervise doctoral dissertations. Salaries for the 162,000 full professors averaged $63,450 in 1994–95; average total compensation was $78,890.

STUDENTS AND INSTRUCTORS IN HIGHER EDUCATION, 1980–95			
Category	1980	1990	1995
Undergraduate Students	10,475,000	11,959,100	12,231,700
Graduate Students	1,521,000	1,586,200	1,732,500
All Students	11,996,000	13,818,600	14,261,800
Instructors	686,000	826,000	915,000

SOURCE: U.S. Department of Education, *Digest of Education Statistics, 1997* (1998).

Since 1980, there have been two developments that reflect important changes in the wage and salary practices in the colleges and universities. The first is the necessity of paying science, computer science, engineering, and business teachers more money than those in other disciplines to prevent them from seeking careers in private industry. While the results of this practice won't be known for several years, it is probably safe to predict that the complaints from professors in the humanities and social sciences will be long, loud, and probably of a legal nature.

The second change worth noting centers on the role played by the so-called adjunct professor, a part-time employee of just about every institution of higher learning. About 40 percent of all college teaching jobs are held by adjuncts, up from 22 percent in 1970. Adjuncts are usually young, always untenured, and they work without fringe benefits, job security, or a guarantee of advancement. The going rate across the country is $1,200 to $1,500 per semester course, so the possibility of earning even $15,000 a year is fairly remote.

The following tables list average salaries for all four ranks, arranged according to type of institution. Although many of the schools included are private institutions, they all receive so much public funding in the form of federal grants, state aid, etc., that it is not inappropriate to include their facilities under the rubric of the public payroll. The source for these figures is the 1994–95 salary survey conducted by the American Association of University Professors.

THE IVY LEAGUE				
University, Location	Professor	Associate	Assistant	Instructor
Brown University, Providence, RI	$85,900	$58,200	$49,700	—
Columbia University, NY, NY	103,600	65,200	52,500	$67,700
Cornell University, Ithaca, NY	89,900	64,200	56,200	44,800
Dartmouth College, Hanover, NH	88,700	60,700	51,800	—
Harvard University, Cambridge, MA	116,800	64,300	60,900	45,700

THE IVY LEAGUE

University, Location	Professor	Associate	Assistant	Instructor
University of Pennsylvania, Philadelphia, PA	$ 83,100	$56,000	$45,800	$31,600
Princeton University, Princeton, NJ	110,300	65,400	51,000	43,100
Yale University, New Haven, CT	108,400	60,500	49,700	—

SOURCE: American Association of University Professors, *Annual Report on the Economic Status of the Profession, 1997–1998.* Reprinted by permission.

MAJOR PRIVATE UNIVERSITIES

University, Location	Professor	Associate	Assistant	Instructor
Baylor University, Waco, TX	$ 70,600	$64,400	$42,500	—
Brandeis University, Waltham, MA	75,000	54,600	46,900	—
Brigham Young University, Provo, UT	63,800	49,700	43,300	$35,800
Case Western Reserve University, Cleveland, OH	83,700	60,700	51,100	42,100
Clark University, Worcester, MA	71,600	52,200	45,700	—
Clemson University, Clemson, SC	68,800	51,500	42,000	24,900
Colgate University, Hamilton, NY	82,300	61,600	45,700	—
Duke University, Durham, NC	100,900	65,800	54,300	—
Emory University, Atlanta, GA	96,400	63,100	51,400	—
Howard University, Washington, DC	68,800	49,400	42,200	38,400
Johns Hopkins University, Baltimore, MD	91,100	61,200	51,300	46,300
Marquette University, Milwaukee, WI	73,500	56,200	45,800	—
New York University, New York, NY	106,400	68,400	57,200	40,200
Northwestern University, Evanston, IL	101,400	67,400	58,500	—
Old Dominion University, Norfolk, VA	69,400	51,400	43,500	31,400
Lehigh University, Bethlehem, PA	83,300	59,000	47,000	—
Purdue University, West Lafayette, IN	57,400	44,600	39,900	26,600

MAJOR PRIVATE UNIVERSITIES

University, Location	Professor	Associate	Assistant	Instructor
Rice University, Houston, TX	$ 92,600	$60,700	$52,600	$35,700
Southern Methodist University, Dallas, TX	83,800	56,300	49,100	—
Stanford University, Palo Alto, CA	111,000	75,300	60,100	—
Syracuse University, Syracuse, NY	70,400	53,500	43,700	43,800
Temple University, Philadelphia, PA	86,000	65,300	47,200	38,300
Tufts University, Medford, MA	83,400	62,600	48,300	41,900
Tulane University, New Orleans, LA	85,400	56,700	48,300	—
University of Chicago, Chicago, IL	106,000	68,000	61,400	39,500
Vanderbilt University, Nashville, TN	93,200	61,700	48,700	46,400
Wake Forest University, Winston-Salem, NC	81,300	61,200	45,100	33,900
Washington and Lee University, Lexington, VA	78,800	55,800	43,100	—
Washington University, St. Louis, MO	91,000	59,300	55,200	—
Wesleyan University, Middletown, CT	81,500	55,100	45,400	—

SOURCE: American Association of University Professors, *Annual Report on the Economic Status of the Profession, 1997–98.* Reprinted by permission.

MAJOR STATE UNIVERSITIES

University, Location	Professor	Associate	Assistant	Instructor
University of Alabama, Tuscaloosa	$66,300	$48,900	$40,500	$27,200
University of Alaska, Fairbanks	67,000	55,100	44,300	33,500
Arizona State University, Tempe	74,200	55,000	45,700	28,800
University of Arizona, Tucson	75,000	52,500	46,500	—
University of Arkansas, Fayetteville	66,000	49,700	42,200	29,000
University of California, Berkeley	92,700	61,100	52,000	—
University of California, Los Angeles	92,600	60,700	52,000	—
University of Colorado, Boulder	75,900	55,100	46,000	36,700
University of Connecticut, Storrs	88,000	64,500	50,000	41,500
University of Delaware, Newark	86,300	61,000	48,400	36,300

MAJOR STATE UNIVERSITIES

University, Location	Professor	Associate	Assistant	Instructor
University of Florida, Gainesville	$72,300	$51,500	$45,400	$39,500
Florida State University, Tallahassee	67,800	50,200	45,400	22,100
University of Georgia, Athens	76,400	54,200	47,400	29,100
University of Hawaii, Manoa	75,500	57,000	48,900	35,700
University of Idaho, Moscow	57,700	46,000	40,900	32,700
University of Illinois, Urbana	83,600	58,400	51,200	—
Indiana University, Bloomington	77,400	54,200	43,600	—
University of Iowa, Ames	80,700	55,900	48,400	38,900
University of Kansas, Lawrence	66,900	48,800	42,800	—
University of Kentucky, Lexington	71,200	53,000	45,300	—
Louisiana State University, Baton Rouge	67,500	50,500	42,600	29,600
University of Maine, Orono	61,500	49,800	41,700	31,900
University of Maryland, College Park	81,000	56,100	49,300	37,900
University of Masssachusetts, Amherst	79,300	60,500	49,500	—
Michigan State University, East Lansing	74,200	55,800	46,500	33,200
University of Michigan, Ann Arbor	91,900	65,900	53,000	42,300
University of Minnesota, Minneapolis-St. Paul	81,000	57,500	48,600	39,800
University of Mississippi, University	64,000	49,500	41,300	27,200
University of Missouri, Columbia	76,000	56,900	47,500	36,600
University of Montana, Missoula	60,200	48,700	40,500	30,100
University of Nebraska, Lincoln	73,700	52,000	43,000	32,400
University of Nevada, Reno	78,700	57,300	45,700	—
Rutgers State University, New Brunswick, NJ	89,600	64,600	47,800	30,600
New Mexico State University, Las Cruces	57,100	47,000	39,100	24,900
State University of New York at Albany	76,400	54,600	43,300	—
State University of New York at Buffalo	81,400	57,900	45,500	30,900
University of North Carolina, Chapel Hill	86,000	61,800	49,200	39,000
North Carolina State University, Raleigh	79,900	57,200	50,600	39,300
University of North Dakota, Grand Forks	51,200	42,300	37,200	33,200
Ohio State University, Columbus	81,800	56,300	47,400	37,200
University of Oklahoma, Norman	71,000	48,700	39,800	28,100
University of Oregon, Eugene	64,300	48,300	42,300	32,000
Penn State University, State College	83,100	56,000	45,800	31,600
University of Rhode Island, Kingston	70,400	52,900	44,100	—
University of South Carolina, Columbia	70,700	52,800	43,400	32,700

MAJOR STATE UNIVERSITIES

University, Location	Professor	Associate	Assistant	Instructor
University of South Dakota, Vermillion	$52,200	$40,900	$35,000	$25,100
University of Tennessee, Knoxville	67,400	51,800	42,300	28,000
University of Texas, Austin	82,400	53,700	49,700	42,600
Texas A&M University, College Station	73,400	52,400	45,800	—
University of Utah, Salt Lake City	66,100	47,400	40,100	29,200
University of Vermont, Burlington	67,000	50,900	40,900	—
University of Virginia, Charlottesville	90,900	61,300	48,900	36,300
William and Mary, Williamsburg, VA	79,000	57,700	45,300	34,700
University of Washington, Seattle	73,000	52,900	47,600	31,900
West Virginia University, Morgantown	62,600	50,400	40,200	33,300
University of Wisconsin, Madison	73,900	55,500	50,600	38,700
University of Wyoming, Laramie	57,400	45,300	40,900	43,300

SOURCE: American Association of University Professors, *Annual Report on the Economic Status of the Profession, 1997–98.* Reprinted by permission.

WELL-KNOWN PRIVATE COLLEGES

University	Professor	Associate	Assistant	Instructor
Amherst College, Amherst, MA	$82,300	$57,700	$48,100	—
Barnard College, New York, NY[1]	87,500	59,200	46,600	—
Bowdoin College, Brunswick, ME	82,100	59,400	45,500	—
Bryn Mawr College, Bryn Mawr, PA	77,400	57,100	45,600	—
Carleton College, Northfield, MN	73,100	55,800	44,600	$39,100
Colby College, Waterville, ME	87,900	59,100	42,800	—
Colorado College, Colorado Springs, CO	71,000	55,000	44,600	—
Franklin and Marshall College, Lancaster, PA	74,800	52,100	41,000	36,100
Haverford College, Haverford, PA	77,400	58,200	46,600	—
Lafayette College, Easton, PA	75,300	57,200	44,800	—
Middlebury College, Burlington, VT	79,200	55,700	45,700	42,300
Mills College, Oakland, CA[1]	68,100	50,400	44,400	—
Mount Holyoke College, South Hadley, MA[1]	76,900	56,900	43,700	—
Skidmore College, Saratoga Springs, NY	70,200	54,900	42,200	—
Smith College, Northampton, MA[1]	85,900	58,700	47,000	38,000
Swarthmore College, Swarthmore, PA	87,000	63,500	49,000	—

WELL-KNOWN PRIVATE COLLEGES

University	Professor	Associate	Assistant	Instructor
Vassar College, Poughkeepsie, NY	$77,700	$59,300	$46,200	—
Wellesley College, Wellesley, MA[1]	89,200	63,000	51,000	—
Williams College, Williamstown, MA	86,500	57,300	46,900	—

[1]Women's college.
SOURCE: American Association of University Professors, *Annual Report on the Economic Status of the Profession, 1997–98.* Reprinted by permission.

MAJOR CATHOLIC COLLEGES AND UNIVERSITIES

University	Professor	Associate	Assistant	Instructor
Boston College, Chestnut Hill, MA	$95,300	$66,500	$59,000	$46,100
Catholic University, Washington, DC	67,600	49,100	41,600	38,700
College of the Holy Cross, Worcester, MA	76,900	57,200	45,400	—
DePaul University, Chicago, IL	79,600	60,500	46,200	38,500
DePauw University, Greencastle, IN	59,400	48,900	38,100	—
Duquesne University, Pittsburgh, PA	67,400	53,800	42,700	36,900
Fordham University, New York, NY	85,500	65,700	50,800	38,300
Georgetown University, Washington, DC	99,000	61,900	48,000	41,800
Loyola University, Chicago, IL	82,700	57,200	46,700	—
University of Notre Dame, South Bend, IN	94,100	63,500	53,300	53,500

SOURCE: American Association of University Professors, *Annual Report on the Economic Status of the Profession, 1997–98.* Reprinted by permission.

INSTITUTES OF TECHNOLOGY

University	Professor	Associate	Assistant	Instructor
California Institute of Technology, Pasadena	$110,200	$77,900	$63,500	—
Carnegie-Mellon University, Pittsburgh	93,900	66,100	56,200	—
Georgia Institute of Technology, Atlanta	88,600	64,600	56,000	$30,100
Massachusetts Institute of Technology, Cambridge	104,200	70,300	61,000	35,600
Rensselaer Polytechnic Institute, Troy, NY	85,300	61,100	53,900	—

INSTITUTES OF TECHNOLOGY

University	Professor	Associate	Assistant	Instructor
Rochester Institute of Technology, Rochester, NY	$71,300	$56,000	$47,300	$41,300
Texas Tech University, Lubbock	72,100	50,900	40,600	29,300
Virginia Polytechnic Institute, Blacksburg	74,100	53,700	47,000	28,800

SOURCE: American Association of University Professors, *Annual Report on the Economic Status of the Profession, 1997–98*. Reprinted by permission.

AVERAGE SALARIES OF COLLEGE PROFESSORS BY DISCIPLINE

Discipline	Professor	Associate	Assistant	Instructor
Agricultural Business and Production	$ 69,712	$52,899	$44,778	$35,080
Architecture and Related Programs	69,295	51,271	42,055	34,495
Biological Sciences/Life Sciences	71,704	51,325	43,855	31,973
Business Management	93,610	71,686	66,795	39,644
Communications	67,651	49,584	41,166	31,508
Computer and Information Sciences	87,600	65,060	57,480	35,307
Education	66,653	49,627	40,578	32,570
Engineering	86,249	63,083	54,120	37,309
English Language and Literature/Letters	67,216	46,851	38,447	26,455
Foreign Languages and Literatures	67,129	47,005	38,140	28,339
Health Professions and Related Sciences	90,147	65,373	59,067	42,584
Home Economics	66,786	50,039	41,658	32,233
Law and Legal Studies	105,279	75,670	67,587	38,816
Liberal Arts and Sciences, General Studies and Humanities	65,270	46,044	39,798	29,489
Library Science	69,415	50,423	41,075	30,555
Mathematics	73,922	51,820	44,252	30,645
Philosophy and Religion	66,949	47,260	37,890	29,360
Physical Sciences	77,429	52,449	44,842	34,312
Psychology	73,783	49,678	42,154	32,055
Public Administration and Services	74,303	52,882	42,381	39,373
Social Sciences and History	73,664	50,384	42,222	34,606
Visual and Performing Arts	60,807	45,474	36,807	30,459
Average for all disciplines	**$76,309**	**$54,684**	**$47,488**	**$33,908**

SOURCE: Oklahoma State University, Office of Planning and Budget and Institutional Research, *1997–98 Faculty Salary Survey*. Reprinted by permission.

University and College Administrators

The growth of education has naturally led to an increase in the number of people needed to oversee the maintenance and development of individual institutions on a daily as well as a long-term basis. In most universities, the organizational structure established to carry out these tasks resembles those found in large corporations: chancellors and presidents—frequently referred to as CEOs—are advised by several vice presidents, each of whom is responsible for a particular university activity and for overseeing the work of the deans, who, in a sense, serve as plant or unit managers. These include business officers, public relations officers, registrars, etc. While the presidents make the most money the chief academic officer (often called the provost) and the head business officer earn well over $100,000 at the best and the largest institutions. Student services directors always make significantly less.

In 1995–96, according to the College and University Personnel Association, as reported to the U.S. Bureau of Labor Statistics, median annual salaries for selected administrators in higher education were as follows:

Academic deans	
Medicine	$201,200
Law	141,400
Engineering	112,800
Arts and sciences	82,500
Business	81,700
Education	80,000
Social sciences	61,800
Mathematics	59,900
Student services directors	
Admissions and registrar	$50,700
Student financial aid	45,400
Student activities	34,500

Because administrators now function as a managerial class, their salaries, especially in relation to those of senior faculty members, have never been higher. At some universities, the salary of a dean in a nontechnical area will be $20,000 higher than that of the average full professor in the same school of study.

JOB TITLES AND RESPONSIBILITIES OF
COLLEGE AND UNIVERSITY ADMINISTRATORS

Chief Executive Officer of a System (multicampus operation—frequently called a chancellor, sometimes a president)—He or she is the principal administrative official responsible for the direction of all operations for all units of the system. He or she reports to a governing board.

Chief Executive Officer of a Single Institution—(usually called a president)— He or she directs entire campus operation.

Executive Vice President—The principal administrative official reporting directly to the CEO.

Chief Academic Officer—Often called the provost, he or she is responsible for the direction of the academic program. All matters concerning the faculty, research, curriculum, admissions, and library fall under this office's jurisdiction.

Chief Business Officer—Responsible for the direction of business and financial affairs, including supervision of purchasing, physical plant management, personnel services, accounting, and investments.

Chief Financial Officer—Responsible for investments, accounting, budgets, and related matters.

Chief Planning Officer—Responsible for long-range planning and allocation of resources, including budget planning, sponsoring institutional research, and building additional facilities; frequently implements state and federal regulations.

Chief Budgeting Officer—Responsible for current budgetary operations.

Chief Development Officer—Responsible for institutional development and fund-raising programs; frequently oversees alumni relations and public relations departments.

Chief Public Relations Officer—Responsible for all relations with the public, the media, alumni, and legislators.

Director of Alumni Affairs—Coordinates contacts and services for alumni; develops mailing lists and organizes alumni activities and events.

Chief Student Affairs Officer—Responsible for the direction of all student services and student life programs, including student counseling and testing, career development and placement, student activities, residence life, and minority support programs.

Chief Admissions Officer—Responsible for the admission of undergraduates and, in some institutions, graduate and professional students. May also oversee administration of scholarships.

Registrar—Responsible for student registrations and records. Schedules classes and classrooms, maintains grades for graduation clearance.

Director of Student Financial Aid—Directs the administration of all forms of student aid, including loans and scholarships. Administers all loan programs and awards fellowships.

Director of Career Development and Placement—Provides job placement and counseling services to undergraduates, graduates, and alumni.

Director of Student Counseling—Provides counseling and testing services for all students.

University and College Presidents

It's been a long time since anyone was naive enough to believe that the men and women who run our best institutions of higher learning do so for some Platonic ideal derived from the love of learning or the care and concern for the youth of the world. No, it turns out that the drive for higher and higher compensation designed to bring someone to that nirvana occupied by all those in the top 1 percent of all salaried persons in America has become part of the landscape in the groves of academe as much as it has on Wall Street. The only difference is the sanctimonious posturing of academics who pretend to see no correlation between public disgust with higher education and their salaries. When tuition levels soar to heights no average middle-class family can absorb without mortgaging their future, these enormous salaries stand out as vivid testimony to the shifting values of even our most educated citizens.

The median salary for presidents of major research universities rose to $351,453 in 1996–97, according to the *Chronicle of Higher Education*, and no fewer than thirteen presidents earned over $400,000. At well-known universities with a commitment to graduate education (Dartmouth, Texas Christian University, for example) the median was $207,337, and at four-year colleges it was $179,322.

HIGHEST PAID UNIVERSITY AND COLLEGE PRESIDENTS

Name	University	Total Compensation[1]
Torsten N. Wiesel	Rockefeller University	$546,966
Joe B. Wyatt	Vanderbilt University	525,496
Judith S. Rodin	University of Pennsylvania	514,878
George Rupp	Columbia University	458,480
L. Jay Olivia	New York University	451,643
Richard C. Levin	Yale University	447,265
James M. Stuart	Hofstra University	438,554
William Brody	Johns Hopkins University	435,592
Stephen J. Trachtenberg	George Washington University	425,041
Thomas K. Hearn, Jr.	Wake Forest University	423,871
James O. Freedman	Dartmouth College	410,756
Thomas E. Verhart	California Institute of Technology	399,147
Gerhard Casper	Stanford University	397,995
Steven Sample	University of Southern California	379,126
John E. Murray	Duquesne University	371,833
William Tucker	Texas Christian University	368,360

[1]Includes benefits.
SOURCE: *Chronicle of Higher Education,* October 1998.

II

In the Public Eye and Behind the Scenes

This section is devoted to the world of entertainment, to the whole spectrum of public performance. Included here are famous actors, athletes, and television personalities, as well as highly acclaimed ballet dancers, classical musicians, and stars of the Metropolitan Opera. In each category, we provide salary information for almost every level from union-established minimums to the highest echelon of what today is called "superstardom." In the section on television personalities, for example, you'll find nationally known names such as Tom Brokaw and Ted Koppel, but you'll also learn about anchors in Des Moines and Green Bay. Another example is the section on models, in which Cindy Crawford and Claudia Schiffer are intermingled with unknowns who work in showrooms and at studios, or who appear in the pages of *Playboy*.

Of course, only a small number of people hold these jobs. Combining statistics from the Department of Labor with those from the major associations and unions representing athletes and performers, a generous estimate would be 160,000 all together. There are, however, more than twice that number working behind the scenes to ensure the smooth functioning of the entertainment system. This includes television technicians, film directors, costume designers, stagehands, fashion photographers, athletic coaches, story analysts, choreographers, and many others. In order to show the occupational and economic relationships between the public performers and the support staff, we kept them together in one integrated section. The juxtaposition resulted in a picture that resembles the basic structure of the

American pay system, with the highest salaries being 10, 20, even 30 times higher than those of the overwhelming majority of employees.

Most of us are so dazzled by the vast sums paid to film stars, TV talk-show hosts, and professional athletes that we think of their salaries as aberrations having no relation whatsoever to the everyday world of work and pay. And as aberrations many people assume that these high salaries have no effect on pay levels outside the world of entertainment. Not only are both these assumptions false, they also preclude any exploration of just what the limits of pay in relation to work might be.

Whether any one person's work can actually be worth $14 million or more a year is in itself an interesting and at least debatable question. But when the subjects are athletes, entertainers, talk-show hosts, and news commentators, the value of their work in relation to their pay simply cannot stand up under even the mildest forms of scrutiny. For no matter how much we admire the pitching prowess of a David Cone or the verbal skills of a Dan Rather, and no matter how many millions watch David Letterman, it is difficult, at best, to think of what they do as being worth 50 or 100 times more than the work of the best scientists, the best engineers, most doctors, and all justices of the Supreme Court.

No wonder high-salaried people who have great responsibilities (chief executives at large corporations, for example) or those who have mastered a large body of complicated knowledge (criminal lawyers or high-powered accountants) frequently justify their earnings by pointing to those of people in show business.

In fact, as shown by the tables on the following pages, the top-paid corporate executives did not earn as much as the top-earning entertainers in 1996–97; but, their earnings far outstripped those in professional sports. Whether it is more difficult to run a large corporation than it is to become heavyweight champion of the world or a world-famous rock star is, of course, subject to debate. So is the question of who might return greater value to society per dollar earned. Certainly when the figure in question is $20 million or more, attempts to justify such compensation strain credibility. But when one considers that NBC reportedly pays Tom Brokaw $7 million to read the news, the salaries of corporate executives seem perfectly reasonable.

Such comparisons have the value of highlighting the way large salaries of public performers can drive up those in the world of business. But the comparisons should not obscure the more interesting fact that the highest salaries in big business and show business come from the same source, America's largest corporations. Just a glance through the pages in this part will show that television is the most lucrative medium for any performer. Moreover, the economic power of the television industry is so pervasive that it affects salary levels in areas seemingly outside it perimeters. The astronom-

THE HIGHEST PAID ENTERTAINERS, 1996–97	
Name	**Average Income, 1996–97**
Steven Spielberg	$313,000,000
George Lucas	241,000,000
Oprah Winfrey	201,000,000
Michael Crichton	102,000,000
The Beatles	98,000,000
Jerry Seinfeld	94,000,000
David Copperfield	85,000,000
Stephen King	84,000,000

SOURCE: *Forbes* magazine

ical sums guaranteed to movie stars, for example, are frequently predicated on the sales of films to television, frequently before production has begun. More often than not, in fact, the deal to make a film is based on guaranteed dollars from a television network.

The escalating salaries of professional athletes over the last decade can also be traced to revenues generated from television. Sure, baseball owners have raised ticket prices, but certainly not enough to pay the average player a million dollars a year, not to mention the 25 or so players who receive more than $5 million a year. As long as the fees for broadcasting ball games can be raised, the owners can keep increasing players' pay and the smart ones can still make a profit themselves. Conversely, if money dries up, there is less to spend on player salaries without raising ticket prices. The proof of this was seen in 1994, when CBS realized it spent far too much for the rights to broadcast major league baseball games. Without this cash infusion, the owners attempted to impose a salary cap on the players in an attempt to fix the other side of the ledger sheet, which prompted the players to go out on strike for 234 days, the longest work stoppage in sports history.

In a similar vein, in 1998 the NBA signed a $3 billion television deal but while offering significant pay increases also demanded that players cut back the percentage of revenues they receive as salary. When the players' union refused, the owners locked them out, saying essentially that they, the owners, deserved a greater return on their investment. In the absurd world of television-dominated sports the players were turning down tens of million of dollars on the basis of fairness.

But let's not belabor the point; to think only in financial terms misses the point. The essential question is whether these multimillion-dollar salaries are creating a new kind of American aristocracy whose economic security is based not on an ancestral blood connection nor on the booty left by more talented or ruthless forebears, but on the wealth acquired by being famous And not famous for an achievement, an accomplishment, a discovery, a daring feat, or any other traditional reason, but simply because of what one does on television.

While most Americans do not begrudge these individuals these large sums of money, they are keenly aware of the inherent injustices in a system that allows celebrities to earn so much more than intelligent, productive members of society. Whether anything can ever be done about it remains, at least at this time in our history, a very academic question.

IN THE PUBLIC EYE

ACTORS

Acting is an enormously seductive occupation, and thousands of young people succumb to its magic and mystery every year. Most of them can be found in New York or Los Angeles working as typists, messengers, waitresses, clerks, or busboys, jobs that allow some flexibility in terms of hours. This enables them to take acting classes, go to auditions, and appear in nonpaying showcase productions while still earning a living. The notion that some of America's most famous and accomplished actors started just his way, from Henry Fonda and Jimmy Stewart to Tom Hanks and Susan Sarandon, keeps the dream of success alive.

From a pedestrian, career-minded point of view, of course, these people are simply wasting their time, since the odds of ever finding work are extremely low. Approximately 60,000 actors a year are paid for their efforts, but there are at least 140,000 professionals looking for jobs. According to all three major unions representing actors, the unemployment rate among their members is extremely high and is likely to remain so.

For example, the Actors' Equity Association (AEA), which represents all stage actors, including Broadway, off-Broadway, off-off-Broadway, and regional theatrical stage actors all over the country had 33,836 total members during the 1996–97 season. Only 15,215 were employed. Those AEA members who did find work worked an average of 17.4 weeks and earned an average annual salary of $13,967. Of the 90,000 members of the Screen Actors Guild, (SAG), nearly 80 percent earned less than $5,000 in 1996.

Members of the American Federation of Television and Radio Artists (AFTRA) number approximately 80,000, yet dramatic serials, including such major television shows as *ER,* employ only 2,000 principal actors, extras, and occasional players per year. Radio shows, television commercials, and other broadcasts using AFTRA performers employ even fewer persons.

There are many actors who belong to both SAG and AFTRA or to all three of the major unions for performers, so the number of the unemployed reported by each does not represent a total of nonworking actors. Those who do finally get that break, be it big or small, will find that the unions do a good job of taking care of their own, and remuneration for actors is often rewarding, though the art of propelling oneself into high-paying jobs sometimes takes more practice and concentration than is actually required by the coveted role. Despite the grim statistics, Los Angeles alone is forecasting the creation of 16,000 additional entertainment jobs in this $20 billion-a-year industry due to a growing demand for films and television.

Stage Actors

On Broadway, actors are guaranteed weekly minimum salaries of $1,090. The average top salary is much higher—approximately $4,000 weekly—and stars receive even more.

In so-called off-Broadway theaters, actors' wages are dependent on the size of the theater. Off-Broadway theaters are those New York City theaters that have the capability of seating between 100 and 499 persons. According to the 1998 Actors' Equity contract for off-Broadway performers, salaries are graduated between $396 and $678 weekly, with stars always receiving more as negotiated in their own contracts.

Off-off Broadway theaters are those with fewer than 100 seats. Salaries for actors in off-off Broadway theaters depend upon whether the theater is privately run or is publicly funded and run as a nonprofit organization. Actors performing in funded nonprofit theaters are guaranteed a Fairshare Minimum Reimbursement as determined by the size of the theater and its gross revenues.

Theaters with productions of under $5,000 come under the Basic Showcase Code as nonfunded stage companies. Actors for these off-off Broadway theaters receive no salary but are paid a so-called carfare expense of $3.00 per day. This is awarded for four weeks of rehearsal and twelve to sixteen performances within a four-week period of time.

Regional theaters are the last category but are certainly a growing and important element in the revitalized life of the American stage. Payment for actors in many regional theaters is regulated by the Actors' Equity Association. Regional theaters are divided into categories A–D, according to each theater's gross and their budget for the season. For example, an A theater would be the Tyrone Guthrie in Minneapolis or the American Conservatory Theater in San Francisco. All touring companies, such as the American Conservatory, must pay their actors on either an A or a B level, depending upon

---

MINIMUM WEEKLY SALARIES FOR ACTORS IN REGIONAL THEATER

A theaters	$628
B+ theaters	601
B theaters	577
C theaters	546
D theaters	451

SOURCE: Actors' Equity Association as of March 1998.

the company's gross. The well-known Actors' Theatre of Louisville, Kentucky, where the plays of many of America's newest playwrights have premiered, is a B theater.

Television Actors

All actors appearing on television must be members of the Screen Actors Guild or the American Federation of Radio and Television Artists. Most are members of both. The unions set rules governing basic working conditions, including the minimum pay rates. These rates vary, depending on whether the program is a series shown during the day—e.g., a soap opera—or a series aired during the prime time hours of 8:00 P.M. to 11:00 P.M. (Eastern time). Minimum rates also depend on whether the actor has a series contract or works on a freelance basis. Freelance actors in prime time are paid on either a daily, three-day, or weekly rate; those in soap operas are paid per episode; all minimum rates go up after eighteen months. Finally, there are also minimum rates for bit players, known officially as "five lines or less performers." The basic rates are shown in the accompanying tables.

Stars, of course, earn considerably more than scale. Although well-known television actors rarely come close to making what major film stars do, the pay is very good, and the work is far less demanding.

On the long-running soap operas, for example, the leading characters routinely make over $400,000 a year, and breakout stars earn double that. Susan Lucci—who is better known for her streak of not winning a Daytime Emmy Award than she is for her role as Erica Kane on *All My Children*—is the highest paid TV soap star, according to *TV Guide,* with an annual salary of $1 million. And that doesn't include the money she receives for pitching Ford cars and trucks. Apparently her lack of Emmys never affected her financial rewards.

The highest TV salaries, however, are reserved for the programs that attract the largest audiences, so prime-time players do best of all, as the accompanying charts make clear. When a show runs for years, the actors' values increase proportionately.

The amounts paid to lead actors in hit TV series continue to escalate. In the early 1980s, Linda Evans and Joan Collins reportedly each received $75,000 per episode of *Dynasty.* Alan Alda was the first to break the $200,000 per episode barrier for his work on *M*A*S*H.* The *Seinfeld* costars received $600,000 each an episode. Why the huge paychecks? *Seinfeld* earned NBC more than $200 million a year; the last episode in May 1998 was sad for more than just the fans of the show. Warner Bros. gave the *ER* stars bonus checks worth up to $1 million each. The studio executives were showing their gratitude—they will make $850 million over the course of a three-year deal with NBC. Normally the actors receive only between $50,000 and $150,000 per episode. However, Tim Allen of *Home Improvement* had the top TV salary while that show was on the air. He received $1.25 million per episode. Paul Reiser and Helen Hunt each got $1 million per *Mad About You* episode.

MINIMUM DAILY RATES FOR TELEVISION ACTORS[1]

Program Length	1995–96	1996–97
Day Actor, Dramatic Program		
over 15 to 30 minutes	$ 506	$ 524
over 45 to 60 minutes	681	705
over 60 to 90 minutes	832	861
over 90 to 120 minutes	1,003	1,038
Day Actor, Serials		
over 15 to 30 minutes	$ 466	$ 482
over 45 to 60 minutes	621	643
over 60 to 90 minutes	776	803

MULTIPLE PERFORMANCES IN ONE CALENDAR WEEK[1]

Program Length	1995–96	1996–97
Over 15 to 30 Minutes		
1 performance	$ 316	$ 327
2 performances	584	604
3 performances	819	848
4 performances	976	1,010
5 performances	1,135	1,175
Over 45 to 60 Minutes		
1 performance	$ 660	$ 683
2 performances	1,060	1,097
3 performances	1,260	1,304
4 performances	1,513	1,556
5 performances	1,857	1,922
Over 60 to 90 Minutes		
1 performance	$ 832	$ 861
2 performances	1,199	1,241
3 performances	1,447	1,498
4 performances	1,827	1,891
5 performances	2,331	2,413

MULTIPLE PERFORMANCES IN ONE CALENDAR WEEK[1]		
Program Length	**1995–96**	**1996–97**
Over 90 to 120 Minutes		
1 performance	$1,003	$1,038
2 performances	1,419	1,469
3 performances	1,639	1,696
4 performances	2,125	2,199
5 performances	2,679	2,773

PERFORMERS WHO SPEAK 5 LINES OR LESS[1] (single performance)		
Program Length	**1995–96**	**1996–97**
over 15 to 30 minutes	$ 243	$ 252
over 45 to 60 minutes	301	312
over 60 to 90 minutes	343	355
over 90 to 120 minutes	392	406

Compensation for Overnight Location Work

On any day in which a performer travels to or from an overnight location and performs work on the same day, the time spent in travel, less any meal period, shall be added to the performer's rehearsal hours. On any non-work day, he is entitled to a $75 per diem.

[1]For work on ABC, CBS, and NBC networks. FOX network rates are slightly higher.
SOURCE: AFTRA contracts.

Since American television runs on a twenty-four-hour-a-day schedule, programming must be found to fill up all this time. That's why so many of the same old shows keep cropping up at all hours of the day and night. For many actors this has proved to be a financial windfall. Since 1954, producers have had to pay actors a fee almost every time a program is rerun. By 1979, this was big business. In recent years the Screen Actors Guild has issued checks worth an estimated $50 million to its members for reruns just in the United States.

Known in the business as "residuals," these payments are based on individual agreements between actors and producers. Of course, stars make the most, but there are minimums based on the number of times a series is rerun. The first time a series or an episode from a series is rebroadcast (usually in the spring or summer, after the initial fall and winter airing), all actors receive exactly what they did the first time. Anytime the show is rerun in prime time (a rare occurrence after the first year), all actors are also paid exactly what they were paid the first time. After this, residuals become a complicated matter based on percentages of base salaries and union minimums, usually 50 percent on first reruns not shown in prime time and 40 percent on the second, descending to 5 percent on the thirteenth rerun.

Some famous programs such as *Bonanza* and *Gunsmoke* became so popular around the world that producers found it more economical to purchase the principal actors' residual rights for a lump sum. *Bonanza*'s Lorne Greene supposedly received several million dollars, while James Arness, Amanda Blake, and Milburn Stone of *Gunsmoke* each received $1 million. The cast of *Star Trek,* on the other hand, received residuals for only six reruns and based only on minimum rates. No one could have predicted the show's immense popularity in reruns in the twenty years since it went off the air: *Star Trek* has run in more than one hundred markets and has inspired seven feature-length movies and almost as many sequel series. The actors on the original series received payment only for their participation in the movies.

Today, as entertainment technology expands and new devices for information storage and retrieval spring up year after year, actors find their faces on the fronts of video tapes and on the screens of airport pay-TVs. Under an agreement worked out by the unions and the people who run pay-TV, the actors receive 4.5 percent of the distributor's worldwide gross if the program is played on each of the distributor's pay television systems for ten days out of one year. The same 4.5 percent take on the worldwide gross applies if a videotape producer releases 100,000 cassettes of the actor's show, or if a distributor sells his show to cable television. As the late actor Ted Knight, best known for his role as the anchorman on *The Mary Tyler Moore Show*, said, ". . . anytime they show an actor's face on the screen, he should get paid for it."

Actors in Advertising

If it weren't for radio and television commercials, a great many more actors would be out of work. Over 45,000 TV commercials are made every year, and many actors maintain their livelihoods from the seemingly bottomless purse of advertising. All minimum pay rates are set by SAG or AFTRA, and the following figures are based on 1997–2000 contracts. The basic contracts are very long and, at times exceedingly complex, so the tables printed here are only representative.

TELEVISION COMMERCIALS

Minimum pay rates depend on such obvious factors as whether the actors are on-camera, and whether they speak or sing or only have their hands shown. The union contract also lists minimum payments for different kinds

MINIMUM RATES FOR TV COMMERCIAL SESSIONS[1]	
On-Camera	
Principal performers, stunt performers, solo/duo singers and dancers	$478.70
Group singers/dancers, 3–5	350.45
Group singers/dancers/speakers, 6–8	310.25
Group singers/dancers/speakers, 9 or more	256.60
Off-Camera	
Principal performers, solo/duo singers, and dancers	$359.95
Group singers/speakers, 3–5	203.00
Group singers/speakers, 6–8	176.15
Group singers/speakers, 9 or more	143.65

[1]At the end of the session, principal performers are advised of the number of commercials made and, in addition to session fee, receive the equivalent of a session fee in excess of one.
SOURCE: AFTRA contract, 1997–2000.

of commercials, including "dealer commercials," which are made for local use only, and "program commercials," which pay actors on the basis of how often they are shown.

The most successful actors in commercials can make a great deal of money. What everyone hopes for, of course, is to become a spokesperson for a particular brand name. The name Bill Cosby, for example, became synonymous with Jell-O Pudding after years of touting the company's products to children in a series of commercials for which he earned over $1 million annually. Those ads proved so successful that Kodak among others also enlisted Cosby's services. Candice Bergen has similarly come to represent SPRINT telephone services, while Jerry Seinfeld is now the face of the American Express Card. Officials at both companies are tight-lipped about what they pay for these endorsements, but it is safe to assume the rewards are substantial, given that both actors were major stars in top-rated sitcoms.

MINIMUM DAILY RATES FOR CABLE TV COMMERCIALS

The compensation to each principal performer for each thirteen-week cycle of cable use of a commercial shall be computed by multiplying the applicable unit price by the aggregate unit weight of all cable systems and networks on which the commercial is aired (see below). Although the contract is complicated, what it means is that actors are well paid for commercials. However, in no event shall compensation be less than the session fee, nor,

CABLE UNITS AND PRICES PER UNIT

Cable	Principals On-Camera	Principals Off-Camera	Groups On-Camera 3-5	Groups On-Camera 6-8	Groups On-Camera 9+	Groups Off-Camera 3-5	Groups Off-Camera 6-8	Groups Off-Camera 9+
Minimum	$478.70	$359.95	$350.45	$310.25	$256.60	$203.00	$176.15	$143.65
Units 1–50	4.57	3.43	3.35	2.96	2.45	1.94	1.68	1.37
Units 51–100	3.97	2.99	2.90	2.57	2.12	1.68	1.46	1.19
Units 101–150	3.37	2.53	2.47	2.18	1.81	1.43	1.24	1.01
Units 151–200	2.77	2.09	2.03	1.80	1.49	1.18	1.02	0.83
Units 201–1,000 each	0.35	0.26	0.26	0.23	0.19	0.15	0.13	0.10
Cable Maximum (1000 units)	1,014.00	760.00	745.50	659.50	545.50	431.50	374.00	300.00

SOURCE: 1997–2000 AFTRA TV Recorded Commercials Contract.

PROGRAM USE FEES FOR TV COMMERCIALS

| | Principals | | Groups | | | | | |
| | On-Camera | Off-Camera | On-Camera | | | Off-Camera | | |
			3-5	6-8	9 +	3-5	6-8	9 +
1st Use	$ 478.70	$ 359.95	$ 350.45	$ 310.25	$256.60	$203.00	$176.15	$143.65
2nd Use	122.70	96.00	113.70	97.35	79.65	61.70	53.65	44.00
3rd Use	97.35	76.35	89.00	80.65	65.95	57.65	49.35	40.30
4–13 each use	97.35	76.35	84.00	75.65	62.00	52.65	45.95	37.65
14+ each use	46.65	34.65	29.00	24.65	20.00	21.00	19.70	16.35
13 uses guaranteed	1,445.50	1,119.65	1,201.90	1,073.70	881.85	731.70	636.85	521.10
14–18 each use	92.00	69.88	67.25	58.86	48.07	44.43	40.06	33.02

SOURCE: 1997–2000 AFTRA TV Recorded Commercials Contract.

for the first eighteen months of the contract term, more than the price for 160 units.

RADIO COMMERCIALS

Those reassuring voices on the radio offering promises of fast relief or urging you to run to the local supermarket are compensated in many different ways. There are prime-time contracts and commercial contracts, national contracts and local contracts, but in order to give some idea of the pay rates for this work, we have provided some of the basic minimum rates for radio actors and announcers set by AFTRA. These minimums are applicable whether the commercial is aired nationally, regionally, or to a single small town. Each performer's or announcer's rate of pay depends on how many times the commercial is aired; how many announcers, actors, singers, or dancers are employed in the commercial; and to where and to how many places the advertisement is broadcast.

Celebrities in Advertising

The tradition of using famous names and faces in advertising dates back to the turn of the century. Stars of the first magnitude, including Sarah Bernhardt, Lillian Russell, and Enrico Caruso, were the start of a long line of well-known performers who took part in what is known as the "celebrity endorsement technique" Legendary movie stars from Douglas Fairbanks, Mary Pickford, and Charlie Chaplin to Spencer Tracy, Clark Gable, and Gary Cooper all put their seal of approval on American brand names. So, too, have genuine heroes such as Amelia Earhart, Charles Lindbergh, and Neil Armstrong. Celebrities have always done endorsements because the money was good, while advertisers have discovered that well-known people give their ads a much stronger impact. The same is true today.

Most recipients of this wealth today are formerly well-known actors or personalities who have passed their prime, such as Lauren Bacall or Ed McMahon, or would-be actors who will most likely never reach stardom. Others are active or recently retired athletes trying to cash in on their inevitably short-lived success. As the payments get larger, however, popular actors like James Earl Jones find endorsements hard to resist.

One problem plaguing celebrity endorsements, however, has been the unexpected fall from grace. Allegations of sexual misconduct ended Michael Jackson's long-term contract as creative consultant and performer in Pepsi-Cola commercials—a stint for which he'd been receiving $5 million every three years. And O. J. Simpson's role as defendant in a double murder trial obviously curtailed his other roles as celebrity spokesperson for Hertz Rent-A-Car and Tropicana orange juice.

Another phenomenon that has grown by leaps and bounds is the TV "infomercial." Program-length commercials featuring celebrities as hosts and guests have blossomed into a $750 million business. And although infomercials were once considered the "ugly stepchild of advertising," celebrities are now waiting in line to host them, said Steve Howard, president of Williams Television Time, an infomercial production company. "We used to have to beat down their doors to get them [to participate]; now, they're flocking to us."

The reason, no doubt, is money. A star can make up to $100,000 for shooting an infomercial, in addition to royalties that can be as high as 5 percent of gross sales, according to *Time.* After filming an infomercial for The Perfect Smile tooth whitener, Vanna White received roughly $1 million in royalties in the first four months alone (gross sales reached $20 million during that period). This is probably why Ali MacGraw hawks beauty products, Victoria Principal promotes a skin care line, and Christie Brinkley sells gym products with Chuck Norris.

FEES FOR CELEBRITIES IN ADS AND COMMERCIALS

Cher: The reigning queen of the half-hour infomercial, Cher is reportedly paid $1 million annually to promote Lori Davis Hair Care Products. The stint was so successful, in fact, that the superstar decided to buy and promote her very own line of cosmetics.

Bill Cosby: One of Hollywood's wealthiest men, Cosby has worked for Jell-O, Ford, Del Monte, Coca-Cola, Texas Instruments, E. F. Hutton, Chrysler, and Kodak. His fees are said to be over $1 million per client annually—a very conservative estimate.

Kathie Lee Gifford: Regis Philbin's outspoken morning show cohost has literally been singing the praises of Carnival Cruise lines in TV ads for several years now, reportedly to the tune of $1 million annually.

"They wouldn't think of shilling products back home," reports *People* magazine, but in Japan where "yen for integrity is a steal," America's top box office draws peddle Japanese wares. For $1 million annually, *Eddie Murphy* could be seen kissing a Toyota on Japanese television. For the same price, *Arnold Schwarzenegger* sold soup, *Sylvester Stallone* hustled ham, and brat-packer *Charlie Sheen* plugged Tokyo Air Conditioners; Leonardo di Caprio appears in Japanese commercials for $4 million.

Not all celebrities, though, are willing to cash in on their fame, no matter how tempting the offer. Late night TV's *David Letterman*—who has never publicly endorsed a product—turned down a five-year, $25-million offer to do Purina Dog Food commercials.

Michael Jordan: The All-time King of Endorsements

The greatest basketball player of all time—and an all-around good citizen—deserves a separate listing here because his name and face have been attached to so many products that it's hard to keep track of them all. Media experts estimate that despite his 1999 retirement from the NBA, Jordan will be kept very busy for most of the next decade.

Here's a list of most of Jordan's corporate allies, the length of his agreements, and the estimated payments he receives:

AMF Bowling Worldwide: 1997–2002—They purchased his golf company and agreed to build a new "MJ" golf center; there is to be an orange bowling ball with Jordan's name on it that will sell for $89 (Jordan gets a percentage).

Bijan Fragrances: 1996–2006—Jordan is guaranteed $1 million annually, plus royalties, that could add $4 million a year for "Michael Jordan" cologne. Other products, including items related to shaving, are in the works.

Chicagoland Chevrolet Dealers: Since 1984, Jordan gets about $1 million a year, plus the use of a Corvette.

General Mills: Since 1998, he has appeared on Wheaties boxes seventeen times prior to this contract, which will involve a "tribute" box and some other deals worth an estimated $1 million.

MCI—WorldCom: 1996–2006—Jordan appears in ads, does voice-overs, and nets about $4 million annually in cash and stock options.

Nike: 1995–2020—Probably the longest endorsement contract in history, this provides for Jordan to have a staff of twenty people working for him until 2020. Estimates of his earnings are in the tens of millions since he *is* the company's image.

Oakley Eyewear: 1995–2005—Jordan gets $500,000 to $1 million a year for use of his image in print ads and, as a member of Oakley's board, his "innate sense of style," the company said.

Quaker Oats: 1991–2001—His total deal is $18 million, mostly for use of "his Airness" in TV spots for Gatorade.

Ray-O-Vac: 1995–2005—Jordan receives about $2 million a year for appearing in their ads for batteries, not as an athlete but as "a person."

Sara Lee: 1990–2000—For $2 million a year, Jordan appears in this conglomerate's underwear ads and in their Ball Park Franks commercials; both parties have been very happy with the results.

Sportsline USA: 1996–2006—This Internet-based media company pays Jordan about $2 million a year for ads, promotions, and occasional audio programs and on-line chats with subscribers.

Upper Deck: 1991–2002—This company puts out Jordan's trading cards and claims it has exclusive rights to autographed material; Jordan does signings under its auspices.

Wilson Sporting Goods: 1984 to unspecified date in the future—Jordan gets $1 million a year for his autographed ball, and an undisclosed amount for his endorsement of the company's golf equipment.

Stuntmen and Extras

There are over two thousand stuntmen in the Screen Actors Guild. The men and women who risk life and limb for film are well-rewarded, and rightfully so. Take thirty-two-year-old Dan Robinson, for example, who, in the filming of *Highpoint* went skydiving in a business suit 1,150 feet off Toronto's CN Tower before he opened a safety chute and floated three hundred feet to the ground. Dan received $150,000 for the six-second fall.

For falling off horses, out of cars, and down stairwells and similar antics, stuntpersons command the same minimum price as principal performers. But most professional stuntpeople, especially stunt drivers, make up to $8,000 or $9,000 a day, or from $100,000 to $150,000 a year, if the business at hand is particularly risky.

Even the hordes of nonacting persons who make up the corps of extras in movies and television are guaranteed minimum salaries, and the pay isn't at all bad for standing around in period costume all day and reading comics between takes. If they do something special, such as ride a horse or a motorcycle or just drive a car, they are placed on a higher scale. If they are employed to do special little silent bits, such as deal cards in a major casino scene or even play dead in a battle scene, they are paid a higher rate. Below are the basic minimum daily rates for extras under the 1994–1997 AFTRA Network Television Code:

DAYTIME SERIAL: RATES			
Program Length	Program Fee Principal Performer	Program Fee 5 Lines or Less	Extras
Half-hour program	$482	$228	$ 99
One-hour program	$643	$280	$128

NON-DRAMATIC PROGRAMS: RATES

Program Length	Program Fee Principal Performer	Program Fee 5 Lines or Less
Half-hour program	$ 537	$252
One-hour program	$ 683	$312
One and one-half-hour program	$ 861	$355
Two-hour program	$1,038	$406

PRIME TIME DRAMATIC PROGRAMS

Category of Performer	Principal Performer Program Fee	Extras
Principal performer day rate	$ 559	
3-day rate	$1,415	
Weekly rate	$1,942	
General extra		$75
Special ability extra		$85

EXTRAS: RATES (VARIETY SHOWS)

Program Length	Program Fee
Half-hour program	$106
One-hour program	$134
One and one-half-hour program	$163
Two-hour program	$192

PROGRAMS (Other than Variety or Serials)

Category	Program Fee
General extra	$75
Special ability	$85

SOURCE: AFTRA Contracts.

The Actor as Conglomerate

TV and move personalities have learned to cash in on their celebrity in a multitude of ways. According to *Forbes,* Oprah Winfrey earned about $97 million in 1996 from all sources, which include the production company that owns the rights to Oprah's syndicated talk show. The key to such large

HIGHEST PAID MOVIE ACTORS

Name	Movie	Fee per Film
Bruce Willis	*Die Hard 4*	$35 million
Sylvester Stallone	Three-picture deal	20 million
Jim Carrey	*Liar, Liar*	20 million
Harrison Ford	*Devil's Own*	20 million
Eddie Murphy	*The Nutty Professor*	20 million
Mel Gibson	*Lethal Weapon 4*	20 million
John Travolta	*Primary Colors*	17 million
Nicolas Cage	*Snake Eyes*	16 million
Julia Roberts	*Notting Hill*	15 million
Arnold Schwarzenegger	*Junior*	15 million
Bruce Willis	*Die Hard III*	15 million
Kurt Russell	*Breakdown*	15 million
Tom Cruise	*Interview with the Vampire*	14 million
Demi Moore	*Striptease*	14 million
Will Smith	*Enemy of the State*	14 million
Sandra Bullock	*Speed 2*	12 million
Sean Connery	*The Rock*	12 million
Sigourney Weaver	*Alien: Resurrection*	11 million
Jack Nicholson	*As Good as It Gets*	10 million

SOURCE: Various publications.

earnings, in addition to a winning personality and a modicum of talent, seems to lie in diversification. Top TV stars inevitably try their hands in movies with mixed results. Many appear in commercials; some have their own production companies. It is a safe bet that all have an entourage of accountants, lawyers, and managers to advise them. In its list of the 100 most powerful people in Hollywood, *Premiere* magazine printed several of the following fees for movie actors. Other figures are reprinted from newspapers and other industry publications.

The power of Hollywood actors is undeniable. Those with a proven track record of box office power can command enormous fees, even before it is determined what their next movie will be. Some stars, like Al Pacino, have what is called a "pay-or-play" fee: Pacino won't even look at a script if the movie pays him less than $6 million; Keanu Reeves commands an $8 million pay-or-play fee. The newest players in the game are increasing their worth amazingly quickly, due in part to the tremendous impact an Oscar nomination can have on their career and worth. Matt Damon, star and co-writer of *Good Will Hunting*, received $300,000 for acting in the movie (and

$350,000 for cowriting it with Ben Affleck) and can now expect between $3 and $6 million, according to the *Wall Street Journal*'s Oscar coverage. Leonardo DiCaprio, according to the same sources, received $2 million for *Titanic* in addition to huge bonuses following the film's international success; he can now get between $15 and $20 million for his next film. Jack Nicholson is already a major player. He, like Pacino, has his preset rules: He commands $15 million a picture. In exchange for profit participation, he accepted a mere $10 million for *As Good as It Gets*. It got even better—he won the Oscar for Best Actor for the film. This makes it clear why the average cost of making and marketing a movie, according to the Motion Picture Association of America, rose to nearly $60 million last year.

Many of Hollywood's biggest names also receive a percentage of the box office gross receipts, or "points," as they are known in the industry. This sweetens the deal, and it's safe to assume that most of the stars listed above have gotten such offers. Robert Redford's total of $24 million for starring in *Indecent Proposal* came from a combination of actors' fees and a draw on box office receipts. Jack Nicholson's deal for his participation in the first *Batman* movie was even sweeter: In addition to a seven-figure acting salary, Nicholson received a percentage of the film's receipts as well as a portion of the licensing and merchandising revenue accrued through sales of Batman T-shirts, hats, posters, etc. Among the top female stars, only Julia Roberts and Michelle Pfeiffer can get these kinds of deals.

OTHER PERFORMERS

Dancers

In opera, ballet, musical comedy, or on television variety shows, dancing has been, in step with its tribal, ritualistic origins, a group activity. But it has

MINIMUM TELEVISION PAY FOR DANCERS	
Program Length (group size of 3 or more persons)	Pay
5 minutes or less	$195
5 to 15 minutes	390
Over 15 minutes to 30 minutes	605
Over 30 minutes to 60 minutes	752
Over 90 minutes to 120 minutes	862

SOURCE: AFTRA contracts.

also supported, especially in the twentieth century, the ego demands of solo performers. The flamboyantly ill-fated Nijinsky and Isadora Duncan come immediately to mind, but more recently, relatively stable superstars in leotards such as Mikhail Baryshnikov and the late Rudolf Nureyev have added a new vitality to dance that has helped to increase its following.

But as in any of the performing arts, stars are stars and the rest are just so many hoofers, nameless legs in a Rockettes lineup or a Busby Berkeley fantasy. Broadway stage shows and various ballet troupes across the country always offer spots for a handful of dancers, but it is mainly a young person's vocation, and many drop out or become instructors or choreographers.

In all, only about 8,000 dancers are paid to perform on the stage, screen, and television. Considering the time, practice, and wear and tear on the body that go into perfecting a single routine, dancers are perhaps the most underpaid of all performing artists. For opera and other stage productions, excluding ballet, dancers receive a little over $400 a week, and even though television has been blamed for reducing the availability of these types of dancing forums, it has opened an entirely new and certainly more lucrative source of revenue for dancers. Whether they appear on a regularly scheduled program or on a variety special, their salaries usually depend on the time they spend on-camera, and are a far cry from the salaries the old song-and-dance men made in vaudeville, even if the acts haven't changed all that much.

BALLET

The notion of an economically deprived, self-sacrificing artist is certainly not a foreign one to dancers, particularly those who have confined themselves

MINIMUM WEEKLY SALARY OF BALLET DANCERS UNDER THE AGMA NATIONAL BASIC DANCE AGREEMENT	
1st apprentice	$310
2nd apprentice	465
New	620
Corps de ballet	717
Principal	951

NOTE: Figures do not include standard AGMA benefits such as health coverage, pension, and severance/exit pay.
SOURCE: AGMA National Basic Dance Agreement Contract, 1998–99.

to the ballet. Some would argue that the term "starving artist" best describes the plight of the ballet dancer. But over the past ten or twenty years, the dance world has made a valiant and somewhat successful effort to change this image.

It's no secret that only a dozen or so ballet dancers have ever commanded six-figure incomes. And those such as Natalia Makarova, Mikhail Baryshnikov, and Rudolf Nureyev, whose annual incomes have, at one time or another, exceeded $1 million, can be counted on the fingers of one hand.

While no one goes into ballet for the money, the economic forecast for dancers who have risen through the ranks of ballet companies is considerably brighter than it was just ten years ago. In the past, even those ballet dancers fortunate enough to be with a company were considered lucky if they could secure just forty performances a year. Today, dance companies operating under union contracts like the National Basic Dance Agreement of the AFL-CIO–affiliated American Guild of Musical Artists (AGMA) can guarantee their dancers as many as forty weeks of work a year.

Alexander Dubé, AGMA's administrator for dance, notes that the AGMA contracts provide seniority increases and, in many instances, benefits such as supplemental disability insurance, dental insurance, and vacation pay. This is something quite new and unusual in the world of ballet. Pay scales also have risen considerably.

Most estimates put the annual salaries of principal dancers within the leading ballet companies at $60,000 to $70,000. For long-time principals with the larger New York City companies, estimates are $80,000 to $100,000. Major modern dance companies, whose budgets are considerably smaller than those of ballet troupes, are said to pay closer to the minimum set forth in the AGMA National Basic Dance Agreement.

Additionally, the AGMA base salaries plus the many extras, note one manager, can add up to a very respectable living wage. Corps members who make $18,000 actually get several thousand dollars more each year when you add on the comprehensive health and pension plans, as well as the as-yet-untaxed unemployment benefits dancers are entitled to for the weeks they don't work, and still more with overtime and other extras. AGMA's newest unemployment benefit, noted Dubé, is career-transition counseling for dancers who wish to retire and pursue other careers.

Models

Many of today's best-known faces come not from the worlds of politics, or even from entertainment, but from the world of modeling. They beam at us from billboards and television screens, selling products from cosmetics to candy to Cadillacs.

Modeling can be an exciting and glamourous career for those few people who make it. But the field is extremely competitive, and, once begun,
the model's career is usually short-lived. "Women come in at seventeen and
are usually out by twenty-three or twenty-five," said model Michael Taylor
in *The New York Times.* According to Katie Ford, who has taken over her
parents' agency, new models are only fifteen or sixteen years old because
that is the only time in life when girls have the look that is so popular now:
slender and flat-chested, with no muscles.

An estimated one hundred thousand people, including part-timers, work
as models in the United States. Geographically there are some jobs to be
found in most urban areas, but New York City, the center of the American
fashion industry, is the model's mecca. Anyone who wants to try for the big
time will sooner or later have to crack the Big Apple, where the sixteen top
agencies represent more than ten thousand models. There are a total of fifty-
eight agencies in New York City, and five hundred in the United States,
according to Donna Eller, president of The Models Guild.

It's difficult to determine exact salary figures since the vast majority of
models work freelance through agencies. Earnings roller coaster with the
number of assignments for which a model gets called, and also depend on
the kind of modeling he or she does. The biggest money is in television work,
where hourly rates are high, and models, under union regulations, earn residuals when their commercials are rerun. In addition to doing television and
magazine work, models also work on runways, in fashion shows, in designer
showrooms, and in art classes. Depending on experience and what type of
agency a model works with, a steadily working model can earn $30,000 to
$100,000 annually.

The most successful models are usually household names and become
closely associated with a product or products that are marketed using the
consumer's familiarity with the model: The celebrity personifies the product.
Examples include Cindy Crawford (worth more than $28 million), who has
a multiyear contract with Revlon to pitch its entire line of products for $1.5
million a year (as well as a lucrative deal with Pepsi); Claudia Schiffer (owner
of Fashion Café with Naomi Campbell and Elle MacPherson) and Linda
Evangelista (Schiffer and Evangelista are each worth over $28 million). Elle
MacPherson, according to the British magazine *Business Age,* is the richest
model, with a net worth of more than $38 million. She is thirty-four years
old and has managed to stay in the business through such ventures as the
Fashion Café chain and a line of lingerie and exercise videos. MacPherson
receives $35,000 for a runway session. Most supermodels can earn from
$10,000 to $25,000 a day, as compared with rates of $1,000 to $3,500 for
other professional models. According to *The New York Times,* only 2 percent
of models are supermodels.

FITTING (OR FIT) MODELS

There's nothing like the real thing—so when garment manufacturers have a nearly finished outfit, they call in a fitting model to see how it looks on a real woman or man. Often some final adjustments will have to be made. Fit models don't command the hourly rates that their runway colleagues might, but they tend to work more. And their career can last as long as their shape fills the manufacturer's requirements. One model, Margaret Rogers, known as the queen of the queen-sized models, works exclusively for Lane Bryant, a fashion chain for large-sized women.

Fit models get paid by the hour. Rates range from an average of $50 in Manhattan's garment district to about $150 for a top fit model working for one of the major designers. According to the Eileen Ford Agency, session rates of $250 to $450 are quite common.

SHOW MODELS

These tend to be the tall, lithe creatures of perfect proportions conjured up by the mere word "model." They work at fashion shows put on by designers and department stores, which can involve considerable travel around the country and even around the world. Runway models can earn between $200 and $750 per show, although many are paid with clothing from the show; some have their agents arrange a flat fee for an entire fashion show. Experienced models may command significantly more.

PHOTOGRAPHIC MODELS

These are the superstars. They're hired by magazines, advertising agencies, and freelance photographers. They're used to sell a variety of products, including but not exclusively fashion and beauty. All of them work through agencies. Being signed with one of New York's top five agencies is probably as close to a guarantee of success as anyone can get in this field. (See the section on models' agents in "The Middlemen," in Part IX.)

Editorial work—for fashion or beauty layouts inside a magazine—pays between $150 and $250 per day. Magazine covers sometimes pay even less than the inside pages. Models are often glad to get these assignments because of the exposure they bring. Modeling for billboards yields $2,000 to $10,000 for a six-month period. Daily rates range between $1,500 and $7,500. Television is paid on union scale. According to a spokesman at the Eileen Ford Agency, models in a TV commercial can negotiate $2,000 to $3,000 per eight-hour day.

Commercials—According to representatives from both the Ford and the Wilhelmina agencies, a beauty model can make $20,000 to $50,000 in the run of a commercial, but much less if the commercial is pulled after only a short airing. An exclusive signing to be a spokesperson for a particular product could guarantee $150,000 up to millions up front, but pinning down annual salary figures for these models is almost impossible. Is this industry still dominated by women? Hourly rates are the same for men and women models, but the field remains somewhat more lucrative for women. Things are, however, beginning to change. "Men are catching up to women, though women are still booked more," noted one Wilhelmina executive. According to Donna Eller from The Models Guild, men are making the same rates in modeling as women, but there is often not as much work. Wilhelmina says, "Some men here make over three hundred thousand dollars, and there are more men models around now than before." Tyson Beckford is currently the highest paid male model: He makes $550,000 from Ralph Lauren.

There are several reasons for this disparity. The two main ones are that catalog work, the bread and butter of business, requires far more female than male models; also, the biggest money comes from exclusive contracts, mostly with cosmetic companies, which leaves men out in the cold. However, due to different social standards for male and female beauty, male models can work longer. Men who can make the transition to the appealing, "older, worldly man look" can make their careers last twice as long as that of most women models.

There have been many changes in modeling. Lauren Hutton broke through the age barrier, while Beverly Johnson broke down the walls for black models. Emme, the well-known plus-sized model, has paved the way for larger women to model. While the average model is still between five feet nine and five feet eleven, and the average clothing sample is size six or eight, petite and plus sizes are now more popular and more readily available.

Of course, the ultimate goal of most models is to become a celebrity. One of the most recent famous businesswomen in modeling is Cindy Crawford. She has hosted MTV's *House of Style*, acted, and handled her career like a true professional. In the past, Cheryl Tiegs and Suzanne Somers parlayed modeling careers into successful roles as actresses, and they are no longer unusual for doing so. A number of other former models have gone on to enjoy lucrative careers on the silver screen, including Kirstie Alley, Michelle Pfeiffer, Kim Basinger, Renée Russo, and Cybill Shepherd.

THE CENTERFOLD

Occupational requirements have burgeoned in every field, it seems. Even models (or aspiring models) who pose nude for *Playboy* must be more than just what meets the eye. In these inflationary times, the Playmate must have intangible qualities, too. *Playboy*'s Playmate Promotions Director Bjaye Turner says, "Playmates, in addition to having the girl-next-door quality, have evolved into being ambassadors for *Playboy*'s growing businesses worldwide. The Playmates are involved in a great deal of promotional work for *Playboy* as well as [for] external clients. Their promotional assignments range from trade shows, international promotion and publicity tours, hostess for VIP corporate receptions, and a myriad of charity fund-raisers."

Besides posing for an au naturel pictorial, a *Playboy* centerfold model is often called upon to travel all around the country to attend different events, to become a sort of magazine mascot at a wide variety of promotional functions. She may host store openings and attend auto and boat shows and almost any other convention or event that presents a good promotional opportunity for the sponsoring magazine.

Very often her magazine debut becomes a springboard for a career in modeling, advertising, public relations, or entertainment. Perhaps the most famous Playmate to go on to an acting career is former *Baywatch* star Pamela Anderson Lee, who was Miss February 1990. Other celebrities who first came to national attention through the pages of *Playboy* are actress and Guess? jeans girl Anna Nicole Smith and actress/model Shannon Tweed, Miss November 1981 and 1982's Playmate of the Year.

Just who are these pinups and where are they discovered? *Playboy* has a variety of sources for discovering Playmate candidates. Potential candidates are welcomed to send in their photos to either the Chicago or the Los Angeles office; there are also talent scouts throughout North America. Also, every five years *Playboy* holds Anniversary Playmate searches to find candidates. Playmates of the Year are chosen by *Playboy* publisher Hugh Hefner himself, although readers' responses to the year's array of monthly Playmates are taken into account.

Life as a Playmate can go on for quite some time. Says Turner, "Once a Playmate, always a Playmate, that's the rule of thumb. As our businesses have expanded, promotional and publicity opportunities have been made available to Playmates spanning five decades."

While the prospect of earning $20,000 for posing nude in a national magazine may seem enticing to many an undiscovered model, it takes a lot more money to convince a celebrity to disrobe for *Playboy*'s cameras. The list of already established stars who have posed for *Playboy* ranges from swimsuit model Stephanie Seymour to actress Bo Derek to presidential daughter Patti Davis Reagan. Many intangible factors go into deciding how much money such celebrities receive, but the general rule is that the bigger the celebrity, the greater the payout. Even a minor celebrity earns more than the Playmate of the Year for a nude pictorial. According to *Playboy* spokeswoman Elizabeth Norris, the majority of celebrities who pose for *Playboy*

THE WAGES OF SEX APPEAL

Activity	Fee
Playboy Playmate of the Month	$25,000 for pictorial spread in magazine and appearances on videotape; $750–$2,500 per day for personal appearances
Playboy Playmate of the Year	$100,000 plus a car; $800–$2,000 a day for promotional appearances

SOURCE: Playboy Enterprises, Inc.

---

earn "in the hundreds of thousands of dollars," but far less than the $1 million figure that is often rumored in news accounts.

Musicians

The incomes of musicians vary so widely from person to person that it is difficult to list any precise statistics. The variation is dependent not only on skill and fame but also on geographical location, age, instrument played, and the type of music performed or taught. Even after determining these factors as accurately as possible, variation may still be great.

For example, many musicians actually earn their living through teaching rather than performing. The income of an experienced classical piano teacher in New York City who rarely performs but who possesses a fairly good reputation can be over $250 per hour. Other teachers charge $15–60 an hour. The average, however, is difficult to determine.

According to the Music Educators National Conference, music teachers in public schools earn between $17,000 and $45,000 a year; teachers in parochial schools can expect $16,000 to $35,000 annually; teachers in a college, university, or conservatory earn from $18,000 to $70,000 a year.

The following statistics are by no means intended to be comprehensive but should give some idea of the range and diversity of salaries and incomes for the estimated 274,000 performing musicians in America.

There are very few musicians who can support themselves entirely on fees from performing and teaching; those who do earn considerably more than musicians in the next highest income bracket. The vast majority, who include many well-known and excellent musicians, fall into an even lower income bracket. Minimum salaries in major orchestras ranged from about $22,000 to $90,000 per year; musicians in regional orchestras have salaries ranging from $18,000 to $22,000 a year. Musicians employed in motion

TOP TEN PAID ORCHESTRAS	
Metropolitan Opera (New York)	$92,640
New York Philharmonic	82,160
Chicago Symphony	81,900
Los Angeles Philharmonic	81,900
Philadelphia Orchestra	80,600
Boston Symphony	80,340
San Francisco Symphony	80,340
Cleveland Orchestra	78,000
Detroit Symphony	76,850
Pittsburgh Symphony	75,660

SOURCE: The American Federation of Musicians.

picture or television recording and those employed by recording companies are paid a minimum ranging from about $120 to $250 per service (for three hours of work). It is not news, however, that musicians earn very little; compared with the salaries in the other professions listed in this book, they are usually underpaid in relation to their talents and training. A closer look at the fees and salaries for musicians will clarify this point.

The fee a musician is paid for a performance may, in some instances, seem high. However, this fee frequently must cover expenses, travel, publicity, and a manager's fees (if the artist has an agent). Thus $1,000 earned by a solo artist for one concert may net the musician at most a few hundred dollars after all expenses are paid. A manager's fees alone are usually 20 percent of all concert fees. (Most managers also demand 20 percent of their clients' fees for concerts they did not even contract or handle themselves.)

The final consideration is that many professional musicians will play for no money or will even lose money merely for the experience and exposure. This is true even of very well-known artists, not merely young or unaccomplished performers. The Bösendorfer concert series in New York, for example, features many artists of international renown. Yet this series pays nothing to these artists; they perform for free. Most young musicians must rent a hall and pay for publicity just to get the opportunity to perform and gain exposure. This is almost always a great financial *loss* to the musician. Very few musicians ever make even a small profit from performances.

Singers

About twenty thousand Americans are employed as singers every year. This figure includes all kinds of performers—from those who sing advertising jingles on radio and television, or "The Star-Spangled Banner" in sports arenas, to Metropolitan Opera divas and the current stars of popular music who appear in famous nightclubs and large concert halls across the country. As is true with most entertainers in this section, only a handful of singers achieve anything like fame or success. A few, such as Sinatra, Elvis, or, more recently, Michael Jackson, Bruce Springsteen, Madonna, and the artist formerly known as Prince become living legends as well as corporations worth tens of millions of dollars.

Singing stars at every level make most of their money through record sales, but almost all of them count on personal appearances to boost interest in their recordings. The strain of concert performing is said to be enormous, but the pay's not bad, either. All well-known singers ask for a minimum guarantee before accepting a concert; this figure is then measured against an agreed-upon percentage of the box office receipts, and the performer takes the larger of the two. Some of the very top singers, such as Whitney Houston and Madonna, take a minimum *plus* a percentage.

The largest fees for public appearances are paid by the people who run the casinos in Las Vegas and Atlantic City. Singers usually work on a weekly basis, doing two shows a night for seven nights. By now it is a hallowed show-business tradition for big-name performers to do a week in a casino, and for their agents to publicize the extraordinary fees.

Recent years have been very good for package record deals and for those lucky enough to have secured them. Madonna, for example, signed a $60 million deal with Warner Music in 1992. She and the entertainment giant formed a separate company—Maverick Entertainment—that includes record and music publishing units as well as TV, film, merchandising, and book divisions. She also got a jump in record advances from $3 million to $5 million per album, and an increase in royalties on their sales to 20 percent, among the highest rates in the industry. Janet Jackson signed an $80 million record deal with Virgin for an unspecified number of albums; she will have to sell 50 million albums for Virgin Records to break even.

However, the life span of a superstar can be unpredictible. An album with less than impressive sales, or an event or rumor that tarnishes the reputation of the artist can grind his megastardom to a halt. This is why record companies express caution when making deals with even the largest of stars, often adding clauses that give them an "out" should the superstar's popularity suddenly wane.

And it happens. Michael Jackson, for example, signed the highest entertainment deal ever—$1 billion with Sony—in 1992. This included $65 million for six albums and one film, as well as his own record label. It seemed a promising venture for Sony; the superstar's two releases in the 1980's— *Thriller* and *Bad*—demonstrated record-breaking sales. The former was the best-selling album of all time. However, sales on Jackson's *Dangerous* album were disappointing. His accompanying world tour was cut short by a drug addiction problem and allegations of sexual misconduct, and so, reportedly, was his deal with Sony.

Prince, likewise, made headlines in 1992 when he signed a $100 million deal with Warner Brothers Records, was made a vice president of the company, and was given an office at its Los Angeles headquarters. However, there was a contingency clause: In what is known as a "mini-maxi" deal, he was granted a $10 million advance for his first album, with advances on subsequent albums to depend on the success of the previous release. It was a wise move by Warner Brothers because Prince has since changed his image, his name—to "the artist formerly known as Prince"—and his ability to sell albums to "lukewarm."

ROYALTIES FOR SINGERS

The money you plunk down on the record shop counter has a long road to travel before any of it reaches the pocket of the man or woman who made the recording. Yes, recording artists earn royalties, a percentage of the income from each copy sold. But before there's any profit to be shared with the talent, a lot of money invested must first be recovered.

About half the cover price stays with the distributor. What remains goes to the company, which passes on the artist's percentage after deducting the money it has laid out in production, advertising, and promotion costs—not just on the current release, but on all previous projects that may have flopped. Having received some money (which often takes several albums), the artist has still further deductions to make to his or her producer, manager, and songwriter.

The royalty figure itself varies greatly from artist to artist and is an item of delicate negotiation at contract time. A rate might begin at 10 percent for an unrecorded, untried talent, rising to 12 percent for a well-known performer, or to as high as 25 percent for an acknowledged superstar such as Michael Jackson. As part of her agreement with Warner Music, Madonna receives 20 percent of the royalties on her albums. Arrangements are always subject to change. In the words of one major recording company's vice president for eastern operations, "Joe Unknown becomes a superstar, we renegotiate." Royalties depend, of course, on the number of CDs a company anticipates selling, and it's not unusual for contracts to provide escalating royalty rates that reward a larger than expected sales volume. Alanis Morissette makes about $1 for each copy (20 million so far) of *Jagged Little Pill* sold. She is, however, the owner of her record label.

In the past, companies commonly offered new artists contracts that paid royalties on 90 percent, not 100 percent, of sales income. This was an added way to protect themselves against the financial risk posed by laying out production costs for unproven artists. This practice is changing today, however, probably as a reflection of the increased competition among companies in an era when a star's loyalty to one label is mere nostalgia.

OPERA

The hierarchy of American opera is very simple to define: There's the Metropolitan Opera, and there's everyone else. Most opera singers' minimum salaries are set by the American Guild of Musical Artists (AGMA). The 1998 weekly minimum for a singer in a lead or a feature role is $650. Supplemental and solo bit singers receive minimum weekly pay of $541 plus a per diem. At the Met, on the other hand, the chorus members' salaries are considerably higher; they range from $1,013 to well over $1,266 per week. Star performers at the Met receive $12,000 per performance, which is actually far less than they would in Europe. Less well-known singers at smaller houses can earn $2,000 to $4,000 per performance.

As in other areas of public performance, however, superstar economics keeps driving up the fees to attract singers who will in turn bring in customers. Unlike movies, television, or professional sports, however, opera is already a money-losing enterprise requiring outlandish ticket prices, heavy corporate subsidies, and occasional grants from publicly supported foundations such as the National Endowment for the Arts. Perhaps, as some observers have noted, the music will never die, but the elaborate spectacles may soon be only a memory. After all, the great singers are drawing better than ever for concerts requiring no costumes or sets costing hundreds of thousands of dollars.

TELEVISION AND RADIO

Many aspiring singers try to find work doing television or radio commercials and, if they're lucky, an occasional TV series. Payment for this work is regulated by AFTRA, so a singer is paid the same minimum rate as an actor if he or she sings alone or in a duo or is on- or off-camera. Since most singers get work singing in groups of three or more, the union has established pay scales for their benefit. More often than not, the work involves making singing commercials, so we've included several examples of union rates for this field. The sources for all of these rates are the 1997–98 AFTRA and SAG contracts.

MINIMUM DAILY RATES FOR SINGERS ON TV PROGRAMS

Singers	On-Camera	Off-Camera
Solo and Duo	$603	$522
Groups 3–8	319	276
Groups 9+	277	240

SOURCE: AFTRA Contract, 1997–98.

MINIMUM FEES FOR RADIO COMMERCIALS

Actor, announcer, solo, duo	$200.00
Group singers: 3–5	147.30
6–8	130.35
9 or more	115.70

Producers employ performers on the basis of recording sessions. A recording session is no more than 90 minutes in duration.
SOURCE: AFTRA contract, 1997–2000.

NETWORK PROGRAM COMMERCIALS (13 WEEKS' USE)

	Actors/Announcers/ Solos/Duos	Group Singers (3–5)	Group Singers (6–8)	Group Singers (9+)
Unlimited use	$1,216.40	$935.60	$836.55	$766.40
Use on across-the-board programs	$1,273.75	$979.50	$875.95	$802.50
Limited use–26 uses	$ 608.30	$467.70	$418.25	$382.15
39 uses	$ 916.00	$641.40	$572.50	$520.15

SOURCE: AFTRA contract, 1997–2000.

Television Personalities

Back in the early days of radio, some anonymous person must have been faced with the problem of what to call all those people who, while not actors or singers or comedians or musicians, were still an integral part of broadcasting. After all, Harlow Wilcos, of the *Fibber McGee and Molly* program, and Don Wilson, of Jack Benny's show, were not simply announcers; and Ted Mack was perceived as something more than the person who introduced aspiring amateur performers to the radio audience. These people became popular and famous in their own right, and were very well paid, too. Somewhere along the line they were dubbed "radio personalities," and the term has stuck to their media descendants even today.

Pat Sajak and Alex Trebek are contemporary examples of the television personality. They are MCs of game shows varying in content from the inane to the offensive, and most Americans know their names and faces better than they do those of cabinet members. And, of course, game show hosts earn much more money: Estimates range from $40,000 to $75,000 per program.

The airwaves are filled with people like this—people who have no outstanding talents but do have a certain confidence and ease of manner and can make small talk readily and continuously. So also included under "television personalities" would be hosts of interview-type programs (Oprah Winfrey and Larry King, for example) and the principals on the morning programs that combine news and chatter (*Today* and *Good Morning America*). Sports commentators, as opposed to play-by-play announcers, would also be listed here on the basis that it is essentially their personas, not their expertise, should they possess any, that make them popular (Bob Costas and Dick Vitale are two examples). As the accompanying list makes plain, these personalities are among the highest salaried people in all America.

Some readers may be surprised to see well-known news broadcasters on a list of personalities, but in our opinion, they fit the basic description given above. Only rarely do network anchors write their own material, and even if they did, that feat would hardly qualify them for such astronomical salaries as they receive. They earn so much because they are well-known TV personalities in the same way that Regis Philbin and Kathie Lee Gifford are. They read the news very well and present the appropriate image of Olympian detachment combined with an air of unspoken knowledge and suitable hints of sophistication.

The injection of entertainment values into news programs has not been confined to the networks. During the last decade, local stations learned that news programs, the basic staple of local broadcasting, could be profitable if the numbers of people watching could be increased. But this bottom-line approach meant that everyday news could not be dull, boring, or filled with unrelieved stories of gloom and doom. And so was born the "happy talk" news format in which predictions of imminent economic collapse and updates on the latest murder count are intermingled with stories about community spirit and uplifting episodes of brotherhood, humane treatment of animals, and harmony among the races. All of this is punctuated by lighthearted banter among the personalities who appear every night: the anchorperson(s), the news reporters, the sportscaster, and the weatherperson.

These news personalities are paid on the same basis as everyone else in broadcasting, in relation to the size of the viewing audience. Stations pay anchorpersons an average of $65,520 a year, and $52,562 to weatherper-

ESTIMATED SALARIES OF FAMOUS NETWORK TV PERSONALITIES

Oprah Winfrey	$97 million
David Letterman	14 million
Howard Stern	12.5 million
Barbara Walters	10 million
Katie Couric	7 million
Larry King	7 million
Peter Jennings	7 million
Jay Leno	7 million
Diane Sawyer	7 million
Dan Rather	7 million
Tom Brokaw	7 million
Stone Phillips	5 million

SOURCE: *TV Guide,* assorted magazine articles.

sons; sportscasters average $48,704, and news reporters, always the lowest paid on news shows, make between $25,000 and $30,000, or less if they are just starting out. In the ten largest markets, the salaries are significantly higher, averaging about $500,000 for anchorpersons, and $100,000 to $200,000 for news reporters. (See also the figures in the section "Behind the Scenes in Television.")

To insiders, especially in New York and Los Angeles, these figures will seem very low. But bear in mind that they are averages that include people at the smallest stations. The largest ones, those owned and operated by the networks, always pay the highest. In Chicago, for example, anchors earn several million a year, the same as Chuck Scarborough in New York and Jerry Dumphy in Los Angeles. In other major markets, salaries for anchors are usually $300,000 to $450,000 a year, or two to three times what news reporters make. In New York, for example, popular news reporters on affiliated stations frequently make $100,000 to $200,000 a year.

Individual contracts bristle with perks, personal fee systems, and deferred tax benefits. Dan Rather is not just CBS's premier anchor; he is also managing editor of the *CBS Evening News.* So great is his power that he has handpicked his own stable of correspondents from the CBS pool. People on Rather's "A team" appear much more frequently on the air. Some correspondents who aren't "allowed" on at all drop completely out of sight and eventually slide right off the network. In turn, those chosen benefit from the exposure next time their contracts come up. Those who languish but stay on complain bitterly.

MINIMUM RATES FOR TV SPORTSCASTERS		
	1995–96	**1996–97**
Sportscasters		
Per event	$ 906	$ 938
Per week	2,301	2,382
Assistant sportscasters/color persons		
Per event	$ 557	$ 576
Per week	1,422	1,472
Championship events		
Sportscaster	$ 970	$1,004
Assistant sportscaster	605	626
Major league baseball—doubleheader		
Sportscaster	$ 970	$1,004
Assistant sportscaster	605	626

SOURCE: AFTRA contracts.

Rather is one of the privileged few broadcast millionaires who are the leading men—as well as directors—in America's new national theater, television news. It is not as a figure of speech that agent Hookstratten calls the main men at the networks "the principal players." An ABC correspondent uses similar terms: "image makers" and "facemen." They are, he believes, "vitally important and they are worth their money."

The proof is in the profits. When a ratings point on just one prime-time network news broadcast is worth $70 million, according to industry sources, the anchor who brings in those ratings may be said to be getting no more than his fair share.

"It's the free enterprise system," said a spokesperson for NBC News. "All is fair in the marketplace."

"We journalists exist in an entertainment medium," explains Bill Moyers. "Star quality attracts viewers in the same way marquees attract audiences to the theater." While the idea may "offend journalistic sensibility," Moyers says, "it is the principle of a hired servant getting his due the same way a stockholder does. I think Dan Rather deserves a proportionate share of what he brings to the bank."

Profit is the key word at local markets, too. "The profitability of a local station is a big, silent subject," says New York agent Alfred Gelter. "Owning a television station is like owning a license to steal." The newspeople who help bring in this money, Geller believes, "deserve every penny they get."

"I have no problem in local anchors trying to get as much as they can," says ABC legal correspondent Tim O'Brien, but he thinks "the role" is over-rated. "The problem is with the stations who pay so much. They could find marketable anchors to whom they don't have to pay $600,000 to a million."

In fact, many agents are reportedly fuming over their anchors' low sal-aries, noting that NBC is particularly tough. What they fail to mention, though, is that, like professional ballplayers, newsmen and their agents have been raking in the big money for quite some time. Anchors receive $2 to $4 million a year, important senior correspondents make $500,000 to $740,000, and even the average, run-of-the-mill correspondent earns ap-proximately $150,000.

THE WORLD OF SPORTS

The Pros

There was a day when athletes in the world of pro sports were measured by their statistics on the field of play. For baseball players, it was batting aver-ages, home runs, and earned run averages. For basketball players, scoring averages and rebounds. For golfers, breaking pars and tournaments won.

For some athletes, besides their salaries, there was a little more money to be made through endorsements. But for the most part, the baseball player went home after the season to run a gas station, look after the farm, sell insurance, or learn a job for his postcareer life, knowing his sports money wasn't going to care for him forever. A few major leaguers—the Joe Di-Maggios, the Willie Mayses, the Mickey Mantles—had $100,000 salaries, but not many. That was a magic figure for years in the middle of the twentieth century, and in just a few sports.

Then came the late 1960s, and sports salaries began to explode. The New York Jets signed rookie quarterback Joe Namath to a $427,000 contract and offered two other rookie quarterbacks $200,000 and $100,000 to entice them to sign with the American Football League team instead of a squad in the more established National Football League. The new American Basket-ball Association took on the National Basketball Association with open checkbooks, signing such fancied newcomers as Julius Erving and Spencer Haywood. In 1971, a Hollywood agent stunned old-time boxing promoters by offering Muhammad Ali and Joe Frazier $2.5 million each for a dream match. Big television money bankrolled a surge in golf with the emergence of Arnold Palmer.

With so much money at stake, athletes turned to agents—and vice versa—to negotiate their contracts, and their salaries got bigger.

It took about a quarter of a century to go from Babe Ruth's $80,000 salary to Joe DiMaggio's $100,000 salary. In another quarter century, Jim "Catfish" Hunter became the first of baseball's free agents to raise the bar past $500,000 (to $578,000 in 1975 with the New York Yankees), and the bar has continued to rise ever since. In 1996, it reached $10 million for the top baseball players and showed no signs of stopping.

Still, baseball has a hard time keeping up with other sports in the check-writing department. Basketball pays more and hockey has higher paid players than the top moneymakers in baseball and football—the latter being replenished by a long-term $17.6 billion television contract that should soon race it to the front.

Boxers are making as much as anyone. The following *Forbes* magazine annual survey has three boxers in the top five of its list, and few fighters make big-time endorsement money. And auto racing, once the sport of grease monkeys, is on the rise because of endorsement dollars from manufacturers, gas companies, and auto parts makers. Tennis and golf are more than holding their own.

Big money isn't hard to find: The sport shoe manufacturers and the apparel industry have it. Michael Jordan, the highest paid athlete in the history of sports, earned $40 million for endorsements in 1995 and raised the bar to $47 million in 1997. Grant Hill, a rising basketball star, got a long-term deal from Fila, an upstart in the battle with Nike, for $80 million.

As for the owners who must pay the inflated salaries, they have come up with a great gimmick for building their expensive stadiums and arenas: Shake the taxpayers down to build new facilities or threaten to move their teams. Nearly half the teams in baseball and football have done that and received new sites to meet their "needs." The money saved and earned from new stadium "revenue streams" can go toward the always-escalating salaries.

How far have sports salaries come?

There's an old story about Babe Ruth, dating back to 1930, in which he was told that as baseball's highest priced player he was making more money—$5,000 more—than the president of the United States, Herbert Hoover. "I had a better year than he did," Ruth supposedly replied, referring to the man who headed the country during the early years of the Great Depression. At the time, Ruth was making about $80,000 a season, more than some entire teams. Going into the 1998 season, the *average* salary was $1,437,917, compared to $200,000 for President Clinton.

We'll let you decide how many of the 841 major leaguers who earned more than that $1.4 million average salary had better years than Clinton.

Besides big salary paychecks, major league sports were in a bonus situation in the 1990s. Much of Sergei Federov's whopping six-year, $38 million deal with the NHL Detroit Red Wings was a $28 million first year that contained a huge signing bonus. Colorado Avalanche center Joe Sakic also cashed in a big bonus: The star got $15 million up front for the three-year contract he signed in 1997.

But there are all kinds of bonuses now. For a baseball player, it could be a five-figure bonus for being named Most Valuable Player or for hitting forty home runs or winning sixteen games. A pitcher may get a bonus if he starts thirty-five games, or a football player might earn a bonus for making the Pro Bowl. The bonus provisions are written whichever way the two parties, team and player, agree upon.

This is consistent with the way the Chicago Bulls offered to compensate Dennis Rodman, who had a base salary of $4.5 million, for the 1997–98 basketball season. Rodman, he of the superdyed hair, cross-dressing fashion statements, and unruly behavior on the court, had been known to miss a few games from suspensions in the past. So the Bulls offered a bonus of $4.25 million if he played all eighty-two regular season games ($184,783 for each game after fifty-nine) Rodman played eighty games during the season, to earn almost $4 million.

The team said it would pay him another $1 million if he was in every play-off game. He would get an extra $500,000 if he led the league in re-

HIGHEST PAID SPORTS PERSONALITIES, 1997

Rank, Athlete	Sport	Salary or Winnings in Millions	Endorsements, Other Income	Total Earnings
1. Michael Jordan	Basketball	$31.1	$47.0	$78.3
2. Evander Holyfield	Boxing	53.0	1.3	54.3
3. Oscar De la Hoya	Boxing	37.0	1.0	38.0
4. Michael Schumacher	Auto Racing	25.0	10.0	35.0
5. Mike Tyson	Boxing	27.0	0.0	27.0
6. Tiger Woods	Golf	2.1	24.0	26.1
7. Shaquille O'Neal	Basketball	12.9	12.5	25.4
8. Dale Earnhardt	Auto racing	3.6	15.5	19.1
9. Joe Sakic	Hockey	17.8	0.1	17.9
10. Grant Hill	Basketball	5.0	12.0	17.0
11. Greg Norman	Golf	3.2	13.0	16.2
12. Arnold Palmer	Golf	0.1	16.0	16.1
13. Horace Grant	Basketball	14.5	0.4	14.9
14. George Foreman	Boxing	10.2	4.5	14.7
15. Pete Sampras	Tennis	6.5	8.0	14.5
16. Andre Agassi	Tennis	0.1	14.0	14.1
17. Cal Ripken	Baseball	6.7	6.5	13.2
18. David Robinson	Basketball	11.0	2.0	13.2
19. Ken Griffey	Baseball	8.8	4.2	13.0

HIGHEST PAID SPORTS PERSONALITIES, 1997

Rank, Athlete	Sport	Salary or Winnings	Endorsements & other income	Total Earnings
20. Alonzo Mourning	Basketball	$ 9.5	$3.5	$13.0
21. Michael Chang	Tennis	2.5	9.5	12.0
22. Naseem Hamed	Boxing	9.5	2.5	12.0
23. Juwan Howard	Basketball	10.0	1.2	11.2
24. Gary Payton	Basketball	9.0	2.2	11.2
25. Greg Maddux	Baseball	10.0	0.8	11.0
26. Hakeem Olajuwon	Basketball	9.5	1.5	11.0
27. Dennis Rodman	Basketball	5.0	6.0	11.0
28. Wayne Gretzky	Hockey	5.9	5.0	10.9
29. Mike Piazza	Baseball	7.0	3.6	10.6
30. Reggie Miller	Basketball	9.2	1.2	10.4
31. Albert Belle	Baseball	10.0	0.4	10.4
32. Jeff Gordon	Auto racing	3.8	6.5	10.3
33. Barry Sanders	Football	8.4	1.8	10.2
34. Chris Gratton	Hockey	10.0	0.1	10.1
35. Lennox Lewis	Boxing	9.5	0.2	9.7
36. Michael Moorer	Boxing	9.6	0.0	9.6
37. Sammy Sosa	Baseball	9.3	0.2	9.7
38. Jack Nicklaus	Golf	0.3	9.0	9.3
39. Frank Thomas	Baseball	7.2	2.1	9.3
40. Brett Favre	Football	5.6	3.6	9.2

SOURCE: *Forbes* magazine, December 15, 1997. Reprinted by permission. This table counts signing bonuses and other upfront money in the year in which they were given, rather than averaging them out over the life of a contract.

bounding, which he did. If he made 66 percent of his free-throw attempts, he would get another $100,000. Alas, not even money could increase Rodman's proficiency from the free throw line: He shot 54 percent. Yet before the play-offs commenced, Rodman had collected $4.48 million out of a possible $6 million in bonus awards.

Major League Baseball

During the 1997 baseball season, Wayne Huizenga, owner of the Florida Marlins, was the architect of that year's World Series victory. With his checkbook he built a team that won the championship in only its third year of existence. He set out to prove you could do it if you spent enough—and he did. The Marlins put together their champions by hiring expensive free agents, to the tune of a 1997 payroll of about $53.5 million. The Montreal

Expos, the lowest paying team in baseball, had a payroll of $18.4 million. In the middle of the pack in payrolls were the Cincinnati Reds: $37 million.

When reality set in before the 1998 season, those teams began to slash. At the start of the season, Huizenga the architect became Huizenga the demolition expert. He cut $20 million from his payroll by trading players or not contesting for his own free agents, much less someone else's. The Expos cut their payroll in half, to less than $10 million. The Reds sliced and sliced salaries enough to get below $22 million.

Does that mean baseball is going through a depression? Hardly.

Baseball salaries have been going up, except during World War II, since the Great Depression of the 1920s. And they have been going up steadily and at faster rates in the past three decades. In fact, for the 1998 season, three players—Albert Belle of the Chicago White Sox, Greg Maddux of the Atlanta Braves, and Gary Sheffield, one of the few stars not trimmed by the Marlins—were *each* earning more money than the entire Montreal payroll. The New York Yankees, baseball's highest paid team in 1997 at $65 million, were paying almost the same. But the Baltimore Orioles were paying more— and the most—at a record $70.4 million.

More than half the teams in baseball had payrolls of $40 million and up. All but two of the thirty teams were paying $20 million or more. The first-year Arizona Diamondbacks were paying more than $30 million; they were already twenty-third on the major league list.

The *average* major league player's salary for 1998 was $1,437,917— up from $1.2 million in 1997. And that did not include play-off earnings or extras such as bonuses for being named Most Valuable Player, finishing in the top three in the Cy Young voting, or leading the league in batting, home runs, or pitching victories.

The *minimum* salary, which was $3,500 when it was instituted in the 1950s, was now $170,000, up from $150,000 the year before.

The first man in baseball to make a six-figure salary (exactly $100,000) was Hank Greenberg with the Pittsburgh Pirates a half century ago. With free agency in the mid-1970s, Jim "Catfish" Hunter of the Yankees topped a half million (at $578,000) in 1975. Before the decade was over, Nolan Ryan of the Houston Astros topped a million (at $1,130,000). Today, less than a quarter century later, that's not even as much as the average salary.

Greg Maddux, the Cy Young–winning pitcher of the Atlanta Braves, reached seven figures at an even $10 million in 1997. Belle and Sheffield matched that in 1998, but it was left to another Cy Young–winning pitcher, Pedro Martinez, to take salaries higher. Before the 1998 season, he signed a deal with Boston that would pay him an average of $12.5 million per year for five years. At the close of the 1998 season, a catcher took the lead: The

New York Mets signed Mike Piazza to a seven-year, $91 million deal that will pay Piazza an average of $13 million per year.

Often team payrolls can be misleading. For example, the White Sox had a payroll of $36.8 million, which was in the lower half of the big league list. Even then, four players—Albert Belle ($10 million), Frank Thomas ($7 million), Robin Ventura ($6.1 million), and Jaime Navarro ($5 million)—comprised about three quarters of that figure. The Marlins began the 1998 season with nine players earning the baseball minimum.

But baseball owners, in general, find no reluctance to spend for talent—or would-be talent. The Yankees signed Japanese pitcher Hideki Irabu for a long-term $12.8 million package in 1997. Then they came back and added Orlando Hernandez for a four-year $6.6 million deal in 1998. Never mind that the pitcher Hernandez, who was listed at twenty-eight years old but may have been as old as thirty-two, had no professional experience, though he was the top player in Cuba's fast-paced so-called amateur system.

In 1998, the Philadelphia Phillies tore up the contract of Scott Rolen, the National League rookie of the year the previous season. The new deal awarded him $10 million over four years. Not bad for a twenty-two-year-old with a .263 batting average. Rolen's contract is written in a way that will give him $750,000 in 1998, a million in 1999, $2.5 million in 2000, and a whopping $5.5 million in 2001.

Of course, by the year 2000, such salaries may be pittance.

Although Albert Belle is already making $10 million, it's only part of a five-year deal that pays him $55 million, so somewhere along the line he has to get some handsome raises from the $45 million balance. Jerry Reinsdorf, the White Sox owner, didn't blink an eye when he made that deal, even though he slashed the team payroll for 1998: "We're not in a fiscal crisis, because we can afford it." He said the team needed to win back fans after attendance fell from 2.9 million in 1991 to 1.6 million in 1996 when the deal was made. Reinsdorf, also the owner of basketball's Chicago Bulls, was already paying Michael Jordan $30.14 million a year.

And Frank Thomas, the team's former high-roller and a two-time Most Valuable Player, didn't flinch, either, at someone topping his $29 million four-year deal. He said Belle deserved it. After all, players like to see other players make big, big dollars. Then, when they have a better season than the high paid star, they—through their agents—can ask for more, too.

MAJOR LEAGUE AVERAGE SALARIES—BY POSITION

The following average salaries, as measured by the Major League Baseball Players Association, are current as of August 31, 1997. They are based on starters' pay, at a date just before the rosters were increased from twenty-five to forty players, including players on the disabled list. The criteria set by the union is for regulars who have appeared in at least 100 games; starting pitchers with nineteen or more starts and other pitchers who have ten or fewer starts or twenty-five or more relief appearances. The number in parentheses is the number of players who fit into one of those categories.

PITCHERS		AVERAGE SALARY 1997 (in millions)
First baseman	(22)	$3.7
Second baseman	(21)	2.4
Third baseman	(23)	2.3
Shortstops	(25)	1.7
Outfielders	(66)	2.6
Catchers	(20)	1.9
Designated hitters	(7)	3.6
Starting pitchers	(116)	2.0
Relief pitchers	(174)	0.7

Source: Major League Baseball Players Association.

BASEBALL'S MINIMUM SALARY—AN EVOLUTION

The minimum salary for a player who is with the team all year long, or on the disabled list, began at $3,500 in the 1950s, when the union was organized. It took jumps to $5,000 and $7,500 before long. The figures below, furnished by the Major League Commissioner's office, are an evolution since 1969.

YEAR	
1969	$ 10,000
1975	16,000
1985	60,000
1990	100,000
1997	150,000

SOURCE: Major League Baseball, 1998.

Date signed	Player and Team	Average Salary (in millions)
April 9, 1990	Don Mattingly, Yankees	$ 3.8
June 27, 1990	Jose Canseco, Athletics	4.7
February 8, 1991	Roger Clemens, Red Sox	5.4
December 2, 1991	Bobby Bonilla, Mets	5.8
March 2, 1992	Ryne Sandberg, Cubs	7.1
December 5, 1992	Barry Bonds, Giants	7.3
January 31, 1996	Ken Griffey, Jr., Mariners	8.5
November 19, 1996	Albert Belle, White Sox	11.0
February 20, 1997	Barry Bonds, Giants	11.45
August 10, 1997	Greg Maddux, Braves	11.5
December 11, 1998	Kevin Brown, Dodgers	15.0

SOURCE: *The New York Times.*

BASEBALL'S HIGHEST PAID PLAYER—AN EVOLUTION

Year	Player	Team	Annual Salary
1923	Babe Ruth	New York Yankees	$ 50,000
1947	Hank Greenberg	Pittsburgh Pirates	100,000
1959	Ted Williams	Boston Red Sox	125,000
1975	Jim "Catfish" Hunter	New York Yankees	578,000
1979	Nolan Ryan	Houston Astros	1,130,000
1981	Dave Winfield	New York Yankees	2,200,000
1989	Kirby Puckett	Minnesota Twins	3,000,000
1990	Jose Canseco	Oakland Athletics	4,700,000
1991	Roger Clemens	Boston Red Sox	5,380,000
1991	Bobby Bonilla	New York Mets	5,800,000
1992	Ryne Sandberg	Chicago Cubs	7,100,000
1992	Barry Bonds	San Francisco Giants	7,290,000
1996	Ken Griffey, Jr.	Seattle Mariners	8,500,000
1997	Greg Maddux	Atlanta Braves	10,000,000
1998	Albert Belle	Chicago White Sox	10,000,000
1998	Ken Griffey, Jr.	Seattle Mariners	10,000,000
1999	Mo Vaughn	Anaheim Angels	13,300,000
1999	Kevin Brown	Los Angeles Dodgers	15,000,000

BASEBALL ANNUAL AVERAGE SALARIES

This list is an evolution of baseball's highest average salaries, those paid for a contract over a period of years. Note, as mentioned before, that Albert Belle was being paid $10 million in 1998, though he had a contract for five years at $55 million. Thus, players are not necessarily making the average for *each* year of their contracts. With the exception of Greg Maddux, Don Mattingly, and Jose Canseco, all of the contracts were signed in the off-season. Some of the earlier contracts have since been rewritten; some of the players are no longer with the teams that signed them.

SALARY ARBITRATION

In order to bring a semblance of order to the free agent market, baseball owners and players agreed in 1974 to a system of binding arbitration. Under this system, the players and the teams each submit suggested salaries for the coming year to an impartial arbitrator who chooses between the two alternatives. For many years, the salaries players received through arbitration were overshadowed by the gigantic dollar amounts landed by free agents. But during the "collusion" years, when owners collectively refused to sign the big free agents, the players turned more and more to arbitration as a way of augmenting their compensation. Until 1990, the top salary won by a player in an arbitration hearing was the $1.975 million first baseman Don Mattingly wrested from the New York Yankees in 1987. But after leading their team to its first division title in ten years, Pittsburgh pitcher Doug Drabek and slugger Bobby Bonilla took the Pirates to arbitration and shattered that record. Drabek walked away with $3.35 million in his victory; Bonilla lost but still earned a hefty raise to $2.4 million, based on the team's arbitration offer.

Since then, arbitration awards have kept pace with baseball's spiraling salaries, mainly because of the big money being paid free agents (the owners started spending for the big free agents again in 1991 after arbitration found them guilty of collusion). Texas Rangers outfielder Ruben Sierra broke the $5 million barrier in 1992. Seattle Mariners outfielder Ken Griffey, Jr., topped $6 million in 1993. Detroit Tigers first baseman Cecil Fielder reached $7 million in 1996.

By 1999 the pressure on all major league teams to produce a winning team led to another surge in star players' salaries. In addition, most of the big deals were long-term arrangements usually binding teams and players together for five or six years. According to the Associated Press the largest deals of this kind were:

Player	Team	Term	Total Pay
Kevin Brown	Los Angeles Dodgers	6 years	$105 million
Mike Piazza	New York Mets	6 years	91 million
Bernie Williams	New York Yankees	6 years	87.5 million
Mo Vaughn	Anaheim Angels	5 years	80.0 million
Pedro Martinez	Boston Red Sox	5 years	75.0 million
Gary Sheffield	Los Angeles Dodgers	5 years	68.0 million
Albert Belle	Baltimore Orioles	5 years	65.0 million
Greg Maddux	Atlanta Braves	5 years	57.5 million
Randy Johnson	Arizona Diamondbacks	3 years	52.4 million

MAJOR LEAGUE TEAM PAYROLLS, 1998
(Based on 25-man rosters and the disabled list. Includes prorated shares of signing bonuses for 841 major leaguers.)

Team	Payroll (millions)
Baltimore Orioles	$70.4
New York Yankees	63.2
Atlanta Braves	59.5
Cleveland Indians	58.4
Texas Rangers	54.7
St. Louis Cardinals	52.6
Seattle Mariners	52.1
Boston Red Sox	51.6
New York Mets	49.9
Chicago Cubs	49.4
Toronto Blue Jays	48.4
Los Angeles Dodgers	47.5
Colorado Rockies	47.4
San Diego Padres	45.4
Houston Astros	40.6
San Francisco Giants	40.3
Anaheim Angels	38.5
Chicago White Sox	36.8
Philadelphia Phillies	34.4
Florida Marlins	33.4
Kansas City Royals	33.0
Milwaukee Brewers	32.1
Arizona Diamondbacks	30.3
Minnesota Twins	26.5
Tampa Bay Devil Rays	25.1
Detroit Tigers	22.7
Cincinnati Reds	22.0

MAJOR LEAGUE TEAM PAYROLLS, 1998
(Based on 25-man rosters and the disabled list. Includes
prorated shares of signing bonuses for 841
major leaguers.)

Team	Payroll (millions)
Oakland Athletics	$20.0
Pittsburgh Pirates	13.8
Montreal Expos	9.2

SOURCE: Major League Baseball.

National Football League

The $17.6 billion television package that the National Football League re-
ceived from three television networks in January 1998 will prove that football
salaries, as well as footballs, bounce in funny ways.

In 1993, the NFL became the second major sport to institute a salary
cap (the NBA was first). The cap was designed to limit the amount teams
would be able to spend on players, and thus maintain competitive balance
between the big city markets, like New York, and the smaller ones, like
Green Bay. But through clever accounting maneuvers, such as spreading out
a signing bonus over several years, a team may spend more than the cap
allows.

To date, the salary cap era has seemed to work for the league. Small-
market teams, like Green Bay and Denver, have won Super Bowl titles since
the cap was instituted.

The cap currently is based on 62 percent (it started at 64 percent) of a
team's income from attendance, television money, and so on. In 1994, the
cap was $34.6 million. Because of the rise in ticket prices and other factors,
the cap rose to about $41 million in 1997, but then the stunning television
pact was signed. The 1998 cap will increase to $52.328 million, providing
a bonanza for free agent players and those players who will reach free agent
status in the coming years.

Here are some examples from the few weeks after the cap was raised:

- The Minnesota Vikings, in an effort to hold on to Robert Smith, John
  Randle, and Todd Steussie, contracted those players to long-term
  deals worth a total of $79.5 million.
- The Washington Redskins, hurting on the defensive line, signed two
  free agent tackles, Dana Stubblefield and Dan Wilkinson. Stubblefield got $36 million for six years, and Wilkinson got $21.4 million.

- The Buffalo Bills, burned by free agent losses in the past, signed nose tackle Ted Washington for $27.3 million over five years, the largest contract in franchise history.
- The San Francisco 49ers tore up Steve Young's contract and gave the star quarterback a new, six-season deal, beginning at a league-high (to date) salary of $8.2 million for the 1998 season.
- The Philadelphia Eagles signed defensive end Hugh Douglas, a free agent, to a $25 million deal over six years, including a $6.2 million signing bonus.

In less than two months after the television deal was made and the salary cap raised, at nine positions the salary was higher than it had ever been in the history of the league. Even a punter, Craig Hentrich of the Tennessee Oilers, became the first kicker to sign for more than $1 million a season.

In the 1997 season, Steve Young was the highest paid player in the game for that season, making $5.87 million. Drew Bledsoe, another quarterback, was the only other player over $5 million. Only seven players made upward of $4 million, and six of them were quarterbacks.

Strangely enough, next to quarterbacks, linebackers and offensive linemen were the highest paid players in 1997. Running backs, led by Detroit's Barry Sanders (at $3.23 million), were in the middle of the pack.

But even with the surge in big money, pro football players seem to fall short of the huge amounts of money made in other sports. Part of this is due to the large rosters a team must carry—fifty players in all, forty-five of whom are active at any one time. Baseball teams carry twenty-five players, and basketball teams a mere twelve.

A Lou Harris poll in 1998 showed that 28 percent of Americans considered pro football their favorite sport, ahead of baseball (17 percent) and pro basketball (13 percent). This means, probably, a better chance for endorsements for football players, but then again there are more of them to share it.

TOP PAID PLAYERS BY POSITION IN NFL, 1997 SEASON		
Name	**Team**	**Salary (in millions)**
Quarterbacks		
Troy Aikman	Dallas Cowboys	$5.87
Drew Bledsoe	New England Patriots	5.193
Trent Dilfer	Tampa Bay Buccaneers	4.53
Dan Marino	Miami Dolphins	4.34
Brett Favre	Green Bay Packers	4.12

TOP PAID PLAYERS BY POSITION IN NFL, 1997 SEASON

Name	Team	Salary (in millions)
Running Backs		
Barry Sanders	Detroit Lions	$3.23
Jerome Bettis	Pittsburgh Steelers	2.70
Chris Warren	Seattle Seahawks	2.70
Terry Allen	Washington Redskins	2.57
Larry Centers	Arizona Cardinals	2.5
Emmitt Smith	Dallas Cowboys	2.5
Wide Receivers		
Jake Reed	Minnesota Vikings	3.23
Rob Moore	Arizona Cardinals	2.85
Carl Pickens	Cincinnati Bengals	2.85
Isaac Bruce	St. Louis Rams	2.65
Jerry Rice	San Francisco 49ers	2.62
Tight Ends		
Shannon Sharpe	Denver Broncos	1.75
Ben Coates	New England Patriots	1.70
Jackie Harris	Tampa Bay Buccaneers	1.70
Mark Chmura	Green Bay Packers	1.60
Rickey Dudley	Oakland Raiders	1.40
Offensive Linemen		
Richmond Webb	Miami Dolphins	3.40
Paul Gruber	Tampa Bay Buccaneers	3.07
Lomas Brown	Arizona Cardinals	3.00
Bruce Matthews	Tennessee Oilers	2.98
Mark Stepnoski	Tennessee Oilers	2.85
Defensive Ends		
Leslie O'Neal	St. Louis Rams	3.17
Marco Coleman	San Diego Chargers	3.16
Bruce Smith	Buffalo Bills	2.07
Alonzo Spellman	Chicago Bears	2.90
Tony Bennett	Indianapolis Colts	2.76
Defensive Tackles		
Eric Swann	Arizona Cardinals	3.50
John Randle	Minnesota Vikings	3.19
Dana Stubblefield	San Francisco 49ers	2.94
Cortez Kennedy	Seattle Seahawks	2.64
Robert Harris	New York Giants	2.14

TOP PAID PLAYERS BY POSITION IN NFL, 1997 SEASON

Name	Team	Salary (in millions)
Linebackers		
Junior Seau	San Diego Chargers	$3.78
Hardy Nickerson	Tampa Bay Buccaneers	3.55
Quentin Corvatt	Indianapolis Colts	3.50
Cornelius Bennett	Atlanta Falcons	3.25
Bryan Cox	Chicago Bears	3.25
Cornerbacks		
Ray Buchanan	Atlanta Falcons	4.00
Aeneas Williams	Arizona Cardinals	3.40
Eric Allen	New Orleans Saints	3.35
Eric Davis	Carolina Panthers	2.75
Troy Vincent	Philadelphia Eagles	2.60
Safeties		
LeRoy Butler	Green Bay Packers	2.55
Henry Jones	Buffalo Bills	2.40
Carnell Lake	Pittsburgh Steelers	2.40
Stanley Richard	Washington Redskins	2.37
Steve Atwater	Denver Broncos	2.26
Kickers/punters		
Steve Christie	Buffalo Bills	0.90
Jon Kasay	Carolina Panthers	0.90
Morten Andersen	Atlanta Falcons	0.86
Bryan Baker	Jacksonville Jaguars	0.82
Matt Stover	Baltimore Ravens	0.74

SOURCE: NFL Players Association.

NFL 1999 FREE AGENT SIGNINGS

Player, Position	New Team	Previous Team	Contract
Tony Bertl, OT	Denver	San Diego	$400,000 for 1 year
Kyle Brady, TE	Jacksonville	New York Jets	14.4 mil. for 6 years
Orlando Brown, OT	Cleveland	Baltimore	27 mil. for 6 years
Devin Bush, S	St. Louis	Atlanta	7.2 mil. for 4 years
Dale Carter, CB	Denver	Kansas City	34.8 mil. for 6 years
Chad Cota, S	Indianapolis	New Orleans	9.6 mil. for 4 years
Charles Evans, FB	Baltimore	Minnesota	3 mil. for 3 years

NFL 1999 FREE AGENT SIGNINGS

Player, Position	New Team	Previous Team	Contract
Corey Fuller, CB	Cleveland	Minnesota	$20.6 mil. for 5 years
Rich Gannon, QB	Oakland	Kansas City	31 mil. for 7 years
Chris Gardocki, P	Cleveland	Indianapolis	6 mil. for 5 years
Eric Green, TE	New York Jets	Baltimore	7.5 mil. for 4 years
Trent Green, QB	St. Louis	Washington	16.5 mil. for 4 years
Charles Johnson, WR	Philadelphia	Pittsburgh	15 mil. for 5 years
Dontae Jones, LB	Carolina	Pittsburgh	6.4 mil. for 4 years
James Jones, DT	Detroit	Baltimore	26 mil. for 6 years
Shawn King, DE	Indianapolis	Carolina	6 mil. for 3 years
Carnell Lake, S	Jacksonville	Pittsburgh	18 mil for 4 years
Doug Pederson, QB	Philadelphia	Green Bay	4.5 mil. for 3 years
Clyde Simmons, DE	Chicago	Cincinnati	4 mil. for 2 years
Torrance Small, WR	Philadelphia	Indianapolis	9 mil. for 4 years
Adam Timmerman, G	St. Louis	Green Bay	19 mil. for 5 years
Steve Tovar, LB	Carolina	San Diego	3.9 mil. for 3 years
Tom Tupa, P	New York Jets	New England	6.1 mil. for 4 years
Gary Walker, G	Jacksonville	Tennessee	18 mil. for 5 years
Wally Williams, G	New Orleans	Baltimore	18.5 mil. for 5 years
Dave Wohlabaugh, C	Cleveland	New England	26.4 mil. for 7 years

SOURCE: NFL Players Association.

NFL FREE AGENTS RE-SIGNING WITH SAME TEAMS, 1999

Player	Position	Team	Contract
Mark Bruener	TE	Pittsburgh	$10M for 4 years
Santana Dotson	DT	Green Bay	26M for 5 years
Lee Flowers	S	Pittsburgh	10M for 4 years
George Koonce	LB	Green Bay	11.3M for 4 years
Mike Mamula	DE	Philadelphia	11.5M for 4 years
Jerry Ostroski	G	Buffalo	12.5M for 4 years
Zach Thomas	LB	Miami	22.5M for 5 years
Corey Widmer	LB	New York Giants	11.2M for 4 years
Dan Williams	DE	Kansas City	28M for 6 years

SOURCE: NFL Players Association.

TOP SALARIES OF NFL HEAD COACHES, 1999

Coach	Team	Salary
Paul Holmgren	Seattle Seahawks	$4 million
George Seifert	Carolina Panthers	2.5 million
Jimmy Johnson	Miami Dolphins	2 million
Steve Mariucci	San Francisco 49ers	2 million
Bill Parcells	New York Jets	2 million
Pete Carrol	New England Patriots	1.5 million
Mike Ditka	New Orleans Saints	1.5 million
Dennis Green	Minnesota Vikings	1.5 million

SOURCE: Associated Press reports.

National Basketball Association

Michael Jordan epitomizes pro basketball, and maybe all of pro sports. In the 1990s, he has earned about $300 million in salary and endorsements. He bagged $47 million in off-court earnings in 1997, more money than any athlete ever made playing his sport. And at age thirty-four, his profits don't appear to be letting up.

But even with an astronomical salary of $33.1 million for the 1997–98 season—or a figure near that, depending on where you do your research—is he the highest paid player in basketball? Based on his annual salary, yes. But based on the total value of his contract, maybe not.

The nay-sayers only have to turn to Kevin Garnett, who jumped from high school right to the Minnesota Timberwolves a couple of years ago. Though Garnett, a spindly forward who probably was not yet the best player on his team for the 1997–98 season, was living on a $2.1 million base salary at age twenty for the 1997–98 season, he had signed a six-year, $126 million contract before the start of the season, which should hold him financially until he hits his peak at age twenty-six or twenty-seven.

Not only did Garnett set a record for the largest contract ever in pro sports, he also turned down a huge one. Garnett told the Timberwolves a clear "no" when they made him an offer of $110 million at the same negotiating table. He held out for the $126 million and got it. It just proves you don't have to go to college to learn how to make money.

Garnett's contract broke the record of another proven pro, Shaquille O'Neal of the Los Angeles Lakers, who had dropped out of college to turn pro and to turn his value into a $120 million player (over seven seasons), but only after becoming an all-star player.

The money in pro basketball is almost too much to fathom.

So, too, is the whole idea that in the midst of all these enormous piles of money, the NBA players actually refused to play in 1998 and caused half the season to be lost. The club owners were determined to get some control over the ever-escalating salaries of star players and to retain the rights to rookies they put under contract for a longer period of time. The players' union refused to accept any serious limitations on the freedom of players to negotiate the best possible deals, and a six-month lockout resulted. In early January 1999, the players caved in to most of the owners' demands, and an abbreviated fifty-game schedule was announced. The key elements in the six-year deal (the owners have an option for a seventh year) include:

Maximum salary levels:	$9 million a year for players with five or fewer years' experience; $11 million for those with six to nine years; and $14 million for those with 10 or more years' experience.
Maximum annual raises:	12 percent for players signing as a free agent with the same team; 10 percent for all others.
Maximum annual salaries:	Rookies $287,000
	One year $350,000
	Two years $425,000
	Three years $450,000
	Four years $475,000
	Five years $537,500
	Six years $600,000
	Seven years $662,500
	Eight years $725,000
	Nine years $850,000
	Ten years $1 million
Rookies:	They cannot become free agents until after five years (formerly it was three), and they are "restricted" free agents since their team has the right of first refusal.
Percentage of revenues to be devoted to players' salaries:	In the first three years of the contract, no fixed number, but in years four, five, and six, the percentage will be 55 percent, and in year seven 57 percent (if the owners exercise their option for a seventh year).

The total compensation for about 400 players was $968 million for the 1997–98 season—and that was about $140 million more than the season before. In 1992, Patrick Ewing of the New York Knicks signed the first contract to top $5 million a year when he agreed to play for $33 million over

TOP PAID PLAYERS IN THE NBA, 1997–98 SEASON

Player	Team	Average Annual Salary
Michael Jordan	Chicago Bulls	$33,140,000
Patrick Ewing	New York Knicks	20,500,000
Horace Grant	Orlando Magic	14,285,000
Shaquille O'Neal	Los Angeles Lakers	12,550,000
David Robinson	San Antonio Spurs	12,379,000
Alonzo Mourning	Miami Heat	11,255,000
Juwan Howard	Washington Wizards	11,250,000
Hakeem Olajuwon	Houston Rockets	11,158,000
Gary Payton	Seattle SuperSonics	10,514,000
Dikembe Mutombo	Atlanta Hawks	9,610,000
Reggie Miller	Indiana Pacers	9,000,000
Chris Webber	Washington Wizards	9,000,000
Larry Johnson	New York Knicks	8,460,000
Derrick Coleman	Philadelphia 76ers	8,002,000
Allan Houston	New York Knicks	8,000,000
Kevin Johnson	Phoenix Suns	8,000,000
Shawn Kemp	Cleveland Cavaliers	7,700,000
Elden Campbell	Los Angeles Lakers	7,000,000
Penny Hardaway	Orlando Magic	7,000,000
Danny Manning	Phoenix Suns	6,830,000
Robert Horry	Los Angeles Lakers	6,000,000
Shawn Bradley	Dallas Mavericks	5,940,000
Otis Thorpe	Sacramento Kings	5,700,000
Glenn Robinson	Milwaukee Bucks	5,510,000
Clyde Drexler	Houston Rockets	5,500,000
Grant Hill	Detroit Pistons	5,500,000
Tom Gugliotta	Minnesota Timberwolves	5,500,000
Steve Smith	Atlanta Hawks	5,400,000
Christian Laettner	Atlanta Hawks	5,350,000
Sean Elliott	San Antonio Spurs	5,333,000
Dale Davis	Indiana Pacers	5,273,000
Jason Kidd	Phoenix Suns	5,223,000
Karl Malone	Utah Jazz	5,119,000
John Starks	New York Knicks	5,100,000
A.C. Green	Dallas Mavericks	5,095,000
Kenny Anderson	Boston Celtics	5,010,000
Brian Grant	Portland Trail Blazers	5,000,000

SOURCE: NBA Players Association.

NBA TEAM PAYROLLS, 1997–98 SEASON

Team	Player Payroll
Chicago Bulls	$61,729,000
New York Knicks	58,534,000
Orlando Magic	45,782,000
San Antonio Spurs	42,865,000
Phoenix Suns	42,117,000
Washington Wizards	40,890,000
Indiana Pacers	38,845,000
Seattle SuperSoncis	36,684,000
Los Angeles Lakers	35,590,000
Miami Heat	34,555,000
Golden State Warriors	34,209,000
Atlanta Hawks	32,116,000
Philadelphia 76ers	28,456,000
Portland Trail Blazers	28,476,000
Utah Jazz	28,470,000
Houston Rockets	27,988,000
Cleveland Cavaliers	27,798,000
Charlotte Hornets	27,760,000
Boston Celtics	27,369,000
Minnesota Timberwolves	27,277,000
Detroit Pistons	27,140,000
Sacramento Kings	27,102,000
Dallas Mavericks	27,042,000
Denver Nuggets	25,859,000
Vancouver Grizzlies	25,473,000
Toronto Raptors	25,272,000
Milwaukee Bucks	24,939,000
Los Angeles Clippers	24,057,000

SOURCE: NBA.

six seasons. Today, $5 million is commonplace. For the 1997–98 season, a total of thirty-eight players had a salary of more than $5 million. Ewing's salary was up to $20.5 million, second only to Jordan's. Nine players made more than $10 million, and more than twenty have long-term contracts of $50 million or more.

The league did come up with something called "the salary cap," which was supposed to put a harness on the free-wheeling big-market franchises back in 1984. The idea was to allow all teams a maximum of how much they could pay their total team. That way, the smaller-market teams would not have to compete dollar-for-dollar with the rich teams. And, supposedly, it would end the raid of the smaller-market team's free agents.

At first, the league's health returned. But after a while, teams began to complain that the salary caps limited the teams from making trades with certain other teams and with the movement of free agents. Before the salary cap, small-market teams—Seattle, Portland, Milwaukee—were winning their share of championships. Nowadays, the teams with the highest payrolls are usually the teams in the chase. In the 1997–98 season, Chicago and New York had the biggest payrolls by far (about $61.7 million for the Bulls and $58.5 for the Knicks). The Knicks signed Larry Johnson and Allan Houston away from other teams for huge deals to get into the hunt.

As pro basketball's popularity has continued to grow, television reared its all-powerful pocketbook in 1998 and came up with a multi*billion*-dollar deal, which the players quickly saw as an opportunity to increase their salaries. The owners agreed but demanded that the players' total share of total revenues be predetermined by contract. When the players refused, the owners locked them out and effectively killed the entire 1998–99 season.

TOP LONG-TERM CONTRACTS IN THE NBA, 1997–98 SEASON

Player	Team	Contract (years, amount in millions)	Expires
Kevin Garnett	Minnesota Timberwolves	6—$126	2004
Shaquille O'Neal	Los Angeles Lakers	7—$120	2002
Alonzo Mourning	Miami Heat	7—$105	2003
Juwan Howard	Washington Wizards	7—$105	2003
Shawn Kemp	Cleveland Cavaliers	7—$ 99.5	2004
Larry Johnson	New York Knicks	12—$ 84	2006
Penny Hardaway	Orlando Magic	7—$ 70	2002
Glenn Robinson	Milwaukee Bucks	10—$ 68.2	2004
Patrick Ewing	New York Knicks	6—$ 68	2001
Gary Payton	Seattle SuperSonics	7—$ 66	2000
David Robinson	San Antonio Spurs	6—$ 66	2000

SOURCE: Various newspaper reports.

TOP COACHING SALARIES IN NBA, 1997–98 SEASON

Name	Team	Avg. Annual Salary (in millions)
Pat Riley	Miami Heat	$8.0
Rick Pitino	Boston Celtics	7.0
Phil Jackson	Chicago Bulls	6.0
Lenny Wilkens	Atlanta Hawks	5.63
Larry Brown	Philadelphia 76ers	5.0
Mike Fratello	Cleveland Cavaliers	5.0
Chuck Daly	Orlando Magic	4.8
Larry Bird	Indiana Pacers	4.7
Rudy Tomjanovich	Houston Rockets	4.5
Don Nelson	Dallas Mavericks	4.0

SOURCE: Various newspaper reports.

National Hockey League

In February 1998, the Detroit Red Wings, who had steadfastly insisted earlier in the month that they could not pay holdout star Sergei Federov more than $5.5 million a season, signed the Russian-born star to a six-year, $38 million contract with $28 million to be paid for the 1997–98 season—or what was left of it: There were only twenty-three more regular-season games, plus play-offs, to be played.

At twenty eight years old, Federov had hit the jackpot.

Earlier, the Carolina Hurricanes had offered Federov a $38 million package. The Red Wings, who had won the Stanley Cup with Federov in the lineup the last time he played, decided, out of desperation, to match it. By union-management agreement, the Red Wings could then retain him.

Said Federov: "I have used the collective bargaining agreement to secure the contract I now have. So, too, have the Red Wings used the agreement to retain my rights."

That simple.

Before the season began, the Colorado Avalanche had used pretty much the same procedure to make Joe Sakic a $17 million man for the 1997–98 season. The New York Rangers had dangled that figure in front of Sakic, but the Avalanche matched it. Sakic's $17.0 million for the 1997–98 season was partial payment of a three-year $21 million package.

The average salary in the National Hockey League has risen from $158,000 to more than a million in the past dozen years, and shows no sign of letting up. But Federov still didn't have the biggest package in hockey.

Jaromir Jagr of the Pittsburgh Penguins had a six-year deal that could be worth $48.0 million. Jagr was to make $5.1 million in 1997–98, and $4.75 in 1998–99 before his salary reached $9.5 million in 1999–2000, and $10.4 million in 2003–04.

Along with Federov, the other player who found Gold during the 1997–98 season was goalie Dominik Hasek, who led the Czech Republic to a stunning Gold Medal in the 1998 Winter Olympic Games. The Buffalo Sabres netminder was given a two-year extension to his contract—worth $18.5 million—after the Games, plus an option that would pay him another $9 million for the 2001–02 season. Until that deal, the Colorado Avalanche's Patrick Roy was the highest paid goalie at $4.46 million.

Even with no substantial television contract with the big three networks (ABC, NBC, or CBS), hockey players are making a mint. If and when they get one, who is to say how much they will be making?

TOP PAID PLAYERS IN THE NHL, 1997–98[1]

Rank	Player	Team	Average Annual Salary (in millions)
1.	Joe Sakic	Colorado Avalanche	$17.0
2.	Chris Gratton	Philadelphia Flyers	10.0
3.	Eric Lindros	Philadelphia Flyers	7.5
4.	Wayne Gretzky	New York Rangers	6.5
5.	Mark Messier	Vancouver Canucks	6.0
6.	Pavel Bure	Vancouver Canucks	5.5
7.	Paul Kariya	Anaheim Mighty Ducks	5.5
8.	Jaromir Jagr	Pittsburgh Penguins	5.1
9.	Steve Yzerman	Detroit Red Wings	5.1
10.	Pat La Fontaine	New York Rangers	4.8

[1]These were salaries going into the season. In 1998, the Detroit Red Wings paid their season-long holdout, Sergei Fedorov, $28 million in salary and bonuses for the final twenty-three regular-season games and play-offs of the 1997–98 season.
SOURCE: NHL Players Association.

AVERAGE SALARY IN THE NHL		
Season	Average Salary	Percent Increase
1986–87	$158,000	—
1987–88	172,000	8.9%
1988–89	188,000	9.3
1989–90	211,000	12.2
1990–91	271,000	28.4
1991–92	368,000	35.8
1992–93	467,000	26.9
1993–94	562,000	20.3
1994–95	733,000	30.4
1995–96	892,000	21.7
1996–97	981,000	10.0

SOURCE: NHL Players Association

Boxing

The problem with boxing is that it is ephemeral. The money goes as fast as it comes. Rich one day, poor the next. The money comes in bunches.

A boxer like Mike Tyson has made, according to published reports, $182 million in the 1990s, by the time he was thirty-one years old. But because of his suspension for biting the ear of Evander Holyfield during their championship bout in 1997, he was indefinitely suspended from the sport, and his average annual earnings will sink from $26 million a year to zero. That's some bite out of the paycheck.

But boxers are still among the top moneymakers in sports, thanks to lucrative television contracts. Boxers don't draw salaries like most team sports but must depend on their fight-to-fight income. For years, that meant that their next fight depended upon their last one. The promoters set the splits, with challengers usually getting the short—sometimes very short—end. Television has boosted the gate and the security for boxers, but who knows how much their managers and/or promoters are taking? Tyson was embroiled with his manager, Don King, over back money—millions of it—as we went to press, just as King was embroiled with federal prosecutors over a strange insurance claim on another fighter.

There is nothing new in boxing in that regard over the years.

But the big money is fairly new in the past quarter century, dating back to the 1971 "Fight of the Century," when Muhammad Ali and Joe Frazier fought their heavyweight title bout for $2.5 million each. The bulk of that money was made from closed-circuit television, which has become a thing of the past.

Closed-circuit TV—shown at movie theaters, auditoriums, and places that could draw moderately good-sized crowds for a per-person or a group fee—has given way to cablevision, or pay-TV, which is much more lucrative with just a portion of the logistics fees. And with the growth of television in the 1980s and 1990s, there seems to be no shortage of outlets.

A good boxer now can sign a multifight deal with television rights, guaranteeing him a nice financial package, win or lose. It has made Naseem Hamed, a featherweight from Great Britain via Yemen, one of the richest people in sports. Featherweights never made much money before.

Because of television and its need for bouts, all the rich boxers these days aren't just the heavyweights and a handful of others such as Sugar Ray Leonard or Marvin Hagler. In fact, the second highest paid boxer in 1997 was a welterweight, Oscar De la Hoya, a twenty-four-year-old who earned $37 million in the ring. In his five 1997 fights, he had two paydays in the eight-figure class.

But the champ, money-wise and otherwise, is Evander Holyfield, who pulled in $33 million for the 1997 Tyson fight alone, and $20 million more for his remaining agenda. With Tyson out indefinitely, and Holyfield remaining on top, those figures may only get higher.

For all the big money in boxing, most bouts are staged between boxers taking the same risks as Holyfield but making only $10,000 or less a bout. Even a promising heavyweight like Andrew Golota, who started his pro career with twenty-eight straight victories and then some bouts with Lennox Lewis and Riddick Bowe, can be brought back to earth to fight for $20,000 or so.

EARNINGS OF TOP BOXERS, 1997

Name	Division	Ring Earnings (millions)
Evander Holyfield	Heavyweight	$53.0
Oscar De la Hoya	Welterweight	37.0
Mike Tyson	Heavyweight	27.0
George Foreman	Heavyweight	10.2
Michael Moorer	Heavyweight	9.6
Naseem Hamed	Featherweight	9.5

SOURCE: *Ring* Magazine.

Tennis

Tennis is unique among professional sports in regard to money winnings by women compared to men. Although the ladies don't make as much as the men do, they stand far closer. True, there are no women tennis players on the *Forbes* highest paid forty pro sports list (in fact, there are no women at all on the list), though three male tennis players are in the top twenty-one. Yet three female tennis players made more than $1 million a year as early as 1994.

One woman, Martina Navratilova, made more than $20 million in her career, and Steffi Graf is closing in on that figure. Only four men have topped $20 million, and no others are close. Endorsements of clothing, shoes, and other businesses are as appealing for women players as they are for men. Women have closed the gaps in all other sports, but it is hard to conceive them matching the monies earned by men. Not so with tennis.

Still, as tennis's premier moneymaking machine, it is a man who stands above the rest. Since his emergence as the top player in 1990, Pete Sampras has been the leading money-winner five times in eight years (through 1997) and finished second, third, and fifth the other years. He is pulling away from second-place Boris Becker on the all-time earnings list and has collected nearly ten times as much prize money as Becker in 1997. His $6.5 million

EARNINGS OF THE TOP TENNIS PLAYERS, 1997

Name	Earnings
Pete Sampras	$6,498.311
Yevgeny Kafelnikov	$3,207,757
Patrick Rafter	$2,923,519
Michael Chang	$2,541,830
Thomas Muster	$2,166,590
Thomas Bjorkman	$1,950,375
Gustavo Kuerten	$1,580,753
Peter Korda	$1,515,483
Greg Rusedski	$1,515,473
Goran Ivanisevic	$1,458,257
Richard Krajicek	$1,434,564
Marcelo Rios	$1,387,445
Todd Woodbridge	$1,335,918
Sergi Bruguera	$1,227,428
Alex Corretja	$1,182,807

SOURCE: Association of Tennis Professionals.

take in 1997 broke the previous yearly earnings record, set by Becker in 1996, by a whopping $2.2 million. In that year he more than doubled the winnings of the runner-up, Yevgeny Kafelnikov.

Sampras, of course, is blessed by the cash rolls of modern times. It wasn't until the late 1980s that tennis players made as much as $2 million in prizes for the season. Sampras made that much in September 1997, when he won the Grand Slam Cup in Munich, Germany. In addition, Sampras earned $8 million in endorsement money in 1997.

TOP PRIZEWINNERS, ALL TIME (IN MILLIONS)
(through September 30, 1997)

Men	Earnings
Pete Sampras	$26.5
Boris Becker	$24.2
Ivan Lendl	$21.3
Stefan Edberg	$20.6
Goran Ivanisevic	$15.6
Michael Chang	$15.0

Women	Earnings
Martina Navratilova	$20.3
Steffi Graf	$19.3
Arantxa Sanchez Vicario	$11.2
Chris Evert	$ 8.9
Monica Seles	$ 8.9
Gabriela Sabatini	$ 8.8

SOURCE: Association of Tennis Professionals; Women's Tennis Association.

EVOLUTION IN ANNUAL MEN'S TENNIS EARNINGS
(through 1997)

1968	$ 83,504	Tony Roche
1977	$ 768,065	Guillermo Vilas
1979	$1,008,742	Bjorn Borg
1982	$2,028,850	Ivan Lendl
1990	$2,900,057	Pete Sampras
1993	$4,579,325	Pete Sampras
1995	$5,415,066	Boris Becker
1997	$6,498,311	Pete Sampras

SOURCE: Association of Tennis Professionals

Golf

Professional golf is unique among money sports because of the staying power of its athletes. Not only can the pros play for more years—and they have their fifty-and-older Seniors Tour to prove it—some can actually play on the regular tour longer. The 1998 Masters Tournament, one of golf's Big Four, saw not only Mark O'Meara winning his first major tournament at age forty-one, but also fifty-eight-year-old Jack Nicklaus finishing in fifth place, and sixty-two-year-old Gary Player making the final cut and playing for the championship on the final two days.

The year before, Nicklaus's winnings were more than $300,000, though he was listed thirty-eight on the *Forbes* magazine list of top moneymakers in sports because of an additional $9 million in sports-related endorsements and earnings. For his fifth place in the Masters alone, he made $111,200. Winner O'Meara, a top pro on the regular circuit, had made $1,124,600 in 1997, and then made more than half of that again ($576,000) with his four-day triumph in the 1998 Masters.

Golf lends itself to endorsements, as the *Forbes* list shows. Of the four top moneymakers, three are fifty-eight and older (Nicklaus, Player, and Arnold Palmer, who ranked second among golfers only to Tiger Woods, though he won only about $100,000 on the links).

Golf has been good to the seniors. That and shuffleboard are probably

EARNINGS OF TOP GOLFERS, 1997

Men	Earnings	Women	Earnings
Tiger Woods	$2.06	Annika Sorenstam	$1.24
David Duval	1.88	Karrie Webb	0.98
Davis Love III	1.66	Kelly Bobbins	0.91
Jim Furyk	1.61	Chris Johnson	0.72
Justin Leonard	1.59	Tammie Green	0.59
Scott Hoch	1.39	Juli Inkster	0.58
Greg Norman	1.35	Liselotte Neumann	0.49
Steve Elkington	1.33	Laura Davies	0.48
Ernie Els	1.24	Nancy Lopez	0.47
Brad Faxon	1.23	Betsy King	0.47
Phil Mickelson	1.22	Lori Kane	0.42
Jesper Parnevik	1.21	Michelle McGann	0.42
Mark O'Meara	1.12	Donna Andrews	0.39
Mark Calcavecchia	1.11	Colleen Walker	0.38
Loren Roberts	1.09	Rosie Jones	0.38

SOURCE: Professional Golfers' Association, Ladies Professional Golfers' Association

the most popular sports for the retired set. But the shuffleboarders make virtually nothing, if anything, while a good Senior PGA golfer like Gil Morgan can already rack up nearly half a million dollars by April 1 on the 1998 tour.

On the regular tour, a half-million for winning one major tournament has become the norm. The U.S. Open paid $465,000 to its winner, Ernie Els, in 1997.

The women pros, without the high TV exposure of men, can't do nearly as well. Eighteen men made $1 million or more in prizes in 1997 but only one woman, Annika Sorenstam, did. But the women's prizes are going up steadily, just like the men's. Sorenstam's prizewinnings of $1,236,789 were nearly double what the leader made in 1994. Tiger Woods's lead among men was about one-third more than the leader in 1994, and he became golf's first player to break the $2 million mark.

Horse Racing

The jockeys in horse racing make their money on volume—the number of races they run in and the cut they get for their finishes. In general, jockeys get only 10 percent of the cut from what their horses win in a race, but it has been said that the only top jockeys who die poor are the ones who bet on somebody else's races. In addition to their winnings, a handful of elite jockeys from time to time will have special guarantees for riding a certain horse for an owner.

EARNING OF TOP JOCKEYS, 1998

Jockey	Earnings	Jockey	Earnings
Pat Day	$1,724,465	Robbie Davis	$713,004
Jerry Bailey	1,708,640	C. H. Borel	696,667
Gary Stevens	1,671,279	D. R. Flores	694,309
Kent Desormeaux	1,456,715	Eddie Delahoussaye	649,830
Corey Nakatani	1,347,012	M. E. Smith	628,303
Shane Sellers	1,271,236	M. Guidry	570,707
Chris McCarron	1,079,719	G. K. Gomez	446,940
Alex Solis	1,040,785	M. St. Julien	432,453
Robbie Albarado	936,349	J. K. Court	430,264
Willie Martinez	737,348	T. K. Kabel	428,174

SOURCE: *Daily Racing Form.*

Auto Racing

There are three kinds of auto racing in the big-money brackets: CART, or the oval type of racing you see at the Indianapolis 500; NASCAR, or stock car racing; and Formula One, the international circuit highlighted each year at races such as the Grand Prix of Monaco.

Auto racing has always been an expensive sport, but one with big earnings. The Indy 500 is an event that ranks right up with premier American sports events such as the baseball's World Series and golf's U.S. Open. The NASCAR circuit has become extremely popular in recent years, and there are signs that stock car racing is finding an appeal beyond its traditional southern base. Formula One is the most popular racing circuit outside of the United States, and enjoys worldwide cachet.

There is money to be made from the prize pool, and the annual NASCAR season winners take home millions. Formula One drivers make more: On the *Forbes* list of the highest paid sporting figures in 1997, Ferrari driver

NASCAR ALL-TIME EARNINGS	
Driver	**Earnings (in millions)[1]**
Dale Earnhardt	$29.5
Bill Elliott	17.4
Terry Labonte	16.1
Darrell Waltrip	16.0
Rusty Wallace	15.6
Jeff Gordon	14.2
Geoff Bodine	13.4

[1]As of September, 1997.
SOURCE: NASCAR.

WINSTON'S CUP DRIVER'S EARNINGS, 1997	
Driver	**Earnings (in millions)**
Terry Labonte	$4.0
Jeff Gordon	3.4
Dale Jarrett	3.0
Dale Earnhardt	2.3
Mark Martin	1.9
Ernie Irvan	1.7
Rusty Wallace	1.7

SOURCE: NASCAR.

Michael Schumacher placed fourth, just ahead of Mike Tyson, and earned $35 million in prizes and endorsements.

In a sport backed by auto manufacturers, tire companies, and fuel suppliers, tons more money is to be made in endorsements. It's a dangerous sport, but it breeds many, many millionaires.

College Coaches

After the 1998 NCAA men's basketball tournament finished, there was the usual flurry of coaching changes due to retirements, firings, promotions, and job shifts. One coach turned down what seemed to be a lucrative promotion because, it was alleged, he did not want to leave a Reebok school for a Nike school. Interpretation: He was being paid so much money on the side by Reebok that he would be taking a pay cut to go to a Nike school.

In the 1990s, a handful of college basketball coaches have made a million dollars or more a season—Rick Pitino at Kentucky, Dean Smith at North Carolina, Mike Krzyzewski at Duke. These were jobs that hardly paid $40,000 or $50,000 about fifteen years before.

Near the end of the 1997 college football season, *USA Today* did an exhaustive survey of the salaries paid to the coaches of teams that were, at that point, in the paper's top twenty-five rankings. Here are the earnings of the top twelve coaches in the survey.

TOP-EARNING COLLEGE FOOTBALL COACHES, 1997

Name	School	Base Salary	Related Income[1]	Total
Bobby Bowden	Florida State	$157,500	$ 847,500	$1,000,000
Lloyd Carr	Michigan	266,512	144,500	411,012
Tom Osborne	Nebraska	175,000	225,000	400,000
John Cooper	Ohio State	165,000	543,550	708,550
Phil Fulmer	Tennessee	135,000	383,568	518,569
Joe Paterno	Penn State	Refused	600,000	600,000
Bill Snyder	Kansas State	170,000	365,000	535,000
Mack Brown	North Carolina	165,375	60,000	225,375
Bob Toledo	UCLA	150,000	253,000	403,000
Steve Spurrier	Florida	168,850	1,800,000	1,968,850
Mike Price	Washington State	112,970	140,000	252,970
Bruce Snyder	Arizona State	500,000	33,500	533,500

[1]Income from apparel manufacturers, football camps, speeches, radio shows, etc.
SOURCE: *USA Today*, November 21, 1997. Reprinted by permission.

Bowling

Compared with other sports on these pages, bowling payouts are like the longtime television show *Bowling for Dollars*. Because bowling alleys are small and can attract only small audiences, much of the bowling money comes from television, which also attracts small, but very loyal audiences. Total purses per event of less than $100,000 are the norm, and they have to be shared by many players.

But bowlers roll on. The big money for most of them comes from endorsements of bowling equipment, and there are a lot of bowlers buying such products in America and the world.

The male bowlers make about twice as much as the women on the major tours by the (men's) Pro Bowlers Association and the Ladies Pro Bowling Tour.

PROFESSIONAL BOWLERS ASSOCIATION ALL-TIME EARNINGS	
Men	**Earnings (in millions)**
Walter Ray Williams, Jr.	$2.0
Pete Weber	2.0
Mike Aulby	1.8
Marshall Homan	1.7
Brian Voss	1.6
Women	**Earnings (in thousands)**
Aleta Sill	$821
Tish Johnson	786
Lisa Wagner	701
Robin Romero	617
Anne Marie Duggan	608

SOURCE: PBA.

The Professional Amateurs

When distance-runner Paavo Nurmi, the Finnish Olympic champion, was at his peak in the 1920s, he was invited to New York to run in an indoor meet. Although Nurmi was technically an amateur, the promoters offered him $1,000, very good money at the time, for his appearance. When he got to New York, the promoters handed him only $750 and said that's all they could pay him.

Nurmi was scheduled to run the mile race at Madison Square Garden. He raced, took a very good lead, then dropped out on his own at the three-quarter mark. The promoters were irate.

He said to them, "You paid me three-quarters of what you said you would, so I ran three-quarters of what I said I would."

"Amateur" athletes have known how to play the money game for years. Amateurs were making so much money on the tennis tour that the elitist sport became professional in the 1960s. Pete Sampras, who would have been an amateur forty years ago, made more than $6 million as a pro in 1997.

The ancient Olympic Games were discontinued about 2,000 years ago because the Romans had violated the original amateur ideals with too many gold coins. Even in the modern Olympics, which date back to 1896, there have been constant accusations of under-the-table payments. The Americans accused the Soviet Union of masking their athletes on the Red Army team as twenty-nine-year-old physical education students. The Russians accused the Americans of harboring professional athletes in college athletic programs. Western Europeans and American track athletes were forever being fed money stuffed in track shoes given to them by feuding footwear companies that set up shop in Olympic villages.

Nurmi, Jesse Owens (the American sprinter), and Jim Thorpe (the American who won the 1912 Olympic decathlon) were all banned, as great as they were, by the Olympic movement. Olympic skiiers were banned when their uniforms looked like human billboards for ski equipment companies. East Germany built a sports complex in Leipzig, closed to the public, that housed and drugged its athletes from the time they were children. Little East Germany became the third most powerful Olympic nation, after the United States and the Soviet Union, in the post–World War II era.

Of course, American college sports have always been tainted, way back to the turn of the century, when football players would compete for alma maters on Saturdays, then play under pseudonyms for semiprofessional teams on Sundays. It was nothing to have half the Notre Dame team, including the legendary Knute Rockne, lined up against half the University of Illinois squad for a Sunday game between town teams. It was Hugh Mc-Elhenney, the great University of Washington halfback of the 1950s, who said, "I had to take a pay cut to turn pro."

With the power of television money, the Olympic movement has become increasingly professional. The International Olympic Committee decided in the 1980s that it was up to each sports federation (basketball and boxing, for example) to establish its own standards. Among the major sports, basketball, ice hockey, and track and field allowed pros.

In the United States, a basketball player or football player can turn to the NBA or NFL whenever he wants, after a couple years of college or even upon finishing high school. About half of the high first-round draft choices of the NBA are players who didn't finish four years of college.

Colleges, which have been called "farm clubs" for the pros, are finding that title to be more appropriate. There has been a growing movement to pay college athletes, and this is something that may been seen in the future.

Athletic Directors

The importance of athletics in college and university programs is clearly reflected in the salaries paid to athletic directors at these institutions of higher education. With an average salary of about $65,000 (over $75,000 in large public universities), athletic directors are some of the highest paid student services officials, according to the College and University Personnel Association's *Administrative Compensation Survey.* Among administrators whose purpose it is to serve students directly, only the Chief Student Affairs Officer, the Director of Student Health Services (who is also a physician), and the Chief of Enrollment Management earn higher salaries. Gender discrimination is in evidence in this job category as well. At institutions where the athletic director's job is divided between men's and women's sports, the director of men's athletic programs earns about 10 percent more than the director of women's athletic programs, regardless of the sex of the office holder. This inequity continues despite federal legislation (Title IX) requiring colleges to devote equal funding to men's and women's athletic programs.

At many institutions where men's football or basketball programs consistently attract national attention (for example, Indiana in basketball; Penn State in football), the coach of the featured team also serves as athletic director. This not only makes the coach responsible to nobody except the head of the university but also effectively insures that the premier sport gets more of the athletic director's attention than any other sport at the institution.

AVERAGE SALARIES OF ATHLETIC DIRECTORS IN HIGHER EDUCATION

Type of Institution	
Large public universities	$75,000
Large private universities	65,000
Private religious institutions	60,000
All institutions	65,000

SOURCE: Estimates based on figures from College and University Personnel Association.

BEHIND THE SCENES

BEHIND THE SCENES IN TELEVISION

Some people still think television is a vast wasteland of worthless entertainment and offensive commercials; others view the tube as a quasidivine instrument bringing mankind together in a "global village." No one, however, questions the simple fact that television has changed people's daily routines, while at the same time expanded their knowledge in ways not imagined a few short decades ago. In America, this has been accomplished essentially by a business-sponsored broadcasting system.

There are about 1,000 television stations in the United States. Of these, about 260 are run by nonprofit organizations, many located in universities, which is why they are usually referred to as "educational" stations. The others are called "commercial" stations because their owners make a profit from selling broadcast time to advertisers. Most of these commercial stations are linked together every night into four separate networks (ABC, CBS, NBC, and Fox) in order to provide advertisers with larger audiences, and audiences with better programming.

Despite the size and scope of the industry, and the important role television plays in our daily lives, the business employs only about 100,000 people, 15,000 of whom work at the major networks. As in any business, most jobs are clerical or secretarial in the accounting and data processing departments. Only a handful of people, perhaps 40,000, are directly involved with getting the news or entertainment onto our sets. For this reason there is intense competition for jobs in television, especially in large cities. However, the Department of Labor foresees expanded job opportunities in the field over the next decade because of the explosion in cable TV systems and the bright prospects for videotapes.

Broadcasting requires the skills and talents of many different kinds of people, from writers and directors to stagehands and lighting experts. Most of these jobs require union membership, but for that reason, salary levels are relatively high. The most important television unions representing technicians at the networks and at major market stations are the International Brotherhood of Electrical Workers (IBEW), the National Association of Broadcast Employees and Technicians (NABET), and the International Alliance of Theatrical Stage Employees (IATSE). Nontechnical, behind-the-scenes people who are not considered management belong to the Directors Guild of America (DGA) or the Writers Guild of America (WGA).

Union contracts can be negotiated either with individual stations or with a network and its owned and operated station for all staff jobs. Although there are differences between compensation at the networks and at local stations, most technical people are paid close to the same rates. Salaries for other staff members will fluctuate, sometimes dramatically, from city to city or, in broadcasting lingo, market to market. And since most jobs in broadcasting exist on the local level, the job descriptions and salaries that follow are based on the organization of those stations. A few network salary figures are included (from the NAB/BCFM Television Employee Compensation and Fringe Benefits Report). These figures are based on an average of *all markets and all stations.* We cannot stress enough that salaries fluctuate wildly depending on what market the station is in.

Management

Every television station has at least three key managerial positions: general manager (also called station manager), sales manager, and program director. Although their duties will differ from station to station, the following general descriptions provide a clear idea of what each job entails. All of these positions usually carry with them very hefty expense accounts.

General Manager/Station Manager—Basic responsibility is to run the station on a day-to-day as well as a long-term basis. Has final decision-making power on all issues—from budgeting to programming—which affects the station's operation. All department managers or directors answer to him.

    The average salary for station managers is $137,811 a year, with a bonus of $50,322. Except in the smallest markets, almost all make over $60,000. The top people earn $200,000 or more.

Sales Manager—Commercial stations make all of their profits through advertising, and the sales manager supervises the men and women who sell broadcast time to sponsors. This is frequently done through advertising agencies that represent large sponsors seeking local coverage. At large stations there are usually three sales managers: one for local sales, one for national sales, and one in charge of the entire sales operation, who is known as the general sales manager.

    As you might expect, market size greatly influences salaries. In New York, $100,000 to $150,000 is not unheard of, but the average in all markets for the general sales manager is $87,481, with other compensation averaging $38, 841.

Program Director—Initiates the development of all broadcasts for the station and then oversee their budgets and production. The producers of each program are answerable to the program director, who reports directly to the station manager.

Again, the size of the station and the market determine salary. An independent station tends to pay more because it does more of its own programming than stations affiliated with a network. The average salary for program directors is $47,828, with an average bonus of $6,549. In the top ten markets, however, most make over $80,000. Top pay in these areas is said to be between $100,000 and $150,000.

Producers and Directors

Producer—Every show, whether it originates locally or comes from a network, has one person who is ultimately responsible for almost every phase of the program, from concept to finished product. The producer selects and works with the talent, instructs the director, and is frequently in charge of the show's budget. On major programs, including all those on the network, there is also an *executive producer* who is responsible for long-range planning and making sure the show does well in the ratings game. Big-time network programs such as *Today, 60 Minutes,* and *Good Morning America* will have producers and associate producers for each segment.

According to the National Association of Broadcasting, salaries for producers at local stations are the same as those for directors: The national average is about $30,794, but top markets often pay three times that amount (see the section on news producers). Since the networks reach much larger audiences, they hire the most talented people. The salaries, therefore, are much higher. Some of the best known even have agents. According to several New York–based agents, executive producers on networks can make over $300,000 a year.

Director—On all live and taped shows (news, soap operas, game shows, interview programs, sporting events), the director sits at a long console and faces a row of television monitors that show him what is going on in the studio or on the field of play from different camera positions. On news broadcasts, there are also closed-circuit monitors where tape or film that has been edited that day will appear at the director's cue. The director's job is to choreograph all the elements of the broadcast: cue the studio cameras; give instructions to the stage manager on the floor to cue the talent; call for slides, film, or tape to be inserted in the control room and implement them on the floor.

There is a base salary for directors negotiated with the DGA, but there is no ceiling. Depending on demand, talent, and experience, a director can negotiate a handsome salary. Established soap opera directors, for example, can be paid $2,000 or more per episode. But the soaps are produced by networks, and the average salaries at local stations are much lower.

Associate Director—Sits next to the director and informs him what comes next in the broadcast. The AD keeps running time of the entire broadcast, and on news shows counts down when videotape machines should roll tape. The AD informs the director when a commercial is coming up and how long it will run. After the broadcast, the AD arranges for tapes to be made.

    Salaries vary from market to market. At most network-owned-and-operated stations, the base salary is about $25,000 to start and rises to around $50,000 after three years.

Technicians

There are several specialized kinds of technicians needed at every station. Most network technicians earn about $20,000 to start, with a top of about $35,000 after three years. Supervisors make $40,000 and up.

Technical Director—Physically implements the director's instructions at his cue by pushing a set of complex buttons on the console in front of him; i.e., he rolls tape machines, and picks up camera shots. Salaries at networks and at the major stations in large cities are in the $35,000 to $55,000 range. The average in all markets and all stations is $26,840.

Audio—Sits in a separate booth in the control room. The audio person wires the talent in the studio, tests and monitors their levels, and raises and lowers audio levels at the director's cue.

Video—Adjusts color levels and balances picture so that it is of air-quality.

Chyron Operator—Types out the names of people to be superimposed on the screen into a special machine and, at the director's cue, punches them up.

The ENG Crew—"Electronic news gathering" today uses a camera crew to shoot tape, not film, because it is cheaper and faster. The ENG crew consists of two people: One records the image, and the other records the sounds. These two positions can be interchangeable, although it is not all that common. Since the tape crew is always on call, their union contract provides for substantial overtime and holiday pay. Most tape technicians earn a good deal above their base salary. In most shops, they are in the same union as other technicians. Many stations hire freelance people, who receive about $200 a day.

Tape Editor—Screens the material on an electronic editing system. In news, unlike in documentaries, the editor does not make major editorial decisions but takes notes on where the writer/associate producer or reporter wants the cut and which sound bites they want to use, and pieces it all together with cover footage for narration. Again, tape editors are in the same union as technicians in most major market stations.

News Division

A large percentage of any station's payroll goes to supporting the people who bring us the local news. Below are the job descriptions and salaries for most of these positions. As with all jobs in broadcasting, salaries vary widely based on the size of the market where the station is located.

News Director—Ultimately responsible for the image, format, and content of all news broadcasts. He or she answers directly to the general manager of the station. News directors' duties differ from station to station, depending on the size of the news staff, but they are usually involved with budgets, hiring the talent (reporters and anchorpersons), and acting as editor-in-chief in the newsroom. In the top markets (Los Angeles, Chicago, etc.) their jobs are almost solely dependent on ratings, so there's a high turnover rate. Their salaries reflect this: The average base salary in all markets is $73,298, with a bonus of $8,619. According to several agents, news directors in New York City earn $70,000 at the smaller stations, and as much as $100,000 to $150,000 at the major stations.

News Producer—On local news shows the producer decides on the order of presentation (the "lineup") for all the stories. He or she is responsible for making sure stories are complete and that they are properly integrated into the program. During the live broadcast, the producer sits in the control room with the director; any last-minute changes or on-the-air readjustments are the producer's responsibility. The average salary for news producers in all markets is $28,433. In New York, Chicago, and Los Angeles, insiders claim, the producers of the evening news earn $100,000 or more. In these major markets there is also an *executive producer of news,* who takes responsibility for all local news broadcasts. Salaries range from $100,000 to $200,000 or more per year.

News Editors—Sometimes called *assignment editors* because they assign writers to particular stories. They also edit all copy that is scheduled for broadcast, including reporters' scripts, and write all necessary transitional copy to keep the show moving. In major markets they are all members of the Writers Guild, which establishes the base salaries. In New York, for example, the salary base is about $35,000, and news editors also receive a 15 percent premium for working nights. The average, however, is $31,245.

News Writers—Members of the Writers Guild of America. At a top market station, writers of thirty-minute broadcasts for five-day-a-week strips earn between $97,810 and $141,668. In smaller markets, they make between $37,000 and $50,000, including overtime. According to inside sources, the top writers in big markets earn over $150,000.

News Desk Assistants—Situated in the middle of the newsroom, their responsibilities include fielding incoming phone calls from the public, the press, public relations people, etc. They also check the newswires and distribute copy to key newsroom personnel. Their job often also entails getting supplies, having machines repaired, etc. They are, in short, considered the newsroom gofers. Desk assistants do not usually make over $22,000 a year.

Other Key Personnel

At the end of almost every program, a list of credits rolls up, usually too quickly to read, but below is a list of titles and descriptions most of us will recognize. It should be noted, however, that the rates for feature films or nighttime versus daytime television rates can vary wildly.

Graphic Artists—Throughout the day, the artists in graphics prepare visual elements that augment the broadcast—i.e., slides, charts, graphs, logos, etc. They prepare original material as well as duplicate or enlarge other artwork so that it is first-rate broadcast-quality. They also work with specialists on animation projects. Union agreements call for a base pay of $431 a day. The average salary for a graphic artist at a major top-market station is about $36,000 a year, including overtime.

Lighting Director—Responsible for preplanning the lighting in the studio and ensuring that it is properly executed either during a taping or a live broadcast. The most recent IATSE figures show that LDs earn $969.46 per week.

Scenic Designers—Although they are highly paid, SDs rarely work on a daily basis. They can design sets for special broadcasts, new shows, etc., as well as redesign old sets. Because of the nature of their work, they may not be needed daily. The average pay for a scenic designer on network television is about $300 per day. Contracts, however, vary according to the network, and those working on evening programming, which is usually on film, not video, make considerably more. The art director for *Law and Order,* for example, made $2,529 per week in 1996.

Scenic Artists—Do any necessary painting or primping of the set. The most recent United Scenic Artists Union rates for feature films are $348.97 per day, but the pay can vary depending upon the type of work done and when it is broadcast. Journeymen made $284.57 per day in 1996.

Makeup Artists—Apply makeup and fix the hair of the news correspondents and anchorpeople in every broadcast. They work on the actors and actresses in the soaps, talk show guests, etc. Anyone who goes before a camera should be made up. According to IATSE in 1995, the average daily rate paid according to IATSE to stylists was $690 for television commercials, one of the highest paying segments of the business.

Stagehands—It is a union regulation that the studio cannot open up without three stagehands present. There are three types: electricians, carpenters, and prop people. They are basically responsible for checking sets and equipment before the broadcast begins, bringing props into the studio and moving them when necessary, etc. The most recent IATSE rate paid for studio head stagehands is $792.78 per week, or $46,274 annually. The average minimum rate for an assistant stagehand was $694.80 per week or $36,180 annually in 1996.

Stage Managers—Are on the floor of the studio and make sure that everything runs smoothly. He or she receives cues from the director and in turn cues the talent as to when to get off and on the set, when to start a news report, etc. In nonnews broadcasts, the stage manager is responsible for supervising set changes. In large-market stations, the stage manager is usually a member of the Directors' Guild, which negotiates minimum wage rates. Average salaries ranged from $16,800 to $31,500 in 1996.

Researchers—At local stations, researchers usually work in news. His or her job is to initiate stories, develop contacts, spot-check facts, and provide writers, reporters, and management with background information. They gather relevant audiovisual material to be incorporated into the broadcast; they also find interesting people to interview. They can work in the library, newsroom, and in the field. Although it is considered an entry-level job in the field of news, it can sometimes lead to an associate producer's or a writer's job.

Networks utilize many kinds of researchers. Some provide information on ratings, audience analysis, marketing, etc.; others work on particular shows, finding background material, setting up interviews, even helping to develop new ideas.

At local stations, researchers still earn only $300 to $500 a week. The networks pay better, and one inside source says that senior research people earn as much as $45,000 to $50,000 a year, including overtime.

Production Assistants—Work on the daily rundown of a program, typing up the routine of the show, including the timing of each segment, the type of piece (film, tape) to be used, and any other production details that should be known. If the show is not seen daily, the production assistant works on long-range planning of the show until each piece fits into place. During the actual broadcast, he or she will sit in the control room and time the show.

On news programs, the production assistant is occupied throughout the day with coordinating graphics, slides, and names of people interviewed in each story to be superimposed on the screen during the report. The PA must coordinate the information he or she gets from the reporters, associate producers, etc., with the story lineup. As the day progresses and the show gets closer to airtime, the production assistant is responsible for "breaking script," i.e., distributing a copy to everyone in the control room. Production assistants at CBS-owned-and-operated stations are members of the Directors' Guild, so salaries are set by contractual agreement. Minimum salaries are approximately $18,000 to start, and $22,000 after thirty months.

WHO MAKES WHAT IN THE FILM INDUSTRY

Are star actors being paid too much? Some analysts think so. Yet a basic rule is in operation. Steven Spielberg once put it this way, "Whatever they're paying you, it's not enough." If the producers of *Waterworld* allowed Kevin Costner to run the movie's budget up over $150 million, it's because they expected to make even more than that as a direct result of his presence in the film. (They were wrong, of course.) This has been true since the earliest days of the movie industry. In the teens, Mary Pickford, Douglas Fairbanks, and Charles Chaplin (with D. W. Griffith) formed their own production company, United Artists, at least in part because their legitimate fees were so extraordinarily high that other production companies couldn't pay them. For thirty years, long-terms contracts helped to keep star salaries under control, but now that actors are free agents once again and movies are making money once again, the stars ask for *and get* large fees. The producers, however, make even more. All of the fingers in the pot have driven up the average cost of making movies to over $60 million in 1997. In many cases, it is still true that a star *is* the movie.

Crew members and technicians make what appear to be good salaries (see the figures that follow), but remember that freelance work is different in nature from full-time employment. A cinematographer on a feature film can easily expect to make $2,000 or $3,000 per week, but this doesn't mean he or she is making $100,000 to $150,000 a year. The real annual income may be much less than half that since the average shooting schedule for a film only lasts twelve weeks, and even the successful freelancer may very well receive no more than two assignments a year.

Remember, too, that of the thousands of people that belong to any particular craft union, the majority are usually out of work. It's traditionally said that 85 percent of the Screen Actors Guild is unemployed at any one time.

With those provisos in mind, here are some of the basic pay rates for the various crafts and professions in the film industry.

Actors and Stars

The Screen Actors Guild represents extras: people who appear in movies and television shows and don't talk. There are only two minimum pay rates for extras, and it's nearly impossible to make a career out of the job. General Extras are paid a minimum of $99 per day as of 1997 under the Hollywood SAG contract. "Special Ability" Extras who can, for example, ride a horse, earn $109 per day.

The Screen Actors Guild also represents people who talk in movies. The basic day rate is $559.

If an actor is hired for a full week's work, that basic rate is $1,942. There is also a special three-day minimum of $1,415 for television work.

Multiple-pictures players (actors hired for more than one appearance) work for a starting salary that depends on the type of show:

30 minutes	$1,436 per week
1 hour	1,436

| 90 minutes | $1,688 |
| 2 hours | 1,992 |

Term players who get hired for the run of a half-hour production earn $1,942 a week for a guaranteed thirteen out of thirteen weeks; or $2,605 a week for a guaranteed minimum of six out of thirteen weeks; and $3,046 a week for six weeks or less. For a one-hour production, the weekly rates are $2,334 for thirteen out of thirteen weeks; $2,603 a week for a minimum of six out of thirteen weeks; and $3,046 a week for six weeks or less.

Of course, these figures represent only the minimum allowed by contract. Many actors besides outright stars will be paid higher rates than these.

Salaries for the stars are, fittingly, astronomical. During the mid-1970s, Steve McQueen set a record by asking $3 million for any performance. He didn't work very often, but when he did, he got paid what he asked.

Many other star actors operate as coproducers and thus earn money as "bosses" as well as "workers." Any well-known actor will ask for and usually receive a percentage of the profits of the film, known in the trade as "points." Directors and even a few writers also commonly receive points. Other craftspeople haven't reached that level yet.

Brad Pitt, Sylvester Stallone, Tom Hanks, Tom Cruise, Jack Nicholson, Robin Williams, Adam Sandler, Leonardo DiCaprio, and Bruce Willis are generally regarded as the highest priced male stars. These actors garner as much as $20 million for a feature film (plus a hefty percentage of profits). Nicholson received $5 million for ten days' work on *A Few Good Men*. Young Macauley Culkin was paid $5 million plus 5 percent of the gross (a total of $16 million) for *Home Alone 2*.

Just a few years ago Demi Moore, generally regarded as one of the highest priced female stars, received $14 million (plus a hefty percentage of profits) for *Strip Tease*, while Barbra Streisand received $3.5 million plus a percentage of profits for ten weeks' work on *All Night Long*. Later she got $6 million per film, as did *Basic Instinct* star Sharon Stone. By 1999 the top female stars, Jodie Foster, Meg Ryan, and Julia Roberts, were edging toward $15 million per film.

Actors and others who receive a percentage of the profits, by the way, are always careful that the contract reads in terms of percentages of the gross income from a film.[1] "Net points"—percentages of profits after the studio and producers have deducted their expenses—always have a way of evaporating, even on very successful films.

Actors are also interested in the expanding uses of film product. Since 1960, every member of the Screen Actors Guild has shared in profits from television broadcasts of films he or she has appeared in. "Residuals" can provide a small but steady income. The main point of the SAG strike of 1980 was to achieve a similar share of a producer's profits from "supplementary markets"—videodiscs, videotape, pay-TV, cable, satellite, and so on. The actors won, and are now paid 3.6 percent of distributors' worldwide grosses on each film.

Writers

The Writers Guild of America sets standards and minimums for writers in film and television. Writers are the last in the chain to share directly in profits from a film (after producers, actors, and directors). Winston Groom, for example, sold the rights to his novel *Forrest Gump* to Paramount for $350,000 and 3 percent of the net profits. But even though *Gump* earned more than $350 million in 1994 alone, Groom didn't see a dime past his advance, as the studio claimed a $62 million loss on the film. Groom, understandably, has sued the studio for this all-too-common bookkeeping sleight of hand. Writers' fees are also often split. A writer who adapts a book or a play to the screen will be paid less than the writer of an original screenplay. A writer for a popular TV show like *The Simpsons* can earn a substantial salary. According to *The New York Times*, a story editor—a junior position—makes $110,000, while the executive producer, the top writing job, earns $700,000 to $3 million. The writer behind *Frasier*, Christopher Lloyd, is earning $9 million over the span of a four-year contract. Writers, unlike directors, often work in teams and split fees.

WRITERS GUILD OF AMERICA'S BASIC MINIMUM AGREEMENT				
	1995–96		1996–97	
	High	Low	High	Low
Original screenplay and treatment	$73,992	$39,076	$76,582	$40,444
Original screenplay only	54,267	26,260	56,166	27,179
Nonoriginal screenplay and treatment	64,207	34,198	66,454	35,395
Nonoriginal screenplay only	44,399	21,369	45,953	22,117
Story or treatment	19,736	12,822	20,427	13,271
Original treatment	29,603	17,707	30,639	18,327
Rewrite of screenplay	19,736	12,822	20,427	13,271
Polish of screenplay	9,867	6,413	10,212	6,637

SOURCE: Writers Guild of America.

TELEVISION

Experienced television writers receive the following minimums under the WGA contract:

	1995–96		1996–97	
	Prime Time	Nonprime Time	Prime Time[1]	Nonprime Time[2]
30 minutes	$15,627	$8,099	$16,095	$8,382
1 hour	22,984	14,720	23,674	15,235
90 minutes	33,308	22,121	32,338	22,895
2 hours	43,822	28,991	42,546	30,006

[1]For 1997–98 rates, add 3 percent.
[2]For 1997–98 rates, add 4 percent.

Writers on weekly salaries at networks earn at least $2,500 per week, but there are few professionals in this category now. For both features and television, fees commonly exceed these bare minimums. A $200,000 salary is not uncommon for screenwriters with a track record; experienced screenwriters command three or four times that fee for feature films. Writers are less likely to get points than are directors, actors, or producers, but it does happen. Increasingly, writers are turning to producing in order to redress the financial imbalance between writer and director.

Studio Executives

Increasingly, studio executives have either started out in the industry as agents or as MBAs, and they tend to pay themselves quite well. A salary of less than $150,000 is now regarded as fit only for second- and third-level employees, and the many vice presidents at the studios earn much more than that. Average salaries for the heads of production at major film companies exceed $500,000. The top executives at all the big studios earn over $2 million a year, and with stocks and stock options they are worth five to ten times that amount. You can see why studios insist on a 35 percent cut as a distribution fee; this sort of overhead mounts up.

The merger and acquisitions mania of the last decade came to Hollywood and, as in other business areas, had the effect of escalating salaries for key high-level personnel. It also helped to make some very high salaries part of the public record.

In 1989, the Sony Corporation agreed to pay Peter Guber and Jon Peters $750 million over five years to run Columbia Pictures, which it had just purchased for $5 billion. Although this team had produced two huge hits (*Batman* and *Rain Man*), they, in fact, had never run a studio before. But what's often overlooked is the enormous sums earned by the executives at Columbia, a dismal failure in the year immediately prior to the sale. One industry source reported that the president received over $20 million, his second in command $13.5 million, another executive $10 million, and nine others at least $1 million, and that was ten years ago. In 1998, when Frank Biondi, Jr., lost his CEO job at Universal, his settlement was $30 million. So failure at the top of the movie business can have its rewards.

U.S. FILM INDUSTRY EMPLOYMENT AND SALARIES

Employment of actors, directors, and producers is expected to grow faster than the average for all occupations through the year 2006, according to the Bureau of Labor Statistics. And industry analysts say the number of people working on motion pictures is probably even higher because of the growing role of independent contractors, which is hard to track. Of course, the prime beneficiaries of this explosion in the movie industry are the actors, directors, producers, editors, lighting technicians, stagehands, and electricians hired to work on feature films. The following figures show the minimum weekly salaries for those engaged in film production. (Note that these salaries are very rarely earned throughout the year—production work can be sporadic in the best of times.)

MINIMUM WEEKLY SALARIES FOR FILM WORK

Profession	Minimum Weekly Salary[1]
Director (film with budget over $1,500,000)	$9,469
Director (film with budget $500,000–$1,500,000)	6,763
Director (film with budget under $500,000)	5,951
Art Director	2,524
Director of Photography	2,469
Costume Designer	2,040
Editor	1,927
Sound or Music Editor	1,405
Unit Production Manager	2,813
First Assistant Director	2,672
Key Second Assistant Director	1,791

[1]All figures are for a standard working week.
SOURCES: Industry unions; 1995 contracts.

Directors

The Directors Guild of America negotiates for film and television directors. Their contracts with the film industry provide for minimum rates of pay, as shown in the previous table. Most directors earn considerably more than the minimum rates of pay. Straight $2 million salaries are not unheard of for well-known directors; highly successful directors now get much more. James Cameron reportedly received $6 million for *Terminator II,* and Richard Donner got $4 million for *Lethal Weapon 3.* (Cameron parlayed his success into an ownership agreement for *Titanic.*) Like actors, star directors can also earn huge sums from the films in which they participate.

Television directors, like TV actors, are paid by the category of show.

Television directors will not command star salaries like feature film directors, but twice the minimum is not an uncommon salary. And there are substantial residuals. Directors of prime-time network shows get roughly 57 percent of their original fee each time the show is rerun. And aside from their work fee, feature film directors get a percentage of box office and videocassette sales.

MINIMUM WEEKLY PAY—DIRECTORS

Prime Time	Pay Rate
30 minutes	$15,819 for minimum 7 days
1 hour	$26,864 for minimum 15 days
90 minutes	$44,773 for minimum 25 days
2 hours	$75,215 for minimum 42 days

SOURCE: Directors Guild of America, 1998 Contracts.

MINIMUM WEEKLY PAY—DIRECTORS' ASSISTANTS

Title	Minimum Weekly Pay
Unit Production Manager	$3,013
First Assistant Director	2,863
Key Second Assistant Director	1,919
2nd Second Assistant Director	1,811
Additional Second Assistant Director	1,102

SOURCE: Directors Guild of America, July 1998.

Cinematographers

For several years now, cinematographers—the people who actually photograph moving pictures—have been angling for admission to the charmed circle of producers, directors, writers, and actors. They haven't yet achieved this in terms of pay scales and percentages, but they are getting there in terms of publicity. Often the key bargaining points in a cinematographer's contract these days will have to do with getting their own mobile vans on location and guaranteed paid advertising rather than with salary.

The base rate for a director of photography is $508 per diem, but recognized, experienced cinematographers work for much more than that. Top cinematographers are able to earn $20,000–25,000 per week (for about twenty weeks), a salary that is comparable with that of decently paid writers; $25,000 per week with points is not unheard of.

Measured in terms of daily wages, cinematographers who work on television commercials do as well as or better than nearly all feature film DPs, even if they aren't as well known. Their rates go as high as $7,500 a day.

Editors

Editors have as much to do with the ultimate effect of a film as cinematographers, but they don't yet have the clout as a craft. This is reflected in lower pay scales. Film editors earn a minimum of $2,044.41 per week under the Motion Pictures Editors Guild contract, effective through May 1999. Assistants earn a minimum of $1,188.59. Sound effects and music editors earn at least $1,490.27. While it is possible for well-known editors to earn much more than this, it is not common.

Composers and Musicians

Like cinematographers and editors, composers have been fighting for a larger share of the film pie in recent years. Like the Producers Guild, the Composers and Lyricists Guild is still fighting for recognition.

Top film composers like John Williams or Jerry Goldsmith will earn a minimum of $60,000 per feature film. Most composers earn half that, and low-budget features will go for as little as $25,000. A lyricist can expect $8,000 for a song, and leading lyricists like Alan and Marilyn Bergman get much more.

For television, composers earn relatively more than you might expect, a reflection of the fact that so many television shows are produced with "wall-to-wall" music, unlike feature films, where music is now usually intermittent. A half-hour sitcom will yield perhaps $2,500, a movie-of-the-week $12,000 to $15,000, and a four-hour miniseries $30,000.

Composers also share in performance royalties but actually receive only half of this money (unlike their counterparts in the outside world); half goes to the producer.

Musicians are covered by an American Federation of Musicians agreement, which guarantees them a minimum ranging from $120 to $250 per service (for three hours of work) as of 1996. A conductor will get double this amount. Different minimum rates exist for pay cable television, public television, documentary film, and basic cable television.

Film Designers and Artists

The recent success of animated full-length features (especially those from Disney) have put a premium on the skills of yet another group of players in Hollywood: the animators. Disney's success in this arena—*The Lion King* alone is expected to generate profits, including merchandising, of nearly $1 billion—has persuaded every major Hollywood studio to jump into the business of creating animated films. As a result, the once-sleepy field of animation has become one of the hottest career tracks in Hollywood. With the pool of talented animators too small to handle the burgeoning work, salaries

WEEKLY PAY RATES FOR DESIGNERS AND ARTISTS IN FILM AND TELEVISION

	Minimum Weekly Salary	
Position	Feature Film	Television
Art Director	$2,529.91	$2,350.00
Assistant Art Director (daily)	1,950.00	413.43
Costume Designer	2,045.51	1,952.00
Assistant Costume Designer (daily)	232.80	233.21
Charge Scenic Artist (daily)	348.97	326.65
Journey Scenic Artist (daily)	284.50	266.34
Shop Person (daily)	163.03	190.88

SOURCE: United Scenic Artists Union, May 1998.

MINIMUM DAILY RATES FOR DESIGNERS AND ARTISTS IN TELEVISION COMMERCIALS

Position	Period	Rate
Art Director	day	$900.00
Stylist	day	700.00
Charge Scenic Artist	7 hours	400.00
Journey Scenic Artist	7 hours	365.00

SOURCE: United Scenic Artists Union, May 1998.

for animators have skyrocketed. According to Tom Sito, president of the cartoonists' union that represents most Hollywood animators, average weekly salaries for animators with five years of experience has just about doubled, from $1,000 in 1992 to close to $2,000 today. The top animators (such as those chosen to draw central characters like Pocahontas or the Little Mermaid) earn closer to $20,000.

Salary rates for other types of designers and artists in film and television are listed above.

Entry-Level Jobs

People who work in the offices of film companies often earn less than people of comparable skills would earn in other businesses. The competition even for secretarial positions is intense since the job is regarded as prestigious and glamourous.

Traditionally, one of the best ways to break into the industry (besides entry-level secretarial positions) is as the job of *story analyst*. All production companies have to deal with thousands of scripts and novels each year. It is the job of the story analyst to read, summarize, and evaluate these potential properties. Very few story analysts have staff positions. Most are freelance, and the pay scale is minimal, ranging from $35 to $100 per script or book covered. Since the coverage involves reading the property and writing two to twenty pages of summary and evaluation, even efficient story analysts earn less than established secretaries—and there are no fringe benefits. In the following piece, *New York Observer* writer George Gurley exposes the myth of the glamorous job in the film biz.

NEW YORK'S HOLLYWOOD SLAVES:
BITTER, JADED AND SO YOUNG
Reading for Money on Film Industry's Lowest Rung
●

by George Gurley

It's one of the most seductive jobs in Manhattan. You get to read for a living, be your own boss, set your own hours and make as much as $40,000 a year (if you're diligent and perceptive), and there's even some slight chance for advancement in the movie business.

If you're just getting started and manage to read, say, eight manuscripts a week, you can still make around $20,000 a year. And that means you can start your workday at around 6 P.M., if you felt like it, and read until 1 A.M., and still have the entire day free to hang out at Starbucks between visits to the video store. But before you plant your foot on this lowest rung in the film industry, know that reading for movie companies is probably the loneliest job in New York.

The job can also leave you absurdly bitter at a young age. You find yourself reading all trash all the time, and, inevitably, you think, *I can do better than this.* Of course, the reason you were attracted to this job in the first place is that you believe you might be the next Waldo Salt. You—the next Waldo Salt! You—the next Robert Towne! The next . . . Quentin Tarantino! And yet, here you are, reading trash, trash, trash. It's really an affront to your sense of your own talents, isn't it?

So meet Josh Safran. At the tender age of 22, he is a dean of Manhattan readers, having gotten in on the game of giving his opinion to big-shot producers at the age of 10, when he was discovered incessantly talking film with his mother at a nail salon. While his friends were being taken to matinees by their uncles, Mr. Safran was pushing especially hard for a project he loved, a now forgotten movie called *Space Camp.*

"I really loved it," Mr. Safran recalled, standing in his East Village apartment. "But they delayed it for six months after the *Challenger* exploded and when it opened, it bombed. I thought it was, like, my fault.

He regained confidence when TriStar Pictures asked for his 12-year-old's take on the robot comedy *Short Circuit 2.* Since then, he has read "thousands of scripts" and has even doctored a few just before they rolled.

Now here he is, in a $900-a-month studio on East 10th Street. The floor, which you could not *see,* was covered with overflowing makeshift ashtrays and hundreds of screenplays, manuscripts, videos and laser disks. Mr. Safran was smoking one Marlboro Light after another and ranting about the trade.

"As any reader will tell you, every script sucks," he said. "Every single script you read is a horror. There's always something very innately wrong with it and it starts to get you down. All the readers are students or wannabe writers who want to be producers and they all will tell you it totally wears you down . . .

"As a reader, if you say to your boss, 'I didn't like this,' they will read our coverage and decide not to read it themselves and call up the agency and pretend they didn't like it. They're just reading off the coverage—they will literally read what you said.

"I remember coming home and not wanting to look at the scripts in my bag because then they wouldn't exist. I'd take them out, put them on the table, regard them curiously, go out with friends for an hour, and then at 3 A.M. you come home, see them on the table and *freak out.* They're your most hated enemies. You've read so much crap, and so you know . . . you have to . . . get to . . . the end. There's no escape.

"My body has processed it, all this shit I went through, all the people who treated me like shit, like a peon, as an intern. It does turn into creative energy. I will show them. My body has processed it, from revenge into energy." With his eyes bulging slightly and his crew cut standing on end, Mr. Safran seemed to be morphing into a psycho. "I just wrote a serial-killer screenplay," he said, leering, "where most of the victims are named after people I've worked for."

Here's how it works. Someone writes a screenplay, or a book with film potential. Then the writer's agent sends the manuscript to a development office at Paramount Pictures, Miramax Films, Universal Pictures, Jersey Films, all of them. Then the story editors at the studios call up the freelance reader. Any good reader already has stacks of scripts in the apartment, but good readers rarely say No to a job, even an overnight 600-page manuscript for another $60.

So you turn off the phone, and the answering machine starts clicking, but you must read. Oh, you don't sleep. You will stay up, indoors, by yourself, starved for conversation. And when you're about to go to the office to deliver your four pages of written remarks, the "coverage," you're ready to cling to any warm body. You hop the subway and ride to the studio, where you tell the receptionist your whole existence is cramming—the last week of graduate school as a way of life! As you walk away, you think, *I am a reading genius!* Law school would be a breeze. Med school? A breeze.

In your absence, the receptionist says to her friend on the phone, "Oh, it was just some idiot dropping off another manuscript."

Now and then, one of the idiots escapes the reader's pit to find a table at Morton's. Lynda Obst is one such creature, a former development girl who now has the power to greenlight a project as head of Lynda Obst Productions, an offshoot of 20th Century Fox Film Corporation.

At E&O restaurant on East Houston Street the other night, Ms. Obst, hawking her book *Hello, He Lied,* was the guest of honor. In casual suits, gossip doyenne Liz Smith and Ms. Obst staged an animated chat for a camera crew and then joined their hosts, film director Nora Ephron and *Interview* magazine editor Ingrid Sischy.

"It's a great irony, these script readers," Ms. Obst said a bit later. "On the one hand, you've got kids fresh out of college anonymously making decisions about people's fates in movies. But by the same token, they're treated like dog-doo."

After working as an editor at *The New York Times Magazine* in the 70's, Ms. Obst read for producer Peter Guber for four years. Since then she estimates she has read more than 2,000 scripts. Any advice for the bitter New York readers, who don't have the union benefits or the lofty job title ("story analysts") of their Los Angeles counterparts?

"Sadly, the truth is, you have to go to L.A.," she said. "If you want the union benefits, I'd say put in your time and give up this fabulous capital of culture and be in that dreary universe of monomania with the rest of us."

In Los Angeles, covering more than five scripts a week is unheard of, but $100,000 a year is not. So some New York readers do fantasize about going West, but most trudge on from gig to gig, like aluminum-can gatherers with Ph.D.'s.

In *The Sun Dialogues,* a play by David Hollander that was recently produced on both coasts, the main character is a reader named Walter Blount. He's a "script assassin" who has panned 999 scripts in 19 months. "I resent my job," he says. "My relationship to scripts is like a heroin addict's relationship to his needles: I hate them with every ounce of my being but need them to stay alive. There are, however, two benefits to being a reader: I get to sleep late and I get to sit around in my underwear all day."

Walter could easily be confused with James, who would not give his last name and who said he has just turned in a report he figured was *his* thousandth. But James is an anomaly, having landed a job as an assistant to a producer. Now he'll be able to hire his own readers. He was even beginning to sound like an asshole executive as he entered his fifth-floor walk-up: "Get the fuck out of my office!" he said, and raced to his Power Mac to click off something on the screen.

Then he explained his routine: "Around Thursday, it starts getting really difficult, because if you take anything, it's due Monday. You don't just read weekends, weekends is when you do most of your work. During the summer on Fridays, you must get your work done by 2 o'clock because everyone goes to the Hamptons, and you're exhausted because more often than not, you've stayed up all night on Thursday. If you don't get it in by Friday, you're in deep shit. Then, you've got more weekend reading material, plus you tell them, 'I've got three scripts, a book, my weekend's full.' They say, 'O.K., how about Tuesday? By the time Monday rolls around, you have stuff due Tuesday and Wednesday, but you still take the calls, and, whenever possible, you don't turn material down, because when you do, even if you are reading regularly, if the person hears 'I can't take it,' and they hear this a bunch of times, they say, 'What are you doing with your time?' If you get sick and take a week off, you go broke. The rent's due, so what do you do? Read more than you ever read before. If you're lucky, you get to go to a premiere or some funky party, the little bones they throw you along the way."

Veteran reader Melissa Miller said she has been living in the fifth circle of hell lately. She said she took Claritin-D for a sinus infection and got only two hours of sleep the night before.

"I've often thought—I don't know if women's prison would be the worst thing for me," Ms. Miller said. "I'd go to a gym, I'd write all the time, free health care, no work, I could learn a trade and read a lot."

The little things get to you when you're a reader. "I'm completely traumatized that Q104 is no longer a radio station," she said, between nibbles of a fruit plate at a sports bar on Park Avenue South. "It was the best alternative station and now it's like classic rock. They play this Bob Seger song every morning, "Katmandu," and I just . . . can't . . . do it. Bob Seger is a pig."

In the absence of a good station, she has to deal with something else that sickens her, sexist scripts: "This one script was sort of like a man's fantasy of a woman acting out sexually, like prostitution, stripping and stuff. And why? Because she had, like, a nice ass. It's like the Joe Eszterhas school of writing," she said, referring to the writer of *Basic Instinct* and *Showgirls*. "I just loathe him. He's despicable. Uh-eccchhhhh! Gives me the willies."

Look to Susan Milrod, all ye hopeless wretches. She's a star reader at 41. How good is she? She turned around David Foster Wallace's 1,079-page *Infinite Jest* in two days. "That's not a big deal. That's what we do, all the time," she said in a cafe near her apartment. What sets her apart from the readers who are bitter because of their secret ambitions is that she *cares.* "I am very protective," she said. "Their blood is on the page. I may laugh to myself when someone writes 'I'm coming to take your soul' and spells it s-o-l-e, but it makes me sad for these writers who never will be writers."

As she made her way across Prince Street, walking with a cane, she cheerfully explained that "reading is a little like Broadway gypsy dancers: You move from show to show. It's a good gig." But later, seated on a park bench, she said, "It's a very, very isolating job."

Still, it has its rewards. For instance, *L'Escargot,* one of the most notorious scripts ever to have made the rounds. It's about a house full of trapped couples having sex with each other while being attacked by atomic snails. Snails that can only be killed by what? Strawberry douches.

"One of the great things about being a reader is you never know when you're going to run into another *L'Escargot.* That's one of my favorite scripts," Ms. Milrod said.

But for every Susan Milrod, there are probably 100 Shipperd Reeds. Mr. Reed reads for New Line Cinema and Paramount, but he's "sick of it." As he walked by the projects next to his place on 100th Street, his angular goatee gave him a devilish air. In a Broadway diner, he was swigging decaf and spouting: "I'm, like, 'What the fuck am I doing reading scripts for a living?' It causes me constant anxiety. It's solitary, so I miss interacting with people."

Another decaf. Mr. Reed, a graduate of the Columbia University film school, said he has high hopes for his optioned script about a New York surgeon abducted by a David Koresh type while attending a Montana wilderness school. Then he got a wild-eyed expression. "I have reader friends who've been paid a million dollars for their scripts," he said. "Overnight. It's kinda sick how those big numbers in *Variety* can make you hungry." Later, burning, he said, "I want more out of life. I want to sell a screenplay. I want to direct."

Five blocks away, a few days later, somebody was saying, "I'm glad I'm not going to be 32 and reading, because I'd get incredibly jaded and bitter, yelling 'Everything sucks!' " It was Emily Gorman, 21, in a white T-shirt, khakis and Doc Martens.

"One of the greatest things I learned at N.Y.U. was that I don't want to be in film," she said. "Now I feel a sort of visceral disdain for the film industry."

It may have been all those birdbrains trying to get the six-picture deal with Columbia before they graduated. Or when she came across something producer Scott Rudin said about how what Hollywood wants is something "uniquely generic" in a script. But a few weeks ago, she quit her reading job at Stanley Jaffe Productions, where she could be relied on to devour a 900-page book in six hours.

"I decided this writer was trying to be serious, but I couldn't believe it," she said about one of the last things she read. "It was about a big brown bear and his adventures with his human buddy in New York. He walked around with a hat and an overcoat, and was really melancholy and philosophical—pages and pages of him talking about jazz—I mean the bear would play the sax at jazz clubs, get in trouble with the cops, and he ended up moving to upstate New York with his lover, a woman—not a bear. It wasn't a children's movie, nor satirical on any level. It was *ridiculous*."

Ms. Gorman said she's looking forward to getting her Ph.D. in English and perhaps teaching her favorite writer, William Faulkner, whose experience in Hollywood once provoked him to write: "I feel bad, depressed, dreadful sense of wasting time, I imagine most of the symptoms of some kind of blowup or collapse."

Source: *The New York Observer*, July 20, 1998. Reprinted by permission.

BACKSTAGE

Behind the scenes of every play, whether it's staged on Broadway or in the local church basement, are all those unseen people who enable the show to go on. Some perform utilitarian tasks like moving scenery or making sure all the props are in order, while others are central to the creation of the world of verisimilitude that is the heart of theater: They design costumes, invent dance routines, and illuminate the stage and the actors in imaginative ways. Where they work and how much they get paid depends on where they are, what kind of theater the play is being performed in, and, for the creative staff, what degree of fame they have attained.

Stage Workers

This designation refers to almost everyone who works backstage, under the stage, high over the stage, behind the lights, or in the sound booth. Stage workers include skilled carpenters and electricians, as well as painters and people who only move scenery.

The International Alliance of Theatrical Stage Employees (IATSE) represents just over 60,000 stage workers throughout the country. Every professional theater, whether it houses a variety of art forms or specializes in opera, ballet, or theater, must hire union personnel. The minimum rates vary according to city and regions. New York City and Los Angeles are given below.

MINIMUM DAILY RATES FOR STAGE WORKERS IN NEW YORK AND LOS ANGELES		
Position	**Weekly**	**Hourly**
Department Heads	$1,047	$36.75
Assistant Department Heads	923	30.31
Sound Crew	872	27.63
Lighting Crew	872	27.63
General Stagehands	800	24.85

SOURCE: IATSE, 1995. Rates effective through 1998.

Note that the designation "Department Head" refers to head carpenter, head electrician, etc.

Stage Managers

Stage managers, simply put, make sure that everything during rehearsals and performances runs smoothly on stage and off.

The first part of their job on a new play is to read the play and become familiar with it. After that, they help arrange for the theater, expedite auditions, coordinate rehearsals, supervise the hiring of the crew, and work with department heads and with the directors and designers. After the play opens, the stage manager does everything from handling union problems to prompting the cast during the performance. In effect, as far as the actors are concerned, the stage manager is director in absentia.

The rates below are the scale for stage managers who are represented by the Actors' Equity Association. The scale is minimum; with experience, a stage manager can get from $50 to $150 a week more than scale, especially if he or she has worked over and over again with the same director.

MINIMUM WEEKLY PAY FOR STAGE MANAGERS ON BROADWAY

	Musical	Drama
Stage Manager	$1,643	$1,413
First Assistant Stage Manager	1,300	1,154
Second Assistant Stage Manager	1,086	NA

Rates effective through 1998.

MINIMUM WEEKLY PAY RATES FOR STAGE MANAGERS IN REGIONAL THEATERS

Type of Theater	Stage Manager		Assistant Stage Manager	
	Repertory	Nonrepertory	Repertory	Nonrepertory
A	$858	$858	$720	$717
B	728	658	657	558
C	683	629	581	529
D	614	543	509	447

NOTE: Rates effective through 1998. For an explanation of A, B, C, and D designations, see the earlier section, "Actors."

Designers

A Broadway theater: The curtain opens, and filtered night light glows on a bedraggled young woman selling flowers in front of a London playhouse. The music plays softly, Eliza Doolittle comes to life, and the audience becomes engrossed in *My Fair Lady*. But the ambiance of the play is created by more than just the actors. What's before the audience is the result of a collaboration of many people, with a major role played by unsung heroes— the scenic, lighting, and costume designers.

These are the creative artists who help translate the playwright's words and choreographer's directions into a play and a ballet. Although their names appear in tiny type at the bottom of the *Playbill,* they are essential to successful theater.

Designers are usually trained in special schools or universities or through apprenticeships. They start out with small regional theaters or repertory companies and, if they're lucky and very talented, work their way to Broadway.

Most of the designers are represented by the United Scenic Artists Union. The pay tables that follow give the scale, which usually applies to beginners only. After some experience, designers can command a little more. The big names, of course, negotiate for as much as they can get.

Where the potential for big money comes in depends on royalties, which are fixed or variable. The fixed royalties generally apply to beginners and middle-level designers. For each week the show runs, the designer gets a royalty of from $100 to $300 on Broadway and in big-city theaters, and from $35 to $75 in off-Broadway and smaller theaters around the country. The royalty applies to the original show as well as to any road companies, foreign tours, or dinner theaters.

Instead of a fixed royalty, the top names can command a percentage, usually from 0.5 to 1 percent, of the show's weekly gross. On a big Broadway musical that can be $5,000 a week or more. As with the fixed royalty, the top names get a percentage of the gross on any road companies or tours.

Added to this, the top designers usually work on as many as four or five shows a season. Frequently a "hot" designer will do Broadway as well as off-Broadway, where he or she can experiment more.

SET DESIGNERS

The best set designers are not simply interior decorators; they do not just paint pictures against which ballets are danced and dramas are acted. Whether it's building a drinking saloon in *Hello, Dolly!,* creating the image of Norma Desmond in *Sunset Boulevard,* or evoking a steamy summer night

MINIMUM PAY RATES FOR SET DESIGNERS

Broadway

Drama, single set	$ 7,801
Drama, multiset	11,084
Musical, single set	8,113
Musical, multiset	25,789

Off-Broadway

	Seating Capacity		
	199 or less	200–299	300–499
Single set	$1,495	$2,244	$4,215
Multiset	1,767	2,715	6,203
Unit set with phases	1,767	2,715	7,686

Regional Theater

	Seating Capacity				
	199 or less	200–299	300–499	500–999	Over 1,000
Single set	$1,495	$2,048	$2,704	$3,353	$3,705
Two sets	1,657	2,373	3,167	4,327	4,915
Unit set with phases	1,718	2,384	3,240	4,024	4,450
Each additional set	57	97	207	531	548

Ballet

	American Ballet Theater New York City Ballet	Standard Companies
First set	$5,289	$3,749
Second set	1,555	974
Each additional set	1,035	729
Unit set	5,294	3,584
Next 9 phases	1,163	729

SOURCE: United Scenic Artists Union, 1998.

for an Alvin Ailey number, the designer's job is to create a particular mood to blend with the acting.

Set designers, like lighting and costume designers, work closely with the director, deciding how to provide a suitable yet unobtrusive background for the action. They are also skilled in planning how scenery can be changed quickly with a minimum of noise and difficulty, as well as how to create different scenes with only one basic set.

The legendary name in scenic design is Oliver Smith, who created the sets for *My Fair Lady, Hello, Dolly!,* and *West Side Story.* Today, Robin Wagner is one of the current crop of most-sought-after set designers. He has done *Hair, Annie, A Chorus Line, 42nd Street, and Dream Girls.*

COSTUME DESIGNERS

Whether it's a Shakespearean costume for a revival of *Hamlet,* a flowing dress for *Swan Lake,* or turn-of-the-century dresses for *The Heiress,* the costume designer has the task of carefully planning the clothes for both the play's character and for the individual actor. Costumes play a major role in creating a character, and the designer's main job is to enhance the character without drawing too much attention to the clothes themselves.

A designer is well versed in different periods of clothing, which materials will hold up well or move well with dancers, how the outfit will look from the first as well as from the last row, and most important, how to use clothes to create a certain mood.

The amount of clothing a designer must plan can be staggering, especially in productions with thirty or forty actors, singers, and dancers, many of whom change costumes for each act.

The best-known costume designer is Theoni V. Aldredge, who has done dozens of Broadway shows. At one time, she had four Broadway hits playing simultaneously: *A Chorus Line, Annie, Barnum,* and *42nd Street.* A conservative estimate of her royalties from those shows was $15,000 per week.

MINIMUM PAY RATES FOR COSTUME DESIGNERS	
Broadway Drama	
Number of Characters	**Pay**
1–3	$ 4,229
4–7	4,229 + 330 each
8–15	7,145
16–20	7,145 + 340 each

MINIMUM PAY RATES FOR COSTUME DESIGNERS

Broadway Drama

Number of Characters	Pay
21–30	$ 9,771
31–35	9,771 + 340 each
36 and over	12,398

Broadway Musical

Number of Persons Onstage	Pay
1–15	$ 8,797
16–20	8,797 + 409 each
21–30	17,593
31–35	17,593 + 409 each
36 and over	25,789

Regional Theaters

	Number of Costumes			
Theater Size	10 or Fewer	11–20 Each	21–30 Each	31 or Over Each
199 or less	$1,495	$ 31	$31	$31
200–299	2,048	57	32	32
300–499	2,597	71	45	45
500–999	2,961	97	71	50
Over 1,000	3,705	121	80	71

Off-Broadway

Number of Characters	Seating Capacity		
	199 or Less	200–299	300–499
Drama			
1–3	10 or less = $1,414	10 or less = $2,009	$ 2,293
4–7		1,005	187 each
8–15	More than 10 = 1,767	More than 10 = 2,362	3,846
16–20			187 each
21–30			5,216
31–35			187 each
36+			6,893
Musical			
1–15	NA	NA	$ 4,611
16–20	NA	NA	225 each

MINIMUM PAY RATES FOR COSTUME DESIGNERS

Off Broadway

Number of Characters	Seating Capacity		
	199 or Less	**200–299**	**300–499**
21–30	NA	NA	9,223
31–35	NA	NA	225 each
36+	NA	NA	13,765

Ballet

	American Ballet Theater New York City Ballet	Standard Companies
Minimum per ballet	$2,625	$875
1–10 each	Minimum[1]	Minimum[2]
11–25 each	Minimum[1]	Minimum[2]
11–25 each	175.00 each	120 each
26–50 each	120.00 each	100 each
51 and over each	95.00 each	78 each
Repeats each	52.50 each	57 each

[1]$265 each, whichever is greater.
[2]Or $190 each, whichever is greater.
SOURCE: United Scenic Artists Union, 1995.

LIGHTING DESIGNERS

After the sets and costumes have been designed, the next people called in are the lighting designers, who do a lot more than just decide where the lights will be hung. They work closely with the directors to plan lighting that will be exactly right for each moment of the play, enhancing the action, mood, and meaning. Lighting is even more important in ballet and dance, where scenery and costumes may be minimal.

Lighting design is selecting what the audience, faced with an entire stage, will see at each moment, whether it's the crook of a finger, a smiling face, or the star in a big production number. The designer plots where the lights—what types and in what intensities—will be hung in a theater. He then cues the lights for every action so that after he completes his job, an electrician can do the actual work during the run of the play.

Jules Fisher is one of the top lighting designers. He's done *Hair, Pippin,* and *Dancin'.* Tharon Musser is noted for creating *A Chorus Line's* computerized lighting as well as that of *The Wiz.*

MINIMUM PAY RATES FOR LIGHTING DESIGNERS

Broadway

Drama
Single set	$ 5,851
Multiset	8,314
Single set with phases	10,717

Musical
Single set	$ 6,085
Single set with phases	11,146
Multiset	19,342

Off-Broadway

	Seating Capacity		
	199 or less	**200–299**	**300–499**
Drama			
Single set	$1,414	$2,009	$ 2,951
Multiset	1,767	2,362	4,338
Unit set with phases	NA	NA	5,383
Musical			
Single set	NA	NA	$ 4,215
Multiset	NA	NA	13,765
Unit set with phases	NA	NA	7,686

Regional Theaters

	Seating Capacity				
	199 or less	**200–299**	**300–499**	**500–999**	**Over 1,000**
Single set	$1,495	$1,852	$2,445	$2,961	$3,705
Multisets or phases	1,657	2,083	2,754	3,420	4,366

Ballet

	Standard Companies
Full-length ballet	$3,350
More than 1/3 of an evening	2,210
1/3 of an evening	1,100
Pas de un/trois	835

SOURCE: United Scenic Artists Union, 1995.

DESIGN ASSISTANTS

Most productions on Broadway or those staged by major ballet companies are so elaborate, they require trained personnel to help the various designers. The union regulates their rates, too.

MINIMUM WEEKLY PAY RATES FOR DESIGN ASSISTANTS		
	Broadway	**Standard Ballet**
Scenic	$947	$675
Costume	947	675
Lighting	947	675

SOURCE: United Scenic Artists Union, 1998.

Directors and Choreographers

The director's task, whether for dinner theater or a Broadway show, is to transform written dialogue and scenes into a lively art. Usually hired by the producer, the director is involved in the play from the very beginning. He functions as an artist, a teacher, and an executive. As an artist, he extracts the meaning from the play and changes it into physical action. As a teacher, he guides the actors through their paces. As an executive, he oversees and collaborates with the lighting, set, and costume designers, the makeup artists, and all the other craftspeople.

The director has the final say on who gets the lead, how the scenery is arranged, when the lights dim, how the actor crosses the stage, and all the other thousands of elements that go into bringing a play to life.

If the play is a musical, the director may also be the choreographer, like the late Bob Fosse (*Chicago, Dancin'*), the late Jerome Robbins (*West Side Story, Fiddler on the Roof, Gypsy*), or the late Gower Champion (*Hello, Dolly!, 42nd Street*). The choreographer plots and coordinates all the dance numbers in a musical. Like a composer, the choreographer notes each step exactly so the number is performed the same on Broadway as it is years later in a summer theater.

The pay for directors and choreographers is a combination of a fee and a percentage of the weekly box office gross. The fees listed below are minimums and can go much higher, especially for name directors like Hal Prince, Mike Nichols, and Gene Saks. The percentage starts at 0.75 percent and can go as high as 5 percent for a sought-after director or choreographer.

BASIC PAY RATES FOR DIRECTORS AND CHOREOGRAPHERS

	Broadway	Off-Broadway			
		"A" Theater (400–499 seats)	"B" Theater (300–399 seats)	"C" Theater (200–299 seats)	"D" Theater (100–199 seats)
Director	$44,675	$10,968	$8,911	$7,539	$6,169
Choreographer	37,130	8,744	7,130	6,034	4,936
Director-choreographer	81,805	19,191	15,596	13,139	10,796

SOURCE: Society of Stage Directors and Choreographers, 1998.

This amount can be substantial, as the weekly gross on a Broadway show can range between $150,000 and $400,000. If the director stages the national theater companies, he gets an additional fee as well as a cut of the box office gross. The choreographer also gets his weekly royalty from any touring companies.

Off-Broadway fees vary by theater size in the range shown above.

Photographers

Lots of people have a knack with a Nikon. But if you can break out of the weddings-and graduation-photo racket, there's good money to be earned in high-fashion, magazine, and other commercial photography. But although the pay is pleasing, the field is extremely difficult to break into. It's competitive, and the money's far from steady.

Putting caveats aside, the work is creative and challenging. Generally hired by magazines or advertising agencies, photographers help develop illustration or campaign ideas and then shoot them. The bulk of jobs are in magazine illustration and in advertising and marketing, with a variety of possible assignments that include television commercials, billboards, catalogs, and packaging. Think of the scope of freelance work possible next time you plow through glossy magazine ads, buy dog food, or choose a book by its cover.

"Probably the best place to break into photography is in magazine

RATE GUIDELINES FOR PROFESSIONAL PHOTOGRAPHERS			
	Lower Range	**Average**	**Upper Range**
Advertising			
Consumer magazines			
National	$ 795–1,325	$1,590–2,650	$2,120–3,577
Trade magazines	530–715	1,060–1,431	1,431–1,908
Newspapers			
National	1,272	1,749–2,173	2,809+
Local	477–742	795–1,060	1,325+
Billboards			
National	1,484	1,961–2,252	2,650+
Local	583	742–875	980
Stills for TV commercial			
National	530	1,060	1,590
Local	291	425	530–795

RATE GUIDELINES FOR PROFESSIONAL PHOTOGRAPHERS

	Lower Range	Average	Upper Range
Brochures			
National	$ 397–477	$ 795–927	$1,590–1,855
Regional	238–344	477–662	954–1,325
Local	185–212	371–424	530–795
Corporate/industrial			
Annual reports	$ 636	$ 742–901	$1,378+
Brochures	424	530–848	1,272+
Film strips	424	636	954+
Record-album covers	477	1,431	1,696+
Editorial			
Editorial illustrations (fashion, home products, magazine and book covers, etc.)	$ 371	$ 477–848	$1,484+
Under 2 hours; magazines under 200,000 circulation	265	318	371+
General documentary (geography, travel, etc.)	371	424–530	742+
Publicity and Promotions			
Basic press kits	$ 265–318	$ 318–371	$ 636–795
Motion-picture specials	265–318	371–477	530–636
Senior executive portraits (PR sittings)	318	530–795	1,060–1,590
Catalogs/brochures			
Covers (per version)	$ 636–795	$1,325	$1,590–2,120
Fashion catalogs			
Per single figure	91	132–185	265–318
Per day	795	1,325	1,590–2,120
Still-life catalogs			
Per single product	79	159–319	1,060+
Per day	7952	1,325	1,590–2,120
Per still life	79–106	159–318	1,060+
Per single full figure	133–159	212–265	318–371
Miscellaneous media			
Posters			
Promotional	$ 371	$ 663	$ 1007
Retail	318	450	609+
Calendars			
Advertising or promotional	398	625	1,007
Retail	345	500	848

RATE GUIDELINES FOR PROFESSIONAL PHOTOGRAPHERS

	Lower Range	Average	Upper Range
Greeting cards			
Advertising and promotional	$318		$ 662
Retail	238		450
Murals (varies widely depending on size and placement)	583		2,650+
Jigsaw puzzles	398		556

SOURCE: American Society of Magazine Photographers. Reprinted by permission.

PAY RATES FOR FREELANCE PHOTOGRAPHERS AT LARGE CONSUMER MAGAZINES

Magazine	Rate
Barron's	$150–$300 day rate
Esquire	$750 for color photo
Golf Digest	$100–$300 for transparencies
Good Housekeeping	$150–$1,000 for color transparencies
Harper's	$50 to $500 per photo
Motor Trend	$25–$500 for transparencies
Ms.	$75–200 per photo
National Wildlife	$300–$800 per photo
The New York Times Magazine	$75 minimum for black-and-white photo
Sierra	$300 maximum for transparencies; more for cover
Ski	$75–$300 per photo
Sports Parade	$35 for transparencies; $50 for cover
Star	$150–$1,000 for color transparencies

SOURCE: *The Freelancer.*

work," says Patti Harris, director of New York City's Freelancer, a placement service for freelance photographers, illustrators, copywriters, and other artists. Which means that, geographically, New York, followed by Los Angeles and Chicago, holds the best opportunities for work in this field. New York also offers the advantage of being the nation's fashion capital. Jobs can also be found in other major cities with concentrations of advertising agencies.

From what she's seen, Harris says, "Most photographers try to specialize in one area." Areas of concentration can include medical reports, fashion, people, still life, travel, editorial, and reportage.

An estimated 95,000 Americans work in all kinds of photography out of commercial studios. Since many photographers work as independent businesspeople, there seems to be no available information on their annual incomes. We do know that the government employs 3,000 photographers in different capacities (including work for the armed forces), for whom the average salary is $24,000. For information on newspaper photographers, please see the section "The Newspaper," in Part VI.

High-fashion photography is undoubtedly the highest paid sector of the profession, with famous photographers receiving over $6,000 a job. These are closely followed by travel pictures and then still-life product shots. Most photographers work freelance, even the full-timers, often utilizing more than one agent or service to scout out and arrange jobs. The rates above usually do not include the typical 25 to 45 percent additional markup for the agent's commission. Furthermore, additionally billable expenses include all film and processing, location and transportation expenses, assistants, insurance, special equipment, overtime, and talent used in the shoot.

The current financial situation for magazine photographers is mixed at best. For while most magazines have been flourishing and ad revenues have increased steadily, the so-called day rate of $350 has remained virtually unchanged since 1988. According to *Photo District News*, a publication for professional photographers, magazines are also demanding the right to reuse pictures for only a small amount of additional compensation; *National Geographic,* which pays $400 a day, recently began paying photographers only $100 for use of pictures in its numerous foreign editions.

The reason for these developments is quite simple, said photographer and journalist David Walker: supply and demand. "As long as there are young photographers out there who will take these terms, photographers will be stuck with them."

III

The Five Standard Professions

In today's parlance, the term "professional" is applied to all kinds of people from the highly trained or educated (engineers and teachers, for example) to those who have completed a short course of study required by the state (beauticians and real estate brokers, among others). Sometimes "professional" is used as a term of approbation referring to someone who is particularly good at his or her job, or to someone who acts with cool detachment when things go wrong on the job: "She didn't complain about the transfer to Boise; after all, she's a . . ." There are other uses, too, but these should suffice to indicate why we decided to buck the contemporary trend and lump together the five occupations that have commonly been referred to as "professions" for most of this century: accountants, architects, dentists, doctors, and lawyers.

Only 2 percent of the workforce, about 3 million people, are actively engaged in these occupations. With the exception of accountants, they have all had to complete several years of rigorous postgraduate training, followed by a period of low-paid apprenticeship. More often than not, they open their own offices and join an organization that sets standards for professional practice and provides essential information, including advice on setting fees. The latter is rather important because, with the exception of architects, membership in these professions virtually guarantees an income substantially above the national norm, frequently placing members among the top 10 percent of all income-earning families in America.

In the past, the wealth and status of these professionals went unchallenged, the value of their work to society unquestioned. Only foreign radicals like George Bernard Shaw would refer to the professions as "conspiracies against the laity." The figures found in this section may lead you to the same conclusion, especially if you are a nuclear engineer, a physicist, a senior college professor, or in any occupation that requires years of preparation. If you are young and looking toward a career, however, these five professions are almost certain to remain sure roads to economic security despite shifting public opinion. One reason is that the norm for wages and income is established by people in private practice. So even if you work as a lawyer or accountant for a corporation or government agency, your salary is based— unofficially, of course—on what people earn on their own. Since there are no signs that Congress or the courts would sanction any legal limitations on fees for professional services, salary levels should remain very high.

ACCOUNTANTS

Gone is the old stereotype of the accountant with the eyeshade and bifocals sitting, hunched, with pencil in hand, over pages of tiny figures. Accountants today come equipped with calculators, computers, sophisticated management techniques, and, more often than not, advanced degrees. Over 1 million accountants work in the United States, and almost all of them work in the corporate sector. As the accountant's role becomes increasingly important to strategic business operations, and as accounting professionals develop more specialized skills, both salaries and hiring are on the rise. According to an annual survey by Robert Half International, the strong economy and record-low unemployment levels mean companies are hiring accounting and finance personnel in every region of the country and at every job level. The Bureau of Labor Statistics has projected employment in accounting to grow as fast as the average for all occupations through the year 2006. The biggest beneficiaries of this growth should be professionals who have obtained certification or licensure. A growing trend among states is to require 150 semester hours of college coursework—thirty more than traditionally required for a bachelor's degree—to be eligible for CPA certification, according to the Bureau of Labor Statistics. This requirement, which makes it more difficult to obtain the certification, should boost demand for CPAs, and salaries should rise accordingly. Additionally, applicants who have strong computer skills, specifically with accounting and auditing software, will have an advantage in the competitive marketplace. The same will be true for those with specialized business and communications skills, as accountants become more involved in overall corporate operations. According to Robert Half, many accounting firms are speeding their hiring process in their race with other recruiters to attract the most qualified candidates. In addition, many are offering referral incentives and generous signing bonuses.

To keep payrolls at a lower level, both corporations and public firms are relying on staff or junior accountants with one to five years' experience rather than more highly paid middle managers. Other companies are hiring accountants on a part-time basis only. After laying off large numbers of people, the companies are finding they don't have enough accountants to get their work done, so they have to hire on a per diem basis.

In the most basic terms, what accountants do is prepare and analyze financial reports that provide managers with the information they need to make decisions. Within a company, for example, an industrial accountant can perform the following tasks, ranging from the simple to the complex: do bookkeeping in various departments, complete tax returns and audit reports, prepare cost analyses for new projects, determine cutoff return investments, and advise on mergers and corporate growth policy. On higher levels, such as that of the treasurer, the accountant will make broad policy decisions on all financial operations.

In public accounting, most of the duties revolve around audits (examining a client's financial records and reports to judge their compliance with standards of preparation and reporting). These tasks include reconciling cash, confirming receivables, observing and testing the taking of inventory, testing internal control and accounting records, preparing tax returns, researching and counseling clients on tax problems, and providing management consulting in the development of all financial operations and frequently in personnel policies, production, and computer-based information systems.

The accounting field is divided into four segments: About 60 percent of accounting professionals work in industrial accounting, about 25 percent in public accounting, about 12 percent in government, and about 3 percent in education.

Industrial accounting—also called management, corporation, or internal accounting—goes on in businesses from multinational corporations to small companies where in-house accountants perform all the financial operations: the treasury, controllership, and internal-audit functions.

Titles and responsibilities vary from company to company, but in general, the lower- and middle-level jobs include cost accountant, internal auditor, plant accountant, data processing specialist, systems and procedures manager, financial analyst, chief accountant, and budget director. Higher up the ladder are assistant controller, controller, treasurer, secretary, vice president of finance, president, and chairman of the board. Every recent survey has found that about 30 percent of the chief executive officers of the largest U.S. corporations had accounting and financial backgrounds, more than in any other business specialty.

Within industrial accounting, the position of certified internal auditor is gaining more importance because of the increase in shareholder lawsuits resulting from alleged inaccurate financial reporting. The approximately

17,000 Certified Internal Auditors in the United States have college degrees, have completed a three-year apprenticeship in internal auditing, and have passed a four-part national exam.

Becoming a certified public accountant is not necessary in industrial accounting as it is in public accounting, but the CPA certificate usually commands a 10 percent salary increase over non-CPAs in comparable positions. CPAs must also serve an apprenticeship and pass a four-part national exam to be certified.

Public accounting in general is slightly more lucrative than industrial. Many of the 400,000 CPAs in the United States work for public accounting firms, ranging from giant worldwide firms with thousands of employees to small one-man offices. The public accountant's work entails financial audits, tax advice, and tax preparation, and often management consulting. The audits require frequent travel to the client's headquarters or branches and long hours examining the company's books and records, usually with a team of experts from the public accounting firm.

Many of the big accounting firms want new employees to have at least a college degree in accounting, and preferably an M.B.A., especially for management consulting; or a law degree, especially for taxation specialization. The career path starts with the junior or staff accountant position, and progresses, if all goes very well, to senior accountant, to manager, to partner and, finally, to senior partner.

Personnel specialist Robert Half estimates that about 60 percent of public accountants leave their first job after three to five years if they fail to attain a supervisory position. After another ten to fifteen years, a large group exits without making partner. Source Finance, another personnel agency, estimates that only about 2 percent of the accountants who join a public accounting firm will make partner. Those who leave will generally go to good positions in industrial accounting. In a big corporation, the CPA who made the switch can eventually earn as much or more than a partner at his old firm.

The approximately 110,000 accountants who work for municipal, county, state, and federal governments are usually not as well paid. Their duties are much the same as those of industrial accountants, except that the "company" is the government. A college degree and the passing of a civil service exam are both required for many government accounting positions.

All these accountants get their original training in schools and colleges from the 3 percent of accountants who are teachers. Many teach part-time and supplement their incomes with consultancy work and by serving on professional organization committees.

As in so many other areas, the number of women entering the accounting field has grown considerably over the last few years. In fact, starting in the late 1980s, more women than men earned bachelor's degrees in accounting. The Robert Half Agency has found that, unlike in some other professions, female accountants are easier to place than their male counterparts. Women were chosen over men, the agency found, three times out of four for a hundred different job openings paying between $15,000 and $50,000.

Top-Level Accountants in Finance

The Robert Half Agency of New York provides the following national survey of high-level salary ranges in the financial field. Geographic differences can mean from 2 to 5 percent more or less, except for a few states like Alaska (+10 percent), Florida (–10 percent), or Arizona, New Mexico, Tennessee, and West Virginia (all of which are –9 percent). Within each state, an accountant who works in a city of 1 million or more people generally earns 5 percent more; if extensive travel is required, the job generally pays an additional 5 percent.

ANNUAL SALARY RANGES FOR TOP-LEVEL JOBS IN FINANCE

Title	Company Volume (in millions)	1998 Salary Range
Chief Financial Officer/Treasurer	to $ 50	$ 65,000–$90,000
	50–100	78,500–100,000
	100–250[1]	97,000–152,000
	250–500[1]	148,000–250,000
	500+[1]	240,000–316,000
Corporate Controller	to $ 10[2]	47,500–63,500
	10–50	55,000–74,500
	50–250[3]	70,000–93,000
	250+	86,000–140,000
Assistant Controller, Divisional Controller,	to $ 10[2]	41,000–54,000
Plant Controller or Assistant Treasurer	10–50[2,3]	45,000–57,000
	50–250[3]	52,000–67,000
	250+	60,000–84,000
Corporate Tax Managers	$50–250	59,000–76,000
	250+	71,000–112,000

[1]Bonus and incentive compensation reflect an increasingly large part of an overall pay package at these levels.
[2]Add 10% for CPAs.
[3]Add 10% for CMAs.
SOURCE: Robert Half International, *1998 Salary Guide*. Reprinted by permission.

Industrial and Public Accountants

The following survey of private industry covers the salaries of accountants on six different levels. Accountant I, a beginning level job, includes such tasks as examining a variety of financial statements for completeness, reconciling reports and financial data with statements already on file, and preparing relatively simple financial statements. Accountant II is more experienced and performs such tasks as preparing routine working papers, schedules, exhibits, and summaries on financial conditions, and examines a variety of accounting documents for accuracy. Accountant III usually has charge of a segment of an accounting system or of an entire system. Duties entail developing nonstandard reports and statements, interpreting financial trends, projecting data, and predicting effects of change in operating programs. Accountant IV is usually in charge of an accounting operation and makes recommendations for new accounts, revisions in account structure, and changes in accounting procedures. Accountant V has duties similar to accountant IV, but the department is larger and/or more complex. Duties include developing and coordinating new accounting systems, assuring accounting reporting systems are in compliance, and identifying and suggesting solutions for problem areas. Accountant VI does much the same except the department he supervises has unusually difficult and complicated problems. He also usually has complete responsibility for his department.

Median Salaries of Accountants and Analysts in Public and Internal Firms

The following survey gives salary ranges of internal and public accountants and of analysts in small, medium, and large firms. Large firms have more than $250 million in sales; medium firms have between $25 and $250 million in sales; small firms have less than $25 million in sales. Internal accountants perform general, audit, and cost work; public accountants perform audits and tax management services; analysts do financial, budget, and cost work.

PREVAILING STARTING SALARIES OF ACCOUNTANTS			
Title	1998 Salary Range	Title	1998 Salary Range
General Audit and Cost Accountants, Internal—Large Firms[1]			
0–1 year experience	$29,500–$32,750	Senior	$38,500–$48,000
1–3 years experience	32,000– 39,000	Manager	47,000– 67,000

Title	1998 Salary Range	Title	1998 Salary Range
General Audit and Cost Accountants, Internal—Medium Firms[1]			
0–1 year experience	27,000– 31,000	Senior	38,000– 45,000
1–3 years experience	30,000– 38,000	Manager	41,000– 51,000
General Audit and Cost Accountants, Internal—Small Firms[1]			
0–1 year experience	25,250– 29,000	Senior	35,000– 42,500
1–3 years experience	27,500– 36,000	Manager	41,000– 47,000
Financial, Budget, and Cost Analysts—Large Firms[1]			
0–1 year experience	28,500– 32,000	Senior	39,750– 50,000
1–3 years experience	32,000– 43,000	Manager	48,000– 69,000
Analysts—Medium Firms[1]			
0–1 year experience	27,000– 31,000	Senior	37,000– 45,000
1–3 years experience	30,000– 39,000	Manager	46,000– 57,000
Analysts—Small Firms[1]			
0–1 year experience	25,000– 29,000	Senior	35,000– 41,000
1–3 years experience	29,000– 35,000	Manager	41,000– 54,000
Audit, Tax, and Management Services Public Accountants—Large Firms[2]			
0–1 year experience	30,000– 35,000	Manager	46,000– 67,750
1–3 years experience	32,000– 38,500	Manager/Director[3]	59,000– 89,000
Senior	36,500– 47,000		
Audit, Tax, and Management Services Public Accountants—Medium Firms[2]			
0–1 year experience	27,000– 30,500	Manager[3]	46,000– 65,000
1–3 years experience	29,500– 37,000	Manager/Director[3]	58,000– 85,000
Senior	35,000– 47,000		
Audit, Tax, and Management Services Public Accountants—Small Firms[2]			
0–1 year experience	25,000– 29,000	Manager[3]	45,000– 60,000
1–3 years experience	29,000– 35,000	Manager/Director[3]	55,750– 77,750
Senior	33,000– 45,000		

[1]Add 10 percent for a graduate degree; an additional 10 percent for a CPA; and an additional 5 percent for substantial travel.
[2]Add 5 percent for a graduate degree; add 10 percent for a CPA.
[3]Subtract 5 percent if not a CPA.
SOURCE: Robert Half International, *1998 Salary Guide.* Reprinted by permission.

ARCHITECTS

Architecture, law, and medicine each promise a certain status as a profession within our society. But in terms of financial reward, architecture is very much the poor relation. Moreover, the end of the building boom of the 1980s has meant that the situation is not likely to get any better in the near future.

Several theories exist to explain why remuneration is not commensurate with the prestige offered by the architecture profession. One of the more persuasive arguments is that architecture is a process, rather than a product, and as such, is not essential to the construction of a building. The role of the architect has been reduced by the introduction of design builders, contractors, and construction managers into the building process. Indeed, it has been claimed that only 20 percent of all building is from architects' designs. Architects need to become either indispensable to the building process or increasingly entrepreneurial, and hence, control the building process. Architecture can be viewed as a generalizing profession; architects typically provide planning and consulting in addition to design services. A more extreme manifestation is the shift of architects toward entrepreneurship—as owners, developers, financiers, builders, or construction managers.

Traditionally, the field of architecture has been caught between the gentleman's art and the artisan's craft. As a profession, architecture is not quite 200 years old, the image of professionalism being established by Benjamin Latrobe at the turn of the nineteenth century. The introduction of the first architecture school in 1865 at MIT paralleled the development of architecture as a profession.

Today, nationally accredited schools enroll some 20,000 students in both undergraduate and graduate programs, and award professional degrees to some 3,000 students annually. The American Institute of Architects represents the profession and estimates that there are currently 85,000 licensed architects in the United States. The AIA boasts roughly 59,000 members, 86 percent of whom are licensed. Of their members, 50,700 are regular members, and 8,000 are associate members—those who are waiting to become registered.

An architecture degree or registration does not necessitate a career as an architect, and what it means to be an architect seems to be undergoing fundamental changes. It has been claimed that close to 50 percent of architecture students end up in other fields. And although this figure is disputed, the decreasing role of the architect would suggest that it will be harder and harder for architecture graduates to find work until their numbers start decreasing as well. With tough competition for firm jobs, those graduates with internship experience and/or training in technology such as computer-aided design (CAD) will have an advantage.

To this day, architecture tends to remain locally based. Even in an age of increasing national and global business, most architecture firms are small (one-third are solo operations, while another third have two to four employees) and closely linked to their local economies and contacts within their communities. Despite the booming economy of the late 90s, some areas of the country are stronger than others when it comes to architecture jobs, and many must relocate to find work. The strongest area in the country for architecture firms is the southwest, where nearly one quarter of jobs in the field can be found, and the average architecture salary is almost 4 percent higher than the national average. California boasts more architecture jobs than any other state, and is home to almost twice as many firms as New York, which is the second largest market in the country. Salaries are lowest in the west south central (Arkansas, Louisiana, Oklahoma, and Texas), where salaries lag behind those of the rest of the nation by over 7 percent, according to the AIA. An increasing number of states are beginning to accept standardized licensing requirements for architects, thereby facilitating relocation.

Over the past six years, salaries at U.S. architectural firms have kept pace with those of other professions. The AIA reports an increase of 22 percent in overall salary for staff architects and interns since 1990, with yearly increases averaging about 2 percent from 1990–93 and almost 5 percent since 1994. Landscape architects, interior designers, CAD operators, drafters, and other technical staff have seen the greatest salary gains over the last six years—but that whopping 30 percent increase is an increase from low base starting salaries.

BASE SALARIES OF ARCHITECTS

Title	Average Salary	First Quartile	Third Quartile
Managing Partner/Principal	$86,307	$60,000	$100,000
Partner/Principal	75,864	60,000	90,000
Chief Architect/Director of Operations	68,643	58,000	77,000
Director of Contract Administration	57,430	51,000	65,000
Project Manager	53,316	43,400	62,225
Architect Level I	25,586	20,800	26,624
Architect Level II	28,491	25,000	31,545
Architect Level III	33,226	28,500	35,173
Architect Level IV	38,076	33,050	42,705
Architect Level V	45,031	36,868	49,000
Architect Level VI	50,539	41,600	56,480
Architect Level VII	58,636	47,418	66,872
Architect Level VIII	69,120	54,600	75,000
Architect, Department Head	66,262	58,718	73,000

SOURCE: D. Dietrich Associates, Phoenixville, PA. Copyright © 1996; reprinted by permission.

The salaries outlined in the table are meant to reflect the broad salary structure of those employed in architecture or architecture/engineering firms. Salaries will vary for those in allied design professions or in other alternate careers. For example, in government service, architects are hired at federal, state, and local levels. In the federal government, architects are generally GS-11, 12, or 13 levels, where average salaries range from $42,000–$60,000. Regional differences in salary become marked at state and local levels.

As a caveat, the following figures represent general salary ranges across a spectrum of firms. There can be no pretense that these figures are comprehensive. The variables within the industry (firms range from less than five employees to over a hundred) are too great to be summarized. Aside from variations in firms' sizes, locations, and business cycles, there are fundamental differences in how the cost of an architect's services to a client can be determined. The American Institute of Architects recognizes several, including lump sum; direct cost, plus compensation for overhead and profit; percentage of construction cost (varying with size and complexity of the particular job); cost, plus fixed fees; and per diem rates.

Undoubtedly there are those earning less than the figures indicate, and it is generally acknowledged in the profession, as in other professions, that the top people—principals, partners, and owners—at the top firms are better compensated than might be suggested by these figures.

Job Descriptions for Architects and Draftsmen

Architect I—The entry-level of professional work, requiring a bachelor's degree in architecture and no experience, or the equivalent (to a degree) in architecture and no experience.

Architect II—At this continuing development level, routine architectural assignments is performed under direct supervision. Works from the designs of others, compiles data, performs design computations, makes quantity takeoffs and prepares estimates, prepares architectural plans and renderings, consults manufacturers, evaluates materials, writes architectural specifications, and inspects architectural features of structures in the field. Limited exercise of judgment is required on details of work in making preliminary elections and adaptations of alternatives.

Architect III—Independently evaluates, selects, and applies standard architectural techniques, procedures, and criteria, using judgment in making minor adaptations and modifications. Assignments have clear and specified objectives and require the investigation of a limited number of variables. Performance at this level generally requires a minimum of one year of architect II or related work experience.

Architect IV—A fully competent architect in all conventional aspects of the subject matter in the functional areas of the assignments: Plans and conducts work requiring judgment in the independent evaluation, selection, and substantial adaptation and modification of standard techniques, procedures, and criteria; devises new approaches to problems encountered. Generally requires a minimum of two years of architect III or related experience. Registration as a licensed architect may be a requirement for certain positions.

Architect V—Applies sound and diversified knowledge of architectural principles and practices in broad areas of assignments and related fields. Makes decisions independently on architectural problems and methods. Requires the use of advanced techniques, and the modification and extension of theories, precepts, and practices in his field. Registration as a licensed architect is a requirement for most positions.

Architect VI—Has full responsibility for interpreting, organizing, executing, and coordinating assignments. Plans and develops architectural projects concerned with unique or controversial problems that have an important effect on major company programs. This involves exploration of subject area; definition of scope; selection of problems for investigation; and development of novel concepts and approaches. Maintains liaison with individuals and units within or outside organization, with responsibility for acting independently on technical matters pertaining to his field. Registration as a licensed architect is a requirement.

Architect VII—Makes decisions and recommendations that are recognized as authoritative and have an important impact on extensive architectural activities. Initiates and maintains extensive contacts with key architects and officials of other organizations and companies, requiring skill in persuasion and negotiation of critical issues. At this level, must exercise individual judgment in anticipating and solving unprecedented architectural problems, determining program objectives and requirements, organizing programs and projects, and developing standards and guides for diverse architectural activities. Registration as a licensed architect is a requirement.

Architect VIII—Makes decisions and recommendations that are recognized as authoritative and that have a far-reaching impact on extensive architectural and related activities of the company. Negotiates critical and controversial issues with top-level architects, engineers, and officers of other organizations and companies. Individuals at this level demonstrate a high degree of creativity, foresight, and mature judgment in planning, organizing, and guiding extensive architectural programs and activities of outstanding novelty and/or importance.

Architect Department Head (Nonpartner/Principal)—Provides technical and administrative supervision to the department to assure that the technical administrative, man-hour, and schedule targets of the department are met within the framework of established corporate policy and in accordance with applicable professional standards, design control procedures, corporate and division procedures, and design guides.

Junior Draftsman (Draftsman, Junior Technician, Professional Trainee)—A beginner requiring close, continuous supervision, whose work is reviewed carefully upon completion for conformity to office standards. Normally a high school graduate with some drafting training, but less than two years' experience.

Junior Designer (Architectural Designer, Designer/Draftsman)—A design-sensitive draftsman handling design and/or drafting assignments on segments of a project under the direction and review of a more experienced designer. A recent graduate with limited (two to five years') training or experience.

Draftsman (Intermediate Draftsman, Architectural Draftsman)—A draftsman with sufficient work experience and/or technical training to work without supervision. The normal entry-level position for an inexperienced architectural graduate.

Designer (Architectural Designer, Design Development, Intermediate Designer, Project Designer)—Involved with segments of larger projects or smaller, less complex jobs, and with minimal supervisory responsibilities. Generally two to six years' experience with sufficient training and ability.

Senior Draftsman (Senior Architectural Draftsman, Assistant Job Captain)—Able to handle assignments of greater scope and complexity with minimum supervision. Several years (six or more) of progressively responsible experience.

SALARIES OF ARCHITECTURAL DRAFTERS AND DESIGNERS

Title	Average Salary	First Quartile	Third Quartile
Drafting Apprentice	$15,600	NA	NA
Drafter Level I	16,719	$15,600	$20,799
Drafter Level II	22,834	21,000	24,000
Drafter Level III	27,120	23,961	30,510
Senior Drafter	31,961	28,080	34,890
Job Captain	35,950	31,200	39,518
Junior Designer "A"	29,725	27,000	33,360
Junior Designer "B"	35,409	31,616	40,320
Designer	40,122	33,830	47,528
Project Designer	52,115	43,347	58,100

SOURCE: D. Dietrich Associates, Phoenixville, PA. Copyright ©, 1996; reprinted by permission.

Senior Designer (Design Job Captain, Project Designer)—Directs other designers on a project and consults regularly with the project manager, the officer or partner in charge of the project, and the client on matters concerning design. May fill a dual project manager role on some projects of limited scope and complexity. Normally six or more years of experience.

Job Captain (Project Captain)—Responsible for producing the working drawings on projects and exercising independent professional judgment, but job teams assigned to his projects are small. Assists project manager and may also act as senior draftsman on some projects.

Senior Job Captain (Deputy Project Manager, Project Manager)—Requires the exercise of independent professional judgment in coordinating the production of construction documents. Supervises a job team of consultants, draftsmen, and specification writers assigned to assist on a project. Normally possesses an architecture degree and may be registered.

Project Manager (Associate, Project Director, Project Architect)—Coordinates the efforts of technical and professional employees and manages the administrative and budget requirements of a job. Ten or more years of diversified experience in the field of architecture and typically an architecture degree and professional registration (although neither is absolutely essential).

HOURLY WAGE RATES FOR DESIGNERS AND DRAFTERS

Title	Average Hourly Rate	First Quartile	Third Quartile
Drafting			
Level I	$ 9.74	$ 7.83	$10.91
Level II	10.55	9.50	12.57
Level III	12.74	11.30	14.70
Level IV	15.40	13.32	16.53
Drafting Supervisor	15.54	14.22	20.36
Designer			
Level I	$16.19	$14.65	$16.55
Level II	17.92	16.00	19.54
Level III	20.01	18.78	21.34
Level IV	25.36	21.20	26.32
Design Manager	26.52	23.31	29.17
CAD			
Applications Analyst	$21.13	$18.25	$23.32
Autographics Supervisor	20.46	17.50	23.60
Lead Operator	17.68	16.30	20.09
Senior Operator	16.69	13.00	18.27
Operator	13.28	11.92	14.90
Assistant Operator	10.44	8.82	12.39
Clerk	10.13	8.80	11.08

SOURCE: D. Dietrich Associates, Phoenixville, PA. Copyright © 1996; reprinted by permission.

Senior Project Manager (Senior Project Architect, Project Administrator)— Like a project manager, coordinates programming, design, production, and construction phases of a project but does so on a larger scale and for substantially greater compensation.

Principal Designer (Associate, Director of Design, Senior Project Designer, Director or Design Development)—One of a limited number of top-level, nonprincipal, design-oriented professional personnel in an office. May act as project manager or as overall project designer on the largest jobs, and participate in departmental staffing, in training and evaluation of design personnel, and in establishing design quality standards within the office. Generally has a degree and registration.

Increasingly Management-Oriented Titles

Program Coordinator—Develops functional and architectural programs for projects as required.

Chief of Design—Coordinates development of project from initial schematic stage through design developmental stages.

Executive Architect—Concerned with coordination and administration of all technical aspects of a project, client contact, and generation of new projects.

Related or Associated Job Titles

Specification Writer—Responsible for writing complete specifications and associated contract documents on a project. Collaborates with the job captain and project designer in establishing the content and format of the specifications and consults with the project team during the construction phase to ensure the proper execution of the work.

Field Superintendent (Field Representative, Construction Administrator)— Represents the architect and client on a job site to ensure construction meets the intent of the contract documents, generally in consultation with the job captain, project designer, and project manager.

Clerk of the Works (Field Superintendent)—Similar to the field superintendent in terms of experience and responsibilities, but allegiance is to the owner/client and compensation is controlled by the client.

Project Administrator—In charge of coordination and administration of all nontechnical aspects of a project, including contracts, fee schedules, selection of consultants, etc.

DENTISTS

Among the five professions in this section, only dentists seem to have an inherent inferiority complex. And not without reason. For most adult Americans, a visit to the dentist is associated either with middle-aged decay or with the remembrance of childhood terrors. Despite the fact that we know how important their work is, how vital to good health, dentists are rarely afforded the same respect as doctors or even lawyers.

NET INCOME OF INDEPENDENT DENTISTS BY REGION, 1996

General Practitioners	1st Quartile	Median	3rd Quartile
New England	$ 76,500	$105,000	$175,000
Middle Atlantic	84,500	122,500	165,500
South Atlantic	88,000	122,500	175,000
Mountain	65,000	119,000	175,000
Pacific	64,770	109,000	153,000
TOTAL U.S.	**70,000**	**112,000**	**159,740**
Specialists			
New England	$100,000	$165,000	$276,590
Middle Atlantic	88,000	155,000	222,500
South Atlantic	102,260	180,000	243,500
Mountain	146,000	210,000	307,000
Pacific	100,000	163,000	255,000
TOTAL U.S.	**100,000**	**175,000**	**250,000**

SOURCE: American Dental Association, *Survey of Dental Practice* (1997).

One thing that does remain high for America's 183,000 professionally active dentists is the size of their incomes. The median net income of dentists in general practice was just under $120,000, according to a 1994 survey by *Dental Economics*. This is before-tax income and represents about 40 percent of the total money brought into the dentist's office (meaning that 60 percent of a dentist's gross income goes toward overhead). Incomes for dentists have increased by about 7 percent each year since 1991, or close to triple the rate of inflation over the same period. The survey also found that the median solo practitioner (representing more than three quarters of all dentists) is forty-four years old, practices thirty-five hours per week, has been in practice seventeen years, and sees fifty patients per week. The median group practitioner is somewhat older (fifty-one), works about the same number of hours (thirty-six), sees about the same number of patients per week (fifty-three), but has been in business much longer (twenty-seven years) and earns correspondingly more ($180,000 for the group practitioner compared with $117,000 for the solo dentist).

The advantages of incorporation are equally clear to dentists as they are to doctors: Incorporated dentists averaged $138,231, while unincorporated dentists averaged only $89,639, according to a separate survey conducted by *Dental Management* magazine. Nevertheless, only about one-third of all dentists are incorporated. It also pays to specialize. Although the vast majority of dentists (91 percent) are generalists, those that specialize in areas like oral surgery, orthodonture, and endodonture make about 50 percent more than do dentists in general practice. And periodontists, who treat gums and the bones that support teeth, earn twice the average salary. But even general practice dentists earn extremely good money relative to other professions, higher even than the average lawyer's income (though salaries at the very top of the lawyer profession can be much higher than the earnings of the best-paid dentists). Considering that dental training lasts only four years, with one or two more for a specialty, dentists' incomes compare very favorably to that of many doctors. And patients rarely call in the middle of the night or complain about a lack of house calls.

The number of dentists increased appreciably in the 1970s after the federal government made a commitment to expanding the nation's dental schools. But starting in 1979, keen competition for jobs has led to a continuing decline of dental school enrollments, meaning that jobs (and more importantly, patients) should be somewhat easier to come by in the 1990s. Dentistry remains a man's world—only 8 percent of dentists are women, according to the American Dental Association—but women's numbers are increasing at a rapid pace. Women dentists' incomes are also growing rapidly—about twice as fast as for men—but they still lag far behind their male counterparts. According to the *Dental Economics* survey, women netted $82,300, compared with $119,997 for men. Of course, the median number of years in practice was only ten years for women, compared to seventeen years for men.

It may seem that dentists are constantly trying to put themselves out of business by encouraging their patients to brush, floss, and gargle regularly, thus decreasing their need for dental care. But these efforts are more than offset by the growth of an elderly population that are more likely to retain their teeth than their predecessors. These older patients are much more likely to need maintenance on complicated dental work like bridges and implants. Dentists' prospects are also likely to be improved by the increasing number of people with dental insurance (up 300 percent since 1975!). And since half the population still fails to visit a dentist on a regular basis, the market for dental services is virtually endless.

DOCTORS

Following the turmoil the health-care industry experienced in the early 1990s—culminating in 1993 with a drop in physicians' earnings for the first time in five decades—recent years have shown a heartening, if not dramatic, economic rebound for doctors. According to a survey of over 11,000 doctors by the journal *Medical Economics,* both gross and net[1] incomes were up in 1996. What is not immediately obvious when looking at the positive numbers is that skyrocketing practice expenses and steadily rising inflation combine to make the overall picture much less bright. The survey showed doctors' median net earnings rising 4.7 percent to $160,740 in 1996—not a bad number. But this rise is tempered by a 5 percent increase in median practice expenses—costing physicians about 36 percent of gross earnings—as well as a 3.3 percent rise in inflation.

Rising practice expenses hit primary care physicians especially hard, according to *Medical Economics.* Family practitioners, who weathered the storm in 1993 and gained 6.3 percent net while overall physicians' earnings were dropping, actually showed a less than 1 percent net increase in 1996.

Surgeons earn about 50 percent more than nonsurgeons. Among the surgeons, the best paid are neurosurgeons, who number 5,164, according to the American Medical Association, and whose median annual salary was $296,870 in 1996, according to *Medical Economics.* Cardio/thoracic surgeons, numbering 2,213, had median earnings of $278,000, an incredible 11 percent jump from 1995. The 22,871 orthopedic surgeons were placed next on the list, with a median salary of $258,110, followed by cardiologists ($240,780) and plastic surgeons ($231,590).

Most people are surprised to learn that the nation's 33,900 anesthesiologists rank very high in the income hierarchy, with an annual average salary of $211,030. The anesthesiologist's tasks are much more complicated than the layman thinks, and other doctors claim that it is tension-filled work, which in times of emergency can be the key to whether or not a patient survives an operation. Still, the figure seems very high and is perhaps best explained by the anesthesiologist's proximity to the surgeon.

One interesting development noted by the *Medical Economics* survey was a shrinking difference in median incomes among doctors who participate in at least one HMO from those who do not. Historically, doctors participating in managed-care programs have had significantly higher median earnings. While gross earnings increased equally for both groups in 1996, HMO participants enjoyed substantially smaller increases in median net earnings—largely due to the additional administrative expenses involved with managed care.

[1]Net refers to earnings after tax-deductible practice expenses and before income taxes, for unincorporated physicians. For incorporated physicians, net is total compensation from practice, before income taxes.

PHYSICIANS' MEDIAN NET INCOME AFTER EXPENSES BEFORE TAXES

Type of Physician	Median Income
All Surgeons	$215,490
Orthopedic Surgeons	258,110
Obstetric/Gynecological Specialists	207,410
Gastroenterologists	206,170
Cardiologists	240,780
Anesthesiologists	211,030
Ophthalmologists	197,430
General surgeons	185,170
All Nonsurgeons	141,840
Internists	126,410
Pediatricians	128,860
Psychiatrists	110,640
Family Practitioners	124,490
General Practitioners	105,360
All Doctors	160,740

SOURCE: *Medical Economics,* September 12, 1997. Reprinted by permission.

DOCTORS' MEDIAN OFFICE VISIT FEES, 1997

Type of Doctor	Fees for Established Patients	Fees for New Patients
General/Family Practice	$45.00	$65.00
General Internal Medicine	58.00	110.00
General Surgery	50.00	85.00
Pediatrics	50.00	65.00
OB/GYN	70.00	100.00

SOURCE: American Medical Association, *Physician Marketplace Statistics, 1997/98.* Reprinted by permission.

SALARY RANGES OF PHYSICIANS AND DENTISTS IN THE VETERANS' ADMINISTRATION

Grade	Starting Salary	Maximum Salary
Director Grade	$83,147	$103,261
Executive Grade	76,777	97,849
Chief Grade	70,894	92,161
Senior Grade	60,270	78,351
Intermediate Grade	51,003	66,303
Full Grade	42,890	55,760
Associate Grade	35,786	46,523

SOURCE: U.S. Office of Personnel Management, *Pay Structure of the Federal Civil Service 1997* (1998).

With all the current talk about controlling the costs of health care, it's not surprising that some people are convinced that there are too many doctors in the United States. In fact, predictions of a doctor glut date back to the mid-1960s, when there were fewer than 300,000 practicing physicians, or one doctor for every 625 people. By 1996, the number of doctors had more than doubled to 737,764, according to the American Medical Association, with one doctor for every 365 people. In fact, some medical experts blame the decline in doctors' incomes on a surplus of physicians: Too many doctors are competing for too few patient dollars. The Department of Labor predicts rapid growth in the number of doctors over the next ten years, since the number of medical school applicants and graduates continue to set all-time highs each year. These figures have sparked renewed calls to limit the number of doctors.

In February 1997, the American Medical Association warned that the United States was on the verge of a serious oversupply of physicians, and said that the number should be cut by at least 20 percent. The current number of medical residents, approximately 25,000, should be much lower, according to the AMA—and they proposed a reduction of federal subsidies for teaching hospitals to bring that number down.

Some argue that attempts to limit the number of doctors will exacerbate what is already an inequitable distribution of medical care. Massachusetts, for example, had 431 doctors per 100,000 residents in 1997 (a function of the many teaching hospitals in Boston), while Maryland, New York, Pennsylvania, and Connecticut each had well over 300. By contrast, Idaho, South Dakota, and Wyoming all had 200 doctors or less for every 100,000 residents. The heavy concentration of doctors in large metropolitan areas insures that people in rural and poor areas have far fewer doctors per capita and,

DOCTORS' NET EARNINGS, 1996

Category	Median Salary
By Type of Practice	
Solo	$137,610
Expense-sharing	182,040
Partnership and groups of 2 physicians	166,810
Partnership and groups of 3 physicians	174,400
Partnership and groups of 4 physicians	227,720
Partnership and groups of 5–9 physicians	211,860
Partnership and groups of 10–24 physicians	212,950
Partnership and groups of 25–49 physicians	203,690
Partnership and groups of 50 or more physicians	175,500
Single specialty groups	219,260
Multispecialty groups	162,240
By Years in Practice	
1–2	$101,260
3–5	153,410
6–10	166,590
11–20	177,940
21–30	160,230
Over 30	120,070
By Age	
30–34	$132,090
35–39	155,730
40–44	171,760
45–49	178,720
50–54	178,690
55–59	157,230
60–64	147,880
65–69	125,350
70 or over	88,830
By Managed Care Participation	
Doctor participates in at least one HMO	$169,480
Doctor does not participate in at least one HMO	$140,030

SOURCE: *Medical Economics,* September 8, 1997. Reprinted by permission.

DOCTORS' NET EARNINGS BY AREA AND REGION

Category	Median Salary
By Area	
Urban	$165,640
Suburban	166,060
Rural	156,630
Inner City	126,080
By Region	
New England (ME, NH, VT, RI, MA, CT)	$154,520
Mid-East (NY, NJ, PA)	159,550
South Atlantic (DE, DC, FL, GA, MD, NC, SC, VA, WV)	165,160
Mid-South (AL, KY, MS, TN)	172,980
Southwest (AR, LA, OK, TX)	175,100
Great Plains (IA, KS, MN, MO, NB, ND, SD)	163,210
Great Lakes region (IL, IN, MI, OH, WI)	158,000
Rocky Mountain region (AZ, CO, ID, MT, NV, NM, UT, WY)	163,540
Far West (AK, CA, HI, OR, WA)	144,490

SOURCE: *Medical Economics*, September 8, 1997. Reprinted by permission.

consequently, receive inferior medical care. Salaries are also lower in rural areas than in urban and suburban areas, thus perpetuating this imbalance.

According to the AMA, however, there is no clear indication that flooding the economy with doctors will improve this situation. They claim that government incentives for medical schools and doctors in inner cities and rural areas can be used to redistribute medical care. The federal government has already set up a National Health Service Corps to repay the medical school loans (up to $20,000 per year for four years) of any doctor willing to undertake primary care duties in rural areas known as Health Manpower Shortage Areas. Since most medical school students have $60,000 to $80,000 in loans, it's easy to understand the attraction. Funding for these incentives can come, at least in part, from a reduction of government spending on teaching hospitals, which currently subsidize the training of not only 17,000 American medical school graduates but also of 8,000 foreign national residents annually. Many in the medical establishment feel strongly that, while training for foreign medical school graduates was beneficial at a time when the United States had a shortage of doctors, it is now not only unnecessary but is harmful to our economy and to the medical industry.

MEDIAN NET EARNINGS OF DOCTORS, 1996

Net Earnings	Percent of Doctors Earning This Amount
$600,000 or more	1%
500,000–599,999	1
400,000–499,999	3
300,000–399,999	6
250,000–299,999	11
200,000–249,999	14
150,000–199,999	18
125,000–149,999	12
100,000–124,999	14
90,000–99,999	4
80,000–89,999	4
70,000–79,999	3
60,000–69,999	3
Less than $60,000	7

SOURCE: *Medical Economics,* September 8, 1997. Reprinted by permission.

To some degree, the law of supply and demand will help correct the inequity of medical care. Younger physicians are looking toward rapidly growing areas in the south and west, where the patient pool is sure to expand and where competition won't be as strong as it is in established cities like New York and Chicago. Other less obvious considerations can also affect where doctors settle. In Washington DC, for example, there are almost five times as many psychiatrists per capita as the national average. This is not a reflection of the sanity of our nation's leaders but the result of federal workers being reimbursed for psychiatric care under their medical insurance. So, add to the rule of supply and demand the fact that doctors settle where they can be sure of payment.

The number of medical specialists needed is changing as a result of the government's determination that it is specialization that drives up the costs of medicine. More and more new doctors are being steered into general practice to serve as "gatekeepers" and diagnosticians. By providing financial incentives in the form of debt forgiveness for doctors who opt for family and general practice, federal and state governments will continue to fuel this development. Despite these efforts, however, the number of specialists continues to grow. It seems that students are weighing higher salary potential against a competitive job market and deciding to take their chances.

A doctor's own business decisions also have a significant impact on earnings. Most accountants recommend that doctors incorporate to save money. Currently, about half of all doctors have done so, according to *Medical Economics*. More are expected to do so, as the financial advantages as well as the growing trend toward group practice will encourage incorporation.

Keep in mind that these are all average figures, and that a good number of doctors still earn upward of $500,000 (especially well-known surgeons, anesthesiologists, and radiologists in large hospitals). Most doctors who work on hospital staffs earn salaries greater than $100,000 (directors and chiefs of services generally earn about 25 percent more), but most also have income from outside practices and consultations.

But all such discussion of doctors' incomes can be very misleading. Just thumbing through this book will reveal that many people earn just as much or more for work that is less demanding and certainly less valuable. No money has never been, and probably never will be, the sole reason for enduring the often brutal regimentation that begins in premedical training and lasts through internship and residency, when new doctors earn $30,000 a year for working twelve to eighteen hours a day. Even after they establish a solid practice (usually not until after the age of thirty), doctors lead abnormally stressful lives. They often work twice as many hours as most people, are subjected to constant interruptions of their free time, and are always expected to win the battle against disease and death.

While greed surely afflicts some doctors, many more forsake for years or even decades the pleasures and privileges their high-income status could bring. The vast majority of doctors provide some kind of charity care, such as free or reduced-fee care to indigent patients. According to the AMA, nearly two-thirds of all doctors—but surprisingly only about half of pediatricians—participate in some form of charity care. On average, they spend three hours a week providing free care, and 3.6 hours a week providing care at reduced fees.

Physicians remain members of an occupation that continues to be held in the highest esteem. Doctors almost always rank near the top in Gallup Polls of the most respected professions (though pharmacists and clergymen usually rank higher). This fraternity also remains an overwhelmingly male enclave: 79 percent of doctors are men. A recent study of 4,500 physicians conducted by Emory University's School of Medicine reflects this male-dominated culture. More than a third of participating female doctors stated that they believe they have been sexually harassed, and nearly half said they have experienced gender-based harassment. The highest incidence of harassment occurred with young female medical students, interns, and residents. While the university noted that the numbers are likely to be reflective of young women's sensitivity to gender-related issues, they do demonstrate the continued existence of a male power structure that is often hostile toward women. Women are making inroads, though: as opposed to 21 percent overall, 36 percent of doctors under the age of thirty-five are now women. They are making similar progress on the salary front, although progress made in surgical fields has fallen off somewhat. While in 1993 female surgeons netted about 90 percent of what male surgeons were netting, in 1996 the figure was only 79 percent, according to *Medical Economics*. In nonsurgical fields, where women are twice as numerous, their net earnings are only 73 percent of what men take home. That's nearly the same as the national average for all jobs: 73.8 female cents for every male dollar in 1996, according to the U.S. Department of Labor.

About two out of three doctors are in private practice, while 20 percent work full-time in hospitals as interns, residents, or hospital-based specialists, like anesthesiologists. The remainder are engaged in teaching and research, or work for government agencies, including the Veterans Administration, National Institutes of Health, and the armed forces.

WOMEN IN MEDICINE:
A Road to Compromise

•

by Jennifer Steinhauer

By all rights, this should be the perfect time to be a woman in medicine.

The days of women toiling as a mostly unwelcome presence in the country's medical schools are long over: women now account for roughly 45 percent of all medical students, up from about 25 percent in 1980.

And once they graduate, they are in high demand: many patients, especially women, now request female doctors because, among other reasons, they are perceived as spending more time with patients. Further, women's health issues—breast and ovarian cancer most prominently—are front and center in medical research and political agendas, fostering star-studded fundraisers, road races and the like in every major city in the country.

But despite these gains, the top tiers of medicine have remained inaccessible to many women, largely, experts say, because they are unwilling or unable to find a balance between the years of study those specialties require and a life outside of medicine.

"Basically, the picture is bad," said Dr. Wendy Chavkin, editor of the Journal of the American Medical Women's Association. "Women comprise very few dean and tenured faculty positions, and there are a lack of them in surgical specialties." The main reason, Dr. Chavkin said, is that in medicine, "there are still issues about career pathways that are the least bit off track, like taking time off for child rearing."

But rather than giving up their medical careers for their families, as so many of their predecessors felt forced to do, or forgoing motherhood altogether, more female doctors today are finding ways to practice medicine part time—as some women in law, journalism, finance and other demanding fields have been doing for years.

They are joining multi-physician practices, or working as employees for practices run by managed-care companies that give them a chance for an office life that is closer to 9 to 5, willingly sacrificing higher salaries for a flexibility that until recently was virtually unheard of in medicine.

In a recent study, the Commonwealth Fund, a large private philanthropic and research organization in New York, found that 25 percent of female doctors who were surveyed said that they worked fewer than 40 hours a week, compared with 12 percent of male doctors. And 17 percent of female doctors said they worked 30 hours a week or fewer, compared with only 8 percent of males.

In New York State, the trend of women working fewer hours is borne out most dramatically among younger doctors. Over all, female doctors work 9 percent fewer hours than male doctors. But among female doctors under 45, the number jumps to 15 percent, said Edward Salsberg, director of the Center for Health Workforce Studies at the State University of New York at Albany.

"The emergence of managed care has introduced the idea that you can be an employee," said Dr. Erica Frank, an assistant professor at the Emory School of Medicine in Atlanta, and the principal investigator of the Women Physicians' Health Study, the largest national study of female doctors.

"This can mean more flexible hours and fewer of them, and the ability to think about medicine as a profession that doesn't require complete consumption," Dr. Frank said. "And clearly women are leading the way. The pay is lower. But this might be acceptable to some people to have more of a life."

Dr. Rayze Simonson works as an obstetrician in a six-person practice on the Upper West Side. The practice is run by St. Luke's-Roosevelt Hospital Center, which takes care of administrative tasks like billings, relieving the doctors—five of whom are women with children—and of some of the time-consuming hassles of running a medical office.

"The idea was that in a larger group you could balance more your life and career," Dr. Simonson said. "We are only on call every sixth night and every sixth weekend, which in ob-gyn is huge flexibility." Her husband is a journalist, and they rely heavily on a baby sitter.

Accepting Less in Pay and Prestige

Yet while this kind of work has become a welcome option for some doctors looking for more balanced lives, experts say that it has created an increasing "pink-collar" level of medicine—in which more women are concentrated in the lowest-paying, least prestigious specialties.

Indeed, while the number of women practicing medicine has more than tripled in the last 20 years, female doctors still earn roughly two-thirds of their male counterparts' salaries, largely because they work fewer hours a week and because there are far fewer of them in the most prestigious and highest-paid specialties.

Of the 34,882 female residents in the country in 1997, one-tenth of one percent were in the surgical subspecialties. Or, looked at another way, of all residents studying surgical specialties, only 17.2 percent of them were women.

And while the average male doctor in private practice in the United States makes $273,690 a year, his female counterpart makes $155,590 on average, according to Medical Economics, a trade journal. Further, 50 percent of female doctors surveyed by the Commonwealth Fund reported incomes of $100,000 or less, compared with 22 percent of men.

Although health experts, including many women, said there was still sexism in medicine, particularly in the top echelons of academia, they cited the difficulty in combining a demanding profession with a family life as the biggest hindrance most female doctors faced in rising higher in their fields.

"I think a lot of male doctors still have housewives at home," said Dr. Simonson, who has four children, one of them a newborn. "They can stay at work until 10 P.M., and when they get home, their kids are bathed and there is food in the house."

"I just don't have the luxury of staying at work late," she added, saying that means a lower income.

Outside of the financial penalties for women, there may be a loss to medicine generally when they are withheld from its top ranks.

"The gains of women help to contribute to an ongoing focus on women's health," said Dr. Karen Scott Collins, a vice president of the Commonwealth Fund. "What they bring is additional important concerns. For example, there is more focus on domestic violence as a medical problem, a lot of attention to counseling for menopause, a focus on reproductive health and so on."

Harsh Demands of Medicine

Women in other high-intensity fields face similar challenges although medicine presents conflicts for women that appear more intractable, experts said.

There are years of study and grueling hospital training programs, followed by demanding schedules and unpredictable patients. And unlike, say, investment banking, there are constant critical advances in medicine: stay out of the field for two years to raise children, and one would miss out on entire bodies of research and treatment developments vital to patients' health.

As a result, many women are attracted to pediatrics and primary care "simply because there is not as much training," said Dr. Holly Andersen, a 36-year-old cardiologist on the Upper East Side, especially since most of that training coincides with a woman's prime child-bearing years.

"Why do men care about this?" she said. "They can always marry 25-year-olds."

Dr. Gail Bauchman got her first taste of compromise in medical school in the 1980's. Although her dream had been to specialize in obstetrics, she felt that she would have a hard time managing a family life while tending to patients in labor on weekends and in the middle of the night. So she chose family medicine instead, and built a bustling private practice on the Upper West Side.

At 36, she decided to try to get pregnant. "I realized it was now or never," she said. But after she gave birth to twins, Avital and Natalia, in August 1997, compromises turned to disappointments.

She tried to return to her full-time practice, but found life unmanageable. So she looked for a part-time position. "Most practices said, 'You work full time or you don't work here,' " Dr. Bauchman said.

Her solution was to take a part-time job at the Mount Sinai Adolescent Health Center, for a fraction of her earnings as a private practice doctor. She said the situation works for her, but was hardly what she had hoped for.

"There is this problem with finding the middle ground," Dr. Bauchman said. "I shouldn't be struggling to find part-time work. And if these practices close their doors to part timers, they don't have the benefit of having a female doctor, and therefore you lose patients, because patients say that they want that."

Growing Demand for Personal Approach

Even while they are earning less on average, female physicians are more in demand than ever, experts say, particularly in specialties that cater to female patients.

Dr. Alison Estabrook, a prominent breast surgeon and associate director of the breast center at St. Luke's, remembers sitting around her family's kitchen table just a decade ago, listening to her mother's friend say that she would never let a female surgeon touch her.

Today, a female breast surgeon can "basically write her own ticket," Dr. Estabrook said. "As more women patients are seeking power in their own care they are attracted to strong women doctors," she said.

Dr. Estabrook concedes that part of the market value of female surgeons is based on supply and demand, because far fewer women than men are willing to devote their lives to surgery. "Surgery creates tremendous conflicts," said Dr. Estabrook, who is 47 and married to another doctor. She deliberately chose not to have children, she says, because she could not imagine where she could trim her professional day.

The demand for female doctors is not limited to specialties that serve women, hospital administrators say. "The minute we put a female physician in a practice," said Dr. Myron L. Weisfeldt, chairman of medicine at New York Presbyterian Hospital, "the appointment book becomes fully booked.

"It is not only women who appreciate these physicians," Dr. Weisfeldt added. "I think it deals with professional attitudes." He said that studies have shown that women tend to spend more time with patients and to focus on them as people rather than on the procedures they need.

With Children, Going Part Time

Some women find that when they become mothers, they need to scale back or forgo jobs with prestigious academic medical centers, and instead choose work in large practices, often ones that serve a high H.M.O. base.

Dr. Genevieve Lambert worked for eight years at the Bronx-Lebanon Hospital Center, mostly in the Pediatric H.I.V. unit. After giving birth to each of her two children, she cut back one work day. As she awaits her third, she has given up her career at the hospital altogether to loosen her schedule and has joined a private practice on Long Island where she works two and a half days a week and is paid per diem.

"At least half of my female friends from medical school are working part time now," said Dr. Lambert, who is 41. The women, she said, are generally not doing this willingly, but because society as a whole still makes child rearing primarily a mother's responsibility.

"Medicine is fairly egalitarian in that a woman who chooses to rise to the top of medicine can do so now," she said. "The issue of how to bring women to parity with men in the workplace is finding ways to relieve women as primary care givers to children."

Dr. Andersen, who was chief medical resident at Cornell in 1994–95 and is now one of only a handful of female cardiologists in Manhattan, said she is beginning to appreciate the conflicts she will face if she chooses to have a family.

"Being a woman in medicine, there are not that many paradigms we

can look to and say, 'This is how they did it, this is the way I can do it, too,' "
Dr. Andersen said. "You have to work on it yourself."

Source: *The New York Times*, March 1, 1999. Reprinted by permission.

LAWYERS

Toward the end of Shakespeare's *Henry VI, Part Two,* Dick the butcher, one of the rebels against the king, utters the secret wish of so many plain folk throughout Western history. When they get power, Dick says, "The first thing we do, let's kill all the lawyers." While many people in contemporary America may still share Dick's sentiments, the task grows more difficult every year as the number of lawyers continues to increase at a rate much faster than that of the general population.

In 1950, when America's population was about 150 million, about 200,000 people (98 percent of them men) practiced law here—or one lawyer for every 750 people. By 1970, the great population boom added 50 million more people to the total, only 80,000 of them lawyers. But between 1970 and 1980, when the population increased by another 20 million, the number of lawyers more than doubled: The entry of 400,000 people into the legal profession led to their being one lawyer for every 323 people. Growth in the number of law school graduates slowed in the mid-80s, then began to rise again in the late 80s and early 90s. In recent years, the growth leveled off somewhat as it became increasingly clear that there were not enough jobs to support all the prospective lawyers. The current number of lawyers working in the United States is approximately 622,000, according to the Department of Labor.

The explosion in the number of lawyers is due in large part to the fact that this can be a very lucrative profession. Median compensation for lawyers nationwide was $60,000 in 1996, more than double that of most other occupations. Lawyers' incomes are 12 percent higher even than doctors' salaries. The average 1996 law school graduate took home $40,000 in his or her first year on the job, according to the National Association for Law Placement, going a long way toward repaying law school loans.

Although the bleeding that led many firms to lay off huge numbers of lawyers during the 1991–92 recession appears to have been stanched, the effects have been felt down the line. The number of lawyers isn't yet decreasing, but the rate of increase is finally slowing. Applications to law schools dropped to 78,000 in 1995, down from 94,000 as recently as in 1991. And six months after graduation, 15 percent of 1994 graduates were still unemployed, compared with 9 percent in 1990, according to the National Association for Law Placement. The recession also led many firms outside of New York to move away from lockstep pay structures, making pay scales and bonuses more dependent on productivity and performance than simply on the number of years a lawyer has been with the firm.

Most single practitioners and small law firms deal with everyday legal problems like wills and trusts, small real estate deals, divorce and child custody, criminal matters, and incorporations. As the amount of work and money involved grows, the lawyers become more specialized and more expensive. Depending on the competition for clients, a lawyer's skill and prestige, and the complexity of the case, fees can range from $25 to $750 an hour, and vary widely even for the same work. *American Lawyer* magazine surveyed nine law firms on how much they would charge to sue a jewelry store for losing a wedding ring. The estimated costs ranged from $45 to $2,122.

A Maryland survey of lawyers' incomes ranked specialties on the basis of income; the results generally hold true nationwide. The most lucrative legal specialties, in descending order, were: labor law, insurance law, taxation, negligence-defendant, real property, corporate and business, administrative agencies, commercial bankruptcy, negligence-plaintiff, banking, savings and loan, wills, estates and probate, domestic relations, municipal government, and criminal law. Lawyers in private practices are earning more than ever while those working for the government and in teaching positions find their salaries increasing at a much slower pace. Public-interest attorneys still make the least amount—starting as low as $28,000 and topping out at $150,000.

For all the high-priced lawyers, there are still thousands trying to get along in small private practices, making an average of $25,000 or less. Even in the growing field of legal clinics, lawyers are not well paid. Jacoby and Meyers, one of the largest such clinics, employs about 300 lawyers in 120 offices in six states: Arizona, California, Connecticut, New Jersey, New York, and Pennsylvania. Initial consultation fees at legal clinics range from about $25 to $35. The simplest legal procedures, like a personal bankruptcy or an uncontested divorce, costs about $1,000.

Women and the Law

Despite significant inroads by women, the legal profession remains very much a man's world. In 1995, 23 percent of all of the lawyers in the country were women, up significantly from the 3 percent they constituted in 1971. But a Price Waterhouse survey demonstrated that female lawyers earned less than their male counterparts at every level, despite comparable years of experience, billing hours, and practice settings. And although women constitute more than 40 percent of the people entering the profession, fewer than one in five new partners is female. This may be blamed in part on choices made by women, but according to a report by the American Bar Association, plain old gender discrimination exists: Lawyers of both sexes told the ABA's Commission on Women in the Profession that women lawyers were viewed as "insufficiently aggressive, uncomfortably forthright, [and] too emotional." The extremely popular television series *Ally McBeal* can't be helping that stereotype, but perhaps the most telling statistic is that 70 percent of male ABA members, but only 40 percent of female members, believe women have equal opportunities in the profession.

Lawyers with Corporations

Over the past decade, spurred by complex litigation, high outside legal fees, and new government regulations, corporate law departments have grown by leaps and bounds. Corporate lawyers often specialize within their companies in energy, antitrust, or environmental law as well as in employment discrimination, product liability, toxic waste disposal, and pension funds. Pay at these corporations varies greatly with the kind of legal work performed and the nature of the company. For example, Philippe P. Dauman, the deputy chairman, executive vice president, chief administrative officer, and general counsel for Viacom, earned $1.1 million in 1997 plus a $2.75 million bonus. Benjamin W. Heineman, Jr., senior vice president, general counsel, and secretary at General Electric Co., makes a salary of $933,333 with a bonus of $1.1 million. In an area of the law that was once thought to be strictly the domain of those who failed to make partner at a major firm, none of these people can be said to be poor.

Lawyers with Law Firms

The highest salaries for freshly minted lawyers are traditionally paid by large law firms in the major cities: Boston, New York, Washington, DC., Chicago, Atlanta, Houston, and Los Angeles. Associate salaries have risen on the kite tails of their firm's profitability. Last year, the top salary for a first-year associate, class of 1996, was $89,000, at New York's Chadbourne & Parke L.L.P. This year, some firms have broken the $100,000-per-year mark. New York's Cleary, Gottlieb, Steen & Hamilton pays $102,000 to a first-year associate; that city's Dewey Ballantine pays $98,000 in salary and a $3,000 bonus. But to win such an offer, a lawyer must be in the top 10 percent of his or her class at one of the nation's elite law schools.

After signing on, associates usually work on a specialty like tax, labor, corporation, securities, real estate, entertainment, antitrust, estate, banking, or commercial law. After about eight years, associates are told whether or

LAWYERS' EARNINGS AND THEIR EXPERIENCE LEVEL

Associate Year	Median Base Associate Salaries by Firm Size					
	2–10	11–25	26–50	51–100	101–250	250+
First	$40,000	$52,000	$50,000	$60,000	$65,000	$71,502
Second	41,000	55,000	52,500	61,800	66,000	72,750
Third	40,000	57,750	56,000	63,800	69,000	75,850
Fourth	47,500	62,750	60,308	66,250	71,000	81,000
Fifth	53,818	69,000	66,175	72,000	76,000	86,500
Sixth	63,000	70,400	70,197	76,000	82,000	92,000
Seventh	N/A	80,000	74,750	78,000	85,000	98,000

SOURCE: *National Association for Law Placement,* 1997 Associate Salary Survey.

IN-HOUSE BASE SALARY BY LEVEL

Staff Level	Average	Median
Chief Legal Officer	$308,733	$288,483
General Counsel	$258,976	$245,000
Chief Assistant	$179,404	$175,000
Subsidiary General Counsel	$151,631	$137,286
Section Head	$144,993	$143,300
Senior Counsel	$118,144	$116,300
Expert Counsel	$114,310	$114,100
Attorney	$ 91,407	$ 90,000
Junior Attorney	$ 62,568	$ 60,934

SOURCE: Price Waterhouse L.L.P., 1997 Law Department Spending Survey.

not they have made partner. At this juncture, their salaries (which have on average nearly doubled since their first year) may jump dramatically into the high six-figure range, accompanied by better benefits and lots of prestige. As the accompanying table demonstrates, profits per partner at every law firm in the *National Law Journal*'s 1998 Salary Survey topped $200,000. And that survey didn't even include some of the most profitable New York firms, where profits per partner routinely top $1 million per year. Those who don't make partner sometimes stay on with the firm as associates, join a corporate law staff or government agency, or move to another firm.

PARTNER INCOME AT 30 LARGE LAW FIRMS

Firm Name and Principal Location	Number of Lawyers/ Partners	Gross Revenues	Profits per Partner
Baker & McKenzie	2091/509	$700,000,000	$460,000
Bryan Cave L.L.P.	545/128	173,099,000	345,000
Brobeck, Phleger & Harrison L.L.P. (San Francisco)	552/120	214,000,000	560,000
Choate, Hall & Stewart (Boston)	180/79	79,000,000	445,000
Cooley Godward L.L.P. (Palo Alto, CA)	374/100	143,996,000	505,000
Covington and Burlington (Washington, DC)	304/119	143,131,000	456,200
Dickstein, Shapiro, Morin & Oshinsky L.L.P. (Washington, DC)	230/94	90,000,000	482,000
Dorsey & Whitney (Minneapolis)	431/198	148,500,000	298,000
Dykema Gossett P.L.L.C. (Detroit)	216/97	366,207	241,616
Epstein, Becker & Green P.C. (New York)	257/79	83,000,436	387,424
Foley & Lardner	635/276	234,000,000	346,000
Gibson, Dunn & Crutcher L.L.P. (Los Angeles)	626/229	336,000,000	710,000
Hale & Dorr L.L.P. (Boston)	318/116	160,000,000	565,000

Firm			
Heller, Ehrman, White & McAuliffe	338/138	141,400,000	380,000
Latham & Watkins	823/259	421,000,000	824,000
Liddell, Sapp, Zivley, Hill & Laboon L.L.P. (Houston)	181/70	60,739,970	365,924
Manatt, Phelps and Phillips, L.L.P. (Los Angeles)	167/541	64,320,000	341,000
McDermott, Will & Emery (Chicago)	713/410	333,000,000	700,000
Nelson, Millins, Riley & Scarborough L.L.P. (Columbia, SC)	192/104	62,890,710	292,527
O'Melveny & Myers L.L.P.	605/196	284,461,000	615,300
Patton Boggs L.L.P. (Washington, DC)	242/125	83,176,000	360,000
Paul, Hastings, Janofsky & Walker L.L.P. (Los Angeles)	475/158	219,000,000	540,000
Piper & Marbury L.L.P. (Baltimore)	329/135	116,324,000	363,000
Rivkin, Radler & Kremer (Uniondale, NY)	172/20	43,600,000	360,000
Rogers & Wells (New York)	374/84	187,660,090	635,417
Schnader, Harrison, Segal & Lewis L.L.P. (Philadelphia)	191/72	61,429,000	264,000
Sills, Cummis, Zuckerman, Radin, Tischman, Epstein & Gross (Newark, NJ)	141/57	52,000,000	370,370
Sonnenschein Nath & Rosenthal (Chicago)	490/213	174,828,000	350,000
Thelen, Marrin, Johnson & Bridges L.L.P. (San Francisco)	195/99	77,500,000	375,000
Wildman, Harrold, Allen & Dixon (Chicago)	180/86	49,253,889	217,622

SOURCE: *National Law Journal,* June 1, 1998.

ASSOCIATES' SALARIES AT SELECTED LAW FIRMS

Firm Name and Principal Location	First Year	Fourth Year	Seventh Year[1]
Andrews & Kurth L.L.P. (Houston)	$66,000 plus $7,100 bonus	$74,000 plus $10,688 bonus	$100,000 plus $10,000 bonus
Brown & Bain P.A. (Phoenix)	60,000	75,000	95,000
Choate, Hall & Stewart (Boston)	83,000	113,000	117,000
Cleary, Gottlieb, Steen & Hamilton (New York)	102,000	156,000	207,000
Dewey Ballantine (New York)	98,000 plus 3,000 bonus	134,000 plus 16,000 bonus	178,500 plus 26,500 bonus
Greenberg Traurig (Miami	70,000–101,000	83,000–145,000	114,000–165,000
Holland & Hart L.L.P. (Denver)	57,000	65,500	80,000
Hunton & Williams (Richmond, VA)	73,000 plus 8–20% bonus	87,000 plus 8–20% bonus	108,000 plus 8–20% bonus
Jenner & Block (Chicago)	80,000	97,000	127,000
Lewis, Rice & Fingersh L.C. (St. Louis)	61,000 plus 3,000 stipend	64,000	67,000
Locke Purnell Rain Harrell P.C. (Dallas)	68,000	88,000–90,000	95,000–107,000
Nixon, Hargrave, Devans & Doyle L.L.P. (Rochester, NY)	55,000	63,000	74,000
O'Melveny & Myers L.L.P. (Los Angeles)	90,000 plus 5,000 bonus	110,000 plus 15,000 bonus	147,000 plus 30,000 bonus
Orrick, Herrington & Sutcliffe L.L.P. (San Francisco)	94,000	130,000	155,000
Patton Boggs L.L.P. (Washington, DC)	80,000	93,000	108,000
Perkins Coie (Seattle)	60,000	66,500–74,500	75,000–83,500
Piper & Marbury L.L.P. (Baltimore)	71,000	81,000 plus bonus	92,000 plus bonus

NOTE: Salaries include bonuses where applicable.
[1]Seventh-year associates are nonequity partners.
SOURCE: *National Law Journal*, accurate as of June 1, 1998.

SALARIES OF PROFESSORS AT SELECTED LAW SCHOOLS, 1998

Law School	Assistant Professor	Associate Professor	Full Professor
Brooklyn Law School	$95,100	$103,200	$ 129,125
Catholic University of America, Columbus School of Law	71,054	90,184	116,269
College of William and Mary, Marshall-Wythe School of Law	81,000	82,700	108,200
De Paul University College of Law	NA	74,987	94,010
Florida State University College of Law	68,048	84,286	101,684
Southern Illinois University School of Law	55,800	78,894	93,654
The University of Texas School of Law	90,067	NA	136,184
Touro College, Jacob D. Fuchsberg Law Center	NA	92,976	114,549
University of Arkansas, Fayetteville, Leflar Law Center	63,409	78,047	89,274
University of California, Hastings College of Law	77,592	90,000	114,060
University of Hawaii, William S. Richardson School of Law	61,000	70,000	83,000
University of Kansas School of Law	NA	66,566	96,336
University of Louisville School of Law	67,024	77,457	97,250
University of Michigan Law School	99,500	NA	158,000
University of Missouri-Columbia School of Law	NA	77,093	106,646
University of Nebraska College of Law	63,500	NA	108,576
University of Pittsburgh School of Law	50,006	76,495	104,964
University of Wisconsin Law School	68,970	80,577	97,030–100,480
Villanova University School of Law	NA	87,000	138,200
Wayne State University Law School	72,301	87,438	106,495
Median salary	**$62,600**	**$ 72,000**	**$ 91,600**

SOURCE: *National Law Journal*, accurate as of June 1, 1998.

SALARIES OF ATTORNEYS GENERAL IN SELECTED STATES, 1998

State	Entry-level Position	Attorney General
Alabama	$ 32,968	$115,695
California	38,400	107,100
Florida	25,000–31,000	110,263
Idaho	32,500	75,000
Iowa	32,947	96,484
Maine	33,280	81,827
Mississippi	32,000	90,800
Missouri	27,500	93,000
New York	33,922–38,749	110,000
South Dakota	33,000	71,972

SOURCE: *National Law Journal,* accurate as of June 1, 1998.

SALARIES OF PUBLIC DEFENDERS IN SELECTED CITIES, 1998

City	Salary Range
Anchorage, AK	$44,916– 92,844
Dallas	32,498–118,300
Denver	34,188– 84,516
Great Falls, MT	38,593–118,400
Honolulu	35,000–130,000
Los Angeles	33,534–118,400
Madison, WI	37,087– 93,108
Sacramento, CA	38,400–129,149
St. Louis	30,400–118,400
Trenton, NJ	39,588–129,149

SOURCE: *National Law Journal,* accurate as of June 1, 1998.

SALARIES OF PROSECUTORS IN SELECTED COUNTIES, 1998

County (Major City), and State	Salary Range
Cape and Island Districts, MA	$25,000– 95,710
Door County, WI	37,087– 65,494
Dutchess County, NY	35,658–104,000
11th Judicial District, TN	27,864– 94,864
Humboldt County, NV	46,679– 76,540
Jefferson County, KY	23,000– 81,210
Johnson County, TX	35,000–110,000
Lackawanna County, PA	23,680–108,898
Multnomah County, OR	43,242– 90,064
Orange County, CA	51,813–126,214
Orleans Parish, LA	30,000–104,904
U.S. Attorneys	**$ 118,400**
Assistant U.S. Attorneys	**$35,800–109,000**

SOURCE: Department of Justice Public Affairs Office, Washington, D.C. Salaries are for 1998.

SALARIES OF CITY ATTORNEYS IN SELECTED CITIES

City	City Attorney	Assistant City Attorney
Buffalo, NY	$ 75,036	$48,566–60,413
Cincinnati	120,000	34,000–84,500
Des Moines, IA	112,375	42,258–79,419
Los Angeles	117,684	47,272–63,099
Miami	125,000	40,000+
Mobile, AL	Contractual	43,344–67,248
New York	136,990	41,121–70,000
Saginaw, MI	72,238	41,205–52,196
Salt Lake City	105,699	57,000–90,180

SOURCE: *National Law Journal*, accurate as of June 1, 1998.

SALARIES OF LEGAL SERVICES LAWYERS, 1995

Service and Location	Staff Attorney	Executive Director
Idaho Legal Aid Services (Boise)	$22,000–27,000	$ 59,000
Ohio State Legal Services (Columbus)	28,782+	86,872
New Hampshire Legal Assistance (Concord)	25,570–50,750	53,000
Legal Aid Society of Metro Denver (Denver)	29,052–61,209	84,000
Nevada Legal Services (Las Vegas)	36,700–45,900	100,000
Legal Services Corp. of Alabama, Inc. (Montgomery)	24,196+	64,938
Legal Aid Society of Middle Tennessee (Nashville)	25,500+	67,853
Legal Aid of Western Oklahoma (Oklahoma City)	24,398+	71,021
Western Kentucky Legal Services	24,000+	50,000
Prairie State Legal Services Inc. (Rockford, IL)	26,000–43,000	90,000
Advocates for Basic Legal Equality (Toledo, OH)	28,000–54,000	80,000

SOURCE: *National Law Journal,* accurate as of June 1, 1998.

SALARIES OF PUBLIC INTEREST LAWYERS

Organization and Location	Starting Salary	Top Salary
Center for Individual Rights (Washington, DC)	$36,000	$ 85,000
Center for the Community Interest (New York)	30,000	80,000
Chicago Lawyers Committee for Civil Rights Under Law	33,800	104,000
Equal Justice Initiative of Alabama (Montgomery)	28,000	31,000
Media Access Project (Washington, DC)	40,000	80,000
National Abortion and Reproductive Rights Action League (Washington, DC)	32,000	105,000
National Center for Youth Law (San Francisco)	32,500	80,000
Native American Rights Fund (Boulder, CO)	48,061	116,513
Pacific Legal Foundation (Sacramento)	30,000	150,000
People for the American Way (Washington, DC)	28,000	90,000
Public Citizen Litigation Group (Washington, DC)	27,000	74,000
Southeastern Legal Foundation (Atlanta, GA)	40,000	70,000
Workplace Project (Hempstead, NY)	28,000	34,000

SOURCE: *National Law Journal,* accurate as of June 1, 1998.

Legal Assistants (Paralegals)

Whatever kind of legal document you need—a will, a contract, a separation agreement—chances are that if you go to a law firm for the service, the legal work will be done not by a lawyer but by a legal assistant. Legal assistants, also known as paralegals, perform all the same duties as lawyers except setting fees, giving advice, signing up new clients, or trying a case in court.

About 113,000 people are currently employed as legal assistants, and thanks to the mushrooming demand for legal services, the field is growing rapidly. The Bureau of Labor Statistics ranks it as one of the fastest-growing professional occupations in America, and projects growth that is much faster than the average between now and 2006. The supply of paralegals has finally caught up to the intense demand for their services. So while the number of openings for legal assistants will continue to increase rapidly, competition for the jobs will be keen over the next decade. Whereas a significant number of currently employed legal assistants have only an associate's degree, there seems to be a trend toward more educational background as competition for these jobs grows.

According to the National Association of Legal Assistants, most job opportunities will be in major cities where the largest private law firms are centered. There will also be a great demand for paralegals in the federal government, especially in the Departments of Justice, Treasury, Interior, Health and Human Services, and in the General Services Administration. While the majority of paralegals are employed directly by law firms or by government agencies, there is a growing trend toward the use of contract paralegals. As a result, an ever-increasing number of paralegal firms are appearing—which place workers in law firms or agencies during busy periods.

The chief reason for the popularity of paralegals in both the public and private sector is economics: Paralegals can do most of the same work as lawyers, but for a lot less money. Even the most inexperienced first-year associate earns more than double what a paralegal earns in an hour. The more work performed by paralegals, the greater the savings a firm can pass on to its clients.

Specifically, paralegals help draft legal documents like wills, mortgages, divorce papers, and trusts. They perform legal research; organize, index, and summarize documents and files; prepare different types of tax forms; draft organizational documents for corporations; and assist in all aspects of pretrial work for criminal and civil cases. Some paralegals are generalists, working on a civil case disposition one day and writing a brief for a felony trial the next. At large law firms, paralegals tend to specialize (as do lawyers) in one area, like real estate, labor law, litigation, corporate law, estates, or trusts. So prevalent is the use of paralegals that twenty-five states now have guidelines delineating the types of work they may and may not perform.

More and more people who work as paralegals are going through some kind of postgraduate training program, which can last anywhere from a few months to four years. The number of these programs is growing as rapidly as the profession—from about 300 in 1993 to more than 800 today. The American Bar Association has approved 214 of these programs; graduates of such certified programs clearly have an advantage when it comes to finding jobs. In addition, the National Association of Legal Assistants offers a certification program culminating in a two-day exam. Salaries of paralegals certified by this test are about $2,000 higher on average than other legal assistants.

While paralegals don't earn wages comparable to those of lawyers, they can eventually make a good living. According to the Labor Department, salaries nationwide averaged $32,900 a year; starting salaries averaged $29,300. A few senior paralegals, who manage entire departments in a big corporate firm, earn upward of $50,000. The federal government paid paralegals $44,400 on average in 1997. Paralegals also received an average bonus of $1,900 per year, in addition to life and health insurance benefits. Employers of most paralegals also contribute to retirement or pension plans on their behalf.

Many large corporations have set up a paralegal services function within their law departments. According to the Administrative Management Society, the person in charge of that area is known as a "Legal Assistant Services Manager," and he or she is usually in charge of planning and coordinating the use of the paralegals, training new employees, and motivating and evaluating the entire staff.

IV

Science and Technology

Over the past fifty years the American economy has created hundreds of thousands of jobs for scientists, engineers, and computer experts. Virtually everyone who entered these fields after securing a college degree found a good job and began a rewarding career. Even in the early 1990s, when a short but harsh recession led to cutbacks in federal funding for scientific research and a reduction in business investment made life difficult for new engineers, the career problems for these talented people were greatly exaggerated. Despite many reports in the media describing the difficulties scientists and engineers were experiencing, unemployment rates for these groups remained at less than 2 percent in most parts of the country. Today, in the surging economy of 1997–99, a college degree in a technical specialty virtually guarantees the holder a first-rate, good-paying job.

Most of the occupations in this section are concerned with the practical—that is to say, business—applications of mathematical and scientific laws and theories. Whether these laws are applied in an established and venerable field such as civil engineering or in a new field like environmental engineering, the one common denominator of all those in these fields is a high level of intelligence and intellectual curiosity. The salary levels for jobs in science and technology do not seem to give recognition to this requirement for higher than average brainpower, however; rather, salaries seem to move strictly by the laws of supply and demand. For instance, a drop in the price of oil to under $15 a barrel will have the predictable effect of putting many petroleum engineers out of work. Likewise, events have cooled the demand for nuclear fuel and, with it, the prospects for nuclear engineers, although by the year 2020, few would be surprised if nuclear power generation were to make a comeback. In the meantime, environmental science and technology promises to be the fastest growing area of opportunity through the turn of the millennium.

The moral of the story is that aspiring engineers and scientists with high earnings expectations should pick their fields with a view toward ones that are likely to grow, because a degree in science or engineering is not necessarily a ticket to a lifetime of high earnings. In fact, while engineers and scientists tend to receive higher starting salaries than other college graduates, they do not, on average, earn more throughout their careers. Many reach a moderate earnings plateau relatively early in their working lives. This may be partly due to the fact that many in the field are project-oriented and do not relish the supervisory and managerial roles that come with higher pay. It may also be that the caricature of the absentminded scientist is at least partly true: Many very good scientists are not very good at the practical requirements of running a business. In this day of high technology, those who are good may end up running great ventures; however, whatever the case may be, the first priority of scientists and engineers is their science and their work, which they usually do very well and without due recognition. For instance, the accomplishments of the Hubble Space Telescope in beaming back pictures from the deepest recesses of space are viewed rather matter-of-factly by most, illustrating that our society takes its scientific community largely for granted.

THE DISCIPLINES OF SCIENCE

The popular view of the American scientists is based on well-known caricatures. In the movies, or on television, scientists are usually depicted as absentminded or evil-minded, muddleheaded or pigheaded. If they are Americans, they are portrayed as easygoing but brilliant; Germans, humorless but brilliant; Russians, devious but brilliant. Whether their motives are humane or sinister, scientists are always shown to be in awe of their subject and of their own extraordinary powers. Skillful writers can blend all of these elements to reflect the ambivalent feelings most Americans have toward scientists.

On the one hand, our respect for scientific work borders on reverence, an attitude fostered by our early leadership in atomic and nuclear weaponry. But this reverence is tempered by our fear that scientists may have unlocked powers that could lead to our own destruction. Add to such fundamental misgivings a strong dose of ignorance concerning scientific methods and aims, and our ambiguous position becomes more understandable. How these factors might affect the relatively low compensation rates for scientists seems never to have been explored.

Only some 500,000 people in America are professionally engaged in nonmedical scientific activities. Many of these are in universities where they teach or do research and are paid under their school's established salary scale. Even at the best schools this means less than $100,000 a year for full professors. (See the section "University and College Professors," in Part 1.) Some top-level researchers at prestigious institutions such as MIT and Cal Tech may control millions of dollars in federal research funds, but their personal compensation remains—at least according to the public record—based on their university salaries.

In the following pages are salary figures for scientists in private industry and public utilities, as well as in state and federal government. Although scientists are paid well at every level, their salaries should be compared to those in other occupations that require the same amount of educational experience (lawyers, accountants, and engineers, for example). This may lead some readers to raise questions about the way work is rewarded in America: Why, for example, do top-level chemists and physicists make less than junior partners in large accounting firms? Should the work of the lawyer be better rewarded than that of the scientist?

It is certainly not within the province of this book to offer answers or to make recommendations regarding such questions. But it is necessary to point out what, in our opinion, are clear-cut inequalities in pay structures. Salaries of scientists are sure to increase over the next decade, but whether they will reach the same levels as some jobs requiring less training and education remains to be seen.

Scientists' Salaries: An Overview

The range of salaries associated with a specific level—say, the entry rate for a scientist with a bacheor's degree—is somewhat narrow; the choice of scientific discipline, however, should not depend on anticipated earnings as much as on personal desire. This narrow range of salaries exists especially in the early years of a career. Later, the differences become almost entirely a function of personal professional worth and employer need.

With this in mind, an excellent summary is available in the form of an annual publication prepared by D. Dietrich Associates, Inc., of Phoenixville, Pennsylvania, entitled *Survey of Scientific Salaries*. They have surveyed almost 10,000 scientists in both private industry and the federal government in virtually every part of the country. The table that follows summarizes some of their findings. They categorize scientists into eight levels—from the new college graduate to the department head.

A Scientist I is someone with a bachelor's degree and no experience. Scientist II includes those with one year as a Scientist I, or no experience and a master's degree. A Scientist III is a Scientist II after about one year's

Title	Average Salary	First Quartile	Median Salary	Third Quartile
Scientist I	$26,912	$25,020	$28,140	$30,760
Scientist II	33,287	30,700	35,402	38,230
Scientist III	39,880	35,969	41,027	44,784
Scientist IV	49,425	41,900	46,350	55,147
Scientist V	58,936	48,540	53,560	63,073
Scientist VI	69,312	57,480	62,640	74,837
Scientist VII	86,638	65,800	74,774	90,000
Department Head	93,349	79,500	86,200	98,350

AVERAGE ANNUAL SALARIES OF SCIENTISTS BY LEVEL OF RESPONSIBILITY

SOURCE: D. Dietrich Associates, Inc., Phoenixville, PA, Copyright © 1996.

experience, or a Ph.D. with no experience. A Scientist IV is one who has been the equivalent of a Scientist III for a year or two and has begun to prove himself capable of independent efforts with little to no day-to-day technical supervision. A Scientist V is recognized as an expert in his field—he usually supervises a small group of lower-level professionals and contributes to higher-level decisions. A Scientist VI supervises Scientists I through V and has considerable responsibility for directing complex tasks. A Scientist VII makes decisions and recommendations on an authoritative level and is a leader and authority in his company. The Department Head provides overall supervision with regard to the technical, administrative, and scheduling aspects of the major programs in the company.

Chemists

Most chemists hold jobs in teaching, research, sales/marketing, and production/inspection. A bachelor's degree is needed for most positions in teaching or research. Over the next decade, the job outlook for chemists is especially good in fields related to energy, pollution control, and health care.

There are four main fields of specialization: *analytical chemists* determine the structure, composition, and nature of substances and develop new techniques; *organic chemists* study the structure of all carbon compounds; *inorganic chemists* study compounds other than carbon; *physical chemists* study energy transformations to find new and better energy sources.

At this time, there are about 92,000 chemists in the United States. Approximately 20,000 of them are in teaching. The rest work for manufacturing firms, state and local governments, as well as the federal government (especially the Departments of Defense, Health and Human Services, and Agriculture).

With no experience, a chemist with a bachelor's degree can expect to start in the federal government at about $25,000; with a master's degree, at about $30,000; and with a Ph.D., at about $45,000. The annual average salary in the federal government for experienced chemists is $60,000. The average starting salary in the private sector is $40,000 with a bachelor's. With experience, a bachelor's degree brings about $49,000; a master's $56,000, and $71,000 for a Ph.D.

Salaries of chemists in private industry are always included in an annual survey of pay conducted by the Bureau of Labor Statistics (BLS). Above are figures based on the salaries of over 40,000 chemists classified according to job levels as defined by the BLS. Generally speaking, these levels are based on experience, complexity of tasks, and supervisory responsibilities. Levels I and II, for example, are beginning positions in which chemists do routine testing and, although they may have the help of technicians, do not directly supervise anyone's work. Chemists at Levels III and IV, by far the largest number in the survey, are experienced employees who have specialized knowledge and who are expected to show "ingenuity" in evaluating unexpected problems. Chemists V and VI are the beginning of the supervisory chain of command where problem-solving and "originality" are the key elements of the job; these people frequently head small teams of researchers. At Level VII are chemists who in large companies, supervise an entire segment of research; in smaller companies, they supervise the entire program. Others at this level are recognized as outstanding "creative" researchers who select problems and then supervise their analysis and solution. Level VIII chemists are usually top supervisory people, probably part of the upper echelon of management; not surprisingly, the government could not obtain sufficient salary data for this level.

Geologists

Geology is the study of the structure, composition, and history of the earth's crust. Most geologists' work centers on judging the suitability of construction sites and locating oil and other minerals and, to a lesser degree, predicting the possibility of earthquakes and their probable magnitudes. There are about 49,000 geologists in the United States today. Approximately 33,000 work in private industry, 6,400 work in the federal government, and 10,000 teach in colleges and universities. The outlook is good, since new energy sources must be found and waste disposal sites and methods must be realized; but job growth will be about average for all occupations.

The main branches of geology are earth materials, earth processes, earth history, and what can be called new fields. There are several subdivisions of each. *Economic geologists*, for example, locate various minerals and solid fuels; *petroleum geologists* attempt to find oil and natural gas; *mineralogists* analyze and classify minerals and gems by composition and structure; *geochemists* study the chemical composition and changes in minerals and rocks; *palynologists* locate oil deposits by studying tiny organic fossils.

Geologists concerned with earth processes study the varied forces in the earth. *Volcanologists* study active and inactive volcanoes; *geomorphologists* study such forces as erosion and glaciation.

Among the earth historians, *paleontologists* study plant and animal fossils found in geological formations; *geochronologists* determine the age of geological formations by the radioactive decay of their elements; *stratigraphers* study the distribution and arrangement of sedimentary rock layers.

New jobs in geology include the *astrogeologist*, who studies the geological conditions on other planets, and the *geological oceanographer*, who studies the sedimentary and other rock on the ocean floor and continental shelf.

In private industry (e.g., oil companies, mining companies, construction firms), starting salaries average about $38,000 per year with a bachelor's degree, and $45,000 with a master's. The federal government (e.g., the Department of the Interior and the Bureau of Mines) start those with bachelor's degrees at about $32,000 per year, those with master's at about $36,000, and those with Ph.D.s at about $40,000. The average salary for geologists in the federal government is $60,000.

Life Scientists

Life scientists are so called because they study all aspects of living organisms. Most life scientists have jobs in zoos or botanical gardens, or are involved in medical research and food and drug testing. A bachelor's degree is at best an introduction to the field; a master's is the minimum requirement for most positions; and a doctorate is a necessity for advanced work.

The main branches of life science are the agricultural, the biological, and the medical. In most cases, however, life scientists take their job titles from the type of organism they study and by the activity they perform. Here are some examples:

The *botanist* deals primarily with plants and their environment; the *agronomist* is concerned with the mass development of plants by deriving new growth methods or by controlling diseases, pests, and weeks; the *horticulturist* works with orchard and garden plants.

Zoologists study the various aspects of animal life—its origin, behavior, and life processes. *Animal scientists* do research on the breeding, feeding, and diseases of domestic farm animals. *Anatomists* study the structure of organisms, from cell structure to the formation of tissues and organs. *Ecologists* explore the relationship between organisms and their environments. *Embryologists* study the development of an animal from a fertilized egg through the eventual birth. *Microbiologists* study microscopic organisms such as bacteria, viruses, and molds. *Physiologists* examine the various life functions of plants and animals under normal and abnormal conditions. *Toxicologists* and *pharmacologists* study the effects of drugs, gases, poisons, and other substances on the functioning of tissues and organs. *Pathologists* study the effects of diseases, parasites, and insects on human cells, tissues, and organs. *Health physicists* study the effects of toxic substances and nuclear radiation on humans and other animals, and direct employers in the proper safeguards in the use of both.

There are about 150,000 life scientists in the country today. The agricultural sciences employ about 28,000; the biological sciences about 61,000; forestry and conservation sciences about 24,000; and the medical sciences about 27,000. About 24,000 are employed in teaching, while 52,000 work in government, especially in the Department of Agriculture. The remainder are employed in private industry, mostly in pharmaceutical, chemical, and food-processing firms.

Starting salaries in the federal government are about $24,000 to $30,000, and $45,000 with a bachelor's, master's, and doctorate, respectively. Private industry pays less than 10 percent higher for life scientists; there is a slight salary bias toward the biological over the agricultural sciences. The outlook is good for those with advanced degrees, especially in environmental fields, but quite poor for those with only a bachelor's degree.

Physicists

Physics is the study of the mathematical nature and structure of the universe and the interaction of matter and energy in it. Most people in the field do some form of research. An advanced degree is virtually a necessity; those with only a bachelor's usually go into a related field such as engineering. All nonteaching physicists specialize in one or more specific branches. Some concentrate on the basic forces and particles in nature. These are the nuclear physicists, the atomic physicists, the elementary particle physicists, the molecular physicists, the plasma physicists. Some deal with a bigger picture. These specialize in optics, acoustics, fluids, electricity, magnetism, or thermodynamics.

There are about 22,000 physicists in the United States today, about 14,000 of whom teach and about 4,000 of whom are in private industry (manufacturers of chemicals, electrical equipment, aircraft, and missiles) and a few, less than 4,000, with the Department of Defense. The outlook is less than favorable for advanced-degree physicists in research and development.

In private industry, a physicist with a master's degree and no experience will start at about $40,000 per year; a Ph.D. will start at about $55,000. In the federal government, starting salaries are about $30,000, $33,000, and $45,000 per year for physicists with bachelor's, master's, and doctoral degrees respectively; the average salary for an experienced physicist in the federal government is $72,000. In private industry, the average is about $80,000.

INTERDISCIPLINARY SCIENCES

Just as there are many subdivisions of each category, so there are many overlappings. Paradoxically, as specialization becomes the way of the world in science, that community has become more and more aware of the interactions among all scientific disciplines.

Biological Scientists

Biological scientists study living organisms and the relationship of animals and plants to their environment. Most of the 62,000 people in this occupation specialize in some area such as ornithology (the study of birds) or microbiology (the study of microscopic organisms). About half of all biological scientists work in research and development.

According to the College Placement Council, beginning salary offers in private industry to bachelor's degree recipients in biological science averaged about $27,000 a year in 1998. Biological scientists in the federal government averaged $52,000 a year in 1998. Only 10 percent of biological scientists earned over $70,000 in 1998.

Geophysicists

Geophysicists study the composition and physical aspects of the earth and its electric, magnetic, and gravitational fields. A bachelor's degree is usually sufficient to embark on a career in some branch of geophysics. The main branches of the field are the specialties of those who devote themselves to the solid earth, the fluid earth, the upper atmosphere, and other planets. *Exploration geophysicists* use seismic prospecting techniques to locate oil and other minerals; *seismologists* study the earth's interior and vibrations caused by man-made explosions; *geodesists* explore the size, shape, and gravitational field of the earth and other planets. *Hydrologists* study the distribution, circulation, and physical properties of underground and surface waters. *Geomagneticians* study the earth's magnetic field; *paleomagneticians* study the past magnetic fields from rocks or lava flows. *Planetologists* study the composition and atmosphere of the moon, planets, and other bodies in the solar system.

Increasingly, all of these occupations are becoming known under the umbrella term *geoscientists,* which more accurately describes these scientists' roles in studying all aspects of the earth.

There are about 48,000 geophysicists or geoscientists in the United States today. About 20,000 of them are in private industry, especially in the petroleum and natural gas fields, and some are in mining or in private consulting. The rest are with the federal government as part of the U.S. Geological Survey, the National Oceanic and Atmospheric Administration (NOAA), or the Department of Defense. Starting salaries in private industries are $30,000 per year with a bachelor's degree; $35,000 with a master's degree; and $45,000 with a Ph.D. In the federal government, starting annual salaries for all geologists in managerial, supervisory, and nonsupervisory positions was $50,000; for all geophysicists, it was $55,000; for all hydrologists, it was $47,000; and for oceanographers at NOAA, it was $55,000.

Meteorologists

Meteorology is the study of the atmosphere, its physical characteristics, motions, and processes, and the ways it affects the rest of the physical environment. Meteorologists usually work at jobs related to weather forecasting, air-pollution control, and prediction of climatic trends. Meterologists who are devoted to the weather are called *synoptic meteorologists,* those devoted to research are *physical meteorologists,* and *climatologists* study the general trends of climate.

There are about 6,100 meteorologists in the United States today. Approximately 1,000 of them work in colleges and universities; private industry (e.g., airlines, weather consulting firms, meteorological instrumentation companies) employs about 3,000. The rest are employed in the federal government, mainly by NOAA.

In the federal government, an inexperienced meteorologist with a bachelor's degree can expect to start at $22,000 to $24,000 per year; with a master's degree, $30,000, and with a Ph.D., $42,000. An experienced meteorologist with the federal government will earn about $60,000 per year. Private industry starts meteorologists about 20 percent higher for each degree, and the annual salary range for experienced meteorologists is $60,000 to $70,000 per year. The outlook for meteorologists with advanced degrees is good, with jobs at the National Weather Service and in private industry expected to grow. The outlook for those with less than advanced degrees is poor.

Oceanographers

Oceanography is the study of the movements, physical properties, and plant and animal life of the oceans. Oceanographers usually hold jobs in fisheries development, mining and ocean resources, and weather forecasting. The minimum degree employable is a bachelor's, though a master's is preferable, and a Ph.D. is often required for high-level jobs.

There are two main branches of oceanography—biological and physical. *Marine biologists* study plant and animal life in the ocean; *limnologists* study freshwater aquatic life. *Physical oceanographers* study the physical properties of the ocean, such as waves, tides, and currents; *geological oceanographers* study the ocean's underwater mountain ranges, rocks, and sediments; and *chemical oceanographers* study the chemical composition of ocean water and sediments, as well as chemical reactions in the sea.

There are only about 3,600 oceanographers in the country today, more than half of whom teach in colleges and universities. About 700 are employed by the federal government (the U.S. Navy and NOAA); the rest are in private industry, and state and local fisheries. The annual average salary of an oceanographer in the federal government was about $60,000 in 1998. The immediate outlook for employment in oceanography is not very good, with most openings being limited to replacement of those who are retiring.

Agricultural Scientists

Agricultural scientists study farm crops and animals and develop ways of improving their quantity and quality. They have played a vital part in the country's ever-rising agricultural productivity. Agricultural scientists normally practice in one of the following specialties: *agronomy*—the study of how crops grow; *animal science*—the study of livestock and poultry; *food technology*—the study of the chemical, physical, and biological nature of food; *horticulture*—the study of fruits, vegetables, and plants; *soil science*—the study of the characteristics of the soil; and *entomology*—the study of insects and their relation to plant and animal life.

There are over twenty-five thousand agricultural scientists in the United States today. According to the College Placement Council, beginning salaries for graduates with a bachelor's degree averaged $27,000 to $30,000 in

1998. The average agricultural scientist employed by the federal government earned $60,000 in 1998.

JOB OPPORTUNITIES FOR SCIENTISTS

The job outlook for scientists will depend partly on two powerful and contradictory trends. On the one hand, the United States remains a highly technological culture dependent in many ways on its scientists' expertise. On the other hand, in the early 1990s, U.S. investment in research and development (R&D) declined for the first time since the 1970s, and only in 1998 were there signs that this trend would be reversed. With the economy in high gear and the forces of globalization moving quickly to form overseas markets, U.S. business leaders have begun to increase the amount of money that goes to R&D.

Certain specific fields will be affected more than others. According to Betty Vetter, executive director of the Commission of Professionals in Science and Technology, the most promising fields are electronics, lasers, and biotechnology: "There's particularly intense excitement in the biological sciences, especially with the new work in genetic engineering." In addition, she said that growing concerns about the natural environment will prompt scientific research and applications to solve problems of pollution and resource depletion.

Chemists—Although the government predicts that only 1,000 *new* jobs will be added annually through 2005, job opportunities should be strong for the field overall for these reasons:

- The number of degrees granted in chemistry will not meet future demand.
- Research and development will greatly expand.
- Demands for environmental protection will require increased attention from industry.
- The chemical industry is much healthier today than it was ten or fifteen years ago.
- Demand for innovative pharmaceuticals, biotechnology, and other technological breakthroughs will increase.

Geologists and Geophysicists—In the past, most of this country's geologists have generally worked for the petroleum industry. Low oil and gas prices during the past decade have consequently suppressed need for scientists in this field. The U.S. Bureau of Labor Statistics anticipates that employment for geologists will grow only as fast as the average for all occupations through the year 2000. However, any substantial increase in oil and gas prices will create strong incentives for petroleum corporations to hire scientists once again. In addition, other job opportunities may occur in areas of groundwater monitoring, toxic waste management and cleanup, and geophysical research into other environmental issues.

Physicists and Astronomers—Slightly fewer than half of the nation's physicists are academic faculty members; the rest work for independent research and development laboratories; for the federal government; and for aerospace firms, electrical equipment manufacturers, engineering service firms, and the automobile industry. The job outlook for scientists in all these areas appears to be moderate. Many physicists—both academic and nonacademic—received their degrees during the 1960s and thus will approach retirement late in the present decade. On the other hand, the end of the Cold War and subsequent cuts in the U.S. defense budget has meant cutbacks in weapons-related R&D, with obvious implications for physicists in related fields.

Biological Scientists and Biotechnologists—Of the approximately 100,000 biological scientists in the United States at the previous decade's end, roughly one-half held faculty positions in colleges and universities. Some 40 percent of the nonfaculty scientists work for federal, state, or local governments; most of the rest work for commercial or nonprofit research and development labs, hospitals, or the drug industry. For all these job categories, the job outlook is unusually bright. Biotechnology remains one of the most innovative fields anywhere in the sciences. Recombinant DNA and other techniques promise breakthroughs in agriculture, the pharmaceutical industry, medicine, and the environment. Most job growth will occur in the private sector.

Meteorologists—The overall outlook for scientists in this field is good for two main reasons. First, the National Weather Service, which employs most U.S. meteorologists, plans to increase its hiring during the next ten years. Second, the private sector will create many new jobs in response to needs for private weather forecasting services by farmers, commodity investors, transportation and construction firms, and radio and TV stations.

Agricultural Scientists—Over 40 percent of nonfaculty agricultural scientists work for federal, state, or local governments. Nonacademic agricultural scientists in the private sector generally work for commercial research and development laboratories, service companies, wholesale distributors, and seed or food products companies. The job outlook for agricultural scientists is good for several reasons: Enrollments in related curriculums have dropped considerably in recent years; a disproportionate number of current workers will be leaving the workforce; and advances in biotechnology will heighten the need for employees within the private sector.

ENGINEERING

•

by *Robert L. Spring*

Plato, in his *Theaetetus,* called a person with a hyperactive sense of wonder a potential philosopher. He never used the term "scientist." But a pure scientist is not so different from a philosopher. They both must have started with and retained that same inquisitive sense of wonder. While the philosopher is content to remain in the abstract, however, the scientist has an urge to scratch away at the concrete. The philosopher sticks with "roundness"; the scientist talks of spheres and elliptic hyperboloids.

The pure scientist gets closer to the world, but he still never quite talks about the one that we know. He's concerned with atoms and potential energy and entropy and relative time, and he is perfectly content to wallow there as long as he can prove his own theories and disprove everybody else's. A pure scientist has no more desire to build a bigger bridge or a smaller computer than the philosopher wants to quantify the electromagnetic forces binding the nucleus of the niobium atom. But they both wonder "why?"

While the philosopher and the pure scientist are questioning everything, a distant cousin is asking fewer questions and concentrating on answers. This person is known as the applied scientist. To the layman, applied science must sound redundant: What good is science if you cannot apply it? The applied scientist takes the world of the pure scientist and blends it with that of the layman. The applied scientist gave us television, stereo, and nuclear power; he quickened our travel, air-conditioned our homes, and put a man on the moon. An applied scientist is an engineer, the one who works to put it all together. He designs what the scientists say *can* work and the layman says should work.

In recent years, engineers have been regarded as saviors and killers, and everything in between, depending on where and when you went to school, who you voted for, and how much and which of the media you believe. During the 1960s, they were the golden boys who would help us catch up with the Russians; later they were the geniuses needed, as Tom Lehrer explained, to put "some clown on the moon." But during the Age of Aquarius people noticed that the air was becoming visible, and the water walkable. Anyone who smelled of "establishment"—and the engineer did—took the brunt of the blame. The 1970s then saw the advent of environmental engineering, especially as related to power engineering. The 1980s saw the power or energy production field as, in one way or the other, a major employer of engineers. It is certainly a rather large microcosm of the engineering world in general with respect to kinds of engineers employed and salaries paid. The 1990s have been a bleaker decade for a variety of engineers. None of the traditional fields are booming, and most are streamlining and concentrating on maintenance, good operations, and plant life extension. Environmental engineering is experiencing a major comeback and fire protection engineering has bloomed as a major new field.

But first, what is engineering? The *Encyclopedia Britannica* offers an excellent definition: Engineering is "the professional art of applying science to the optimum conversion of the resources of nature to benefit man." You may be surprised to see the word "art" in the brief, carefully worded definition, and most engineers would be too. Consider, however, a broader sense of "art" and "science." Science is an organized body of knowledge derived through observation of cause and effect; art, a systematic application of knowledge or skill in effecting a desired result. An engineer is as dependent on his judgment and imagination for solving problems as he is on his knowledge of physics, chemistry, mathematics, etc. The engineer must be both a scientist and an artist. He must possess the store of technical knowledge or science but he must also be imaginative enough to apply it to a particular problem as needed. And it must be done, as our definition above states, as an optimum application and benefit to man.

For example, automobiles would be fancier and cheaper if no safety factors were included; on the other hand, they could be built with near-zero risk inherent in their use if an astronomical price tag could be placed on them. In the simplest of considerations, safety here is played against cost until a mixture is realized that is salable to the public and profitable to the seller. Social factors, economic factors, and health and safety factors must in all cases be interwoven with technical expertise to yield a final design. The engineer must weigh the importance of all these factors, plus a host of others (deadlines, regulations, resource availability, etc.) and play them against each other until the final product is the optimal blend.

So, essentially, the engineer exists to take the world of science, which is nature itself, and somehow apply it to accomplish a particular effect and to satisfy a particular need. The engineer does not generalize; he particularizes.

Let us hypothesize. In the suburbs of a very large American city, it has been forecast that, in ten years, more electrical power will be needed. Along with the lawyers, the politicians, the executives, and the other relevant people, the engineers are called in for expert advice and opinions. Society has a need and the engineers must come up with a solution. Build a power plant to supply, let's say, 1,000 more megawatts of electricity to the existing system serving Newburbia. The site must be found—an easy job if the plant is invisible and undetectable, in everyone else's backyard, and rates will not go up. What kind of fuel will be burned? Oil? Coal? Uranium? In the old days the engineers had a good deal of influence in this decision. Today, it's minimal, but they contribute technical support to the political, legal, environmental, and economic determination.

Now the Environmental Impact Statement must be written—and these have been known to fill small rooms. Plant design gets under way. Turbines, pumps, relays, boilers, thousands of feet of piping, tubing, wiring. The specifications are very complex: Is the equipment safety-related? Environmentally related? What special "extras" are needed? If it's a coal plant, design accessible storage space. If oil, ditto. If nuclear, make it capable of withstanding an earthquake, a tornado, a tsunami (seriously). There are still controls and instrumentation, redundant fail-safe components, inspections, quality assurance, fire protection, security, waste treatment, and, for coal or nuclear plants, waste packaging and shipment.

Now the structures must be built to house all this. What kind of flow do we put in to hold up a multiton turbine? The transmission lines must be designed to get the power where it's wanted. Don't forget the beautification plan and the permits and licenses and public-hearing testimony and checks and rechecks, and paper, paper, paper. The engineer survives and has, in turn, succeeded despite the "system."

Continuing within the framework of the example above, hundreds of engineers of various disciplines must be called on for their routine and not-so-routine problem-solving capabilities. Today's complex needs and desires demand a high degree of coordinated, specialized expertise. An individual can no longer stay abreast of rapid changes in a plethora of technological fields. He must concentrate on one aspect of engineering and stay more than superficially aware of what's going on in related fields; he can afford interest in unrelated fields little more than as a hobby. This was not always so.

In the distant past, in what not only Charlemagne but Caesar, Homer, and even King Tut would call the old days, there was civil engineering. The earliest engineer whose name has survived to our times was a civil engineer; he is Imhotep and he designed and supervised the construction of the Step Pyramid complex (a tomb plus associated temples and other buildings) for the third dynasty Egyptian pharaoh Djoser, also known as Horus Neterirykhet. That was 4,500 years ago; we still only theorize how it was all done. In later life Imhotep became a philosopher and was eventually deified.

Some Descriptions of Engineering Titles

Imhotep probably did all the conceptual work for Djoser's pyramid himself. He didn't consider himself a civil engineer—he was an engineer, a fulfiller of man's (albeit a man's) desire or, as the case may have been or appeared, need. He had a knowledge of physical science and the ability to apply that knowledge to a particular need. Granted, he needed only limited know-how; awareness of atomic structure would not have yielded a better pyramid, and, of course, it didn't have to fly or stay afloat. For thousands of years, civil engineers provided their citizenry, and coincidentally, later generation, with the Sphinx in Egypt, the temples and "well-walled" cities of ancient Greece, the Coliseum and the aqueducts of Rome, the castles and cathedrals of medieval Europe, and more.

By the nineteenth century, the Industrial Revolution expanded the range of engineering to include mechanical engineering and, even later, chemical engineering and electrical engineering. Further hierarchies of specialization now include petroleum engineering, metallurgical and materials engineering, industrial engineering, and mining engineering. Each of these fields again splits up into more and more specialized branches of engineering.

To meet the needs of today, they all must work together, each on that aspect of the job for which he has been educated and trained but with knowledge of his own limitations and his fellow engineers' contributory efforts. Not only can no one branch of engineering expertise result in a finished product such as an automobile, a power plant, a spaceship, or even a fully functional modern office building, but the degree and complexity of the specialized knowledge needed for any of them is such that only a person skilled in a particular engineering discipline can, in truth, be beneficially utilized.

To get all of these highly trained experts to work together without getting in each other's way, without overemphasizing their own discipline and without ignoring important concerns outside their own area of expertise, is the job of *project engineer,* or *coordinating engineer.* He must have overall knowledge of what must be done, by whom, in what order, and on what detailed schedule. He could have been educated in any of the engineering fields of specialization; he should be experienced enough to have seen many projects come to fruition, successfully and unsuccessfully; he must possess at least superficial knowledge of the functions of all the disciplines that will be used. He must keep the mechanical and electrical engineers working on the same goal.

The *mechanical engineer* designs engines and motors and the turbine mentioned before. He sizes and lays out pipes that are needed to transport water, air, fine powders, or hghly viscous liquid metals from one place to another for one reason or another. He considers the temperatures and pressures that he must deal with and finds or designs equipment with materials that are not only compatible but most efficient.

The *electrical engineer,* in as simple a statement as possible, is concerned with the most efficient way of getting electric power from one place to another. We've all seen transmission lines, electric circuits around the house, and maybe the insides of our televisions or stereos. They were all designed by the electrical engineer. He may not know what electricity is. He may not even care. But you can be sure he knows *how* it works. There's a lot of what he does that we've only heard of, such as supplying power to the instruments on the likes of the *Apollo* project, recovering from a widespread urban blackout (what the utility business calls a "system disturbance"), and arriving at what we used to call an electronic brain.

The *civil engineer,* as mentioned above, gets things built. He takes on structures such as the Empire State Building, the Eiffel Tower, the Golden Gate Bridge, and the Statue of Liberty. Why don't these structures fall in a good wind, a small earthquake, or a plane crash? Because of the civil engineer. We never see much of what he does. The steel structure in a building of any size is designed by him. Such a problem varies in complexity: How do you do it on the San Andreas Fault? Did you know that the World Trade Center towers sway? How must you build a wall or a floor if it's half a mile under the Pentagon and it's supposed to withstand an all-out nuclear attack?

According to some people, much of this technology we've been talking about is polluting the earth. This is partially the realm of the *chemical engineer,* who takes the world of the chemist and utilizes his own artistic talents to apply it to the problems and needs of the everyday world around us. He knows that the water and the air can be made cleaner, and he knows how to do it. The chemical engineer does not concern himself solely with the cleanup, but he applies his technology to satisfy our whims and needs in ways that do not pollute the environment.

The other branches of engineering are, for the most part, smaller subsets of those we have been discussing. *Petroleum engineers* are specialized chemical engineers. *Environmental engineers* come from a variety of education backgrounds, especially chemical and mechanical engineering. They devote their efforts to air and water quality as well as to land use. *Metallurgical* and *material engineers* are mechanical engineers who study the internal structure of matter to be sure that materials are utilized to their fullest capabilities efficiently, and, more importantly, that they are not misused in design. *Aeronautical* and *astronautical engineers* do for planes and rockets and other space-travel components what *marine engineers* do for ships. Airplanes must be lighter than air; boats must be lighter than water; rockets must be able to counteract gravity for a sustained period of time. An important subdivision of mechanical engineering is *HVAC Engineering.* The letters stand for Heating, Ventilation, and Air-conditioning. If your office is like most, and the Arts Center works great in December and is like a sauna in August, call up the HVAC engineer, who will explain how wonderfully it's designed and how poorly it's maintained. Not all temperature control is for the comfort of humans in office buildings. The HVAC engineer also works on computer rooms, museum displays, and spacecraft habitability.

Nuclear engineers, like environmental engineers, come from various engineering backgrounds. Many have been educated in physics or chemistry; more are mechanical, civil, or electrical engineers devoted to the design and/or operation of nuclear power plants. A combination of on-the-job training and further specialized education prepares them for the work. A fewer number are educated at the bachelor's level in nuclear engineering. The primary reason for the need of expanded training is that nuclear radiation inherent in such a heat source must be contained to the plant with no adverse health effects on the public or plant operating personnel. A nuclear engineer is, de facto, a nuclear *safety* engineer.

Fire protection engineers combine the talents of a variety of engineering disciplines. The fire protection engineer designs fire detection and suppression systems, is instrumental in providing fire prevention measures, and is often involved with the preparation of and compliance with relevant insurance and government codes and regulations. He evaluates the fire resistance of barriers such as walls and floors and will place limits on combustibles to be stored or used in specific sections of structures. Some of the tools of the fire protection engineer are mathematical modeling, computer simulation, and full-scale testing.

The list of engineering categories could go on forever—both legitimate categories and spurious ones. The trend is not to be a joiner of an existing engineering field but to invent a new field that is specifically devoted to your purposes. Some are abstractions like *process engineer, applications engineer,* or *systems engineer,* others pinpoint the function with titles like *traffic engineer, mining engineer,* and, believe it or not, *low-level nuclear rad waste engineer.* A purist may argue, but these are legitimate. Despite the fine-tuning of categorization, they are all engineers. They have been trained to be engineers by reason of their education and/or their job functions. Not so with many that are inaccurately called *engineers* by employing euphemisms such as *sanitary engineer,* who is in fact a plumber; *operating engineer,* who is a crane operator; and the *security engineer,* who is a night watchman or sells padlocks. Honorable professions all, but call them what they are and reserve the title *engineer* for those who do *engineering.*

An engineer has a college or university degree or the equivalent. These days, that pretty much means he *has* a college degree—a bachelor's, master's, or a Ph.D. The degree is usually called some kind of engineering as the field discussed above, but not always. Physicists, chemists, and mathematicians have been known to "turn engineer," and at least a few major schools give a Bachelor of Applied Science degree for what most would call engineering. The significant thing is that the college-level training with certain basic coursework is there.

An engineer must be well trained in math. It is the language of science and engineering. Arithmetic and basic algebra are not sufficient; calculus is needed. The physical sciences are essential. General physics, electricity, magnetism, atomic structure, optics, statics and dynamics, thermodynamics, and general chemistry are basic. Elective courses provide the specialization necessary for the specific degree, such as electrical, civil, mechanical, etc.

Salaries of Engineers

Let's consider the engineer working as an engineer—no line supervisory responsibilities, no commissions, just the salaried engineer.

In 1998, he or she came out of college with a bachelor's degree and started at about $40,000 a year. The successful companies paid more; the poorer ones paid less. The span ran from about $30,000 to around $45,000. Theoretically, there was a small range in each company in which to take care of the top student, middle student, and the poorer student that no one admits to having a policy of hiring. Most come in at the high end of the range allowed by each company. In 1998, the entry rate at what we'll call the Sunshine Electric Utility, a large metropolitan supplier of electricity generated by nuclear and fossil fuels, was about 15 percent higher than it was three years before. This pretty much held true throughout the industry. Career Services officials at top-notch schools like RPI, MIT, and Columbia report that $50,000 was not an uncommon salary offer to graduates in 1998.

Engineers have done well over the years, but very few go on to extraordinary high salaries. With the exception of the aftermath of the *Apollo* Project fiasco and the relatively gloomy situation today, engineers have rarely lacked for their choice of jobs at a living wage. The salaries are competitive, but at the imaginary utility, the quasisocialist benefits add to the picture. Engineering salaries do and will continue to go up year after year. Today, new engineers just out of school do better against inflation in terms of yearly increases. Experienced engineers stay above water, but barely. Let's not lose perspective: They do better in absolute magnitude than many, probably most, occupations, but they are not by any stretch of the imagination living off the gravy. They work for the money they bring home; they're dedicated, so they often put in more hours than they are theoretically paid for; but, as we've said, they do make a living wage, and they will do better than many. In 1998, an engineer who has been at it for five years, probably at the same company, was earning anywhere from $45,000 to $60,000 a year.

A very significant point is that one can very easily become an engineer and advance little over the years in terms of salary. An engineer who does not do good engineering will not get good raises, and rightly so. On the other hand, a hotshot will do better. It's not a union job (yet); engineers are not paid for merely surviving. They must produce. They must use imagination. They should have good representation skills. They must be able to tackle a job and come to a conclusion—not just a technically feasible one, but a safe, economical, and practical one. In every sense, the better an engineer is at this art, the better the financial reward. If more than good engineering talent is shown, he or she will go on to supervisory engineering work. As with other professions, this means seeing a bigger picture. Time spent behind the computer is minimized. Supervising means managing and handling people more than numbers. The well-roundedness of the engineer is called on to its fullest. A few more bucks are involved; on the average, say 30 to 40 percent more than the good, not the best, engineer will see. In 1998, engineers with managerial responsibilities averaged about $100,000 per year.

A little summary: Engineering can be a rewarding profession. It will pay well. It can pay very well. It is not a millionaire-maker. It can, however, lay the groundwork for getting there. There's nothing or, at least, very little, that is automatic about it. A poorly planned education and/or a poor performance on the job will result in a lower but fair salary. Get that good education or make up for it later and apply common sense, sound engineering technology, imagination, good judgment, and decision-making ability, reasonable presentation skills, and the rewards will be there—monetary rewards, the rewards of internal self-satisfaction, and a feeling of professionalism.

At this time the demand in many disciplines for newly graduated, inexperienced engineers is well below average. Employment in the engineering industry traditionally follows a "peaks and valleys" course. Recall that the engineer is called on to fulfill a need or desire of a segment of society at a particular time. Such needs and desires naturally fluctuate, so engineering opportunities and salaries, while not likely to see absolutely depressed conditions, will vary with economic circumstances.

Aerospace Engineers: Average staring salary is $36,000
After five years, the average salary for aeronautical and astronautical engineers is about $44,000 and after ten years about $50,000. With a master's degree, their salary does not tend to increase much, if at all, with five to ten years of experience; a Ph.D. will earn about 15 percent more than lesser degrees in this field. According to the Bureau of Labor Statistics, 73,000 aeronautical and astronautical engineers work in the United States today. A booming field thirty years ago, few young people are entering this field now, a situation that will make them a highly sought after commodity in the event of a surge in the U.S. aerospace program, which might be a while off due to reduced federal budgets.

Chemical Engineers: Average starting salary $43,000
After about five years working as a chemical engineer, one with a bach-

elor's degree earns about $50,000 yearly; after ten years a similarly educated chemical engineer with little to no supervisory responsibilities earns about $63,000. A master's degree does not appear to increase these figures significantly. One extra year of work brings a raise equivalent to the differential awarded the higher degrees. A Ph.D., however can expect to earn 15 to 20 percent more than either. There are now about 50,000 chemical engineers in the United States. The chemical engineer will be assured of steady, interesting, and challenging work in the years ahead by reason of the large effort directed toward the minimization, cleanup, and eventual disposal—or, ultimately, recycling—of toxic wastes, and the development of synthetic fuels.

Civil Engineers: Average starting salary $36,000
A typical civil engineer without an advanced degree earns about $43,000 annually after five years in the field; after ten years, about $55,000. An advanced degree will mean a higher starting salary (usually about 10 to 15 percent) at the beginning of a career, but after a few years it has little, if any, economic effect. There are about 199,000 civil engineers in various industries in the United States today. Until the day when all buildings are built and we need no more or better roads or bridges or subways, etc., the civil engineer will be as needed as ever. New materials, and the problems of constructing modern architecture in the future's high-population-density, limited-space environment will provide sufficient challenge to novices.

Electrical and Electronic Engineers: Average starting salary $41,000
After working for about five years as an electrical engineer with a bachelor's or master's degree, one earns about $50,000 per year. A Ph.D. in electrical engineering earns about $55,000 about five years after obtaining his degree. After ten years, these salaries increase to about $55,000 and $60,000 respectively, assuming no supervisory resonsibilities. There are approximately 427,000 electrical/electronic engineers in the country today; this is by far the largest single engineering field in the United States—over 25 percent of all the engineers working in this country today are electrical or electronic engineers. Electricity is with us, and will be for quite a while, so those who can design the most efficient and progressive systems have a secure and profitable future.

Mechanical Engineers: Average starting salary $38,000
A mechanical engineer with no advanced degree and about five years of experience is earning about $47,000 annually; a master's degree picks this up a little but not much; a Ph.D. does less than would be expected, earning about $55,000 after an equivalent time since earning

the bachelor's degree. After ten years, the Ph.D. seems to make about $63,000, while the lesser degreed ones make about 10 percent less, or about $57,000 a year. Mechanical engineers are plentiful—the Bureau of Labor estimates that about 233,000 of them are working in the United States today. The outlook is, as it has been for years, very good. Despite what seems like a nuclear and electronic age, the mechanical engineer still tells us how to make things go. Most of our life continues to depend on mechanical goods; we just plug them in nowadays instead of wind them up.

Metallurgical and Materials Engineer: Average starting salary $39,000

After five years in one of these fields, one's salary is about $44,000 to $48,000, the higher figure more reflective of those with master's degrees. A Ph.D. is earning slightly more but has been working somewhat less than five years. After ten years, the metallurgical or materials engineer with a B.S. is up to about $55,000, with a master's to about $60,000 to $65,000, with the metallurgical engineer on the high side and the material engineer on the low side; the Ph.D. in either would not be much higher. All of this assumes no supervisory responsibilities. There are about 18,000 metallurgical and materials engineers in the United States today, and the field has been increasing of late. In aerospace technology, and now certainly in the power production field, among others, materials are being used under pressures and temperatures so high that metallurgists and material engineers have their work cut out for them indeed.

Nuclear Engineer: Average starting salary $38,000

After about five years in the industry, a nuclear reactor engineer's salary is up to about $43,000 to $46,000; after ten years, this increases to $56,000. Advanced degrees affect starting salaries as much as 10 to 15 percent but appear to have little direct effect on salary as the years of experience increase. There are about 18,000 nuclear engineers in the country today. In the early seventies, they were a highly sought-after commodity. The accident at Three Mile Island and the enormous publicity that followed had brought a flood of new regulations and, along with it, more jobs and higher salaries for the relatively few who could fill them. That same accident, however, virtually halted new orders for reactors and cancelled many existing ones, and the disaster at Chernobyl made things worse. As a result, nuclear engineers not employed by utilities or by the Nuclear Regulatory Commission are not faring very well in this relatively depressed job market.

Petroleum Engineer: Average starting salary $43,000

   After five years of professional experience, a petroleum engineer is earning about $53,000; after ten years, about $67,000 per year. The difference in salary between a bachelor's degree and a master's is not apparent; a doctorate, however, is worth about 15 percent in terms of higher salary for nonsupervisory work. There are about 17,000 petroleum engineers in the United States today, 5,000 fewer than five years ago because the United States could not compete with lower priced foreign oil. The long-term trend may be away from oil in electric power production, but the transportation industry alone will support an enormous domestic petroleum industry, and prices should rise sufficiently to bring back a resurgence in the production of U.S. oil.

Fire Protection Engineer: Average starting salary $37,000

   This is a relatively new engineering discipline, and information on salaries of veteran fire protection engineers is sparse. At this time, a bachelor's degree commands a starting salary of about $30,000 to $37,000, and a master's would start at $37,000 to $42,000. There are about 3,000 fire protection engineers in the United States today, and the number is growing at a faster than average pace. Opportunities exist for fire protection engineers in industries such as insurance, power, automotive, chemical, construction, government, etc. The outlook is excellent since the supply is still small and the demand is growing rapidly.

Engineers in Private Industry: A Government Survey

Every year the U.S. Bureau of Labor Statistics surveys a wide variety of jobs in private industry. The study delineates various levels of experience and achievement for each occupation and provides detailed job descriptions and salary information for all levels. For engineers, eight levels are recognized in the survey. Here's a brief summary of the government's descriptions:

Engineer I—This is the entry-level of professional work, requiring a bachelor's degree in engineering and no experience.

Engineer II—A continuing developmental level. Person performs routine engineering work requiring application of standard techniques, procedures, and criteria in carrying out a sequence of related engineering tasks. Requires work experience acquired at an entry-level position or appropriate graduate-level study.

Title	Average Salary	First Quartile	Median Salary	Third Quartile
ANNUAL SALARIES OF ENGINEERS IN THE PRIVATE INDUSTRY				
Engineer I	$35,044	$31,750	$34,200	$ 36,400
Engineer II	39,575	35,800	38,532	42,130
Engineer III	46,344	41,808	45,357	48,870
Engineer IV	53,182	47,252	52,759	57,242
Engineer V	60,910	55,230	60,912	66,549
Engineer VI	70,924	64,376	71,160	76,755
Engineer VII	80,053	70,000	80,700	89,190
Engineer VIII	83,986	76,004	84,151	95,200
Department Head	90,842	79,326	89,665	103,000

SOURCE: D. Dietrich Associates, Inc., *Fall 1996 Engineering Salaries Survey,* Copyrighted 1996. Reprinted with permission.

Engineer III—Independently evaluates, selects, and applies standard engineering techniques, procedures, and criteria, using judgment in making minor adaptations and modifications. Assignments usually include one or more of the following: equipment design and development, test of materials, preparation of specifications, process study, research investigations, and report preparation. Sometimes supervises or coordinates the work of drafters and technicians.

Engineer IV—Plans and conducts work requiring judgment in the independent evaluation, selection, and substantial adaptation and modification of standard techniques, procedures, and criteria. Devises new approaches to problems encountered. Work requires a broad knowledge of precedents in the specialty area and a good knowledge of principles and practices of related specialties. Usually works with only general supervisory instructions, and may oversee the work of a few other engineers.

Engineer V—Applies intensive and diversified knowledge of engineering principles and practices in broad areas of assignments and related fields. Makes decisions independently on engineering problems and methods and represents the organization in conferences to resolve important questions and to plan and coordinate work. Supervises, coordinates, and reviews the work of a small staff of engineers and technicians.

Engineer VI—Plans and develops engineering projects concerned with unique or controversial problems that have an important effect on major company programs. Plans, organizes, and supervises the work of a staff of engineers and technicians. As an independent researcher, he or she often serves as a specialist in advanced theories to the entire staff.

Engineer VII—Makes decisions and recommendations that are authoritative and have an important impact on many engineering activities. Individuals have demonstrated creativity, foresight, and mature engineering judgment in anticipating and solving unprecedented engineering problems, determining program objectives and requirements, organizing programs and projects, and developing standards and guides for diverse engineering activities. Directs several subordinate supervisors or team leaders.

Engineer VIII—Makes authoritative decisions and recommendations that have far-reaching impact on extensive engineering activities. Negotiates critical and controversial issues with top-level engineers and officers of other organizations and companies. Often supervises the entire engineering program of a medium-sized company or an important segment of an extensive engineering program within a large corporation.

Department Head—Provides technical and administrative supervision, insuring that technical, administrative, and schedule targets of the department are met in accordance with professional standards, design control procedures, and engineering design guidelines.

Job Opportunities for Engineers

Not too long ago, the outlook for today's 1.5 million engineers was not so much mixed as it was murky and confused. Because of the collapse of the Soviet Union and the slow but inevitable reduction of America's bloated defense budgets, thousands of engineering jobs, especially those in aerospace, were lost, but extraordinary economic growth in the mid-1990s has made job opportunities better than ever. In addition, the passage of a gargantuan transportation bill in 1995 and a highway restoration bill unleashed tens of billions of federal dollars to local economies and created many jobs for civil engineers, design engineers, and the like.

According to many experts, the most promising fields for engineering at the turn of the century will be those related to the protection of the environment. Literally tens of thousands of engineering jobs are being created for the management of solid waste, the cleansing of toxic waste sites, as well as the monitoring and controlling of industrial pollution. (Of course, older engineers will remember that in the 1960s, nuclear power was the place to be, while in the 1970s, petroleum engineers were in the greatest demand, both fields with limited demand today.) According to the Association of Environmental Engineering Professors, the universities are currently producing only about 2,000 of the 5,000 new engineers needed each year in this field. Employment opportunities exist throughout the country in both private industry (including the large corporations involved in oil exploration, chemical production, and several major environmental engineering firms such as CH2M Hill in Denver as well) and at the federal, state, and local levels of government as the enforcement of stricter pollution laws becomes essential for our future. Even the recent assault on environmental regulation launched by conservative Republicans in Congress has not reversed public opinion about this issue.

Chemical engineers will also benefit greatly from the "green movement." Many industries will be looking to chemical engineers to provide environmental experts, corrosion experts, etc., to supplement their staffs in the future.

For mechanical engineers the job market also looks encouraging, although the Bureau of Labor Statistics believes that most opportunities will result from the need to replace many retiring engineers rather than from the creation of new jobs. Not surprisingly, then, most of the literally hundreds of ads for mechanical engineers we found in 1998 were for those with five or more years of experience.

While the outlook is not exuberant, there are more employment opportunities for experienced electrical and electronics engineers than for most other engineering disciplines. The power industry—utilities, independent power producers, and their suppliers—has been stagnant for some time, but some parts of the country are hiring. Two other strong fields for electrical engineers include medical electronics and telecommunications.

Aerospace engineering and the companies devoted to it are as depressed as one would expect given diminishing defense and space-related budgets. It will be a while before these industries recover and become strong sources of employment, but it will happen.

The nuclear engineering field, which employs a wide variety of engineering disciplines, as well as those with nuclear training and experience, has been in a lull but is starting to bounce back. The power reactor business has, over the last twenty-five years, been the principal employer of nuclear engineers. However, since no new units have been ordered since the Three Mile Island accident and several under construction have been cancelled, licensees (the owners and operators of the reactors) have not increased their need for nuclear engineers except in the areas of operations and maintenance. They have, however, maintained that need for a high-quality engineering staff, since safety and downtime are of vital importance.

The Nuclear Regulatory Commission (NRC), the overseeing regulator of the industry, has been seeking and hiring engineers in anticipation of the retirement of existing personnel who joined them in large numbers in the 1950s and 1960s, when the business was starting in earnest, and then again in the 1970s, when a multitude of engineers became available at the end of the *Apollo* Project.

Within the next five to ten years, the NRC expects a rebirth of activity in the regulatory arena due to the need to review plans for new units of a standardized design as well as applications for renewal of existing forty-year licenses, which will start to expire around the turn of the century. Both these activities will require a large resource allotment by the NRC and the utilities as well as by contractors to both.

The Department of Energy is also seeking to hire nuclear engineers for both the cleanup of the waste generated by government reactors used to produce weapons-grade material and for safe, renewed operation of reactors (e.g., the Savannah River in South Carolina) to be used for such in the future.

Engineering Technicians, Science Technicians, and Drafters

The ever-increasing importance of science and technology in all areas of the workplace has helped to create a strong job market for engineering technicians, science technicians, and electrical and electronic technicians. These people assist scientists and engineers in research and development of various equipment by setting up experiments and calculating results. Technicians in production test product quality and monitor procedures. Some work as manufacturers' field reps, advising buyers on the installation or maintenance of complex machinery. Others simply sell or service the equipment.

Engineering and science technicians usually require a post–high school training, often in a technical institute or a junior or community college. Many receive on-the-job training while serving in the armed forces. Others, especially science technicians, attend a four-year college.

Related to the work of science technicians and engineers is drafting. Drafters prepare detailed drawings from the rough sketches and specifications made by scientists, engineers, architects, and designers. They are also expected to specify materials to be used, procedures to be followed, and any other information needed to carry out the job. Drafters usually specialize in a particular field, such as mechanical, electrical, aeronautical, civil, or architectural drafting.

Applicants for drafting positions are expected to have two years of post–high school training in a technical institute, or a junior or community college.

Some receive their experience in the armed forces. Pertinent courses for a career in drafting include mathematics, physical sciences, and mechanical drawing, with some training in engineering and industrial technology a plus.

Increasingly complex design problems associated with the information age will greatly increase the demand for drafting services in the coming decade, although some say this growth may be offset by the rising use of CAD (computer-aided design) systems, which cut down a drafter's work time. So far, however, the predicted layoffs have not for the most part occurred, and drafting remains a field worthy of serious consideration.

Below are salary figures compiled by D. Dietrich Associates for drafters at five different levels. Drafter I works under close supervision, traces or copies finished drawings, and makes revisions. Drafter II prepares drawings of simple, easily visualized parts or equipment from sketches or marked-up prints. Drafter III prepares various drawings of parts and assemblies, including sectional profiles, irregular or reverse curves, hidden lines, and intricate details. Drafter IV prepares complete sets of drawings that include multiple views, detail drawings, and assembly drawings. Drafter V performs unusually difficult assignments requiring considerable initiative, resourcefulness, and drafting expertise.

Job Descriptions for Drafters

DRAFTING/DESIGNER POSITION CLASSIFICATION DESCRIPTIONS

Drafting, Apprentice—Trainee assignment to learn the basic drafting skills and techniques.

Drafting, Level I—Entry level with high school drafting training or other appropriate basic-level drafting experience. Copies sketches, layouts, and drawings prepared by others.

Drafting, Level II—Entry level for individual with some specialized technology relating to drafting or engineering such as associate degree or experience as Level I. Copies detailed plans and drawings.

Drafting, Level III—Experienced draftsperson able to perform nonroutine and complex drafting assignments that require the application of standardized drawing techniques. Works independently with occasional advice from supervisor and may direct the efforts of less experienced draftspersons.

HOURLY WAGE RATES FOR DESIGNERS AND DRAFTERS, FALL 1996

Title	Average Hourly Rate	First Quartile	Median Salary	Third Quartile
Drafting				
Level I	$ 9.74	$ 7.83	$ 8.50	$10.91
Level II	10.55	9.50	10.96	12.57
Level III	12.74	11.30	12.65	14.70
Level IV	15.40	13.32	15.21	16.53
Drafting Supervisor	15.54	14.22	15.20	20.36
Designer				
Level I	$16.19	$14.65	$15.86	$16.55
Level II	17.92	16.00	17.76	19.54
Level III	20.01	18.78	19.66	21.34
Level IV	25.36	21.20	24.16	26.32
Design Manager	26.52	23.31	26.44	29.17
CAD				
Applications Analyst	$21.13	$18.25	$22.00	$23.32
Autographics Supervisor	20.46	17.50	20.46	23.60
Lead Operator	17.68	16.30	17.70	20.09
Senior Operator	16.69	13.00	16.05	18.27
Operator	13.28	11.92	13.30	14.90
Assistant Operator	10.44	8.82	9.74	12.39
Clerk	10.13	8.80	9.50	11.08

SOURCE: Dietrich Associates Inc., Phoenixville, PA. Copyrighted 1996.

Drafting, Level IV—Involved in planning the graphic presentation of complex items having distinctive design features that can differ significantly from established drafting precedents. May recommend minor design changes. May direct the preparation of drawings by other drafting personnel of lesser experience.

Drafting Supervisor—Coordinates the work activities of a group of five or more drafters of various levels of capability to ensure that time schedules and quality of work are maintained. Works with professional staff in scheduling work and assigning drafting support staff to their projects. Normally requires an experienced drafter with ten or more years of experience.

Designer—Involved in application of engineering fundamentals to engineering design; will select and recommend procedures in design and prepare preliminary designs for engineer's approval. Works independently on design projects in support of design engineer and will often coordinate drafting efforts on projects.

Senior Designer—A designer with significant years of engineering experience and proficiency.

COMPUTER-AIDED GRAPHICS DRAFTING GROUP CLASSIFICATION DESCRIPTIONS

Application Analyst—Explore, develop, and administer electronic graphics coupled with associated data for the production of design computer drafting. Train and assist workstation users in drawing techniques, input sketch preparation, clarification of standards, drawing verification, and revision and checking of output. Requires degree in engineering graphics or associate degree with four years of computer graphics experience.

Supervisor, Autographics—Responsible for quality and productivity of subordinate operators and the review of work for conformance to standards. Implements new methods and procedures. Provides coordination of operations with source departments for equipment utilization, drawing development, and work processing. Requires three to five years of computer graphics experience with drafting or graphics course work at technical school or college level.

Lead Operator, Autographics—Provides supervisor with assistance in maintaining efficient daily operations by resolving problems of other operators and handling difficult operating tasks. May analyze incoming material and develop drafting methods for most efficient production. Should have three years of computer graphics experience with some applicable technical schooling.

Senior Operator, Autographics—With minimal supervision will operate autographics input station using digitizer, console unit, disk storage, and preprogrammed material to develop finished drawings. Able to maintain and increase proficiency in operations and recommend new methods and procedures. Accuracy, quality, completeness, and schedule adherence can be independently maintained at this level of experience. Requires two to three years of experience in computer graphics, with some technical schooling.

Operator, Autographics—Under general supervision will operate with proficiency autographics input station using digitizer, console units, disk storage, and preprogrammed material to develop finished drawings. Can analyze sketches, notes, and other input material to determine best approach to complete drawing. Will operate plotter to transfer developed drawings from disk or tape storage to reproducible medium. Responsible for input-output of drawings from mag tape and/or disk. Requires one and a half to two years of computer graphics experience with some technical schooling.

Assistant Operator, Autographics—Under close supervision and instruction will learn proficiency in operation of autographics input station. Assignments should progress in difficulty as proficiency is increased. All work at this level will be fully reviewed and checked. Requires one year of drafting experience.

Clerk, Autographics—Responsible for logging in/out work requests and maintaining all records and files of work requests. Maintain files and records within the group and provide typing and clerical skills of competent proficiency.

COMPUTER TECHNOLOGISTS AND PROFESSIONALS

Computer technologists and professionals are among the most sought-after workers in the nation today. While the early 1990s were marked by a downsizing trend among large high-tech employers such as IBM, recent years have shown explosive growth and a rising shortage of qualified applicants.

According to *The New York Times,* in January 1998, some 200,000 to 400,000 jobs in the computer software industry were vacant because of a lack of skilled applicants. This void is likely to worsen as an increasing number of software and Internet start-up companies appear in the marketplace. As a result of the shortage, many companies are offering extremely high salaries and perks to potential employees in order to hire them and keep them from being stolen by the competition.

There are two primary reasons for the shortage of workers in the computer industry. The first is the obvious increase in demand for computer professionals. The growth of the industry has spread the pool of qualified professionals very thin—it is no longer only large software companies that are hiring. The emergence of the Internet and related companies, as well as the transition that almost all major corporations have made into the world of databases and networks, have created intense competition among employers.

The second, more troubling, reason is the reduction in students specializing in the field. *U.S. News and World Report* stated that the number of college graduates receiving a degree in computer science dropped 43 percent between 1986 and 1994. The explanation for this drop is not entirely clear—but many blame the downsizing at the beginning of the decade for discouraging students from choosing computer science as a career. Others point to the grueling and antisocial nature of the work. An average workday for a programmer consists of long hours in front of a computer monitor, writing endless strings of code, suffering from eyestrain, boredom, and a lack of human interaction. Those who love programming defend their work by explaining that job satisfaction comes from the thrill of "solving a puzzle"—of "outsmarting the computer." Unfortunately, this thrill isn't enough for everyone—and it is clear that the number of jobs in computer programming will continue to outnumber qualified applicants in years to come.

Industry leaders and economists have expressed such concern that this situation will lead to the United States falling behind other countries in the high-tech industry that President Clinton has promised to allocate some $28 million to pay for training and promoting the computer industry as a career choice.

In 1998, Congress and the president pushed through a bill enabling tens of thousands of foreign workers with expertise in computer technology to emigrate to the United States almost immediately. Most experts doubt that even this strategy will be able to fill the growing demand for so-called IT ("Information Technology") workers.

According to the U.S. Department of Commerce, by the year 2006, the nation will need 1.3 million more computer scientists, systems analysts, and computer programmers. Here's the breakdown:

Job	Jobs in 1996	Vacancies in Existing Jobs	New Jobs	2006 Employment
Computer Scientists and Engineers	506,000	34,000	520,000	1,026,000
Systems Analysts	427,000	33,000	485,000	912,000
Computer Programmers	568,000	177,000	129,000	697,000

The law of supply and demand will continue to drive up salaries for all these jobs. As more and more corporations expand their demands for computer services, the Information Technology expert will reap substantial benefits.

Where the Jobs Are by Region

Given the growth in the high-technology industry, jobs in this field can be found virtually anywhere. There are still some stand-out regions of the country, however, that are particularly dense with high-tech companies. Silicon Valley, the region in California between San Francisco and San Jose, remains the biggest employer of technology professionals. Despite some setbacks resulting from industry resizing—this area has proven to be resilient—riding the waves of evolution within the industry and coming back stronger than before. The newest development—the Internet revolution—has its roots in the Silicon Valley region, and new Internet start-ups are appearing there by the day. Semiconductor, computer hardware, and software companies still have a strong presence in this region.

Austin, Texas, is quickly becoming a rival to Silicon Valley. Dell Computer company is headquartered there, as are hundreds of small software and semiconductor companies. Many young computer professionals prefer this area to Northern California. In Austin, the attitude is more laid-back, the real estate is more affordable, and in general a higher premium is placed on a happy, relaxed lifestyle than in the cutthroat, fast-paced Silicon Valley.

New York City, although never thought of as a center for high-technology, has acquired a new identity thanks to the information revolution. Those working in the new media industry in Manhattan have dubbed the area "Silicon Alley." Always the home of advertising, design, publishing, and the arts, New York now has start-up Internet companies, interactive design firms, and on-line publishing companies popping up all over the place to lead these traditional businesses into the on-line world. The reason this high-technology boom can take place in a city with such limited real estate is that most of the business takes place in the "virtual" world. A small shop in a single tiny SoHo office can produce Web sites for hundreds of companies. With so much creative talent in place, New York is the natural meeting place for art, communication, and technology.

Other growing regions for high-tech jobs include: Boston—although the area has struggled with industry upsets, the presence of MIT to feed companies with highly skilled computer professionals has helped to keep the region alive; northern Virginia and Maryland—the area along the Beltway outside Washington, DC, has been referred to as the "technology corridor"—this area is also the home of America Online, the nation's largest commercial on-line service; and the Seattle area—home to Microsoft Corporation.

Computer Systems Analysts

The increasing use of computers by businesses of all kinds means that demand for systems analysts should grow much faster than the national average for all jobs by the year 2006. However, increasing specialization within this field means that competition for jobs will increase, threatening those who do not have specialized computer training or experience. Nevertheless, the number of systems analysts is expected to grow nearly 80 percent, to 912,000 by the year 2006, up from 463,000 in 1990.

Starting salaries for computer scientists or computer engineers with a bachelor's degree can be significantly higher than starting salaries of bachelor's degree graduates in many other fields. According to the National Association of Colleges and Employers, starting salary offers for graduates with a bachelor's degree in computer engineering averaged about $39,722 a year in 1997; those with a master's degree, $44,734 a year; and those with a Ph.D., $63,367. Starting offers for graduates with a bachelor's degree in computer science averaged about $36,597 a year; in information sciences, about $35,407 a year; and in systems analysis, about $43,800 a year in 1997. Offers for those with the bachelor's degree vary by functional area for all types of employers, as shown in the following tabulation.

Computer programming	$35,167
Information systems	34,689
Systems analysis and design	36,261
Software design and development	39,190
Hardware design and development	41,237

Offers for graduates with a master's degree in computer science in 1997 averaged $45,853 a year; and those with a Ph.D. in computer and information sciences, $61,306.

According to Robert Half International Inc., starting salaries in 1997 for systems analysts employed by large establishments employing more than fifty staff members ranged from $46,000 to $57,500. Salaries for those employed in small establishments ranged from $38,000 to $48,000. Salaries for programmer-analysts ranged from $39,000 to $50,000 in large establishments, and $33,500 to $43,000 in small establishments. Starting salaries ranged from $54,000 to $67,500 for database administrators, from $36,000 to $55,000 for network administrators, from $25,000 to $36,500 for help desk support technicians, and from $49,000 to $67,500 for software development specialists.

In the federal government, the entrance salary for systems analysts who are recent college graduates with a bachelor's degree was about $19,520 a year in early 1997; for those with a superior academic record, $24,180. The average annual salary for computer engineers in the federal government in nonsupervisory, supervisory, and managerial positions was $62,900 in early 1997.

Computer Programmers

Further automation of offices and factories, coupled with advances in health and medicine, made the job of programmer ever more important through the 1990s. Jobs for programmers should grow much faster than the national average by the year 2006, according to the Department of Labor. Competition for jobs is high. Jobs for both systems and applications programmers should be particularly plentiful in data processing service firms, software houses, and computer consulting businesses.

There were 565,000 computer programmers in 1990; the number is expected to swell to 697,000 by the year 2006. Like systems analysts, programmers must keep abreast of changing technology and train and retrain constantly. Most of them can find work in every area of the country.

The advances in prepackaged software has the projections for the number of programmers over the next decade. According to the Bureau of Labor Statistics, starting salary offers for graduates with a bachelor's degree in the area of computer programming averaged about $35,167 a year in private industry in 1997. Programmers working in the west and northeast earned somewhat more than those working in the south and midwest. On average, systems programmers earn more than applications programmers.

A survey of workplaces in 160 metropolitan areas reported that beginning programmers had median annual earnings of about $27,000 in 1995. Experienced midlevel programmers with some supervisory responsibilities had median annual earnings of about $40,000. Median annual earnings for programmers at the supervisory or team leader level were about $55,000.

According to Robert Half International Inc., starting salaries ranged from $32,500 to $39,000 for programmers, and $47,500 to $60,000 for systems programmers in large establishments in 1997. Starting salaries for programmers in small establishments ranged from $28,000 to $37,000.

In the federal government, the entrance salary for programmers with a college degree or qualifying experience was about $19,520 a year in early 1997; for those with a superior academic record, $24,180.

Operations Research Analysts

This job combines business savvy with extensive knowledge of computers. Generally speaking, these people are problem solvers who utilize mathematical models to present managers with a series of possible outcomes that will help them make more informed decisions. They are employed in most industries, and their numbers are expected to increase by over 70 percent, from 57,000 in 1990 to 100,000 by 2006. Salaries range from $50,000 to $100,000. The requirements for employment are a fairly rigorous training in mathematics or quantitative methods with a strong knowledge of computer programming.

Job Descriptions in Data Processing

First, an overview of the three basic divisions in DP.

Systems Analysts—The systems analyst provides management with the information and computer processes necessary to meet different organizational goals. Systems analysts design or improve operational systems and periodically evaluate and revise existing ones. They prepare detailed descriptions of the tasks a computer system will have to perform—for example, estimating the stress during monsoon season on a bridge to be built in the tropics.

Computer Programmers—Once the systems analyst details what the computer's tasks are to be, programmers tell it how to do them. To continue with our bridge project, the programmer is told that the computer will have to retrieve data stored in another computer, organize it in a certain way, and perform needed calculations. He or she then breaks down each of those steps into a series of instructions coded in one of the computer languages.

Computer Operators—These specialized workers physically operate the computer console, entering data to be processed with instructions to the computer ("input") and retrieving final results ("output"). They run the program, producing the numbers needed in order to build that bridge.

Job Descriptions in Data Processing: By Title

MANAGEMENT

Corporation Director of Data Processing—The top executive for all computer processing.

Manager of Database Systems—Plans, organizes, and controls all activities of database systems, their design, and integration.

Manager of Data Processing—Directly supervises personnel, administration, and data processing. Oversees all three divisions of data processing work.

Assistant Manager of Data Processing—Assists in planning, organizing, and controlling the three divisions of DP.

Project/Team Leader—Plans, organizes, and controls all facets of work on a particular assigned project.

SYSTEMS ANALYSIS AND PROGRAMMING

Manager of Systems Analysis/Programming; Lead Systems Analyst/Programmer; Senior Systems Analyst/Programmer; Systems Analyst/Programmer; Systems Analyst/Programmer Trainee—These positions cover both the analysis and programming functions.

SYSTEMS ANALYSIS

Manager of Systems Analysis—Analyzes how data processing is applied to user problems; designs effective and efficient solutions.

Senior Systems Analyst—Confers with users to define data processing projects, formulates problems, designs solutions.

Systems Analyst—Assists in devising computer system specifications and record layouts, with guidance and instruction.

APPLICATIONS PROGRAMMING

Manager of Applications Programming—Responsible for the development of effective, efficient, well-documented programs.

Lead Applications Programmer—Assists in planning, organizing, and controlling section activities.

Senior Applications Programmer—Works with program designs or specifications.

Junior Applications Programmer—Assists in the review and analysis of detailed systems specifications and the preparation of the program instructions.

Applications Programmer Trainee—Learns to program, working under direct supervision. This is the entry level.

SYSTEMS PROGRAMMING

Manager of Systems Programming—Plans and directs the activities of the operating system–programming section; assigns personnel to projects.

Lead Systems Programmer—Assists in planning, organizing, and controlling the activities of the operating system–programming section.

Senior Systems Programmer—May specialize in the support, maintenance, and use of one or more major operating systems; is able to work at the highest level of programming.

Systems Programmer—Assists in the review and analysis of detailed systems specifications and the preparation of the program instructions.

Trainee—Learns programming and other routine work of the department, under direct supervision. This is the entry level.

Data Communications Manager—Responsible for design of data communications networks and installation and operation of data links.

Data Communications Operator—Operates and/or monitors, under supervision, various communication devices related to the information-processing system.

COMPUTER OPERATIONS

Manager of Computer Operations—Responsible for the operation of computers, including scheduling, assignment of operators, and monitoring of efficiency.

Lead Operator—May be responsible for the operation of large-scale computers during a complete eight-hour shift or for the operation of a remote site.

AVERAGE ANNUAL SALARIES OF COMPUTER PROFESSIONALS BY LOCATION

Title	National Average	Washington, DC	Boston	New York	Florida	Chicago	Texas	Los Angeles	San Francisco
CIO/VP	$111,495	$99,000	$112,679	$109,265	$92,095	$103,460	$103,500	$153,385	$113,583
Director	76,380	73,805	83,184	70,519	68,730	74,818	71,957	84,526	86,898
Manager/Supervisor	57,246	55,709	59,625	57,080	49,678	57,058	49,248	62,562	65,440
Application Development Manager	61,006	59,052	67,792	58,773	55,071	57,397	54,712	65,341	69,962
Application Designer	51,408	58,000	53,300	48,389	46,815	44,686	45,688	55,526	58,760
Application Developer	47,210	47,080	53,364	45,055	42,092	41,360	41,011	51,242	52,085
Project Manager	55,691	55,453	63,345	53,058	50,065	52,364	53,904	56,731	58,541
Project Leader	52,667	51,138	68,727	47,278	45,927	49,925	46,456	56,263	55,034
Senior Systems Analyst	49,621	50,250	59,683	48,406	43,172	47,301	44,263	50,297	53,697
Systems Analyst	42,166	40,926	47,545	41,532	35,795	41,021	38,690	42,895	47,990
Senior Programmer Analyst	43,912	43,375	47,858	42,136	38,615	40,132	40,592	49,249	48,505
Programmer	35,481	34,693	40,063	33,430	30,340	32,905	33,025	40,781	39,404
Computer Operator	26,130	27,056	30,593	23,451	21,597	24,095	23,677	29,633	29,896
Data Entry Clerk	20,821	19,016	22,250	19,075	17,700	20,416	19,430	23,254	23,964
Administrator	52,508	48,940	64,556	55,316	40,738	50,679	45,736	52,618	56,691
Database Analyst	46,410	44,923	55,000	49,427	41,838	41,042	40,585	46,045	50,687
Network Manager (LAN/WAN)	50,466	49,932	55,227	51,400	43,740	50,267	44,749	50,981	54,704
LAN Manager	45,460	43,494	51,345	43,826	39,865	43,094	44,081	47,574	49,059
Network Engineer	42,471	39,917	44,000	40,714	38,231	43,364	38,463	42,760	49,253
Help Desk Manager	42,624	38,000	41,572	42,138	40,027	40,973	38,350	43,840	51,926
Technical Support Analyst	36,559	33,126	40,828	33,943	35,729	38,366	35,602	36,567	39,323
Computer Hardware Engineer	39,638	34,200	39,143	39,074	39,700	37,692	36,033	40,643	48,866
PC Technician	31,614	27,696	35,909	29,847	29,259	31,160	29,413	32,188	36,902

SOURCE: *Datamation* magazine, annual salary survey, October 15, 1994. Reprinted by permission.

Senior Computer Operator—May be responsible for all operations on a medium-scale computer or for console operator of a large machine.

Computer Operator—Assists in computer monitoring and control; able to work on own on several phases of operation.

Computer Operator Trainee—Usually assigned to mounting magnetic media, loading printers, or working on a peripheral subsystem, always under direct supervision.

Computer Input/Output Control Manager—Schedules and controls all data entering the DP system, and the editing and balancing of reports coming from the system.

JOBS IN NEW MEDIA

Since 1995 there has been an explosion in the newest and most rapidly developing sector of the computer industry—"the new media." The new media business includes the Internet and World Wide Web, as well as "off-line" interactive technology such as multimedia CD-ROMs.

The growth of new media has had a dramatic effect on corporate America. While only 16 percent of American adults currently access the Internet on a regular basis, the figures for American business are much different. In 1997, 80 percent of *Fortune* 500 companies were on-line—and that number has been growing steadily. Additionally, because the cost involved is relatively low, many small businesses are making a success out of "cyber commerce"—selling their products and services on-line.

New media extends well beyond the scope of the business world. Interactive games and "edutainment" CD-ROMs and multimedia Web sites are changing the way children learn. The publishing industry is exploring new ways to expand the content of traditional books, newspapers, and magazines to take advantage of multimedia technology and a "real-time" on-line format.

With the business of new media growing and evolving by the day, there is a constant demand for qualified professionals who can keep up with the trends. In the New York metropolitan area's "Silicon Alley" alone, the number of jobs in new media was estimated at 106,000 in mid-1997—representing a 48 percent increase in only two years.

Because of the evolving nature of the business, there is an infinite number of job titles within new media—and those titles can be difficult to define. When looking for a position in this field, it is necessary to review the job duties and required skills rather than focus on titles—as each company defines a job in its own way. The breakdown that follows provides an overview of the various fields within new media and some common job descriptions in those fields.

The Corporate Web Site

With the rise of new media, businesses and nonprofit organizations have rushed to "get on-line." The amount of time and money spent on corporate Web sites is as varied as the companies themselves—there are those created by a single employee in his or her spare time, and others with elaborate business plans and teams working on the Web project. Most fall somewhere in between.

Many companies and organizations have an "intranet"—an internal system by which company communications, human resources activities, and proprietary content can be accessed by employees. The technology behind the intranet is essentially the same as that of the Internet: The difference is that an intranet is not accessible to the outside world. Many companies prefer intranets for security purposes, and to better control the information available to employees. For consistency, this section refers to corporate Web sites— but many of these job descriptions would also apply to corporate intranet systems.

One of the most common job titles for a corporate Web site is the *webmaster*. Generally speaking, *webmaster* is a catch-all term used to describe the person who has overall authority for the Web site of a company or organization. Job requirements usually include a strong knowledge of HTML (hypertext markup language), the coding language used to create Web pages, as well as familiarity with Web browser software and server technology. Frequently, a webmaster will also be expected to know more complicated programming languages, such as JavaScript, Perl, C++, and graphics applications such as Adobe Photoshop and Illustrator for design purposes. Additionally, the webmaster often serves as content editor for the site.

By contrast, some companies take an entirely different approach to the webmaster position. In some large organizations, the webmaster is not required to have expert technical knowledge but rather is expected to act as coordinator, managing the activities of an in-house technical staff, outside designers, and various contributors to ensure the quality of all aspects of the Web site. Some companies use the title *Web Site Manager* for this role.

Depending on the size and budget of the company or organization, the webmaster may take on all or some of the following roles:

Web Designer (Graphic Designer/Artist)—Plans the look of the site, creates graphics. Standard requirements include a traditional graphic design background, experience with graphics software such as Adobe Photoshop and Adobe Illustrator, and some knowledge of Web development including HTML. Multimedia tools such as Macromedia's Director and Shockwave can be helpful.

Web Programmer (Developer)—Builds interactive Web applications using advanced HTML, Java, Javascript, CGI scripting, Perl, C++, etc. It can be helpful to have experience in operating systems such as UNIX or NT, and database systems such as Oracle.

Online Editor—Rewrites and proofreads content before it is published on the Web site; adapts content for on-line format. HTML skills are a plus, but not always necessary.

Network Administrator (Network Manager)—Sets up, administers, and provides technical support for the Web server and network—the "backend" system on which the Web data is stored and by which the information is transmitted. Unix, NT administration skills necessary; database skills such as Oracle are a big plus.

Internet Consultant—A generalist, an Internet consultant usually works for an outside firm or on a freelance basis, brought in by a company that lacks the technical expertise in-house. Requires a thorough knowledge of all aspects of designing and managing a Web site, as well as other Internet tools such as e-mail, etc.

The Interactive Studio

Many commercial, educational, and information Web sites as well as multimedia CD-ROMs are created at private companies specializing in new media technology. Additionally, many large advertising agencies are creating interactive departments. Their primary purpose is to serve businesses who want to take advantage of new media technology but don't have the resources or expertise to do the work in-house. These companies/departments usually work on a project by project basis, and often on several projects simultaneously. As a result, the working environment is more varied, and sometimes more stressful, than working on a corporate Web site. For example, a team of producers may be working on an interactive cookbook on CD-ROM, a Web site for a tax publisher, and an educational children's Web site focusing on space exploration, all at the same time. This type of work can be fun and exciting but requires an individual who can juggle many projects at once, and can switch gears between widely varying subjects quickly.

Creative Director—Supervises all design and production, making sure that the final product meets the company's standards and budget. The creative director usually has strong technical skills and a fine creative mind.

Project Manager—Responsible for the production of a specific CD-ROM or Web site. Working under the creative director, the project manager orchestrates the entire production effort, supervising (and often hiring) the designers, writers, artists, and programmers and making sure the project is finished on time and on budget. Sometimes a producer will take on the project management role.

Producer (also Associate Producer, Assistant Producer)—Responsible for the actual hands-on production of a Web site or CD-ROM. Often works with a team of other producers and the project manager to conceptualize how the product will look and perform, then produces the product with the help of designers and programmers. In some cases the producer is responsible for project management duties such as setting the production schedule and meeting deadline and budget requirements.

Game Designer/Instructional Designer—A specialist in the design of games or educational software. For the latter, a background in education, educational psychology, or instructional technology is particularly useful.

Writer/Editor—Writes or edits the script or text. A game may require a script to be narrated by actors; a nonfiction work will require a text, often adapted from a book. Research and fact-checking is often necessary, particularly with educational or informational Web sites.

Graphic Artist (Designer)—Creates the artwork. Graphic artists usually specialize; some do animation, others static graphics, and still others video. Graphic artists must be adept with such applications as Adobe Photoshop, which is widely used to modify photographs, and Adobe Illustrator, used to create graphics. Multimedia tools such as Macromedia's Director and Shockwave are also helpful.

Software Designer/Programmer (Software Engineer)—Writes the software code that makes everything work. A good programmer usually knows several programming languages, such as Lingo, C, C++, Perl, Javascript, and a variety of authoring applications, such as Macromedia Director.

Production Assistant—Assists the producers. An entry-level position, the production assistant performs functions such as basic HTML coding, fact-checking, scanning images, testing for bugs, and sometimes administrative duties.

Audio Engineer—Creates the sound for a Web site or interactive application.

Electronic Publishing

A couple of years ago, electronic publishing meant nothing more than books on CD-ROM. While this is still a component of the industry, the field has expanded to include interactive newspapers, magazines, and books on the Internet. Through the World Wide Web and on-line subscription services such as America Online, these traditional publications have begun to adapt their content for a real-time, on-line format.

There are significant differences between print publications and their electronic counterparts, especially in the case of periodicals. A monthly magazine, and even a daily newspaper, has a limit to how much information it can provide, and to how current that information can be. On the Internet, the publication never "closes." New information can be added by the hour—even by the minute. A well-connected Web customer can get news faster on a Web site than on television.

The content itself is also different. A challenge faced by many publishers is that the kind of content that works on paper will not necessarily translate into an on-line format. An on-line magazine article cannot be too text-heavy—or people won't read it. It needs to take advantage of the technology to include images, even sound and video, to break up the text. An on-line publication needs to be arranged in a nonlinear format—so that readers can use links to "jump around" between related content items. The responsibility of those working in electronic publishing is to adapt print content for the on-line format, as well as to create new content, solely for the on-line customer.

Despite the growing trend, this is still uncharted territory for many publishers. Although most magazines have at least some presence on the Web, some are very slowly and carefully getting their feet wet. Many magazines have not yet decided how to approach the format, so they are using their sites as "teasers," providing a few brief samples of the contents of their current issue, subscription information, and little else. Book publishers are also uncomfortable with going on-line, where they have much less control than in the CD-ROM format. While not all traditional publishers are ready to plunge in, a large sector within electronic publishing is made up of content written specifically for the Web—in webzines (on-line magazines) and e-books (on-line books), for example. As a result there is a rising demand for qualified individuals looking to combine their publishing and new media skills.

Director, New Media (New Media Publisher; Executive Producer)—Creates the company's strategic plan for a multimedia product/on-line publication. Defines company's market and product mix. Staffs and manages department. Takes a lead role in business development, including acquisitions and partnerships.

Producer (Content Producer; Associate Producer)—Manages a team of internal and external programmers, graphic and interface designers, writers, editors, and others to produce a particular multimedia product or on-line publication. Defines budgets and schedules. Assumes overall responsibility for the product.

Writer/Editor (Online Editor)—Adapts text for on-line/multimedia format. Writes and edits original text.

Licensing/Permissisons Manager—Obtains electronic rights for reproduction of printed articles and books. Coordinates licensing process.

Design Director (Art Director)—Creates the visual "look and feel" of new media publication. Oversees a team of graphic designers.

Other New Media Opportunities

Opportunities within the new media business are being created by the day. The three categories discussed above only scratch the surface of the industry. Here are some examples of other new media opportunities:

- On-line subscription services—such as America Online—that are in constant demand for all types of new media professionals, from highly technical programmers, to marketing professionals, to creative types like writers and graphic artists.
- New media training/education—at all levels of education, from elementary school to adult education technical centers for professionals looking to build their skills. People with an education background and/or a high level of expertise in some area of new media are needed for teaching positions.
- Electronic commerce—the business of selling products and services on-line has created new jobs in on-line marketing, advertising, etc.
- Archiving experts—many companies have large libraries of digital files, images, and media objects. Professionals with expertise in databases and archiving systems are in demand.

- Technical writers.
- On-line market analysts/researchers.

Making the Decision to Work in New Media

Although the growth of new media offers many exciting new opportunities, there are some drawbacks to pursuing a career in this field. Because it is still a young industry, many companies view it as a gamble and are unwilling to invest the money they do in their other ventures. Other companies are start-ups, with very little money and even less stability. As a result, a large number of available jobs are either part-time or freelance (one study showed the number to be as high as 44 percent of all jobs in the new media industry), and thus do not offer benefits. This means the necessities such as health insurance come out of the pocket of the employee. This might change as the industry becomes more established, and as the start-ups start making profits—but for now, the safety of a full-time, full-benefit position is difficult to come by.

Additionally, there is much speculation that new media salaries are inflated to a level that cannot be maintained. While technical experts will always be in demand, and probably will have no trouble continuing to pull down big salaries, others in the industry might be in for a disappointment. Professionals in electronic publishing, for example, are currently making much more than their print counterparts. This is because no one really knows what they should be making—or how much revenue they will generate. Once companies start to make real profits—or lose money—on their new media ventures, and as more workers make the transition into new media and crowd the job market, salaries will level out.

The new media industry is not for everyone. It is exciting, growing, on the cutting edge of technology. By the same token, it is unstable, demanding, and unpredictable. To succeed in new media, an employee must be extremely flexible and constantly be willing to learn and build skills in order to keep up with technology.

THE EMERGING DIGITAL ECONOMY

In 1998, the U.S. Department of Commerce published a study of the rapid changes taking place in the American economy and their effects on business and the labor force. In the pages below are the most relevant parts of the "Executive Summary" of the report and all of the chapter entitled "Workers in the Digital Age."

The Digital Revolution

In recent years, the U.S. economy has performed beyond most expectations. A shrinking budget deficit, low interest rates, a stable macroeconomic environment, expanding international trade with fewer barriers, and effective private sector management are all credited with playing a role. While the full economic impact of information technology cannot yet be precisely evaluated, its impact has been significant.

- Information technology industries have been growing at more than double the rate of the overall economy; they now represent 8.2 percent of GDP, up from 4.9 percent in 1985.
- IT industries by themselves have driven over one quarter of total real economic growth (not including any indirect effects) on average over each of the last five years.
- Without information technology, overall inflation would have been 3.1 percent in 1997—more than a full percentage point higher than the 2.0 percent it was.
- Companies throughout the economy are betting on IT to boost productivity. In the 1960s, business spending on IT equipment represented only 3 percent of total business equipment investment. In 1996, IT's share rose to 45 percent.
- In 1996, 7.4 million people worked in the IT sector and in IT-related jobs across the economy. These workers earned just under $46,000 per year, compared to an average of $28,000 for the private sector as a whole.
- At almost $56,000 per year, workers in the software and services industries were the highest wage earners. Earnings have been growing at a rate of 6.6 percent per year, versus 3.8 percent for total private sector employment. In 1985, 557,000 people worked in these industries. By 1996, the figure had more than doubled to reach 1.2 million workers.

Building Out the Internet

Where advances in telecommunications and computing largely occurred side by side in the past, today, they converge in the Internet. Soon, virtually all information technology investment will be part of interlinked communications systems, whether internal to a business, between businesses, between individuals and businesses, or individual to individual.

- The Internet's pace of adoption eclipses all other technologies that preceded it. Radio was in existence thirty-eight years before 50 million people tuned in; TV took thirteen years to reach that benchmark. Once it was opened to the general public, the Internet crossed that line in four years.
- In 1994, 3 million people were connected to the Internet. By the end of 1997, more than 100 million people were using the Internet.
- Traffic on the Internet has been doubling every 100 days.
- The number of names registered in the domain name system grew from 26,000 in July 1993 to 1.3 million in July 1997. Over the same period, the number of hosts connected to the Internet expanded from under 1.8 million to 19.5 million.
- Consumer electronics companies, media giants, phone companies, computer companies, software firms, satellite builders, cell phone businesses, Internet service providers, and television cable companies are aggressively investing to build out the Internet. Within the next five years, the vast majority of Americans should be able to interact with the Internet from their television sets, or watch television on their PCs, and make telephone calls from both devices.

Electronic Commerce Between Businesses

Internet commerce is growing fastest among businesses. Businesses use the Internet to lower purchasing costs, reduce inventories and cycle times, provide more efficient and effective customer service, lower sales and marketing costs, and realize new sales opportunities. By 2002, Internet commerce between businesses will likely surpass $300 billion.

- General Electric uses the Internet for procurement. Its lighting division has lowered its purchasing labor costs by 30 percent and its material costs by up to 20 percent. By the year 2000, GE aims to have all twelve of its business units purchasing materials via the Internet, for a total of $5 billion. Doing so could save the company $500–$700 million over the next three years.
- At the beginning of 1997, Dell was selling $1 million worth of computers via the Internet each day. By the end of the year, Dell regularly sold over $3 million per day via the Internet, and even reached $6 million during December. Dell estimates that it saves several million dollars a year by having basic customer service and technical support functions available on the Internet. Fifty percent of small businesses that bought from Dell's Web site in 1997 had never before purchased

from Dell. Dell expects to do half its business on the Internet by the year 2000.

- Boeing spare parts business allows its airline customers around the world to check parts availability and pricing, order parts, and track the status of their orders on the Internet. Less than a year after this service was launched, about 50 percent of Boeing's customers used it for 9 percent of all parts orders and a much larger percentage of customer service inquiries. Because of the Internet, Boeing was able to process roughly 20 percent more shipments per month in 1997 than in 1996 with the same number of data entry people.

- Cisco Systems has saved $363 million (approximately 17.5 percent of total operating costs) by putting key business applications on the Internet. Its technical support productivity has increased by 200 to 300 percent per year, lowering technical support staff costs by $125 million. Customers download new software releases directly from Cisco's site, saving the company $180 million in distribution, packaging, and duplicating costs. Having product and pricing information on the Web and Web-based CD-ROMs saves Cisco $50 million in printing and distributing catalogs and marketing materials.

- W. W. Grainger's (a leading wholesaler of manufacturing supplies in North America) revenues from its Web site have been growing 100 percent quarter over quarter. Over 30 percent of its on-line sales are to new customers or incremental sales to existing customers. More than half of all on-line orders are made when Grainger stores are closed.

- Two-thirds of Federal Express's shipping transactions are transmitted and received using on-line services. The company's own proprietary network handles 54 million transactions a day, allowing it to keep track of every package FedEx delivers, every step of the way. Using this system, National Semiconductor, a FedEx logistics customer, has seen a reduction of its average customer delivery cycle from four weeks to one week, and its distribution costs drop from 2.9 percent of sales to 1.2 percent.

Digital Delivery of Goods and Services

Software programs, newspapers, airline tickets, and music CDs no longer need to be packaged and delivered to stores, homes, or news kiosks. They can be delivered electronically over the Internet.

- Lower sales and marketing costs, increased consumer choice, and convenience are driving the Internet's increased use in news and entertainment, travel, software distribution, securities trading, banking, and insurance.

- Nearly 90 percent of Web users go on-line to get news and information.
- More than 2,700 newspapers and 800 TV stations, and all but three of the top fifty magazines have a Web presence.
- Up until three years ago, print revenues made up 85 percent of McGraw-Hill financial information service's sales. Today, digital products account for more than 50 percent of the division's sales.
- Airlines are able to drive down costs and generate new revenues through the Internet. Commissions paid to on-line travel agents are about half the commission paid to traditional agents. Through auctions and special "cyberfares" offered to Internet customers, airlines can sell seats that otherwise would go unsold. American Airlines' NetSAAver program has generated tens of millions of incremental revenues since its launch in March 1996.
- Travelocity and EasySABRE book $4 million in travel sales each week, up from $1 million in January 1996. Two years after its launch, Travelocity has 2 million registered members.
- By the year 2000, on-line travel sales could reach $5 billion, or close to 7 percent of U.S. airlines' revenues for passenger air travel.
- It costs about a penny to conduct a banking transaction using the Internet, and more than one dollar if handled by a teller at a branch of a bank. In 1997, 4.5 million households were banking on-line. By the year 2000, as many as 16 million households are expected to do so.
- Connecting billers and payers electronically could save as much as $19–46 billion each year in check-processing costs.
- By 2001, $1.1 billion of insurance premiums will be generated via the Internet.
- Nearly 5 million people actively trade stocks on-line and pay $8–30 per trade, versus an average of $80 paid to traditional brokers. In 1997, $614 million in broker commissions were generated on-line, representing 29 percent of all commissions paid to discount brokers last year.

Retail Sales of Tangible Goods

Increasing demands on leisure time and the improvement of overnight and second-day delivery services that spurred the growth of catalog shopping in the 1980s and 1990s are now leading people to shop over the Internet.

- By the end of 1997, 10 million people in the United States and Canada had purchased something on the Web, up from 7.4 million six months earlier.
- 1-800-FLOWERS sold $30 million on-line in 1997. While this represents only 10 percent of the company's total revenues, its profit contribution to the overall business is nearly that of its store-based business, which is twice as large.
- Amazon.com offers a selection of 2 million book titles to Internet customers (traditional bookstores have about 150,000 titles). In 1996, the company recorded sales of less than $16 million. In 1997, its sales reached $148 million.
- Sixteen percent of all new car and truck buyers used the Internet as part of their shopping process in 1997, up from 10 percent in 1996. By 2000, the Internet will likely be used in at least 21 percent of all new car and truck purchases.
- Auto-by-Tel, a Web-based automotive marketplace, processed an average of about 29,000 purchase requests for autos each month in 1996. At the end of 1997, the Web site was generating $500 million a month in auto sales ($6 billion annualized) and processing over 100,000 purchase requests each month.
- In order for the full potential of Internet retail sales to be realized, consumers must be more comfortable that credit card and personal information given on-line will not be tampered with, stolen, or misused. The U.S. government is encouraging the private sector to establish codes of conduct and self-regulation in order to empower consumers to have control of their own personal information.

Challenges Ahead

IT and electronic commerce can be expected to drive economic growth for many years to come. To realize this potential, however, the private sector and government face a number of challenges.

- The pace of technological development and the borderless environment created by the Internet drives a new paradigm for government and private sector responsibilities.
- Where possible, rules should result from private collective action, not government regulation.
- Governments must allow electronic commerce to grow up in an environment driven by markets, not burdened with extensive regulation, taxation, or censorship. Government has a role to play in supporting the creation of a predictable legal framework for doing

business on the Internet—a role that must be exercised in a non-bureaucratic manner.

● Greater competition in telecommunications and broadcast industries should be encouraged so that high-band-width services are brought to homes and offices around the world.

● Information technology has already begun to create demand for highly skilled workers. As electronic commerce becomes more wide-spread, it will drive further changes in the labor market. Countries that have an insufficient supply of skilled workers will see high-skilled, high-paying jobs migrate to countries that can supply the needed talent. The private sector and the government must work together to create new human resources policies that better prepare students and workers to meet the challenges of the emerging digital economy.

WORKERS IN THE DIGITAL AGE

The rapid growth of the computing and telecommunications industries has already created a large and growing demand for programmers, systems analysts, computer scientists, and engineers. If electronic commerce begins to substitute for more conventional sales and services, it will shift employment from traditional occupations to those requiring IT skills and, in many instances, other higher-level cognitive reasoning abilities. Electronic commerce is very much part of a broader national trend that requires more skills in the workplace and an improved basic education in mathematics and science.

The digital age will also create greater opportunities for telecommuting, and already strong trends toward globalization will accelerate.

Changing Skill Requirements

Demand for workers in IT industries and workers with occupations focused on the design, programming, maintenance, and repair of the computing and communications infrastructure will continue to grow. In 1996, more than 7 million people worked in these jobs, and they earned an average annual wage of just under $46,000. Over the next ten years, the Bureau of Labor Statistics (BLS) projects that an additional 2 million workers will be needed to fill these jobs. Companies already report difficulties in filling these positions today.

Workers with information technology skills are needed across the economy. An analysis of IT occupations shows that the demand for workers to fill higher skilled IT jobs (computer engineers, scientists, and systems analysts) is expected to grow from 874,000 in 1996 to 1.8 million by 2006.[1] These positions typically require a four-year undergraduate degree, often in a field of science, mathematics, or engineering, and in many cases, advanced training or a graduate degree. Employment in lesser skilled jobs like computer operators and duplicating machine operators is expected to decline from 481,000 in 1996 to 342,000 by 2006.

As electronic commerce becomes more widespread, it, too, will likely drive changes in the labor market. In most cases, the share of sales generated by a company's Web business is still only a small fraction of the company's total business. As it increases, however, the composition of the workforce required to produce and deliver a product or service may shift.

For instance, if on-line delivery of news services replaces some portion of the conventionally delivered news, workers may gradually shift away from the printing or delivery of newspapers to the creation of content or managing of computers. Workers manning printing presses, driving trucks, and staffing newsstands have no role in on-line news distribution. Their function is performed by new workers responsible for programming, operating, and maintaining the computer servers that "distribute" the news to Web readers.

The same could be true for retail as on-line sales begin to substitute for in-store sales. Today, a superstore might be staffed by a few hundred employees. Warehouse personnel receive new merchandise into the store and keep the shelves and bins filled. Salespeople advise customers on product features, check availability of merchandise not found on the shop floor, and book special orders. Cashiers ring up the sale and bag the goods. Back-office staff keep track of inventory and sales patterns, pay vendors and payroll, deposit sales receipts, and manage the day-to-day store operations. Other workers keep the store and its grounds clean and well-maintained. A retail sale via the Internet does not require the presence of a physical store or the same intensity of staff in order to generate the sale. Virtual retailers will hire people with IT skills to develop and program software, and operate and maintain computer servers and networks. They will also need marketing staff, accounting departments, customer service representatives, and people skilled in graphic design to keep their Web site, or "storefront," attractive and user-friendly.

Whether a retailer handles the physical distribution of its own products or contracts with another company to perform that function, warehouse and distribution personnel will continue to be necessary to transport products

---

[1] These numbers represent wage and salary employment only, not self-employed and unpaid family workers. Total employment figures that include wage and salary, self-employed, and unpaid family workers are slightly higher.

from the manufacturer's site to the customer's home. Retailers with an existing store infrastructure are likely to position the on-line business as complementary to their traditional store business, at least in the near term. Until on-line sales are of a size to warrant a dedicated distribution strategy, traditional retailers may choose to deliver goods to Web customers from the nearest store location, adding to the workload of existing warehouse personnel. Other retailers may choose to have manufacturers package and mail or "drop-ship" goods directly to customers without going through any intermediate steps. Or, they may outsource the entire logistics process for the on-line business to a third party. In any of these scenarios, few store personnel would be involved in an on-line sale.

Jobs characterized by a transfer of information from one party to another—travel agents, insurance agents, stockbrokers, customer service representatives—will likely see routine tasks like order taking disappear, and more complicated tasks replacing them. For instance, a leisure traveler making plans to go home for the holidays usually knows all the carriers flying that route and simply needs to make the reservation and pay for the flight. That would be a case of order taking, a function as easily performed on-line as by calling the airline or a travel agent. On the other hand, a couple planning a trip to South Africa might seek the advice of someone who has been to the region, who can recommend hotels in the wine country near Cape Town and safaris in Kruger. Similarly, someone purchasing a term life insurance policy with a face value of $400,000 may feel comfortable enough researching and purchasing that policy on-line. To help make the decision of whether to buy a whole or variable life insurance policy or put the money into an Individual Retirement Account or other investment vehicle, however, he or she might prefer to consult an expert in person.

Workforce Flexibility

Workforce flexibility refers to a company's ability to produce products and services with less rigid organizational structures. It also refers to a worker's ability to work without being tied to a desk or an office. The growth in information technology has played an important role in both driving the need for a new workforce and in enabling greater flexibility in the workplace.

In the old model of industrial organization, production workers performed tasks by rote, over and over again throughout a shift. A car frame rolled down an assembly line, a worker attached a part, it proceeded to the next worker who performed the next process, and on it continued until a completed car emerged at the other end. A bank teller opened accounts, accepted deposits, and provided account balance information. Someone else handled transactions involving Certificates of Deposit, Money Market Accounts, and safety deposit boxes.

Bureaucratic work organizations are giving way to flexible "cells" and teams that cross the once-rigid lines of job description, management reporting structures, and business units. This transformation often results from a corporate objective to implement total quality management (TQM) and Six Sigma (a benchmark of nearly zero defects) systems throughout their organizations. Reducing errors and return rates, lowering cycle times, and reducing costs means getting it done right the first time. People on the "front lines"—the factory floor, the sales department, the customer service organization—need to have the education and information to make decisions and solve problems. Companies with successful TQM and Six Sigma initiatives invest heavily in training and education. They also give employees the tools they need: clearly stated objectives and real-time feedback on how well those objectives are being met. A robust computer network with on-line training and support tools can reinforce (or substitute for) in-classroom training sessions. It also keeps workers up-to-date with the latest forecasts, the current day's production or sales requirements, materials shortages, and other information in order to better perform the day's tasks and anticipate future needs.

As more companies move to this method of work organization, the need to share information and knowledge across the enterprise will increase. Internal corporate networks and the Internet will play an important role in enabling this transition.

Thanks to personal computers, fax machines, modems, and cellular phones, as many as 7 million workers in the United States work at home in "virtual offices."[2] The Department of Transportation estimates that up to 15 million workers may be telecommuting in the next decade.

Organizations with telecommuting programs report an increase in productivity, faster completion of assignments, fewer sick or absent days, better time management, and increased morale and commitment to the company. They also benefit from reduced office space needs and associated costs, an enhanced ability to attract and retain quality employees, and improved customer service.[3]

---

[2]The U.S. Department of Transportation reports that 2–7 million people telecommute. See: "Successful Telecommuting Programs in the Public and Private Sectors: A Report to Congress." U.S. Department of Transportation, August 1997, pp. 3–5.

A recent survey of 2,000 U.S. households by Find/SVP suggests that the figure might even be higher. Their results find that the number of telecommuters in the United States jumped to 11.1 million in 1997, up from 9.7 million in 1996. Three out of four telecommuters own home computers, and 43 percent have multiple phone lines. Thirty-five percent of today's telecommuters use the Internet and e-mail. Http://www.etrg.findsvp.com:80/prls/pr97/telecomm.html.

[3]"Successful Telecommuting Programs in the Public and Private Sectors: A Report to Congress." U.S. Department of Transportation, August 1997, pp. 3–5.

Telecommuting benefits employees, as well. For those who need to balance work commitments with family commitments, telecommuting provides the means for working and communicating with coworkers and clients from home. Employees working part-time can manage their time more effectively, spend less time driving to one or more offices, and instead focus on completing work assignments.

Globalization

Information technology has opened up new opportunities for global commerce. The signals transmitted over the Internet do not recognize national borders. Work on the same project can be done in several places or several countries without workers having to physically relocate.

Organizations can now deploy resources and operations around the world. Information about new product introductions, corporate earnings, forecasted sales patterns, and materials requirements can be shared almost instantaneously via corporate e-mail systems and value-added networks, and now, over the Internet.

Developing software, designing a car, and providing consulting services to a client can be done collaboratively by teams of employees from different parts of the world. For instance, an engineer in California can send an e-mail at the close of her business day to a colleague in Singapore, asking him to look over the attached design specifications for a new product. By the time she arrives for work the next morning, a reply could be sitting in her in-box with a marked-up set of specifications. With these kinds of opportunities come serious challenges. Countries that have an insufficient supply of skilled workers will see high-skilled, high-paying jobs migrate to countries that can supply the needed talent. Those that have a surplus will find job opportunities opening for their workers in overseas organizations. Even though the United States has led the world into the digital age, we face these same realities. Without a concerted effort to develop students and workers to meet the new challenges of the digital economy, the United States could face a migration of high-skilled, high-wage jobs to other countries.

V

Key White-Collar Jobs

At first glance, the occupations contained in this section may appear to be an unorthodox grouping, especially if one is accustomed to standard delineations of white-collar jobs and blue-collar jobs, or service-sector and production-sector jobs. Those designations *are* helpful to economists and sociologists. But the characteristics common to the jobs found here make this section especially relevant to those planning a career. These jobs usually require a college education, they pay well, they exist in every major corporation, and the government predicts good opportunities for all of them over the next decade. Most important, in today's booming economy the unemployment rate for people in these jobs has sunk to less than 2 percent, a level not seen since the mid-1980s.

This career orientation requires extensive entries that include job descriptions and salary information for entry-level to senior and vice president–level positions. Where it was possible, we also included salary figures from different industries. Special attention was given to government pay levels in personnel and purchasing since they are large and essential areas in the public employment sector. Interested readers should also be sure to consult the sections on accountants (in Part III) and computer professionals (in Part IV).

The section begins with a look at those executives who have made it to the top levels of the corporation. A detailed list of compensation figures for leaders of America's major corporations highlights this profile.

We devote the next section to describing typical white-collar jobs at large and midsized companies. At one point, these jobs were synonymous with ironclad job security and rising salaries. However, beginning in the 1980s, white-collar jobs became targets for corporate cost cutting, starting with so-called staff and support jobs. White-collar operating jobs became the target of further cost cutting in the 1990s as methods such as "increasing spans of control"; "outsourcing basic support service"; and "reengineering processes" found their way into management's lexicon. Many supervisory and managerial jobs were eliminated as a result. In fact, white-collar workers were laid off as often as blue-collar workers were during the last recession, and those jobs have not come back in many cases, or have come back at lower salary levels. There are numerous case histories about $100,000 managers becoming entrepreneurs struggling to break even or reentering the corporate world at one half to two thirds of their former salaries.

In today's environment, the white-collar worker must develop transportable skills and knowledge within his or her functional area. For example, an ideal plant manager today is one who understands and can apply modern quality theory, not one whose chief skill is managing people. The ideal inventory control manager is one who can manipulate data to perform "just in time" techniques effectively. Among the most desirable human resource specialists are those who can design and administer diversity programs. Administrative and people skills are still required, but they must be closely tied into specific expertise for two reasons. First, the skilled white-collar generalist, the "manager" of yesterday, is on the endangered list, having been declared a surplus species at least five years ago. Second, with job security a tenuous proposition at best in today's work environment, and with large numbers of white-collar workers pounding the pavement at any given time, employers are more pointedly specifying the skills and experience they need in filling a vacancy and are using lack of these as a disqualifying factor in the hiring decision. Also, having special skills can help promote one's career with the service companies to whom the corporations are outsourcing, as well as enable the white-collar worker to move into a smaller company environment or strike out on his or her own.

Ironically, while this reengineering of the corporate landscape has done much to change the vocabulary and job skills of the white-collar worker, there is growing evidence that downsizing has done little if anything to improve corporate bottom lines. According to a 1995 study by the San Francisco–based Wyatt Co. of 531 downsizing companies, only 46 percent increased earnings, only 34 percent increased productivity, and a mere 33 percent improved customer service. Kenneth DeMeuse, a business professor at the University of Wisconsin in Eau Claire, performed a similar study and found that companies that downsized had no better (and in many cases had worse) profit margins than similarly situated companies that did not reengineer their workplaces.

THE AMERICAN CHIEF EXECUTIVE

Our look at executive compensation starts at the top. There is probably no subject in the field of compensation that has been more controversial over the past ten years than the growing compensation of the chief executive officers of America's top corporations. According to Graef S. Crystal, a vocal critic of CEO pay, the pay of American CEOs increased by 400 percent from 1970 to 1990. This has created a vast gulf between CEO pay and the pay of all other workers. According to *The Wall Street Journal,* in 1995 chief executive officers received an 11.7 percent increase in salaries and bonuses. In 1996, the median salaries and bonuses for top executives climbed to $1,596,667 from $1,471,250, a 5 percent increase.

This gap is evident in the following statistics cited by Crystal in his book, *In Search of Excess,* published in 1991. After adjusting for inflation, the average pay of the American worker declined by 14 percent over the twenty-year period, 1970 to 1990. (Even during the 1980s, a period not marked by the runaway inflation of the previous decade, the average worker's pay still declined 5 percent.) Over the same twenty-year period, and in the same inflation-adjusted dollars, the average CEO's pay tripled. In 1974, the typical CEO earned thirty-five times the pay of the average manufacturing worker. In 1990, that same CEO earned roughly 120 times the pay of the average manufacturing worker, and about 150 times the pay of the average worker in manufacturing and service combined. Taking changes in the tax code into account, CEO compensation has increased by 400 percent, while real worker pay has declined slightly less than 13 percent. According to Crystal, the average CEO in Japan in 1990 earned sixteen times the average worker; in Germany, twenty-one times. Such comparisons raise many issues.

Crystal has cited three trends that are driving American executive compensation to such dizzying heights:

- U.S. senior executives are paid so much in excess of U.S. workers that it raises questions of equity, even decency. The imbalance has continued to grow in the 1990s.
- U.S. senior executives are paid far in excess of their counterparts in other countries—and that gap has continued to grow, although there is some evidence that Canadian and European executives have started adopting inflated American-style compensation plans.
- U.S. senior executives are insulating themselves from pay risks to an alarming degree. Even though CEO compensation plans are drawing the ire of large institutional stakeholders such as Calpers, there are very few scenarios in corporations today that could devastate the CEO's pay package. Meanwhile, there are an almost infinite number of scenarios that could enrich the top executive.

Bowing to pressure from the public, as well as from influential share-holders, more corporations in the 1990s have adopted a pay-for-performance approach that shifts a greater proportion of the CEO's compensation into stock options. *Business Week* reports that boards of directors are also moving toward rewarding chief executives using a formula that ties compensation to stock appreciation. Increased stock options or a percentage of stock appreciation can yield an even greater upside for CEOs, while their base annual compensation package may be expected to remain extremely high in most cases. For example, Lawrence Bossidy, chairman of AlliedSignal, was working under a contract that provided him with a base of $2 million in salary and a guaranteed minimum bonus of $1.85 million. In addition, Bossidy's potential gain on stock options is estimated to be more than $100 million over 10 years.

According to *Business Week*, Travelers chairman and CEO Sanford Weill had one of the most generous compensation packages. Weill earned $12.2 million in salary and bonus in 1994 and has an unusual "reload" feature in his stock option plan. Each time he exercises an option, he receives a new one to replace the one exercised. Between 1991 and 1993, Weill received options on 6.9 million shares. In 1994, he was given a reload on about 525,000 of those shares. (By contrast, typical CEO option grants range from 100,000 to 250,000 in any given year.) This has resulted in estimated "paper profits" to Weill of $185 million from options granted between 1991 and 1993. On the other hand, Travelers' market value under Weill's stewardship has risen from $1 billion in 1986 to $12.3 billion. Weill's defenders say that he has a right to a cut of the shareholders' gains because without him the company's performance would have been less impressive. Weill *can* show that the company has prospered. That cannot be said of some of his peers on the highest paid list. For example, Jerry Sanders, CEO of Advanced Micro Devices, did not make any noticeable improvement at his company, yet received $50 million in stock options.

Regardless of the debate over executive compensation, the clear trend is ever upward. *The Wall Street Journal* reported this in a special supplement on April 13, 1995. The *Journal* attributed the current upward trend to "rising profits, directors' pursuit of outside talent, and reduced public criticism." The *Journal* reported that the median increase in CEO cash compensation in 1994 was 11.4 percent, following an 8.1 percent increase in 1993. The average increase for all white-collar workers, by contrast, was a mere 4.2 percent.

What seems to be missing from that report is a sense of proportion on the part of boards. It's the compensation committee of the board of directors that sets CEO pay. These committees are usually quick to point out that fat pay packages are necessary to hold on to executives who otherwise would be moving to greener pastures. According to a recent article in *The New York Times:* "Boards justify raises by saying they have to pay their chief executives 'competitively' in order to retain them, even if those executives are underperforming." But is the average CEO really that mobile? Does an extra half-million dollars, or even a million, mean that much when the CEO is earning so much already?

One suspects that ego is the major driver in CEO compensation. CEOs are highly competitive people with huge egos for whom being tops in their industry or tops in compensation in America may be a tangible, satisfying goal. In general, the bigger the company, the more lucrative the CEO's compensation package. The CEOs also usually select the compensation consultant who advises the compensation committee. In cases where a CEO's current contract doesn't seem sufficiently generous, it must actually be bought out before it can be altered. *The New York Times* reported that Occidental Petroleum Corporation paid its CEO, Ray R. Irani, $95 million to buy out his current contract so as to create a new agreement more closely linking pay and performance. After such a payout, how could he even care what was in the new contract?

These days, even executives at levels below CEO are earning salaries to make even the best-paid baseball player jealous. Of course, the most celebrated of lieutenants is Michael Ovitz, who left the helm of his own Creative Artists Agency to take a job at Disney. His pay package was valued at approximately $100 million over five years. According to *The Wall Street Journal,* many companies are now offering substantial salaries, bonuses, and stock compensation to the CEO's heir apparent. These lieutenants are targets for headhunters; for the future of the company, something must be done to entice them to stay.

Whatever forces drive CEO pay, it seems safe to assume that while wages for the average American worker are losing ground to inflation, CEO compensation will continue to soar. A recent headline in *Newsday* summed up the differing perspectives of the corporate top dog and the rank and file thusly: "Citicorp's Reed Gets a Crummy 5 Percent Raise." The accompanying article points out that John S. Reed, Citicorp's Chairman and CEO, received a raise of less than 5 percent in 1994, despite the fact that the bank had record earnings. The pay included a $1.275 million annual salary and a cash bonus of $3 million, which means that Mr. Reed's "crummy" raise surely exceeded what 99 percent of Citicorp's workers made all year in 1994. To his credit, Mr. Reed was not quoted as calling his increase "crummy," and he may even admit that there have been years in which he was overcompensated, given Citicorp's past roller-coaster results. But this does sum up the attitude of many CEOs, and it may help to account for Reed's 1998

Executive/Company	Estimated Value of Nonexercised Stock Options (millions of dollars)
Henry Silverman/Cendant	$832.9
Michael Eisner/Walt Disney	590.5
Eckhard Pfeiffer/Compaq Computer	242.4
Richard Scrushy/Healthsouth	216.1
Lawrence Ellison/Oracle	200.9
Charles Wang/Computer Associates	187.3
John Welch/General Electric	182.2
Millard Drexler/The Gap	177.5
Reuben Mark/Colgate-Palmolive	149.2
Louis Gerstner/IBM	143.7
M. Douglas Ivester/Coca-Cola	142.9
Eli Broad/SunAmerica	141.3
Charles Heimbold/Bristol-Myers Squibb	139.4
Summerfield Johnston/Coca-Cola Enterprises	131.9
Eugene Isenberg/Nabors Industries	125.0
Steven Burd/Safeway	120.5
Stephen Case/America Online	119.8
Joseph Nacchio/Qwest Communications	112.5
Randall Tobias/Eli Lilly	108.3
John Chambers/Cisco Systems	100.4

THE TOP 20 CEOs IN TERMS OF LONG-TERM COMPENSATION, 1997

SOURCE: *Business Week,* April 20, 1998.

decision to merge with Travelers to create the world's largest financial institution (and guarantee himself at least $40 or $50 million).

The following tables list the top 20 CEOs in terms of total long-term and short-term pay for 1997, the top 10 non-CEOs compensation-wise, and the first- and second-in-command at 100 of America's largest corporations.

THE AMERICAN EXECUTIVE COMPENSATION SYSTEM

Lest our look at executive compensation become totally jaundiced by the megapay of the corporate elite, we will now take a more balanced look at executive compensation.

THE 20 HIGHEST PAID CEOs in 1997 . . .

(numbers in thousands of dollars)

Name	Company	1997 Salary and Bonus	Long-term Compensation	Total Pay
Sanford Weill	Travelers Group	$ 7,453	$223,272	$230,725
Roberto Goizueta	Coca-Cola	4,052	107,781	111,832
Richard Scrushy	HealthSouth	13,399	93,391	106,790
Ray Irani	Occidental Petroleum	3,849	97,657	101,505
Eugene Isenberg	Nabors Industries	1,675	82,872	84,547
Joseph Costello	Cadence Design Systems	584	66,258	66,842
Andrew Grove	Intel	3,255	48,958	52,214
Charles McCall	HBO & Co.	1,725	49,684	51,409
Philip Purcell	Morgan Stanley Dean Witter	11,274	39,533	50,807
Robert Shapiro	Monsanto	1,834	47,491	49,326
John Welch	General Electric	8,069	31,825	39,894
Harvey Golub	American Express	3,469	29,989	33,457
William Schoen	Health-Management Associates	1,041	29,905	30,945
Charles Heimbold	Bristol-Myers Squibb	2,803	26,409	29,211
Shailesh Mehta	Providian Financial	2,066	26,298	28,365
Lawrence Bossidy	Allied Signal	5,155	23,082	28,237
William Steer	Pfizer	3,880	24,240	28,120
Stephen Case	America Online	271	26,642	26,913
Robert Lipp	Travelers Property Casualty	3,730	22,570	26,301
Reuben Mark	Colgate-Palmolive	3,847	21,544	25,390

SOURCE: *Business Week*, 1998. Reprinted by permission.

AND 10 WHO AREN'T CEOs

| Name | Company | (numbers in thousands of dollars) | | |
		1997 Salary and Bonus	Long-term Compensation	Total Pay
James Crowe	Worldcom	$ 151	$ 68,913	$ 69,064
Anthony Petrello	Nabors Industries	575	47,722	48,297
James Dimon	Travelers Group	5,255	39,005	44,260
Lawrence Lasser	Marsh & McLennan	12,870	24,585	37,455
J. Carter Bacot	Bank of New York	8,302	23,193	31,495
Henry Silverman	Cendant	61	27,058	27,119
Charles Cawley	MBNA	4,623	22,461	27,084
Thomas Schneider	Morgan Stanley Dean Witter	2,460	21,242	23,702
Paolo Fresco	General Electric	3,700	19,064	22,764
Gerry Cameron	U.S. Bancorp	2,116	18,897	21,013

SOURCE: *Business Week*, 1998.

TOP EXECUTIVE PAY AT MAJOR AMERICAN CORPORATIONS

Company	Type of Business	Title	1997 Compensation (salary + bonus)	Long-term Compensation (in thousands of dollars)
AETNA	Nonbank financial	Chairman, CEO	$ 1,614	$ 3,709
		Executive VP	939	83
ALUMINUM CO. OF AMERICA	Metals, mining	Chairman, CEO	2,100	2,713
		President, COO	1,460	8,113
AMERICA ONLINE	Office equipment and computers	Chairman, President, CEO	271	26,642
AMERITECH	Telecommunications	Chairman, President, CEO	2,642	405
		Executive VP, CFO	1,014	0
AMOCO	Natural resources	Chairman, CEO	1,946	1,756
		President	1,229	308
AMR	Airlines	Chairman, CEO, President	806	1,471
		Executive VP	648	0
ANHEUSER-BUSCH	Beverages	Chairman, President, CEO	1,799	7,191
		VP	950	2,576
AT&T	Telecommunications	Chairman, CEO	3,275	4,823
		President	2,078	320
ATLANTIC RICHFIELD	Natural resources	Chairman, CEO	2,350	907
		President	1,115	967
BANKAMERICA	Banks and bank holding companies	Chairman, CEO	5,238	1,444
		President	2,575	4,698
BEAR STEARNS	Nonbank financial	President, CEO	10,376	9,616
		Chairman	14,332	4,708

TOP EXECUTIVE PAY AT MAJOR AMERICAN CORPORATIONS

Company	Type of Business	Title	1997 Compensation (salary + bonus)	Long-term Compensation (in thousands of dollars)
BELL ATLANTIC	Telecommunications	Chairman, CEO	$ 2,653	$ 4,378
		President	2,771	3,989
BOEING	Aerospace and defense	Chairman, CEO	1,331	2,347
		President, COO	3,719	12,318
BRISTOL-MYERS SQUIBB	Drugs	Chairman, CEO	2,803	26,409
		Executive VP	1,194	8,578
CATERPILLAR	General and special machinery	Chairman, CEO	2,530	1,125
		Group President	884	375
CBS	Publishing, radio, and television broadcasting	Chairman, CEO	3,058	86
		President-subsidiary	4,154	0
CHASE MANHATTAN	Banks and bank holdings companies	Chairman, CEO	6,148	5,137
		President, COO	5,660	5,936
CHEVRON	Natural resources	Chairman, CEO	2,795	7,466
		Vice Chairman	1,476	1,413
CHUBB	Nonbank financial	Chairman, CEO	2,424	1,240
		President	928	445
CIGNA	Nonbank financial	Chairman, CEO	3,270	9,068
		Executive VP, CFO	1,283	5,979
CISCO SYSTEMS	Office equipment and computers	President, CEO	558	0
		VP	493	0
CITICORP	Banks and bank holding companies	Chairman, CEO	4,000	90
		Executive VP	1,442	6,322

Company	Industry	Title		
COCA-COLA	Beverages	Chairman, CEO (died 10/18/97)	$ 4,052	$107,781
		Chairman, CEO (succeeded 10/18/97)	2,856	9,920
COLGATE-PALMOLIVE	Personal care products	Chairman, CEO	3,847	21,544
		President, COO	2,259	16,742
COMPAQ COMPUTER	Office equipment and computers	President, CEO	4,500	0
		Senior VP	1,787	15,809
COMPUTER ASSOCIATES INTERNATIONAL	Office equipment and computers	Chairman, CEO	6,000	11,589
		President, COO	4,150	6,552
CORNING	Miscellaneous manufacturing	Chairman, CEO	2,004	3,768
		Vice Chairman	1,461	3,997
CVS	Retailing, nonfood	Chairman, CEO	2,575	1,243
		Vice Chairman, COO	1,753	1,778
DEERE	General and special machinery	Chairman, CEO	2,264	2,330
		President	846	410
DELTA AIRLINES	Airlines	Chairman, CEO, President	577	4,758
		Executive VP	554	1,350
DISNEY	Leisure time industries	Chairman, CEO	10,650	0
		Senior Executive VP	2,225	0
DOW CHEMICAL	Chemicals	President, CEO	1,835	3,128
		Executive VP	1,107	1,158
DUPONT	Chemicals	CEO	3,075	11,141
		Executive VP	2,118	431
EASTMAN KODAK	Leisure time industries	Chairman, President, CEO	2,000	15,045
		President, COO	730	39
EXXON	Natural resources	Chairman, CEO	3,276	19,273
		Senior VP	1,314	4,096

TOP EXECUTIVE PAY AT MAJOR AMERICAN CORPORATIONS

Company	Type of Business	Title	1997 Compensation (salary + bonus)	Long-term Compensation (in thousands of dollars)
FIFTH THIRD BANCORP	Banks and bank holdings companies	President, CEO	$ 1,679	$ 1,560
THE GAP	Retailing, nonfood	Executive VP	722	780
		President, CEO	3,736	0
		Executive VP	1,762	0
GENERAL DYNAMICS	Aerospace and defense	Chairman, CEO	1,962	1,224
GENERAL ELECTRIC	Conglomerate	Chairman	1,241	9,613
		Chairman, CEO	8,069	31,825
		Vice Chairman	3,700	19,064
GENERAL MILLS	Food processing	Chairman, CEO	1,062	109
		Vice Chairman	1,040	135
GEORGIA-PACIFIC	Paper and forest products	Chairman, President, CEO	2,138	0
		Executive VP	864	0
GILLETTE	Personal care products	Chairman, CEO	3,417	5,311
		President, COO	1,358	0
GOODYEAR TIRE & RUBBER	Tire and rubber	Chairman, President, CEO	1,906	1,185
		President-subsidiary	874	3,729
GTE	Telecommunications	Chairman, CEO,	2,608	3,247
		President	1,913	1,926
HALIBURTON	Oil service and supply	Chairman, CEO	3,080	0
		President, COO	1,150	3,869

Company	Industry	Title		
HBO & CO.	Office equipment and computers	President, CEO	$ 1,725	$49,684
		President, co-COO	626	4,390
HEINZ (H.J.)	Food processing	Chairman, CEO	2,405	0
		Executive VP	993	530
HEWLETT-PACKARD	Office equipment and computers	Chairman, President, CEO	1,811	8,052
		Executive VP, CFO	1,032	5,594
HONEYWELL	Instruments	Chairman, CEO	2,020	1,907
		President, COO	1,207	2,265
IBM	Office equipment and computers	Chairman, CEO	6,000	8,799
		Senior VP	1,400	10,503
INTEL	Electrical, electronics	Chairman, CEO	3,255	48,958
		President, COO	2,555	0
INTERNATIONAL PAPER	Paper and forest products	CEO	1,713	2,995
		Executive VP	775	1,217
ITT INDUSTRIES	Conglomerate	Chairman, President, CEO	1,793	1,854
		Senior VP	707	851
JOHNSON & JOHNSON	Drugs	Chairman, CEO	3,574	8,431
		Vice Chairman	2,662	7,737
LILLY (ELI)	Drugs	Chairman, CEO	2,679	1,661
		President, COO	1,634	2,824
LOEWS	Nonbank financial	Co-Chairman, co-CEO	2,115	26
		Co-Chairman, co-CEO	2,559	26
MATTELL	Leisure time industries	Chairman, CEO	1,546	9,140
		President-subsidiary	1,667	200
MBNA	Banks and bank holdings companies	Chairman, CEO	4,500	1,564
McGRAW-HILL	Publishing, radio, and television broadcasting	President	4,623	22,461
		Chairman, CEO	2,398	12,419
		President, COO	1,422	1,406

TOP EXECUTIVE PAY AT MAJOR AMERICAN CORPORATIONS

Company	Type of Business	Title	1997 Compensation (salary + bonus)	Long-term Compensation (in thousands of dollars)
MERRILL LYNCH	Nonbank financial	Chairman, CEO	$ 7,729	$15,923
		President, COO	6,140	10,947
MICROSOFT	Office equipment and computers	Chairman, CEO	591	0
		Executive VP, COO	1,209	0
MINNESOTA MINING & MFG.	Miscellaneous manufacturing	Chairman, CEO	1,694	4,986
		Vice Chairman, Executive VVP	1,041	1,869
MOBIL	Natural resources	Chairman, CEO	2,064	3,564
		Executive VP	1,176	2,655
MOTOROLA	Electrical, electronics	CEO	1,951	0
		Chairman	1,855	0
THE NEW YORK TIMES	Publishing, radio, and television broadcasting	Chairman emeritus	1,423	4,772
		President, CEO	1,163	1,868
NIKE	Textiles, apparel	Chairman, CEO	2,117	0
		President, COO	1,498	1,923
NORFOLK SOUTHERN	Railroads	Chairman, President, CEO	1,988	2,473
		Executive VP	851	848
OCCIDENTAL PETROLEUM	Natural resources	President, CEO	3,849	97,657
		President	1,907	17,327
PEPSICO	Beverages	Chairman, CEO	2,807	0
		Chairman, CEO Pepsi-Cola	2,018	8,196

Company	Industry	Title		
PFIZER	Drugs	Chairman, CEO	$ 3,880	$24,240
		Executive VP	1,796	7,791
PHILIP MORRIS	Tobacco	Chairman, CEO	3,418	8,938
		Vice Chairman	1,957	7,934
PHILLIPS PETROLEUM	Natural resources	Chairman, CEO	1,975	568
		President, COO	1,364	1,056
PROCTER & GAMBLE	Personal care products	Chairman, CEO	1,180	1,661
		President, COO	1,035	1,278
RITE AID	Retailing, nonfood	Chairman, CEO	1,900	0
		President, COO	1,330	0
RJR NABISCO HOLDINGS	Tobacco	Chairman, President, CEO	4,739	0
		President-subsidiary	1,952	333
SARA LEE	Food processing	Chairman, CEO	2,259	3,523
		President	1,311	2,311
SCHWAB (CHARLES)	Nonbank financial	Chairman, CEO	7,162	0
		President, COO	5,014	0
TEXACO	Natural resources	Chairman, CEO	1,876	3,666
		President, COO	737	1,881
TEXAS INSTRUMENTS	Electrical, electronics	President, CEO	2,146	0
		Executive VP	1,459	0
TIME WARNER	Publishing, radio, and television broadcasting	Chairman, CEO	7,749	1,689
		Vice Chairman	6,050	0
UNION CARBIDE	Chemicals	Chairman, President, CEO	1,809	1,086
		VP	690	0

TOP EXECUTIVE PAY AT MAJOR AMERICAN CORPORATIONS

Company	Type of Business	Title	1997 Compensation (salary + bonus)	Long-term Compensation (in thousands of dollars)
UNITED HEALTHCARE	Service industries	CEO	$ 1,271	$ 7,233
		COO	515	2,930
WORLDCOM	Telecommunications	President, CEO	18,031	0
		CFO	4,000	5,581

SOURCE: Company proxy statements.

The Total Compensation Package

For the top officers of every corporation, salary is only one aspect of what is referred to as the total compensation package.

TYPICAL EXECUTIVE COMPENSATION PACKAGES IN LARGE CORPORATIONS		
	Top Management	**Middle Management**	**Lower Management**
Title	Chief Operating Officer	Division Manager	Division Controller
Base Salary	$750,000	$200,000 to $300,000	$80,000 to $120,000
Annual Bonus Expected Maximum	50 percent of base to 100 percent of base	40 percent of base to 80 percent of base	25 percent of base to 50 percent of base
Capital Accumulation	25,000 nonqualified stock options plus 50,000 performance units	7,500 nonqualified stock options	2,000 nonqualified stock options
Retirement Benefits	Company pension plus supplemental benefits to equal 65 percent of final average 5-year gross pay (salary plus bonus)	40 to 50 percent of final average 5-year gross pay	40 to 50 percent of final average 5-year gross pay
Life Insurance	Three times base	1.5 times base	1.5 times base
Major Medical and Dental	Company group plan plus supplemental	Company group plan	Company group plan
Perks	Car, luncheon club, country club, personal tax and financial planning advice	Possibly a car, a luncheon club or a country club	None

SOURCE: Peat, Marwick, Mitchell & Co.

EXECUTIVE COMPENSATION: AN ACTUAL SAMPLE

(Executive recruited into company)

Age:	53
Company:	Fashion industry related, with $650 million in sales
Contract:	3 years, 8 months
Annual salary:	$300,000
Front-end bonus:	$175,000 with cash or deferred-payment option. (Cash was taken.)
Annual incentive bonus:	0 to 50 percent of salary, determined by success in meeting mutually determined goals.
Stock grant:	30,000 shares given at market value of NYSE closing price on the first day of work.
Pension:	Guaranteed annual pension of 65 percent of final year's pay starting at age 65. No vesting for first three years of employment; 40 percent vesting at start of fourth year; additional added vesting at 10 percent annually thereafter.
Miscellaneous:	Personal choice of leased, Cadillac-value car, all expenses included. Membership in luncheon or athletic club of choice.
Insurance:	Fully paid medical insurance; plus all other medical expenses for family not covered with maximum of $10,000 a year. Group life insurance of $750,000. Long-term disability insurance of $5,000 a month, exclusive of social security benefits. Travel insurance: $600,000.

Personal Accounting and Legal Services:	Up to $5,000 a year.
Termination Agreement:	If contract not renewed by company, executive receives $50,000 a year for ten years, plus additional vesting in pension plan to equal 6 years, or 60 percent of benefits at age 65.
Relocation:	All expenses with mortgage provision to keep payment constant. Company also agreed to lend up to $100,000 as down payment with interest rate of 5 percent. No principal payment for three years at which point the loan could be rolled over.

SOURCE: Wells Management. Reprinted by permission.

Elements of the Compensation Package

Executive compensation depends, predictably enough, on the size of the corporation and the kind of business that it does. In theory, the most talented people end up working for the largest companies, so they usually earn the most money. Historically, the automobile, oil, and food industries paid their top people the most, but today aerospace, electronics, communications, computers, and entertainment are right up there with them and may have surpassed them in some cases. The common elements of these industries' compensation packages are described below.

SALARIES AND BONUSES

While every person's contract is different, almost all of them contain a provision for compensation over and above base salary. The most common form of additional cash payment is the annual bonus, which is at least partially tied to how well the company performs. Most top executives, however, have minimum bonus clauses that pay off regardless of their employer's overall performance.

Different companies use bonuses in different ways. At some firms, base salaries are deliberately kept low, with so-called at-risk compensation as high as 200 percent of base pay. This ties performance directly to compensation.

At other companies, salaries are set higher to reward average-to-good executive performance. Bonuses are reserved for outstanding achievement. Still another method is to tie the bonus to a five-year performance goal, which if met, brings a very big payoff.

STOCK OPTIONS AND STOCK APPRECIATION RIGHTS

Nine out of ten companies provide stock-related plans, but usually only 1 to 3 percent of the company's employees receive these perks. Stock options provide the recipient the right, at some future date, to purchase a specified amount of stock at today's price. The time limit for exercising the option is almost always ten years with restrictions placed on exercising the option during the first three or four years. If the stock price rises, the executive can make a substantial profit by exercising his or her options at the appropriate time. If the stock price declines, he or she simply chooses not to exercise the option, and loses nothing. A stock appreciation right is usually part of a long-term plan in which a unit of so-called phantom stock is held at a specific market price by an executive. If the stock price rises above that level, the executive can cash in on the gain without having to put up any money. With stock options, the executive must provide cash for the purchase of the shares. Chairman and Chief Executive of Walt Disney Co. Michael D. Eisner exercised 7.3 million stock options and immediately sold four million shares in private placement. His profits exceeded $300 million before taxes and $100 million after taxes.

DEFERRED PAYMENTS

It is not uncommon today for executives to receive other deferred payments besides stock options. The amounts are normally expressed as a percentage of base compensation, typically ranging from 25 to 50 percent of combined salary plus cash bonus. This is not a deferral of the base pay, though. Rather, it is an addition to be paid in future years. According to The New York Times, the number of executives who participate in deferred-compensation plans is unknown but is definitely growing. In the past twenty-five years, IBM has increased the number of participants from 3 to 1,000, and some large companies offer such plans to more than 3 percent of their workforce. The benefit of this type of compensation is that taxes are postponed until payouts are made—sometimes decades from now. For example, Roberto Goizueta of Coca-Cola paid taxes on $75 million in compensation over the past seventeen years, but deferred taxes on about $1 billion.

RETIREMENT PAY AND TERMINATION PAY

When successful executives come to the end of their careers, the possibility of hefty earnings does not necessarily fade away. In addition to their pensions and retirement plans, many executives have deferred payments still owed to them, sometimes tied to stock and sometimes tied to base compensation. At the very top of the executive ladder, moreover, retired executives have the potential to be rehired as consultants by the very corporations they just left. For instance, when Harold F. Geneen retired as CEO of ITT more than a decade ago, he received a retirement package of more than $450,000. It consisted of $250,000 in consulting fees, $112,000 in deferred payment as called for in his employment contract, and $130,000 from the company's retirement plan. Today every chairman who retires receives at least $2 million.

However, the biggest retirement perk for executives is when companies enlarge the compensation formula to include both base salary and bonuses.

In a relatively new method of compensating a retiring CEO, RJR Nabisco reportedly bought Charles Harper an annuity with a principal estimated at $11 million. Because the annuity was taxable, RJR also paid Harper's $5.5 million tax bill. This munificence was in addition to his cash compensation of $10.5 million for 1994 and his regular pension payout of $1 million annually.

Compensation consultants commented that this arrangement is unusual. Normally a fund is set up in-house and is taxable only when proceeds flow to the retired executive. The risk to beneficiaries is that the fund can be terminated if they are fired or leave of their own volition prior to retirement. But Harper owns the annuity outright. A similar annuity was set up for Louis Gerstner while he was at RJR. Presumably he took it with him to IBM. William Alley, CEO of American Brands, is one of the few other CEOs with a similar arrangement. Alley's annuity is estimated to be worth $9.5 million, and American Brands is said to have paid about $4.7 million in taxes on his behalf.

What if an executive does not stay at a corporation until the day of retirement? Today most executives have termination pay clauses written into their contracts. These usually pay as much as two years' salary if the executive is fired within three to five years. This relatively new form of executive compensation is a result of the increasingly precarious nature of life at the top of the corporate ladder. In 1997, according to *The New York Times Magazine*, the new president of AT&T, John Walter, was given a pink slip just nine months into his tenure. He was also handed a check for $26 million. That comes to $92,300 for each day he came to work. Similarly, Gilbert Amelio was paid $7 million to leave Apple Computer, perhaps because the company lost $1.5 million on his watch. Failure to meet goals, "bad chemistry" with the board, and the current tough business climate are all cited as reasons for the sharp increase in executives who have been booted out after periods of as short as a few months. But there's really no distinction between competency and incompetency. An executive fired for failing to perform is treated no differently from one who is laid off because of an acquisition.

Finally, many fired executives also get a chance to work for their former company as management consultants. Although the given rationale is that the fired executive is an excellent planner but a poor implementer, the true reason for offering consulting work is to secure the executive's secrecy in confidential corporate affairs. And then there's Ronald T. LeMay, who got "made whole" twice. According to *The Wall Street Journal*, LeMay was hired away from his job as president of Sprint to become CEO of Waste Management. He returned to the number two position at Sprint just three months later. The process of being made "whole" involves the employer matching stock holdings and payouts that the executive is giving up to join the new company. In LeMay's case, he collected twice. Ultimately he ended up receiving a package valued at $20.5 million to return to Sprint.

PERKS: HIDDEN COMPENSATION

Derived from the word "perquisite," the meaning of "perk" has evolved since the Renaissance from something that could be demanded to something over and above what is deserved. Especially at the executive level, "perk" has become a standard part of today's business language. Managers at every level of the corporate pyramid receive extra rewards beyond salary and bonus. The most common perks given to executives today include the following:

- Company car and free parking facilities (the very top executives in large corporations always have chauffeurs)
- Free use of corporate-owned apartments and vacation homes
- Country club memberships and fees
- Luncheon club memberships and/or expense account for entertaining
- Personal financial counseling
- Low-interest loans
- Travel expenses for spouse on business trips
- Free insurance: life insurance up to $1 million and more, 100 percent medical and dental coverage, up to $5,000-a-month disability
- Pension: up to 65 percent of the average pay over the final five years of work

Not too long ago, perks were simply considered tax-free amenities that helped to ensure the loyalty of the corporation's most prized employees. In today's highly unstable business world, however, perks have become less of a factor in attracting people or convincing employees to stay. Still, perks are expected. Once given, they are difficult to take away. Nevertheless, in the new era of cost cutting, many companies have taken steps not only to trim executive jobs but also to slim down executive perks.

GOLDEN PARACHUTES

During the acquisition and buyout fever of the 1980s, golden parachutes became a subject that sparked as much debate as the level of executive compensation does today. Corporations that felt vulnerable to takeover drafted for their top executives special "termination compensation agreements," more commonly known as "golden parachutes." The purpose of a parachute is to cushion the fall of a corporate executive pushed out the door. The cushion is usually a deep pile of cash and benefits. Two to three years' salary, and, in some cases, hefty bonuses are now common.

Golden parachutes have made many executives millionaires many times over. They have also raised substantial issues concerning conflict of interest and greed. In one of the earliest examples, F. Ross Johnson and E. A. Horrigan, respectively CEO and vice chairman of RJR Nabisco, reportedly received parachutes estimated at $53.8 million and $45.7 in the late 1980s when the company was sold to Kolberg, Kravis and Roberts, a New York investment firm. The sale was actually set in motion when a management group led by Johnson made an offer to do a leveraged buyout at a price below what was considered fair market value and substantially below the price finally realized. The insiders' offer may well have been accepted without question had it not been for a few diligent outside directors. In the end, the shareholders of RJR Nabisco realized higher value, but the whole affair raised some serious questions. For instance, can a group of executives objectively evaluate alternatives to selling their company when they know they will personally profit handsomely from the sale? What if they are personally involved in the bidding? Does the existence of a golden parachute represent a temptation to put the company into play? Also, can shareholders of other companies expect their boards to behave like RJR's board in insuring an optimum selling price?

EXCESSIVE EXECUTIVE PERKS

In the not-too-distant past, corporate boards would simply look the other way when confronted with reports of excessive executive perks. Ross Johnson was legendary in the 1980s for his personal use of corporate jets as well as flying his personal chef all over the world at company expense. However, the unrivaled king of perks was Steve Ross, the late CEO of Time-Warner. Ross lavished gifts on his corporate officers and directors, friends, and himself, all paid for by the company treasury. Ross reportedly even paid (with Time-Warner funds) for expensive art selected by his wife to hang in their apartment. Given that a strong CEO can dominate a company board and that the CEO's business and personal life frequently blur in the course of day-to-day activities, it is relatively easy for directors to rationalize almost any expenditure as being for the good of the company. In the cases above, the directors did just that.

But in 1995, directors at Morrison Knudsen, an engineering and construction firm based in Boise, Idaho, took a very different tack and staged a coup. The directors forced the resignation of CEO William Agee. The case is said to epitomize two principles of CEO power. First, once installed, it is extremely difficult to dislodge a CEO. Mr. Agee was said to have managed the company into near insolvency. Yet his compensation kept rising, and up until 1994, there was not a whimper of protest from the board, which consisted, with one exception, of Agee's friends. Second, a CEO with a friendly, docile board has a license to abuse corporate resources for his own comfort and aggrandisement: Agee reportedly ran the company a majority of the time from his estate in Pebble Beach, California. He reportedly spent company money ($7,050) for a near-life-sized portrait of himself and his wife, which hung at company headquarters in Boise. He is also said to have had Morrison Knudsen pay for legal expenses incurred by his wife, to have used the corporate jet for personal purposes on many occasions, and to have charged the company for many of the expenses associated with maintaining his home in California. Still, Mr. Agee lost his job because of bad business results and a loss of confidence by his senior managers, not because he had plunged his hand too deeply into the corporate till. Even though rumors of Mr. Agee's excesses had existed for years, it is doubtful that his board would have pulled back the extra perks that he had taken as long as profits continued to flow.

Executive Compensation in Midsized Companies

The compensation statistics below are from a study of midsized companies in California conducted by *California Business* and KPMG Peat Marwick published in 1990. While some allowances must be made for regional differences, the results present a comprehensive view of compensation in companies with $100 million of revenue or less. While this study has not been updated, we believe the relative differences still to be valid.

TOTAL CEO COMPENSATION BY COMPANY SIZE[1]

Revenues (millions of dollars)	Percentile (thousands)		
	25th	50th	75th
5–10	$105.0	$150.0	$217.3
10.1–15	105.8	143.0	199.8
15.1–25	120.0	163.0	250.0
25.1–50	123.0	175.0	309.0
50.1–100	168.0	220.09	295.0

[1]Financial institutions excluded.

TOTAL CEO COMPENSATION BY INDUSTRY

Industry	Percentile (thousands)		
	25th	50th	75th
High-tech manufacturing	$120.0	$170.0	$247.0
Other manufacturing	110.0	144.0	210.0
Wholesale/retail trade	93.0	132.0	223.0
Financial services	92.0	151.5	192.8
Other	108.8	154.0	225.0

SENIOR EXECUTIVES TOTAL COMPENSATION BY COMPANY SIZE

Median Compensation Revenues (millions of dollars)	COO[1]	(thousands) CFO[2]	CMO[3]
5–10	$ 87.5	$ 60.0	$ 70.0
10.1–15	90.0	70.0	83.0
15.1–25	113.8	78.5	90.0
25.1–50	110.0	90.0	100.0
50.1–100	123.5	104.0	117.0

[1]Chief Operating Officer. [2]Chief Financial Officer. [3]Chief Marketing Officer.

SENIOR EXECUTIVES TOTAL COMPENSATION BY INDUSTRY

Industry	COO	Median Compensation (thousands) CFO	CMO
High-tech manufacturing	$104.0	$90.0	$95.0
Other manufacturing	100.0	70.0	92.5
Wholesale/retail trade	92.0	66.5	80.0
Financial services	64.0	76.0	62.0
Other	117.5	91.0	86.0

PROFILE OF THE MEDIUM-SIZED COMPANY CEO

Median total compensation	$150,000
Median base salary	$120,000
Percent receiving bonus	70.9%
Median bonus (of those receiving one)	$45,000
Percent receiving long-term incentives	30.5%
Median age	51 years old
Median years as CEO	8 years
Median years with company	14 years
Median number of positions with company	2
Median number of employers last 10 years	1
Formal Titles:	
Percent CEO	50.9%
Percent Chairman of the Board	20.9
Percent President	69.8
Percent shareholders in company	69.7
Percent owning 50 percent or more of company	26.5
Percent owning 100 percent of company	9.5

Compensation of the Chief Financial Officer

CFOs have been making similarly high salaries and overall earnings. Among the highest-paid CFOs is General Electric Co.'s Dennis Dammerman. In 1996, he received a salary and bonus of $2 million, 18 percent more than the $1.7 million he received in 1995. In addition to that, Dammerman received $4.9 million under GE's long-term incentive program. The CFO of the securities firm Donaldson, Lufkin & Jenrette Inc., Anthony F. Daddino made more than $10 million, including a $3 million bonus and $7 million under DLJ's long-term incentive plan.

CFO SURVEY HIGHLIGHTS

	CFO Salary	CFO Bonus*	Total Compensation
Top 10%	$350,000	$286,300	$554,800
Average	$227,300	$133,100	$319,000
Bottom 10%	$125,000	$24,400	$134,600

*Bonus-paying companies only.
SOURCE: *CFO Magazine,* September 1996.

AT THE TOP: HOW EXECUTIVES COMPARE

	CEO	COO	CFO
Compensation: Salary	$489,000	$328,500	$227,300
Bonus	$389,100	$208,100	$133,100
Base salary increases 1995–96	3.1%	(3.5%)	51.1%
Base salary increases 1992–96	10%	8%	16.7%
Bonus as % of salary	68.1%	55.2%	50.1%
Bonus targets as % of salary: 1995	58.2%	52.3%	41.5%
Bonus targets as % of salary: 1996	57.1%	59.1%	43.9%
Total compensation increases 1992–96	18.2%	12.5%	24.8%

SOURCE: *CFO Magazine,* September 1996.

BOARDS OF DIRECTORS

Every large corporation has a board of directors whose essential function is to give advice and consent to the management team. The power and influence of this board varies from company to company, ranging from purely ceremonial to almost dictatorial. The size and composition of most boards are, however, fairly uniform.

According to the Korn/Ferry annual survey, the average company had eleven directors in 1998. On average, two directors come from within the company, and the other nine come from outside. These outside directors usually have very similar backgrounds and experience. Senior executives of other large corporations sat on 82 percent of all boards of directors; retired corporate executives sat on 88 percent. Former government officials sat on 53 percent, and commercial bankers sat on 20 percent, a 14 percent decline since 1994. Women's presence on corporate boards continues to grow, as 72 percent of boards had at least one woman director in 1998, up from 52 percent in 1987, and 10 percent in 1973. Ethnic minorities increased from 44 percent in 1995 to 55 percent in 1998.

Most corporations pay their directors an annual retainer as well as a per-meeting fee ($1,035 in 1998). Many companies pay the directors the fee even if they don't attend the meetings. Average total compensation for directors was $37,924 in 1998, up from $26,190 in 1992. More than 90 percent of the companies in the Korn/Ferry study paid directors additional amounts for serving on any of several board committees. Committee fees averaged about $1,000 per meeting; committee chairmen generally received a retainer of $4,000–5,000 per year. When committee fees are taken into account, board members averaged $40,651 in total corporate largesse for their services. Half of the boards surveyed allow directors to defer their fees until retirement (mostly for tax purposes), and 78 percent provide stock options and/or stock grants.

Some celebrated examples made even more money for sitting on corporate boards. At American Express, directors including Henry Kissinger received $64,000 retainers in 1994, plus 1,000 shares of stock, an annual $30,000 pension, $50,000 in free life insurance, $300,000 of accidental death coverage, and a half million-dollar gift to a chosen charity upon death. If this were not enough, board committee chairmen received an additional $10,000. All of this beneficence is needed in the eyes of the company to attract and retain a top-notch slate of directors. At Baltimore Gas & Electric, nonemployee directors receive lifetime pensions equal to their annual retainer of $18,000; at Sprint, directors get a $35,000 annual retainer paid for up to ten years *after they retired from the board.* In anticipation of shareholder protests, some companies are changing their directors' compensation programs. Travelers now pays its directors a flat fee. But the amount, $75,000, isn't likely to keep any of its directors from buying that new Range Rover this year.

So what do these companies get in return for showering their directors with amounts that must be considered extravagant by even white-collar standards, but are a pittance when compared to the annual compensation packages these directors receive at their own companies? Companies in the Korn/Ferry survey averaged eight board meetings a year in 1994, up from seven in 1993. Outside directors spent an average of 159 hours per year attending, preparing to attend, and traveling to and from board meetings. That comes out to roughly $255 per hour, per director. For the company, the costs are even higher, since average payments don't include the amounts spent on life insurance, pension plans, charitable donations, and flying the directors to company headquarters eight times a year. This last item can be quite expensive, especially considering that 17 percent of boards paid for a spouse to come along.

WHERE THE BUCKS ARE:
FINANCE EXECUTIVE PAY AS A FUNCTION OF INDUSTRY

	Base Salary	Bonus	Total Compensation
Construction/mining—CFO:	$199,500	$175,200	$345,500
Controller:	$101,900	$ 46,200	$141,500
Education—CFO:	$169,300	N/A	$184,600
Controller:	$102,500	N/A	$102,800
Financial services—CFO:	$244,600	$188,600	$391,000
Controller:	$131,300	$ 46,000	$168,000
Treasurer:	$158,100	$ 90,100	$241,300
Government—CFO:	$ 98,300	N/A	$ 98,300
Controller:	$ 87,500	N/A	$ 87,500
Health care—CFO:	$194,200	$ 52,900	$227,500
Controller:	$110,600	$ 20,600	$120,300
Treasurer:	$109,500	N/A	$117,000
Insurance—CFO:	$235,500	$141,900	$345,100
Controller:	$132,500	$ 48,400	$174,200
Treasurer:	$134,400	$ 52,300	$177,500
Manufacturing (durable)—CFO:	$236,900	$137,800	$351,700
Controller:	$133,200	$ 58,300	$174,200
Treasurer:	$142,500	$ 66,900	$195,000
Manufacturing (nondurable)—CFO:	$250,100	$140,300	$362,700
Controller:	$141,000	$ 60,800	$191,200
Treasurer:	$148,500	$ 64,700	$204,500
Service-profit—CFO:	$251,400	$135,400	$349,200
Controller:	$143,400	$ 54,900	$182,800
Treasurer:	$149,700	$ 55,000	$187,400
Transportation—CFO:	$217,600	$ 95,700	$265,500
Controller:	$133,200	$ 35,600	$154,500
Treasurer:	$132,000	N/A	$149,100
Utilities—CFO:	$212,100	$ 86,700	$272,800
Controller:	$124,100	$ 33,600	$147,300
Treasurer:	$138,000	$ 35,300	$163,900
Wholesale/trade distribution—CFO:	$224,900	$102,900	$286,600
Controller:	$121,600	$ 38,500	$143,500
Treasurer:	$131,400	$ 43,500	$161,400

SOURCE: *CFO Magazine,* September 1996.

TOP EARNING CFOs, 1996

Name	Company	Salary	Cash Bonus	Total Annual Compensation
Barry D. Romeril	Xerox	$413,341	$1,005,080	$1,418,421
James G. Stewart	Cigna	501,900	800,000	1,301,900
Gary C. Valade	Chrysler	456,250	800,000	1,256,250
Harry L. Kavetas	Eastman Kodak	567,231	581,561	1,148,792
Ronald J. Arnault	Atlantic Richfield	665,229	480,000	1,145,229
Robert M. Hernandez	USX	475,000	550,000	1,025,000
Robert G. Dettmer	Pepsico	521,539	486,280	1,007,819
Charles L. Henry	DuPont	436,000	540,000	976,000
Edward E. Matthews	American International Group	466,924	470,000	936,924
Marcus C. Bennett	Lockheed Martin	464,615	443,500	908,115
William C. Lusk	Shaw Industires	588,000	315,000	903,000
Stephen F. Page	United Technologies	497,917	400,000	897,917
Clark H. Johnson	Johnson & Johnson	437,500	457,000	894,500
Robert P. Wayman	Hewlett Packard	725,000	82,105	807,105
Robert S. Roath	RJR Nabisco	357,250	419,500	776,750
Donald L. Waite	Seagate Technology	400,005	373,500	773,505
J. Pedro Reinhard	Dow Chemical	346,674	412,500	759,174
Julian C. Day	Safeway	365,000	367,000	732,000
Thomas C. DeLoach	Mobil	470,000	260,000	730,000
Jack L. Stahl	Coca-Cola	401,583	290,000	691,583

SOURCE: *CFO Magazine,* September 1996.

AVERAGE PAYMENTS TO MEMBERS OF BOARD OF DIRECTORS, 1998

Type and Size of Company	Annual Retainer Plus Per-Meeting Fee	Committee Meeting Fee	Committee Chairman's Retainer	1998 Total Compensation
Under $1 billion	$28,059	$ 874	$3,928	$33,157
$1 billion–$2.999 billion	31,348	992	3,752	35,125
$3 billion–$4.999 billion	35,157	1,040	4,212	38,611
$5 billion–9.999 billion	38,014	1,053	5,398	41,000
$10 billion–19,999 billion	46,370	1,141	6,902	48,622
$20 billion and over	50,978	1,204	7,309	56,592

AVERAGE PAYMENTS TO MEMBERS OF BOARD OF DIRECTORS, 1998

Type and Size of Company	Annual Retainer Plus Per-Meeting Fee	Committee Meeting Fee	Committee Chairman's Retainer	1998 Total Compensation
Industrials	$35,313	$1,072	$4,192	$42,876
Banks	35,068	1,018	5,492	43,185
Other financial institutions	41,196	1,158	7,594	42,500
Insurance companies	35,868	940	6,400	45,107
Consumer products	37,241	1,021	5,353	40,153
Retailers	32,538	921	3,946	35,645
Advanced technology	36,526	1,145	4,226	41,081
Aerospace	47,070	1,003	7,093	51,625
Energy	33,877	993	4,101	39,698
Health-care provider	38,631	1,084	8,471	40,125
Pharmaceuticals	46,738	1,265	6,160	49,666
Entertainment companies	48,470	1,029	3,500	50,000
Other service companies	33,395	1,014	4,694	41,600
Average of all companies	**$37,924**	**$1,035**	**$5,237**	**$40,651**

SOURCE: Korn/Ferry International, *Board of Directors, 25th Annual Study*, 1998. Reprinted by permission.

HUMAN RESOURCES

Human resources (HR), once known simply as personnel, encompasses all areas of a company's dealings and relationships with its employees, from the hiring of new staff members to planning programs that assist people when they leave the company. Human resources also covers training, compensation and benefits (including but not limited to health care), labor relations, corporate safety and security, and, in many companies, in-house communications.

More than 550,000 individuals are employed in this field, which has grown dramatically in status and importance over the last decade. And despite all the corporate downsizing in the early 1990s, the human resources field experienced significant growth. That's because more and more corporate managers and executives began to realize that the best-run, most successful large companies in America were those that took special care of their employees' needs. This attitude has become more prevalent as unemployment has dropped to record lows—now companies are finding themselves constantly in search of new ways to make their employees happy, comfortable, and less likely to defect to a competitor with a higher salary bid. Human resources specialists are playing key roles in the establishment of unique employee benefit plans that range from casual dress codes to on-site child care and health facilities.

The increasing importance of the training staff within human resources departments is another example of management's changing views. Teaching standardized company procedures to all levels of employees, from clerks to middle-level managers, helps corporations cope with high turnover rates and frees veteran employees from an instructional burden that often hampers their own work. Frequently, employers look for people with educational or teaching backgrounds to fill these slots. "The need and importance of keeping workers abreast of changing technologies has required companies to maintain and enforce their entire corporate training and development programs," says Helen Bensimon of the American Society of Training. In addition, many companies hire training people on a freelance basis (see the separate entry called "The Training Staff" in this section).

According to the Bureau of Labor Statistics, the human resources job market will likely remain competitive between now and 2006. The projected large number of job openings will be offset by an abundant supply of qualified college graduates entering the marketplace. While the field is constantly changing, over the next decade the strongest demand should be for those specializing in recruiting and retention of employees, occupational safety and health, equal employment opportunity administration, and employee benefits. Labor relations, international human resources management, and HR information systems should also see substantial growth. The field is likely to feel the negative impact of corporate downsizing and restructuring as well as improvements in information systems technology that make some workers obsolete.

Salaries in human resources continue to vary widely, probably because of the variety of positions contained under this grouping—the following chart provides salary information for a total of fifty-eight different positions in human resources—and because of the variety of industries in which these people work. The median 1995 salary for specialists in human resources with limited experience was $25,700; for supervisors/managers it was $59,000. Salaries for personnel specialists in the federal government in 1997 started at $19,500 for a person with a bachelor's degree or three years of experience in human resources. Federal government personnel specialists averaged $52,900 in 1997; personnel managers averaged $55,400.

Below is a wide range of salary levels compiled from several sources, including the federal and state governments and the Society for Human Resources Management. In conjunction with William M. Mercer Inc., of Deerfield, Illinois, the Society produces the best and most accurate survey of salaries in personnel every year, as well as an excellent set of job descriptions and salary information for mostly large corporate personnel departments.

AVERAGE ANNUAL SALARIES IN CORPORATE HUMAN RESOURCE DEPARTMENTS

Title	Average Salary	Average Minimum[1]	Average Maximum[1]
Vice President, Administration[2]	$169,400	$128,500	$205,700
Top Human Resources Management Executive[2] (with industrial relations)	157,900	116,400	190,200
Top Human Resources Management Executive[2] (without industrial relations)	148,200	114,500	185,600
International Top Human Resources Management Executive[2]	126,900	91,100	148,100
Top Corporate Labor/Industrial Relations Executive[2]	109,200	82,900	126,100
Top Corporate Organizational Development Executive	109,000	79,800	128,300
Top Corporate Compensation and Benefits Executive	102,100	76,800	121,600
Total Top Quality Executive	101,500	80,800	126,900
Top Division, Subsidiary or Regional Human Resources Executive	94,100	69,100	110,500
Human Resources Director (in small organization)	90,900	70,400	110,200
Top Corporate Employee Relations Executive	89,300	69,000	111,100
Executive Compensation Manager	88,400	71,100	114,400
International Compensation and Benefits Manager	83,700	66,000	105,400
Top Corporate Security Manager	80,900	61,700	97,300
Human Resources Planning Manager	78,900	58,100	94,600
Training and Organizational Development Manager	75,900	59,100	93,300
Labor Relations Supervisor	74,800	56,900	88,000
Top Corporate Safety Manager	74,000	57,400	88,700
Compensation Manager	71,600	55,200	87,200
Employee Benefits Manager	69,200	53,600	84,200
Plant/Branch Human Resources Manager (union facility)	69,200	55,200	85,500
Equal Employment Opportunity/Diversity Manager	68,100	57,100	90,800
Human Resources Information System Manager	67,700	51,800	81,800
Management Development Manager	67,300	53,600	86,100
Employee Assistance Program Manager	66,200	45,900	71,500
Employee Communications Manager	66,000	53,200	84,200
Employment and Recruiting Manager	65,600	51,500	81,000
Total Quality Manager	65,500	51,200	80,000

AVERAGE ANNUAL SALARIES IN CORPORATE HUMAN RESOURCE DEPARTMENTS

Title	Average Salary	Average Minimum[1]	Average Maximum[1]
Group Insurance Manager	$ 65,100	$ 50,200	$ 78,800
Plant/Branch Human Resources Manager (nonunion facility)	65,000	52,100	84,900
Employee Training Manager	61,500	49,000	77,100
Managerial and Executive Recruitment Specialist	56,200	44,200	69,800
Work and Family Program Manager	56,100	42,500	67,300
Manager, Office Services	54,900	44,400	69,600
Workers' Compensation Supervisor	54,400	42,500	66,100
Labor Relations Generalist	53,300	42,400	63,800
Safety/Security Supervisor	51,700	41,500	64,100
Senior Compensation Analyst	50,700	39,500	60,900
Safety Specialist	50,000	38,500	59,100
Wellness Program Manager	48,700	37,700	57,900
Senior Training Specialist	48,200	38,600	60,000
Generalist	47,200	36,300	56,300
Benefits Planning Analyst	46,100	39,400	61,700
Human Resource Information System Specialist	45,900	34,600	53,100
Professional/Technical Recruitment Specialist	45,500	36,400	56,400
Equal Employment Opportunity/Diversity Specialist	44,600	38,900	60,300
Plant/Branch Human Resources Administrator	43,500	37,700	58,500
Employee Assistance Program Counselor	42,800	35,600	54,000
Compensation and Benefits Administrator	41,800	35,300	54,100
Benefits Administrator	41,500	31,600	48,200
Associate Training Specialist	41,100	31,600	48,200
Nurse	39,400	29,500	47,200
Compensation Analyst	38,900	32,400	50,100
Entry Level Generalist	34,900	28,500	43,600
Recruiter	34,500	30,400	46,600
Security Specialist	30,900	34,000	52,300
Benefits Clerk	27,600	22,500	33,700
Personnel Assistant	27,000	22,100	33,500

[1]Not all companies report minimum and maximum salaries, so figures in this column may be based on smaller sample sizes than the average salary column.
[2]Salary does not reflect bonus, which reflects a large percentage (more than 25 percent) of total compensation.
SOURCE: William M. Mercer Inc., *1997 Human Resource Management Compensation Survey.* Effective date for all data is 1997.

Job Descriptions

UPPER MANAGEMENT

Vice President, Administration—Responsible for planning and directing corporate staff functions in support of operations. Specific responsibilities may include human resources, purchasing, management information systems, long-range planning, budgeting, and finance. Manages administration activities for corporate properties and facilities. May act as chief adviser or liaison to executive vice president, president, and/or chief operating officer in order to plan, evaluate, and recommend overall corporate strategies.

Top Human Resource Management Executive—Develops, implements, and coordinates policies and programs encompassing all, or nearly all, aspects of human resources management, including employment, labor relations, wage and salary administration, training, placement, safety and health, benefits, and employee services. Originates policies and monitors activities affecting all operations and locations of the company. May be responsible for community and/or public relations activities.

Top Corporate Personnel Executive—Develops, implements, and coordinates policies and programs encompassing all, or nearly all, aspects of personnel for salaried (nonunion) employees, including employment, salary administration, training placement, manpower planning and development, employee benefits, and affirmative action programs. Originates policies and monitors activities affecting all operations and locations of the company. May report to top human resources management executive, the CEO, or other corporate general management.

MANAGEMENT

International Top Human Resources Executive—Develops, implements, and coordinates policies and programs encompassing all, or nearly all, aspects of international human resource management, including employment, labor relations, wage and salary administration, training, placement, safety and health, benefits, and employee services. Originates policies and monitors activities affecting all international operations and locations of the company.

Top Divisional/Regional Human Resources Executive—Develops and implements human resources policies and programs within the policy guidelines formulated by the top corporate human resources executive and top management. Usually receives guidance and counsel from the corporate human resources function.

Top Corporate Security Manager—Develops and administers policies to protect corporate facilities, properties, and employees, which may include computer security systems and employee identification card systems. Selects and supervises outside protective services contractors and in-house security guards. Typically reports to human resources executive or corporate management. This job does not include safety responsibilities.

Top Corporate Safety Manager—Develops and administers policies and programs to ensure all facilities are in compliance with OSHA and other safety and health requirements and that employee safety programs are developed and carried out. May also be responsible for highway safety where applicable. Typically reports to human resources executive or corporate management. This job does not include security responsibilities.

Top Corporate Employee Relations Executive—Directs the establishment and maintenance of satisfactory labor-management relations, union avoidance and decertification efforts, and the formulation and administration of the company's labor relations policy, subject to top management guidance and approval. Represents management in labor relations, including the negotiation, interpretation, and administration of collective bargaining agreements, directly or through subordinates and administration of grievance procedures. May include responsibilities for programs designed to improve the quality of work life and employee satisfaction. Typically reports to top unit or corporate human resources executive.

Top Corporate Organizational Development Executive—Directs the development and implementation of corporate programs to better develop and utilize human resources. Major responsibilities may include: (1) internal consulting; (2) management assessment and development; (3) performance measurement; (4) management utilization and development needs; (5) consultation with managers on motivational strategies, human performance problems, personal career development, and stress reactions; (6) employment research and attitude surveys; (7) job enrichment applications; and (8) long-term human resources plan and management succession. May supervise employment and recruiting function. Typically reports to top corporate human resources executive or top corporate personnel executive.

Top Corporate Compensation and Benefits Executive—Responsible for all compensation and benefits programs for all employees, including design implementation and administration of programs. Compensation duties often include job descriptions, job evaluation, performance appraisal, merit and other salary increases, wage and salary surveys, incentive plans, and stock option and other executive programs. Benefits responsibilities often include life, health, and disability insurance programs, profit-sharing and retirement programs, and personnel practices. Often responsible for selection and supervision of benefits consultants, brokers, trustees, and necessary legal assistance.

Human Resources Director—Develops and administers policies and programs covering several or all of the following: recruitment, wage and salary administration, training, safety and security benefits and services, employee and labor relations, and personnel research. Supervises small human resources department in small- to medium-sized firm. Typically reports to senior management.

LABOR RELATIONS

Labor Relations Supervisor—Establishes and maintains satisfactory labor-management relations, formulates and administers the company's labor relations policy subject to top management guidance and approval, and represents management in labor relations, including the negotiation, interpretation, and administration of collective bargaining agreements. Responsible for administering grievance procedures. May be responsible for developing union-avoidance programs at nonunion facilities and for coordinating decertification activities at union facilities. May include supervision of quality of work-life programs.

Labor Relations Generalist—Assists in administration of company's labor relations policies. May be involved in negotiations, administration of collective bargaining agreements, and administration of grievance procedures. This exempt position typically reports to plant/branch human resources manager or labor relations supervisor.

EMPLOYEE RELATIONS

Equal Employment Opportunity/Diversity Manager—Develops, implements, and recommends equal employment and affirmative action programs that are in keeping with corporate objectives and that ensure compliance with the current legal requirements. Maintains statistics necessary to monitor the effectiveness of the programs and alerts top management to difficulties encountered in attaining and maintaining compliance with established policies. Communicates policies and affirmative action programs to employees, top management, the public, and government agencies. May direct processing of complaints and company defense before administrative or judicial proceedings. Typically reports to top employee relations or top corporate personnel executive.

Human Resources Information System Manager—Designs, develops, tests, and directs ongoing administration of the human resources information system, including selection of software and hardware. Supervises maintenance and processing of employee records. Human resources information system may be on microcomputer, minicomputer, mainframe, or a combination. Develops recurring or special reports as requested. Typically reports to top employee relations executive or top unit or corporate human resources executive.

Employee Assistance Program Manager—Develops, implements, and directs company-wide employee assistance programs. Researches, investigates, and evaluates existing methods and approaches in the field of employee assistance programs. May also investigate treatment facilities and their staffs in order to maintain an up-to-date reference resource and information on current treatment philosophy. May design and implement own programs and procedures. Produces in-house publication of information on corporate employee assistance programs and procedures. May assist in effectively resolving employee job performance problems through performance evaluation, documentation, and counseling. Typically reports to top corporate employee relations executive.

Employee Communications Manager—Manages the company's employee communications programs. Areas of responsibility may include preparation and publication of several or most of the following: company newsletters, management reports, brochures, employee handbooks, materials for employee conferences and seminars, internal directories, etc. May provide assistance in management speechwriting. May also be involved in corporate public/community relations programs. Normally reports to top employee relations executive.

ORGANIZATIONAL DEVELOPMENT

Employment and Recruiting Manager—Establishes procedures for recruitment and placement. Directs the exempt and nonexempt recruiting, interviewing, selection, and placement of applicants for employment. Directs design and placement of employment advertising. Responsible for relations with outside employment agencies and recruiters. Supervises testing and training programs. Assures that Equal Employment Opportunity goals are attained. May direct new employee orientation, in-processing, exit interviews, outplacement, and employee counseling.

Recruitment Specialist—Interviews and recommends placement of candidates for entry-level and experienced positions. Seeks out sources of candidates, including colleges, technical schools, and job fairs. May travel extensively. Typically reports to employment and recruiting manager or top human resources executive of own organizational unit.

Human Resources Planning Manager—Develops short- and long-range strategic plans for effective recruitment, development, and utilization of human resources. Projects current and future companywide staffing and organizational requirements. Establishes and maintains human resources planning, control, and reporting activities. Advises with departmental managers on the preparation of departmental human resources plans. May also contribute to top corporate strategic planning process. Typically reports to the top corporate organizational development executive.

Training/Organizational Development Manager—Analyzes and determines training needs of the company and formulates and develops plans, procedures, and programs to meet specific training needs and problems. Develops and constructs training manuals and training aids or may supervise their development by outside suppliers. Plans, conducts, and coordinates management inventories, appraisals, placement, counseling, and training, and coordinates participation in outside training programs by company employees. Typically reports to top organizational development executive or top human resources executive (corporate or own unit).

Employee Training Managers—Analyzes and determines training needs and administers plans, procedures, and programs to meet training needs and problems. Constructs training manuals and aids. Supervises or conducts special courses designed for training selected groups of company employees. Typically reports to training/organizational development manager, top organizational development executive, or top unit or corporate human resources executive.

Management Development Manager—Plans, conducts, and coordinates special studies of existing management staff and possible replacements. Conducts investigations to ascertain the executive training and developmental needs. Develops and directs approved management training programs. Typically reports to training/organizational development manager, top organizational development executives, or top unit or corporate human resources executive.

COMPENSATION AND BENEFITS

Executive Compensation Manager—Designs, implements, and administers compensation programs for officers and key executives. Programs may include perquisites, short- and long-term incentive plans, stock option plans, long-term capital accumulation, special benefits programs for executives (such as deferred compensation, supplemental life insurance, and low-interest loans), in addition to executive salaries. May coordinate financial

ANNUAL SALARIES OF STATE PERSONNEL DIRECTORS

State	Salary	State	Salary
Alabama	$106,407	Nebraska	$ 65,616
Alaska	80,244	Nevada	73,570
Arizona	62,400	New Hampshire	53,375
Arkansas	76,790	New Jersey	100,225
California	107,939	New Mexico	70,695
Colorado	95,640	New York	90,832
Connecticut	90,420	North Carolina	92,378
Delaware	89,900	North Dakota	58,560
Florida	84,549	Ohio	82,888
Georgia	100,242	Oklahoma	61,661
Hawaii	85,302	Oregon	78,624
Idaho	73,528	Pennsylvania	95,100
Illinois	71,796	Rhode Island	72,283
Indiana	73,467	South Carolina	72,154
Iowa	82,620	South Dakota	70,795
Kansas	73,984	Tennessee	81,264
Kentucky	82,688	Texas	55,834
Louisiana	88,920	Utah	84,000
Maine	68,557	Vermont	60,008
Maryland	70,912	Virginia	82,417
Massachusetts	73,156	Washington	93,659
Michigan	97,405	West Virginia	50,000
Minnesota	67,505	Wisconsin	90,124
Mississippi	75,000	Wyoming	57,120
Missouri	67,548	U.S. Virgin Islands	65,000
Montana	50,425		

SOURCE: Council of State Governments, *The Book of States*, 1998–99.

counseling, executive relocation, and tax-return preparation for executives. Conducts and participates in surveys of competitive executive compensation.

International Compensation and Benefits Manager—Develops, implements, and administers compensation programs for international personnel, to include expatriates and third-country nationals (may be responsible for local nationals). Programs include salary administration, tax equalization, differentials, allowances, and employee benefits. Provides guidance to international management and may take policy-level direction from them. Typically reports to top compensation and benefits executive, top international human resources executive, or top corporate human resources executive.

Employee Benefits Manager—Designs and administers retirement, profit sharing, thrift, group medical-surgical, disability, and life plans. Often responsible for selection and supervision of benefits consultants, brokers, trustees, and necessary legal assistance. Ensures that the firm retains a competitive benefits posture in the marketplace. Typically reports to top corporate compensation and benefits executive or top unit or corporate human resources executive.

Compensation and Benefits Administrator—Administers compensation and benefits programs. May administer any or all of the following programs: life, health, and disability insurance programs, profit sharing, pension, and other retirement programs. Typically reports to top corporate compensation and benefits executive or local human resources management.

Compensation Manager—Directs the design, implementation, and administration of compensation programs, including job evaluation, salary administration, annual and long-term management cash incentives, sales compensation and differential incentive, and perquisite and supplemental pay programs. May coordinate stock option, perquisite, deferred compensation, and other executive programs. Administers performance appraisal and salary administration programs.

The Training Staff

In 1940, a small group of sales executives wanted to change attitudes toward buying in the United States. Realizing the need for good teaching personnel to ensure companies of ethical yet highly persuasive salesmanship, they founded the first national society of training directors. The American Society of Training Directors (ASTD) was formed in 1945 and today (under the name American Society of Training and Development) has over 70,000 members. It also publishes a journal and provides one- and two-week courses of instruction at its own institutes.

Originally the ASTD's emphasis was on the training of manufacturing and marketing personnel. While training in those two fields continues, many other fields of employment now have training programs as well, including government, utilities, and finance. The programs range in scope from introductory sales techniques to safety courses for school bus drivers, and from basic office procedures to lessons in word processing techniques. Some training personnel even teach stress management with Zen and yoga methods. Corporate awareness of the need for carefully planned training programs to provide essential instruction to employees has grown, and the increased costs of mismanaging human resources has become apparent. These factors have led companies to place greater value on the function of the trainer and to increase the number of training positions available.

AVERAGE ANNUAL SALARIES OF THE TRAINING STAFF BY POSITION

Title	Average Salary
Executive-level training/HRD manager	$81,802
Manager of a training/HRD department (with five or more full-time training professionals)	62,658
Manager of a training/HRD department (with one to four full-time training professionals)	54,655
One-person training department	46,948
Classroom instructor	42,974
Instructional designer	47,658
Management development, career development or organization development specialist	52,293
Personnel director	54,309
Line or staff manager/specialist other than training or personnel	63,610

SOURCE: *TRAINING* magazine. Copyright © 1997. Lakewoood Publications, Minneapolis, MN. Reprinted by permission.

Trainers work with on-the-job trainees both at the actual corporation site and at training centers, to which corporations send their employees. The optimum training system is one that encompasses instruction, evaluation, and implementation; therefore, trainers' jobs consist of elements within all these areas. The most common training job titles are listed above, followed by each title's annual salary range.

During the 1990s, the training occupation changed substantially as responsibilities and spheres of involvement expanded due to the increased demand for their services within both traditional fields and new fields of employment. In all probability, the training occupation will continue to grow markedly in upcoming years, as will trainers' salaries.

MANAGEMENT CONSULTANTS

As with many sectors of the job market in the late 1990s, the management consulting industry is plagued—or blessed, depending on your point of view—with more work than there are qualified employees to handle. In fact, some estimates predict 16 percent growth for management consulting in the next few years. While this boom in business is creating tremendous opportunities for would-be consultants, and while an abundant supply of college graduates is entering the marketplace each year, competition for the best jobs remains tight. The simple explanation for this is that not everyone has what it takes to make it in the consulting business.

Consultants are the gypsies of the business world, moving from assignment to assignment without putting down roots. This creates problems. To the career consultant, there is no permanency. He or she is hired for the expertise and objectivity he or she brings to a situation. After performing the task at hand, the consultant is summarily let go while the client goes about using or implementing the particular product of the consultant's work. So consultants cannot point to any particular enterprise other than the project work performed as their own. From the client side there can be a mistrust of consultants because, at least in theory, they are not held closely accountable for their work. The idea that the consultant just pushes ideas, meaningful or not, is a lament that can stem from poor consulting work or can be an excuse for not cooperating with the consultant.

The role of the consultant is to come into a situation in which a client is unsure or inexpert and recommend actions or provide assessments. There are many different types of situations, so the specific use of consultants can vary widely. Therefore, there are many different shapes and sizes of consultants. At the top of the list are the well-known, old-line management consulting firms such as Andersen Consulting and McKinsey & Co., who practice consulting on a broad list of business operating and strategic issues. There are also firms, large and small, as well as individuals whose practice centers on single aspects of business, such as sales productivity or marketing strategy. And there are firms that may specialize in specific disciplines, such as MIS function.

A wide variety of practitioners exists. Anyone with some degree of business experience or expertise in a field can hang out a consulting shingle. The number of one- to two-person consulting operations may well exceed a hundred thousand. Many small firms also exist, filling special niches and usually serving medium- and small-sized companies. These may serve specialized needs like engineering studies or providing expert opinion, or they may give generalized advice. There are also consulting divisions in larger companies, such as the major accounting firms, which use the special expertise of the organization as a wedge to get other kinds of consulting work. The largest firms have national and international practices with staffs that number in the thousands.

The top general management consulting firms are very exclusive clubs. These firms normally hire consultants directly from the top graduate schools of business and then train them in their own methodology and traditions. Competition for the best graduates is stiff, and starting salaries in the $65,000 to $75,000 range are common. The new consultant then has five to seven years to make it to the first partnership level or leave. Not more than one in five is expected to pass the test.

While the titles of the working levels in a consulting firm are different from firm to firm, the pecking order follows a logical progression that indicates length of experience and relative ranking. What follows is a discussion of a typical structure in a top-rate consulting firm. The titles are not a foolproof indication of either standing or compensation. Some well-known firms have few partners, perhaps only the founders; yet the same titles are used. Use the information accordingly.

A brand-new consultant may be referred to as an associate for the first two years or so. The progression is then to senior associate, a title that indicates three to five years of experience and the ability to do more complex and independent work. The senior associate may supervise others as well. Around the five-year mark, the consultant who is making satisfactory progress may become an engagement manager, with the responsibility to lead a consulting team on a particular client project. The best may then become a senior engagement manager, leading several study teams or a very large project team. This is a prelude to being considered for junior partnership. Around the seven-year mark, the very best will be considered for appointment as a junior partner, sometimes titled principal. Partnership brings with it responsibility for marketing the firm and its services as well as the leadership of client projects. The final step some time later is to senior partnership or director.

Compensation for the few who run the full course can be extremely rewarding. As mentioned, starting salaries at the best firms can easily exceed $70,000. A bonus opportunity of up to 40 percent and noncontributory profit sharing may be included. Progress up the entry-level ranks brings generous increases in base salary. In general, more experience means that the firms can charge more for an individual's services, and therefore the individual shares in the increasing fee structure. Junior partnership brings a salary often in the $150,000 range plus bonus and the right to purchase shares in the firm. These shares give the partner a claim against the assets of the firm. The shares can be sold when the individual leaves. Senior partners may earn a base compensation in excess of $250,000, plus the other compensation incentives.

Independent consultants work on a different structure. They are self-employed, although much of their work may come from established firms on a subcontract basis. Generally these consultants can command fees between $400 and $1,000 a day. Some well-known professionals may receive over $2,000 a day. Most are on the lower end of the scale. When the independent works on his or her own, the fee is maximized because there is no one to split it with. Of course, self-employed is one step away from being unemployed, so many hedge their bets by working in close association with others as subcontractors. By pooling talents, marketing is easier, more resources can be brought to bear on an assignment, and different talents and backgrounds are made available. So there are advantages, even though a portion of the fee (up to 50 percent) may be sacrificed.

By working for themselves, consultants also sacrifice benefits provided by the large firms, so the fees gained are not free and clear. To cover these overheads as well as protect against lost cash flow during idle periods, the independent is in a constant struggle to maximize fees. Still, despite the insecurity, independents exist because they are not the type of people who are comfortable working for large organizations. They like the intellectual challenge of consulting as well as the personal freedom of movement the independent road brings.

When thinking about career consultants, remember a familiar but corrupted form of the old Bernard Shaw saw, "He who can does; he who cannot consults." Consultants seem to get much of their satisfaction from advising rather than doing. New MBA graduates who get into the profession do so because it is normally a ticket to a good second job high in the management ranks of a client company. Those who remain consultants or who return to the profession are unique individuals. (Here we distinguish between the truly professional consultants and those who are doing the work because they can't find anything else.)

Consultants are different most of all because they normally have been blessed with higher than average intelligence. These highly intelligent people also possess a great deal of self-confidence and have faith in their ability to handle any situation presented. They are very analytical and objective by nature. They thrive on exposure to the lofty areas of corporate policy and executive decision-making. Many career consultants are workaholics who may spend undue amounts of time on the road. To many, a fourteen-to-sixteen-hour workday is common.

While some may bill themselves as general management consultants and others as specialists, all have certain areas where they are normally more expert. Some may have special knowledge or experience in a specific industry or group of industries. Others may be expert on specific functions such as advertising or compensation. All the good ones are quick to learn and keep their knowledge updated.

Consulting also requires a great deal of tact, even while debating a point or telling someone he or she has misinterpreted data. A consultant must be good at making presentations and quick on his or her feet, able to refute objections with finality. And he or she must be able to enlist cooperation while exerting leadership. Part of this overall ability to handle people and situations arises from the expertise and experience of the consultant, but part of it is a talent that can't be taught.

While consulting is a potentially lucrative profession, it is not an easy one in which to prosper. It requires a disposition toward the intellectual side of business, a natural curiosity about how things are working and how they should work. This must be coupled with an ability to be unbiased and analytical. For those who have the talent, the rewards are substantial.

There are many large consulting firms that have gained national prominence over the years. Some generalist firms like McKinsey & Company and Booz, Allen, Hamilton are multinational in scope with offices around the world. Other large firms like John Diebold and Associates, which specialize in specific fields, are also very large and broad in reach. In the 1980s, large accounting firms such as Coopers & Lybrand and Peat Marwick Main Hurdman started large consulting practices. Employment opportunities vary among the large firms. Some will hire research associates directly out of college and provide a career path into consultancy for the best and brightest of these people. Others hire only from graduate schools into consultant-level positions. These accounting firms usually require an accounting background, even on the part of their consultants. Some are looking for industry-specific or functional expertise, such as computer systems or inventory management, on which they can leverage. All are looking for very bright, imaginative people.

Beyond the very large and well-known firms are literally thousands of smaller firms with a wide variety of needs. These consulting companies tend to specialize in specific areas of knowledge and expertise and do not usually hire trainees. To land a job with any of these requires a demonstrated track record in an industry or a functional area and, in most cases, prior consulting experience.

Among the consulting specialties most in demand are computers, human resources, marketing research, inventory control, telecommunications, and manufacturing efficiency. Consultants who specialize in computers advise clients on the use of computer systems, the development of programs and applications, and, generally, how to use computer systems to enhance operating efficiency. Consultants in human resources perform a wide variety of services from doing comparative compensation studies to designing training programs. Marketing research is a very large and specialized area that is described below. Experts in inventory control advise companies on modern-day techniques for reducing inventory costs, such as just-in-time inventory stocking. Telecommunications consultants aid businesses in selecting telephone and data communications equipment and services. They also monitor expenditures and make recommendations on reducing costs. Consultants in the area of manufacturing efficiency advise clients on making their equipment and manufacturing processes as efficient as possible. There are many other specialties as well.

Compensation for specialists averages close to $1,000 per day. Unless the specialty is particularly arcane or the specialist is well-known, specialists generally earn less than generalists who practice strategy consulting.

AVERAGE COMPENSATION OF CONSULTANTS, 1997

Position/Firm Size	Base Salary	Bonus
Senior Partner		
less than $1 million	$100,047	$ 36,314
$1–4 million	150,306	93,162
$4–25 million	201,372	113,141
over $25 million	215,750	125,000
Junior Partner		
less than $1 million	51,143	38,525
$1–4 million	99,285	79,758
$4–25 million	120,354	51,232
over $25 million	152,250	46,300
Senior Consultant		
less than $1 million	59,978	13,746
$1–4 million	69,076	15,400
$4–25 million	90,774	26,842
over $25 million	107,750	26,050
Management Consultant		
less than $1 million	43,632	2,329
$1–4 million	50,825	8,202
$4–25 million	69,822	13,015
over $25 million	70,950	13,550
Entry-Level Consultant		
less than $1 million	33,600	2,000
$1–4 million	37,375	8,266
$4–25 million	51,690	7,166
over $25 million	43,450	6,075

SOURCE: Association of Management Consulting Firms. Reprinted by permission.

CONSULTANTS: RECRUITING, TURNOVER, AND PROMOTIONS

Position	% Hired from Outside	% Leaving	% Likely to Be Promoted
Senior partner	0%	4%	N.A.
Junior partner	0	6	20%
Senior Consultant	25	15	25
Management consultant	53	18	50

SOURCE: Association of Managment Consulting Firms (1997 data).

TOP 10 MANGEMENT CONSULTING FIRMS

	World Revenue 1996	U.S. Revenue 1996
1. Andersen Consulting	$3,115.3	$1,590.0
2. McKinsey & Co.	2,100.0	800.0
3. Ernst & Young	2,100.0	1,400.0
4. Coopers & Lybrand Consulting	1,918.0	1,005.0
5. KPMG Peat Marwick	1,380.0	770.0
6. Arthur Andersen	1,379.6	766.2
7. Deloitte & Touche	1,303.0	821.0
8. Mercer Consulting Group	1,159.0	707.0
9. Towers Perrin	903.0	659.0
10. A. T. Kearney	870.0	530.0

SOURCE: Association of Management Consulting Firms.

MARKET RESEARCHERS

When C. Wright Mills wrote of the changing world of business after World War II in *White Collar* (1951), he mentioned market research only in passing and did not cite the field as a major category in the book's Index. However, the future importance of market research was clearly indicated in the following passage from *White Collar:* "Before high-pressure salesmanship, emphasis was upon the salesman's knowledge of the product, a sales knowledge grounded in apprenticeship; after it, the focus is upon hypnotizing the prospect, an art provided by psychology."

The underpinning of the "hypnosis" of the American buying public is frequently provided by market research analysts—a work force of approximately 40,000 men and women employed not only in independent market research organizations but also in manufacturing companies, advertising agencies, media enterprises, university research units, and governmental agencies.

Independent market research organizations may be found in large- and medium-sized cities—wherever there are central sales and manufacturing offices—but the largest tend to cluster in major cities, especially New York, Chicago, and Los Angeles.

The market researcher provides businesses with information about the needs and desires of the buying public, attempting at the same time to shape that information into future trends. The basic tools for this information-gathering and trend-projecting are surveys, interviews, and focus groups. The market researcher collaborates with statisticians and trained interviewers—all working together to monitor and shape not only buying habits but basic thinking and motivation as well. After the information and data have been collected and analyzed, the market researcher determines what action should be taken: Changes in advertising to improve sales, searches for new markets, efforts to reach a new segment of the population, attempts to improve the public's discernment of the faltering image of anything from a bar of soap to a soapbox politician.

A market research trainee usually has a bachelor's degree in marketing or economics, with a strong background in mathematics, statistic survey design, and computer science. To advance, graduate work in business administration or a related field is frequently required. Some marketing positions require specialized knowledge or skills related to the particular product or service being promoted. Finally, for more and more market research work, strong training in computer technology is helpful.

Market research trainees usually perform a great deal of clerical work along with basic research—transcribing data and tabulating questionnaire and survey results. Junior analysts help to conduct surveys and questionnaires, along with writing reports on the results. Senior analysts assume responsibility for specific market research projects. At the top of the ladder is the manager and then the director, who have overall supervisory responsibility.

Market research requires considerable quantitative skill along with the creativity to break new ground by analyzing buying habits and the underlying motivation. As the backseat driver for business, the market researcher must also be skilled in written and oral communication. The salary in this field starts at $28,000–$30,000 and, with experience, can go as high as $75,000 after ten or fifteen years.

Job Descriptions in Marketing Research

Account Executive/Director of Marketing—Services the client account directly, solicits business, and oversees its completion. A background in marketing research; analytical, selling and interpersonal skills are required.

Data Processor, Tabulation Specialist, Programmer—Responsible for programming, developing, and reviewing data, interpreting codes, data entry layout, and tabulation specifications, as well as preparing the final data tables. Design, math, and statistical skills as well as basic business knowledge and interpersonal skills are needed.

Moderator, Qualitative Consultant—Facilitates focus group discussions to discern consumer interests, opinions, ideas, etc. Analyzes the synthesis and identifies issues. Writing and interpersonal skills are required; usually a psychology or sociology background is required.

Project Manager, Project Director, Field Manager, Field Director, Project Supervisor, Field Supervisor—Defines the study as received from the Account Executive creating the specifications and detailing instructions for executing the research for the client. A degree in business and/or marketing research is usually required.

Research Analyst/Supervisor/Manager—Designs and analyzes marketing research studies. Often a math or statistics background is helpful. Conceptual writing and presentation skills are needed.

Sampling Specialist—Develops the sample for a proposed study with attention to meeting client demographic requirements. Math and statistical skills are helpful as are basic computer skills.

Source: Marketing Research Association.

AVERAGE COMPENSATION[1] FOR TOP MARKETING EXECUTIVES BY TYPE OF PRODUCT AND SERVICE AND BY COMPANY SIZE, 1996

By Product and Service		By Company Size	
Consumer products	$101,300	*Under $5 million*	$77,200
Consumer services	89,000	*$5 million–$25 million*	96,200
Industrial products	104,000	*$25 million–$100 million*	109,700
Industrial services	107,000	*$100 million–$250 million*	110,700
Office products	110,000	*Over $250 million*	140,900
Office services	104,000		

[1]Includes base salary and bonus.
SOURCE: The Dartnell Corporation.

PUBLIC RELATIONS

In his 1952 book on the growing field he helped develop, Edward Bernays wrote: "Public relations is vitally important today because modern social science has found that the adjustment of individuals, groups, and institutions to life is necessary for the well-being of all." He explained that "because technology has advanced more rapidly than human relations, society has been unable to cope with accelerated technological advances." Public relations, he concluded, is "the new profession of adjustment."

Since then, the growth of the public relations (PR) industry has more than kept pace with technological advancement. Public relations workers may, for example, act on behalf of medical research institutes in bringing possible new cancer cures like interferon to public attention. They may present the pros and cons of nuclear power to the press and public in the energy debate. Whatever the organization being represented, the public relations department is the place where technical concerns and developments are filtered through communications experts for public dissemination, usually via the mass media.

What in 1952 was a field struggling for respectability is now a part of the American way of life that employs over 110,000 people, mostly in large media-center cities. They work for nonprofit organizations, large corporations, and independent consulting firms. Jobs in the management and public relations services industry are expected to grow by 55 percent by the year 2006, making PR among the most rapidly growing industries.

But "public relations" is a term that covers a wide range of communications functions. PR people act as two-way information centers, promoting their clients to the targeted public through the media and also providing feedback to the clients along with advice on how a particular move might impress the public. PR workers are concerned with publicity, trying to keep their employers in the limelight, or, in the case of certain big companies and their executives, out of it. Their work is closely allied with the news media and actually accounts for a significant percentage of news stories and features. Today's press release can be and often is tomorrow's newspaper article.

PR representatives can be book, record, or film promoters; government or corporate spokespersons; college fund-raisers; or lobbyists in Washington. Whatever subject matter they handle, they must be strong communicators, dealing with telephone inquiries, maintaining thriving press contacts, and otherwise interacting with the public in a way that is courteous, creative and, one hopes, informative. The hottest areas in public relations today are health care, high-tech industries, financial services, pharmaceuticals, the food and beverage industry, and telecommunications. Some of the top public relations agencies are N. W. Ayer & Partners, BmC Strategies, Inc., Burson-Marsteller, Cerrell Associates, Inc., Charles Ryan Associates, Clarke & Co., CMG&Z Public Relations, Cohn & Wolfe, Cone Communications, and Cunningham Communications, Inc.

The traditional entry into public relations was via journalism, and today media training is still an advantage to the PR job-seeker. But many people also enter the field with educational backgrounds in English, sociology, economics, political science, or business administration. Some corporations look for PR representatives with expertise in the business of the company itself, such as finance, energy, or heavy industry.

A 1996 survey by the Public Relations Society of America (PRSA) showed the following earnings by job groupings:

MEDIAN PR SALARIES BY JOB TITLE AND REGION				
	Region			
Title	Northeast	Midwest	South	West
Account executives	$34,449	$28,760	$33,275	$38,016
Supervisors	57,054	50,627	50,253	60,216
Senior managment	88,705	71,534	62,423	90,420

MEDIAN PR SALARY BY AREA OF PUBLIC RELATIONS, 1996

Industry	Salary	Industry	Salary
Investor relations	$72,484	Research	$51,519
International	63,964	Employee relations	51,032
Environmental affairs	65,881	Media relations	50,797
Issues management	66,300	Special events	49,450
Technology	52,114	Marketing	48,869
Government relations	65,367	Community relations	49,157
Crisis managment	59,523	Publicity	48,886
Public affairs	55,916	Advertising	45,577
Corporate communications	53,508	Other	53,514
Generalist	54,600		

SOURCE: Public Relations Society of America. *1996 Salary Survey.* Reprinted by permission.

Women in PR

The PRSA survey reveals a surprising disparity between the salaries of men and women. Despite an overall feeling of satisfaction with their career choices, some 63 percent of female respondents said they felt undercompensated. And well they should, considering the fact that the median salary for men was 45 percent higher in 1996 than that of women. While the association explains that women earn less in part because they are younger and less experienced, it has no clear reasoning for why women with equal experience to that of male coworkers also earn substantially less. This is true for all levels of experience, from entry-level employees to professionals with over twenty years in the business. In addition, men were shown to receive considerably more in cash bonuses—as much as double what women received—at almost every level of experience.

Part of the blame for the tremendous difference in earnings comes from the fact that women are overrepresented in low-paying areas such as health care and education. Certainly as women make more inroads into the higher-paying traditional male arenas, their salaries should rise. There is an "old boys' network" that still exists in the higher echelons of the industry, and as women take more senior positions, the situation for those coming up within the business should improve. What is disturbing, however, is that such a large variance in salary exists between men and women with less than five

MEDIAN ENTRY-LEVEL PR SALARIES, 1996

Type of Employer	Salary
Corporation	$23,550
Nonprofit	23,210
Public relations firm	21,110
All respondents	23,030

SOURCE: PRSA, 1996 Salary Survey. Reprinted by permission.

HIGHEST PAID PR DIRECTORS, 1997

Name	Company	Salary and Bonus
Ronald Hoffman	Aluminum Co. of America	$795,200
J. E. Jacob	Anheuser Busch	582,000
Dean Cherry	World Color Press	578,057
Ben Peternell	Harrah's Entertainment	346,948

SOURCE: Executive Compensatory Advisory Services, Springfield, VA.

MEDIAN PR SALARIES BY SEX, AGE, AND EXPERIENCE

Category	Median Salary	
	Men	Women
All experience levels	$59,463	$41,108
1–4 years experience	48,162	29,726
5–9 years experience	47,888	41,141
10–14 years experience	54,457	44,941
15–19 years experience	69,120	49,270
20–plus years experience	70,476	52,870

SOURCE: Public Relations Society of America, Salary Survey 1996. Reprinted by permission.

years' experience—women are earning 62 percent of what men earn at that level. This means that young men just starting out already have a huge jump on their female colleagues when it comes to compensation. Such a disadvantage is going to be difficult to overcome.

Nonprofit Organizations

Into this category falls an alphabet soup of groups and foundations, colleges and universities, hospitals, and the largest employer of them all: federal, state, and local governments. Close to a third of all public relations personnel work for government on all levels. In the federal government their average salary was $52,540 in 1996, although at major departments (State, Defense, etc.) and agencies they are often classified at the GS-15 level, which carries an average salary of over $83,000. In state and city governments, press aides, or "directors of communications," for governors and mayors frequently earn over $50,000, depending on the size of the government.

Public relations specialists are also finding well-paying positions in colleges and universities. According to a detailed salary survey published annually by the College and University Personnel Association, the chief PR officer at large public universities (over 20,000 students) usually earns in excess of $70,000, while the director of the university's information office makes more than $60,000.

For the most part, salaries are lower in the nonprofit area. The nonprofit agency can be a good place to begin a career in public relations. It's a way to receive valuable training and experience before moving into more competitive—and lucrative—jobs in agencies or large corporations. Of course, many people choose to remain in this sector of the occupation. Applying their communications skills to an organization whose goals and work personally interest them—a consumer group, for example, or a health research foundation—can bring great job satisfaction. And in the top-level jobs, salaries are very respectable, often surpassing $100,000. Work in nonprofit organizations, as well as in government, also brings with it certain advantages not usually found in agencies or corporations—a high level of job stability, predictable (usually nine to five) hours, and generous benefits, all of which can make the salary difference less significant.

Independent Agencies

About 17 percent of those answering the PRSA survey work in PR counseling firms. Not surprisingly, New York City is the major center for public relations firms: Of the 4,000 PR firms listed in the national Yellow Pages, 700 are in Manhattan. Other large cities—such as Los Angeles, with 300; Washington, DC., with 250; Chicago, with 225; and San Francisco, with 150—are strong areas for jobs in public relations.

In 1996, the median salary at PR counseling firms was $64,364. People working in the PR section of advertising agencies commanded a median salary of $40,426. Solo practitioners reported a median of $51,298.

The entry-level position is that of assistant account executive, with a typical salary between $20,000 and $24,999. These workers mainly write press releases "pitching" their client, then follow them up with telephone calls. They're also on hand to help with the legwork in campaigns planned by senior consultants. That could involve activities ranging from hand-delivering releases to making arrangements for a promotional luncheon.

After three years or so, promotion to account executive may come, with a median salary expectation of $32,582. Employees at this level deal exclusively with clients and propose and plan publicity campaigns. Promotion to the next level, account supervisor, can bring a median salary in the neighborhood of $52,861. Vice presidents tend to earn roughly $76,791, although some go as high as $90,000. Presidents and CEOs working in consumer products earn about $200,000, and in the high-tech field around $265,000 in New York City, according to Marshall Consultants.

And don't forget the so-called "superflacks," individual public relations consultants handling big clients in such publicity-conscious spheres as show business and politics. Media whiz kids have kept Broadway shows from closing after poor reviews and gotten unusual films like *Ulee's Gold* national attention (and good box-office receipts). Superflacks handle clients on monthly retainers that run from $3,000 to $10,000, sometimes more.

Corporations

The largest number of people in public relations work for corporations, with top salaries in many large companies inching their way toward dizzying heights.

In the nation's largest corporations (over $2 billion in sales), PR executives are part of management's highest echelon. PR directors earn an average of $115,000 to $160,000 annually. Vice presidents in charge of corporate communications make between $145,000 and $250,000. The an-

MEDIAN PR SALARY BY INDUSTRY, 1996

Industry	Salary
Industrial/manufacturing	$53,029
Utility	65,609
Scientific/technical	47,744
Public relations counseling firm	64,364
Media/communications	37,097
Financial/insurance	66,284
Government	48,928
Solo practitioner	51,298
Association/foundation	42,496
Health care	47,871
Transportation/hotels/resorts/entertainment	55,640
Professional services	50,666
Education	39,042
Advertising agency	40,426
Religious/charitable	42,705
Other	51,883

SOURCE: PRSA, 1996 Salary Survey. Reprinted by permission.

nual compensation package for a senior vice president at a *large corporation* can run as much as $200,000 to $300,000.

The corporation is not the place to start but to consider after several years of organization or agency experience. "Corporations for the most part do not offer entry-level positions," says Marshall Consultants' Judith Cushman. "They want applicants who have some background and experience so they can handle the structure and constraints of a corporation." The job includes corporate communications (such as writing brochures and company newsletters); handling employee, government, investor, and press relations; involvement with community affairs; attention to international issues; and any other facets of the company's public dealings and actions.

The Speechwriter

Most of the *Fortune* 1000 companies have a need for people who can craft words for their top executives when they are in the public eye speaking at trade shows and conventions, or before business and charitable organizations, or in other public arenas such as committees of Congress. Somewhere around 50 percent of these companies employ full-time speechwriters. Others use people provided by their public relations firms or independent speechwriters. Typically speechwriters are also charged with producing text for the company's annual reports and other special publications. Salaries for in-house speechwriters range from $70,000 to more than $120,000. Free-lance speechwriters may command from $1,000 to $10,000 for a thirty-minute speech.

SOURCES: *PR Reporter;* Public Relations Society of America; Marshall Consultants (New York); Wesley-Brown Enterprises; Charet & Associates; *Public Relations Journal; O'Dwyer's Newsletters.*

PURCHASING AGENTS

According to the CEO of a major industrial corporation, the three most important characteristics of the purchasing agent are honesty, integrity, and unpopularity. The reason becomes apparent when one realizes that purchasing people, on average, spend half the income of the company for which they work.

About 650,000 people are employed in purchasing in the United States today. These individuals are responsible for buying the goods and services necessary for the running of their company; regardless of its type and size, every company must make certain purchases nearly every day. It is the purchasing agent's job to procure materials, supplies, and equipment of high quality for the best price. Additionally, a purchasing department may monitor other departments to see that they stay within budget when purchasing supplies. Purchasers constantly work to reduce costs.

The outlook for purchasing employment is mixed. The federal government projects employment in this field to grow more slowly than average through the year 2006, though this can largely be attributed to technological advances that have eliminated the need for some low-level positions. Those with college degrees and some industry experience and/or technical knowledge should have an advantage in hiring. Salaries in purchasing reflect an occupation that has grown in size and importance in the past ten years. A 1997 survey conducted by *Purchasing* magazine showed a 36 percent increase in the average salary for the profession over the last decade. The findings of the survey suggest that talent counts more than title in determining compensation. Although salaries vary from industry to industry and according to the size of the firm, a large firm does not always promise a larger paycheck. What usually matters, especially at the executive levels, is the volume of purchases necessary.

Studies show that about 46 percent of purchasing personnel receive regular bonuses, and these beneficiaries include buyers, not just top management. Thus, bonuses, averaging over 11 percent of the base salary, are a major factor to be considered in assessing purchasers' compensation.

The National Association of Purchasing Management delineates five categories of "buyers," the broadest job title within purchasing. These areas are general products buyer; construction buyer; production materials or components buyer; raw material or commodity buyer; and governmental and institutional buyer. The type of work and qualifications for purchasers in the public sector are not necessarily different from those in private industry, but most government positions are regulated by Civil Service requirements. Moreover, because federal, state, and local governments spend almost $100 billion a year acquiring goods and services; opportunities for purchasers abound there. Most federal purchasing is concentrated in the military and the General Services Administration; the local level has state, municipal, and county buyers.

Jobs in Purchasing

Duties within purchasing jobs often are not strictly confined to a designated job title. Depending on the size of the purchasing department, titles may vary from company to company while duties will overlap. Often the title purchasing agent serves as a general term for any position in a purchasing department. Listed below are job descriptions for the most commonly used titles in the field. These titles supply a guideline to a purchasing department ladder, but keep in mind that a multitude of responsibilities can be assigned to employees with the titles purchasing agent or buyer.

Vice President/Director of Purchasing—Depending upon the size of the company, the top purchasing position usually bears one of these titles. Primarily an administrative position, responsible for coordinating, directing, and planning all aspects of the purchasing department.

Materials Manager/Purchasing Manager—These positions usually combine two functions: buying and supervising subordinates' buying activities. In addition to their own buying responsibilities, they also train new buyers and advise assistant purchasing managers.

Purchasing Agent—Responsible for inventories and supplies of necessary materials, for buying goods and services, and for determining the best sources from which to buy. Often the purchasing agent will confer directly with manufacturers and suppliers.

ANNUAL SALARIES OF STATE DIRECTORS OF PURCHASING

State	Salary	State	Salary
Alabama	$53,976	Nebraska	NA
Alaska	84,484	Nevada	$44,073
Arizona	77,576	New Hampshire	37,850
Arkansas	71,640	New Jersey	86,100
California	107,939	New Mexico	62,795
Colorado	84,660	New York	NA
Connecticut	60,000	North Carolina	81,120
Delaware	62,200	North Dakota	42,024
Florida	85,951	Ohio	82,867
Georgia	67,782	Oklahoma	70,520
Hawaii	77,964	Oregon	71,256
Idaho	NA	Pennsylvania	54,142
Illinois	64,932	Rhode Island	78,191
Indiana	52,362	South Carolina	44,157
Iowa	68,744	South Dakota	40,456
Kansas	65,680	Tennessee	68,016
Kentucky	NA	Texas	74,965
Louisiana	57,564	Utah	73,498
Maine	59,218	Vermont	53,144
Maryland	65,660	Virginia	82,417
Massachusetts	73,156	Washington	67,956
Michigan	60,761	West Virginia	NA
Minnesota	67,505	Wisconsin	70,572
Mississippi	51,406	Wyoming	44,676
Missouri	67,548	U.S. Virgin Islands	65,000
Montana	43,095		

SOURCE: Council of State Governments, *The Book of States*, 1998–99.

Purchasing Analyst—Compiles and analyzes data to determine the feasibility of purchasing products, determines price objectives, keeps up-to-date on price trends and manufacturing processes.

Buyers—Many levels of buyers exist, and responsibilities of a particular buyer will depend upon the size of the company and the experience of the buyer. In general, buyers will perform some or all of the aspects required in determining, analyzing, negotiating, delivering, supplying, and procuring necessary goods and services. Most companies have senior buyers, buyers, and junior buyers positions.

AVERAGE SALARIES BY REGION

Region	Average Salary, 1997	Percent Increase Since 1996
New England (CT, ME, MA, NH, RI, VT)	$53,300	+.2%
Middle Atlantic (DE, DC, NJ, NY, PA)	50,800	+3.2%
Southeast (AL, AR, FL, GA, KY, LA, MS, NC, SC, TN, VA, WV)	50,100	−.2%
Great Lakes (IL, IN, MI, OH, WI)	50,800	+3.2%
Plains States (IA, KS, NE, MN, MO, ND, SD)	49,700	+6.4%
Southwest (AZ, NM, OK, TX)	53,400	+6.6%
West (AK, CA, CO, HI, ID, MT, NV, OR, UT, WA, WY)	54,200	+4.4%

SOURCE: *Purchasing* magazine, December 11, 1997. Copyright © Cahners Publishing Co. Reprinted by permission.

AVERAGE SALARIES IN PURCHASING BY CITY, 1997

City	Average Salary	City	Average Salary
Highest Salaries		**Lowest Salaries**	
Miami, FL	$80,600	Williamsport, PA	$29,400
San Jose, CA	76,800	Springfield, IL	30,600
New Haven, CT	74,700	Norfolk, VA	31,900
New York, NY	72,700	Washington, IN	32,300
Wilmington, DE	69,800	Lynchburg, VA	33,800
Muncie, IN	69,400	Mankato, MN	34,600
San Francisco, CA	68,900	Iron Mountain, MI	35,100
New Orleans, LA	66,500	Evansville, IN	35,800
Peoria, IL	66,500	Frederick, MD	36,500
Youngstown, OH	64,700	Sioux Falls, SD	36,700
Waterbury, CT	63,600	Marion, OH	37,500
Newark, NJ	62,700	Huntsville, AL	37,500
Stamford, CT	62,200	Baltimore, MD	38,400
New Brunswick, NJ	62,000	Erie, PA	38,600
Oakland, CA	62,000	Rock Island, IA	38,800

SOURCE: *Purchasing* magazine, December 11, 1997. Copyright © Cahners Publishing Co. Reprinted by permission.

Average Salaries in Purchasing

The best salary survey in the field is published by *Purchasing,* a monthly periodical devoted to the ins and outs of the business. The 1997 *Purchasing* survey found that the average salary in purchasing was $52,500, up 3.4 percent from 1996's average of $50,500. Salaries were highest in the west (the average buyer salary in San Jose, California, was $76,800) and lowest in the Plains states (buyer salaries in Mankato, Minnesota, averaged $34,600). Purchasing remains very much a man's world both in numbers— men outnumber women three to one—and in earnings. In 1997, men earned nearly 40 percent more than women in purchasing. While some women have broken through the glass ceiling and risen to the top executive ranks (twelve women in the 1997 *Purchasing* survey reported earnings over $100,000, compared with only one in 1996), progress overall has been slow. Women's salaries have increased more slowly than those of men in the past year, further widening the gender gap. *Purchasing* points out that although women on the whole are younger and less experienced than men in this industry, when the salaries of men and women with comparable experience and responsibilities are compared, the average compensation among women is considerably less than that of men. Education and certification also played a large role in purchasing salaries. Purchasing professionals with a college degree, as well as "certified purchasing managers," each earned nearly $14,000 more than their less educated or noncertified counterparts.

PURCHASING SALARIES, 1997

Category	Average Salary		
	All	Men	Women
Job Title			
Buyer	$35,000	$37,700	$31,900
Senior buyer	47,200	49,000	43,900
Purchasing agent	41,200	44,900	34,200
Purchasing manager	56,100	58,400	48,700
Materials manager	59,500	61,500	47,500
Materials director	79,800	81,400	62,200
Subcontract administrator	57,100	59,300	47,900
Purchasing director	81,300	85,700	62,200
Vice president of purchasing	125,800	127,200	75,500
Age			
20–24	$31,400	$34,100	$27,100
25–29	36,300	39,800	32,300
30–34	43,100	45,800	39,000
35–40	50,200	54,200	41,500
41–50	54,400	59,700	42,100

PURCHASING SALARIES, 1997

Category	Average Salary		
	All	Men	Women
Age			
51–60	$ 59,700	$ 64,800	$ 43,400
Over 61	55,700	58,300	39,100
Experience (in years)			
3 or fewer	$ 42,100	$ 47,200	$ 33,300
4–6	44,500	49,300	36,000
7–10	49,900	54,900	40,800
11–15	53,300	57,800	43,200
More than 15	60,200	64,500	46,300
Education Level			
No degree	$43,000	$47,700	$36,700
B.S. (liberal arts)	50,300	53,700	44,200
B.S. (business)	53,200	56,600	42,100
B.S. (technical)	59,700	63,000	43,200
M.B.A.	76,800	79,600	61,800
Other graduate degree	56,200	62,100	44,600
Company Size (sales)			
Less than $2 million	$ 39,200	$ 42,400	$ 35,500
$2–$10 million	39,200	44,000	31,000
$11–$20 million	40,400	44,000	34,000
$21–$50 million	46,700	51,000	38,300
$51–$125 million	50,400	53,400	43,000
$126–$250 million	56,800	60,600	45,800
$251–$500 million	55,700	61,900	41,700
$501 million–$1 billion	57,800	61,900	47,300
More than $1 billion	66,800	71,200	51,700
Industry			
Energy	$ 66,700	$ 71,100	$ 46,300
Petroleum	64,200	68,700	50,700
Chemicals	62,200	68,200	47,400
Public utilities	58,900	60,300	49,100
Food, tobacco	58,700	61,900	50,100
Transportation	58,500	62,300	46,700
Primary metals	56,900	59,900	45,700
Transportation equipment	55,800	58,800	40,400
Construction	54,900	60,300	39,500
Financial services	54,200	61,100	40,000
Printing, publishing	53,800	58,500	45,700
Electrical equipment	53,600	59,400	40,100
Textiles, leather	51,400	57,100	40,800
Stone/glass/clay	51,300	54,200	34,700
Paper	49,700	55,000	38,300
Wholesale	49,400	53,600	37,300
Rubber	48,600	56,800	33,500

PURCHASING SALARIES, 1997

Category	Average Salary		
	All	Men	Women
Industry			
Instruments	$ 48,200	$ 52,300	$ 40,000
Lumber	48,000	62,300	26,500
Fabricated metals	47,700	51,000	35,800
Machinery (excluding electric)	47,100	50,000	38,800
Miscellaneous manufacturing	47,000	53,400	38,600
Furniture	45,000	50,900	32,900

SOURCE: *Purchasing* magazine, December 11, 1997. Copyright © Cahners Publishing Co. Reprinted by permission.

THE SALES FORCE

One of the largest occupational groupings in the United States, sales has undergone dramatic growth throughout the 1990s. In 1990, there were 3.6 million people employed in retail sales. By 1996, the number had grown to over 4.5 million, according to the Department of Labor.

The rewards of sales vary widely by industry, ability, and geography. Starting salaries for part-time retail sales jobs is minimum wage, but in areas where employers have trouble attracting and retaining workers, wages are much higher. Here are median weekly earnings for sales workers in six industries.

Information on many of these jobs—those in real estate and financial services, for example—can be found in other parts of this book. In this section we will be dealing exclusively with sales personnel in manufacturing and service industries.

Industry	Median Weekly Earnings
Motor vehicles and boats	$593
Radio, television, hi-fi, and appliances	423
Parts	409
Furniture and home furnishings	403
Hardware and building supplies	372
Apparel	265

SOURCE: U.S. Bureau of Labor Statistics, *Occupational Outlook Handbook*, 1998–99.

The Sales Professional

For thirty years, Willy Loman, Arthur Miller's confused and pathetic character in the play *Death of a Salesman*, has been regarded as the prototype of the American salesman. But the days of the drummer, like Willy "riding on a shoeshine and a smile," have long since passed. According to a survey by the Dartnell Corporation, today's salesperson:

- Is male (only 24.1 percent of salespeople are women, up from 22.8 percent in 1994, but down from 26 percent in 1992).
- Is 36.8 years old (the median age of the entire population is 44).
- Has a college degree (65 percent).
- Will stay with his or her current company for an average of 7.4 years.
- Makes 3.3 sales calls or visits per day.
- Works about 46.9 hours per week.
- Earns $39,800 in an entry-level job, $50,700 as an intermediate salesperson, and $68,300 as a senior-level salesperson.
- Receives an average of $7,548 in benefits from his or her employer.

The earnings of sales professionals have obviously also changed dramatically, as businesses have come to realize the importance of competent, well-trained people, especially in highly competitive industries. The following table lists base salaries and total compensation levels for ten sales positions by product type and company size.

Salary vs. Commission

In any corporate sales job the role of commissions cannot be ignored, since virtually every company attempts to reward its sales staff for any increase in volume. Even when the company's official policy is to pay salespeople a straight salary, it usually has some short-term incentives such as a small bonus or a free trip. According to the Dartnell Corporation, the straight salary plan works best when it is difficult for management to determine which person on the staff actually made the sale, or when the product involved has a broad, cyclical sales pattern, which would leave the sales staff with virtually no income during the fallow periods if only a commission were used. Unfortunately, this plan also rewards nonproducers.

Those corporations using a straight commission plan usually want to provide the greatest incentive to their salespeople while maintaining a predictable sales cost in relation to sales volume. This method of compensation has fallen out of favor recently because it leads to high personnel turnover

AVERAGE TOTAL CASH COMPENSATION[1] FOR SALES PERSONNEL BY TYPE OF PRODUCT OR SERVICE AND BY COMPANY

Group	Top Sales Executive	Regional Sales Manager	District Sales Manager	Senior Sales Rep	Intermediate Sales Rep	Entry-Level Sales Rep	National/ Major Account Manager	National Account Rep
By Type of Product or Service								
Consumer products	$ 99,000	$ 66,400/ 76,800	$62,300/ 68,000	$47,200/ 54,500	$35,700/ 42,600	$29,600/ 32,500	$64,500/ 71,800	$72,700/ 60,200
Consumer services	81,300	59,600/ 70,900	52,300/ 67,000	49,600/ 48,600	28,900/ 36,700	24,200/ 29,500	49,000/ 62,400	48,100/ 59,000
Industrial products	98,500	60,800/ 79,700	57,200/ 73,400	41,300/ 58,400	31,800/ 45,500	27,500/ 35,700	58,400/ 75,600	51,600/ 64,500
Industrial services	97,700	67,300/ 80,200	52,800/ 74,700	45,000/ 59,300	31,200/ 44,300	26,300/ 32,400	58,700/ 79,400	51,300/ 57,900
Office products	106,900	71,600/ 90,500	59,100/ 82,800	47,800/ 57,000	31,400/ 43,000	27,100/ 32,100	52,500/ 79,700	49,700/ 68,200
Office services	91,900	75,500/ 86,500	55,500/ 76,600	46,100/ 53,200	32,000/ 41,500	26,800/ 32,200	58,900/ 76,200	51,900/ 68,100

By Company Size

Under $5 million	$66,600	$40,000/ 56,800	$34,300/ 52,900	$33,200/ 47,500	$27,800/ 38,200	$19,600/ 25,900	$60,000/ 63,300	$40,000/ 53,200
$5 million—$25 million	82,100	49,600/ 68,800	46,200/ 64,100	31,300/ 50,800	25,800/ 39,500	22,800/ 31,300	60,200/ 65,300	39,100/ 55,800
$25 million—$100 million	130,500	65,200/ 77,100	56,300/ 63,700	44,300/ 60,500	34,400/ 45,400	30,700/ 34,900	60,500/ 76,000	60,000/ 61,600
$100 million—$250 million	130,500	58,600/ 82,400	54,000/ 68,600	38,100/ 52,700	30,000/ 49,000	26,400/ 36,300	58,300/ 74,000	45,300/ 59,000
Over $250 million	158,300	96,500/ 105,400	72,400/ 85,100	66,100/ 66,700	46,100/ 50,000	35,700/ 38,900	68,200/ 84,700	80,000/ 72,700

¹Includes base salary and bonus.
SOURCE: The Dartnell Corporation, *Dartnell's 29th Sales Force Compensation Survey 1996–97*. Copyright © 1996 The Dartnell Corporation.

and a downgrading of the service aspects of selling—a key element for strongly established companies.

For these reasons, many corporations have installed a combination plan that provides a fixed salary plus an incentive feature. This helps to establish continuity in the sales force, yet allows the top producers to earn more and encourages everyone to develop new business. The figures that follow show that such plans are now prevalent throughout American businesses. On average, those on the hybrid plan earn slightly more than those working solely for commission. Salespeople on salary only earn significantly less. Outstanding sales personnel on commission or straight commission usually achieve markedly higher compensation at the high end of the scale, but they must prove themselves anew each year.

Most salespeople working for corporations get the same fringe benefits as other employees, and many get additional ones that are important to their work and beneficial to their personal and family lives as well. The most common of these special benefits is a company car, but many salespeople also get fringe benefits worth as much as 40 percent of their pay.

After learning the business, some salespeople choose self-employment. Many insurance agents work for themselves, selling policies written by various firms. (See the section on insurance in Part VI.) Manufacturers' representatives work the same way, handling products that complement one another but do not compete.

Self-employment has the benefit of independence, the risks associated with working solely on a commission basis (no sales, no pay), and the prospect of substantial income if all goes well. Typically, the manufacturer who turns to agencies to sell its products sees immediate market penetration as a major benefit. An agency in place with established customers can bring in business almost immediately. Also, manufacturers see longevity as an important factor. Manufacturers' agents are business partners who grow with their principals and maintain a steady presence in a territory. Compared with the fairly rapid turnover seen with salaried factory people, this stability is a critical factor today, as competition is intense and getting worse.

The Manufacturers' Agents National Association, a trade group in Laguna Hills, California, periodically surveys its members about the commissions they earn. The figures in the second table are reprinted from the Association's 1992 Survey of Sales Commissions. It is important to understand, however, that there is no such thing as a "standard" commission, nor should there be. Commission rates vary widely from industry to industry, and even within individual industries. For example, some products require special installation and service; when this is part of the picture, commission rates are higher. Many agents also do more than simply sell products for the companies they represent. Some provide warehousing facilities, while others do extensive engineering consulting. On the other hand, products in the mature part of the marketing cycle require less effort to sell them. And, of course, regardless of overall trends, there are usually considerable variations for the same product from territory to territory because of unique competitive conditions. Thus, the accompanying figures represent not a standard but a snapshot, or an average based on considerable national and territorial variations.

AVERAGE COMPENSATION LEVELS
FOR SENIOR SALES REPRESENTATIVES, BY INDUSTRY

	Average Performer		Best Performer	
Industry	Average Base Salary for Bonus-Eligible Individuals	Average Total Cash Compensation for All Plans	Average Base Salary for Bonus-Eligible Individuals	Average Total Cash Compensation for All Plans
Agriculture, forestry, and fishing	$42,700	$40,500	NA	$66,700
Banking	48,800	44,200	NA	59,500
Business services	40,400	56,000	53,500	111,400
Chemicals	42,700	53,100	80,300	103,800
Communications	43,000	71,800	56,700	95,000
Construction	27,500	57,000	32,500	103,300
Electronics	48,400	69,800	61,700	112,100
Electronic components	47,500	55,700	50,000	54,000
Fabricated metals	39,500	52,100	42,200	71,700
Food products	40,000	65,000	49,000	NA
Health services	61,800	66,600	43,000	91,500
Holding and other investment offices	50,000	63,200	NA	NA
Instruments	40,000	66,200	NA	80,000
Insurance	NA	74,400	NA	210,700
Manufacturing	31,000	47,700	NA	80,000
Office equipment	43,900	67,600	66,200	97,800
Paper and allied products	40,000	68,700	55,000	NA
Pharmaceuticals	47,200	57,100	61,500	74,600
Primary metal products	65,000	49,700	93,000	NA
Retail	34,100	48,400	80,000	65,000
Rubber/plastics	53,700	65,100	82,500	99,500
Utilities	36,800	52,700	NA	NA
Wholesale (Consumer goods)	70,000	45,900	NA	63,000
Overall	**$44,200**	**$ 55,600**	**$57,800**	**$ 81,700**

SOURCE: The Dartnell Corporation, *Dartnell's 29th Sales Force Compensation Survey, 1996–97.* Reprinted by permission.

AVERAGE COMMISSIONS FOR MANUFACTURER'S REPRESENTATIVES

Product Market	Selling to (average percentages):		
	End User	OEM	Distributor
Abrasives	9.44%	8.87%	7.40%
Advertising products and services	15.25	6.50	4.00
Aerospace and aviation	9.44	6.27	7.27
Agriculture/chemicals	10.60	8.93	6.87
Agriculture/equipment and machinery	7.32	6.09	6.72
Appliances	6.54	5.36	5.50
Architects and interior designers	9.30	5.06	8.62
Arts and crafts	18.12	10.00	7.39
Automation/robotics	9.51	8.69	8.86
Automotive/aftermarket	7.84	6.85	7.85
Automotive/OEM	9.18	4.74	6.75
Builders/contractors	10.01	6.27	7.14
Building materials and supplies	8.85	5.68	6.88
Castings and forgings	7.05	5.05	4.83
Chemicals/industrial	12.50	9.12	9.12
Chemicals/maintenance	17.70	7.56	8.80
Coatings	11.71	8.22	9.12
Computer/hardware, software, and peripheral equipment and supplies	13.10	6.09	7.10
Construction equipment and machinery	9.00	5.57	7.41
Controls and instrumentation	15.01	9.31	13.51
Electrical/consumer	9.93	6.31	6.32
Electrical/technical and industrial	9.66	7.58	8.42
Electronic/communications, audio-visual, and professional products	8.27	5.96	6.79
Electronic/components and materials	9.20	6.32	6.68
Electronic/consumer products	5.94	7.95	4.92
Electronic/technical products	11.87	7.57	8.65
Energy	10.68	7.36	7.66
Engineering/design	10.13	7.82	10.00
Environmental	12.59	8.76	10.95
Fasteners	6.20	5.07	5.84
Floor and wall coverings	9.44	11.00	6.94
Food/beverage chemicals	13.27	8.75	9.08
Food/beverage processing	12.91	9.00	9.25
Food/beverage products and services	15.75	8.88	6.29
Food/beverage service equipment	9.94	7.62	7.46
Furniture and furnishings	7.97	4.87	7.35
Gas, oil, and petroleum products and services	13.07	7.93	8.29
Glass industry/raw materials and products	11.59	6.78	6.28
Government	11.33	8.75	11.25

AVERAGE COMMISSIONS FOR MANUFACTURER'S REPRESENTATIVES

Product Market	Selling to (average percentages):		
	End User	OEM	Distributor
Graphics/printing equipment, and supplies	12.28%	7.71%	7.56%
Hardware/houseware	9.47	5.47	6.92
Hazardous waste/material handling	12.86	7.44	8.07
Health and beauty aids	8.75	7.16	7.33
Heating, ventilation, air-conditioning	13.47	7.72	8.92
Heavy-duty truck-trailer equipment	8.72	5.40	7.64
Home improvement	10.75	5.53	6.00
Import-export	11.04	7.92	7.59
Industrial equipment and machinery	11.49	9.00	8.46
Industrial supplies	12.67	7.92	7.72
Injection molding, parts, and supplies	9.63	5.69	6.75
Jewelry	6.50	9.35	8.25
Kitchen/bath	4.00	4.79	6.21
Lawn and garden	8.50	5.29	5.83
Lighting	9.75	6.08	6.70
Lubricants	12.75	11.67	8.50
Lumber industry	11.00	7.95	6.08
Machining equipment and services	7.94	6.64	7.89
Maintenance supplies	14.72	12.83	8.90
Marine	11.20	7.11	7.80
Material handling	10.03	7.92	7.59
Medical equipment, supplies, and services	10.73	6.29	8.23
Metals/processing, fabricating, assemblies, and products	8.22	5.73	5.80
Metals/raw materials	6.90	4.92	2.98
Mining	11.42	11.10	8.10
Mobile homes, accessories, and supplies	6.66	5.60	7.50
Office supplies and equipment	10.00	6.00	4.80
Optical equipment and supplies	9.37	6.33	7.00
Packaging and plastics	9.23	7.99	6.26
Paints and varnishes	10.91	7.50	7.73
Paper industry	11.30	7.43	6.42
Pharmaceutical	13.44	9.14	8.50
Photographic equipment and supplies	9.58	7.63	9.08
Plastics	8.33	6.10	6.26
Plumbing	7.66	5.52	7.25
Pollution and purification products and services	12.69	12.46	14.42
Powdered metal/parts and components	9.59	5.08	5.41
Power transmission	8.38	7.25	7.63
Process equipment	11.50	9.46	10.31
Pumps	13.39	7.63	8.46

AVERAGE COMMISSIONS FOR MANUFACTURER'S REPRESENTATIVES

Product Market	Selling to (average percentages):		
	End User	OEM	Distributor
Recreational vehicle/aftermarket and OEM	6.75%	5.54%	9.25%
Recreational water products/services	5.58	5.75	6.50
Recycling	10.71	7.50	4.87
Refractories	10.29	8.35	9.12
Refrigeration and cold storage	10.54	6.87	6.36
Rental equipment and supplies	NA	NA	8.53
Retail consumer products and services	7.30	7.83	7.00
Roofing materials and supplies	8.48	5.55	5.53
Rubber products	8.88	6.31	6.19
Safety, emergency, and security products	12.51	7.08	7.68
Scientific research equipment and supplies	15.14	8.66	18.75
Screw machine products	6.65	5.44	5.68
Special services	14.00	30.00	NA
Sporting goods, supplies, and accessories	7.35	6.78	6.87
Stampings	6.33	5.02	5.30
Steel mills and foundries	10.67	6.46	7.42
Telecommunications equipment, services, and supplies	8.27	6.34	9.44
Textile/apparel trade	15.10	5.92	5.33
Textile/industrial	12.20	5.06	7.19
Toys, gifts, and novelties	9.30	8.22	8.29
Transportation	8.22	5.62	5.70
Tubing	6.48	4.35	4.20
Utilities	10.35	11.10	8.93
Veterinary	7.50	7.50	7.12
Waste handling/processing	10.47	9.11	12.32
Water/wastewater treatment equipment products and services	12.41	10.53	10.71
Welding	12.17	7.06	7.91
Wood/woodworking	13.16	4.94	5.99

The Marketing Staff

While businesses rely on their salespeople to bring in revenues, salespersons in large companies are normally supported by a marketing staff that does everything from preparing fancy sales brochures to designing sales promotion programs to developing new or improved products and much more. In general, the larger the company, the larger the marketing organization and the more important the marketing role. Typical management positions in marketing include brand or product manager, sales promotion or support manager, advertising manager, and market-research manager. The orientation of the work done by the marketing staff tends to be more strategic than the tactical orientation of the sales force.

There are basically two distinct career paths in marketing: one involving direct entry into the marketing disciplines; the other gaining entry via the sales function. In small- and medium-sized companies there are likely to be no separately identified marketing functions. In these companies salespeople perform the marketing functions on a part-time basis. The roles of sales and marketing are thus combined, and selling receives most of the emphasis. Also, in these companies the career path for someone with a bent for marketing definitely has a sales bias: i.e., while the need for marketing skills may be recognized by the organization, people are promoted largely based on their sales abilities.

Employees of large companies may also find themselves on a career path toward marketing via sales. At IBM or Xerox, for example, an aspiring marketing manager will usually find himself or herself in the field selling long before getting the opportunity to work in a marketing capacity. This approach makes sense in situations where products and markets are highly complex. Managers in such markets are expected to understand products and markets from the ground up. By starting as salespeople, they acquire a detailed understanding of what makes people buy, and this understanding permits them to then function effectively in the marketing role.

In consumer product companies, where the emphasis in marketing is on the ultimate user of the product, it is common to hire and train product and brand managers directly from graduate school. Procter & Gamble is particularly renowned for hiring and training professional product and brand managers. Its development program, which is very intense and packed with pressure to perform, has been the envy of the consumer products industry for years. P & G's approach has in fact been copied by more than one of its rivals.

These companies typically hire MBAs as assistant brand managers at starting salaries of $40,000 to $60,000. Basically these managers are responsible for increasing sales of their assigned product or brand. This means planning and executing retail and trade promotions as well as advertising campaigns; evaluating product packaging, and positioning; assessing the potential of product improvements and new products; tracking and analyzing sales; etc. The brand manager must pull all of these elements together into a cohesive program, sell that program to various parts of the company, and then implement it. This requires a great deal of analytical ability, a capability to distill large volumes of data into meaningful groupings of information, a personal style that communicates persuasively orally and in writing and, most of all, an underlying feel for the intangible forces that affect relative success or failure in highly competitive markets.

The challenge to those beginning their careers in consumer marketing is to rise from assistant manager to manager within two to three years. A brand or product manager wields much power and influence. Budgets can run into millions of dollars. Those who are successful in attaining manager level can earn $100,000 or more before the age of thirty. While this is not financial success of 1990s Wall Street dimensions, it is still substantial compensation for someone who has been in the business world for only a few years. Also, progression through the product and brand management ranks can lead directly to very high compensation levels. In 1998 Marshall Consultants, Inc. in New York surveyed 1,000 marketing executives and found that senior vice presidents of marketing averaged over $300,000 a year in high-tech companies and health care and over $250,000 in financial services and consumer products companies. Moreover, in a recent poll, more than 40 percent of today's CEOs cited sales and marketing as the best route to the top ranks of American business.

ECONOMISTS

According to the *Wall Street Journal* the so-called "dismal science" of economics is in vogue again on college campuses across the country. Once considered the major MEGO ("My Eyes Glaze Over") of the undergraduate curriculum, economics is now seen as a necessity for even modest success in our money-centered culture. According to university officials, the booming financial industry and the surging stock and bond markets of the last few years have been the chief reasons for this renewal.

Economists study how society should best use its limited supply of resources to satisfy the demands of consumers. Economists generally come in several varieties. Some economists are primarily concerned with teaching and research at the university level. Many economics professors also do consulting work part-time and publish research in economic journals. Business economists earn their living working for banks, securities firms, or corporations; many work for market research firms. Other economists work for local, state, or federal government in a wide variety of jobs ranging from studying inner-city unemployment rates to analyzing the economies of foreign countries for the CIA. Many economists spend time devising methods of and procedures for obtaining data that will allow them to make inferences regarding the economic outlook.

Most economists, whether employed in the public sector, private sector, or in academia, have masters or Ph.D.–level degrees in economics. An individual's studies in economics at the graduate level are often highly specialized and focus in an area such as econometrics, labor economics, or international economics. Today American economists tend to be relatively conservative in their economic beliefs as socialism and communism have less appeal in our consumer-oriented society.

Some observers believe the demand for economists in the private sector will see somewhat of a decline in the next few years in part because of the rapid escalation in the number of bank mergers. Additionally confidence in economic forecasts is at a low with the sudden crash of the Asian economy in 1998. Demand should remain steady, however, in universities and in government jobs. Additionally, many high schools are now beginning to offer economics courses, and this is creating new opportunities for those with at least undergraduate economics degrees. New technology such as computer software will let economists spend less time doing research and more time forecasting.

Economists working in the private sector make more money than other economists. All business economists have a median salary of $73,000, plus about $15,000 in bonuses. Economists working for securities firms have an average base salary of $100,000. Those working for banks have an average salary of about $93,000. Many economists working in the private sector also receive bonuses of up to $60,000 a year. For the salaries for college and university economists, see Part II.

VI

Jobs and Salaries in Representative Businesses

This section contains job descriptions and salary information for occupations that exist only in specialized businesses. Actuary, bank teller, flight attendant, and media planner, for example, are jobs found only in the insurance, banking, airline, and advertising businesses respectively. Obviously not every distinct enterprise could be included, but we did manage to get a good mix of large industries employing hundreds of thousands of workers with relatively small businesses that are recognized as extremely powerful and influential (the brokerage firm and the advertising agency, for example).

Note that office jobs found in every business establishment, such as secretary, typist, and keypunch operator, are not included here. See the section "Office Staff," in Part VIII.

THE ADVERTISING AGENCY

Few facts reveal the extraordinary growth of America's so-called mass consumption society as vividly as those dealing with the advertising business. In 1950, as the postwar economy began to heat up, American business spent $5.7 billion to advertise its goods and services, just about double the 1930 figure. By the late 1980s, the total money spent on advertising had increased to over $120 billion. And by 1998, total advertising spending was over $185 billion. Advertising has in fact become such an integral part of our business system that nearly 100 corporations now spend over $100 million a year to place their ads and commercials in broadcast, print, and outdoor media. The vast majority of these dollars get filtered through that uniquely American business known as the advertising agency.

According to *Advertising Age* magazine, there are about 6,000 large and small agencies currently in operation and employing most of the 125,000 people engaged directly in advertising. Most agencies make the bulk of their money by charging their clients a commission of 15 percent of the total fees billed by the newspaper, magazine, radio, or television station. This can amount to quite an impressive sum, since a large advertiser like Procter and Gamble spends about $20 million a year just on Crest toothpaste; Bristol-Myers about $15 million on Excedrin; and General Foods spends $10 million for Jell-O pudding. The three biggest U.S. advertisers in recent years (Procter and Gamble, General Motors, and Philip Morris) each spent more than $2 billion dollars advertising their various products.

While the late 80s and early 90s were marked by merger mania and, as a result, substantial job loss throughout advertising, the current economic boom has turned the industry around. With competition ever increasing, ad budgets are at all-time highs, and hiring is projected to be faster than average for the next decade. One notable late-90s trend is the merging of established ad agencies with interactive media companies—a logical move considering that on-line advertising is currently the fastest-growing segment of the industry. On-line ad revenues reached $340 million for the first half of 1997, which represented over 300 percent growth from the same period the year before. Because the merging companies are opting, for the most part, to keep the groups functioning as separate units, there hasn't been a problem with job overlap and elimination. On the contrary, bringing the newest technology to established client bases is creating more work than most agencies are staffed to handle.

JOBS WITHIN ADVERTISING AGENCIES

To understand the hierarchy of an advertising agency, one must understand the advertising and marketing process. When a client places advertising for its product into review, each ad agency's accounts and marketing departments evaluate the product's potential in the marketplace. If the agency wins the account, the heads of the accounts, marketing, and creative departments formulate an advertising plan or campaign, which involves an advertising concept, schedule, and budget. Each department then assumes responsibility for designated tasks (see below for detailed description of those responsibilities) and goals. All three departments are regulated by a fourth department:

office management and finance. That group makes sure the three groups adhere to their schedules and budgets and integrates all efforts to reach a mutual end, which is the introduction or sale of a product.

Governing the four agency arms—creative, accounts, marketing, and office management—is the agency president and board of directors. These executives are customarily seasoned veterans of the Madison Avenue wars. The structure of the presidency and governing board is specific to each agency and determined by the size of the agency, the dollar volume in which it trades, and the diversity of its accounts and interests.

What follows is a department-by-department breakdown of agency jobs, progressing from department head down the company ladder.

Accounts Department

This department is responsible for dealing with the client in all aspects of the campaign; it is the agency's "public face" and, in terms of expense accounts and the social sphere, is the most visible department.

Accounts Manager—Responsible for overseeing and guiding the course of new business and accounts and supervising the management of existing accounts by working with a staff of account executives. Helps create budgets and project schedules, answers to board of directors or agency president.

Accounts Supervisor—Mediates between account executives and management; works with other department supervisors to meet schedules and agency goals. In a large agency, supervisors may be responsible for related items (e.g., packaged goods or food accounts) or for one client's spectrum of products (e.g., Procter and Gamble's soaps, lotions, and instant coffee).

Account Executive (AE)—As a liaison between client and agency, the AE meets client needs without compromising the agency's creative concepts or budget. Part of the job entails wooing (and winning) prospective accounts, as well as maintaining happy relations with existing accounts. This is a high-visibility position, and good AEs advance quickly in the corporate ranks. There is a high turnover of AEs, as an account succeeds or fails. A good AE is a valuable agency asset; as a result, perquisites, performance incentives, and bonuses are granted in accord with the AE's track record.

Senior AE and Junior AE—Titles which, in larger agencies, denote greater (or lesser) experience or expertise. Senior AEs are usually responsible for a staff. Salaries are scaled according to rank.

AE Trainee—Largely a little-thanks, prove-yourself position for an individual who has excelled in an entry-level spot and wants to rise in the agency. Projects are assigned rather than self-determined.

Account Planner—A relatively new job title in the American ad business, a planner conducts an in-depth study of potential consumer markets, often in a less than traditional way. Using interviews, psychoanalysis, and other offbeat methods, they determine how consumers think and what they respond to, then provide this information to the creative team to invent an ad concept. Planners come from all backgrounds, and are required to be inquisitive above all other characteristics, and to have the ability to make logical extrapolations from their findings. Ad agencies are increasingly utilizing the services of planners to provide insights that can not be gained from traditional statistical studies.

Marketing Department

This department is responsible for market analysis, consumer research, product evaluation, and ultimately providing the data and statistical insight to create an advertising campaign.

Marketing Manager—Integrates the media research and sales promotion department efforts; works with staff to implement ads that maximize existing market potential and utilize agency resources; works with creative and accounts managers to formulate campaign. Answers to agency president and/or board of directors.

Media Director—Responsible for supervision of staff, planning, and scheduling; authorizes the purchase of airtime on television and radio, or newspaper and magazine space for ads; usually works with AEs and clients to develop ad plan.

Media Planner—Responsible for specific medium; e.g., television, radio, print, or specialty advertising (display, direct response, etc.). Analyzes media options and selects best ad forum; develops media plans and strategies. Frequently the titles *associate* or *assistant media director* are used.

Media Buyer—Negotiates and procures time and space, deals with media representatives, evaluates and selects media markets (networks, programs) to suit a campaign.

Operational Media Staff—In close conjunction with buyers, they handle agency paperwork (requisitions, invoices, memos, etc.) and media correspondence. This is often an entry-level position.

Research Director—Responsible for the accumulation, preparation, and presentation of research findings, statistics, and market analysis data to marketing and accounts staff (and occasionally to the client). Supervises and assigns research staff projects.

Research Analyst—Responsible for the design and execution of statistical analysis of a product's salability; they also supply data to corroborate ad claims, and perform product-related tests and studies.

Market Researcher—Analyzes existing market and projects market potential; advises media and creative staff on ad choices; provides statistics on the consumer, general economics, and the marketplace.

Media Researcher—Analyzes media options, then suggests most effective media to sell the product; projects media trends.

Junior/Senior Research Analyst—Again, these titles denote seniority in the agency and reflect a salary variance equivalent to the rank. Senior staff usually head a group and supervise group effort.

Sales Promotion Manager—Supervises and coordinates sales and promotion staffs; designs sales strategy once market has been targeted.

Sales Representative—Responsible for ad sales (both projected and actual) in an assigned region. Operating on national, regional, and local scales, working with sales staff, sales representatives implement sales strategies previously outlined by the sales manager and the client, in conjunction with the AE. Sales reps are also valuable agency members, and experienced individuals accumulate contacts that simplify negotiations and give the agency a favorable position in good markets. Sales reps are on salary and receive commissions that act as production incentives.

Promotion Staff—These individuals, working with AEs and creative department staff, design, manage, and enact promotional events, direct-response mail campaigns, consumer incentives (coupons, special "deals"), and in-store and display ads, as well as manufacture elaborate schemes and public events designed to draw attention (and business) to the product.

Creative Department

The creative department is the most diverse and complicated facet of the agency. Following is a skeleton structure of a hypothetical creative department. In the industry, no two departments are identical, but they all fill the same function: to create, design, and produce advertising art and copy.

Creative Director—Responsible for all copy, art, and production work; works with marketing and accounts directors (and, rarely, the client) to formalize ad concept; guides department staff to meet goals.

Copy Supervisor/Group Head—Helps create advertising languages, supervises writing staff, develops ideas with art director, writes copy for select accounts, or creates central ideas to be written out in detail by copy staff.

Copywriter—Writes advertising for print media, scripts for radio and television commercials, and sales promotional material for sales department. In larger agencies there is also a *senior copywriter* responsible to copy supervisor and creative director for ad copy on one or a series of related accounts; supervises copy staff. Works in conjunction with senior art staff members to integrate copy and art for presentation to management and client. A *junior copywriter* proofreads ad copy and may write incidental copy or participate in group writing projects; this is an entry-level position.

Art Director—Works with copy supervisor, AE, and art staff to produce ad art, storyboards (for television commercials), magazine layouts, and other visual media (specialty advertising).

Commercial Artists, Designers—Perform the actual drawing of ads; design and layout ad pages; work with photos, copy, and other visuals to create ads.

Paste-up, Mechanical Artists—Construct (paste up) boards for print media; construct models and dummy material for client and management review and approval.

Storyboard Artists—Create television storyboards—frame-by-frame setups of the television commercial as it will be shot, incorporating director's camera angles, set designer's specifications, and other production variables.

Commercial Production Staff—Each agency has its own system for commercial production. A large Madison Avenue agency may employ a full-time casting department (*casting director* and *assistants*) and a television and radio commercial production department (in-house *directors, producers,* and *technicians*). A smaller or regional agency may bring in casting and production personnel for a specific commercial; still others maintain steady freelance relationships with a roster of commercial talent.

Traffic Department Staff—The size of the traffic department depends on agency size; usually a *traffic supervisor* is responsible for a traffic staff. In larger agencies, of course, the staff is more diverse; in smaller houses, one or two people may be the entire department. Essentially, traffic personnel tie together all the odd threads of the creative department to keep the ad on schedule and reasonably within budget. They handle paperwork flow, keep tabs on the progress of creative department projects, coordinate department efforts, and handle freelance assignments and internal memoranda.

Office Management and Finance Department

This department is responsible for inner agency workings as well as paying outstanding accounts and billing for agency services; oversees total agency expenditures and maintains budgets.

Department Manager—Responsible for internal agency checks and balances: keeping departments within budgets and on schedule. Oversees agency financial operations, including payments to media and expense accounts; employee relations and personnel; and general administration.

Estimators—Estimate print, radio, and television spot advertising costs; generalize network and production estimates.

Planners—Anticipate and plan for new business, agency expansion; adjust existing schedules to reflect actual timetables. Planners can be responsible for a facet of a department (for instance, the copy end of the Creative Department) or for the entire department.

Senior Planners—Supervise and guide a planning team and integrate individual plans to formulate a total projection for management; their salary is commensurate with their responsibility, seniority, and expertise.

Broadcast Forwarders—Working with shipping estimates and schedules, responsible for trafficking broadcast copy to various media outlets.

Coordinators—Plan, schedule, and coordinate media traffic flow; buy office and art supplies; coordinate use of marketing, sales/promotional, and creative materials.

Talent Payments Staff—Pay commercial and freelance design talent: actors, directors, artists, technicians, etc.

Billers—Bill clients for agency services (e.g., commercial production costs, advertising pages, newspaper copy).

Some Entry-Level Positions

The advertising industry is mercurial, with a high turnover in agency staff, creating a serious and competitive job market. Entry-level positions exist throughout the industry, but they can be tough to get because of stiff competition. If an entry-level spot is open, the most prized skill across the board is, alas, typing. Candidates are sought who are meticulous and detail-minded, as well as strong in language and math skills. Usually a first agency job will be working as an assistant (or a glorified "gofer"), learning department operations and looking after the loose odds and ends of a superior's efforts. Some examples of entry-level positions follow.

Creative Department, Production Assistant—Gal/guy Friday with general office skills; positions offer the opportunity to learn print, television, and/or radio production, as well as art production; growth potential.

Creative Department, Assistant Copywriter—Clerical and editorial (proofreading) work; strong language skills needed for limited writing; career interest fostered.

Marketing Department, Advertising Assistant, Sales—Heavy telephone work and typing, work with sales reps, some client contact.

Marketing Department, Media Assistant—Trainee can learn media operations, buying, planning, and scheduling; job involves preparation of graphs and client presentations.

AVERAGE BASE SALARIES IN ADVERTISING BY AGENCY SIZE, 1997

Agency size[1]	Less than $3.6 million	$3.7–7.5 million	$7.6–15 million	$15.1–45 million[2]
CEO	$108,700	$180,100	$225,000	$250,000
COO	95,600	146,600	174,900	241,700
CFO	56,700	79,400	110,700	135,600
Creative director	75,700	108,000	134,000	156,200
Art director	46,500	52,800	57,900	57,100
Copywriter	42,000	52,900	54,900	60,000
Media director	42,100	67,000	78,800	92,400
Senior account executive	62,400	68,800	86,000	54,900
Account executive	36,200	39,000	45,800	37,100

[1]In millions of gross income. [2]Numbers are subject to skews due to the small number of responses from agencies in the $15 million to $45 million range.
SOURCE: AM&G survey for *Advertising Age* magazine. Reprinted by permission.

ENTRY-LEVEL SALARIES IN ADVERTISING, 1997

Agency

Assistant media planner/traffic coordinator	$17,500–$22,500
Assistant account executive	20,000– 25,000
Account executive/media desk coordinator	27,500– 32,500

Advertiser

Marketing assistant	$22,500– 27,500
Assistant brand manager	27,500– 32,500
Assistant product specialist	32,500– 37,500

Media

Reporter, print or broadcast	$17,500– 22,500
Production assistant	20,000– 25,000
Assistant copy editor	22,500– 27,500

SOURCE: *Advertising Age* magazine. Reprinted by permission.

THE AIRLINES

Early in the 1990s, prospects seemed gloomy for the airline industry. In fact, throughout 1990–94, the industry operated at a loss—losing more than $13 billion in all, according to the Air Transport Association (ATA). This was due to numerous factors including a weakened economy, high fuel costs, out-of-control "fare wars," and political issues such as fear of terrorism. In recent years, however, the industry has experienced a dramatic turnaround. Each year since 1995 has shown an increase in passenger traffic on both domestic and international flights, and most U.S. carriers have been showing year-end profits. While the increase in traffic and profits hasn't come without a price— many airline employees were furloughed in a downsizing trend—the positive turn in the industry bodes well for the future.

The airline industry has been in almost constant upheaval ever since the passage of the Airline Deregulation Act in 1978. No longer compelled by the Federal Aviation Administration (FAA) to fly unprofitable low-density routes, airlines dropped them in favor of competing for the more heavily traveled and profitable routes. The less-traveled routes have been filled by commuter airlines that fly smaller planes in short hops between regional airfields and the major airport hubs. In most cases, the major airlines have bought up these smaller carriers.

The business rationale for deregulation was to allow the major airlines to fly hub to hub in order to improve profitability. But in the end, cutthroat competition led to mountainous losses, widespread labor unrest, and the eventual destruction of several companies that had been mainstays of the airline industry, including Eastern, Pan Am, and Braniff. Many other carriers were forced to seek bankruptcy protection in order to stay operational (America West, TWA, Continental, and Northwest, among others). Today, the three strongest airlines in the United States are American, United, and Delta—and each is now an international carrier with well-established routes purchased from the defunct airlines. Despite extraordinary losses of billions of dollars during the early 1990s, these three companies are again thriving in the strengthening economy. Other carriers like US Airways (USAir changed its name in 1997 as a symbol of its emergence as a global carrier) and Continental have struggled with high operating costs and fare wars with "bargain" airlines, but have continued to grow with the economy and are operating at near-full capacity on most of their routes.

As the economy becomes increasingly global, the airlines are rushing to form strategic alliances with foreign airlines in order to gain market share. These alliances, which offer smoother, more efficient travel to international passengers, are the beginnings of what some analysts believe will become "megacarriers"—a handful of giant airlines that will control air travel around the world.

The impact of the recent growth on job opportunities has been quite favorable, as more flights require more mechanics, more pilots, and more attendants, both on the ground and in the air. Keep in mind, however, that the competition for these jobs remains very strong. Airline employees who were furloughed during the economic slump are returning to work—and the number of qualified applicants for airline positions continues to exceed the number of jobs being created.

Working for the airlines has several positive aspects, including good benefits and very inexpensive travel opportunities. But unless you are a pilot or first officer, the pay is moderate at best, a condition that is not likely to be ameliorated by intense competition for scarce jobs.

Pilots

The Airline Pilots Association (ALPA), which represents pilots at most major airlines (American, which has an in-house union, is one exception) estimates that some 66,000 active pilots fly for the scheduled airlines.

Being a pilot is a competitive, demanding job. The preparation involved is extensive. Many commercial pilots begin their careers in the military, where they receive their flight training for free, and have the opportunity to accumulate the flight hours required to be hired by the airlines. While choosing the military route has obvious benefits, it is not the only path to an airline career. In fact, with the tightening of military budgets in recent years, flying in the military is not an option for many aspiring airline pilots.

Earning the required flight training and experience as a civilian takes a great deal of time, money, and commitment. Today, nearly all commercial airlines require their pilots to have a four-year college degree. Beyond college, completing flight training and building flight time can take years and cost in the range of $30,000. Some of the cost of ratings is occasionally absorbed by the hiring airlines; however, given the fierce competition among new commercial pilots, this is increasingly uncommon. Along the road to becoming qualified for the major air carriers, a pilot will spend years working in relatively low-paying positions such as flight instructor; or corporate, cargo, or regional pilot—jobs that demand a great deal of time and provide little in the way of benefits.

Once hired by a major airline (and completing a probationary period), a pilot is usually rewarded by generous pay increases, benefits, and flexibility in scheduling. However, advancement comes on a strict seniority basis and can be slow, depending on the growth of the airline and the economy.

The following is the Airline Pilots Association's breakdown of the training required and estimated costs for a commercial airline pilot:

Student pilot solo	$1,100
Private pilot's license	2,000
Cross country	2,250
Instrument rating	3,500
Additional flight time	6,460
Commercial pilot's license	2,000
Multiengine rating	1,500
Certified flight instructor rating	1,600
Certified flight instructor instrument rating	1,200
Airline transport pilot rating	1,000
Type rating	7,000
TOTAL:	$29,610

Two main positions control the cockpit. The captain, also called the pilot in command, has overall responsibility for the safety of the craft, crew, passengers, and cargo. The first officer, or copilot, assists and relieves the captain in the operation of the aircraft. He shares a percentage of the flying and monitors certain systems during the flight. While most modern aircraft have sophisticated computer systems and require only a two-person flight crew, some of the large, older airplanes still have a third crew member—the flight engineer, or second officer. The flight engineer rarely engages in any actual flying. The monitoring of the aircraft's electronic and mechanical systems is his responsibility.

The average starting salary for pilots in the major airlines was $26,290 in 1996, according to the Future Aviation Professionals of America (FAPA). Salaries rise dramatically for pilots after the first year on the job. Average earnings for pilots with six years' experience reached nearly $76,800 at the biggest airlines, and the most senior captains on the largest aircraft earned upward of $200,000. Generally pilots who work outside the commercial airlines earn lower salaries. Pilots who fly jet aircraft earn higher salaries than pilots who fly propeller planes.

Employment of pilots is sensitive to cyclical swings in the economy. During recessions, when declines in air travel force airlines to curtail their number of flights, they may temporarily furlough pilots. Even given recent strengthening within the industry, competition for pilot jobs is expected to remain heavy for the next few years. It is important to note, however, that a large portion of the pilot population was hired during the late 1960s (the last major industry growth period) and is headed toward retirement age within the next decade, since the federal government mandates retirement of commercial pilots at age sixty. As a result, the Bureau of Labor Statistics is projecting several thousand pilot job openings each year during this period.

Airline pilots' salaries vary greatly, depending upon seniority and type

REPRESENTATIVE ANNUAL SALARIES OF CAPTAINS AND FIRST OFFICERS AT MAJOR AIRLINES

		Captain, Boeing 737	First Offier, Boeing 737
Delta Airlines	2nd year	$134,160	$ 31,680
	12th year	148,205	101,222
Southwest Airlines	2nd year	124,926	37,021
	12th year	140,041	92,428
United Airlines	2nd year	119,022	35,696
	12th year	131,303	89,860
USAirways	2nd year	149,318	34,333
	12th year	164,730	112,506

Note: Yearly pay calculated from hourly wage rates, according to standard monthly hours flown. Standard monthly flight hours vary among airlines, ranging from 80 to 94.
SOURCE: Airline Pilot's Association contracts, effective as of December 1997.

of aircraft flown, as well as upon contracts negotiated between the pilots' unions and individual companies. The information in the following table is included as a sampling of pilots' salaries—using the Boeing 737 as an example. The 737 is a medium-sized airplane, the most commonly flown commercial aircraft today.

Flight Attendants

After much fuss and many lawsuits, the stewardess has become a flight attendant—chosen without regard to sex, race, religion, marital status, or even the amount of makeup worn. Flight attendants are considered the airline's personal representatives. They greet passengers as they board the plane, serve meals and beverages, assist with information concerning connecting flights, and, at the end of the flight, complete paperwork relating to cabin maintenance, inflight catering and sales, and, if necessary, incidents.

Nearly 100,000 flight attendants work on the scheduled airlines, logging an average of seventy-five to eighty-five hours in flight each month. These hours do not include time spent on the ground en route or in preflight checking of supplies. Furthermore, before acquiring a regular run, all flight attendants serve on reserve duty, lasting from three months to two years, during which time they must be on constant call.

Salaries for flight attendants are outlined in the following table.

REPRESENTATIVE MONTHLY AND YEARLY SALARIES OF FLIGHT ATTENDANTS

Airline	Base Starting Salary		6th-Year Salary		Highest Year Salary (After number of years)	
	Monthly	Yearly	Monthly	Yearly	Monthly	Yearly
Majors						
American	$1,390	$16,697	$2,220	$26,637	$3,160 (15)	$37,920 (15)
United	1,429	17,145	2,464	29,565	3,076 (14)	36,918 (14)
TWA	1,157	13,887	1,651	19,818	2,059 (12)	24,705 (12)
Nationals						
Hawaiian	$1,064	$12,762	$1,882	$22,581	$2,327 (20)	$27,927 (20)
Air Wisconsin	916	10,998	1,504	18,045	2,020 (18)	24,246 (18)
Regionals						
Piedmont	$1,184	$14,211	$1,706	$20,475	$2,030 (15)	$24,363 (15)
Allegheny	1,063	12,762	1,669	20,025	1,993 (15)	23,913 (15)
PSA	988	11,853	1,422	17,064	1,576 (10)	18,909 (10)

NOTE: All rates effective January 1998, based on seventy-five hours of flying per month. Domestic rates shown. International rates are higher.
SOURCE: Association of Flight Attendants.

Airplane Mechanics

The roughly 82,000 industry mechanics perform scheduled maintenance on all aircraft systems and equipment at periodic intervals. They put each aircraft through a checklist of functions before each flight, and complete inspections required by the FAA. Several levels of advancement exist within this occupation, which is represented by the International Association of Machinists and Aerospace Workers.

The shortage of mechanics has grown more serious in recent years, and several major airlines have started training programs in high schools while Delta has started financing students in four-year aviation schools. The outlook for job opportunities looks very good over the next decade.

In 1996, the median salary of aircraft mechanics was about $35,000. Mechanics who worked on jets generally earned more than those working on other aircraft. The top 10 percent of all aircraft mechanics earned over $48,000 a year. Airline employees and their immediate families receive reduced-fare transportation on their own and on most other airlines. Beginning aircraft mechanics employed by the airlines earned from $18 to $22 an hour. Earnings of experienced mechanics ranged from $25 to $32 an hour. Added to these base figures are license premiums, which can add from $.50 per hour for the first license held, to a maximum of approximately $2.60 for holding several, depending on the airline. Also, shift premiums can add $.51 to $.58 per hour for working night or rotating shifts. There are across-the-board cost-of-living increases almost each year.

Mechanic—Their job is as described above. Mechanics are responsible for their own work but do not supervise others; nor are they required to test and inspect parts on completed aircraft except as necessary to test their own work.

Lead Mechanic—A mechanic who, as a working member of a group, leads, directs, and approves the work of other employees. Must hold valid federal licenses.

Lead Inspector—Assigned at maintenance bases to the work of overall inspection of aircraft during major repairs and overhauls. At the airport, lead inspectors handle preliminary and final inspection during heavy maintenance checks. They perform the required "critical item inspection" before takeoff at airport stations. Must hold valid federal licenses.

Reservation or Ticket Agents

In recent years these two jobs have been consolidated into one. Agents may be based in large central offices or at ticket counters in airports and sales offices. They answer telephone inquiries and book customer reservations on a computer terminal on which they record passenger reservation information. At the airport, they accept luggage, ticket it, and issue boarding passes. Agents also stand at the gate, helping passengers board and working with flight attendants to ensure that all necessary equipment is onboard the flight.

The Bureau of Labor Statistics estimated the average weekly earnings of reservations and ticket agents to be $421 in 1996. As with other airline employees, agents receive free or greatly reduced-fare travel privileges for themselves and their families.

Employment for reservations and ticket agents is expected to decline slightly through the year 2006. The primary reason for this is the development of computerized ticketing and other technology that significantly reduces the workload of agents. Since entry-level requirements are relatively minimal (a high school diploma is almost always sufficient), and since the benefits of working for an airline are enticing, competition is always strong for these positions.

Baggage Handlers and Skycaps

Known officially as station agents, these people work for the different airlines, not for the airport. Station agents handle the loading and unloading of baggage and air freight; assign passengers with baggage, wheelchairs, and the like; place the disembarking ramp for passengers and freight; and aid the aircraft into position at the ramp.

Baggage handlers earn in the range of $7.25 to $15.60 per hour. Salaries vary greatly depending on the size of the airline, seniority, and shift schedule. Night work generally receives extra pay.

THE BANK

Banking is a major American enterprise whose activities influence the daily lives of all of us. Just about everybody has a bank account, and anyone who works gets paid through one. Bank accounts are used for everything from simple identification to proof of one's credit standing. The bank itself is a source of capital for anything from a family home to a company's production plant. Banks stand for prosperity and thrift, as well as conservatism in everything from interest rates and dress codes to the salaries of their employees.

The spectacular savings and loan debacle of the late 1980s and the recession of the early 1990s pitched the banking industry into depression early in this decade. But since 1992, low interest rates have kept banks riding a wave of good fortune. The drop in banking employment—the Bureau of Labor Statistics estimates that 50,000 jobs were lost in 1991 alone—leveled off in the middle of the decade. In 1997, employment in commercial banks rose just over 1 percent—the first such rise since 1989. An estimated 1.5 million people in the United States work in some form of banking, the majority for America's approximately 9,500 commercial banks, making banks one of the largest employers of American workers.

The predictions of massive job loss resulting from bank closings and mergers have so far been, thankfully, overstated. While the government is projecting employment for most positions within the banking industry to decline slightly between now and 2006, there is also good news. Growth in other areas of the financial industry, such as investment and real estate, is offsetting the job loss from bank downsizing. People with banking experience are finding good opportunities in these areas. What's more, one group within banking is expected to grow faster than the national average over the next decade—loan officers and counselors. With the growth of the economy and the population, the demand for loans, and thus, loan officers, will rise. Loans are a principal source of income for banks, and since loan officers work largely on commission, they are affordable even during cost-cutting times.

More than 80 percent of banking jobs are tedious, low-paying clerical jobs like teller, accounting clerk, or proof machine operator. The federal government projects that a great number of the job openings in the banking industry will come in these areas, not because of job growth, but because of the high turnover rates. And no wonder. Banks usually pay their clerks less than those in other industries, and the work is hardly stimulating. The Bureau of Labor Statistics describes the teller's job succinctly as "a series of repetitive tasks and prolonged standing." Those workers particularly in demand will be those willing to work part-time. Banks are increasingly transitioning their teller staff to part-time positions to cut the costs of benefits.

Bank clerks and tellers are usually required to have a high school diploma, but exceptions are made. The lowest-paid 10 percent of tellers earned less than $11,900 in 1996; the highest paid earned just over $24,800. If clerks or tellers stay with a bank for a long period of time, they can attain a supervisory role in some branch of operations. But unless they seek further education, their chances of joining the ranks of professional bank officers are nonexistent.

Bank officers are hand-picked from colleges, universities, and sometimes from graduate schools, and are then trained within the bank for up to two years. They begin on a different pay scale from clerks and ascend a different ladder of advancement.

The information that follows was gathered from a number of industry and government sources and pertains to commercial banks alone, which comprise the largest segment of the industry. In general, Federal Reserve banks pay about the same as commercial banks, but mutual savings banks and savings and loan institutions pay less. Salaries for similar jobs can vary from 5 to 20 percent between savings and loan associations and commercial banks.

Bank Officers

The standard unwritten rules governing salary levels apply to bank officers as much as to anyone: The older you are, the more years of education you have, and the more years of service you have, the more you get paid. And as the figures demonstrate, the size of the bank, in terms of total assets, also affects officers' salaries significantly.

A word of caution: Don't be surprised by the paltry figures. Bank officers' salaries are known to be comparatively low. Excellent benefits and job security, combined with work that is not considered very high-pressured, are the compensatory elements. In addition, like all bank employees, officers are virtually guaranteed mortgage loans and personal loans, and at a slightly reduced rate of interest.

Below are job descriptions for just about every kind of bank officer, derived from those given by the Bank Administration Institute. The chief executive officer and second-ranking officer are not included on the grounds that their functions are managerial in the broadest sense of the term.

Bank Investment Officer (Senior)—Overall responsibility for investment of bank funds.

Bond Department Manager—Acquisition of treasury and agency securities; maintains the bank's portfolio.

Branch Manager (Small, Medium, Large)—Responsible for all phases of branch operation, including personnel, business transactions, customer relations, and branch finance.

Business Development Officer (Senior)—Same as new accounts. A sales representative for the bank. Solicits new accounts; sells new services to old and new accounts, such as payroll preparation and time deposits.

Commercial Credit Department Manager—Develops credit studies for loan officers, financial analysis, review and control of loan portfolio.

Correspondent Bank Officer (Senior)—Establishes and coordinates acquisition of demand deposit accounts with correspondent banks. (For example, when a bank in Indiana wants to clear checks through or borrow cash from a New York bank, it contacts the correspondent bank officer.)

Financial Officer (Chief)—Prepares and interprets reports for top management, fiscal reports, federal reserve and government reports, and internal budgets.

Installment Loan Collection (Collector, Manager)—Day-to-day personal accounting; reviews credit ratings and applications; deals with delinquent accounts.

Installment Loan Department Manager Officer—Services customers seeking car loans, boat loans, trailer loans, etc.

SALARY RANGES FOR BANKING PERSONNEL, 1998[1]

Position	Salary Range, 1998	% Change from 1997
Senior vice president/head of lending	$200,000–$215,000	1.0%
Lending division head/lender	95,000– 133,500	1.1
Commercial lender		
1–3 years' experience	45,000– 60,000	5.0
3 or more years' experience	60,000– 88,000	3.5
Commercial real estate mortgage lender	54,000– 74,000	1.6
Residential real estate mortgage lender	37,000– 47,000	3.7
Consumer loan officer	35,000– 49,000	2.4
Investment merchant banker	55,000– 75,000	0.8
Executive professional lender		
1–3 years' experience	38,000– 50,000	2.3
3 or more years' experience	51,000– 69,000	2.6
Loan review officer	48,000– 59,500	1.7
Loan workout officer	60,000– 82,000	0.7
Branch manager	38,000– 50,000	2.6
Branch administrator	45,000– 57,000	2.0
Marketing director	73,000– 98,000	1.5
Asset/liability investment manager	59,000– 81,000	2.4
Operations officer	40,000– 51,000	1.1
Corporate trust officer	41,000– 52,000	2.2
Personal trust officer	37,000– 48,000	1.2
Employee benefits trust officer	38,000– 48,000	2.4
Trust investment officer	47,000– 58,000	1.0

[1]Figures are for banks with assets of $1 billion or more. Deduct 5% for banks with assets of $500 million to $1 billion; deduct 10% for banks with assets of $100 million to $500 million; deduct 15% for banks with assets of $100 million or less.
SOURCE: Robert Half International, *1998 Salary Guide*.

International Banking Officer (Senior)—Recommends overall policy for international division; develops new and existing services to accounts overseas and intergovernmental loans.

Loan Officer, Commercial—Makes and services loans to businesses.

Loan Officer, General—In smaller banks, this one person makes and services a variety of business and individual incorporated loans.

AVERAGE BASE SALARIES OF OFFICERS IN LARGE BANKS[1]

Job Title	Weighted Average Salary	Percentile	
		25th	75th
Management			
Chief executive officer	$323,500	$220,000	$405,400
Chief operating officer	198,500	124,300	208,600
Chief financial officer	147,700	105,000	175,100
Director of marketing	75,900	57,100	89,100
Business development officer	43,100	36,800	50,000
Bank investment officer	84,500	62,700	100,100
Head of data processing/information services	90,300	63,000	107,100
Head of operations	86,700	67,500	110,100
Head of retail banking	121,600	90,100	147,100
Branch administration manager	68,700	58,600	79,000
Branch manager I	34,300	29,800	39,700
Branch manager II	43,900	35,300	48,200
Loan Department			
Commercial loan department manager	$96,300	$ 72,600	$108,800
Senior commercial loan officer	63,400	58,100	74,800
Commercial loan officer	45,800	40,000	49,400
Consumer loan department manager	75,400	63,700	89,300
Senior consumer loan officer	39,400	39,300	52,500
Consumer loan officer	29,000	27,400	37,400
Mortgage loan department manager	79,500	52,300	102,300
Senior mortgage loan officer	40,700	35,100	58,900
Mortgage loan officer	27,900	25,000	38,300
Trust Department			
Head of trust	$122,400	$90,100	$142,800
Senior personal trust officer	56,900	48,500	62,000
Corporate trust officer	36,400	37,700	53,000
Junior Officers			
Assistant branch manager I	$27,100	$23,500	$29,200
Assistant branch manager II	33,100	25,300	35,100

[1]Banks with assets of more than $1 billion.
SOURCE: Bank Administration Institute, *Cash Compensation Survey 1997*. Reprinted by permission.

AVERAGE BASE SALARIES OF OFFICERS IN SMALL BANKS[1]

Job Title	Average Weighted Salary	Percentile	
		25th	75th
Management			
Chief executive officer	$123,600	$100,800	$143,300
Chief operating officer	77,600	60,000	92,600
Chief financial officer	73,900	60,000	85,000
Director of marketing	43,800	34,400	49,700
Business development officer	43,700	29,300	52,500
Bank investment officer	48,200	35,800	55,000
Head of data processing/information services	44,200	34,100	54,900
Head of operations	45,600	35,000	54,600
Head of retail banking	52,700	42,100	65,000
Branch administration manager	43,300	35,100	55,000
Branch manager I	30,800	24,500	35,000
Branch manager II	37,900	31,600	41,100
Loan Department			
Commercial loan department manager	$64,100	$54,200	$72,900
Senior commercial loan officer	59,000	48,000	61,800
Commercial loan officer	44,800	33,600	48,100
Consumer loan department manager	48,900	37,100	56,800
Senior consumer loan officer	38,200	34,400	44,000
Consumer loan officer	29,300	25,000	33,500
Mortgage loan department manager	48,300	39,500	52,800
Senior mortgage loan officer	39,000	31,500	47,300
Mortgage loan officer	29,200	23,800	33,500
Trust Department			
Head of trust	$62,600	$50,000	$67,700
Senior personal trust officer	39,400	30,300	47,200
Corporate trust officer	33,800	25,600	39,900
Junior Officers			
Assistant branch manager I	$24,800	$20,900	$33,500
Assistant branch manager II	28,400	23,000	33,500

[1]Banks with assets of $100–$249 million.
SOURCE: Bank Administration Institute, *Cash Compensation Survey, 1997*. Reprinted by permission.

Loan Officer, Mortgage (Department Manager, Jr.)—Studies risk and then approves or rejects mortgage loans, either personal or commercial or both.

New Accounts Officer/Representative—See business development officer.

Personal Banking Manager Officer—Sits on "the platform" in a branch office across from the tellers; provides customers with information; certifies checks; waives overdrafts for individual customers; sometimes acts in a supervisory capacity.

Trust Department Officer (Senior)—Oversees personal and corporate trusts and securities administration. Develops new trust business and coordinates investments.

Most of the salary figures that follow have been extracted from a salary survey published annually by the Bank Administration Institute. Salaries have been rounded off to the nearest 100 and do not include annual bonuses. Nationally, bonuses average from about 5.5 percent of base salary (for an officer trainee with a bachelor's degree in a bank with assets of $73.5 million) to nearly 50 percent of base salary (for the chief executive of a bank with over $1 billion in assets). There are three tables: one listing salary ranges in banks; a second showing average base salaries of officers of banks with assets over $1 billion; and a third listing average base salaries of officers in banks with assets of $100 to $249 million.

Tellers and Clerks

Ever since the arrival of the automated teller machine (ATM) or cash machine, the human teller has become a dying breed. Today, about one quarter of bank transactions are conducted at ATMs, and 56 percent take place at the teller window. With the ever-increasing numbers of ATMs (there are currently 150,000 in the United States), the need for tellers is certain to decrease further. The mathematics aren't hard to fathom: It costs the average bank 28 cents to process an ATM withdrawal (65 cents if the ATM transaction is at a networked bank), while that same transaction costs an average of $1.15 with a human teller.

Human tellers haven't quite gone (and probably won't ever go) the way of the full-service filling station or the neighborhood drugstore. In the summer of 1995, customers raised a fierce protest when Citibank attempted to impose teller fees for customers who insisted on using a human teller for transactions they could have performed at an ATM. And some tellers will always be needed to perform tasks like changing money, issuing certified checks, and accepting coin deposits.

Some banks, including Citibank, are extending free electronic banking services to their customers to encourage them to do their banking over the Internet. Others are seeking to expand their use of direct deposit, which reduces their need for tellers to cash checks. First National Bank of Chicago succeeded in foisting a $3 fee on customers for teller transactions. As the business changes, with banks decreasing in number while increasing in size, the role of the teller will undoubtedly change as well. Those who remain will be required to expand their skills in areas such as customer service to best serve the needs of the cost-cutting banks.

There are several different kinds of tellers and a wide variety of clerks serving various functions. The best-paid tellers are the *note tellers,* who draft contracts, calculate renewal notes and mortgages, and pay dividends. *Commercial tellers,* also known as paying and receiving tellers, are the most common type. They cash checks and handle deposits and withdrawals. *Head tellers* are supervisory personnel who help train new paying and receiving tellers and who answer most of the difficult questions. According to the Bank Administration Institute, they earn an average of $17,300–21,100 per year.

There are also different kinds of bank clerks, and the pay scale is generally the same for all of them: low. The more a clerk knows about processing and recording information, the better his or her salary should be, regardless of the job titles. The Bureau of Labor Statistics lists the following clerical categories.

Country Collection Clerks—Sort thousands of pieces of mail daily and determine which items must be held at the main office and which should be routed to branch banks.

Exchange Clerks—Service foreign deposit accounts.

Interest Clerks—Keep records on interest-bearing items.

Mortgage Clerks—Type legal papers dealing with real estate upon which money has been loaned.

Proof-Machine Operators—Use equipment that sorts check and deposit slips, add their amounts, and record the tabulations.

Reconcilement Clerks—Process financial statements from other banks to reconcile differences.

AVERAGE ANNUAL EARNINGS OF BANK CLERKS AND TELLERS

Job Title	Large Banks[1]			Small Banks[2]		
	Weighted Average	Percentile		Weighted Average	Percentile	
		25th	75th		25th	75th
Accounting clerk I	$17,700	$16,900	$21,300	$18,700	$16,400	$20,500
Accounting clerk II	20,500	20,200	25,800	21,300	18,400	24,500
Loan officer I	28,200	26,800	34,000	32,300	26,900	37,000
Loan officer II	37,500	32,600	59,200	47,900	40,300	56,000
Clerk/processor						
Loan department	20,400	18,100	22,000	18,700	16,400	21,900
Mortgage department	21,800	19,800	23,800	20,500	17,800	22,500
Commercial loan	21,500	18,700	23,500	20,800	17,200	24,000

Bookkeeping and operations

Clerk I	17,000	20,200	16,300	13,900	18,000
Clerk II	20,300	22,700	18,800	16,700	21,300
File statement clerk	15,200	16,500	15,200	13,200	17,300
Check processing clerk	17,800	19,300	16,300	14,500	18,500
Safe deposit clerk	17,700	18,900	17,000	14,500	19,100
Data entry clerk	15,500	17,700	17,300	14,000	19,200
Head teller	21,100	21,300	19,300	17,300	22,300
Teller I	15,600	16,800	14,800	13,400	15,900
Teller II	16,900	18,700	16,200	15,000	18,200
Teller, ATM	18,000	20,100	15,700	14,000	17,600
Teller, note loan	16,500	22,000	18,900	15,200	21,000
Teller, vault	18,700	20,300	17,700	15,600	19,700
Teller, part-time	15,600	17,000	14,900	13,500	16,600

¹Large=banks with assets of more than $1 billion. ²Small=banks with assets of $100 to $249 million.

SOURCE: Banking Administration Institute, *Cash Compensation Survey, 1997.* Reprinted by permission.

Sorters—Separate checks, deposit slips, etc., into different batches and tabulate them.

Transit Clerks—Sort checks and drafts on other banks.

Trust Securities Clerks—Post investment transactions made by trust officers on behalf of bank customers.

THE BROKERAGE FIRM

Think of brokerage houses as department stores for stocks, bonds, mutual funds, and other investment vehicles. Full-service brokerage houses such as Merrill Lynch are the Bloomingdale's of the industry, providing a host of services such as equity analysis and portfolio management. Not surprisingly, quality service equals hefty commissions. Meanwhile, discount brokerages such as Charles Schwab can be likened to Wal-Mart: no frills, low commissions. An increasing number of discount brokers such as E-Trade and Datek are setting up shop on the Internet.

Working a brokerage house can be a lucrative career but it is available to only a small number of people. The entire securities industry employs roughly 500,000 people, many of them in the 5,500 firms registered with the National Association of Securities Dealers. Both the number of employees and number of firms fell precipitously after the 1987 stock market crash. When the stock market rebounded, so did employment, which has been increasing along with the Dow Jones industrial average since 1990.

Brokerages vary in size from well-known giants like Salomon Smith Barney to small two-room office operations whose names are familiar only to a handful of investors. The majority of major firms are located in New York City. The number of employees in the big national full-line firms has fluctuated from year to year, depending largely on the performance of the stock market.

Anyone who has had experience looking for a job in this business, especially on Wall Street itself, knows there are two related obstacles to finding one: the relatively small size of the industry, and the blatant nepotism that pervades every area. Because the pay is so good (even retail brokers now average more than $150,000 a year), and the work is clean and mostly respectable—the frequent scandals notwithstanding—it's not surprising that relatives of those on the inside have the first crack at these jobs.

The job market looks better today than it has since October, 1987, when the Dow plunged more than 500 points and the industry began a major contraction, reducing the workforce by 50,000 over the next three years. Since then, the Dow Jones Index has surged to record levels and helped bring greatly increased pretax profits to most securities firms. Increased global business also brought hefty profits and helped the market see new possibilities. Setbacks in 1997, especially in emerging markets, hurt profits and caused sporadic layoffs. But generally speaking, the surge in market activity should keep employment levels rising.

A very important reason for the dramatic increase in market activity was the lowering of prime interest rates. Many investors began taking their money out of banks, where it was earning less than 5 percent interest, and sought higher returns in stocks, mutual funds, collateralized mortgages, and a whole host of products that were once the province of only the most sophisticated players. As a result, many of the largest firms, including Prudential and Dean Witter, have been increasing their staffs of retail brokers. Others have resumed their training programs to meet future needs.

The most prestigious and best-paying jobs are in sales, trading, research, and what might be broadly termed as investment banking. In fact, average salaries in these areas are probably the highest of any nonprofessional group in the country. In other words, a person can make a great deal of money in a brokerage firm without an advanced degree or long, arduous training. Although an M.B.A. has become a prerequisite in research and certain areas of investment banking, savvy, guts, and the ability to work long hours remain the best qualifications for the high-paying, pressure-packed jobs of trader and broker.

Brokers

Brokers act as agents for people buying or selling securities. They collect a fee for that service. Brokers are known in the industry as registered representatives, or account executives, and sometimes simply as salespersons. Brokers usually specialize in one type of investment vehicle and are therefore known as stockbrokers, bond brokers, etc. They also specialize in either retail or institutional sales. Retail brokers work with individual investors. Institutional brokers help corporations, mutual funds, pensions, and foundations to place orders and invest money. Most large brokerage houses also have a few brokers who work on the floor of the major exchanges placing orders. They are called, appropriately enough, floor brokers.

Brokers receive a commission on the fee their firms charge for all transactions. Because a firm's fee varies with the type of security and the size of the transaction, so does the broker's commission. Retail brokers usually collect about 40 percent of the gross fee; institutional brokers collect a lower percentage because they deal with larger blocks of security, but they also get large bonuses. First Boston, for example, pays 15 percent, and Merrill Lynch 13 percent to its brokers. The bonuses handed out by firms can make straight salary seem meager. Senior executives' bonuses rose 20 to 30 percent in 1997, according to *the Wall Street Journal.* Bear Stearns paid $87 million to its top five officers. The large bonuses also often include stock options and restricted stock that can equal more than half of the employee's total pay.

Beginning brokers usually start with a salary and lower commission. As they become experienced, the commission rises and the salary remains the same or drops, often to a point at which a broker is working on a straight commission. Because pay depends on an individual's production, income for brokers varies widely. But average starting salary for a retail broker is around $50,000; for institutional brokers, more like $60,000. Midcareer, both retail and institution brokers make six-figure incomes, ranging as high as $750,000. Truly stellar performers can make $1 million-plus. Floor brokers are on a similar salary track.

As salaries have risen, so have the number of brokers. There are currently 116,000 in the United States, according to the Securities Industry Data Bank, compared to only 73,700 in 1987. Industry watchers predict that the demand for brokers will further increase as more and more employees are asked to make their own retirement decisions, a role often filled by employers in the past. Many retail brokers have become more like financial advisers according to *The New York Times.* They are helping investors manage their money and earn most of their income from fees rather than from straight commission.

Sales Assistants

Sales assistants support the brokers by providing clerical help and acting as a liaison between the clients and the broker. Because this industry is so time-sensitive, all calls that come in while the market is open must be taken. Sales assistants handle the calls that come in during those hours and keep the broker free to talk with established clients. They also do most of the paperwork, keeping records of transactions and account activity. A sales assistant may become registered to place orders for his or her broker. This increases the value of the sales assistant greatly and is reflected in compensation. Sales assistants make between $35,000 and $80,000 a year, depending on experience. Bonuses vary from 1 to 3 percent courtesy of the broker; the firm usually pays a small bonus as well.

Traders

Traders use their firm's capital to buy and sell securities and earn money on fluctuations in the marketplace. There are traders for different types of securities: corporate bonds, municipal bonds, etc. Most traders are paid a salary plus bonus, but because the industry places heavy emphasis on individual performance, that bonus can run anywhere from 10 percent to 200 percent of one's salary.

A bonus is meant to reflect the amount of money a trader makes for a firm. Some brokerage houses pay a "production bonus," which is a fixed percentage of a trader's annual output. If a firm's production bonus is 10 percent and a trader makes $600,00 for the firm, then he or she will make $60,000 as a bonus. In some firms, bonuses are more arbitrary and less systematic. A 50 percent bonus might be granted to all traders in a good year, regardless of each trader's performance. There is at least one firm in New York that offers bonuses strictly on the basis of seniority. In general, large firms tend to pay higher salaries and lower bonuses, and small firms tend to do just the opposite.

The pitfalls of this bonus system were exposed in February 1995, when twenty-eight-year-old Nicholas Leeson risked more than $29 billion on the Japanese stock market in an attempt to win huge profits for his firm and a correspondingly gigantic bonus for himself. But he lost $750 million on the trade. Leeson fled to Germany before anybody realized what he had done. His monumental miscalculations caused the collapse of his firm, Barings PLC, Britain's oldest and one of its most venerable investment firms. To forestall such a collapse in the United States, federal banking regulators issued a set of guidelines in late 1995 that limit the pay of traders who take excessive risks. The guidelines don't make trading in derivatives and emerging markets any less volatile or risky, but they should deter individual traders from making large, speculative bets in hopes of earning a hefty bonus.

The average total compensation (salary plus bonus) for an entry-level trader ranges from $60,000 to $120,000. The average midcareer salary is around $300,000 to $500,000 a year. Once again, the top of the pay scale is off the charts: several million in some cases. At large firms such as Salomon Smith Barney, this is certainly the case. During the 1992 scandal at Salomon Brothers, for example, it became public knowledge that senior partners (all of whom were traders) made no less than $2 million each, and there was at least one $6 million man.

Research

Behind every broker who makes the big sale and every trader who makes the right move stands a small group of experts working in the research department. Their job consists of studying stocks and bonds, usually in specific areas such as automobiles, oil, or steel. Known as security analysts or stock analysts, they issue reports on the current value of these securities, and predict the effects of national economic trends on their growth potential.

In today's extraordinarily competitive marketplace, the importance of analysts has never been greater. This is why, when prestigious Wall Street firms decide to spend millions of dollars on television advertising, they often single out the work of their excellent research departments in the commercials. Tough competition also explains the rise of independent investment counselors devoted only to research. Some analysts such as Goldman Sachs' Abbey Joseph Cohen have achieved such fame and respect among investors that their predictions are eagerly awaited.

Analysts receive training on the job, but an increasing number now come into the business armed with an M.B.A. This trend has helped increase starting compensation to around $100,000 for "junior analysts" and "research analysts" and well into six-figures for those with a few years' experience. The midcareer average is $500,000 according to one Wall Street recruiter.

In the past few years, as corporate takeovers, leveraged buyouts, and merger-mania have made research ever more important, the elite analysts have been able to induce the big houses into bidding wars for their services, sending their salaries skyrocketing. "When analysts are instrumental in pulling in underwriting business, they get big bonuses," former analyst Nancy Zambell told the *Wall Street Journal.* "Then they're no longer making $250,000. They're making $1 million and up." Merrill Lynch paid three analysts $1.2 million each to lure them away from other firms. Jack B. Grubman, one of Wall Street's top telecommunications analysts, received a two-year, $5 million deal for jumping from Paine Webber to Salomon in 1994.

Investment Banking

Large brokerage houses employ large staffs of corporate finance experts, usually lumped under the broad rubric of investment bankers. Investment bankers help work out the financial details when two companies merge and also help a company to value a business unit that it plans to sell. Given the heavy volume of mergers in recent years, this has been a real boon to Wall Street firms. Investment bankers also help companies and municipalities to figure out canny ways to invest their cash reserves. Most companies and municipalities have some available cash on hand. Investment bankers dream up all kinds of esoteric ways of investing this cash such as swaptions and derivatives.

One of the major functions of investment bankers is underwriting. When a brokerage house purchases an entire new issue of stocks or bonds from a corporation or the government in order to distribute them in the marketplace, the brokerage is said to "underwrite" those securities, thus guaranteeing their sale. For this service, the investment bankers who handle the transactions take a commission of, say, .05 percent. Of course when you deal with sums in the hundreds of millions of dollars, even such a small percentage can translate into substantial amounts of money.

Another underwriting service provided by investment bankers: initial public offerings or (IPOs). This is when a new company issues its first block of stock. Along with merger-mania, the country has also been seized by IPO fever. High-profile IPOs of recent years include such technology startups as Amazon.com, Netscape, and Yahoo. Underwriting IPOs requires knowledge of finance and a thorough understanding of larger economic trends. For this reason, virtually all investment bankers entering the field today have an M.B.A. degree or broad experience in several phases of the business. Compensation is commensurate with specialized knowledge. Fresh out of school, an investment banker can make $90,000 easily. Midcareer, $1 million is not out of the question. Remember, this is the field that carries the adage: "If you're not a millionaire by thirty, you're a failure." Stars in this field command salaries in the multiple millions. Bonuses account for most of an investment banker's compensation, though. When the market tumbles, so does an investment banker's pay.

THE RETAIL TRADE

The department store, once the definitive symbol of American consumerism, stood until the late 1980s as the cornerstone of retailing. As a monolith of consumerism that was unique to America, the department store dominated the urban and suburban landscapes as the center of convenience in a culture where people depend so heavily on their cars. In recent times the department store has declined only to be replaced by large chains and discounters as well as specialty retailers. Large chain stores such as K-Mart and Wal-Mart, with their broad selection of merchandise at discounted prices, as well as specialty chains such as The Gap and The Limited, dominate national retailing today the way department stores like Macy's and Nordstrom's dominated regional retailing in their heydays.

The local mall has become what the department store was for years: a one-stop shopping center that conveniently saves time, gas, and money. The typical mall with its large anchor store—more often now a discount "superstore"—may house specialty stores, old-fashioned department stores, and chain stores, all competing for the same customers. In this environment, department stores have narrowed the number of products they carry and refocused on high margin products. They have resorted to frequent markdowns to keep their customers loyal, selling 60 percent to 80 percent of their merchandise on sale in 1994. Despite these efforts, even affluent shoppers have moved away from the department stores to the specialty stores and large discount chains. The latter stores have taken advantage of the weaknesses of the department stores' approach to merchandising. The specialty stores typically sell within a narrow product range (e.g., Footlocker sells only sneakers) but offer a far wider selection within their specialty categories. The discount stores offer less service and fewer upscale products but take advantage of a reborn cost consciousness in the American consumer of the 1990s.

Despite these changes in the retailing landscape, which place a premium on lowering costs such as inventory building, merchandising, and selling, job growth in the retail trade remains strong. Today there are over 20 million workers in the U.S. retail industry—more than in the entire U.S. manufacturing sector. And this is not surprising when you consider the $2.2 trillion in retail sales in the United States alone in 1997. While many of these jobs are at the low-wage sales associate level, there are many opportunities to move up the ranks. The salary ranges for the following job descriptions were provided by the National Retail Federation, and the data was compiled as a part of an annual survey of specialty retail chains. Therefore we will concentrate here on the specialty chain in discussing these career opportunities. The titles, job descriptions, and salaries/wages shown are generally similar across all retailing.

In most specialty chains, the buying decisions and merchandising decisions are made at company headquarters and not at the store level. There are several levels of management in these organizations, and they are divided into two distinct categories of activities: merchandising and operations. Merchandising management positions include general merchandising managers, divisional merchandising managers, buyers, and assistant buyers. In addition to these corporate merchandising positions, those positions that are actually involved in the operation of the stores are regional or zone managers, district or area managers, store managers, assistant managers, visual merchandisers, and the sales staff.

For management positions in retail, a college degree is preferred but not required. Prior experience in retail is also looked upon favorably.

Jobs in Merchandising

General Merchandise Manager (GMM)—GMMs have vice presidential status and have overall responsibility for one of the three divisions above. While not involved in actual buying, they coordinate buying and selling activities. They plan sales promotions, determine the quantity of merchandise to be stocked, and decide markups and markdowns. GMMs report directly to the store's chief executive officer.

Divisional Merchandise Manager (DMM)—Reporting directly to the GMM, the divisional merchandise manager is responsible for one or more classifications of merchandise. For example, there's a DMM in charge of juniors (coats, dresses, sportswear); a DMM overseeing furniture, carpeting, and lamps; another for cosmetics and accessories, and so on. The DMM's first duty is to achieve the profits and sales set for his or her department by management. With the help of the three to seven buyers under his or her supervision, the DMM keeps stock of merchandise, its display, replenishment, and sales movement.

Both GMMs and DMMs are usually college graduates these days, some with degrees in fashion merchandising, others simply with years of experience as buyers, the usual path of advancement. Salaries vary widely, with the biggest difference due to the store's volume. In a large majority of stores, executives' annual earnings include a bonus for meeting or exceeding sales goals.

According to the National Retail Federation survey, DMMs made in the range of $91,500 (25th percentile) and $141,000 (75th percentile) before bonus in 1997.

Buyer—Buyers seek out and purchase all the items stocked by a retail store, from canned soup to mothballs to Christian Dior suits. They do often lead glamourous lives, traveling four to five days each month or more to trade and fashion shows, sometimes around the world. They return with items that past experience, market research, or their own fashion instincts indicate will sell at way above original cost. About 150,000 buyers work in retail stores around the country, mostly in major metropolitan areas. Generally they have college degrees, although their training comes from the store where they start out as assistant buyers. Earnings vary by location and volume, but most buyers made a base salary of between $50,000 (25th percentile) and $72,000 (75th percentile) in 1997.

Assistant Buyers—While training (usually for about a year) to become buyers, assistant buyers must also grapple with much of their division's daily paperwork: processing purchase orders, checking invoices on material received, keeping account of stock. The lowest quartile of assistant buyers were earning base salaries of just over $30,000 in 1997, while the upper quartile averaged over $37,000.

Jobs in Retail Operations

Zone or Regional Managers—In large regional or nationwide retail operations, zone or regional managers supervise large geographic regions composed of two or more districts or areas. They mainly oversee the activities of the district or area managers who report to them. They also implement and oversee company policies and enforce company standards. By virtue of their experience, zone or regional managers also perform troubleshooting in their operations. Average total pay for zone managers was $150,257 in 1997; for regional managers, $97,103. Note that these figures include bonuses that can represent upward of 30 percent of base salary.

District or Area Managers—District or area managers are in charge of a group of stores, usually ranging from three to ten stores. District managers supervise store managers and define their responsibilities. They channel corporate information to their stores. They also help solve any problems that the store manager may be having trouble dealing with. District managers meet frequently with store managers and their staffs to insure that the stores are being run to company standards. They set and track the stores' sales and budget goals, and suggest and help implement merchandising techniques to promote sales. District managers average base salaries were in the range of $44,200 (25th percentile) to $55,857 (75th percentile) in 1997. Incentive programs may add to these salaries.

Store Managers—Store managers are in charge of all aspects of daily operations within the store. Along with the district or zone manager, they set the sales and budget goals and make sure the staff is achieving these goals. Store managers are also in charge of employee incentive programs to keep their staffs motivated. Store managers work closely with their assistant managers, defining their responsibilities and delegating the daily activities of the store. A major part of the store manager's job consists of educating the staff on performing their jobs and on matters of corporate policy. Average base salaries for store managers were in the range of $24,614 (25th percentile) to $32,200 (75th percentile) in 1997. Companies also frequently incentivize store managers in achieving or beating their sales goals.

Assistant Store Managers—Assistant managers basically help with the day-to-day operations of the store, like merchandising, supervising, scheduling, serving customers, and assuring that customer service guidelines are followed. They also help with the implementation of company programs. Assistant managers supervise those employees who do pricing, ticketing, and restocking. Some assistant managers are paid on a salary basis, but most are paid on an hourly basis. The wages usually range from $7.50 to $11.00 per hour, depending on the size of the store, its location, and the experience level of the assistant manager. Some companies also offer incentive programs to assistant managers.

Merchandisers—Some very large retail stores have merchandising managers within the store; in others, merchandisers travel from store to store within a district or area. Usually working with a company recommended store and display layout, merchandisers create displays that appeal to customers. This job is very important because the placement and display of goods has a big impact on customer buying patterns. Merchandisers must have a special talent: the ability to visualize displays that will attract customer interest and make the merchandise attractive. Hourly wages are in the range of $7.50 to $11.00, but those who travel from store to store receive salaries ranging from $23,000 to $33,000.

Sales Staff—Retail businesses of all types employ over 4.5 million salespeople in the United States. Sales workers' major priorities are customer service and selling. They present product features and benefits and answer any questions. They also help with the daily maintenance of the store as well as unpack goods, price ticketing, and place them on the display floor. Sales staffs are normally paid on an hourly basis with a hiring rate generally just above the federal minimum wage of $5.15 per hour. The average total pay of full-time sales workers was $7.12 per hour in 1997. Some companies also pay commissions on sales. In some cases, commissions can double earnings.

HOTELS AND MOTELS

More than 1.1 million people work in hotels and motels—a figure that continues to rise along with the growth of tourism and business travel. The range of salaries is enormous. Bellhops make as little as $3.31 an hour before tips; general managers make well over $100,000 a year after bonuses. More than half of the employees work in the service area, which includes food service, housekeeping, and personal services. About 20 percent do clerical work as telephone operators, secretaries, and front office staff. General managers, restaurant managers, bar managers, and executive housekeepers make up another 13 percent, and the rest work as salespersons, skilled workers (electricians, plumbers, etc.), and general staff.

One's education and the size and whereabouts of the hotel or motel affect salaries. A laundry worker in New York, for example, can make twice as much as a telephone operator in Atlanta. The manager of a hotel with over 1,000 rooms might make three times as much as the manager of a motel

HOTEL OCCUPANCY AND ROOM RATES, 1993–97

Category	Occupancy Rate		Average Room Rate	
	1993	1997	1993	1997
By Region				
New England	59.3%	66.6%	$ 74.53	$ 86.69
Middle Atlantic	64.2	69.0	78.79	100.07
South Atlantic	64.0	66.8	60.47	73.48
East North Central	60.3	62.6	56.28	69.91
East South Central	63.0	61.6	47.14	56.21
West North Central	63.1	60.9	48.76	58.30
West South Central	62.3	63.2	53.86	65.00
Mountain	65.2	68.2	58.41	71.33
Pacific	62.5	69.3	71.17	87.25
By Price Category				
Luxury	69.7%	75.2%	$105.70	$129.12
Upscale	66.8	69.0	72.05	88.59
Midprice	63.9	66.1	54.99	68.09
Economy	61.3	61.8	42.66	52.17
Budget	61.0	61.0	32.74	42.55
U.S. AVERAGE	**63.1%**	**65.9%**	**$ 61.30**	**$ 75.29**

SOURCE: American Hotel and Motel Association, *Lodging Outlook Survey*, December 1993 and November 1997.

with sixty rooms. Graduates of a hotel management school typically earn salaries in the high teens to low twenties in their first job.

Like the rest of the travel industry, jobs in the hotel and motel industry are subject to fluctuations in the economy's health. Business travel, which accounts for the majority of hotel stays, is one of the first items to be cut from corporate budgets during a recession, thus creating even harder times for people who work in hotels and motels. This trend is illustrated by hotel occupancy rates, which dropped to 60.9 percent during the 1991 recession but rebounded to 65.2 percent in 1994 and have held steady ever since; the 1997 occupancy rate was 65.9 percent. This rate is still below the 68 percent occupancy rate considered the baseline for sustained profitability, but the industry continues to show signs that it is in good health despite the turmoil brought on by recent mergers and consolidations. For one, the higher the cost of the hotel, the higher the occupancy rate. This is in contrast with the situation at the beginning of the decade, when occupancy rates were highest among economy hotels and lowest among basic and upscale hotels, suggesting that travelers were cutting down the scale of their trips rather than canceling them outright.

Room rates are another reflection of the health of the hotel industry, and they too are on the rise. They jumped 6.1 percent, from $70.94 in 1996 to $75.29 in 1997. As might be expected, rates are highest in urban areas and in the geographic areas (i.e., New York in the Middle Atlantic; Los Angeles and San Francisco in the Pacific region), where the biggest and most expensive cities are located. These areas all enjoy higher than average occupancy rates and are targeted for increased growth within the hotel industry.

Jobs in Hotel and Motel Management

Job descriptions in the services area—maids, bellhops, and laundry workers—are really unnecessary, but some of the managerial positions should be defined.

General Manager—Managers, through subordinate managers, all aspects of the hotel's or motel's activities.

Resident Manager—Lives on the premises, reports to the general manager, and supervises all hotel activities except those of the food and beverage department.

Food and Beverage Manager—Reports to the general manager. Supervises food, banquet, and beverage service through subordinate managers.

Front Office Manager—Supervises front office personnel. Compiles daily a revised weekly, monthly, and yearly room forecast. Handles guest complaints; schedules employees' work assignments.

Front Office Reservations Manager—Reports to the front office manager. Responsible for reservations, operations, and coordination of rooms forecast.

Controller—Supervises accounting personnel, cashiers, auditors; in charge of payroll, credit, and accounting departments. Compiles financial statements.

Executive Housekeeper—Supervises all maids, porters, cleaners, and window washers. Orders supplies and fabrics. Determines room redecorations and prepares work schedules.

Chief Engineer—Supervises all mechanics, tradesmen, and other maintenance personnel. Purchases maintenance and fire equipment.

Sales Manager—Supervises a sales force to promote maximum transient, convention group, and banquet business. Prepares sales reports and plans sales quotas.

ANNUAL SALARIES OF HOTEL/MOTEL MANAGERS, 1997

Position	First Class Hotels	Midpriced Hotels	Economy Hotels
General Manager (live-in)			
25th quartile	$ 59,800	$45,900	$35,400
75th quartile	115,800	67,500	50,000
General Manager (non-live-in)			
25th quartile	60,000	38,000	31,400
75th quartile	105,200	65,000	53,000
Resident Manager			
25th quartile	39,100	23,500	NA
75th quartile	60,000	40,800	NA
Front Office Manager			
25th quartile	25,300	20,000	18,200
75th quartile	36,500	30,000	24,000
Reservations Manager			
25th quartile	22,000	20,000	19,100
75th quartile	33,000	29,000	22,400
Controller			
25th quartile	33,300	27,300	23,200
75th quartile	64,500	45,000	33,000
Executive Housekeeper			
25th quartile	25,100	19,300	17,200
75th quartile	40,400	30,000	23,200
Chief Engineer			
25th quartile	32,600	22,100	20,000
75th quartile	54,600	34,000	25,000
Director of Sales and Marketing			
25th quartile	45,000	28,000	24,000
75th quartile	65,000	40,000	38,000

ANNUAL SALARIES OF HOTEL/MOTEL MANAGERS, 1997

Position	First Class Hotels	Midpriced Hotels	Economy Hotels
Senior Sales Manager			
25th quartile	$32,200	$28,300	NA
75th quartile	49,400	42,200	NA
Sales Manager			
25th quartile	26,000	22,000	NA
75th quartile	35,000	29,100	NA
Security Director			
25th quartile	26,000	22,300	NA
75th quartile	43,400	31,400	NA
Personnel Director			
25th quartile	31,000	24,000	NA
75th quartile	52,200	42,200	NA
Director of Food and Beverages			
25th quartile	41,100	30,000	NA
75th quartile	65,000	44,000	NA
Executive Chef			
25th quartile	38,000	28,100	NA
75th quartile	62,600	45,500	NA
Executive Steward			
25th quartile	26,000	12,300	NA
75th quartile	36,300	26,200	NA
Restaurant Manager			
25th quartile	25,100	18,500	NA
75th quartile	34,400	30,700	NA

SOURCE: American Hotel and Motel Association, *Hospitality Industry Compensation Survey* (1997). Reprinted by permission.

THE INSURANCE INDUSTRY

The insurance industry is a vast and financially powerful sector of the U.S. economy. The industry is also one of the largest employers in the country, with just under 2.5 million people employed, approximately half of them in clerical positions.

The early 1990s were a time of major consolidation and downsizing within the insurance industry, as in so many sectors of the economy. The resulting reduction of the insurance workforce led many to leave the field permanently. In recent years, while the merging of major insurance companies continues, the strength of the economy has led to increased demand for insurance services and, as a result, experienced insurance professionals— particularly in specialized markets.

Demographic variables—conspicuously the aging of the baby boom generation—have sharply increased demand for products that provide retirement income and health care insurance. Health insurance continues to provide one of the strongest sectors of growth. Elected officials now voice concern over the plight of uninsured and underinsured citizens; even Americans with adequate coverage may upgrade their policies in response to escalating health care costs. Underwriters, adjusters, investigators, and claim workers seem likely to benefit from ongoing growth in this sector of the industry. Since insurance companies require large clerical staffs to function, growth in clerical job categories is also probable. In all of these cases, however, the increased demand for services coincides with an increased use of highly efficient computer software systems and other modern techniques that increase the productivity of individual workers—thus lowering demand for new employees.

Actuaries

Actuaries are the architects of the insurance industry. Insurance agreements of every kind—life, casualty, and health—as well as industry pension plans are all the designs of insurance actuaries. If you ever got hot under the collar because as a twenty-five-year-old your automobile insurance rates were nearly twice as high as those of a friend only three years older, then you have actuaries to blame. They are the ones who have studied and assimilated the statistics that prove that drivers under twenty-five are apt to pay more attention to the radio than to the road. But whatever they decide, their findings are the results of an incredible amount of research and deduction. Probabilities of injury, sickness, death, and unemployment in certain industries and certain surroundings, situations, and living conditions, and property loss from fire, theft, or natural disaster, are all carefully studied by actuaries, and their calculations of loss determine what premium rates for insurance policies should be. This task is not easy, since rates must be fair and competitive but still sufficiently high to cover all possible claims and expenses.

About one-half of all actuaries work in the insurance industry, with the rest employed by consulting firms and rating bureaus to gather information for smaller insurance companies that don't employ actuaries of their own; for the government; or, in a few cases, with software companies creating actuarial software applications. Most actuaries work in life insurance; the rest work in casualty, property, and other types of insurance.

Actuaries are the highest paid professionals in the insurance field, with an average salary of $36,500 for those who have a bachelor's degree and have completed both actuary exams. According to the Life Office Management Association, Inc., associate actuaries (midlevel professionals who have demonstrated leadership) average $78,600 a year, and senior level actuaries, $93,500.

There are approximately 16,000 actuaries working in the U.S. today. Job growth for actuaries is predicted to be slower than the average for all industries over the next decade. Those who will fare the best will be actuarial consultants, as more insurance companies of all sizes are turning to consultants to help cut costs, and those in health services, as the growth of managed-care programs will provide increasing opportunities. The worst off will be the least experienced actuaries—corporate downsizing has made competition for entry-level positions tougher than ever.

Claim Representatives

Under the title *claim representative,* also called *claim approver,* there are actually two separate and distinct jobs. A claim representative is either a *claim adjuster* or a *claim examiner.* Each works toward a speedy and agreeable settlement of all claims, but there the similarity ends. Basically, examiners have desk jobs. They settle claims by using various reports, physical evidence, and testimony of witnesses. But adjusters are assigned to the investigation of questionable claims or those that exceed reasonable amounts; they work in the field. Their method is much the same as a police investigator's or a private eye's. They interview medical specialists and in other ways check for accuracy and honesty.

About 250,000 people work as claim representatives, and the majority of these work for insurance companies that sell property and liability coverage. Unlike many other occupations within the insurance field, the job market for claim representatives is projected to grow faster than the average through the year 2006. The increased demand will be a direct result of the increased need for insurance of all types and the resulting rise in claims. The Department of Labor estimated the median weekly earnings of claim adjusters and examiners to be $440.00 in 1996. Adjusters are also usually provided with a company car, or reimbursed for the use of their own car. Because adjusters often work independently, their income largely depends on the number of claims they investigate. Ironically, for those in the property and casualty field, a major disaster such as a hurricane can mean a huge boost in business and, consequently, income.

Underwriters

The persons who examine and decide which risks their company will take are called underwriters. They must analyze numerous sources—applications, backgrounds, medical reports, actuarial studies—and then make the decision themselves. It is one of the most responsible positions a person can have in the industry. Underwriters may correspond with policyholders and their agents, and they may frequently accompany the agents when they call on their clients. Nearly 100,000 people hold this position in the insurance field, and about 75 percent of them are property and liability underwriters. Underwriters with life insurance companies, however, make more money.

The median salary for all underwriters in 1996 was $31,400, while senior underwriters earned over $52,000. Hiring is projected to slow over the next decade, not because of a reduction in business but because of an increased use of computer software applications to perform typical underwriters' duties such as analysis of applications. In order to stay competitive in the changing job market, experienced underwriters will need to expand their skills to enable them to perform marketing and customer service duties. It will also help to have "specialty" skills, or experience creating customized insurance packages, as companies become more focused on individual client needs.

Agents and Brokers

Insurance agents and brokers are the persons who actually sell the policies to the individuals and businesses that wish to insure themselves against future losses and accidents. About 410,000 agents and brokers sell some kind of insurance in the United States. About half are in life insurance, and most of the remainder sell property and liability insurance. They are employed either as agents of insurance companies or as brokers, independent insurance business people who may represent one or more insurance companies in order to place their clients with policies that best meet their particular needs. Three out of ten agents and brokers are self-employed.

Following a training period of approximately six months, most agents are paid on a commission that is dependent on the type and amount of insurance they sell. The median salary for agents and brokers in 1996 was $31,500. The top 10 percent earned a median of over $76,900. A few highly successful ones (about one in five of those with over ten years of experience)

THE TOP 10 LIFE INSURANCE COMPANIES IN AMERICAN, 1997

Company	Assets (in billions)
1. Prudential of America	$178.62
2. Metropolitan Life	162.48
3. Teachers Insurance and Annuity	86.36
4. New York Life	62.73
5. Northwestern Mutual Life	62.68
6. Connecticut General Life	62.28
7. Principal Mutual Life	56.84
8. Equitable Life Insurance	54.74
9. John Hancock Mutual Life	53.59
10. Massachusetts Mutual Life	53.35

SOURCE: A.M. Best Company.

SALARIES AND BONUSES OF MANAGERS AT LIFE INSURANCE FIRMS

Position	Salary	Annual Bonus
Chief executive officer	$446,638	$334,252
Chief operating officer	295,094	193,845
Executive vice president	208,401	92,775
Top administrative executive	116,537	37,351
Top financial executive	201,666	108,300
Treasurer	114,764	36,981
Controller	116,185	37,387
Top actuarial executive	152,335	60,738
Top investment executive	230,776	128,618
Top legal executive	172,836	79,302
Top marketing executive	166,228	63,020
Top agency executive	137,103	45,525
Top claims executive	92,223	27,641
Top underwriting executive	102,627	24,568
Top policyholder sales executive	115,219	38,907
Top information resources executive	137,284	48,023
Top human resources executive	123,403	45,499
Top group life/health executive	210,029	86,703
Top property/casualty executive	167,580	59,195
Top compliance officer	115,137	33,091

SOURCE: Life Office Management Association, Inc., *1997 LOMA U.S. Executive Compensation Survey.* Reprinted by permission.

bring home over $150,000 a year. More than in any other position in the insurance field, the salary for agents and brokers can be self-determined. As with underwriters, the projected job growth for agents and brokers is slower than the average through the year 2006, according to the Bureau of Labor Statistics. Again, this is largely due to the increased use of computer systems that enable individual brokers to handle sales more efficiently and take on more clients.

Clerical Workers

Those who hold clerical positions within the insurance industry basically perform the same duties as they would in the administrative offices of any business. Records must be kept so premium payments, services, and benefits are all up-to-date. For this purpose, secretaries, accounting clerks, typists, computer operators, and general office workers are all needed. Some companies use titles such as *premiums ledger card clerk* (a bookkeeping function usually equivalent to accounting clerk), or *policy evaluation clerk* (typing and proofreading approved policies), but the pay scales are the same as for standard office jobs.

Altogether, they make up about 50 percent of all the people employed in the industry. Pay for clerical workers in the insurance field varies from city to city, company to company, and position to position. In 1996, file clerks earned a median salary of $17,000; accounting, bookkeeping, and auditing clerks, $20,700; and computer operators, $22,400. Clerical supervisors earned a median salary of $28,900. (For more information on the salaries of office workers, see the section "The Office Staff," in Part VIII.)

THE MAGAZINE

In the glamorous world of magazine publishing, the supply of eager young workers will always outstrip demand, but the employment picture for this industry is no longer quite so bleak as it was during the recession of the early 90s. It is possible to find employment with magazines, due either to high attrition among entry-level staff or the staff's constant movement between magazine titles. Numerous nearly horizontal moves from magazine to magazine is the norm among the young and ambitious as they position themselves to capture better titles and more enjoyable responsibilities. Loyalty to a single magazine is, in general, unrewarded. Turnover in entry-level positions is high as starry-eyed twenty-somethings enter the field, and then, frustrated by heavy clerical duties and low salaries, exit.

Competition is high not only between employees, but also between magazine titles themselves. No one is complacent, although overall in the industry, advertising and sales have had healthy increases. In 1997, newsstand dollar sales broke records with a rise of 8 percent, while ad pages were up 5.2 percent through September. But the industry feels it must defend its claims to advertisers against not only TV but also Internet sites, not to mention fighting tooth-and-nail amongst themselves. The early '90s taught the industry some difficult lessons in modern capitalism as, in order to survive, magazines cut staffs and watched venerable titles such as *House and Garden* fold due to dropping advertising and sales revenues.

From this time, subscribers no longer got an almost-free ride on the backs of advertisers, who refused to pay hefty page rate increases each year. Newsstand buyers found magazine cover prices had skyrocketed to an average cost of $4 an issue. An unthinkable breach a few years ago, now editors regularly join in marketing campaigns, sometimes online or on cable TV shows, in order to attract both advertisers and subscribers.

The way magazines hire has changed, as well. Although they may be hiring again, they're taking on people willing to work as freelancers or consultants. Paid by the hour and without benefits, such workers enjoy greater flexibility than their on-staff counterparts. They can work for a number of different employers and, within limits, set their own hours. Of course, for the magazine this means greater freedom in hiring and firing, as well as saving money that would otherwise be spent on 401Ks or health insurance.

Tight competition in the industry doesn't prevent new magazine titles from joining the pack. Many start-ups, or new titles, are niche publications, magazines concentrated on one interest or audience—for example, *Cat Fancy* or *PC World*. These magazines have the advantage of attracting advertisers with a specific audience while inspiring reader loyalty, according to New York–based employment consultant Jackie Riley.

One way magazine companies can hedge their bets with a start-up is to spin it off from an existing title, probably from a section already in existence—for example, *Travel & Leisure Family*. Such start-ups may not appear each month but may begin as quarterly or bimonthly publications. According to Riley, technology magazines in particular benefit from this strategy. "Introduce an audience to a section, get a strong enough poll on reading it and voilà." Other niches being filled include titles about dogs, hobbies, and sports. As the population ages, new titles will cater to it, focusing on parenting, grandparenting, health care, homes and travel.

Spin-off products are also becoming popular, as magazine companies try to find new ways to profit. Such products may include international editions of a title, books, home videos, and even mail-order merchandise.

International editions may include the new Chinese language edition of *Forbes*, or Spanish-language editions sold both abroad and within the United States. Magazine publishers were not slow to understand the growth of Hispanic buying power in the United States, launching *People en Español* from Time Inc., and *Discover en Español* by Disney, even as smaller publishers, with more established Hispanic-market titles such as *Moderna, Hispanic Magazine* and *Latina* looked on.

Magazines make money through both advertising and circulation. For decades advertising revenues constituted the bulk of the profits, sometimes up to 70 percent, but the recession changed all that. Starting in the mid-'90's, the proportions were closer to fifty-fifty. Magazines make money through circulation by putting together a selective collection of articles and photographs on a weekly, monthly, or quarterly basis, hoping to attract a large number of readers. Magazines sold on newsstands and at supermarkets earn a higher profit for publishers because they share the revenues only with distributors and retailers. Magazines sold through subscription are less profitable because of the high costs to get and keep readers through direct mail. By the time they pay for a direct mail campaign, postage, billing, and other mail costs, publishers very often lose money in the first year of a subscription.

In circulation, both quality and quantity count. The quality refers to the readers, who are measured by both demographics—age, income, education, geographic area—and psychographics—lifestyles, hobbies, intellectual pursuits. Quantity applies to numbers—how many readers the magazine attracts week in and week out.

Magazines use the quality and quantity of their readership to draw advertisers, trying to convince them that their magazine is read by the very same customers the advertisers are trying to attract to their products. With the right quality of reader, even small circulation publications can win advertisers. *American Lawyer,* for example, is attractive to luxury car makers not for its circulation quantity (relatively small) but rather for its quality (average income $350,000).

The reason profits from advertising drastically declined is because advertisers have grown unwilling to pay the "sticker price" for ad rates, demanding instead negotiated page rates. In addition, while advertising budgets have not increased substantially, magazines face increased competition from other new magazines. As an industry, however, magazines seem to be holding their own against TV, radio, the Internet, and other media in the competition for advertising dollars.

Some magazines, called controlled circulation, make money only through advertising. The magazines deliver a highly desirable audience—doctors, business executives, airline passengers, moviegoers—that advertisers want to reach. The readers are generally happy to get a free magazine that contains useful information. Magazines are also divided into two categories by editorial coverage: consumer and trade. Consumer publications, like *TV Guide, Sports Illustrated, Newsweek, Good Housekeeping,* and other magazines most of us receive at home are geared to readers personal interests, and make their money by appealing to a wide general audience. Trade publications, meanwhile, like *Ad Age* and *Publishers Weekly,* are not generally available on newsstands and have a very high subscription price. But because their editorial content is narrowly tailored to an audience that often considers the publication required reading in the industry, trade publications can charge higher rates for their advertising.

Magazine staffs are usually divided between the editorial side and the business side, which consists of the advertising, circulation, and production departments. Thousands of small publications exist where a half dozen or fewer staffers perform both editorial and business duties. About 600 magazines, audited by the Audit Bureau of Circulation, account for more than 75 percent of all magazine circulation and advertising.

The largest consumer magazine companies—Hearst, Time-Warner, and Condé Nast—are all concentrated in New York City, the center of publishing for both books and magazines; New York also boasts the highest salaries in the industry. Editorial salaries are typically augmented by perks, which vary from title to title and company to company, but gifts may range from meals to products to travel. Large magazines provide their senior editors with car service, free meals, gym memberships, and more. They can use assistants, who are paid for by the company, to take care of personal business including picking up laundry and running other errands. This theoretically frees the editor to handle important magazine business and is part of the "boot camp" experience for assistants at the bottom of the magazine ladder. Also, advertisers anxious for a plug in a magazine may shower anyone who might offer them publicity with free beauty products, meals, books, travel, and more. After all, how can a travel editor write about a trip he or she hasn't experienced?

Surveys by *Folio* magazine in 1997 and 1998 showed a trend among magazine employees in editorial, production, and circulation departments. The trend was toward staffers' greater responsibilities for the magazine's Internet sites in maintaining and updating text, design, and subscriptions. Salaries did not reflect these increased responsibilities, employees said.

The following listing describes the typical staff structure at these magazines.

The Executives

Publisher—Supervises all activities of advertising, circulation, and production and manufacturing departments. Involvement with the editorial department is usually minimal unless he or she is also the editor, in which case he or she sets the magazine's editorial policy. Basically the publisher's job is to make sure the magazine makes a profit. If the magazine is incorporated, the publisher is usually president or executive vice president of the corporation as well. At most large consumer magazines where the publisher is a salaried employee, the salary is anywhere from $50,000 to $400,000 a year. Publishers of magazines in the Time/Life Group (*Sports Illustrated, Fortune, People, Entertainment Weekly*, etc.) tend toward the upper end of that range.

Editor—Has ultimate responsibility for the magazine's entire editorial content, including art, text, and cover of the magazine. If publisher is not also editor, plays leading role in determining editorial policy. Along with the managing editor, the editor must make sure each issue of the magazine is acceptable, on time, and within budget. The editor is also the magazine's figurehead. On some major publications where the editor must spend much of his or her time making public appearances and doing other essentially promotional activities, where he or she is in charge of a group of publications, or where he or she is both editor and publisher, the day-to-day operations of the magazine may be turned over to an executive editor.

Managing Editor—Coordinates editorial, art, and production departments to insure that the magazine is put out on time and in an acceptable form. Oversees the copyediting and proofreading staff to make sure the magazine is factually and grammatically correct. The managing editor may also be responsible for keeping the editorial department within its budget, and usually has a large say in the magazine's content.

Art Director—Oversees all art and editorial design work for the magazine, including illustrations and photography. Supervises art staff and controls art budget and works with production manager and printing house to insure that printing quality is acceptable and colors are accurate. Oversees art production and heads photography and illustration departments.

Assistant Art Director—Designs editorial page layouts, supervises illustrators, photographers, and typographers. Works with editors to arrange photography sessions. Pastes up editorial pages and prepares them for the printer.

Editorial Department

Senior Editor—Plans and writes features and other articles. May head editorial features department and may oversee other editorial employees, freelance writers and designers. Keeps abreast of trends and news; responsible for editorial work in assigned subject area.

Circulation Department

Circulation Director—Plans, directs, and coordinates circulation-marketing projects. In charge of budgeting and analyses of single-copy sales and all subscription programs, list rentals, database planning and maintenance.

Circulation Manager—Directly below the circulation director, manages circulation programs for both subscriptions and single-copy sales. For one title or more, deals with all aspects of circulation.

Production and Manufacturing

Manufacturing and Distribution Head—Negotiates contracts with vendors, typesetters, printers, and engravers; supervises and coordinates their activities to make sure agreements are kept and the magazine is manufactured and distributed properly and on time; supervises all activities of the production and manufacturing department.

AVERAGE SALARIES AT LARGE CONSUMER MAGAZINES, 1997

Occupation	Average Salary	After
Section editor	$52,580	flat rate
General editor	42,900	flat rate
Associate editorial director	32,552	flat rate
Writer-editor, staff correspondent	32,500	1 year
Editor	32,214	3 years
Associate editor	31,326	6 years
Art editor	27,040	3 years
Rewrite chief, copy chief	27,040	3 years
Head, subscription and statistical services division	39,534	4 years
Circulation manager	27,917	3 years
Subscription manager	25,155	3 years
Key Punch operator	26,267	3 years
Proofreader	18,980	2 years
Tape librarian	18,980	2 years

SOURCE: The Newspaper Guild, 1997.

AVERAGE SALARIES OF RESEARCHERS AT SELECTED MAGAZINES, 1997

Occupation	Average Salary	After
Consumer Reports	$55,578	4 years
Scientific American	46,709	3 years
Nation	35,663	3 years
Time	33,592	1 year
Newsweek	28,392	3 years

SOURCE: The Newspaper Guild, 1997.

AVERAGE SALARIES FOR EDITORIAL EXECUTIVES, 1997

Category	Editor	Managing Editor	Senior Editor
Region			
Northeast	$60,892	$60,873	$66,464
South	50,194	46,225	44,223
North Central	44,997	45,922	40,801
West	43,365	38,793	53,637
Sex (4–10 years' experience)			
Male	$44,308	$41,217	$56,099
Female	40,099	37,697	50,617
Age			
29 or younger	$42,432	$35,771	$36,271
30–39	47,520	45,446	59,223
40–49	50,034	61,792	66,627
50 or older	59,942	53,377	54,606
Circulation			
20,000–49,999	$48,037	$41,816	$44,643
50,000–99,999	48,464	45,466	40,179
100,000–499,999	61,512	48,172	56,900
500,000 or more	NA	81,737	77,820
Range			
Highest salary	$150,000	$116,000	$130,000
Lowest salary	12,000	22,000	24,000

SOURCE: Magazine Publishers of America, *Folio: 1997 Editorial Salary Survey*. Reprinted by permission.

AVERAGE SALARIES FOR MAGAZINE PRODUCTION EXECUTIVES, 1997

Category	Art Director	Production Director	Production Manager	Circulation Director
Region				
Northeast	$53,440	$ 77,519	$42,943	$ 62,218
South	44,366	54,625	39,147	53,038
North Central	46,272	57,490	37,881	49,824
West	48,145	54,760	37,582	NA
Sex (4–10 years experience)				
Male	$51,815	$ 74,757	$41,794	$ 66,678
Female	45,599	58,710	40,109	55,630
Age				
29 or younger	$32,109	$ 49,317	$31,574	$ 42,323
30–39	50,690	59,485	41,102	59,141
40–49	43,531	67,182	43,533	63,341
50 or older	50,794	75,417	45,234	62,695
Circulation				
20,000–49,999	$45,550	$ 58,233	$39,977	$ 50,480
50,000–99,999	51,008	51,472	38,341	61,900
100,000–499,999	52,420	68,583	43,617	63,450
500,000 or more	74,602	84,411	49,452	NA
Range				
Highest salary	$95,000	$175,000	$75,000	$175,000
Lowest salary	$19,000	28,000	19,000	25,000

SOURCE: Magazine Publishers of America, *Folio: 1997 Circulation Salary Survey.* Reprinted by permission.

THE NEWSPAPER

First came television, then VCRs and cable, now the home computer. For decades, newspapers have competed with formidable foes, all of which have eroded their readership. To stave off these challenges, newspapers have broadened their definition of news, adding sections like "Living," "Home," "Business," and "Science," and have expanded coverage of entertainment, restaurants, and sports. Publishers, many in cities without a competing paper, have been successful in producing profitable newspapers targeted at well-educated, affluent readers sought by advertisers. There are 1,462 dailies and nearly 900 Sunday newspapers, with circulations ranging from a few thousand to well over a million. The number of Sunday editions has been increasing in recent years even as the number of daily papers (and total newspaper circulation) has dropped precipitously. As recently as 1980, there were 1,745 daily papers with a combined circulation of more than 62 million. Circulation of daily papers has dropped every year since 1987; all of the decline has come from folding evening papers, whose numbers and circulation have dropped every year since 1975.

WEEKLY SALARIES OF NEWS STAFF AT SELECTED NEWSPAPERS

Newspaper	Reporter and Photographer Top Minimum (after years employed)
Baltimore Sun	$ 979.00 (5)
Boston Globe	1,179.18 (5)
Buffalo News	962.97 (5)
Chicago Sun-Times	1,087.08 (5)
Denver Post	924.59 (5)
Detroit News	750.54 (4)
Eugene Register-Guard (OR)	852.63 (5)
Harrisburg Patriot, News (PA)	631.90 (4)
Indianapolis Star News	755.03 (6)
Jersey City Journal	735.03 (4)
Lynn Item (MA)	579.60 (4)
Manchester Union Leader (NH)	839.89 (3)
New York Times	1,309.00 (2)
Pawtucket Times (RI)	650.50 (4)
Pottstown Mercury (PA)	763.95 (5)
Providence Journal-Bulletin	922.03 (4)
San Diego Union-Tribune	832.76 (6)
San Francisco Chronicle, Examiner	944.35 (6)
Seattle Times	814.90 (5)
Sioux City Journal (IA)	606.66 (4)
St. Louis Post-Dispatch	1,028.00 (5)
Toledo Blade	932.24 (4)
Washington Post	968.00 (4)

SOURCE: The Newspaper Guild, 1997.

WEEKLY SALARIES OF DISTRICT CIRCULATION MANAGERS
FOR SELECTED NEWSPAPERS

Newspaper	Top Minimum (after years employed)	Newspaper	Top Minimum (after years employed)
The New York Times	$1,309.00 (4)	Denver Post	$842.00 (4)
Toledo Blade	920.00 (4)	Albany Times-Union	750.00 (4)
Minneapolis Star		Portland Press-Herald	796.00 (4)
Tribune	912.00 (5)	Duluth News-Tribune	656.00 (5)
Long Beach Press-		Manchester Union	
Telegram	795.00 (4)	Leader	692.00 (3)
Seattle Times	776.00 (4)	Terre Haute Tribune-	
San Diego Union	775.00 (5)	Star	438.00 (5)
Boston Herald	844.00 (3)		
St. Louis Post-Dispatch	1,028.00 (5)		

SOURCE: The Newspaper Guild, 1997.

In the mid-1990s, newspapers face new competition from cyberspace in the form of on-line services and other outlets on the World Wide Web. In this case, newspapers are not fighting the competition, they're joining them, with their own Internet "home pages" and on-line services. The Newspaper Association of America reports that 75 percent of newspapers in 1998 have on-line services. From the *San Jose Mercury News,* to the *Chicago Tribune,* to the *Tampa Tribune,* to Long Island's *Newsday,* newspapers are providing readers with on-line previews of the next day's paper and extended coverage of top news stories. Readers can "talk" back to editors and reporters about stories as well as access information from previous issues. Most newspaper publishers are uncertain whether the on-line services will be financially successful. But they don't want to be left in a ditch off the information superhighway, so they cruise down a road that could lead nowhere or to a pot of gold.

The on-line newspapers have created hundreds of new jobs, especially for recent journalism grads, who are sought for their ability to navigate the World Wide Web, their computer skills with HTML and Quark XPress, their knowledge of the latest trends, and their willingness to work long, unpredictable hours. These jobs carry titles like content producer, online editor, creative director and webmaster, and the responsibilities vary widely. Some on-line newspapers simply "repurpose" stories written by print reporters, adding Web links and supplemental information. Staffers at other papers—and many specialized on-line services—report using the phone and e-mail,

WEEKLY SALARIES FOR ADMINISTRATIVE POSITIONS FOR SELECTED NEWSPAPERS

Newspaper	Librarian Minimum (after years employed)	Clerk Minimum (after years employed)	Copy and Office Person Minimum (after years employed)
Baltimore Sun	$ 757.00 (5)	$432.00 (5)	$514.00 (5)
Boston Globe	1,094.00 (1)	578.00 (4)	405.00 (3)
Buffalo News	1,011.00 (flat)	374.00 (3)	421.00 (1)
Chicago Sun-Times	814.00 (5)	490.00 (3)	411.00 (1)
Cleveland Plain Dealer	783.00 (3)	561.00 (4)	578.00 (1)
Denver Post	972.00 (5)	384.00 (3.5)	460.00 (3.5)
Detroit Free Press	729.00 (4)	496.00 (4)	NA
Long Beach Press-Telegraph (CA)	817.00 (flat)	433.00 (1)	397.00 (flat)
Manchester Union Leader (NH)	848.00 (1)	567.00 (3)	516.00 (1)
Minneapolis Star Tribune	947.00 (2)	475.00 (4)	441.00 (6 months)
The New York Times	1,440.00 (6 months)	669.00 (2)	515.00 (1)
Philadelphia Inquirer	845.00 (4)	599.00 (4)	561.00 (3)
Pittsburgh Post-Gazette	759.00 (2)	550.00 (3)	429.00 (1)
San Francisco Chronicle	788.00 (2)	489.00 (2)	433.00 (1.5)
Seattle Times	605.00 (4)	445.00 (2)	392.00 (2)
St. Louis Post-Dispatch	1,028.00 (5)	464.00 (3)	376.00 (1)
Toledo Blade	963.00 (flat)	562.00 (2)	605.00 (6 months)
Washington Post	968.00 (2)	443.00 (2)	409.00 (1.5)

SOURCE: The Newspaper Guild, 1997.

and write stories for on-line publication. Many on-line newspapers feature extensive listings of restaurants, bars, and clubs reviewed by the young and restless on-line writers.

The salaries for these positions are among the highest in the newspaper business, beginning at $25,000. Starting salaries in the $30,000 to $40,000 range are not unusual for graduates of journalism MA programs, according to Paul Grabowicz of the University of California at Berkeley, who manages an electronic job listing called J-Jobs. After a few years' experience, an on-line content producer and editor commands $50,000 and up, especially if they have specialized knowledge about business, technology, and other hot topics such as health.

The digital jobs require both old and new journalism skills. On-line employers still want the basics: good news judgment, the ability to report quickly and to write clean, concise copy. In addition, many require new hires to be familiar with spreadsheets and databases, pagination, art software, and Web design.

These requirements are also sought for more traditional jobs. Computer skills are a given; reporters are also expected to use on-line research for everything from searching local real estate records to retrieving U.S. Census documents to checking computerized data banks in Australia. Electronic bulletin boards offer a new way to get comments for stories and to develop sources.

Modern technology is not the only development to leave a lasting mark on the newspaper industry. The women's movement, as well as sex discrimination lawsuits, has also brought change to the business. The number of women in the newsroom has shifted dramatically since 1970, when only a small percentage of reporters and editors were women. Today, more than half of the nation's 54,700 editorial employees are women. Over the past two decades, newspapers have made an effort to recruit more minorities, spurred both by the demands of black, Latino, and Asian organizations and by an acceptance of the notion that a newsroom staff should reflect the readership. Since the late 1970s, the number of minority editorial employees has grown from 4 percent to just over 11 percent. However, only about 8 percent of journalism school graduates find jobs with newspapers, according to the latest annual survey by the Ohio State Journalism Department. About half pursue careers in unrelated fields, while the rest go into corporate communications, public relations, advertising, and broadcasting.

Newspapers' increased attention to the diversity of their editorial staff indicates that women and minorities will find it easier to land a job in the field. The number of editorial employees was 54,700 in 1998, up 700 from the previous year; 25,557 reporters, 10,654 copy editors, 12,724 supervisors, and 5,790 photographers are employed at newspapers. Total newspaper employment—including advertising, circulation, production and other staff— was 478,000 in 1996, an increase after a downturn in the early 90s. Total female employment in all segments of newspaper operations has climbed to 234,000, while male employment has dropped to 244,000 in 1996. These figures suggest that older male employees—typesetters, darkroom assistants, and pressmen—are retiring and being replaced by new technologies like digital photography and desktop publishing. While many new female hires work in the newsroom, they have also made in-roads in other areas such as advertising sales. The U.S. Department of Labor predicts that job growth for newspapers will be about average through the year 2005. Most editorial openings will be created by people leaving to retire or to switch to less stressful, less time-consuming work.

While technology has created new jobs and recast other positions, in many aspects the reporter's worklife remains unchanged. Most reporters start out on small weekly or daily newspapers, where they cover everything from crime to community boards to cooking contests. Newspaper reporting is not a nine to five job; it's a lifestyle that often requires long hours and not very glamorous travel. Editors try to hire reporters with tenacity, initiative, creativity, a nose for news, and an ability to deal with all types of people from the homeless to the famous. A high energy level coupled with strong self-motivation are requirements for success. After several years on a small paper, most reporters move up to either a larger paper or an editing slot. Career advancement depends on good clips (published stories) and good contacts with both newsmakers and editors at other papers.

Small or large, most newspapers operate in the same manner. Reporters generate stories either through their own sources or from assignment editors, who specialize in coverage of different sections of the paper like local, state, or national news, sports, or lifestyles. Reporters cover the story by doing research, which can include reading past stories on the same topic, searching databases of other publications and information sources, or telephoning sources. While many reporters do most of their news gathering over the phone, often they cover a story in person, armed with paper, pen, and tape recorder. Reporters "file" stories either in the office or from an outside location on a laptop computer hooked by modem to the newspaper. In either case, once completed, the story, which is usually of a predetermined length, goes to the desk editor, who works with the assignment editor.

After the editor reads the story and makes the corrections and changes, the copy goes to the copy desk. The job of copy editors has evolved into one with more responsibility during the late 1990s because of several technological improvements. Most newspapers now lay out their pages electronically on a computer screen in a process called pagination. Copy editors have added design and pagination to their job requirements.

Copy editors first check the copy for style, content, grammar, spelling, and libel, cutting the length of the story if necessary to fit the allotted space. They then write a headline, electronically paste up the page, pulling together text, graphics, photos, and other design elements. Because the job requires such diverse skills, from the ability to use Quark XPress to spotting grammatical errors, copy editors are in high demand and are often paid 10 to 20 percent more than reporters. One downside is that at most newspapers a copy editor starts to work in the early evening, finishing late at night or early the next morning, including weekends and holidays.

Experienced reporters working for daily newspapers who were members of the Newspaper Guild had starting salaries ranging from about $27,664 to nearly $68,062 in 1997. Many top reporters at big city dailies earned more. In general, newspaper salaries increase proportionately to the circulation of the newspaper.

Copy editors and assistant editors follow reporters on the salary scale. At many newspapers, these workers make about 10 percent more than the reporters and reach the salary ceiling more quickly. An assistant managing editor responsible for several departments at a large newspaper makes upward of $100,000, while salaries for managing editors at large papers usually top $150,000.

The newspaper industry has always benefited from supply outweighing demand: Young people are attracted to a career where they can earn a living as a writer. And that living, especially on small to midsized papers, has always been low-paid, whether or not at a considerable newspaper. A 1997 Illinois State University study found that new grads hired at small newspapers, with circulations under 20,000, earned a starting salary of $16,564, while at midsized papers they earned between $20,000 and $24,000. New grads very rarely start at larger papers, which require five or more years of experience. However, some industry analysts believe because of the high demand for new college grads, and the competition for journalists from on-line services, many newspapers will be forced to hike their wages across the board to recruit and keep good reporters and other editorial staffers.

WEEKLY SALARIES FOR ADVERTISING SALES STAFF AT SELECTED NEWSPAPERS

| | Top Minimums | | |
Newspaper	Ad Sales, Display	Ad Sales, Classified Outside	Ad Sales, Classified Inside Phone
Albany Times-Union	$ 722.00	$ 722.00	$522.00
Baltimore Sun	995.00	995.00	722.00
Boston Globe	1,179.00	1,212.00	961.00
Denver Post	925.00	721.00	545.00
Duluth News-Tribune	675.00	675.00	409.00
Manchester Union Leader (NH)	845.00	840.00	721.00
Memphis Commercial Appeal	770.00	686.00	584.00
Philadelphia Inquirer	1,110.00	1,110.00	843.00
Sacramento Bee	649.00	649.00	464.00
San Diego Union	833.00	833.00	639.00
San Francisco Chronicle	944.00	944.00	740.00
San Jose Mercury News (CA)	947.00	947.00	740.00
Seattle Times	766.00	766.00	645.00
St. Louis Post-Dispatch	1,028.00	1,028.00	779.00
Toledo Blade (OH)	944.00	932.00	682.00
Washington Post	968.00	968.00	661.00

SOURCE: The Newspaper Guild, 1997.

THE PUBLISHING HOUSE

Despite the ubiquitous presence of books in our lives—think Oprah, Katie, and Rosie—book publishing is a relatively small industry. In 1996, book shipments totaled over $26 billion while employment stood at only about 100,000 nationwide. In recent years, however, the industry has experienced very strong growth. The number of books published increased every year between 1992–96, when it reached an all-time high of 68,175 titles. The reasons for this are that the number of educated Americans continues to increase (almost 24 percent had finished college in 1997 compared with 17 percent in 1980) while the publishing business has developed new and powerful sales and marketing techniques. The advent of the "superstore" has made many more titles available while the Internet has given on-line booksellers—most notably, Amazon.com—a very efficient means of selling any book whatsoever, even out-of-print titles.

Between 1996–98 the merger madness that seized the American business world found its way to book publishing as well. Several major independent houses, including Random House, Farrar Straus, and Henry Holt, were bought by German publishers; earlier huge media conglomerates invaded the book business: Disney started Hyperion, and Time Warner swallowed Little, Brown as well as the Book-of-the-Month Club. So be forewarned: Big-time New York publishing is no longer the Ivy League gentlemen's comfortable game. The people who run publishing are very demanding of their employees and expect bottom-line results not very different from other industries.

While the declining number of large publishing houses in New York and Boston is shrinking the number of available jobs, the explosive growth of small independent publishers throughout the country are adding many more. In general, however, the very low salaries in book publishing usually means there are entry-level jobs available at almost any time.

What the new job-seeker should be aware of is that some sectors of the publishing industry are more profitable now than others, so the opportunities for advancement can be significantly better. In the late 1990s, for example, the baby boomlet of the late 1980s means that there are many more young children in school than there were a decade ago, so educational publishing—both elementary and high school—may be a good place to look. The same is somewhat true of children's publishing, which grew by nearly 40 percent in the early 1990s. Although most major publishers of children's books have struggled in recent years (they published too many books, thinking the pool was bottomless), the future looks fairly strong as more and more parents realize the significance of reading with young children.

Of course, adult trade publishing remains the most attractive part of the industry to most people, because these books garner all the attention from the press and television. If you love to read fiction or hope to have influence over public opinion, this is the arena to do your job search.

Below are descriptions of a wide variety of jobs that exist in all large publishing houses. Most require a bachelor's degree, and virtually all require some knowledge of computers. Anyone seeking employment in this field should acquire as much knowledge of the leading software programs (WordPerfect, Microsoft Word, etc.) as possible. Knowledge of specialized programs such as PageMaker, and QuarkXPress, will also be a major help in securing employment. The anecdotal evidence would indicate that the book publishing industry uses Macs in their art and production departments although most large houses still use IBMs for their accounting and word processing needs.

Of course the most important skill in publishing remains the ability to read critically. It is required of almost everyone—of marketing and sales people, as well as editors. And remember, you'll have to love doing it or you'll find this business oppressive.

Editorial Department

Acquistions Editors—Frequently called *senior editors,* their primary responsibilities are deciding which books the company will publish, negotiating with writers and their agents to decide how much they will be paid, and working with writers to insure that manuscripts are turned in on schedule and in reasonably good condition. Once the manuscript comes in and is accepted, the editor shepherds the book through the various stages of production; he or she also attends sales and publicity meetings to explain why the book deserves more advertising and why the company's sales people should push it harder to bookstore owners. Responsibility for actual editing—i.e., making comments, asking questions about content, etc.—varies considerably from editor to editor.

Assistant and Associate Editors—Work is similar to that of senior editors except that they usually handle fewer books and less prominent authors, and have less autonomy in deciding which books they will acquire and in negotiating fees. The last two functions are often reviewed closely and sometimes taken over by senior editors. In many houses the assistant or associate editor only reads and edits manuscripts that are under contract.

Editorial Assistants—Often they are treated as glorified secretaries, and the main evidence of their glorification is that they are paid less than secretaries. However, many times this position does serve the function of an apprenticeship, which was its original intention. In addition to typing letters and contracts, filing, and related tasks, editorial assistants are sometimes permitted to read unsolicited manuscripts and give their recommendations for rejection or acceptance.

Developmental Editor—Often the impetus to produce a book comes not from an individual author but from the publisher, as in the case of many textbooks and reference books. In this case, the so-called developmental editor takes a much more active role in the writing of the book: He or she will find the writers, explain to them in detail what is required, edit the work closely, and often write some of the material.

Production Editor—Sometimes called a managing editor, coordinates activity between editors, designers, copy editors, typesetters, and other people necessary to prepare a manuscript for printing. He or she establishes a production schedule, makes sure it is followed, and often sets and supervises the editorial budget.

Copy Editor—Reads manuscripts for grammatical accuracy, consistency of style, phrasing, word use, and logical consistency. Also usually proofreads galleys, repro, and mechanicals (the initial boards from which printing plates are made) to see that the typesetters and paste-up artists have followed the editor's instructions.

Advertising, Sales, and Publicity

Publicity Director—It is the publicity director's job to make sure the company's books receive attention in the media. Toward this end he or she sends out copies of newly published books to publications likely to review them, tries to get authors on TV and radio shows, and arranges other engagements for authors, such as autographing sessions in bookstores and lecture tours of colleges.

Publicist—Under the supervision of the publicity director, performs essentially the same job, except that he or she may deal with less important authors and books, or may be restricted to a specific aspect of publicity.

Copywriter—Writes material intended to sell books. This includes advertising copy, press releases, and the laudatory plot synopses found on the inside flaps of book jackets, called "flap copy."

Marketing Director—Is in charge of the overall effort to sell published books. On the basis of projected sales, he or she decides how many copies of a book will be printed and how and where they will be distributed, oversees the sales staff, and decides how and where books will be advertised.

Advertising Director—Places advertisements in selected publications, such as book review supplements of newspapers and journals aimed at the book's intended audience, and in the case of best-sellers and other mass market books, with TV and other media. A few publishers still prepare their own advertising rather than rely on agencies, so here the advertising director also supervises the writing and design of ads and helps set the advertising budget for each book.

Sales Manager—Supervises the sales staff, makes sure they receive all the necessary material such as press releases and news of new publications, receives their reports and orders for new books, and generally coordinates their activities with those of the rest of the company.

Salespersons—Spend most of their time on the road, visiting bookstore owners and gently persuading them to buy as many books as possible and to display them as prominently as possible. They then make follow-up visits to make sure the books and other materials (such as those large cardboard display stands, called "dump bins") have arrived satisfactorily. Salespeople also report back to the main office with their customers' comments on the quality of service, what kinds of books they are asking for, and other information. Because of the knowledge they thus acquire of the book market, salespeople are sometimes promoted to editors.

Subsidiary Rights Director—A book's circulation seldom ends with its hardcover sales. It may be sold to a book club, a movie company, or a paperback publisher, part of it may be reprinted in magazines, or all of the above may happen. The subsidiary rights director, usually in concert with the author's agent, promotes and manages these sales. Over the past decade, as subsidiary rights contracts for top books have climbed into the millions of dollars, "sub-rights" directors have become increasingly important at major publishing houses. They now exercise a strong influence over the acquisition of new books and the advances paid to writers based on the chances of subsequent sub-rights sales.

Subsidiary Rights Assistant—Usually handles a specific area of sub-rights sales, such as magazines, foreign rights, or book clubs.

Production Department

Art Director—Determines what the book will look like. Along with the acquisitions editor and production director, he or she selects the typeface, book size, paper, jacket design, display type, and other elements of the book's design. The art director also procures the necessary illustrations and photographs (which are sometimes supplied by the author) and determines how they will be placed in the book. Finally, he or she supervises illustrators, freelancers, and paste-up artists.

Managing Editor—See Production Editor, under "Editorial Department."

Traffic Manager—Large publishing houses with complex production schedules often require a traffic manager to keep track of everything. The traffic manager oversees the flow of work between the editorial and art departments, the typesetter, and the printer; sets schedules; and keeps records of which stage of development each project is in. The traffic manager's job is similar to the production editor's, and indeed the two often work closely together; but the production editor's concern is primarily with the needs of the editorial department, while the traffic manager coordinates work among all departments.

Production Director—Supervises the work of the production department, sets a budget for the preparation and printing of each book, and negotiates contracts with typesetters, printers, paper manufacturers, and other suppliers.

AVERAGE ANNUAL SALARIES IN PUBLISHING HOUSES, 1997

Department and Title	Company Revenues		
	$1 million–9.9 million	$10 million–99.9 million	$100 million or more
Editorial			
Editorial director/Editor-in-chief	$ 63,801	$ 92,109	$124,455
Executive editor/managing editor	45,336	58,604	88,713
Editor	53,688	52,000	53,830
Associate editor	31,534	28,925	34,850
Production/development editor/acquisitions	NA	48,000	42,450
Copy editor/proofreader	30,000	NA	NA
Editorial assistant	NA	25,000	39,500
Sales and Marketing			
V.P. sales and marketing	$ 78,250	$106,214	$127,400
Publisher	59,200	82,375	136,720
Associate publisher	61,200	NA	90,000
Sales director/manager	61,250	72,208	99,139
Marketing director/manager	49,242	51,600	61,188
Promotion director/manager	36,375	38,013	72,000
Sales rep/account manager	72,000	51,777	67,305
Advertising Director	NA	39,446	66,500
Marketing Assistant	26,972	26,000	30,000
Management			
President/CEO	$128,088	$289,100	$325,000
Owner/director	109,703	166,500	174,000
Executive/senior V-P	85,330	246,000	227,500
V-P General Manager	52,900	71,060	158,000
V-P Finance/Controller	73,390	107,665	277,500
V-P Production/Operations	67,000	120,450	135,000

SOURCE: *Publishers Weekly.* "1997 Salary Survey." Reprinted by permission.

SELECTED EXECUTIVE PUBLISHING SALARIES, 1996–97

Company and Position	Annual Compensation 1997	1996	% Change
Amazon.com			
President	$ 79,797	$ 64,373	23.0%
V-P, CIO	242,045	NA	NA
Advanced Marketing Services			
Chairman	$ 388,294	$ 265,000	46.5%
President, CEO	388,653	251,658	54.4
Barnes & Noble			
Chairman, CEO	$1,440,000	$1,440,000	0%
President	451,154	420,000	7.4
Books-A-Million			
President, CEO	$ 326,700	$ 300,000	8.9%
Senior V-P, Merchandising	$160,400	113,500	41.3
Borders Group			
Chairman, CEO	$1,030,000	$1,040,300	−10.0%
President	800,000	903,900	−11.5
Golden Books Family Entertainment			
Chairman, CEO	$1,437,885	$ 957,558	50.2%
President	618,462	461,354	34.1
Educational Development Corp.			
Chairman, President	$ 120,800	$ 110,000	9.8%
Harcourt, Brace & Co.			
President, CEO	$ 935,385	$ 637,500	46.7%
Houghton Mifflin			
Chairman, president, CEO	$ 831,250	$ 720,875	15.3%
Executive vice president	358,900	324,030	10.8
IDG Books			
CEO	$ 596,975	NA	NA
President and publisher	481,358	NA	NA
McGraw Hill Cos.			
Chairman, CEO	$2,323,016	$1,912,833	21.4%
COO	1,376,409	1,170,809	17.6

SELECTED EXECUTIVE PUBLISHING SALARIES, 1996–97

| Company and Position | Annual Compensation | | % Change |
	1997	1996	
Millbrook Press			
President, CEO	$ 161,539	NA	NA
Senior V-P, publisher	127,916	125,000	2.3%
Scholastic Corp.			
Chairman, president, CEO	$ 600,000	$ 776,938	–22.8%
Executive vice president	500,000	540,477	–7.5
Waverly Inc.			
Chairman	$ 374,200	$ 381,875	–1.8%
President, CEO	413,800	411,250	0.6
John Wiley & Sons			
President, CEO	$ 841,882	$ 749,645	12.3%
Senior V-P	393,370	393,981	–0.1

SOURCE: Company proxy statements.

VII

Jobs and Salaries in Health Care

In 1980, the nation reached a milestone of sorts when for the first time in its history slightly more than half of all its citizens were past the age of thirty. With birth rates and fertility rates remaining at very low levels, the median age of the population has continued to rise throughout the decade: In 1990 it was 33.0 years, and by the year 2000 it will be 36.4. By 2010, 14 percent of the U.S. population will be over sixty-five, up from under 10 percent in 1970, and 11 percent in 1980. A continuously aging society will cause many dramatic changes in the future, not the least of which will be the need for an expanded workforce in the health care field.

Over 6 million people are currently employed in health care jobs. But the U.S. government projects that health care will create almost 5 million new jobs by 2006. Jobs for registered nurses are expected to increase by 700,000; and by 400,000 for licensed practical nurses; 125,000 for medical assistants; over 125,000 for therapists; and 450,000 for nursing aides, orderlies, and attendants. Employment in the health-care field has grown fastest in physicians' and surgeons' offices', which have added 200,000 jobs in the 1990s.

Almost every occupation in health care will have higher than average growth in the next decade, including the highly paid managerial positions. With hospitals forced to deal with cuts in government support, and with new types of health-care maintenance organizations (HMOs) growing across the country, management and accounting skills are more highly valued than ever before. According to the U.S. Department of Labor, the biggest portion of the growth (some 700,000 jobs) will occur in the demand for registered nurses by the year 2006. The demand for licensed practical nurses is expected to grow by 275,000. Other occupations expected to experience triple-figure growth are physicians and surgeons; therapists, nursing aides, orderlies, and attendants; and medical assistants. Almost every occupation in the health-care field will experience higher than average growth in the 1990s.

But it is important to keep in mind that these figures were compiled before the full impact of for-profit medical centers and serious cutbacks in federal funding could be measured. We know now that many hospitals are being forced to reduce staff across the board; some are openly replacing highly trained nurses with licensed practical nurses simply to save money, while other reports indicate that nurses are being asked to perform the tasks of respiratory therapists and the like.

The future pay structure in the industry is hard to predict. No one is quite sure whether wage rates will increase as society places a higher value on health-care work or stay about the same as cost-saving pressures predominate. Although we might normally expect to see some heavy upward pressure on earnings as the demand for workers grows, the need to control the skyrocketing overall cost of health care will possibly exert an equal downward pressure. An increasingly strong union movement among nonprofessional employees (especially in public hospitals) will make for some confrontations regarding wage rates.

At the same time, the importance of hospital administrators (executives, accountants, marketing, and public relations specialists) has grown in direct proportion to the requirement that hospitals and HMOs become part of contemporary corporate culture. As most Americans are forced to accept less health-care service at greater personal cost, the salaries of administrators continue to soar, especially in the publicly held, for-profit health maintenance organizations. In recent years the average cash compensation for chief executives in the HMO industry was about $350,000, but the highest paid executives made over $10 million (some over $40 million) because of their stock option plans (see the entry on "The American Executive" for an explanation of how these plans work). Even Graef Crystal, the foremost executive compensation expert, pronounced these compensation awards "monstrously large, among the highest in any industry." So while many doctors, nurses, and technicians are all asked to take salary reductions, the people demanding that health costs be reduced are reaping huge salaries while providing investors with heavy returns.

The true impact of this peculiarly American approach to caring for the sick and dying may not be known for a while, but for now the anecdotal evidence clearly points to a much reduced system aimed at those with good health-care coverage and with wage rates relatively stable.

HOSPITAL ADMINISTRATORS

At the center of America's health-care system are the approximately 6,649 hospitals that every year admit almost 35 million patients and provide $256 billion worth of services, more than 38 percent of the nation's total health care bill. This is big business by anyone's definition, but every prediction indicates that many hospitals will close and many more will merge their services as the federal government cuts back its financial support for Medicare. The crucial problems most hospitals face today are the same ones that other businesses must cope with, including strict, ever-changing government regulations, stiff competition for patients, and spiraling costs. As in other businesses, too, a new breed of specially trained personnel is bringing important changes to the way hospitals are run.

The complex task of managing a hospital falls to the administrator, sometimes known as president, chief executive officer, or executive vice-president. The administrator's duties and salary vary considerably, according to the size of the hospital. At a small, rural hospital with less than 100 beds, an administrator will earn an average of $90,000 and have a finger in everything from deciding how often the floors should be waxed to planning a redesign of the emergency room. At a big-city medical center with about 500 beds, an administrator will earn $225,000 on average and will spend some of his time managing associate and assistant administrators who take care of the day-to-day operation. Good-sized chunks of time are given to raising funds for new construction; lobbying with local, state, and federal officials; presenting proposals to government watchdog committees; conferring with physicians and the board of directors on whether to buy a multimillion-dollar piece of equipment. At the same time, a good administrator tries to keep the high-priced medical specialists as well as the lowly interns happy. While the administrator spends hours in meetings, his subordinates see that all the departments—from admissions to purchasing to X-ray—are running smoothly. In most hospitals, all the medical departments are also headed by a physician who oversees all the strictly medical areas.

The Department of Labor classifies about 257,000 persons as health-service managers. Under this title fall government and nongovernment hospital administrators as well as managers of nursing homes and health-maintenance organizations. A sizable number are employed by government agencies that analyze regional health-care needs, by insurance agencies, by hospital associations, and by consulting firms. The Department of Labor estimates that job openings in the field will grow much faster than the average through the year 2005. However, depending upon how the managed-care system progresses, there could be quite a decline in administrative and support jobs in hospitals since this trend tends to treat patients on an out-patient basis to cut costs.

Because the medical field has grown increasingly sophisticated in its use of management techniques, many hospitals require job-seekers to have a master's degree in business or health administration. A survey by *Modern Healthcare* magazine found that about 64 percent of hospital administrators held advanced degrees. Salaries among top hospital administrators vary widely by geography—New England executives earn as much as 70 percent more than their counterparts in Arizona, Colorado, Idaho, and other mountain states—and by the type of hospitals they work in. For example, the average salary for a chief executive officer of a psychiatric hospital is only $84,400, according to *Modern Healthcare,* but at a corporate health-care system, the average salary is over $339,000.

One of the fastest-growing new job categories in health care is that of the *compliance officer.* These in-house monitors have the task of overseeing the operations of hospitals and medical schools to ensure they are not involved in health-care fraud, and to help minimize the penalties when infractions are found. Consultants estimate that only 5 percent of the nation's 5,400 hospitals and medical schools have comprehensive compliance departments, but suggest this number could double in the next year.

Traditionally, hospitals have counted on low-level internal auditors to catch problems and report them to senior management. Compliance officers are expected to get involved in potential trouble spots much earlier. They are also expected to flag hospital boards and the government immediately if infractions are found. Perhaps their most important function is to train employees in how to follow the complex and seemingly ever-changing rules associated with the health-care system in the first place.

MEDIAN TOTAL COMPENSATION OF HOSPITAL ADMINISTRATORS, 1995
(in thousands of dollars)

Title	All Facilities	(by number of employees)			
		0–599	600–1199	1200–2199	Over 2200
Medical affairs director	$182.3	$139.6	$150.0	$185.4	$190.3
Administrator/CEO	165.5	110.1	167.4	207.3	233.7
Associate Administrator/ COO	110.0	72.2	106.6	146.3	160.1
Chief financial officer	105.3	76.7	99.3	129.6	151.0
Head of nursing services	88.0	66.2	90.0	101.3	108.2
Head of MIS	71.3	45.2	64.6	75.0	84.6

MEDIAN TOTAL COMPENSATION OF HOSPITAL ADMINISTRATORS, 1995
(in thousands of dollars)

Department Executive/Mgt	1995	1994	Percent Change
	(thousands of dollars)		
Administration			
General counsel	$104.0	$114.2	−8.9%
Public Affairs	86.6	81.7	6.0
Development	75.6	73.3	3.1
Planning	75.0	74.1	1.3
Marketing	63.6	59.7	6.5
Quality assurance	56.5	54.5	3.7
Public relations	51.6	48.0	7.5
Financial			
Controller	$ 70.1	$ 67.9	3.2%
General accounting	50.5	49.5	0.2
Business office	55.4	54.4	1.8
Admitting	40.1	39.8	0.1
Budget planning	50.9	51.0	−0.1
Risk management	51.3	51.4	−0.2
Medical records	50.9	49.2	3.4
General Services			
General services	$ 80.0	$ 77.5	5.8%
Food/dietary services	53.2	52.8	0.8
General service/ supply	40.3	40.0	0.8
Linen services	38.9	36.8	5.7
Patient Care			
Ancillary patient care	$ 85.5	$ 83.8	2.0%
Pharmacy	69.7	67.9	2.6
Clinical lab	58.7	57.9	1.4
Radiology	58.0	57.1	1.6
Nuclear medicine	46.1	45.7	0.1
Rehab services	66.7	62.8	6.2
Physical therapy	58.0	57.2	1.4
Occupational therapy	51.3	50.9	0.1
Speech therapy	49.2	48.5	0.2
Respiratory therapy	52.3	52.0	0.1

MEDIAN TOTAL COMPENSATION OF HOSPITAL ADMINISTRATORS, 1995
(in thousands of dollars)

Department Executive/Mgt	1995 (thousands of Dollars)	1994	Percent Change
Chaplain	$48.8	$47.3	3.2%
Social services	50.7	49.1	3.3
Outpatient services	62.4	57.0	9.5

SOURCE: *Modern Health Care,* executive compensation survey, June 1995. Reprinted by permission.

REGISTERED NURSES

As a nation our commitment to first-rate health care is unrivaled, or at least we believe that to be the case. But today a strong possibility exists that our system of caring for the sick is being threatened by the demands of for-profit industries bent on keeping down the wages of health-care personnel. Their work may have a high social value, but as long as their services are not productive or profitable in the traditional sense, they will always have to struggle for higher wages. No better example of this premise exists than the historic role of nurses in American life.

The image of the kind, saintly women ministering to the needs of the sick and dying has been a constant theme in Western art, and the ideals embodied in those representations are part of our cultural heritage. Over the last century, women continued to play a vital role as leaders in the fight for better health care. Equally important were the services women performed as low-paid workers in financially troubled hospitals. This situation continued into the early 1980s, when salaries for nurses failed to keep up with inflation and many talented, intelligent women fled the nursing profession and sought work in higher paying, less stressful jobs. Throughout the 1980s, there was an acute shortage of nurses with as many as 100,000 vacancies at any given time.

Traditional economic theory says that these circumstances should have immediately driven up the nurses' wages. But in fact this did not happen in any dramatic way. The hospital industry argued that the already staggering costs of modern hospital care wouldn't allow for any dramatic increase in labor costs, especially since the federal government was bearing so much of the cost while struggling to dig its way out of the mountain of debt left by the Reagan administration. Unlike manufacturing or other service industries, increased health-care costs could not be passed on to the consumer.

The era of the HMO—which no longer needs any description—soon

SALARIES OF HOSPITAL NURSES, 1997

Total Income	All Nurses[1]	Nurses on Salary	Nurses Paid Hourly
$60,000 or more	8%	29%	4%
50,000–59,999	13	23	12
47,500–49,999	3	5	2
42,500–47,499	12	11	12
40,000–42,499	11	9	11
37,500–39,999	6	4	6
35,000–37,499	11	7	12
32,500–34,999	6	3	7
30,000–32,499	6	3	7
27,500–29,999	4	1	5
25,000–27,499	5	NA	6
Under 25,000	11	4	12
Average	$41,010	$54,300	$38,650

[1]Includes both full and part-time nurses.
SOURCE: *RN Magazine*, October 1997. Reprinted by permission.

AVERAGE ANNUAL SALARIES OF NURSES BY SETTING, 1997

Setting	Average Annual Income
Acute care hospital	$41,010
Ambulatory care center/HMO	40,300
Community hospital/home health	38,650
Extended care/psych	35,280
Physician's office	30,440

SOURCE: *RN Magazine*, October 1997. Reprinted by permission.

followed, and with it came demands for cost-cutting in every area of medicine (except in administrators' salaries). Nurses have not fared as badly under the new systems as many predicted, but it is still very early in the game. With the Medicare and Medicaid programs in serious need of new financing, the future is less certain than many think.

Still, despite rapid and often wrenching changes in the health-care industry, the employment outlook for nurses remains bright, while the salary levels increase slowly. The Department of Labor continues to project much faster than average growth throughout the year 2006. In fact, one of every five new jobs in the health-care industry will be for nurses. The aging population, which is responsible for fueling most of the growth in the health-care industry, will especially benefit nurses, especially home health-care nurses. Growth will also be strong for nurses in physicians' offices, clinics, HMOs, ambulatory centers, and nursing homes. Hospitals, where two of every three RNs currently work, will experience the slowest growth, as the number of inpatients is not expected to increase. That's primarily a result of fiscal austerity by insurance companies, who are refusing to pay for overnight stays for all but the most serious procedures. One major change in the profession will be the increase in part-time work (without benefits, of course).

Pay Rates for Nurses

As the accompanying tables make clear, several factors affect registered nurses' salaries, including the regions where they work, the kinds of institutions that employ them, and their levels of expertise. While it is clear that nurses' salaries have reached tolerable levels, they still reflect a reluctance to recognize the vital role registered nurses play in the health-care system. After all, many doctors—especially the younger ones—will tell you that in good hospitals, the senior nursing staff is more responsible for the level of care a patient receives than anyone else. Still, the *most* experienced registered nurses are being paid $55,000–65,000 a year, a level hardly comparable to most of the jobs in this book that require three or four years of training, serious responsibilities for sick people, and a frequent acquaintance with death and human suffering over many years.

Several disturbing trends have emerged in recent years that should be noted. Until recently, a bachelor's degree in nursing was seen as a way of professionalizing nursing and creating career paths for those with plans to stay in nursing for many years. Today, however, nurses who take a degree make less than those who attend nursing school, which in the long run is bound to keep all nurses' salaries at a lower level.

Another current concern is the assignment of tasks always done by registered nurses to licensed practical nurses (see below) who have far less training and education. The evidence for this trend may only be anecdotal, but it is clearly a concern nationally and threatens the quality of patient care as well as the pay levels of registered nurses who are forced to compete with lower-paid employees.

Related to this trend is the movement of some experienced nurses into medical areas once reserved exclusively for doctors. In addition to the increasingly familiar physician assistant (see the entry below), the *nurse anesthetist* has become an attractive field for experienced nurses willing to take on more training (a certification process is required). According to a 1997 study by the Hay Group, the median salary for nurse anesthetists in acute

AVERAGE HOURLY PAY RATES FOR NURSES BY REGION, 1997

Region	Hourly Pay Rate
New England	$22.10
Mid-Atlantic	21.15
South Atlantic	18.60
Great Lakes	18.60
Mid-South	17.40
Plains	17.30
Southwest	18.00
Rocky Mountains	18.25
Far West	24.10

SOURCE: *RN Magazine*, October 1997. Reprinted by permission.

AVERAGE PAY FOR NURSES BY AGE, EXPERIENCE, AND EDUCATION, 1997

Age	Average Hourly Pay	Average Annual Income
Under 30	$16.70	$34,630
30–39	18.65	37,650
40–49	20.20	43,080
50 and over	21.50	46,170
Years' experience		
Less than three	$16.10	$31,115
3–5	16.90	36,045
6–10	18.45	39,180
11–15	20.80	41,100
16 or more	21.90	46,525
Education		
Diploma	$20.35	$41,620
BSN	19.95	41,010
Associate degree	18.30	37,910

SOURCE: *RN Magazine*, October 1997. Reprinted by permission.

care hospitals was $82,000 (the middle 50 percent group earned between $74,700 and $90,300). Needless to say, anesthesiologists with M.D. degrees and several years of advanced training have been leading the fight against this development.

There has also been a growing trend, at least among a certain set of people, toward a return to having babies at home. But economic and cultural deprivation, especially in rural areas, have also contributed to an increase in the number of pregnant women who truly need the assistance of trained people, and *nurse-midwives* have helped fill the gap. According to the American College of Nurse-Midwives, about 5,000 trained nurse-midwives are working in the United States today. The average salary range is from $65,000 to $75,000 but may vary depending on the area in which they practice. Midwives in large urban areas command the highest salaries.

Less controversial but still a matter of concern has been the emergence of the *nurse practitioner*, who also must receive advanced training but a bit less rigorous than the nurse anesthetist. Almost all nurse practitioners are employed by HMOs or clinics. They provide basic primary medical care, including treatment of common illnesses and injuries, and the prescribing of medications. In 1996 their median annual base salary was $66,800, and more than half of them earned over $54,000.

The obvious reason for these developments is to drive down the costs of medicine by cutting fees ordinarily paid to medical doctors. Many nurses are surely qualified to take on some of these tasks, but unless they are carefully supervised by doctors, the results could be catastrophic.

Part-Time Work for Nurses

About three out of ten nurses work part-time. Part-timers work an average of twenty-seven hours a week; their hourly salaries are more than $1.00 higher than their full-time counterparts (to make up for their lack of benefits). But they take home an average of only $28,400. A closer look at the demographics of each group helps explain why part-timers can afford to pass up this income. Almost 85 percent of part-time nurses are married, with an average household income of $69,400. These figures suggest that many part-time nurses work because they want to work, not because they need the money. Only 54 percent of full-time nurses are married.

Job Descriptions of Registered Nurses

Registered Nurse—Provides professional nursing care to patients in hospitals, nursing homes, clinics, health units, private residences, and com-

HOURLY PAY RATES FOR PART-TIME NURSES, 1997

Hourly Pay Rate	Percent Earning
$20.00 or more	42%
19.00–19.99	13
18.00–18.99	12
17.00–17.99	9
16.00–16.99	10
15.00–15.99	6
14.00–14.99	3
13.00–13.99	4
Less than $13.00	1
Average	**$20.55**

SOURCE: *RN Magazine*, October 1997. Reprinted by permission.

munity health organizations. Assists physicians with treatment, assesses patient health problems and needs, develops and implements nursing care plans, maintains medical records. May specialize: e.g., nurse anesthetist, nurse practitioner, industrial nurse, psychiatric nurse, clinical nurse specialist.

Nursing Supervisor—A registered professional nurse who directs nursing services in more than one organized nursing unit or operating room. Plans work schedules and assigns duties to nurses and aides, provides or arranges for training, and visits patients to observe nurses and to insure that care is proper. May also insure that records are maintained and that equipment and supplies are ordered.

Head Nurse—A registered professional nurse who is responsible for nursing services and patient care in a single nursing unit.

Hospital Nurse—Forms the largest group of nurses. Provides bedside nursing care and carrys out medical regimens. May also supervise licensed practical nurses and aides. Usually is assigned to one area, such as surgery, maternity, pediatrics, emergency room, intensive care, or treatment of cancer patients, or may rotate among departments.

Office Nurse—Assists physicians in private practice, clinics, surgicenters, emergency medical centers, and HMOs. Prepares patients for and assists with examinations, administers injections and medications, dresses wounds and incisions, assists with minor surgery, and maintains records. May also perform routine laboratory and office work.

Home Health Nurse—Provides periodic services, prescribed by a physician, to patients at home. After assessing patients' home environments cares for and instructs patients and their families. Must be able to work independently and may supervise home health aides.

Nursing Home Nurse—Manages nursing care for residents. Generally spends the most time on administrative and supervisory tasks. Assesses residents' medical conditions, develops treatment plans, supervises licensed practical nurses and nursing aides, and performs difficult procedures such as starting intravenous fluids. May work in specialty-care departments, such as long-term rehabilitation units for strokes and head injuries.

Public Health Nurse—Instructs individuals, families, and other groups in health education, disease prevention, nutrition, and child care. Arranges for immunizations, blood pressure testing, and other health screening. Also works with community leaders, teachers, parents, and physicians in community health education.

Occupational Health or Industrial Nurse—Provides nursing care at worksites to employees, customers, and others with minor injuries and illnesses. Provides emergency care, prepares accident reports, and arranges for further care if necessary. Also offers health counseling, assists with health examinations and inoculations, and assesses work environments to identify potential health or safety problems.

Nurse Anesthetist—Recommends and administers general anesthetics intravenously, topically, by inhalation, or by endotracheal intubation.

Nurse Practitioner—A registered nurse responsible for providing continuous and comprehensive nursing care in collaboration with a physician and/or other members of a health-care team. This position requires additional preparation beyond requirements for licensure, which typically includes an M.A. in nursing science.

Staff Nurse—A registered nurse who employs special skills, knowledge, and judgment in caring for patients within an organized nursing unit. Gives

VETERANS ADMINISTRATION NURSES: Number Employed and Average Salaries		
Grade	Number Employed	Average Salary
I	5,621	$38,166
II	18,940	46,518
III	6,908	57,429
IV	5,576	66,850
V	154	94,040
Total	32,199	48,028

SOURCE: Office of Personnel Management, *Pay Structure of the Federal Civil Service*, March 31, 1997.

medication, administers highly specialized therapy using complicated equipment, observes and reports on a patient's condition, and maintains all medical records therein.

Job-Level Descriptions of Nurses

Level I: Provide standard nursing care.

Level II: Assignments involve comprehensive nursing care.

Level II specialists: Typically work in intensive care or critical care units.

Level III: Provide advanced nursing care beyond specialized patient care.

PHYSICIAN ASSISTANTS

While some nurses, especially the nurse practitioner and the nurse clinician, are carving out roles for themselves that allow a greater participation in patient-care decisions, a small group of health care specialists, called physician assistants, has been doing just that for more than twenty years. The idea of using medically trained people (nurses and military medics, for example) to perform the physician's routine tasks surfaced in the mid-sixties, when dire predictions of a doctor shortage ran rampant. By 1970, there were about 100 specially trained P.A.s (as they are called); by 1982, however, there were about 10,000 of them, with 40 percent of them serving in rural areas (counties of less than 50,000), where doctors are still hard to find. And,

AVERAGE INCOME OF PHYSICIAN ASSISTANTS BY EXPERIENCE, 1996, 1997

	1996	1997	% Change
Total	$61,493	$63,910	3.9%
Under 1 year	52,740	55,081	4.4
1–3 years	55,942	58,494	4.6
4–6 years	59,988	62,346	3.9
7–9 years	62,414	64,753	3.7
10–12 years	64,299	66,791	3.9
13–15 years	65,178	68,225	4.7
16–18 years	66,825	68,911	3.1
Over 18 years	66,578	69,928	5.0

NOTE: Excludes active duty military P.A.s, self-employed P.A.s, and P.A.s who report working fewer than thirty-two hours per week for their primary employer.

today, P.A.s number more than 64,000; about 35 percent of them serve rural areas.

Most P.A.s work under the direct supervision of a licensed physician, although a growing number, now about 40 percent, work in hospitals and clinics. The P.A.'s duties include taking down patient histories, giving physical examinations, ordering laboratory tests, and assisting during compli-

AVERAGE INCOME OF PHYSICIAN ASSISTANTS BY PRIMARY SPECIALTY, 1996, 1997

	1996	1997	% Change
Total	$61,493	$63,910	3.9%
OB/GYN	57,535	59,543	3.5
Pediatric subspecialties	58,780	59,741	1.6
General pediatrics	59,253	59,823	1.0
General internal medicine	57,833	60,051	3.8
Family/general medicine	58,547	61,060	4.3
Other	59,223	62,055	4.7
IM subspecialties	59,895	62,095	3.7
General surgery	62,194	62,975	1.3
Industrial/occupational medicine	63,933	65,966	3.2
Emergency medicine	67,285	70,361	4.6
Surgical subspecialties	68,771	71,384	3.8

NOTE: Excludes active duty military P.A.s, self-employed P.A.s, and P.A.s who report working fewer than thirty-two hours per week for their primary employer.
SOURCE: American Academy of Physician Assistants, 1997 Membership Census Report (December 1997).

cated medical procedures such as cardiac catheterizations. Physician assistants may write prescriptions in thirty-nine states as well as in the District of Columbia. Some P.A.s specialize in assisting surgeons or pediatricians, or working in a hospital emergency room; in those cases, their duties are more elaborate.

Training to be a P.A. takes two years, and almost all states require that new P.A.s complete an accredited, formal education program. In 1997, there were ninety-six such educational programs for physician assistants; fifty-three of these programs offered a baccalaureate degree or a degree option. The rest offered either a certificate, an associate degree, or a master's degree. Most P.A. graduates have at least a bachelor's degree; about 80 percent have had extensive experience in health care, usually as a nurse or medical technician.

Employment opportunities are expected to be excellent for physician assistants, particularly in areas or settings that have difficulty attracting physicians, such as rural and inner city clinics. Employment of P.A.s is expected to grow much faster than the average for all occupations through the year 2006 due to anticipated expansion of the health services industry and an emphasis on cost containment. Physicians and institutions are expected to employ more P.A.s to provide primary care and assist with medical and surgical procedures, because P.A.s are cost-effective and productive members of the health-care team. Physician assistants can relieve physicians of routine duties and procedures. Besides the traditional office-based setting, P.A.s should find a growing number of jobs in institutional settings such as hospitals, academic medical centers, public clinics, and prisons. Additional P.A.s may be needed to augment medical staffing in inpatient teaching hospital settings if the number of physician residents is reduced. In addition, state-imposed legal limitations on the numbers of hours worked by physician residents are increasingly common and encourage hospitals to use P.A.s to supply some physician resident services. Opportunities will be best in states that allow P.A.s a wider scope of practice, such as the ability to prescribe medication.

Given their extensive training and experience, physician assistants, like almost all health-care workers except for doctors, receive relatively low pay. According to the American Academy of Physician Assistants, the mean total income for physician assistants in full-time clinical practice in 1997 was $63,910 ; median income was $61,021. Income varies by specialty, practice setting, geographical location, and years of experience. The average annual salary for physician assistants employed by the federal government was $48,670 in early 1997.

NURSES' AIDES AND ORDERLIES

Over 1.3 million people work as aides, orderlies, or attendants in our hospitals and nursing home facilities. Their tasks include taking temperatures, giving baths, making beds, transporting patients from one part of a facility to another, etc. According to the Department of Labor, median weekly earnings of nurses' aides were about $292 in 1996. The middle 50 percent earned between $233 and $372. Chain nursing homes paid certified nurses' aides median hourly wages of $6.60 in 1996.

LICENSED PRACTICAL NURSES

Over the next decade, this will be one of the fastest-growing jobs in the nation. According to the federal government, jobs for licensed practical nurses (LPNs) will grow by more than 260,000 by the year 2005. There are currently more than 665,000 LPNs working in hospitals, nursing homes, private homes, doctors' offices, and now, more frequently, in HMOs. They do everything from keeping records and giving alcohol rubs to administering prescribed medicines and taking patients' vital signs. Their willingness and ability to perform a wide variety of jobs has made LPNs a crucial part of the emerging lower-paid health-care workforce. In addition, because so much of contemporary medicine is administered in the home, the numbers of part-timers will increase significantly, as in other parts of the American economy.

According to the Bureau of Labor Statistics, hourly wage rates for LPNs vary by region, from $9.00–$10.00 in the south to $13.00–$15.00 in the north and west. Those with more experience earn slightly more. Several other surveys indicate that LPNs earn an average annual salary in the $22,000–$26,000 range, with a top salary of $30,000–$35,000.

HEALTH TECHNICIANS

Almost 550,000 people work as health technicians and technologists in the medical and allied health fields. Health technology is a rapidly growing field. Advances in diagnosis and treatment of disease have created jobs that did not exist ten or fifteen years ago and, given the extent of research going on in this country alone, this trend will clearly continue. In addition, the combination of recent population growth, better medical plans, and the public's greater, if not obsessive, health consciousness has led to an increase in regular physical examinations and the routine tests that are part of them. This has meant excellent job growth for health technicians throughout the 1980s and 1990s.

A technician must complete high school and at least two years of college, or a specialized program in the field. The American Medical Association's Committee on Allied Health Education and Accreditation approves these programs, which are available in vocational schools, junior colleges, and hospitals. On-the-job training is equally important. A cardiopulmonary technologist, for example, needs six to twelve months of training for proficiency in invasive tests (when substances such as chemical dyes or tubes enter the patient's body), and three to six months for proficiency in one noninvasive test.

Technicians can be certified by passing examinations administered by their associations. Most hospitals and clinics prefer to hire registered technicians, and there is some evidence that they receive higher salaries than their nonregistered counterparts. The most striking fact about salaries in this field, however, is the enormous difference between pay on the West Coast as compared to the rest of the country.

Job Descriptions of Health Technicians

It is difficult to standardize job descriptions because the degree of responsibility varies so much depending on the job setting. The descriptions that follow attempt to summarize the usual duties of each technician.

CLINICAL LABORATORY PERSONNEL

Clinical laboratory personnel work in the laboratories of hospitals, clinics, and research institutions, in private laboratories, and in doctors' offices. With the exception of the medical technologist, they work under the supervision of the laboratory director.

Certified Laboratory Assistant—Performs a variety of routine tests and procedures, including collecting blood specimens, typing blood, and preparing slides.

Medical Laboratory Technician—Performs more complex tasks than those handled by the certified laboratory assistant, but only those that do not require a great deal of technical knowledge.

Medical Technologists—A skilled general laboratory scientist who performs the chemical, microscopic, and blood-analysis tests that require the exercise of independent judgment and the responsibility of diagnosis. Often runs private laboratories and may also specialize in one aspect of laboratory research.

SURGICAL TECHNICIANS AND PERFUSIONISTS

These technicians work only in the hospital setting, under the direction of the surgeon performing the operation in which they are involved.

Surgical Technician—Prepares the operating room and organizes the supplies used during surgery. In some instances assists the surgeon by holding instruments and cutting stitches.

Perfusionist (Extracorporeal Technologist)—Operates the heart-lung machines that take over for the patient's own blood circulation during open-heart surgery. Must know the limitations of every piece of equipment and be able to keep it working properly during surgery.

INSTRUMENT TECHNICIANS

The following technicians work with technical instrumentation. They work in hospitals, clinics, and private offices, and are primarily involved with the diagnostic side of medicine. Dialysis technicians, radiation therapy technologists, and nuclear medicine technologists are involved with treatment of disease.

EKG (Electrocardiogram) Technologist—Performs heart testing under a physician's supervision. Attaches the electrodes to the patient's body and adjusts them to obtain different records of heart action.

EEG (Electroencephalograph) Technologist—Uses equipment to measure and record the brain's electrical activity. Attaches the electrodes to the patient's head, monitors the test, and prepares a descriptive report of the tracing for the physician.

Cardiopulmonary Technologist—Performs diagnostic tests on the lungs and heart. In noninvasive procedures the technologist has the same duties as an EKG technologist, but in invasive tests injects the patient with chemical dyes, or inserts tubing. Must carefully monitor the patient to be able to recognize heart or respiratory failure.

Ultrasound Technologist (Diagnostic Medical Sonographer)—Uses complex equipment to direct high-frequency sound waves into specific areas of the body to determine abnormalities. Selects and operates the equipment and must have enough knowledge of anatomy to recognize abnormalities.

X-ray Technician—Takes X-ray film for use in diagnosis of medical problems.

Radiation Therapy Technologist—Assists physicians in treatment of patients with prescribed doses of radiation.

Nuclear Medicine Technologist—Participates in activity involving radioactive drugs used for the diagnosis and treatment of medical problems. Calculates and administers the correct dosages of drugs and is involved with the safety procedures required when using them.

Dialysis Technician—Prepares and maintains the dialyzer that performs kidney functions for the patient. Also takes blood tests and monitors the patient's vital signs.

EMERGENCY MEDICAL TECHNICIANS

Emergency medical technicians are trained to provide immediate care to the critically ill or injured. They are often the first people to treat the victims of an accident or illness and as such must determine the nature of the injury and decide on the sequence of emergency treatment. Depending on their level of training, they may treat shock, control bleeding, apply splints, or assist in childbirth.

**AVERAGE ANNUAL SALARIES OF EMERGENCY MEDICAL TECHNICIANS,
BY TYPE OF EMPLOYER, 1996**

Employer	EMT-Basic	EMT-Paramedic
All employers	$25,051	$30,407
Fire departments	29,859	32,483
Hospital based	18,686	28,373
Private ambulance services	18,617	23,995

SOURCE: *Journal of Emergency Medical Services.*

AVERAGE SALARIES OF HEALTH CARE WORKERS IN THE FEDERAL GOVERNMENT

Title	Number Employed	Average Salary
Physician assistants	2,025	$49,798
Nurses	43,752	45,184
Nursing assistants	13,811	22,089
Occupational therapists	704	43,398
Physical therapists	649	45,367
Corrective therapists	536	37,883
Rehabilitation therapist's assistants	850	24,998
Nuclear medicine technologists	142	36,012
Medical technologists	5,725	38,482
Medical technicians	2,099	24,780
Pathology technicians	499	30,780
Diagnostic radiology technicians	3,166	31,496
Medical instrument technicians	2,156	29,337
Pharmacy technicians	3,618	22,819
Speech pathologists and audiologists	754	50,475
Health system administrators	595	74,729
Medical record technicians	3,269	23,865
Dental assistants	2,704	22,331
Dental hygienists	339	28,677

SOURCE: Office of Personnel Management, *Occupations of Federal White-Collar and Blue-Collar Workers* (1996).

The State Emergency Medical Services Directors estimate that there are 450,000 emergency medical technicians and emergency medical technician-paramedics in the United States, many of whom work on a voluntary basis.

There are three ratings for emergency medical technicians.

Emergency Medical Technician (Non-Ambulance)—Works as nurse, nurse's aide, and orderly. Must complete an eighty-one-hour course in emergency medical care and have three months of patient or health-care experience. There is no evidence that these technicians receive additional compensation for having this training. In fact, many hospitals are requiring their employees, at all levels, to take a certain amount of emergency medical training in order to remain on staff.

Emergency Medical Technician (Ambulance)—Works on ambulance and with rescue or military services. Must complete the eighty-one-hour course plus six months of emergency ambulance rescue service, and must renew certification every two years.

Emergency Medical Technician (Paramedic)—Usually works on mobile intensive care vehicles, under a physician's direction, using voice contact from a medical center. A paramedic must first be registered as an emergency medical technician (ambulance), and then complete a special training program in advanced life support, ranging from 800 to 1,500 hours, and six months of field experience. Paramedics work for police and fire departments, and private and municipal ambulance services. Emergency medical technicians who work for police and fire departments receive the same salary as patrol officers or firefighters.

PHYSICAL THERAPISTS

Physical therapists (PTs) are health-care professionals who evaluate and treat people with health problems resulting from injury or disease, such as muscle, nerve, joint, and bone diseases or injuries. PTs assess joint motion, muscle strength and endurance, function of heart and lungs, and performance of activities required in daily living, among other responsibilities. Physical therapists use various procedures and techniques to relieve pain and strengthen muscles, including therapeutic exercise, massage, electrical stimulation, and cardiovascular endurance training.

Physical therapy is one of the fastest-growing occupations of the 1990s, with job opportunities expected to grow by 76 percent (or 4,000 jobs per year) between 1989 and 2005. As the field expands, it will grow in specialization. Specialty areas include neurology, pulmonary therapy, musculoskeletal therapy, sports medicine, and prevention. In addition to the increasing levels of specialization, the field has also changed in terms of its competency standards.

Over 160 colleges now offer degrees in this field, and the minimum educational requirement is a four-year college degree in physical therapy from an accredited education program. Competition to enter the best programs (the University of Vermont's, for example) is very sharp. The American Physical Therapy Association now requires a postbaccalaureate degree for certification. By January 1, 2002, the M.A. will be the minimum educational requirement for a degree in physical therapy.

Throughout the seventy-seven-year history of physical therapy in the United States there has been a shortage of qualified physical therapists.

The American Physical Therapy Association surveyed its membership and found the typical physical therapist to be a white thirty-one-year-old female with a B.S. in physical therapy working in a hospital, treating fourteen to nineteen patients each day. There are approximately 115,000 physical therapists currently practicing. A physical therapist may be on staff at a facility like a hospital or nursing home, or may be self-employed and contract out work at such a facility for a set fee. Self-employed physical therapists often make more than $30 per hour. Among metropolitan areas studied separately, earnings ranged from $30,794 in St. Louis to $42,682 in San Francisco.

In 1996, median weekly earnings of salaried physical therapists who usually work full-time were $757. The middle 50 percent earned between $577 and $1,055. The top 10 percent earned at least $1,294, and the bottom 10 percent earned less than $400. According to the American Physical Therapy Association, the average annual salary of full-time physical therapists was $55,000 in 1998.

OCCUPATIONAL THERAPISTS

Occupational therapists plan and participate in goal-related therapy for people who are physically or psychologically impaired. They involve patients in activities suited to their individual needs, ranging from jewelry-making and weaving to vocational training. But whatever the activity, the goals are the same: to help the patient adjust to everyday living in spite of his or her handicap. Roughly 60 percent of all 57,000 occupational therapists work with people who have physical disabilities. Their activities are designed to improve motor skills, strength, and endurance. The remaining 40 percent work with patients with psychological problems. The accompanying tables show average annual salaries for occupational therapists and occupational therapy assistants by years of experience, highest educational degree, pri-

ANNUAL SALARIES FOR OCCUPATIONAL THERAPISTS AND OCCUPATIONAL THERAPY ASSISTANTS, 1997

	Average	Median	Low	High
Occupational therapists	$47,095	$45,600	$12,000	$13,000
Occupational therapy assistant	31,126	30,000	10,000	64,000

AVERAGE ANNUAL SALARIES FOR OCCUPATIONAL THERAPISTS AND OCCUPATIONAL THERAPY ASSISTANTS, 1990–97			
	1997	**1993**	**1990**
Occupational therapists	$47,095	$42,245	$25,470
Occupational therapy assistant	31,126	$25,348	$21,282

SOURCE: The American Occupational Therapy Association.

mary function, and employment setting. The average annual base salary for full-time occupational therapists was $42,700 in January 1997.

SPEECH-LANGUAGE PATHOLOGISTS AND AUDIOLOGISTS

Speech-language pathologists and audiologists provide help to people with speech and hearing problems resulting from brain injury, partial or total hearing loss, cleft palate, or emotional illness. A speech-language pathologist diagnoses and evaluates one's speech and language abilities and conducts treatment programs designed to restore or develop a patient's communication skills. He may teach patients to correct a lisp or stutter or to recover speech following a stroke or after a hearing impairment is corrected. An audiologist assesses the degree of hearing impairment and plans and conducts a rehabilitation program. He is involved in hearing-aid selection, auditory training, and teaching speech reading.

Although there are some jobs for people with bachelor's degrees, state and federal agencies as well as school systems and hospitals prefer to hire someone with a master's in one of the specialties. In fact, almost 93 percent of all 93,000 speech-language pathologists and audiologists have a master's degree. Speech-language pathologists and audiologists may have a variety of credentials, including a state license, certification by the American Speech-Language-Hearing Association, and teaching credentials. Because speech and hearing are interrelated, a practitioner must be familiar with both fields to be competent in one. Dual certification in both speech-language pathology and audiology is common; a practitioner holding dual certification generally earns more than one certification in one specialty.

Average salaries in this field are relatively low, considering the level of education required. Median weekly earnings of full-time, salaried speech-language pathologists and audiologists were about $690 in 1996. The middle 50 percent earned between $560 and $880. The lowest 10 percent earned less than $440, and the top 10 percent more than $1,160. According to a 1997 survey by the American Speech-Language-Hearing Association, the median annual salary for full-time certified speech-language pathologists was $44,000; for audiologists, $43,000. Certified speech-language pathologists with one to three years of experience earned a median annual salary of $38,000; licensed audiologists with one to three years of experience earned $32,000. Speech-language pathologists with twenty-two years' experience earned a median annual salary of $52,000, while audiologists with comparable experience earned about $55,000. Salaries also vary according to geographic location and type of employment facility.

Most speech-language pathologists and audiologists in public schools are classified as teachers or special education teachers and are paid accordingly. Teacher salaries vary widely by state—from under $25,000 in North and South Dakota to over $40,000 in New York and New Jersey.

Job-Level Descriptions/Professional and Administrative Workers in Private Hospitals

Physical Therapists I—Works under general supervision; seeks technical advice in solving nonroutine problems; may provide technical direction to nonprofessional staff.

Physical Therapist II—Independently evaluates, plans, and carries out a full range of treatments with complex therapeutic objectives with procedures that require highly specialized knowledge and skill.

Medical Technologist I—Performs a limited variety of standard but specialized medical laboratory tests and nonroutine procedures; reviews, analyzes, and records test results.

Medical Technologist II (Senior or Lead Medical Technologist)—Performs and analyzes wide range of specialized tests and nonroutine procedures; establishes quality controls; troubleshoots and modifies existing procedures; implements protocols for new procedures; may supervise lab technicians.

Job-Level Descriptions for Hospital Technical Support Occupations

Licensed Practical Nurse (LPN) I—Provides standard nursing care requiring some latitude for independent judgment and initiative to perform recurring duties.

LPN II—Provides nursing care requiring an understanding of diseases and illnesses sufficient to communicate with physicians, registered nurses, and patients.

LPN III—Can immediately recognize and respond to serious situations, sometimes prior to notifying a registered nurse, though any deviations from guidelines must be approved by a supervisor.

Nursing Assistant I—Performs simple personal care and housekeeping tasks requiring no previous training.

Nursing Assistant II—Performs common nursing procedures, in addition to providing personal care.

Nursing Assistant III—Performs a variety of common nursing procedures. Work requires prior experience or training and some latitude for exercising independent initiative of limited judgment.

Diagnostic Medical Sonographer—Operates diagnostic equipment that produces ultrasonic patterns and positive pictures of internal organs for use by doctors in diagnosing disease or monitoring pregnancies.

Respiratory Therapist I—Administers a variety of prescribed therapeutic and diagnostic respiratory therapy procedures.

Respiratory Therapist II—Independently administers a variety of complex respiratory therapy treatments and diagnostic procedures.

Medical Laboratory Technician I—Performs routine or standardized tests following detailed written procedures.

Medical Technician II—Performs a variety of complex tests.

PHARMACISTS

Although pharmacists' duties vary depending on their place of employment, their principal responsibility remains the same: to compound and dispense medication ordered by physicians or other authorized prescribers. A pharmacist must be familiar with the effects of drugs on people and have thorough knowledge of the procedures for testing drug purity and strength. Physicians rely heavily on the pharmacist for information on prescription drugs.

To become a pharmacist, one must have at least a B.S. degree in phar-

AVERAGE BASE SALARIES OF PHARMACISTS, BY PRACTICE SETTING, 1996

	Hospital	Independent Pharmacy	Chain
By Region			
East	$51,400	$56,800	$54,600
South	47,400	53,000	53,700
Midwest	47,600	54,700	51,900
West	52,000	57,500	60,500
By Sex			
Male	$50,700	$52,200	$55,200
Female	45,100	53,600	52,300
By Job Title			
Store Manager	$51,100	$55,700	NA
Chief Supervising Pharmacist	52,100	55,700	NA
Staff	46,300	53,300	$49,800
Director	NA	NA	58,600
By Age			
Under 36	$49,300	$54,400	$50,400
36–45	49,200	55,700	56,500
46 and over	48,700	54,600	55,600

SOURCE: *Drug Topics* magazine, 1996. Reprinted by permission.

macy. The bachelor's program involves five years of college study. Some colleges offer an integrated program, which includes liberal arts and professional training, while others require one or two years of preprofessional study before entering the professional college. All states have strict laws about licensing and registering pharmacists, although the regulations vary. All states require graduation from an accredited school of pharmacy, and most states require an internship before being eligible for registration. All pharmacists must pass an examination given by the board of pharmacy in the state where they choose to practice.

Pharmacists held about 172,000 jobs in 1996. About three out of five worked in community pharmacies, either independently owned, part of a drugstore chain, or part of a grocery store, department store, or mass merchandiser. Most community pharmacists were salaried employees, but some were self-employed owners. About one-quarter worked in hospitals, and others worked in clinics, mail-order pharmacies, pharmaceutical wholesalers, home health care agencies, or the federal government. About one in seven pharmacists works only part time. Jobs for pharmacists are expected to grow faster than the national average for all occupations through the year 2005, due in large part to an aging population's increasing need for drugs and medications. Other factors likely to increase the demand for pharmacists through the year 2006 include the likelihood of scientific advances that will make more drug products available, new developments in administering medication, and increasingly sophisticated consumers seeking more information about drugs.

Salaries of pharmacists are influenced by the location, size, and type of employer; the education and professional attributes of the pharmacist; and the duties and responsibilities of the position. Median weekly earnings of full-time, salaried pharmacists were $992 in 1996. Half earned between $827 and $1,177. The lowest 10 percent earned less than $554, and the top 10 percent more than $1,422. According to a survey by *Drug Topics* magazine, published by Medical Economics Inc., average base salaries of full-time, salaried pharmacists were $59,276 per year in 1996. Pharmacists working in chain drugstores had an average base salary of $61,735 per year, while pharmacists working in independent drug stores averaged $52,189, and hospital pharmacists averaged $61,317. Overall, salaries for pharmacists were highest in the west, and second highest in the east. Many pharmacists also receive compensation in the form of bonuses, overtime, and profit-sharing. In hospitals, pharmacists are employed at several levels. There is almost always a chief of pharmaceutical services, several assistant supervisors, and a group of staff pharmacists. Salaries of hospital pharmacists depend on the number of beds in the hospital.

Job-Level Descriptions—Pharmacists

Pharmacist I—Applies pharmaceutical principles and concepts to conventional problems; may perform additional administrative duties and/or supervise nonprofessional pharmacy staff.

Pharmacist II (Senior Pharmacist, Pharmacy Supervisor)—First-line supervisor of pharmacists I, staff pharmacists in a specialty field, and staff generalists with a broad experience in total pharmacy operations.

MEDICAL PRACTITIONERS

There is a wide range of occupations in the field of medicine, from technicians to physicians. Somewhere in between are the four professional groups discussed here: chiropractors, optometrists, podiatrists, and midwives. The first three of these are called "doctors" (Dr. of Chiropractics; Dr. of Optometry, O.D.; and Dr. of Podiatric Medicine, C.P.M.) and earn their degrees by attending professional colleges. Yet they often do not command the same respect or salaries as M.D.s.

Opportunities in these field are increasing, as they are in all health professions. Podiatry is the least crowded of all health occupations, but the demand for podiatric services is steadily rising, no doubt partly because of the nationwide obsession with fitness and its resultant problems. Chiropractors are also seeing more patients than ever before. There is now wider public acceptance of chiropractic treatment, and most insurance plans, including Medicare, Medicaid, and workmen's compensation, provide coverage for these services, leading people to consult chiropractors rather than orthopedists.

Chiropractors

A chiropractor diagnoses a patient's health problems in the same way as a physician: by interviewing the patient and by conducting a physical examination, an X-ray examination, and laboratory tests. It is in the area of treatment where chiropractors differ from medical doctors.

In chiropractics, the emphasis is on the spine and its position. Treatment consists mainly of chiropractic adjustment; that is, the manipulation of the body, especially the spinal column. Chiropractors are not permitted to perform surgery or dispense prescription drugs, although they can advise the patient to begin a nutritional program that always includes vitamins.

The academic training program for chiropractors consists of six years of study. A two-year preprofessional (liberal arts) program must be completed before admission to the chiropractic college. The professional curriculum consists of two years' science courses and two years of clinical work under supervision. All states require chiropractors to be licensed, and many states require practicing chiropractors to take continuing education courses throughout their careers. Job prospects are expected to be good for persons who enter the practice of chiropractics. Employment of chiropractors is expected to grow faster than the average for all occupations through the year 2006 as consumer demand for alternative medicine grows. Chiropractors emphasize the importance of a healthy lifestyle and do not prescribe drugs or perform surgery. As a result, chiropractic care is appealing to many health-conscious Americans. Chiropractic treatment of back, neck, extremities, and other joint damage has become more accepted as a result of recent research and changing attitudes. The rapidly expanding older population, with their increased likelihood of mechanical and structural problems, will also increase demand.

Chiropractors held about 44,000 jobs in 1996. About 70 percent of active chiropractors are in solo practice. The remainder are in group practice or work for other chiropractors. A small number teach, conduct research at chiropractic institutions, or work in hospitals and clinics. In 1995, median income for chiropractors was about $80,000, after expenses, according to the American Chiropractic Association. In chiropractics, as in other types of independent practice, earnings are relatively low in the beginning, and increase as the practice grows. In 1995, the lowest 10 percent of chiropractors had median net incomes of $30,000 or less, and the highest 10 percent earned $170,000 or more.

Optometrists

Optometrists examine, diagnose, and treat conditions of the vision system. They perform a variety of tests to diagnose and treat eye health and vision problems. They prescribe glasses, contact lenses, low vision rehabilitation, vision therapy, and medications as means of treatment.

All schools of optometry require at least two years of college prior to admission, although most students complete all four years of college prior to entering the professional program. Programs leading to the O.D. degree are four years in duration. Optometrists must be licensed in the states in which they choose to practice. Traditionally, most optometrists have been men, but this is changing dramatically. More than half of students in schools of optometry are women. In 1990, the Department of Labor predicted faster than average growth in this field through the next decade; but by 1992, it

AVERAGE SALARIES OF OPTOMETRISTS AND PODIATRISTS IN THE FEDERAL GOVERNMENT

Title and Grade Number	Average Salary
Associate Grade	NA
Full Grade 10	56,005
Intermediate Grade 37	65,585
Senior Grade 60	77,879
Chief Grade 83	94,533
TOTAL: 190	**$81,609**

SOURCE: Office of Personnel Management, *Pay Structure of the Federal Civil Service,* (March 31, 1997).

revised this forecast to indicate only average growth because advances in technology and optometrists' productivity had allowed each optometrist to see more patients. Moreover, this is an industry with an extremely low turnover rate: Almost every job opening in optometry will result from the death or retirement of a practicing optometrist.

Although some optometrists are employed by hospitals, HMOs, clinics, and retail chains, by far the majority of the 41,000 licensed optometrists are self-employed, so salary and income data are limited. According to the American Optometric Association, new optometry graduates in their first year of practice earned median net incomes of $57,500 in 1996. Overall, optometrists earned median net incomes of $80,000.

Podiatrists

According to the American Podiatric Association, there are 147,000 licensed practitioners of the care and treatment of feet. As with other medical practitioners, podiatrists rely on examinations, laboratory tests, and X rays to determine the nature of the problem, which may range from simple corns to fractures and tumors. Unlike the other practitioners in this section, podiatrists do prescribe medication and do surgery on foot bones and muscles even though they are not M.D.s.

A podiatrist has completed two to four years of college and a four-year professional program that includes two years of classroom study and lab work and two years of clinical training. Most podiatrists serve a hospital residency before beginning a practice.

Most podiatrists are self-employed, although a growing number are entering partnerships and group practices. According to a survey by Podiatry Management, median net income of podiatrists was about $91,400 in 1996. Earnings vary according to practice size and location, and years of experience. According to a survey by the American Podiatric Medical Association, average net income for podiatrists in private practice was $108,156 in 1995. Those practicing for less than two years earned an average of $44,662; those practicing sixteen to thirty years earned an average of $141,135. Average net income of podiatrists in 1993 was $100,287 according to a survey by the American Association of Colleges of Podiatric Medicine, a figure that is closer to the salaries earned by doctors than those earned by other types of practitioners discussed in this chapter. However, salaries vary greatly with years of experience and location of practice. For example, in the northeast, where most podiatrists are concentrated, competition for patients is fierce, and lower salaries reflect it. An aging population (with tired feet) will contribute to a demand for podiatrists that will increase faster than the national average through the year 2005. Some estimates put podiatrist growth rates as high as 50 percent over this period. Job openings will result primarily from growth, as very few podiatrists leave the field before they die or retire.

DENTAL ASSISTANTS AND DENTAL HYGIENISTS

The demand for good dental care has increased as the public has become educated about the importance of oral hygiene. In order for dentists to increase their productive capacity, they must rely on the services of dental assistants and dental hygienists. Dental assistants work "chairside," sterilizing instruments, arranging them on trays, and handing them to the dentist as needed. They also prepare solutions and process X rays. It is not unusual for an assistant to perform clerical duties as well, such as keeping patient-treatment records and bookkeeping. A dental assistant may also perform expanded functions, which vary by state and which may include treating teeth to make them more resistant to decay and making impressions of the mouth. In states where it is legal, assistants may also clean and polish teeth and make uncomplicated repairs on dentures.

There are accredited programs for dental assistants in community colleges and vocational schools, but many dentists hire assistants right out of high school and conduct their own training. Certification is optional and not a requirement for employment. There are currently about 202,000 dental assistants in the United States; and the Bureau of Labor Statistics predicts that this number will grow by almost 100,000 by the year 2005. Progress in the field of dental medicine will continue to fuel demand for all dental occupations, because as people retain their natural teeth longer, they will continue to need to clean, maintain, and repair them. The outlook is particularly bright for dental assistants because dentists are relying on them to perform routine tasks that they or their hygienists once had to perform themselves.

Fully one-third of all dental assistants worked only part time, according to the Department of Labor. Median weekly earnings for full-time assistants were $361 in 1996, according to the American Dental Association. A dental hygienist is a more highly trained technician. A hygienist must complete a two-year program after high school or college and must obtain a state license before he or she can be employed. In some states, continuing education is required to maintain licensure.

Dental hygienists working in private practice remove scale from teeth, treat teeth to make them resistant to decay, take X rays, and perform laboratory tests. They also advise the patients on the proper way to take care of their teeth and give instruction about the correct way to brush and use dental floss. Their expanded functions, again governed by the state, may include administering local anesthetics, performing curettage (scraping under the gums), and placement and removal of temporary fillings.

About half of all dental hygienists work part-time—usually fewer than thirty-five hours a week—meaning that only 70,000 to 80,000 hygienists were needed to fill the 133,000 positions available for hygienists in 1996, according to the Department of Labor. Some hygienists work for a different dentist each day of the week. Job growth in this field is expected to be rapid, as dentists turn more tasks over to hygienists. Younger dentists are even more likely than older ones to rely on hygienists. According to the American Dental Association, experienced dental hygienists who worked thirty-two hours a week or more in a private practice averaged about $759 a week in 1995.

PSYCHOLOGISTS

Psychology, the study of the human mind, is, according to its practitioners, a science that provides us with information on intelligence, mental capacity, and the effect of emotions on health and behavior. Over 144,000 people work in the field of psychology, most of them in the areas of research and counseling.

Experimental psychologists are the largest group working in research. These are the people who conduct experiments designed to study some aspect of animal and/or human behavior, such as learning or perception. Though experimental psychologists may work in private laboratories or in industry, they most often hold teaching positions at colleges or universities. Their salaries are listed in Part I in the section "University and College Professors."

The second area of psychology and, not surprisingly, the most familiar to the general public, is counseling. An estimated 34 million Americans annually seek professional help for their problems. In addition to the 40,000 practicing psychiatrists in the United States, there are, according to the American Psychological Association, 58,000 clinical psychologists and psychiatric social workers (see the section "Social Workers" in Part I) and 12,500 counselors vying for the estimated $13 billion spent annually for psychological services.

A clinical psychologist works directly with patients to uncover information that will help them understand and correct their problems. Methods of treatment vary. Some psychologists specialize in psychoanalysis, the Freudian technique of curing neuroses by talking about dreams, fantasies, etc., and by the transference of emotions to the analyst. This type of therapy often involves an unwavering commitment in time and money, since patients must attend sessions weekly, or from two to five times a week, for several years, often for a very high fee. The cost of a fifty-minute session ranges between $50 and $140, depending on the analyst and the city in which he or she practices. Short-term therapies based on Freudian principles are also

ANNUAL SALARIES OF STATE DIRECTORS OF MENTAL HEALTH DEPARTMENTS

State	Salary	State	Salary
Alabama	$102,752	Nebraska	NA
Alaska	69,780	Nevada	$81,520
Arizona	86,221	New Hampshire	59,542
Arkansas	78,333	New Jersey	87,026
California	107,939	New Mexico	NA
Colorado	82,260	New York	NA
Connecticut	NA	North Carolina	94,871
Delaware	NA	North Dakota	49,440
Florida	77,250	Ohio	NA
Georgia	115,014	Oklahoma	92,926
Hawaii	60,600	Oregon	86,616
Idaho	53,040	Pennsylvania	NA
Illinois	97,380	Rhode Island	86,328
Indiana	110,000	South Carolina	94,549
Iowa	86,944	South Dakota	NA
Kansas	84,874	Tennessee	75,000
Louisiana	140,000	Texas	95,000
Maine	77,896	Utah	123,067
Maryland	NA	Vermont	73,216
Massachusetts	NA	Virginia	94,778
Michigan	99,994	Washington	82,776
Minnesota	83,249	West Virginia	70,000
Mississippi	74,720	Wisconsin	51,210
Missouri	86,100	Wyoming	72,000
Montana	61,911		

SOURCE: The Council of State Governments, *The Book of the States, 1998–99.*

available, and psychologists who treat patients in this way usually charge $50 to $120 for a forty-five-minute session. Another method of treatment is called behavior modification. The psychologist attempts to help the patient correct undesirable behavior or habits through conditioning. Fees for an individual session range from $40 to $120, depending again on the therapist and the location of the practice. Group sessions, which are usually used when modifying eating or smoking habits, cost from $25 to $60 per person.

Most opportunities exist for psychologists with doctoral degrees. A clinical psychologist must usually complete an internship in conjunction with his or her program. All states require psychologists to pass licensing examinations, and in order to qualify for the examination one must have a doctorate. All graduates of professional psychological institutes or graduate schools or universities are called therapists, as are all mental health workers, regardless of the degree they hold. There are, however, countless others who call themselves therapists, sex therapists, marriage counselors, and crisis therapists who, on closer inspection, would be found to have little or no professional training. There is no real monitoring system in this profession, and therefore, it is essential for a person seeking help to know as much as possible about a therapist's educational background.

Society's ever-increasing acceptance of the value of psychological counseling has helped to make this one of the fastest-growing occupations in the country. And the U.S. Department of Labor predicts that the spiraling growth will continue through the year 2006, with about 5,000 new positions available each year until then. Most of the jobs will be for clinical psychologists working in community mental health centers, nursing homes, and drug and alcohol abuse programs. And because the high level of education required for entry into this field, turnover in the profession is low, meaning that most jobs will result from growth or the need to replace retiring psychologists. The AIDS epidemic and the public's increasing awareness of the extent of family violence will also bring a stronger demand for specialized psychological services. So, too, will the needs of the aged, whose growing numbers are affecting all health care services.

According to the American Psychological Association, increased opportunities for psychologists are also expected to occur in schools and in corporations as industrial psychology grows in importance in the human resources sector. In addition, with the rise in the willingness of third-party insurers to cover some of the costs of therapy, more and more psychologists are expected to enter private practice (approximately one in six psychologists is self-employed). Finally, a surprising number of college and university teaching positions will be available over the coming years since over 20 percent of the current faculty are over the age of fifty-five.

One note of caution for those not familiar with this profession: All supervisory positions, and most meaningful responsibility, require a doctoral degree; many entry-level positions require a master's degree. On the positive side, the APA estimates that the unemployment rate for psychologists is less than 1 percent.

According to the National Science Foundation, the median earnings of a psychologist with a doctoral degree and 5.9 years of experience is $55,000. The table below shows median annual salaries by place and kind of work. Those with an independent practice usually earn 20 to 30 percent more than the median.

In the federal government, the average starting salary for a psychologist with a bachelor's degree ranged from $19,500 to $24,200 in 1997, depending on academic credentials. Counseling psychologists with a master's degree and a year of counseling experience started at $38,000. Clinical psychologists with a doctorate and one year of internship started at $43,000. The average salary for all psychologists in the federal government was $62,120 in 1997.

MEDIAN SALARIES FOR PSYCHOLOGY INSTRUCTORS WITH DOCTORAL DEGREES, 1997

Setting and Rank	Median Annual Salary
University Psychology Department	
Full professor	$69,000
Associate professor	46,000
Assistant professor	38,000
University Research Center/Institute	
Full professor	$85,000
Four-Year College Psychology Department	
Full professor	$52,000
Associate professor	41,000
Assistant professor	35,000
Two-Year College	
Full professor	$51,000
Associate professor	44,000
Lecturer/instructor	36,000
Medical School Psychiatry Department	
Full professor	$88,000
Associate professor	60,000
Assistant professor	41,000
Freestanding Professional School of Psychology	
Full professor	$60,500
Other Professional School	
Full professor	$56,000
Associate professor	46,000

SOURCE: *1997 Salaries in Psychology*. Research Office, American Psychological Association. 1998.

MEDIAN SALARIES FOR CLINICAL PSYCHOLOGISTS WITH DOCTOR'S DEGREES BY SETTING AND EXPERIENCE, 1997

Setting and Years of Experience	Median Annual Salary
University Counseling Center	
2–4 years	$38,000
5–9 years	42,500
Group Psychological Practice	
2–4 years	$42,000
5–9 years	53,000
10–14 years	70,000
Public general hospital	
2–4 years	$48,000
5–9 years	50,000
Private general hospital	
2–4 years	$51,500
5–9 years	70,000
10–19 years	55,000
20–24 years	72,000
Medical-psychological group practice	
2–4 years	$50,000
5–9 years	57,500
10–14 years	70,000
20–24 years	96,500
Public psychiatric hospital	
2–4 years	$43,000
5–9 years	45,000
10–14 years	48,000
Outpatient Clinic	
2–4 years	$42,000
5–9 years	43,000
Community Mental Health Center	
2–4 years	$40,000
5–9 years	44,000
10–14 years	48,500
15–19 years	51,000

MEDIAN SALARIES FOR CLINICAL PSYCHOLOGISTS WITH DOCTOR'S DEGREES BY SETTING AND EXPERIENCE, 1997

Setting and Years of Experience	Median Annual Salary
VA Hospital	
2–4 years	$55,000
5–9 years	60,000
10–19 years	62,000
20–24 years	65,500
25–29 years	70,000
HMO	
2–4 years	$44,500
5–9 years	56,000
10–14 years	58,000
Individual Private Practice	
2–4 years	$55,000
5–9 years	65,000
10–14 years	75,000
15–19 years	80,000
20–24 years	70,000
25–29 years	75,000
30+ years	75,000
Criminal Justice System	
2–4 years	$48,000
5–9 years	46,500
10–14 years	53,500
Other Human Service Setting	
2–4 years	$42,000

SOURCE: *1997 Salaries in Psychology*. Research Office, American Psychological Association, 1998.

VIII

Jobs and Wages in the Workaday World

The title of this part is our own invention; it has no standing whatsoever with economists, with sociologists, or even with employment agencies. Yet in this section can be found the occupations and wage levels of some 20 million Americans. Most of these jobs are traditionally classified as white-collar or blue-collar; some would be called skilled, but most unskilled; some are unionized, others not; some are held almost exclusively by women, others predominantly by men. But certain essential characteristics common to them all made this present grouping especially appropriate to this book.

First of all, none of these jobs, save electricians, is represented by large, national unions whose power is centered in one industry and which can therefore dramatically affect wage levels. Nor are any of these jobs predominantly in the public sector, where job security and benefits are very good. On the other hand, none of these jobs requires a college degree or extensive formal training, so there is no elaborate hierarchical structure such as what distinguish those occupations commonly referred to as careers. Finally, the pay for these jobs is normally calculated as an hourly or weekly wage rate rather than on an annual salary basis. As a result of all these factors, the annual income from these jobs is very rarely above $40,000 and very frequently below $20,000.

Most of the jobs represented in this section need little or no description, since the work involved will be familiar, at least in a general way, to all readers. Although barbers, electricians, plumbers, etc., follow procedures we're not aware of, most of us know the function these people serve. (Where this is not the case, information is, of course, provided.) The jobs are organized in two different ways. Some of the most common are grouped under general headings: "Building Trades Workers," "The Office Staff," "Restaurant Workers," etc. These are followed by a simple alphabetical listing that should enable quick and easy reference.

For other jobs that fit in this basic category but are located in different sections, see the index for baggage handlers, bank clerks, bank tellers, bell-hops, insurance clerks, farm workers, nurses' aides, and orderlies.

BUILDING TRADES WORKERS

The term "construction worker" actually encompasses workers in as many as a dozen occupations related to the construction of houses and buildings. Together, the country's bricklayers, carpenters, electricians, plumbers, painters, and unskilled construction workers total more than 3.7 million laborers. More than half are unionized, and about one in four is self-employed. Because there is no one employer that dominates the construction industry the way General Motors or U.S. Steel dominate their respective industries, construction unions are largely decentralized. The union headquarters may publish guidelines and average wages for specific areas of the country, but local chapters are free to negotiate their own contracts. All unions (except the building laborers' union) have apprenticeship programs that are usually administered by the locals in conjunction with building contractors. Most apprenticeships last from three to five years.

No other sector of the economy feels the immediate effect of a recession more quickly than construction. In the last recession, people as always stopped buying new houses, so housing starts (a key indicator of the economy's health) declined, and rapidly, too. And with commercial vacancy rates hovering around 20 percent due to a tax code that encouraged wealthy citizens to invest in office space that no one needed, construction jobs dropped by 310,000 in 1991 alone.

Since then, however, the construction industry has rebounded to the point that the Department of Labor predicts average to better than average growth in almost all construction occupations through the year 2005. The demand for new housing soared to record levels in 1997–98, as did federal funding to improve the nation's infrastructure—repairing and maintaining roads, bridges, tunnels, and buildings—creating many new jobs. Still, unemployment among construction workers in the past thirty years has remained fairly consistent at double the overall rate and will continue to in the future. Moreover, because construction work is subject to the whims of weather, most construction workers do not work a full year, As a result, the hourly or weekly wages given in this section cannot be extrapolated to yield average annual incomes. The exception is maintenance construction workers, who work on a full-time basis in buildings or power plants. They usually earn less per hour, but their employment is steady and they work when cold weather stops other construction work. Figures are supplied at the end of the entry.

Bricklayers

Bricklayers, some of whom are represented by the International Union of Bricklayers and Allied Craftsmen and others by the Bricklayers, Masons, and Plasterers International Union of America, number about 142,000, according to the Department of Labor. Median weekly earnings for bricklayers in 1996 were $484. Beginning apprentices are usually paid about 50 percent of the journeyman rate; apprenticeships usually last about three years. Jobs for bricklayers are expected to grow about as fast as the average for all occupations through the year 2006. Population and business growth will create a need for new factories, schools, and hospitals. The popularity of brick exteriors will continue to stimulate demand for bricklayers' work.

Building Laborers

Building laborers unload trucks, carry materials, dig ditches, erect scaffolds, and do other routine tasks to assist more specialized construction workers. There is no apprenticeship, but many laborers do enter training for specific building crafts. There are about more than half a million of them, and they are represented by the Laborers' International Union of North America.

Carpenters

Carpenters are the largest group of building trade workers in the country, numbering just under 1 million. Because wood is such a versatile material, carpentry is divided into many specialties. Construction carpenters are classified as either "rough" carpenters—those who build scaffolds, frameworks, forms for concrete, bridges, and other large structures—or "finish" carpenters—those who build stairs, put up moldings and paneling, lay floors, and so on. Carpenters in factories (making furniture for instance) may specialize in specific machines, such as sanders, trim saws, rip saws, and plywood presses. Carpenters also work with glass, fiberglass, plastic, and other building materials.

About one-third of carpenters are self-employed. Although most employers recommend that prospective carpenters learn their trade through a

formal apprenticeship, the number of programs is limited. Thus, only a small
proportion of carpenters acquire their skills this way. The rest learn through
informal apprenticeships, vocational education, or on-the-job training under
the supervision of experienced workers. The five major carpenters' unions,
the largest of which is the United Brotherhood of Carpenters and Joiners of
America, sponsor and administer three-to-four-year apprenticeship programs
that combine on-the-job training with classroom instruction. First-year apprentices generally make no more than 50 percent of what an experienced
carpenter earns. By their fourth year of apprenticeship, the trainee receives
90 to 95 percent of the journeyman rate. Scheduled increases in salary end
at the end of the apprenticeship, but in general, the more experience a carpenter has, the more money he or she earns. Specialties requiring finer work,
such as cabinetmaking, pay better than other types of carpentry. The union
does not set nationwide pay levels, but rather leaves it up to the local chapters to negotiate each contract individually. This practice results in a wide
range of salaries.

Median weekly earnings of carpenters who were not self-employed was
$476 in 1996. Like other construction occupations, carpentry's growth is
subject to the number of new housing starts. The increased use of prefabri-
cated components should decrease the need for carpenters, meaning that
this field will grow no faster than the average for all occupations. If building
activity picks up dramatically, however, so should carpentry. Moreover, because the industry is large and turnover is high, the number of job openings
for carpenters is usually higher than for other construction and craft occupations.

Electricians

According to the Bureau of Labor Statistics, there were about 575,000 electricians in the United States in 1996. More than half were employed in the
construction industry. Others worked as maintenance electricians in just
about every industry. One-tenth of electricians are self-employed. Almost all
electricians belong to the International Brotherhood of Electrical Workers,
which administers apprenticeship programs for aspiring electricians. A typical apprenticeship program provides at least 144 hours of classroom instruction each year and more than 8,000 hours of on-the-job training. Earnings
for electricians are among the highest earned by skilled workers: Median
weekly earnings for electricians who were not self-employed were $620 in
1996. Maintenance electricians in metropolitan areas earned about $18.78
an hour in 1995.

Electricians' unemployment rate is usually lower than the rate for other
construction workers—at times less than half as high as the rate for brick-

layers, stonemasons, and roofers. Their employment is also less subject to cyclical swings in the weather or the economy. Nevertheless, their jobless rate is still tied to the level of new construction.

Jobs for electricians are expected to grow about as fast as the national average. Increasing use of computers, automation, and robots will necessitate rewiring (or in the case of new construction, prewiring) by experienced electricians. Job turnover in this field is low, but a large number of openings are expected because a large number of electricians are beginning to reach retirement age.

Painters

About half of the country's 449,000 painters and paperhangers are self-employed, or about double the rate for most other construction occupations. Most painters belong to the International Brotherhood of Painters and Allied Trades. Apprenticeships in painting usually involve three to four years of on-the-job training and 144 hours of classroom instruction in topics like color harmony, use and care of tools and equipment, surface preparation, application techniques, paint mixing and matching, blueprint reading, wood finishing, and safety. Median weekly earnings for painters who were not self-employed were about $381 in 1996. Paperhangers generally earn more than painters. Jobs for painters and paperhangers will grow about as fast as the national average through the year 2006.

Plasterers

There are about 32,000 plasterers in the country; about one-fifth of them are self-employed. Their numbers declined in the past as more and more builders switched to drywall construction, which is cheaper than plastering and requires less skill. But that decline has reversed in the 1990s as newer, cheaper, and easier-to-install types of plaster have made the material more attractive to builders.

Two unions represent plasterers: the Operative Plasterers' and Cement Masons' Association of the United States and Canada, and the Bricklayers and Allied Craftsmen International Union. Apprentices, who must work for four years before becoming journeymen, usually start at half the journeyman's base rate. The average plasterer who belonged to a union and worked full-time made between $14.45 and $39.08 an hour in 1997. Plasterers in large cities received the higher wages. In 1996, median weekly earnings for plasterers working full-time were about $531. Jobs for plasterers are expected to increase—albeit slowly—as more people realize that plaster is much more durable and attractive than drywall. Plasterers will also be needed to renovate plasterwork in older structures and create special architectural effects like curved surfaces, which cannot practically be achieved with drywall.

Plumbers and Pipe Fitters

Plumbing, pipe fitting, and steam fitting are often considered the same trade, and people who work primarily in one may easily switch to another. All three involve installing and maintaining conduits for fluid materials. Plumbers, of course, work with water pipes in homes, schools, and so on. Pipe fitters work with industrial pipes that carry a variety of materials like oil, gas, and hot water. Steam fitters obviously specialize in steam pipes. Workers in all three trades number about 389,000.

Apprenticeships usually involve four to five years of on-the-job training and 144 hours of classroom instruction in topics like drafting and blueprint reading, mathematics, applied physics and chemistry, and local plumbing codes and regulations. Apprentices usually begin at about 50 percent of the wage rate paid to experienced plumbers or pipe fitters, and their salaries increase periodically as they improve their skills. Many plumbers and pipe fitters are members of the United Association of Journeymen and Apprentices of the Plumbing and Pipe Fitting Industry of the United States and Canada. Median hourly earnings for plumbers and pipe fitters were $21.46 in 1995. In general, wage rates tend to be higher in the midwest and west than in the northeast and south. Plumbers are expected to be victims of their own efficiency throughout the next decade, because the plastic pipes and fittings now being installed are much easier to use and need less maintenance than their older metal counterparts. The job market for plumbers is less cyclical than for other construction workers because maintenance, rehabilitation, and replacement of existing systems provides jobs for plumbers even when construction activity declines.

Roofers

By definition, roofers work outdoors in all kinds of weather. It is unsurprising, therefore, to find that roofers have the highest accident rates of all construction workers. They risk slipping and falling from scaffolds, ladders, or the roofs themselves and, especially during the summer, they can get burned from the hot roof tar that holds the shingles, insulation, or other coverings in place on the roof. And severely cold, rainy, or snowy weather can reduce the number of days they are able to work.

There were about 138,000 roofers in 1996. Almost all wage and salary roofers work for roofing contractors. About 30 percent of roofers are self-employed, and the majority of self-employed roofers specialize in residential work. Most roofers acquire their training through informal apprenticeships with experienced roofers or through three-year apprenticeship programs administered by locals of the United Union of Roofers, Waterproofers, and Allied Workers. The program requires 144 hours of classroom training in subjects like tool use, arithmetic, and safety, as well as 2,000 hours of on-the-job training.

Turnover among roofers is high because of the hot, dirty, strenuous nature of the work. Many roofers leave the trade for other construction occupations that are less difficult and less dangerous. As a result, job openings for roofers should be plentiful through the year 2006. Roofs need repairing more often than other parts of a building, and therefore keep roofers in business throughout downturns in new construction. About 75 percent of all roofing work is repair.

Median weekly earnings for full-time roofers were $363 a week in 1996. According to a survey by the *Engineering News Record,* average hourly earnings (including benefits) for union roofers were $25.75 in 1997. Salaries were highest in New York City and lowest in Nashville. Apprentices start at about 40 percent of what experienced roofers earn.

Maintenance Mechanics

Most craft workers specialize in one kind of work; general maintenance mechanics are jacks-of-all trades. They repair and maintain mechanical equipment, machines, and buildings; work on plumbing, electrical gear, air-conditioning and heating systems; and install, maintain, and repair specialized equipment and machinery. They also do routine preventive maintenance to correct defects before equipment breaks down or buildings deteriorate.

General maintenance mechanics held about 1.36 million jobs in 1996. Unlike many other jobs in the trades, jobs for maintenance mechanics are expected to grow throughout the 1990s. Earnings in this field vary widely by industry, geographic area, and skill level. The median salary was $9.88 per hour in 1995; it was about $9.90 an hour in manufacturing businesses and about $9.41 in nonmanufacturing businesses. Wages are generally highest in transportation companies and public utilities and lowest in service firms. On average, workers in the midwest and northeast earned more than those in the west and south.

AVERAGE HOURLY RATES OF MAINTENANCE TRADES WORKERS IN FIFTEEN CITIES

City	General Maintenance Workers	Maintenance Electricians	Maintenance Machinery Mechanics	Maintenance Motor Vehicle Mechanics	Maintenance Pipe Fitters
Atlanta	$10.68	NA	$14.92	$17.17	NA
Boston	11.95	$19.10	17.42	17.52	$19.57
Chicago	10.32	20.07	18.15	18.28	23.90
Dallas	8.74	15.49	14.06	15.66	NA
Denver	11.20	18.41	16.16	16.00	NA
Detroit	11.24	21.24	20.00	17.80	21.24
Houston	9.22	18.67	18.46	14.63	NA
Miami	9.02	15.65	15.27	14.44	15.58
Phoenix	9.34	18.96	15.40	15.69	NA
Philadelphia	11.78	17.75	16.92	16.37	18.04
St. Louis	9.86	20.51	17.38	17.32	20.52
San Diego	9.53	18.25	19.28	16.25	NA
San Francisco	10.69	22.43	20.78	20.55	NA
Seattle	11.53	21.59	20.12	19.22	21.68
Washington, DC	10.71	18.36	19.82	17.97	15.79

SOURCE: Bureau of Labor Statistics, *Occupational Compensation Survey, National Summary*, 1996.

THE OFFICE STAFF

In the United States today, the Department of Labor estimates that there are:

- 3.4 million secretaries
- 2.2 million bookkeeping, accounting, and auditing clerks
- 1.1 million typists, word processors, and data entry keyers
- 1,074,000 receptionists
- 335,000 billing clerks
- 319,000 switchboard operators
- 293,000 file clerks
- 124,000 personnel clerks
- 98,000 stenographers, court reporters, and medical transcriptionists

Clerical and secretarial occupations are among the lowest paid white-collar jobs available anywhere. This is no new development, but rather an old and venerated tradition: Bob Cratchit was a clerk for Ebenezer Scrooge; Herman Melville's Bartleby was a scrivener, or copyist. Typical modern sal-

**EMPLOYMENT LEVELS AND PERCENTAGE GROWTH FOR SELECTED
ADMINISTRATIVE SUPPORT OCCUPATIONS, 1992–2005**

Job	Estimated Employment, 1992	Projected Employment, 2005	Percentage change, 1992–2005
Adjusters, investigators, and collectors	1,185,000	1,552,000	31%
Clerical supervisors and managers	1,267,000	1,568,000	24
Computer and peripheral equipment operators	218,000	271,000	24
Credit clerks and authorizers	296,000	174,000	−41
General office clerks	2,688,000	3,342,000	24
Information clerks	1,333,000	1,762,000	32
Hotel and motel desk clerks	122,000	172,000	40
Interviewing and new accounts clerks	175,000	209,000	19
Receptionists	904,000	1,209,000	34
Mail clerks and messengers	271,000	297,000	10
Material recording, scheduling, dispatching, and distributing occupations	3,558,000	4,013,000	13
Dispatchers	222,000	268,000	21
Stock clerks	1,969,000	2,156,000	10
Traffic, shipping, and receiving clerks	824,000	971,000	18
Record clerks	3,573,000	3,777,000	6
Billing clerks	409,000	421,000	3
Bookkeeping, accounting, and auditing clerks	2,112,000	2,185,000	3
Brokerage clerks and statement clerks	88,000	93,900	7
File clerks	257,000	305,000	19
Library assistants and bookmobile drivers	114,000	134,000	18
Order clerks	300,000	313,000	4
Payroll and timekeeping clerks	165,000	165,000	0
Personnel clerks	128,000	160,000	25
Secretaries	3,324,000	3,710,000	12
Stenographers and court reporters	115,000	113,300	−2
Telephone operators	314,000	225,000	−28
Typists, word processors, and data entry keyers	1,238,000	1,192,000	−4

SOURCE: U.S. Department of Labor.

aries range from as low as $12,400 for a clerk in the federal government to $36,000 for a secretary in private industry. It is rare for office workers to make over $40,000, although some executive secretaries, whose duties include much more than the usual typing, filing, and answering the phone (see job descriptions below) can earn upward of $50,000 in private industry. For additional salary statistics based on a nationwide survey, see the table later in this section entitled "Average Annual Salaries of Office Workers in Private Industry."

The largest major occupational group, this collection of office support and clerical jobs is expected to grow at about the same rate as the national average for all jobs. Technological advances are expected to decrease the demand for stenographers, typists, word processors, and data entry keyers, while the demand for information clerks is expected to grow substantially. By the year 2005, jobs for receptionists will grow the fastest, at 47 percent, while the market for general office clerks should increase by the most jobs, 670,000. Typists and word processors will lose more than 100,000 jobs. Overall, the industry should grow about 12 percent, from just under 22 million in 1990 to about 24.84 million in 2005, according to the Department of Labor. The size and rapid turnover within this industry should mean lots of job openings throughout the end of the millennium. Statistics for all jobs within the industry are in the table above.

Secretaries

In the movie *9 to 5,* Dolly Parton played a teased-haired, stiletto-heeled babe who was smarter than her mean, leering boss. She eventually triumphs over him and turns her office into a kinder, gentler workplace. While many secretaries may be smarter than their bosses, the rest of the scenario plays out only in the movies. The workplace has not been kind to secretaries over the past decade.

There were 3.4 million secretaries in the United States in 1996, but that number is expected to decrease by over 80,000 by 2006. Computers, of course, have made the biggest dent in the need for secretaries. The one boss–one secretary ratio no longer exists except in upper management ranks. Now most secretaries work for several bosses, each with competing demands.

In recessionary downsizing, many secretarial jobs were cut, and the trend continues. IBM announced that the first targets in a company-wide salary review would be 120 senior secretaries, some of whom made more than $70,000. They were told to expect pay cuts of up to 36 percent by mid-1996, bringing their pay more in line with that of other corporate secretaries who, according to IBM, earn in the $40,000 range. (Of course, there was no mention of a pay cut for IBM's chairman and chief executive Louis V. Gerstner, Jr., who earned $12.4 million in salary, bonuses, and other compensation in 1994.)

Even the title "secretary," considered sexist or demeaning by some, has changed. Now the preferred titles are "executive assistant" and "clerical staffer." The "assistant" title usually means more money, upward of $30,000 in major cities. The title also means more skills are expected, including working with spreadsheets and database programs. But those high-paying, prestigious jobs are scarce. For most secretaries without advanced skills, the job is generally low-paying and a dead end. The average annual earnings of a secretary with limited experience was $19,700 in 1995, according to the Bureau of Labor Statistics.

Obviously, the more responsibility, the higher the pay.

The Administrative Management Society, one of the best sources for information about salaries and benefits for office employees, makes the following distinctions among the various levels of secretaries:

Executive Sectretary/Administrative Assistant—Performs a full range of secretarial and administrative duties for high-level member of executive staff; handles project-oriented duties and may be held accountable for the timely completion of these tasks; relieves executive of routine administrative details. Position requires an in-depth knowledge of company practice, structure, and a high degree of technical skills.

Secretary, Level A—Performs an unlimited range of secretarial duties for middle-management personnel or for more than one individual; composes and/or takes and transcribes correspondence of a complex and confidential nature. Position requires a knowledge of company policy and procedure, and above-average secretarial and administrative skills.

Secretary, Level B—Performs a limited range of secretarial duties in a small company or for a supervisor in a larger firm; may take dictation and transcribe from notes or dictating equipment with speed and accuracy; screens calls, makes appointments, handles travel arrangements, answers routine correspondence, and maintains filing systems.

Legal Secretary—Performs an unlimited range of secretarial duties for one or more members of the firm, usually a junior, senior, or managing partner; takes and transcribes dictation with a high degree of speed and accuracy. Position requires knowledge of the specific legal terminology within the attorney's area of specialization, i.e., litigation, probate, corporate, etc. May utilize word-processing equipment.

Although jobs for secretaries are expected to grow more slowly than the national average for all jobs, there are always opportunities for well-qualified and experienced secretaries. Several hundred thousand positions turn over each year as secretaries transfer to positions of greater responsibility or leave the labor force. The trend toward secretaries assuming more responsibilities also means that their ranks should grow at the expense of the managers and professionals who formerly performed these duties.

Below are some examples of average salaries in major cities.

AVERAGE WEEKLY SALARIES OF SECRETARIES IN 15 CITIES

City	Level I	Level II	Level III	Level IV	Level V
Atlanta	$389	$448	$551	$621	$771
Boston	447	511	581	677	798
Chicago	455	533	593	699	798
Dallas	432	468	529	632	779
Denver	400	508	553	639	750
Detroit	500	510	620	628	873
Houston	429	496	573	676	808
Miami	398	490	547	645	762
Phoenix	380	430	449	543	639
Philadelphia	NA	472	564	661	744
St. Louis	377	451	532	647	805
San Diego	426	503	585	666	790
San Francisco	NA	600	668	748	840
Seattle	431	491	563	629	766
Washington, DC	459	525	586	699	816

SOURCE: Bureau of Labor Statistics, *Occupational Compensation Survey, National Summary,* 1996.

File Clerks

The work of the file clerk varies in complexity from simple filing to maintaining a large and varied filing system and keeping computerized records of filed materials. Advanced-level file clerks may even supervise a staff of lower-level clerks. File clerks held about 293,000 jobs in 1996. They are found in nearly every sector of the economy, though 90 percent are employed in services, government, finance, insurance, and real estate. In 1996, about one-third of all file clerks worked part-time, and more than a quarter were employed by temporary service firms. The average file clerk earned

AVERAGE WEEKLY SALARIES OF CLERKS IN 15 CITIES

City	Accounting Clerks				General Clerks				Personnel Clerks			
	I	II	III	IV	I	II	III	IV	I	II	III	IV
Atlanta	$335	$413	$462	$534	NA	$332	NA	$504	NA	$442	$554	NA
Boston	NA	421	491	595	NA	NA	$438	NA	NA	437	522	$646
Chicago	NA	406	462	610	$310	356	434	524	NA	425	528	609
Dallas	396	383	442	533	302	319	401	402	$324	401	477	586
Denver	350	399	478	565	311	NA	396	458	NA	452	506	618
Detroit	309	382	475	607	318	NA	433	542	NA	435	492	NA
Houston	409	406	193	580	328	349	479	442	NA	408	NA	NA
Miami	NA	380	468	558	285	NA	397	441	306	423	520	NA
Philadelphia	336	424	480	606	NA	378	419	NA	NA	NA	552	NA
Phoenix	NA	359	411	457	256	309	364	384	NA	NA	NA	NA
St. Louis	392	355	428	527	238	333	388	466	323	385	495	NA
San Diego	NA	392	456	NA	NA	319	414	505	NA	NA	518	NA
San Francisco	NA	454	533	622	NA	396	511	594	NA	NA	638	700
Seattle	NA	406	477	588	369	363	445	510	NA	439	529	591
Washington, DC	343	414	494	565	284	370	416	542	NA	421	521	NA

SOURCE: Bureau of Labor Statistics, *Occupational Compensation Survey, National Summary,* 1996.

$17,100 in 1996 (slightly less in the federal government), though salaries vary considerably by geography, industry, and responsibility.

Accounting Clerks

Accounting clerks record their companies' financial transactions in ledgers, maintain financial records, and are responsible for the accuracy, completeness, and consistency of those records. The Bureau of Labor Statistics divides accounting clerks into four classifications: level I and II clerks perform simple bookkeeping tasks under close supervision, while level III and IV clerk jobs "require a knowledge and understanding of established and standardized bookkeeping and accounting procedures," including double-entry bookkeeping. They may also supervise lower-level accounting clerks. There were more than 2.2 million people working as bookkeeping, accounting, or auditing clerks in 1996. One-fourth of them worked in the wholesale or retail trade industries.

Accounting clerks frequently do the same tasks as bookkeepers, and it would seem likely that the two levels recognized by the Bureau of Labor Statistics would correspond roughly to the titles "Assistant Bookkeeper" and "Full-Charge Bookkeeper" as they are advertised in the newspapers. Oddly, they do not. Whereas an accounting clerk can expect to earn no more than $26,000, a full-charge bookkeeper's salary starts at $26,000 and may range as high as $40,000, according to the Robert Half International Salary Guide (see accompanying table). If one wishes to pursue this profession, it is obviously better to call oneself a bookkeeper than an accounting clerk. For more information, see the "Accountants" entry in Part III: Five Standard Professions.

BOOKEEPERS' SALARIES, 1998	
Title	**Salary Range**
Full Charge/controller (financial statements)	$29,000–40,000
Full charge (general ledger)	26,000–35,000
Bookkeeper/assistant (up to general ledger)	22,000–29,000
Accounting clerk	16,500–26,000
Accounts Receivable/Payable Supervisor	24,000–40,000
Payroll Manager	24,000–42,000
Payroll clerk	20,000–26,500

SOURCE: Robert Half International, *1998. Salary Guide.* Reprinted by permission.

Personnel Clerks/Assistants

The great importance of personnel and/or human resources departments (see also Part V, "The Personnel Staff") has created many new clerical jobs in this area. The Bureau of Labor Statistics defines this job as providing "clerical and technical support to personnel professionals or managers" who deal with all aspects of employment, from recruiting to compensation and benefits, to termination of company employees. The responsibilities of clerks/assistants range from checking that job applications are filled out properly, checking references of new employees, and eventually interviewing prospective job candidates. Senior people must have an excellent knowledge of the company's entire personnel policy. According to the Bureau of Labor Statistics, the median earnings of a full time personnel clerk in 1996 was $23,100.

Purchasing Assistants

People in this job assist the buyers and purchasing agents described in Part V. Like the personnel department, purchasing has become an increasingly vital function in companies of every size and description. The entry-level purchasing assistant's job is primarily a clerical one, requiring fact-checking by rote, routing, and filing functions. After gaining some experience (and depending on the boss's flexibility), assistants handle daily routine ordering and eventually advise the supervisory staff about the suitability of supplies and the quality of materials. At the highest levels, people in these jobs earn over $30,000 a year.

Receptionists and Switchboard Operators

At all but the largest companies, the receptionist and the switchboard operator are the same person. This person is usually required to do some of the typing and light clerical work. Salaries for receptionists are usually on par with those of general clerks and file clerks—about $17,300—though salary progression is uncommon. Many companies use the receptionist position as a stepping-stone to jobs with more responsibilities. Because of this, and because of the tedium involved in this position, turnover among receptionists is high. Many receptionists leave the labor force when they leave their jobs, either to return to school, to tend to household duties, or to retire. There were 1,074,000 receptionists in 1996. Job openings for receptionists should be plentiful in the coming years not only because of the high turnover but also because so many receptionists work in the service industry, which is expected to continue its strong growth through the end of the century. Doctors' and dentists' offices, law firms, temporary help agencies, and consulting firms should all have high demand for receptionists.

In large companies, operating the switchboard is often a full-time job in itself. In 1996, about 319,000 people made answering the phone their primary responsibility. One-fourth of these people worked for national or local phone companies. The remainder were employed in hospitals, hotels, department stores, or other large companies. Telephone operators who worked full-time earned a median weekly salary of $371 in 1996. Operators for the telephone companies like AT&T and the Bell Operating Companies (a.k.a. the Baby Bells) earn considerably more than the other operators. That's primarily because they are almost all members of one of two unions: the Communications Workers of America (CWA) or the International Brotherhood of Electrical Workers. In 1996, salaries for CWA operators averaged $638 a week after five years on the job. Automation is expected to replace much of the work currently performed by operators, so employment prospects in this field are dire.

Computer-Operating Personnel

After the 1 million-plus systems analysts and programmers have drawn up plans and instructions in a language their computers can understand, some 319,000 workers are needed to keep the machines functioning smoothly. Some of these people are key-entry operators, who work at keypunch machines or key-operated magnetic tape or disc encoders that "translate" data into a form suitable for computer processing. The Bureau of Labor Statistics describes the work as "routine and repetitive" at the first level, but requiring "experience and judgment" at the higher level. (From the salary figures in the table later in this section titled "Average Weekly Salaries of Office Workers in Private Industry," these qualities don't seem to be worth much.) Despite the generally strong growth patterns in employment among computer-operating personnel, the future of the key entry operator isn't encouraging. The predictions are that improved technology will eliminate much of their function.

Just the opposite is true for computer operators, who are also commonly known as console operators. Rapidly changing computer technology is not only making these machines more powerful, it is also making them accessible to more and more businesses. The result will be a significant net increase in jobs over the next decade for an occupation many experts said had reached the saturation point.

Computer operators are usually required to have a high school diploma, and most have received special training in the field before they are hired. This training may have been acquired in high school, in a community college, in the military, or in an accredited institution offering courses in this area. In addition, many firms transfer employees from other departments and provide on-the-job training for them.

The Department of Labor recognizes six different levels of expertise among all computer operators. Levels I and II are essentially trainee positions, while Level VI requires knowledge of program language and an ability to assist programmers in developing systems or modifying programs. In between, Levels III to V carry out the basic tasks of computer operating: loading the equipment with tapes, cards, etc.; starting and overseeing the machine; responding to the computer's instructions, including "error messages"; and maintaining a record of work.

Employment is expected to decline sharply as data centers become automated and as more computing is done on personal computers. For salary figures, see the tables at the end of this section. (See also "Computer Technologists and Professionals" in Part IV.)

Typists, Word Processors, and Data Entry Keyers

When the first edition of this book was published, the word processor's job was one of the most important in the modern office. As the majority of the office staff has become computer literate and word processing is integrated into the duties of almost every employee, from receptionist to CEO, this is no longer the case. In offices nationwide, not to mention private homes, the word processor—a catch term that encompasses any piece of computer equipment that electronically captures and stores the keystrokes that create any kind of document a business may need—has replaced the typewriter as the primary instrument of communication. The almost total reliance by companies on their computer systems has meant that secretaries with word processing abilities are in high demand and those who lack this ability often learn it quickly on the job.

The Department of Labor classifies word processors along with typists and data entry keyers when keeping employment statistics. Because so many typists now work on computers, the differences between them are growing more and more slight. Data entry keyers do less literate work like filling out forms that appear on a computer screen or entering lists of items or numbers. Together, these three occupations accounted for nearly 1.2 million jobs in 1992 in every sector of the economy. Forty percent worked in educational institutions, health-care facilities, law offices, temporary agencies, and word processing service bureaus. They earned an average of $20,000 in 1995. Word processors, meanwhile, earned an average of $23,000. In the federal government, clerk-typists and inexperienced data entry keyers started at $15,500 and average $21,500.

Although the amount of text to be processed and entered is tremendous and growing, increasing automation and restructuring of work processes should enable fewer typists, word processors, and data entry keyers to handle the increased workload. There should be little change, therefore, in the total number of people employed in this field. However, job openings should be plentiful since turnover in these jobs is high. The one threatening factor is the amount of work being sent overseas where labor costs are dramatically lower.

AVERAGE WEEKLY SALARIES OF SWITCHBOARD OPERATORS/RECEPTIONISTS AND COMPUTER OPERATING PERSONNEL IN 15 LARGE CITIES

City	Word Processors			Key Entry Operators		Switchboard Operators/ Receptionists
	I	II	III	I	II	
Atlanta	NA	NA	NA	$351	NA	$372
Boston	NA	$497	NA	380	$448	402
Chicago	NA	538	$584	347	435	361
Dallas	NA	486	NA	305	377	337
Denver	NA	NA	NA	362	391	357
Detroit	$420	480	638	349	NA	NA
Houston	392	474	620	341	396	361
Miami	362	456	NA	336	409	335
Philadelphia	415	464	555	369	446	396
Phoenix	416	399	429	310	364	310
St. Louis	NA	413	525	323	374	322
San Diego	380	488	586	339	424	351
San Francisco	NA	589	711	NA	494	438
Washington, DC	413	486	583	346	459	412
Seattle	433	476	615	402	438	400

SOURCE: Bureau of Labor Statistics, *Occupational Compensation Survey, National Summary,* 1996.

AVERAGE WEEKLY SALARIES OF OFFICE WORKERS IN PRIVATE INDUSTRY

Job Title and Level	Number Surveyed	Average Salary
Accounting clerks I	10,997	$308
Accounting clerks II	175,171	370
Accounting clerks III	137,376	459
Accounting clerks IV	34,303	542
Computer operators I	4,250	352
Computer operators II	32,975	440
Computer operators III	23,849	569
Computer operators IV	4,888	681
Computer operators V	393	804
General clerks I	15,218	280
General clerks II	131,364	343
General clerks III	186,245	424
General clerks IV	93,344	494
Key entry operators I	64,939	335
Key entry operators II	37,627	406
Personnel clerks/assistants I	3,207	318
Personnel clerks/assistants II	16,168	396
Personnel clerks/assistants III	17,756	495
Personnel clerks/assistants IV	4,741	590
Secretaries I	72,456	374
Secretaries II	136,726	469
Secretaries III	148,686	550
Secretaries IV	61,817	656
Secretaries V	11,742	795
Switchboard operators/receptionists	106,501	340
Word processors I	13,410	374
Word processors II	24,647	504
Word processors III	5,180	604

SOURCE: Bureau of Labor Statistics, *Occupational Compensation Survey, National Summary,* 1996.

MACHINING OCCUPATIONS

More than 2 million people are employed in machining occupations. Machine tools are used to shape metal and metal parts are the bricks of mass production, since, according to the Bureau of Labor Statistics, "nearly every product of American industry, from cornflakes to turbines, is made either using machine tools or using machines made by machine tools." Machine tools are extremely precise and are often designed for specific tasks by the people who operate them. The design of machines and their functions is the part of machining that is most interesting and lucrative. The operation of machinery after it has been produced and adjusted can be tedious, especially if the machines are designed to do all of the work.

There are four different categories of machine workers, although in smaller shops, the distinctions are not as clear-cut as in large ones. Employment in machining occupations is expected to grow no faster than the average rate for all jobs, and in many cases is expected to decline. As machines become more sophisticated, they will do more of the work themselves. Most jobs are found, of course, in places with lots of factories, such as Los Angeles, Chicago, New York, Philadelphia, Boston, San Francisco, and Houston.

All-Round Machinists

There were about 393,00 machinists and tool programmers in 1996; although the number is expected to decrease due to increased automation, job opportunities are expected to be good as there are increasingly fewer workers with the necessary skills. These are skilled workers who have often completed a four-year formal apprenticeship (about 8,000 shop hours and 570 hours in the classroom). A high school science or vocational degree is preferred by most employers. Workers must be able to operate a variety of machines using a variety of metals. Besides shaping metal, they must also know how to calculate precise measurements (sometimes down to a millionth of an inch) so that the pieces they produce will be perfect.

Working conditions in most machine shops have improved from the sweatshop image that many people still harbor. Work areas are now well-lit and ventilated; more sophisticated equipment makes less noise. However, the enormous energy and cutting speed required to chop up blocks of metal can produce red-hot, molten pieces that sometimes fly through the air. Machinists are required to wear protective clothing and goggles while they work.

Earnings of all-round machinists compare favorably with those of other skilled workers. In 1996, their median weekly earnings were about $550; the top 10 percent made more than $870 a week.

Metalworking and Plastics-Working Machine Operators

These 1.5 million employees can be separated into two groups: Those who set up machines for operation and those who tend the machines while they operate. Setup workers (or setters) need to know how the machines operate, so they generally have more training and are more skilled than those who simply operate the machines. Regular operators are usually identified by the kind of machine they run, for example, a screw machine operator or lathe

tender. Half of these workers are machine tool–cutting and forming machine
setters or operators, and another 8 percent are sheet-metal workers. About
one-third of metalworking and plastics-working machine operators are represented by unions.

Median weekly earnings for metal and plastics working machine operators
were $440 in 1996; the top 10 percent earned over $770. Employees who
worked in the industries of transportation equipment ($760), primary metals
($660), machinery ($590), fabricated metal products ($530), and rubber and
miscellaneous plastics materials and resins ($470) earned considerably more
than the average. Jobs in this area are expected to decline through the year 2005
as firms move factories (and jobs) to other countries where labor is cheaper and
as fewer laborers are needed to tend more machines.

Tool and Die Makers

Tools and dies are the parts of equipment used by other machining workers
to mass-produce metal parts. Tool makers produce "jibs" and fixtures that
hold metal while it is being shaved, and measuring devices to gauge the
precision of the parts produced. Die makers produce metal forms or dies for
stamping out pieces of metal. These jobs are most like those of instrument
makers except that tool-and-die makers specialize in one type of product.
Tool-and-die makers work in machine shops but usually in separate, quieter
areas called toolrooms. Four years of apprenticeship is the norm. The Bureau
of Labor Statistics says that "many tool and die makers become tool designers
and others may open their own tool-and-die shops." About 134,000 people
are employed as tool-and-die makers, a number that is likely to decline as
businesses increase their used of numerically controlled (or automated) machine tools. In 1996, their average weekly earnings were about $720, with
the top 10 percent making over $1,160.

Millwrights

Millwrights install machinery, not just in the production of metal parts but
in all industries, from textiles to printing. Installation includes construction
of foundations and platforms for machines, which means that a millwright
has to read blueprints and be able to use installation tools (torches, crowbars,
power tools, etc.) and direct the operation of cranes and other equipment.
Millwrights sometimes train as apprentices for as many as eight years, but
many follow a four-year course of job and classroom instruction similar to
that of all-round machinists.

Most of the 78,000 millwrights are employed full-time by large manufacturers, but a fair percentage are employed by contractors and construction

AVERAGE HOURLY EARNINGS OF MACHINISTS IN 15 CITIES

City	Maintenance Machinists	Tool and Die Makers
Atlanta	$17.73	NA
Boston	16.90	$17.66
Chicago	18.13	19.47
Dallas	NA	17.27
Denver	17.73	17.32
Detroit	18.51	20.32
Houston	NA	17.22
Miami	16.68	15.21
Philadelphia	18.57	17.73
Phoenix	21.41	18.64
St. Louis	19.69	21.07
San Diego	NA	20.41
San Francisco	19.37	NA
Seattle	20.26	NA
Washington, DC	20.79	NA

SOURCE: Bureau of Labor Statistics, *Occupational Compensation Survey, National Summary,* 1996.

companies, and this means that many are frequently out of work when the economy is in a downward trend. Median earnings of full-time millwrights were $670 in 1996. About 55 percent of millwrights belong to labor unions, one of the highest rates in the country.

MATERIAL MOVEMENT WORKERS

These are the people in the background working to ensure that items move quickly from point A to point B. Material movement workers represent over 3.5 million members of the workforce. Generally members of large unions, workers in these occupations tend to earn wages on a par with, or even better than, national averages for blue-collar jobs. However, the future employment outlook varies for the different occupations in this field because of increased mechanization and automation. Here are descriptions of several of these occupations.

Forklift Operators

Because of strict union regulations, forklift operators don't actually manually load or unload material onto or from ships, trucks, or railroad cars. That job is left to material handlers (see below). Rather, forklift operators stack crates in warehouses and load and unload trucks and boxcars only when their machinery is required. Many forklift operators work in the electronics manufacturing industry, although opportunities also exist on the docks, in freight yards, and in any other field where warehouses are to be found. In 1996, there were 479,00 forklift operators. The employment outlook for this occupation is about average for nonsupervisory positions.

Material Handlers

Many material handlers, also known as stevedores or handling laborers, work in the motor vehicle and equipment manufacturing field. They load and unload parts and raw materials from railroad cars, ships, and trucks. That makes them the first people on the assembly line. Material handlers are members of the UAW (United Automobile, Aerospace, and Agricultural Implement Workers of America).

Warehouse Specialists and Shipping and Receiving Clerks

Sometimes known as stock clerks, warehouse specialists are given a billing with all the part numbers and quantities needed by a customer. They then go through the warehouse filling the order, and then take it to be packed and shipped. Their earnings are generally a bit higher than those of shipping and receiving clerks.

Shipping and receiving clerks record all shipments sent out and received. Shipping clerks have the final responsibility for merchandise before it leaves the company for a customer. They must check to see that an order has been filled correctly and that it is well-packaged and bears the proper postage. Then they must supervise its loading onto delivery trucks.

Receiving clerks handle similar tasks only in reverse. They inspect incoming merchandise to make sure an order has been correctly filled and billed. They may direct goods to the department that ordered them within the company. Receiving clerks must be adept at record-keeping, too, in order to assist with inventory computations.

There are about 759,000 shipping and receiving clerks, and about 1.85 million warehouse specialists in the country. Employment opportunities are expected to grow about as fast as the national average for all jobs. Median weekly earnings in 1996 for these workers were $412. These clerks generally receive no more than standard benefits.

AVERAGE HOURLY WAGES OF MATERIAL MOVEMENT WORKERS IN 15 CITIES

City	Forklift Operators	Material Handling Laborers	Shipping/ Receiving Clerks	Warehouse Specialists	Truckdrivers Light	Medium	Heavy	Tractor- Trailer
Atlanta	$10.60	NA	NA	NA	$ 7.52	$14.38	$14.45	$15.59
Boston	NA	$9.08	NA	NA	10.04	NA	12.30	14.71
Chicago	NA	9.01	$10.15	NA	NA	15.45	18.16	15.66
Dallas	9.95	7.65	10.02	NA	7.53	12.92	9.05	NA
Denver	NA	7.50	9.30	NA	8.73	NA	12.79	15.98
Detroit	15.74	14.34	13.05	NA	NA	NA	NA	15.42
Houston	NA	NA	10.59	NA	NA	15.02	10.25	13.26
Miami	NA	NA	9.10	NA	NA	NA	11.83	NA
Philadelphia	12.33	12.25	10.59	$14.04	NA	15.87	14.15	13.33
Phoenix	10.51	6.69	8.99	10.38	NA	NA	13.01	NA
St. Louis	13.74	NA	11.04	NA	8.21	NA	12.72	17.31
San Diego	NA	NA	7.92	NA	7.54	NA	NA	NA
San Francisco	NA	7.41	11.80	NA	NA	NA	NA	NA
Seattle	NA	NA	NA	NA	NA	NA	15.22	14.35
Washington, DC	NA	NA	11.76	NA	NA	NA	12.68	17.42

SOURCE: Bureau of Labor Statistics, Occupational Compensation Survey, National Summary, 1996.

Truck Drivers

It is not an exaggeration to say that the 3 million plus truck drivers in the United States play a crucial role in our economy and our daily lives. Virtually every product that ends up in our homes, offices, or factories gets there by truck: bread, produce, beer, soda, lumber, gasoline, automobiles, auto parts, computers, express delivery packages, etc. Even if Fed Ex and its competitors have brought a new dimension to the transporting of goods, truck drivers are as essential to the success of those operations as the pilots who fly the planes.

Not surprisingly the outlook for jobs in this area is extremely good. The booming economy has created thousands of new jobs for truck drivers, and some experts are predicting that 40,000 more will be needed over 1999–2000. At the end of 1998, the federal government gave a $1.2 million grant to train dislocated workers as long-haul drivers.

Hourly pay for most truckers is in the $15 to $20 range, but good companies pay as much as $40,000 to $60,000 (plus benefits), although drivers usually have to work long hours. Despite all the negative things that can be said about the Teamsters Union, the fact is their members have always made more money than nonunion drivers.

MECHANICS, INSTALLERS, AND REPAIRERS

It's heartening to know that in this land of disposable everything, there are still large numbers of people whose workday is spent fixing, mending, and repairing. There are quite a few occupations falling under the mechanics and repairers category, in which a total of nearly 4.6 million Americans work. The unemployment rate for mechanics in particular tends to be much lower than that for blue-collar workers generally, so the work is basically steady and less subject to seasonal layoffs. Most of these jobs are not unionized, although there is frequently some licensing qualification. Training usually comes in the form of apprenticeships. Earnings are commensurate with experience, with highly skilled workers earning wages considerably above average for nonsupervisory positions.

Although these jobs tend to have longer than usual work weeks, employees often work with minimal supervision, and many are self-employed.

The various occupations in this category evidence one of the widest fluctuations of growth within a single industry. Increases in the use of data processing equipment and biomedical equipment will bring with them a corresponding need for people to repair and install them. At the same time, labor-saving advances should cause a decline in employment for installers and repairers of telephones, televisions, and other types of communications equipment.

MECHANICS, INSTALLERS, AND REPAIRERS, 1990–1996, BY TYPE

Job	Employment	
	1990	1996
Aircraft mechanics and engine specialists	122,000	137,000
Automotive body repairers	219,000	225,000
Automotive mechanics	757,000	775,000
Diesel (bus and truck) mechanics	268,000	226,000
Electronic equipment repairers, total	370,000	396,000
Computer and office machine repairers	159,000	141,000
Communications equipment mechanics	125,000	116,000
Commercial and industrial electronic equipment repairers	73,000	60,000
Electronic home entertainment equipment repairers	41,000	33,000
Telephone installers and repairers	47,000	37,000
Elevator installers and repairers	19,000	25,000
Farm equipment mechanics	48,000	44,000
General maintenance repairers	1,128,000	1,362,000
Heating, air-conditioning, and refrigeration technicians	219,000	256,000
Home appliance and power tool repairers	71,000	71,000
Industrial machinery mechanics	474,000	459,000
Line installers and cable splicers	133,000	309,000
Millwrights	73,000	78,000
Mobile heavy equipment mechanics	104,000	104,000
Motorcycle, boat, and small engine mechanics	50,000	45,000
Musical instrument repairers and tuners	9,000	9,000
Vending machine servicers and repairers	26,000	21,000
Bicycle repairers	15,000	13,000
Camera and photographic equipment repairers	7,000	14,000
Electric meter installers and repairers	14,000	12,000
Electromedical and biomedical equipment repairers	8,000	9,700
Precision instrument repairers	50,000	38,000
Riggers	14,000	9,300
Tire repairers	81,000	94,000
Watchmakers	7,000	7,400
TOTAL	**4,361,000**	**5,124,400**

SOURCE: Department of Labor, *Occupational Outlook Handbook,* 1998.

Overall, America's 4.5 million mechanics, installers, and repairers should grow 16 percent by the year 2005, according to the Department of Labor. Jobs for computer and office machine repairers should grow by 30 percent; meanwhile, telephone installers and repairers should see their numbers decline by half. Statistics for all jobs within the industry are in the chart above.

Heating, Air Conditioning, and Refrigeration Mechanics

Wherever large numbers of people live, work, or play, some system for keeping them cool in hot weather and warm in cold weather is an integral part of the building and its maintenance. Heating, refrigeration, and air-conditioning mechanics are skilled workers who repair, install, and maintain the complex systems that fill these functions.

Some mechanics specialize with one kind of equipment or a particular task, such as installation or repair. Others handle all facets of a building's climate control system, as well as doing such maintenance work as overhauling the air-conditioning system in the winter and making sure pipes are clear and ducts clean for heating. There are about 256,000 mechanics in this classification; about half of them work for cooling and heating contractors. About 15 percent are self-employed. The remainder are divided among the federal government, hospitals, office buildings, and other organizations that operate large air-conditioning, refrigeration, or heating systems.

Because of the increasing sophistication of air-conditioning, refrigeration, and heating systems, employers are beginning to rely more on mechanics with technical school or apprenticeship training. Apprenticeship programs, lasting four to five years and combining on-the-job training with 144 hours of classroom instruction, are administered by locals of various different unions, including the Air Conditioning Contractors of America, the Mechanical Contractors' Association of America, and the National Association of Plumbers, Pipe Fitters, and Cooling Contractors. In addition, many secondary and postsecondary technical trade schools, junior colleges, and the U.S. Armed Forces now offer one-to-two-year programs in heating, air conditioning, and refrigeration. Despite the development of all these programs, however, a sizable number of heating, air-conditioning, and refrigeration mechanics continue to learn their trade on the job.

Earnings in this field vary with experience, skills, and geographical location. Median weekly earnings in 1996 were $536 for full-time mechanics. And although turnover in this field is very low, job openings are expected to be plentiful as a result of faster than average growth. The continued pattern of U.S. migration from the rust belt to areas in the south and west (where central heating and cooling systems abound) should also help job prospects in this field.

Home Appliance Repairers

Back in nineteenth-century England, a band of workers, fearful they would soon be losing their jobs to machines and frustrated by the newfangled things, joined forces under Ned Ludd and smashed all the equipment they could lay their hands on. The Luddites had their day or two in history, but with time, workers grew accustomed, or at least resigned to, the mechanized workplace; they, and everyone else, eventually saw it happen to their homes as well. American homes are a gadget heaven, with appliances existing to vacuum, clean clothes, wash dishes, make toast, blend food, dry hair, dry lettuce, chop onions, fry perfect hamburgers, mow lawns, and brush teeth— and that's a conservative listing. (With all these time-saving devices, want to guess how much less time a homemaker spends on weekly chores today than did her counterpart ninety years ago? Answer: exactly one minute.)

However, as everyone knows, appliances are fair-weather friends. Some corollary to Murphy's Law dictates that the ice-making machine must break down, with the air conditioner, in July; the blow-dryer on prom night; and so on. Luckily there are heroes in these scenarios. They are appliance repairers.

There are about 71,000 people working as home appliance and power tool repairers, with little change expected over the next two decades. Most repairers are employed by independent appliance stores and repair shops. Many work, too, for gas and elecric utility companies, department stores, and in service centers operated by appliance manufacturers.

Repairers, who often take vocational classes for background training, also receive on-the-job training, sometimes up to three years' worth before becoming fully skilled on very complicated machinery. They must be adept with mechanical and electrical work so as to be able to determine what exactly is wrong with an appliance and how to fix it or replace a used or defective part. Some appliance repairers make house calls, bringing all their tools along to repair an item on the spot, or to install an appliance and explain its use.

According to the Department of Labor, earnings for appliance repairers vary widely by skill level, geographic location, and type of equipment serviced. On average, experienced repairers earned $579 per week in 1996. Trainees earned less and senior technicians earned more than the range extremes. Salaries tend to be highest in large firms and for those servicing gas appliances.

Automobile Mechanics

There are some who consider finding an honest, reliable automobile mechanic more vital than finding a reliable family doctor. Mechanics test-drive a car or use testing equipment to locate a problem on a car that a customer has brought in. Once the problem has been determined, mechanics make the needed repair or adjustment or replace a part that is worn. They also perform such routine maintenance as oil changes and tune-ups.

Probably the vast majority of auto mechanics are generalists, able to deal with just about any kind of car repair. However, some specialize in such narrower areas as automatic transmissions, automobile air-conditioning, automobile radiators, auto glass, brakes, mufflers, oil changes, tune-ups, wheel alignments, and front-end adjustments.

There were 775,000 automobile mechanics in 1996, with job openings expected to increase apace with the national average over the next decade. Qualified mechanics should find work wherever they go, as opportunities exist all over the country. Mechanics with the most training, especially training in basic electronics, should find the most job prospects and the highest salaries.

Most mechanics receive all their training on the job, with their earnings increasing as their skills and experience do. Some independent repair shops and large auto dealers offer apprenticeship programs. The majority of all mechanics are employed by franchised dealerships like Ford or GM service shops, which employ eight or nine mechanics on the average. Other jobs exist in gasoline service stations, auto repair shops, and department stores' automotive service centers.

Median weekly earnings of auto mechanics were $524 in 1996. Many experienced mechanics also receive a commission related to the labor cost charged to the customer. Many employers guarantee a minimum weekly salary in case the amount of work drops in a given week. Auto mechanics belong to one of several unions: the United Auto Workers, the Teamsters, and the International Association of Machinists and Aerospace Workers.

Industrial Machinery Repairers

Industrial machinery repairers work in factories repairing broken machinery and doing preventive maintenance. They're experts in diagnosis, being able to tell by the mere sounds and shakes of a piece of equipment just what is ailing it. They then disassemble it and make the necessary repair or replacement of the damaged part. Since service and general overhauls must go on even if machinery is idle or running at low capacity, industrial machinery repairers are not usually subject to seasonal layoffs or slow work periods.

There are are now about 459,000 workers in this trade. They are employed in a wide variety of industries, ranging from coal to paper to machinery to food products. Work can be found all over the country, although most jobs exist in the more industrialized states. This is a highly unionized occupation, with mechanics belonging to different unions depending on what industry they're working in. Most industrial repairers belong to the United Steelworkers of America, the UAW, the International Association of Machinists and Aerospace Workers, or the International Union of Electrical, Radio, and Machine Workers.

Job opportunities are forecasted to decline as more firms move to automated production equipment. All job openings will result from retirements or the need to replace workers who leave the field or the labor force. According to the Department of Labor, median weekly earnings of most industrial machinery repairers were $570 in 1996.

Shoe Repairers

Here's one trade that profits when economic times are hard—and not because many people look "down at the heel." It's just that people are more interested in repairing or maintaining shoes they already own than in spending money on new ones. Shoe repairers reheel, make new soles, replace insoles, and restyle old shoes by dyeing uppers and changing heels. They also do a miscellany of other tasks, such as mend handbags, tents, and luggage; stretch shoes; and fix zippers.

According to the Bureau of Labor Statistics, shoe and leather workers held about 21,000 jobs in 1996; about 6,000 were self-employed. Inexpensive imports have made the cost of replacing shoes and leather goods cheaper or more convenient than repairing them, thus reducing the demand for shoe and leather repairers. However, repair of more expensive, high-end products will continue to grow, as will demand for repairers of custom-made and orthopedic shoes. An increase in the population over seventy-five years old, the group most likely to need orthopedic shoes, should expand the market for this type of shoemaker and repairer. The trade is nonunionized, with many of its workers running their own shops, often squeezed into tiny spaces in alleyways between other stores. Salary information is therefore limited. Generally, beginning workers earn no more than the minimum wage. Store owners earn substantially more.

RESTAURANT WORKERS

More than 7.5 million people work in the restaurants, bars, pizza places, and chili joints, etc., that seem to have sprung up in every nook and cranny of every little town, large urban area, and suburban mall. Despite recent tough times in the industry, every analyst in every state as well as all the forecasters in Washington, DC, project very strong growth in this sector of the economy. In fact, the Bureau of Labor Statistics expects the category "Food preparation and service workers" to be the fastest-growing set of occupations in the next decade. By the year 2006, fully six percent of U.S. employees (some 8.7 million people) will work in eating and drinking establishments. Average annual growth should top 1.2 million jobs, well above the average for the rest of the labor force. Granted over 40 percent of food preparation workers are on a part-time schedule, reflecting the growth of fast-food restaurants, but this does not mean there won't be tens of thousands of good jobs leading to careers in a solid industry.

The most compelling reason for these increases is the growth in the number of restaurants of all kinds, from fast-food burger joints to the many new ethnic restaurants (Mexican, Vietnamese, Japanese, etc.) to four-star palaces of rarified culinary delights that have sprung up in every major city. Between 1990 and 1995, over 60,000 new establishments opened their doors as more and more Americans found it necessary or simply pleasurable to dine out rather than cook at home. With so many more women working full time these days, this social trend should continue to fuel the rapidly expanding restaurant industry.

Restaurant Managers

About 375,000 people are employed as restaurant managers, many of whom now have college degrees in restaurant and food service management. According to the National Restaurant Association, entry-level trainee jobs in 1995 paid $22,000 to $30,000 while assistant managers averaged $27,000 to $30,000 ($22,000 in fast-food restaurants). Food and beverage directors made over $40,000 with a top level of almost $60,000 with bonuses of $7,000. Earnings for experienced managers run the gamut from $300 a week in small, inexpensive establishments to $1,000 a week at top-end places. Most managers also earned bonuses of $3,000 to $10,000 a year depending on the restaurant's success.

Cooks and Chefs

The Department of Labor counts more than 2.1 million people working as cooks of all kinds, including 804,000 short-order cooks, 727,000 restaurant cooks, and 182,000 pastry bakers. Their wages vary as much as their task, from the $5.25 per hour earned by fast-food fryers to the $40,000 plus per year earned by executive chefs in very good restaurants. In between are cooks, whose median hourly earnings were less than $7.00 in 1995, according to the National Restaurant Association; bread and pastry bakers

AVERAGE ANNUAL SALARIES OF CHEFS AND FOOD MANAGERS IN HOTELS

Category	First Class	Mid-Price Class
Executive chef	$56,800	$41,300
Director of food and beverage	62,400	42,700
Banquet chef	33,800	21,300
Sous chef	32,600	25,400
Executive steward	31,700	19,200
Restaurant manager	33,300	27,900

NOTE: Salaries include bonus.
SOURCE: American Hotel and Motel Association.

whose median earnings were $6.50; assistant cooks, $6.25; and short-order cooks, $6.50. According to a 1998 report in The New York Times, at the very best restaurants, such as Le Cirque, 2,000 trained cooks earn only $12.50 an hour, and they have to work six days.

Chefs who develop a following often end up as partner or sole proprietor of their own restaurant, where their income depends on the establishment's success. Some employers provide their employees with uniforms and free meals, but federal law allows them to deduct the fair value of these meals from their workers' salaries.

To some degree, the number of jobs for cooks and chefs is reliant on a strong economy, as people tend to eat out more often (and in more expensive restaurants) when the economy is healthy. Nevertheless, jobs for chefs and cooks are expected to grow rapidly regardless of the health of the economy because of population growth and increased leisure time. Jobs for cooks and chefs in restaurants, especially those offering more varied menus, are expected to grow the fastest; jobs for cooks and chefs in nursing homes will be equally strong, followed by openings in institutions like schools, hospitals, and other cafeterias.

In recent years the job of the chef has become romanticized and the work glorified beyond reason. As a result, many sons and daughters of the upper middle class have made this their career choice, so of course established chefs have leaped into the breach and created a way to provide credentials to anyone willing to spend $15,000 to $20,000 a year for training. Cooking schools (often called quite grandly "culinary institutes") have sprung up offering two or four year courses of study; some like the French Culinary Institute in New York, offer six-month programs for over $20,000. Graduates of these vocational schools usually earn $21,000 to $24,000 to start and on average take five years to reach the $35,000 level, and ten years to surpass

	Less than $500,000	$500,000 to $1 million	$1 million to $2 million	Over $2 million
	MEDIAN SALARIES OF RESTAURANT CHEFS BY SALES LEVELS, 1995			
Executive chef	$30,000	$35,000	$38,134	$45,000
Chef	22,500	27,000	31,100	35,000
Sous chef	16,640	20,000	25,000	30,000
Pastry chef	16,445	19,500	25,000	30,000

SOURCE: National Restaurant Association. Reprinted by permission.

$50,000. On the other hand, some insiders say all this training can be learned by working for pay, albeit meager, in restaurant kitchens that are almost always looking for inexperienced help.

JOB DESCRIPTIONS FOR CHEFS

Executive chef—Responsible for all kitchens in a food-service establishment or chain operation. Duties include menu planning, portion control, quality standards, and training of employees.

Chef—Responsible for the kitchen operation in a food-service establishment or chain operation. Duties include menu planning, portion control, quality standards, and training of employees.

Sous chef—Responsible for assisting the chef in the kitchen operation in a food-service establishment or chain operation. Duties include menu planning, portion control, quality standards, and training of employees.

Pastry chef—Responsible for pastry production in a food-service organization. Ensures quality standards in conjunction with the executive chef. May be responsible for bakery goods, centerpieces, and other decorative items.

Bartenders, Waiters, and Bus Persons

The vast majority of the nation's 4.8 million bartenders, waiters, and busboys (of both sexes; also called dining room attendants) work part-time. Indeed, few admit to this being their career. Flexible hours and low educational and training requirements make this an attractive option for actors, musicians, writers, and students seeking to pay their rent while pursuing their careers. Most waiters and waitresses are in their late teens or early twenties and have little or no work experience. Bartenders generally have some form of training (usually obtained through a vocational course that may or may not help with job placement) and are expected to be familiar with state and local laws concerning the sale of alcoholic beverages; consequently, they often earn more than waiters and buspersons.

Salaries in all these positions are subject to lower minimum wage requirements than all other jobs because food service workers make such a large proportion of their money from tips. Salaries within each job category vary widely depending on the prices charged by the restaurant, the number of people served, and whether or not waiters share some portion of their tips with the bartenders and/or the busboys. And because so many restaurant workers are paid off the books (and therefore don't necessarily report all their income to the IRS), they may tend to underreport their incomes to Department of Labor interviewers as well. Bear that fact in mind as you read the following median weekly salaries for full-time restaurant workers, according to a 1996 Bureau of Labor Statistics survey:

Position	Median Weekly Earnings
Busboys	$260
Waiters and waitresses	270
Fast food waiters or attendants	220
Bartenders	310

Thus it is clear that for every bartender who boasts of taking home $200 in tips alone on a single Saturday night there are hundreds of restaurant workers toiling at a rate a lot closer to the minimum wage (or at least telling this story to the government).

In addition to their salaries and tips, most restaurant workers receive free meals from their employers (though after working there for a few weeks, many such employees report they'd rather go hungry than eat the food served in their restaurant). But, generally, only full-time workers receive benefits like paid vacation, sick leave, or health insurance. That may change as the service industry continues to expand and restaurants seek to keep qualified workers from jumping ship. For example, Starbucks, the Seattle-based coffee bar giant, provides full medical benefits to any employee who works as little as twenty hours per week. The company has found that the amount it spends on benefits (about $1,275 per year) is far less than the cost of rehiring and training new employees (about $3,000). Restaurant service workers in the largest restaurants and hotels belong to unions, the principal ones being the Hotel and Restaurant Employees International Union and the Service Employees International Union.

REPRESENTATIVE JOBS IN THE WORKADAY WORLD

Precision Assemblers

Assemblers man the production lines, putting together the different parts of manufactured items. Each worker is stationed at a set point along a moving conveyor belt, completing his or her task in the creation of a single, finished product. Assemblers, therefore, all work with different equipment and use different skills. Floor assemblers work on heavy machinery on shop floors and often use power tools, such as power drills or soldering irons, to fasten equipment. Bench assemblers do more detailed work or sometimes are responsible for a complete subassembly, such as the whole motor of a vacuum cleaner.

Out of the 1 million-plus assembly-line workers who assemble the parts of manufactured goods, the elite are the 380,000 who are employed as precision assemblers. Precision assembly requires a great degree of accuracy. The precision assembler must be able to interpret detailed specifications and instructions and apply independent judgment as opposed to the simple repetitive jobs of the majority of assembly-line workers. Precision assemblers are usually involved in the manufacturing of durable goods.

The Department of Labor estimates that jobs for precision assemblers will decline over the next decade as companies automate their factories and move assembly operations to countries like Mexico, the Philippines, and Malaysia, where labor is vastly cheaper. But not all precision assemblers can be replaced by a machine or a third-world laborer. The jobs that require the most precision and skill and the least repetition—and those that involve assembly of irregularly sized parts—will survive best.

Median weekly earnings for precision assemblers of electrical and electronic components were $340 in 1996. Wages were much higher for unionized assemblers working in companies manufacturing automobiles, aircraft, and electronic equipment: median weekly earnings ranged from $400 to $600. The biggest unions representing assemblers are the International Association of Machinists and Aerospace Workers; the International Union of Electrical, Radio and Machine Workers; and the United Automobile, Aerospace, and Agricultural Implement Workers of America.

Barbers and Cosmetologists

The haircutting profession has come a long way since the day when men whistled for "shave and a haircut, two bits." Today, nine out of every ten haircutters are so-called "cosmetologists" who offer many more services than the traditional barber of yesteryear, who seems to be going the way of the candy-striped pole and the 25-cent haircut. In addition to cutting hair, the cosmetologist (also known as a beautician or stylist) shampoos, styles, and colors hair, advises customers how to care for their hair, performs treatments that make straight hair curly or vice versa, and provides scalp massages and treatments. Some also do manicures, makeup, and electrolysis. It is the rare barber (and never a cosmetologist) who still offers a razor-and-strap shave.

The Department of Labor estimates there were 701,000 cosmetologists and barbers in 1996. The vast majority worked in a beauty salon or a "unisex" salon, though most of the 59,000 or so barbers remaining still work in traditional barber shops. About three-quarters of barbers and two-fifths of all cosmetologists are self-employed; about one in three haircutters works part-time. Every state requires barbers and cosmetologists to be licensed, though qualifications for a license vary from an eighth-grade education in some states to rigorous physical and educational requirements in others. Public and private vocational schools offer training programs that last six to twelve months, usually followed by an apprenticeship of one to two years. Reciprocity agreements between many states allow haircutters to practice in a different state without having to retrain.

Jobs for hair stylists should grow about as fast as the national average for all jobs through the year 2006, as population growth and an increasing number of women entering the labor force should increase demand for hairstyling services. Cosmetologists will account for all of these jobs; barbers' employment is expected to decline. Opportunities will be best for haircutters offering the widest array of services, for men and women alike.

Because so many haircutters are self-employed, salaries vary depending on the success of the establishment. Nonself-employed barbers and cosmetologists receive income either from commission (usually 50 to 70 percent of the price of the service) or from wages and tips. In 1996, their median weekly income was $290.

Custodial Workers

There are over 3.2 million people working as building custodians; about one third of them work part-time. Also called janitors or cleaners, custodians keep schools, stores, office buildings, hospitals, factories, and apartment houses clean and in general repair. In addition to such chores as cleaning

AVERAGE HOURLY WAGES OF JANITORS AND GUARDS IN 15 CITIES

City	Janitors	Guards I	Guards II
Atlanta	$ 6.58	$6.62	NA
Boston	9.08	8.04	$11.98
Chicago	9.19	6.84	12.08
Dallas	NA	6.79	14.01
Denver	7.62	6.49	NA
Detroit	9.21	6.75	13.58
Houston	5.40	6.59	10.33
Miami	6.99	6.06	NA
Philadelphia	9.23	7.74	11.71
Phoenix	6.43	6.67	10.29
San Diego	8.85	6.81	14.76
San Francisco	NA	7.81	12.92
Seattle	9.21	6.76	13.89
St. Louis	6.72	NA	13.22
Washington, DC	7.54	NA	11.09

SOURCE: Bureau of Labor Statistics, *Occupational Compensation Survey, National Summary,* 1996.

and waxing floors, vacuuming carpets, dusting and washing windows, custodians also do maintenance tasks including basic painting and carpentry, minor plumbing, lawn mowing, and exterminating.

Good opportunities exist for work as a custodian, especially in part-time and evening shifts. Jobs are found all over the country, but are concentrated in cities with lots of large buildings. As most cleaners learn their skills on the job, no special education or training is required. However, in places where there is more than one maintenance worker, a high school diploma can help improve the chances of promotion to a supervisory job.

Guards

More than 995,000 guards, working for security services or for privately run police forces, provide protection and surveillance for such varied institutions as banks, factories, college campuses, office buildings, hotels, and individuals. This represents an increase of almost 200,000 jobs since 1994. Their duties include visitor registration, traffic control, and identification during business hours. During off-hours, they perform as caretakers, making rounds of buildings and facilities to protect against any number of potential problems from fires to robbery or spying. They may also be the primary suspect when an office or business is robbed, as the long hours they spend trying to outwit potential thieves may tempt them to steal from their own employer. In 1996, the average guard earned $6.50 per hour. Guards who are members of one of the two major guard unions earn slightly more than the average for all guards. Guards with specialized training earn nearly double this amount.

The Bureau of Labor Statistics uses the classifications I and II to differentiate those guards who are specially trained, always armed, and in good physical shape from the run-of-the-mill security person who stands around supermarkets and is rarely (thank God) armed. Since most Class I guards are hired by manufacturing companies and Class II guards by nonmanufacturing companies, we have used only those designations in the preceding table.

Cashiers/Retail Clerks

There are about 3.1 million people working as cashiers, about half of them under the age of twenty-five. As the size of this population continues to shrink throughout the 1990s, openings in this occupation will be plentiful. Cashiers work at the register in a variety of stores as well as in theaters and offices. In addition to working with cash, they may perform bookkeeping functions, wrap and bag purchases, and act as receptionists. The work is entry level, requiring little or no previous work experience or educational requirements, though a high school diploma is preferred.

The United Food and Commercial Workers International Union represents about five percent of cashiers and retail clerks. Their salaries are considerably higher than the vast majority of clerks who earn little more than the federal minimum wage of $5.15 per hour. In addition, more than half of cashiers work only part-time. Their earnings do not figure in the median weekly salary of $247 for full-time cashiers. Because of the shrinking labor pool for cashiers, many employers are using higher wages, additional benefits, and flexible schedules to attract and keep cashiers on staff.

Meat Cutters

Meat cutters, who also cut and debone fish and chicken, work in supermarkets or wholesale food outlets preparing meats for purchase. Tasks include dividing meat into primal cuts, trimming fat, removing bones, and in some stores, stocking meat display cases and serving customers.

There are about 369,000 meat cutters in the United States; 217,000 of them are skilled butchers, the majority of whom work in retail grocery stores. Meat cutters can find work in almost every American town or city; a high school diploma is not even required, though it is preferred. Training is usually on the job, although some trade schools offer apprenticeship programs. Many meat cutters are represented by the United Food and Commercial Workers Union.

Butchers and meat cutters had median weekly earnings of $370 in 1996; the highest 10 percent earned over $740 per week. Meat cutters are usually among the highest paid employees in the grocery store. They also receive paid vacation and sick leave, and health and life insurance. Union meat cutters also have pension plans.

IX

Special Groups

This section has been intentionally designed as a hodgepodge, a catchall that gives the book a broader scope by enabling important topics to be included. How, for example, do the earnings of women and minorities stack up against those of white males? In addition, recent trends in the salary levels of college graduates and newly minted M.B.A.s can also be found here.

THE TEMPORARY WORKER

The task of counting the nation's temporary workers has always been a difficult one, primarily because of the difficulty of defining what makes an employee temporary. Some seasonal work, such as ski instructor or migrant farm worker, is by nature temporary since the job lasts only as long as the weather. Other temporary workers, such as contract engineers or secretaries, may work a full work week every week of the year, but at a different business each week. So it was not until 1995 that the Bureau of Labor Statistics even undertook to estimate the number of temporary workers in the United States and they have not done so since.

Estimates of the number of temporary workers range widely. According to the National Association of Temporary and Staffing Services, there were 2.5 million workers registered with temp agencies in the United States in 1997—that's about 2 percent of the total workforce and over triple the number registered in 1986. Estimates by the Bureau of Labor Statistics put the total number as high as 6 to 7 million. But since there were 8 million people holding at least two jobs in 1997, the government's figure has been called too low. Whatever the exact figure, it is clear that the trend toward temporary employment is growing, and not only for administrative positions. An increasing number of lawyers, computer programmers, and even medical professionals are working in temporary positions. In fact, some point to the rise in temporary employment as a large factor in the sharp drop in unemployment in the late 1990s.

The benefits to a company of using temporary work are obvious: Temps earn slightly more in hourly wages than do full-time employees, but usually do not accrue the benefits that accompany full-time employment. In some companies, a benefits package, including health insurance, disability or workers' compensation, life insurance, and a pension plan, increase the cost of having a full-time worker by as much as 35 percent. The company also has no long-term obligations to temporary workers and can let them go at a moment's notice without having to pay severance or unemployment insurance. Anybody who has tried to fire a union member or other employee with some amount of job security doesn't need to be told how important that flexibility is. So the hiring of temporaries can be a boon for any company where demand for labor is volatile. For years, companies have used temporary workers during periods of peak work and heavy vacation; in the current downsizing labor market, companies that have laid off full-time workers are finding they still need people to do the work and, as a consequence, are resorting to temps.

From the worker's point of view, the temps who choose not to have a permanent position talk about how much they cherish the "convenience" or "freedom" offered by temporary work. They may find themselves in a situation where temporary work is a good source of income while they look for something more permanent. Others may view a temporary assignment as a door opener for permanent work. And there are also workers who value the ability to specify where and when they will work. In all, though, only about one-third of temporary workers said they prefer their situation to a permanent job.

Things are looking up for temporary employees, however. In response to pressure from large companies that rely heavily on temp workers and wish to reduce turnover, an increasing number of temporary agencies are offering comprehensive benefits packages, including medical insurance, paid sick and vacation leave, and even tuition reimbursement or career training courses. These benefits allow "career temps" to build what is referred to as a "portfolio career"—improving their marketability by building a strong skill set rather than by gaining seniority in a company. And in today's changing job market, it is this kind of experience that is most in demand.

Additionally, recent legislation has ensured that equal opportunity laws apply to temporary workers. In the past, employers were not considered liable for unfair treatment of temporary workers because they were not technically their employers. Workers who were once left with no recourse now have the same right to equal pay and fair treatment as do full-time employees under the law. Of course, even given the new laws, many temps do not feel they receive equal treatment. Microsoft Corporation, the software giant that has had more than its share of legal battles lately, has recently come under attack for allegedly taking advantage of temp workers. Like many large corporations, Microsoft employs several thousand temporary workers. A large percentage of these are considered "long-term temps." These temps essentially do the same job as many full-time staff members but, given their temporary status, do not earn benefits. While many enjoy the flexibility their status allows, others complain of being treated as "second-class" employees. While these workers are paid very well to make up for their lack of benefits, many feel they are still missing out on the most important perk of full-time status at Microsoft—stock options. As a result, many workers have taken the company to court to recoup what they considered to be their rightful benefits. This falls into a very murky area of the law, however, and no definitive ruling has been made on the issue as yet.

Of course, the majority of temporary assignments are not of the long-term variety. The average temporary work assignment lasts up to two months with only 14 percent of the assignments lasting longer, according to the Bureau of Labor Statistics. Those that last longer usually involve professional services. Of course, the temporary worker absorbs the loss of income for any downtime between assignments.

AVERAGE HOURLY EARNINGS FOR TEMPORARY WORKERS, BY OCCUPATION, 1994

Position	Number of Workers	Average Hourly Earnings
All Occupations	**1,122,165**	**$ 7.74**
White-collar Occupations	**547,671**	**$ 9.37**
Professional Specialty and Technical Occupations	75,265	17.68
Professional Specialty	33,236	24.11
Commercial/graphic Artists	1,712	17.63
Computer systems analysts	1,779	28.75
Designers	8,351	23.04
Engineers	10,243	28.54
Registered nurses	6,164	21.98
Technical writers	1,377	22.71
Technical	42,029	12.60
Computer programmers	2,492	25.40
Drafters	5,821	13.64
Electrical and electronic technicians	6,853	10.32
Licensed practical nurses	4,908	14.30

AVERAGE HOURLY EARNINGS FOR TEMPORARY WORKERS, BY OCCUPATION, 1994

Position	Number of Workers	Average Hourly Earnings
Executive, Administrative, and Managerial Occupations	9,124	17.22
Accountants and auditors	4,323	13.96
Accountants	4,220	13.96
Auditors	103	13.83
Marketing and Sales Occupations	31,513	6.61
Cashiers	3,397	5.72
Product promoters	9,082	6.43
Telemarketing sales workers	9,041	7.18
Clerical and Administrative Support	431,769	7.96
Bookkeepers, accounting, and auditing clerks	18,332	8.30
Computer aides	249	9.44
Computer operators and printer operators	4,217	10.63
Customer service workers	18,068	7.81
Data entry operators	57,416	7.15
General office clerks	90,182	6.78
Inventory clerks	4,683	6.59
Receptionists	39,733	7.07
Secretaries	61,353	9.49
Typists and word processors	57,173	9.85
Blue-collar Occupations	**444,895**	**$ 6.02**
Precision Production, Craft and Repair	47,354	7.23
Assemblers, electrical and electronic equipment	32,495	6.60
Machine Operators, Assemblers, and Inspectors	111,593	6.26
Assemblers, other than electrical and electronic	73,092	5.97
Transportation and Material Movement Occupations	10,853	7.03
Motor vehicle operators	7,164	7.34
Handlers, Equipment Cleaners, Helpers, and Laborers	275,095	5.67
Construction laborers	10,503	5.39
Helpers	6,768	5.93
Equipment cleaners and vehicle washers	1,282	5.43
Laborers, other than construction	194,030	5.64
Material handlers	62,512	5.80
Service Occupations	**56,624**	**$ 6.28**
Janitors and cleaners	10,220	5.67
Maids and housekeepers	2,912	5.26
Nursing aides, orderlies, and attendants	23,387	7.01
Nursing aides and attendants	28,121	7.02

SOURCE: U.S. Bureau of Labor Statistics, *Occupational Compensation Survey: Temporary Help Supply Services, November 1994* (1995).

Full-time workers at temporary agencies who are responsible for hiring and placing temporary workers generally work on commission. Salary information for these employees, therefore, is highly variable and highly competitive, according to Bruce Steinberg, spokesman for the National Association of Temporary Services. The agent interviews and screens out candidates for temporary positions at large companies and receives a percentage of the temp's earnings. The agency commission can run as high as half of the total cost to the company seeking temporary help. It is not hard to understand, therefore, why some temps are dismayed to learn that they are receiving only $10 per hour when the company is paying the agency $20 for their services. About 20,000 people work full-time in temporary agencies. That number increases (as do the number of temporary workers) around the end of each decade, when the federal government hires large numbers of temporary workers to carry out the decennial census.

CHILD-CARE WORKERS

With the increase in single-parent families and families where both parents work, day care has become a fact of life in almost every American community. Today there are over 2.3 million child-care workers caring for more than 10 million children in America. About four out of ten of these workers are self-employed. The number of child-care workers is expected to grow faster than the average for all industries through the year 2006, largely because of the high numbers of mothers entering the workforce, according to the Bureau of Labor Statistics. In addition, the child-care industry has a very high turnover rate, which contributes to the growing number of opportunities available to those interested in a career in this field.

About one in four child-care establishments is affiliated with a religious institution. The rest are divided among schools and preschools, local and national chains, centers run by business firms for their own employees, and small mom-and-pop operations. Because so many centers are of this last variety (and consequently file no financial reports), total revenues generated in this burgeoning business are not known. Salary information is equally hard to find. In general, though, pay is very low. According to the Bureau of Labor Statistics (BLS), median weekly earnings for full-time salaried child-care workers were $250 in 1996, with the top 10 percent earning at least $390. The National Center for the Early Childhood Work Force, a research and advocacy project in Washington, DC, corroborates these depressing results. The Center found that the highest paid child-care teachers, those with bachelor's degrees and many of whom held certifications in early childhood education, earned an average of $14,500 per year. By comparison, the average salary for men with bachelor's degrees was more than four times that amount at $58,582, and the average for women with bachelor's degrees was $30,344, more than twice that of child-care workers with equal education in 1996. Given these figures, it is no wonder that one-third of child-care workers leave their jobs each year. According to Yasmina Vinci, executive director of the National Association of Child-Care Resource and Referral Agencies, zoo workers are more adequately paid than child-care workers.

In contrast, turnover among public school teachers is less than 6 percent per year. Preschool teachers in public schools with state certification generally earn a salary comparable to kindergarten and elementary school teachers, whose average salary was estimated by the National Education Association to be $37,336 in 1996.

The vast majority of those employed in the child-care industry are women. The following chart from the Department of Labor's Women's Bureau shows the breakdown of occupations within this field.

PERSONS EMPLOYED IN CHILD-CARE OCCUPATIONS, 1996

Child-Care Occupations	Employed	Percent / Women
Family child-care providers	479,000	98.5%
Early childhood teacher's assistants	387,000	95.4
Child-care workers, private household	276,000	97.1
Pre-kindergarten and kindergarten teachers	543,000	98.1
Teacher's aides	623,000	92.1
Total	**2,308,000**	

SOURCE: U.S. Department of Labor, Bureau of Labor Statistics, *Employment and Earnings,* January 1997.

The growing number—and notoriety—of child abuse and molestation scandals surrounding disreputable day-care centers have led many states to adopt licensing requirements that regulate care-giver training. Educational requirements can range from a high school diploma to a college or postgraduate degree in childhood development. Many states require a Childhood Development Associate credential, offered by the Council for Early Childhood Professional Recognition, which also administers a training program. The vast majority of child-care providers in the United States however, are unregulated, and are therefore not held to any particular standards of training or experience.

Child-care workers in private households are even less regulated and well-compensated than those outside of the home. According to the BLS, the median salary for household child-care workers in 1996 was $10,500, and most received little or no benefits. In what was perhaps the most public and

controversial child-care scandal of the 1990s, British au pair Louise Woodward was put on trial in Massachusetts in 1997 for the death of an eighteen-
month-old baby in her care. She was found guilty of second-degree murder
and subsequently had her conviction reduced to involuntary manslaughter
and her sentence limited to time served, all in the midst of a media frenzy.
There was public outrage on all sides, with some of the loudest voices blam-
ing the parents of the dead baby for putting him in the hands of this girl in
the first place. What the case succeeded in doing was shaking to the core
the confidence many parents held in their child-care providers.

Despite the fact that the press referred to the case as the "nanny trial,"
many in the child-care industry spoke out to explain that Ms. Woodward
was not, in fact, a *nanny*, but rather an *au pair*. A foreign au pair is defined
by the international Nanny Association as: "a foreign national in the United
States for up to a year to experience American life. Lives as a part of the host
family and receives a small allowance/salary and helps with child-care and
housework. May or may not have previous child-care experience." The International Nanny Association publishes an *Annual Directory of Nanny
Training Programs, Nanny Placement Agencies and Special Services* to aid
parents in finding suitable care-givers for their children.

A nanny, on the other hand, while not specifically required to have any
special training, has chosen child care as a career. This generally means they
have significant experience, and they often pursue training in the field to
enhance their employability. The controversy lies in parents choosing an au
pair over a professional child-care provider to save money. This case, and
others like it, have led child advocacy groups and lawmakers to reconsider
the current standards of "acceptable" child-care.

During his White House conference on Child Care, President Clinton
announced a new National Child-Care Provider Scholarship Fund that provides over $300 million over five years to up to 50,000 child-care providers
annually who care for over half a million American children. Additional
scholarships and increased pay is available for those continuing to provide
child-care service. In addition, according to a survey by the American Public
Welfare Association in 1997, states are seeking to establish quality child-
care programs as a means to move welfare recipients off assistance and into
the workforce. They also seek to create a universal system providing care to
all eligible families.

In addition, the Child Development Associate (CDA) credential is recognized nationwide in the field as a professional credential awarded to child-
care workers. Over 90,000 providers have the credential, which is
administered by the Council for Early Childhood Professional Recognition,
and each year an additional 10,000 providers apply. Among requirements
to receive the credential are Red Cross or First Aid certification, some coursework in child development, membership in an early childhood professional
organization and at least eighty hours of work experience.

Effectively implementing a sweeping change in the standard of care, however, would necessitate a significant raise in the current levels of compensation. Illustrating this point, a nursery school teacher recently lamented that two other teachers from her school left to take jobs at a fast-food restaurant where they were earning more money and had better benefits. This example does not bode well for the condition of the child-care industry in the future.

FARMERS AND FARMWORKERS

Nothing symbolizes the unparalleled abundance of America more strikingly than the richness and diversity of our food supply. So fertile is the land and so efficient the agricultural system that our farms not only feed almost 270 million Americans and millions more overseas, we actually pay farmers to limit their production so prices won't collapse. Moreover, unlike more agrarian countries where up to 40 percent of the population may work in agriculture, the United States needs less than 2 percent of its people to produce such extraordinary results. In the history of farming, interestingly enough, the principal source of America's industrial strength can be found.

In 1776, when the "embattled farmers" began their revolution against the British, more than 95 percent of the 3 million colonists were directly involved in agriculture. By 1900, only 42 percent of the nation's 70 million people lived on farms. By 1950, the population had doubled to 150 million people, but the farm population had dwindled to 23 million, or just over 15 percent of the total population. Today, fewer than 5 million people live on farms even though the population has nearly doubled again since 1950. The number of people who actually work on farms is even less: In 1996, 2.3 million people worked on farms, about half as many as in 1970.

There are just over 2 million farms in the United States today, covering just under a billion acres of land. While 17 percent of farms are of the giant commercial (averaging 1,513 acres) variety, the vast majority remain moderate-sized family-run operations. While the average farm size continues to increase dramatically, from under 430 acres in 1982 to 471 in 1997, there are more than 1 million farms of less than 200 acres. As such, they remain as vulnerable to the vagaries of weather and politics as they have been throughout history. And unlike most other sectors of the economy, where income generally follows a gradual upward progression, farm income continues to fluctuate dramatically. Since 1986, however, gross and net farm income have both increased gradually every year, even as government payments to farms have decreased. Another positive is that in 1997, the U.S. Department of Agriculture (USDA) reported a median income for farm households that was 98 percent of the median for nonfarm households.

Employment growth in rural industries has been traditionally strong, unemployment has been low, and real earnings have increased. The Bureau of Labor Statistics predicts that 18.6 million new jobs will be created by the year 2006 and 32 million will become available due to replacement needs.

Earnings for farmworkers, which once varied widely by age, race and geographic region, are now fairly uniform across the country. According to the USDA, average hourly earnings for the 848,000 hired farmworkers were $7.36 in 1997, up from $6.78 in 1996. Taken over the last two decades, however, when considering inflation, real earnings of farmworkers have actually dropped—7 percent according to the USDA—closer to 20 percent according to some independent agricultural economists. Part of the reason for this decline might be attributed to the sharp drop in the power of the United Farm Workers of America, whose membership fell from 80,000 in 1970 to 21,000 in 1993, according to *The New York Times* (March 1997). Farmworkers are also feeling the pressure of competition from a rise in the numbers of immigrant workers—resulting in a decrease in their working hours.

THE MIDDLEMEN: AGENTS, AUCTIONEERS, AND BROKERS

A person who makes his or her living by representing the interests of another person to a third party is commonly referred to as a middleman or a go-between. Their job consists of bringing buyers and sellers together (auctioneers and brokers) or of finding outlets for the work of people with special talents (agents). In both cases their chief function is negotiating a fair price or fee, and both earn their money by taking a percentage of that figure. Below are examples of both kinds of jobs, some commonplace, others slightly off-beat.

Executive Recruiters

In Europe they proudly proclaim themselves "headhunters." In America, where the term is considered pejorative, they call themselves "executive search consultants." In either case, the profession is one that has raised a good deal of controversy. Many feel that headhunters are vultures setting out to steal well-trained, relatively happy bodies from their corporations with a siren's song of high pay and unlimited advancement. And, according to the critics, they don't do the job very well, often coaxing naive managers into situations that are doomed to failure. The executive recruiter takes the view that much like the broker he is putting buyer and seller together. One thing is certain, recruiting is a profession that can be very lucrative.

Recruiters get paid for work performed much like the salesman. The recruiting firm usually receives one-third of the total first-year compensation of the selected candidate as its fee. Of this amount the recruiter who actually makes the placement receives 40 percent of the proceeds—or more if he or she brought the search assignment through the door. Much like the large law or consulting firms, compensation may grow if the recruiter plays a supervisory role or is a partner in the firm.

There can be vast differences in compensation and the nature of the work depending on the type of firm and the market for its service. Recruiters always work for the client company, and their fees are paid by the hirer not the hired. This distinguishes recruiting firms from employment agencies. The arrangement with the client differs, however, according to the type of firm— contingency or retainer. Contingency firms operate much like employment agencies. They are given the right along with a number of other firms to search for candidates to fill vacancies. The hiring company pays the fee only to the firm that finds the person finally hired. The retainer firm, on the other hand, is granted an exclusive right to search for appropriate candidates: Progress payments are made, so the retainer firm receives up to 75 percent of its fee regardless of whether it completes the search or not.

As a rule, contingency firms operate at the lower end of the compensation spectrum, where quantity and speed rather than quality are the keys to success. Given the need to perform to get paid, the contingency world is highly competitive, and some may be highly unprincipled in meeting the pressure. On the retainer side, where the search may reach the proportions of finding a new CEO for IBM or American Express and compensation packages may be expressed in the upper 6 or 7 figures, quality, discretion, and judgment are emphasized. Here the process is more deliberate and the potential rewards per search are much higher. This type of search is a careful process of rooting out the most appropriate, best-qualified people to fill demanding positions rather than running a list of qualified people past a client.

Given our rule of thumb on compensation—40 percent of the one-third that the firm receives—ample compensation can be earned on either side of the industry. In general, the contingency recruiter has to make more placements, but there are more to be made. Since contingency firms work at the low end of the market, the average first-year compensation may be only $36,000. So in order for the recruiter to earn $75,000, it would take about sixteen successful placements.

On the retainer side, where the average package is normally in the $100,000 to $200,000 range, it may take only half as many placements to reach the same range of income. An experienced retainer recruiter should be able to complete eight to twelve searches a year. Thus the recruiter who completes eight searches at $100,000 each would make about $100,000. This is about the industry average, according to *Executive Recruiter News,* an industry publication. For partners-level consultants at the upper end, compensation ranges from $300,000 to $500,000. The presidents and CEOs of major firms earned over $2 million in 1998, according to Hurt-Scanlon Consultants. The accompanying chart details revenues and billings per recruiter for the ten largest U.S. firms. The compensation figures are derived by multiplying the billings per recruiter by the 40 percent commission.

Obviously most search firms are smaller than the ten listed in the table, and a majority are operations of less than three people, grossing less than $1 million per year. But the estimates provide a good guide nonetheless, since size of billings in total has very little to do with individual compensation. Of more importance is the average fee value of the searches undertaken. There are many firms where that value exceeds $100,000. Since an experienced recruiter ought to be able to close one search a month, it would not be uncommon for the average professional in a small firm to earn as much or more than those at the larger firms, provided business is good.

REVENUES, BILLINGS, AND EARNINGS AT THE 10 LARGEST U.S. RETAINED SEARCH FIRMS

Firm Name	Total Revenues	Billings per Recruiter	Estimated Compensation per Recruiter[1]
Korn Ferry International	$102,200,000	$577,401	$231,000
Heidrick & Struggles, Inc.	86,900,000	886,735	354,700
SpencerStuart	69,700,000	967,361	386,900
Russell Reynolds Associates	61,700,000	582,075	232,800
Lamalie Amrop International	28,300,000	577,551	231,000
Paul Ray Berndtson	26,500,000	602,273	240,900
A. T. Kearney Executive Search	22,500,000	459,184	183,700
Ward Howell International	16,500,000	458,333	183,300
Egon Zehnder International	14,100,000	742,105	296,800
Witt/Kieffer Ford Hadelman & Lloyd	12,200,000	338,889	133,600

[1]Compensation figures calculated by *The American Almanac of Jobs and Salaries.*
SOURCE: © 1995 *Executive Recruiter News.* Reprinted with permission of Kennedy Publications, Fitzwilliam, NH.

Literary Agents

In a well-known interview from the late 1980s, Perry Knowlton, former head of the Curtis Brown Ltd. Literary Agency, gave a condensed explanation of the agent's role as publishing middleman. "It seems to me that 50 years ago publishers looked down on agents and didn't want to have anything to do with them. Nowadays, publishers would almost rather work with an agent. He leaves the relationship between the editor and the author relatively free of all the nastiness of the business aspects of writing."

Agents represent authors to publishers. They evaluate proposals or manuscripts and, if they deem them salable, submit them to the most suitable publishers for consideration. The right house is not automatically the one offering the highest advance, either: Agents have been known to choose a house offering less if the editor is enthusiastic enough about the product to stay behind it through all phases of the publishing process or if he or she has the right reputation for a special kind of book.

Once upon a time, book projects were submitted to only one publisher at a time. Nowadays, agents routinely send even first novels to several houses simultaneously, complete with response deadlines. Some 20 years ago, "superagent" Scott Meredith revolutionized the business with the introduction of the auction. Since then, it has become common practice to send properties to ten or more publishers, giving them the choice of telephoning a bid on the appointed day or offering an earlier preemptive bid instead.

Once a sale is made, agents run a fine-tooth comb through contracts, which tend to arrive in a standard form that gives the publisher most of the advantages unless marked otherwise. Later, agents often become involved in subsidiary rights sales, such as magazine excerpts, TV and film deals, and paperback contracts. In between, there's a lot of hand-holding and encouragement.

Successful literary agents usually combine a knowledge of book publishing with an instinct for public taste that is often more finely honed than that of many editors. When agent J. Garon took on John Grisham, for example, his work had already been turned down by many publishers. But Garon believed in the author and persevered. After receiving a super deal from Doubleday, through Garon's efforts, Grisham's tepid novels have become international bestsellers in hardcover and paperback, and have been made into high-budget movies as well.

Agents' earnings come from commissions. The standard rate was 10 percent of all the author's earnings from the book, including advance and royalties. Most agents now take 15 percent. Many agents also deduct expenses made on a client's behalf. The individual nature of the business makes it impossible to gauge earnings with any accuracy. It's only safe to say they range enormously, often getting better with time. Literary agenting usually does not pay off for the first year or two, before books sold to publishers are actually printed and capable of earning royalties, and before agents establish the reputation that brings them money-generating clients. But the ultimate possibilities are dazzling.

So-called "super" agents such as Mort Janklow, Lynn Nesbit, and Andrew Wylie (a person known in the business as "the Jackal") represent sure-fire best-seller writers and are reportedly uninterested in advances below $300,000, so they earn $45,000 per initial book contract, not to mention 15 percent of movie and TV offerings.

Another well-known agent is John Brockman, who specializes in obtaining large advances for writers of serious science books. Often these people are well-known scientists who have been accustomed to writing academic monographs for free. Brockman has been known to get $300,000 to $800,000 for these people by tapping into the worldwide interest in science whose major figures today usually write in English. (See also the entry, "Writers," later in this section, for recent book deals of some note.)

Models' Agents and Bookers

Models' agents arrange bookings for their listed models. When advertising agencies, clothing designers, department stores, and others requiring the use of a model have an opening, they contact an agency, sometimes several. The agency then sends the models fitting the client's requirements on what is often termed a "go-see."

The hottest agencies in New York are the Eileen Ford Agency, Elite, Zoli, Click, Next, and Company. All these agencies manage a stable of runway and editorial models who earn from $100,000 to $400,000 a year. Their reputations as the top agencies result because they represent the exclusive group of supermodels who earn from $500,000 to several million dollars a year. These models, who generally have contracts with cosmetic companies and appear routinely on the covers of women's magazines, include Shalom Harlow, Naomi Campbell, Claudia Schiffer, Amber Valetta, Tyra Banks, and Irina.

While the agents earn the top salaries, many models are more loyal to the agencies' bookers than to the owners. Bookers do what their name implies: They book models for shows, magazines, and advertisements. Often the professional becomes personal as the booker juggles the models' schedules and a symbiotic relationship forms. If a booker jumps to a new agency often he or she will take a coterie of models along. A booker typically earns in the range of $80,000; the supermodel bookers can earn in the $200,000 and up range.

The agents wield a double-edged sword in earning their money. Standard commissions are 20 percent from the model, plus 15 percent from the client. In other words, if a booking comes in for a $1,000 assignment, the agency bills the client for $1,100 and also deducts $200 from the check handed the model, who receives $800. When you consider that percentage on a $15,000 assignment, which is what top models earn for a day of fashion shooting or runway work, or on a $100,000 payment for a major fashion show, the net result is a not untidy profit, even after the telephone bills have been paid.

Real Estate Agents and Brokers

Like other types of agents, people in real estate embody the hustle-to-get-ahead nature of hard-core free enterprise. This is the business of the mythical Florida land scheme, and in which one in twenty Californians holds a real estate license.

Previously one of the faster growing occupations, jobs for real estate agents and brokers are not expected to grow any faster than the average rate through the year 2006. There are just under 400,000 agents and brokers in the United States today. The vast majority of these are sales agents, independent sales workers who contract out their services to real estate brokers in return for a portion—usually half—of the agency's commission on the sale of property. Brokers, who number about 75,000, are independent business people who buy and sell real estate for others, and in some cases rent and manage properties for a fee. Brokers may also help prospective buyers line up financing for their purchase in order to facilitate a sale.

An additional 48,000 people work as *real estate appraisers,* who provide unbiased estimates of a property's value and quality. This is the fastest-growing occupation in the real estate industry, with an expected growth of 25 percent by 2006.

All fifty states and the District of Columbia require prospective agents to be a high school graduate, be at least eighteen years old, and pass a written test of their knowledge of property laws and real estate transaction, in order to receive a realtor's license. Most states also require classroom training of at least thirty hours for a sales license and ninety hours for a broker's license. Brokers generally also need anywhere from one to three years of selling experience before they can apply for the broker's license.

The standard commission on the sale of a house is 6 percent. Traditionally this figure is presented to sellers as if it were a legislated rate. However, the commission is negotiable; and in the present climate of frenzied buying and selling, it's often slashed as part of the broker's competition to obtain listings. On the other hand, if a firm can receive an exclusive listing, giving its brokers exclusive showing rights for a set period of time, commissions can rise to 10 to 15 percent. Some agents routinely charge higher commissions on properties valued under $150,000.

The money can be excellent—if you can survive the first year. Newcomers go through brief, intensive training, and then, according to Long Beach, New York, agent Doris Newalk, "You don't get to sell houses until you've been there six months to a year. You handle rentals at first, for a small percentage, but that cannot support you. You need another job or another wage-earner in the family for that first year."

Because industry averages reflect not just the long-time agent but also the large number of people who leave the business after less than a year, salary averages are low. So even though median earnings for full-time agents were about $31,500 a year in 1996, the agent who has been in the business for at least a few years earns a figure closer to $50,000. And as in all sales jobs, what you earn depends on what you sell. According to *The New York times,* top agents selling Manhattan's and Los Angeles's choicest coops, town houses, and condominiums earn upward of $200,000. The top 10 percent of all brokers earned over $75,000 a year in 1996 according to the U.S. Department of Labor.

Sports Agents

Most people representing professional athletes have two things in common: They are lawyers, and they are very well heeled. Just a glimpse at the lists of sports stars' salaries in Part II of this book will reveal why sports agents make so much money. The standard agent's fee for contract negotiation is 5 percent, which amounts to $100,000 on a $2 million contract, a commonplace figure for today's sports superstars. Some agents with several multimillion-dollar athletes in their stable often wield substantial power in professional sports; at times their ability to shape team rosters and payrolls exceeds that of a team's general manager. For example, it was rumored that agent David Falk urged Xavier McDaniel to leave New York and accept an offer from the Boston Celtics because Falk was worried that McDaniel would have turned the Knicks into a serious title threat to the Chicago Bulls, whose star player, Michael Jordan, is Falk's bread and butter. Of course, since Falk also represents Knicks' center Patrick Ewing—who earns about 20 million a year—the rumors were probably little more than conjecture by a few sportswriters, but it's not hard to imagine other agents being motivated solely by the interests of their most profitable clients.

The proliferation of multimillion-dollar contracts for athletes has filled the sports pages with the names of as many agents as stars. Many agents specialize in one particular sport, though they usually have a few clients in each sport. Falk specializes primarily in basketball; Scott Boras, Jerry Kapstein and Richard Moss are among the best known baseball agents; Leigh Steinberg's stable of athletes contains mostly football players, most of whom are quarterbacks.

Boras is the newest star among agents, and his annual income has been estimated at 5 million. He represents Greg Maddux, Bernie Williams, as well as fifty other major leaguers and thirty-five minor leaguers.

Agents in other sports like golf and tennis may not be household names, but when their clients bring in millions of dollars each year, the agents still profit from it. Golf and tennis agents generally receive 10 percent of the player's winnings and as much as 25 percent of endorsement income. For well-known players like Arnold Palmer, who may not be at the top of their games, endorsement income often far outstrips winnings, making the agent's percentage substantial. For more information about endorsements, see the entry in Part II, "In the Public Eye and Behind the Scenes."

There are other middlemen in sports. In boxing, managers usually receive 33 percent of their fighters' prizes, while trainers receive about 10 percent. There are exceptions, however, especially when a fighter hits it big.

Travel Agents

For many years, the deregulation of the airline industry made the professional travel agent irreplaceable. The dizzying array of options that opened to travelers—a simple flight from New York to Los Angeles suddenly could present a choice of four or five airlines and six or seven fare options—almost necessitated exploiting a travel agent's skills at finding the cheapest and most convenient itinerary. And the price to the consumer—nothing—was right.

Ironically, the deregulated airline industry almost sounded the travel agents' death knell. For while deregulation no doubt reduced the cost of air travel, it also resulted in the establishment of three megagiants (American, Delta, and United) that increasingly dictate prices and fees in the industry. So when Delta, American, and Northwest airlines all announced in February 1995 that they would no longer pay travel agents the customary 10 percent commission on airline tickets but would instead cap commissions at $50 for a domestic round-trip ticket, many agents felt powerless to do anything about it.

For several years the business floundered even more noticeably as more and more people became aware that the Internet gave them as much information as a travel agent could.

But the strong economy and an even stronger dollar dragged many Americans out of their homes and made travel one of the most popular activities of the decade. Good agents seized the moment and began doing what individuals couldn't: securing low fares and room rates by guaranteeing sizable numbers of people to the much more competitive marketplace of hotels, resorts, and spas. So while the largest airlines were trying to cut them out, other parts of the industry saw the value of the travel agent's service as invaluable.

Carnival Cruise Lines, for example, said it would raise the agent's take from 10 to 12 percent. Amtrak announced that on short-term promotions, the agent's commission would be as high as 15 percent instead of the 10 percent it now awards. And the Hotel Reservations Network, a nationwide hotel booking service, said it would double its 5 percent agent's commission to 10 percent. Also, commissions on international airfares, which range from 8 to 11 percent, were not affected by the airlines' recent reduction.

It's no wonder, then, that many agents are predicting that selling airline tickets will be a much smaller portion of what they do in the future. According to the American Society of Travel Agents, airline tickets constituted 61 percent of travel agency revenues in 1992. Today, industry officials say, the percentage is closer to the low 50s and it is expected to decline even further. Moreover, with agency commissions running at over $1 billion per year at the biggest airlines (making it their third-biggest expense after salaries and fuel), the airlines may not lament some drop-off in business from travel agents, especially if those same customers book their tickets directly. Currently, only about one in five customers books airline tickets without a travel agent.

There are about 142,000 travel agents working in approximately 30,000 agencies across the United States. And even though close to 3,000 agencies go broke every year (nearly three times as many as in 1987), job opportunities for travel agents are expected to expand much faster than average for all jobs as business and leisure travel continue to grow. Some estimates place growth in this industry at over 80,000 jobs over the next ten years.

The number of jobs in this field is heavily dependent on the health of the economy as travel is one of the first things businesses and individuals cut back on during hard times. Almost 150,000 people worked as travel agents in 1997, a significant increase over the recession years of 1991–92. Most agents at travel agencies are salaried, but some work as independent contractors. Those who have been in the business long enough to develop a following may work at an agency's offices but receive a portion of the agency's commissions (sometimes as high as 50 to 70 percent of what the agency receives). Others may work through, but outside, an agency's offices or as part-timers. These agents may receive 25 to 50 percent of the agency's commission in lieu of salary. About nine out of ten agents work for an agency; the rest are self-employed.

Earnings for travel agents are determined by many factors, including experience, sales ability, and the size and location of the agency. According to *Travel Weekly* magazine, beginning travel agents earned about $16,500 in 1996, while experienced agents earned anywhere from $25,000 to $33,000. Those numbers are not appreciably different from salaries earned by travel agents in 1992. Salaried agents usually have standard benefits like health and disability insurance and paid vacations.

Self-employed agents pay their own benefits, but they make considerably more than the averages printed above. However, the investment required to start an independent travel agency is estimated to be approximately $75,000.

What must be considered, however, are the travel benefits that come with the job. These can include discounts as high as 75 percent off domestic travel, and the same off international flights after one year in the business. Hotels also offer many concessions to agents, including free rooms during off-peak season.

Even with these benefits, the salary and income figures are surprisingly low. A large number of people working as travel agents are women who are not primarily family wage earners but who enjoy the work for the considerable travel benefits offered. Many young people also work for agencies for the same reason.

"Most men in this business are agency owners," says one experienced agent, "and agency owners are the only people in the field who do make good money." As usual, this fact of business life is a tough one to change. In an industry dominated by family operators, many agency owners were brought into the business by relatives who were already in travel. One assumes that, in the future, more daughters will have both the interest and the opportunity to inherit the family business.

Job opportunities for travel agents will be available in most regions of the country, but according to P. Jason King, president of Yours in Travel Personnel Agency, most travel agent jobs will be found on the East Coast, particularly in Boston, New York City, Washington, DC, and Florida. California, Chicago, Dallas, Denver, and Phoenix will also offer good opportunities. Strong growth in managerial, professional, and sales occupations—the people who travel the most on business—should also spark an increase in sales for travel agents, especially those with corporate clients. Travel agents with foreign language skills will also thrive in the coming years.

Agencies that are best able to adapt to the changing travel environment will have the most success in the 1990s. That means creating specialized itineraries to places like Disney World, the Grand Ole Opry, or the Great Barrier Reef. It also means catering to specialized audiences like senior citizens, music aficionados, honeymooners, or the environmentally conscious. They must also use the Internet effectively by showing people that their expertise and knowledge cannot be duplicated just by surfing the Web for bargains.

And it also means cruises, cruises, cruises. Agents typically receive a 12 percent commission on cruises, which sell for several thousand dollars per person. Because of the high-dollar volume involved, more than 800 travel agencies now sell cruises exclusively. As more airlines continue to cut their commissions, this trend can only be expected to continue.

Auctioneers

The auction has long been a popular way of selling all kinds of things from rare works of art to parcels of real estate, household goods, even livestock. The National Auctioneers' Association, a trade group with 6,000 members, estimates that the number of auctioneers has doubled in the last decade. One reason for the increase is the possibility of good pay. The head of a Missouri school of auctioneering estimates annual income to be about $50,000 to $60,000 for a successful auctioneer.

As with all middleman jobs, the auctioneer takes a percentage of the total sale as a commission for his efforts. For real estate the figure is usually 6 percent; for household sales, 20 percent or more.

WRITERS

The term "writer" carries with it a lot of cultural baggage, some of it dragged along from the nineteenth century, some from the era when Fitzgerald and Hemingway were supposedly forging a modern American sensibility. Images of the writer as a lonely artist or indefatigable scholar are ones we all absorbed in school, probably to the detriment of our own development: Who, after all, could measure up? On the other hand, at that age who knew that people actually had jobs as writers that didn't require psychic immolation and an unwavering commitment to Art and Knowledge?

For most professionals, however, today as well as in the past, writing is not so much a creative exercise as it is a skill, a way to make a living, a career like banking or engineering. Writers who work on a freelance basis for magazines, for example, must be able to adapt their styles to the publication's needs. Until the writer has a reputation in a particular subject, he or she will have to cover a variety of topics for several magazines. Technical writers, on the other hand, must acquire knowledge in complex subjects such as chemistry or medicine so that their writing and editing skills can be used to communicate information to the public or to business leaders.

For young college graduates the question of whether to pursue a career as a writer is not a simple one. Some observers say that jobs for writers will be plentiful. In a society where the rudimentary forms of literacy are supposedly declining faster than enrollments in English literature classes, one would think the skill of writing would be marketable. But others insist that the "crisis" in literacy is a media-created myth since the number of books and magazines have proliferated over the last decade in unprecedented fashion. In fact, not only are more people reading more than ever before, more writers are generating more words than society can possibly absorb. Although over 60,000 new books are published each year, publishers tell of receiving literally thousands of unsolicited manuscripts that not only don't get read but frequently are returned unopened. Magazine editors, too, say they receive more articles and suggestions than ever before.

Just how many writers or would-be writers there are may be impossible to ascertain. Professional groups such as the Writers Guild and the Authors Guild, both of which require at least a modicum of success for membership, account for only 15,000 people. But other signs, such as the 100,000-plus circulation of *Writer's Digest* and the brisk sales of an annual publication called *Writer's Marketplace,* indicate that a large number of people are looking for realistic, professional advice about how to make money as a writer. Many of them are, of course, disguised as editorial assistants and copy editors in publishing houses, or as accountants and housewives who work on their computers in spare hours. What they have in common, however, is the tenacity to pursue very demanding work without guarantee of reward.

This section focuses on writers who produce material for books and magazines, and it ends with a short discussion of the fast-growing field of technical writing. For those readers interested in other kinds of writing jobs, see in Part II the sections "Who Makes What in the Film Industry" for script writers and "Behind the Scenes in Television" for television news writers; still more information can be found in Part V in the section "Public Relations," and in Part VI in the section "The Newspaper."

Writers of Books

If you've written your first book, or even part of one, and are looking to find a publisher, the best advice anyone can give you is to find a literary agent who likes your work well enough to represent it (see the previous section, "The Middlemen"). So many manuscripts are being written today that editors find it almost impossible to properly evaluate unsolicited work. Most editors now rely on a small enclave of New York City–based agents to screen the works of would-be writers. But even if you do find a willing agent, there are some basic items in every publisher's contract that every writer should know about, mainly because they all affect one's income. Whether you write fiction or nonfiction, reference books or textbooks, and whether your words appear between cloth or paper covers, the following terms are relevant to your work: *royalties, advances against royalties,* and *subsidiary rights.*

ROYALTIES

In those forms of publishing designed to make a profit, the author usually receives from the publisher a percentage of the take based on the list price of each book. On clothbound trade books (the ones you see in bookstores), the standard royalty clause is 10 percent on the first 5,000 copies sold; 12.5 percent on the next 5,000; and 15 percent on everything after 10,000 copies. So, for example, if a $25 book sold 10,000 copies, the author would earn $28,125; if it sold 50,000 copies, the figure would be $178,125; and if it became a best-seller and sold 200,000 copies, the author would earn $740,625.

Royalties on paperbacks are always lower because the margin of profit is smaller, or at least that's what the publishers say. On trade paperbacks, such as the one you're reading, royalty rates range from 6 percent of the list price to 10 percent, rarely going any higher. Trade paperbacks, the fastest-growing form of publishing, are priced above $8.95 and are usually sold in bookstores or department stores. Mass-market paperbacks are the least expensive and are distributed through candy stores, drugstores, and airport shops as well as traditional book outlets. Royalty rates for mass-market paperbacks vary greatly depending on the author. A standard royalty arrangement for an author not considered a star property is 6 percent of the list price on the first 150,000 copies; 8 percent on 150,000 to 500,000; and 10 percent thereafter. Perennially best-selling authors such as Danielle Steel reportedly receive 15 percent on every paperback copy.

College textbook publishers usually pay royalties based on the book's net price—i.e., what the bookstore paid for it, which is usually 20 percent less than the list price. Standard royalty rates are 12 percent of net, rising to 15 percent and then 18 percent, depending on the projected sales rates. College publishers will frequently try to pay less, but with some prodding most are willing to follow these guidelines.

ADVANCE AGAINST ROYALTIES

When a publisher decides to take on a project, he or she will usually pay the author a lump sum of money called an *advance*. The practice developed to help struggling authors eat and pay the rent while they finished their books. It has evolved into the most important point of negotiation for books sought by several publishers.

Strictly speaking, money given "in advance" of publication is actually a no-interest loan since authors are required to pay it back through their royalties after the book is published. No royalties are paid until the advance has been earned back through actual sales of the book. If the book does not sell in sufficient quantities, however, the author is not required to pay back any of the advance money.

Most advances are paid in two installments: half on signing of the contract; half on delivery of the final manuscript. When the sum exceeds $50,000 or so, it is often paid one-third on signing; one-third on delivery of half the manuscript; and one-third on delivery of the rest.

Authors and their agents are, of course, enamored of large advances, but not just for immediate gain. In theory a big advance means that the publisher will do much more promotional work so that the book sells and the lump sum can be recouped. In today's economic and cultural climate, however, agents claim that the size of the average advance is declining. A very good project rarely brings over $75,000, they say. Supposedly this is because so much big money is going to what publishers believe will be the boffo best-seller, often an imitation of a book already on the best-seller lists. While many publishers keep searching for derivative works, most first novels and serious nonfiction books bring advances of $7,500 to $25,000.

Only recently advances of over $1 million were paid to such established writers as Norman Mailer, John Irving, and Arthur C. Clarke. Today any writer who has had a best-seller commands millions in upfront payments. Robert Ludlum, John Jakes, Len Deighton, Jean Auel, Ken Follett, Mary Higgins Clark, and Jeffrey Archer now sign multibook deals for $10 to $15 million. Barbara Taylor Bradford and Danielle Steel command over $6 million for each book. In 1995 Clive Cussler entered this exclusive circle when he signed a two-book deal for $14 million (for United States and Canadian rights only). Tom Wolfe reportedly received $7 million for his 1998 best-seller, *A Man in Full,* and Sue Grafton and David Baldacci are guaranteed $5 million per book. But even these figures are being overshadowed.

Stephen King and Tom Clancy once commanded $10 million per book. Now they have become partners with their publishers, receiving guarantees of profit participation that could generate over $20 million per book. John Grisham and Michael Crichton are the only writers in the same league, but they also receive enormous sums for the film rights to their books. (Crichton's estimated income in 1998 was $65 million.)

Among nonfiction writers, Kitty Kelley has been the highest paid in recent years. She reportedly received over $2 million for her scathing biography of Nancy Reagan and nearly $5 million for a book about the British royal family. Dick Morris, President Clinton's political guru, got $3 million for a book about politics that sunk like a stone.

Celebrities of any type—actor, athlete, or businessperson—can almost always obtain a substantial advance for their autobiographies. In recent years, Colin Powell ($6 million), Marlon Brando ($5 million), Mia Farrow ($3 million), General Norman Schwarzkopf ($5 million), Magic Johnson ($5 million for two books), and Sam Walton ($4 million) were the biggest money winners. And the O. J. Simpson double murder trial made millionaires of prosecutors of Marcia Clark and Christopher Darden, who, despite failing to win a conviction, signed book deals valued at $4 million and $2 million respectively. Darden's book was a success, but Clark's failed miserably. Even O. J.'s girlfriend, Paula Barbieri, got a $3 million advance, and Denise Brown got $1 million for the story of her sister Nicole, O. J.'s murdered wife. In 1998 Aristotle Onassis's private secretary was given $1 million for a book called *The Onassis Women,* and so was syndicated gossip columnist Liz Smith for a book of her recollections.

In recent years, famous comedians such as Jerry Seinfeld, Jay Leno, and Paul Reiser each received over $4 million advances for their "thoughts" on life and its vicissitudes (only Leno's flopped). Whoopi Goldberg reportedly received $6 million for something called *Book,* which disappeared in three weeks.

In any kind of publishing, the key to obtaining a large advance—say, one over $100,000—is to get more than one publisher interested in the project. The book is then auctioned off to the highest bidder. Even a first-time author (with a skillful agent), can negotiate an advance approaching $1 million if he or she succeeds in getting several publishers to bid against each other. Most trade publishers today often pay higher advances than they could ever realistically expect to recover through sales alone. For books with very good sales prospects, the publisher counts on income from subsidiary rights to make up the difference and then some.

SUBSIDIARY RIGHTS

Most material written to appear in book form can usually have a life outside that medium. All writers should know that in exchange for putting up the capital, publishers expect to share in any income derived from any other printed version of the work.

Magazines and newspapers are obvious examples of media that thrive on reprinting excerpts from books. Sometimes they choose whole chapters, sometimes rewritten summaries of whole sections. The author is almost always paid for this, but the sum depends on the size of the excerpt, the nature and circulation of the periodical or newspaper, and, of course, the reputation of the writer and the topicality of the subject. In addition, if the publication acquires the rights to publish the excerpt before the book appears (these are called "first serial rights"), it usually must pay more than if the book is already available ("second serial rights"). If you are a writer without an agent, you should know that publishers usually split second serial fees fifty-fifty, but for first serial rights, the writer keeps 90 percent.

Two traditional, and frequently very lucrative, sources of subsidiary rights income are simply reprints of the existing work after it is published. First, if a clothbound trade book is picked up by one or more book clubs, especially the two largest, Book-of-the-Month Club and the Literary Guild, the author will receive another advance as well as royalties on every copy of the club's edition. Second, if the publisher licenses another house to do a paperback version of the work, the author receives another advance and royalties. For best-selling books or those expected to be best-sellers, these deals can be very lucrative.

Over the past five years or so the blockbuster paperback sale has diminished in visibility and importance as large hardcover publishing houses have merged with or acquired the major paperback houses. Now almost all of the megadeals include all rights including paperback. The largest paperback sales in recent years were for Terry McMillan's *Waiting to Exhale* ($2.6 million), Robert Harris's *Fatherland* ($1.8 million), Frank McCourt's *Angela's Ashes* ($1 million) and Gail Sheehy's *The Silent Passage* ($1 million).

Of increasing importance to authors is the value of their work overseas. All of the largest publishers—such as Penguin USA and HarperCollins—are now part of international corporations. Bantam Doubleday Dell, St. Martin's, and Random House are owned outright by large German publishers. All these houses seek world rights for their properties and authors (and their agents) and often must struggle to obtain fair market prices for these rights. Most publishers will give the author 75 percent of the monies received from a foreign publisher, but if they are selling books to their own company, be it in London or in Australia, they try to pay the author as little as possible.

As a result, most agents try to retain foreign rights, preferring to hire an agent who specializes in this field. Germany, Japan, the United Kingdom, France, Spain, and Holland are all excellent markets for U.S. titles, and their total advances can reach $100,000 to $300,000 quite easily.

And with Hollywood waiting to capitalize on the success of any bestseller, the movie rights fees for a popular page-turner can often outweigh the earnings from the book. Tom Clancy, Stephen King, John Grisham, and *The Bridges of Madison County* author Robert James Waller have all profited more handsomely from the movie versions than from the books they were based on. But perhaps the most curious example is that of Nicholas Evans, who received a $3.2–million book deal for his novel *The Horse Whisperer* only *after* he had negotiated another $3.2 million from Hollywood Pictures for the film rights.

The other burgeoning subrights areas are audio and electronic publishing. Most publishers try to retain 50 percent of all the monies, but strong resistance has begun to set in as these new media begin to become commonplace. Now publishers who retain these rights are merely acting as the author's agent so a 20 to 50 percent fee should be more than adequate.

Magazine Writers

Most magazine articles are written by freelancers, not staff writers, who produce mostly service copy—blurbs about clothes and other merchandise featured. The reasons are twofold. The first is cost: It is much cheaper to pay a one-shot fee to a freelancer than an annual salary and benefits. The other reason is originality. Editors, chained to their desks, rely on freelancers to spot emerging trends, uncover topical issues, and sniff out stories. The pay for all this work ranges from dismal to dazzling, depending on the circulation and reputation of the magazine.

One of the most difficult aspects of freelance writing is breaking into a magazine. Even established writers have trouble getting magazine editors to answer their letters and phone calls. Magazines that appeal to mass audiences like *Seventeen* and *Rolling Stone* get hundreds of queries a year, most of which end up in a "slush" pile read by college interns. Writers trying to break into the magazine market need a track record, demonstrated by "clips" from smaller publications or newspapers. With 11,000 magazines in the United States covering virtually every field and interest, there are lots of opportunities for writers to begin at small "books." For example, a writer interested in music reviews might start freelancing at one of the small circulation music magazines or in the arts section of a midsized newspaper. Listings of magazines by category with their publication guidelines are available in several reference books including *The Writer's Market*.

To get an assignment, a writer first must understand a magazine's niche. Each of the dozens of magazines aimed at young women believes it carves out an editorial backdrop that no one else does. *Cosmopolitan* looks for chatty, personal articles about relationships and *sex*, while *Glamour*, which attracts basically the same age audience, wants articles that call on experts for advice in these areas. Some magazines publish travel articles and run technology columns, and others don't. That's why it is essential to study a year's worth of back issues of a particular magazine to find the topics that are routinely covered. It's also important to discern the tone and attitude of a particular magazine. *Good Housekeeping*, which appeals to mid-thirties women and up, tends toward an authoritative tone as compared with *Redbook*, which likes a breezy writing style for readers in their late twenties and early thirties. One frequent reason for a rejection letter is that the idea is not targeted to a particular magazine's subject matter or approach. Editors lament, "Do freelancers actually read our magazine?"

Magazine writing requires the ability to come up with fresh, original ideas followed through with good research, reporting, and writing—six months in advance of the issue date. Writers learn to think of winter holiday articles in July. While most fledgling writers are generalists, it's wise to also specialize in at least one area. Writers can spot emerging trends and new developments before they make the mainstream press. Writers trying to break into the mass circulation consumer market can use that expert information to pitch story ideas for a 1,000-word department article, known as a front- or back-of-the-book piece. Once a short piece has run in a magazine, it's much easier to try for a feature of 2,000 words and up in the main editorial "well."

A story is usually proposed in a query letter, which describes the idea, outlines the research and reporting, and gives the writer's credentials. Many magazines will only consider queries, automatically rejecting completed manuscripts. If the idea is accepted, the writer signs a contract agreeing to do the piece for a specified amount on deadline. If the writer is new, often the editor will assign the piece on speculation (or spec), meaning that the magazine will consider the finished piece but is not obligated to buy it.

The payment ranges from 50 cents a word to $4 a word, depending on the writer's reputation and the publication. *The New Yorker* is reported to have paid some marquee writers $25,000 for 10,000-word pieces during Tina Brown's reign as editor. For an established freelancer the going rate at major magazines is usually between $1 to $2 a word. Most magazines also pay for expenses like phone calls and travel. A "kill fee" of 20 to 25 percent is paid for a contracted piece if it is not used.

Magazines pay in two different ways: on acceptance and on publication. On acceptance means when the editors accept the piece (usually after a rewrite and fact-checking), payment is authorized. On publication means when the piece is published. Since magazines often work on issues four to six months in advance, on publication payment is obviously not preferred. However, that's the payment method used by smaller publications where new writers break in.

While some people do make a living writing for magazines, it is a difficult life that requires persistence, hustle, and a high energy level, not to mention talent. Many freelancers supplement their magazine income by writing for corporations, public relations firms, educational publishers, and other less glamourous outlets.

A new outlet for magazine writers is on-line publications, ranging from *Salon* to celebrity fanzines. The on-line publications that pay writers a fee usually take advertising so they are easy to distinguish from the charity cases. The digital magazines work in much the same way as their print counterparts, although they usually have a much shorter lead time because there's no production. Another major difference is that articles are usually a lot shorter (up to 1,000 words) and usually pay less. Also, the writing style tends to resemble e-mailese, with sentence fragments, a casual tone, and lots of hyperlinks. Usually on the magazine's logo is a spot to click for information about the magazine, its staff, and guidelines for freelance submissions.

Below are some current rates for well-known magazines:

Cooking Light	85 cents to $1.26 a word for 2,000 words
Country Living	$300 to $800 for 1,200 words
Men's Journal	$1 to $1.25 a word for up to 2,000 words
Vibe	$1 a word; any length
Family Life	$4,000 for 1,500 to 2,500 words; $1,500 for 1,200-word columns; $400 for 300-word short articles

Ghostwriters

Some call them hacks, some call them godsends, but there's no doubt that many people do call on ghostwriters for assistance in literary ventures. And they have been with us a long time: It's thought that Roman emperor Nero's speeches were ghosted by Seneca, that *The Autobiography of Ulysses S. Grant* was written by Mark Twain, and that even Washington's Farewell Address was prepared by Alexander Hamilton. More recent items of speculation include *The Autobiography of Malcolm X*: How much was written by Alex Haley? And what part was Theodore Sorensen's contribution to John F. Kennedy's *Profiles in Courage*?

Ghostwriters' clients are a varied lot. They include gothic romance publishing houses, politicians, scientists, celebrities, and wealthy narcissists looking to tell their story whether or not anyone will buy it.

Today, many ghostwriters work as part of an agency. S. J. Michelson, seventy-three, employs 200 from his New York–based service. According to *The New York Times*, Robin Moore, credited with *The French Connection*, *The Green Berets*, and *The Happy Hooker*, farmed out most of the forty-five or so books published under his name in the last ten years.

If the credit is elusive, the money is quite tangible in ghosting. Several established writers will tackle most projects for between $1,000 and $6,000 in a flat-fee arrangement. Where books are involved, most ghosts opt for what has become the standard in publishing: 50 percent of the author's earnings. For major books, the ghostwriter frequently receives a large fee or advance. Michael Novak, for example, received $80,000 for *Iacocca* (Iacocca himself made $6 million); Novak, however, has become the most sought-after "ghost" and now gets full billing with the authors (including Tip O'Neill and Nancy Reagan) and probably half the royalties.

Technical Writers

Technical writers work for industry, government, and nonprofit organizations, translating technological terms and facts into easily understood lan-

SALARIES FOR TECHNICAL WRITERS

Category	First Quartile	Median Salary	Third Quartile
Total	$38,500	$46,500	$55,000
Employment Level			
Entry level	$31,800	$35,500	$39,000
Mid-level, nonsupervisory	35,000	41,300	48,350
Mid-level, supervisory	39,930	48,000	52,970
Senior level, nonsupervisory	46,000	54,510	62,800
Senior level, supervisory	46,000	55,000	65,000
Education Level			
Bachelor's degree	$37,650	$44,260	$54,938
Master's degree	38,700	50,000	56,000
Doctorate	NA	59,000	NA
Sex			
Female	$38,000	$45,330	$55,000
Male	39,000	49,500	58,000
Age			
20–29	$33,100	$36,070	$41,510
30–39	38,890	46,000	53,040
40–49	41,550	49,050	58,000
50 years and over	43,250	52,000	61,900
Years of Experience *(in technical communication field)*			
Less than 2 years	$29,950	$35,000	$43,250
2–5 years	35,000	40,000	46,500
6–10 years	41,000	48,000	56,000
11 years or more	45,000	52,880	61,750

SOURCE: Society for Technical Communication, *1995 Salary Survey.* Reprinted by permission.

guage. They produce instructional aides, training manuals, and public relations brochures. Technical writers may also prepare reports to corporate stockholders or work with scientists in preparing complex documents or research papers.

There are more than 35,000 technical writers and editors working in America in just about every industry. Federal, state, and local government agencies employ large numbers of technical writers, as do large companies in the chemical, computer manufacturing, aerospace, aviation, electronics, and pharmaceutical industries.

According to the Society for Technical Communication, a professional organization of more than 22,000 technical writers, the average salary for technical writers and editors was $48,250 in 1998. Starting salaries ranged from $28,600 to $44,800, and top salaries for senior management writers and editors ranged as high as $72,000. Salaries were highest in the Washington, DC, area, New England, Idaho, Utah, and Wyoming. In the federal government they averaged $47,400 in 1996. Technical writing is also a good career for women: They earned 93 cents per men's dollar, compared to an average of 73 cents for all other occupations.

WOMEN'S WAGES

Three decades of affirmative action have opened doors for millions of women, although not as wide as was hoped by many. Now, affirmative action programs are coming under attack not only from the Republican Congress but also from President Clinton, who wants a critical "review" of the legislation. In California, a lobbying group is attempting to abolish the state's "preferential treatment" laws by referendum. And a 1995 *Wall Street Journal/ABC* poll found that two out of three Americans oppose affirmative action.

Is this another form of backlash? Why the opposition to helping women and minorities get ahead? Critics cite varying causes. One is a perception that the groups covered by affirmative action have expanded beyond women and minorities to the disabled, homosexuals, and other underrepresented people. Many executives complain that "white men need not apply" is an unstated requirement in many job openings. Others argue that unqualified women and minorities have been promoted over men. Anecdotes circulate like the (true) tale of the National Forestry Service's quest for "unqualified applicants" to fill $20,000-a-year jobs so it could meet its quota of 43 percent female workers.

Women's groups counter that while substantial progress has been made, there's still a long way to go before they achieve pay and job equity with men. The 1996 median income for all men workers was $32,144, while women's was $23,710. More than 61 percent of working women are mired in low-paying clerical and sales jobs. A 1996 study by the Bureau of Labor Statistics of the twenty leading occupations of employed women demonstrates how the vast majority of working women are still stuck in traditional female, "support position" roles. The number one occupation for women in 1996? Secretary—with over 3 million women employed in this profession; that's nearly a million more than the number two occupation—cashier.

Other job titles that made the top twenty list include the typically female careers of elementary school teacher, nurse, waitress, and receptionist. While there is honor in all of these professions, the one thing they have in common is low pay. More surprising is that even within these female bastions, men who held the same positions received significantly higher compensation. Across the economy as a whole in 1996, working women averaged 73.8 cents for every dollar earned by men.

Since 1982, the wage gap has narrowed by only 12.1 cents. However, 60 percent of the change in the wage gap can be attributed to falling earnings for men rather than increases in women's pay, according to the National Committee of Pay Equity, a lobbying group. For minority women, the disparity is even greater, with black women earning 65 cents and Hispanic women 57 cents for every dollar earned by white men.

One area where women are actually pulling ahead of men is in university administration: Women deans now earn more than their male counterparts. But not all university personnel come close to achieving pay equity. Several of the highest-ranking administrative positions in universities such as CEO, chief academic officer, and chief development officer still pay men more for the same jobs.

While the outlook is grim for women in low-paying jobs, women with education and skills have fared much better. In corporate America, pay for women managers and professionals has risen dramatically in comparison to men's compensation. In many industries, women are narrowing the wage gap by a substantial amount. *Working Woman* magazine reported that female engineers make nearly 94 percent of what men do, female college deans make 96 percent of their male colleagues' salaries, and corporate lawyers make 92 percent. Women are still behind in the fields of accounting, financial services, and various sciences.

Women have successfully navigated middle management, particularly in the finance, real estate, and insurance industries. However, when the name plate reads vice president or above, it's a man behind the title, most likely a white man. While they constitute 46 percent of the workforce, white men hold 95 percent of senior management positions at *Fortune* 500 companies. Only two of the *Fortune* 500 CEOs were women in 1997, and women make up only 2.5 percent of the top earners in the *Fortune* 500. And women who do make it to the top are found most often in female ghettos in personnel and public relations, not in operations or line positions that lead to CEO. They hit the "glass ceiling" of corporate life beyond which they cannot rise. More than 50 percent of managers in a *Working Woman* survey complained of this invisible barrier to their careers. A 1998 study by Catalyst, a women's research group in New York, revealed that 57 top female officers of *Fortune* 500 companies had median cash compensation of $518,596 as compared to the male median of $765,000. Women serving as CFOs make a median of 77 cents for every dollar earned by male CFOs; among senior vice presidents the gap was 91 cents. Even for women with so-called "line" roles that have direct profit responsibilities, the difference in median compensation was more than 10 percent: $592,457 for men; $532,474 for women.

So, while corporations often boast of a commitment to diversity, the reality is very different. Women's careers are limited because they frequently are not chosen for international assignments or training programs, often because male bosses believe that women will not spend large periods of time away from their families or will not relocate. Some of these bosses are not wrong in their perceptions. *The Wall Street Journal* reported that the inability to balance career and family demands has led to a 25 percent turnover among female executives. A Labor Department survey of 250,000 women found that major concerns included reducing job stress and balancing work and family. In an effort to achieve a balance, many women find themselves on the much-maligned mommy track, trading less work time and pay for the Catch-22 of more family time but less career advancement and prestige. Some experts believe that until companies alter their macho take-no-prisoners culture and adopt a gentler, employee-friendly attitude, the glass ceiling will remain shatterproof.

Many women are having difficulty explaining to their children why they work, according to an article in *The New York Times.* Although the family structure has undergone many changes in the last few decades, with child care responsibilities shifting and being shared in different ways, it is still often the mother who is made to feel that she is the one making the decision to leave the house and work. The father is not questioned in the same way. Society still manages to indicate to children that women belong in the traditional position in the home. Most working women still have to deal with the dailiness of home life even though they have full-time jobs, which means they have two full-time jobs to juggle.

In an effort to overcome the sexist bias in major corporations, many women have dropped off the corporate "fast track" to set up their own shops. The number of women-owned businesses grew from 6.3 million in 1992 to 7.7 million in 1995, employing more than 15.5 million people, according to a report by Dun & Bradstreet and the National Foundation for Women Business Owners. Impressive in an era of downsizing is the fact that the number of women-owned businesses with more than 100 employees has grown by nearly 20 percent since 1991. While many of these women "inherited" the companies from their fathers, joined family businesses, or took over after a family member's death, the women remained at the helm, refusing to pass the torch to the next male in line. The increased number of women-owned businesses also reflects the growing trend toward midcareer self-employment.

Encouraging news is found in cyberspace, where many new jobs are being created in software and on-line design. By their nature, software com-

20 LEADING OCCUPATIONS OF EMPLOYED WOMEN
1996 ANNUAL AVERAGES

Occupations	Number Employed (in thousands)	Percent women	Women's Median Weekly Earnings[1]	Ratio of Women's Earnings to Men's Earnings
Total, 16 years and over	58,501	100%	$418	75%
Secretaries	3,119	98.6	406	NA
Cashiers	2,230	78.1	240	87.6
Registered nurses	1,853	93.3	695	95.3
Sales supervisors and proprietors	1,689	37.5	415	68.3
Nursing aides, orderlies, and attendants	1,636	88.4	286	84.4
Bookkeepers, accounting and auditing clerks	1,631	91.9	396	88.0
Elementary school teachers	1,538	83.3	648	90.1
Waiters and waitresses	1,071	77.9	253	82.1
Sales workers, other commodities[2]	1,026	68.4	273	80.3
Handlers, equipment cleaners, helpers, and laborers	971	19.3	295	86.0
Receptionists	930	96.9	333	NA
Machine operators, assorted materials	915	32.1	327	75.7
Cooks	869	42.2	242	86.7
Accountants and auditors	862	56.0	561	72.8
Textile, apparel, and furnishing machine operators	793	74.1	257	82.9
Janitors and cleaners	769	34.9	272	86.9
Administrative support occupations, n.e.c.[3]	697	76.9	450	87.5
Investigators and adjusters, excluding insurance	692	76.3	458	70.6
Secondary school teachers	686	55.9	643	84.6

[1]Wage and salary for full-time workers.
[2]Includes food, drugs, health, and other commodities.
[3]Not elsewhere classified.
NA: Not available where base is less than 50,000 male workers.
SOURCE: U.S. Department of Labor, Bureau of Labor Statistics, February 1997.

panies often have less hierarchical organizational structures in their attempts to encourage creativity. *Working Woman* magazine put "on-line multimedia content developer and services marketer" on the top of its list for best careers for women in the year 2005. Other careers included advanced-practice nurse, physical therapist, practice care manager, human resources manager, special education teacher, bank financial services manager, independent financial planner, hotel general manager, travel agent, paralegal, labor, employment or environmental lawyer, and environmental engineer. These jobs reflect that a third of all new jobs in the next decade will be in health, business services, or social services. The worst careers? Because of both diminished job growth and low satisfaction, the careers that made the list include child and elder care provider, telemarketing sales representative, word processor, switchboard operator, and bank teller.

EMPLOYMENT STATUS OF THE POPULATION BY SEX, 1960–98 (numbers in thousands)

Year	Civilian Noninstitutional Population[1]	Total in Workforce	Percentage of Population	Number Employed	Employment/ Population Ratio[2]	Percentage of Unemployed
			Total			
1960	117,245	69,628	59.4%	65,778	56.1%	5.5%
1965	126,513	74,455	58.9	71,088	56.2	4.5
1970	137,085	82,771	60.4	78,678	57.4	4.9
1975	153,153	93,775	61.2	85,846	56.1	8.5
1980	167,745	106,940	63.8	99,303	59.2	7.1
1985	178,206	115,461	64.8	107,150	60.1	7.2
1990	188,049	124,787	66.4	117,914	62.7	5.5
1991	189,765	125,303	66.0	116,877	61.6	6.7
1992	191,576	126,982	66.3	117,598	61.4	7.4
1993	193,550	128,040	66.2	119,306	61.6	6.8
1994[3]	196,814	131,056	66.6	123,060	62.5	6.1
1997	202,832	135,963	67.0	129,565	63.9	4.7
1998	204,899	137,364	67.0	131,453	64.2	4.3
			Male			
1960	55,662	46,388	83.3%	43,904	78.9%	5.4%
1965	59,782	48,255	80.7	46,340	77.5	4.0
1970	64,304	51,228	79.7	48,990	76.2	4.4
1975	72,291	56,299	77.9	51,857	71.7	7.9
1980	79,398	61,453	77.4	57,186	72.0	6.9
1985	84,469	64,411	76.3	59,891	70.9	7.0

EMPLOYMENT STATUS OF THE POPULATION BY SEX, 1960–98 (numbers in thousands)

Year	Civilian Noninstitutional Population[1]	Total in Workforce	Percentage of Population	Number Employed	Employment/ Population Ratio[2]	Percentage of Unemployed
			Male			
1990	89,650	68,234	76.1%	64,435	71.9%	5.6%
1991	90,552	68,411	75.5	63,593	70.2	7.0
1992	91,541	69,184	75.6	63,805	69.7	7.8
1993	92,620	69,633	75.2	64,700	69.9	7.1
1994[3]	94,355	70,817	75.1	66,450	70.4	6.2
1997	97,559	73,191	75.0	69,968	71.7	4.4
1998	98,591	73,783	74.8	70,685	71.7	4.2
			Female			
1960	61,582	23,240	37.7%	21,874	35.5%	5.9%
1965	66,731	26,200	39.3	24,748	37.1	5.5
1970	72,782	31,543	43.3	29,688	40.8	5.9
1975	80,860	37,475	46.3	33,989	42.0	9.3
1980	88,348	45,487	51.5	42,117	47.7	7.4
1985	93,736	51,050	54.5	47,259	50.4	7.4
1990	98,399	56,554	57.5	53,479	54.3	5.4
1991	99,214	56,893	57.3	53,284	53.7	6.3
1992	100,035	57,798	57.8	53,793	53.9	6.9
1993	100,930	58,407	57.9	54,606	54.1	6.5
1994[3]	102,460	60,239	58.8	56,610	55.3	6.0
1997	105,274	62,772	59.6	59,597	56.6	5.1
1998	106,308	63,581	59.8	60,768	57.2	4.4

[1]Age 16 and over.
[2]Civilians employed as a percentage of the civilian noninstitutional population.
[3]Data for 1994 are not directly comparable with data for previous years because of a major redesign of the Current Population Survey questionnaire and collection methodology and the introduction of 1990 census-based population controls, adjusted for the estimated undercount.
SOURCE: U.S. Department of Labor, Bureau of Labor Statistics, *Employment Status of the Civilian Population by Sex and Age* (1998).

THE BEST PAID WOMEN IN CORPORATE AMERICA, 1997

Rank, Name	Position, Company	Total Compensation[1]
1. Linda Wachner	Chair, CEO, and president/Warnaco Group	$9.28 million
	Chair and CEO/Authentic Fitness	$989,726
	Total =	$10.27 million
2. Jeannette P. Meier	Executive vice president, finance and administration/Sterling Software	10.06 million
	Executive vice president/Sterling Commerce	
3. Jill Barad	Chair and CEO/Mattel	6.62 million
4. Ngaire Cuneo	Executive vice president of corporate development/Conseco	6.51 million
5. Janice Roberts	Senior vice president, marketing and business/3 Com	5.81 million
6. Carol Bartz	Chair and CEO/Autodesk	5.51 million
7. Marion Sandler	Co-Chair and Co-CEO/Golden West Financial Corp.	4.47 million
8. Dorrit Bern	Chair, president, and CEO/Charming Shoppes	3.6 million
9. Amy Lipton	Senior vice president and general counsel/CUC International	3.46 million
10. Rosemarie Greco	Former president/CoreStates Financial Corp.	3.36 million
	Former president and CEO/CoreStates Bank	
11. Irene Miller	Former vice chair and CFO/Barnes & Noble	2.73 million
12. Julliette Tehrani	Executive vice president, CFO, and treasurer/MBIA	2.46 million
13. Pamela Patsley	President and CEO/Paymentech	2.28 million
14. Charlotte Beers	Former chair and CEO/Ogilvy & Mather Worldwide	2.13 million
15. Ellen R. Gordon	President and COO/Tootsie Roll Industries	2.06 milion
16. Janice K. Henry	Vice President, CFO, and treasurer/ Martin Marietta Materials	1.99 million
17. Susan Wang	Senior vice president, CFO, and treasurer/Solectron	1.92 million
18. Beth Ravit	Former president, retail stores and special merchandising/Authentic Fitness	1.85 million
19. Barbara Bednar	Vice president and COO/Renal Treatment Centers	1.84 million

THE BEST PAID WOMEN IN CORPORATE AMERICA, 1997

Rank, Name	Position, Company	Total Compensation[1]
20. Robin Burns	CEO and president/Estée Lauder USA & Canada	1.81 million

[1]This listing consists exclusively of employees of public companies. Earnings include salary, bonuses, and other cash compensation, and value of options exercised.
SOURCE: *Working Woman* magazine, 1998 *Salary Survey*.

FEDERAL WHITE COLLAR WORKERS: AVERAGE ANNUAL SALARIES, BY SEX, 1995

Occupation	Men's Salaries	Women's Salaries
Administrator	$79,531	$61,675
Architect	54,213	50,556
Attorney	77,153	69,942
Cartographer	47,891	46,231
Chaplain	51,193	48,290
Chemist	59,497	50,768
Clerk-typist	23,910	21,040
Computer operator	30,623	28,933
Computer specialist	52,245	47,136
Dentist	83,570	67,882
Doctor	85,169	82,462
Economist	65,530	57,210
Engineer, aerospace	63,256	55,312
Engineer, chemical	58,665	51,835
Engineer, civil	55,914	46,717
Engineer, electrical	55,561	49,135
Engineer, general	67,427	58,557
Engineer, mechanical	55,197	48,765
Engineer, nuclear	64,241	56,071
Engineer, petroleum	58,799	54,571
Engineering technician	40,738	33,798
Internal Revenue agent	53,892	46,471
Librarian	52,336	48,763
Library technician	26,593	25,776
Management and program analyst	57,283	48,514
Mathematician	61,538	55,064
Medical technologist	38,799	38,330
Messenger	21,283	22,055
Museum curator	56,944	49,664
Nurse	44,387	45,294

FEDERAL WHITE COLLAR WORKERS: AVERAGE ANNUAL SALARIES, BY SEX, 1995

Occupation	Men's Salaries	Women's Salaries
Nursing assistant	$21,939	$22,170
Paralegal	44,783	40,049
Pharmacist	52,844	49,644
Photographer	37,072	32,414
Physicist	64,400	54,071
Psychologist	61,271	52,781
Secretary	23,732	26,237
Security guard	24,168	23,519
Social Worker	45,679	42,675
Statistician	60,228	53,163
Veterinary scientist	55,437	51,066

SOURCE: Office of Personnel Management, *Occupations of Federal White-Collar and Blue-Collar Workers,* September 1995.

PERCENT OF FEMALE WORKERS IN SELECTED OCCUPATIONS, 1975–97

Occupation	Women as Percent of Total Employed			
	1975	1985	1996	1997
Airline pilot	NA	2.6%	1.4%	1.2%
Auto mechanic	0.5%	0.6	1.2	1.5
Bartender	35.2	47.9	53.8	57.2
Bus driver	37.7	49.2	46.8	47.8
Cab driver, chauffeur	8.7	10.9	10.7	8.3
Carpenter	0.6	1.2	1.3	1.6
Child-care worker	98.4	96.1	97.1	96.8
Computer programmer	25.6	34.3	30.8	30.0
Computer systems analyst	14.8	28.0	28.1	28.6
Data entry keyer	92.8	90.7	84.5	81.9
Data processing equipment repairer	1.8	10.4	18.3	13.3
Dentist	1.8	6.5	13.7	17.3
Dental assistant	100.0	99.0	97.8	96.7
Economist	13.1	34.5	54.4	52.2
Editor, reporter	44.6	51.7	55.7	51.2
Garage, gas station attendant	4.7	6.8	5.8	9.6
Lawyer, judge	7.1	18.2	29.0	26.7
Librarian	81.1	87.0	82.7	80.5
Mail carrier (Postal Service)	8.7	17.2	28.3	30.7

PERCENT OF FEMALE WORKERS IN SELECTED OCCUPATIONS, 1975–97

Occupation	1975	Women as Percent of Total Employed		
		1985	1996	1997
Office machine repairer	1.7%	5.7%	3.7%	4.6%
Physician	13.0	17.2	26.4	26.2
Registered nurse	97.0	95.1	93.3	93.5
Social worker	60.8	66.7	68.5	69.3
Teacher, college and university	31.1	35.2	43.5	42.7
Teacher, elementary school	85.4	84.0	83.3	73.9
Telephone installer, repairer	4.8	12.8	13.9	13.1
Telephone operator	93.3	88.8	90.5	83.5
Waiter/waitress	91.1	84.0	77.9	77.8
Welder	4.4	4.8	5.0	5.6

NA = Not available.
SOURCE: Bureau of Labor Statistics.

INCOME AND EARNINGS OF MINORITIES

During the booming economy of the late 1990s, the market for low-paying jobs has exploded and as a result, unemployment among minority groups has dropped as has the number of minorities living in poverty. So with all the talk on Capitol Hill and in statehouses across the country about reforming or even dismantling affirmative action programs, one might be tempted to think racial discrimination in the workplace had been eradicated. But while the situation is obviously far better for minorities than it was only ten years ago (not to mention 200 years ago, when the founding fathers declared black slaves to be the equivalent of three-fifths of a person), there are plenty of indicators that employment opportunities and rewards are still greater for whites than for blacks. Whether or not that is an argument for continuing affirmative action in its present form is debatable, but it is surely an argument against completely dismantling programs that open doors to a group of people who continue to be the victims of workplace discrimination. Here are just a few indicators:

● Minorities currently make up 26 percent of the workforce, but in no industry do they make up more than 13 percent of managers, and in many industries fewer than one in 100 managers is a minority, according to the Federal Glass Ceiling Commission, a bipartisan panel studying diversity in the workplace. Overall, minorities hold less than

3 percent of senior level (vice president and above) jobs in corporations.

- Black men's annual earnings are 74 percent of what white men earn, the same as they were in 1975. Hispanic men's earnings are 64.8 percent, down from 72.1 percent in 1975. And while earnings for black and Hispanic women have increased in proportion to white men's salaries over the same time period, they have not increased as fast as their white women counterparts'. Their earnings have therefore decreased in relation to white women's salaries.

- Median family income for blacks was $26,522 in 1996, while for whites it was $44,756. The difference between median incomes of blacks and whites in 1996 was $18,234. Median incomes for Hispanic households declined, from $27,098 (adjusted for inflation) in 1976 to $26,179 in 1996.

- The unemployment rate for blacks is consistently double the rate for whites, regardless of the country's economic prosperity. Black unemployment has been below 10 percent during the economic boom of late 1997 and 1998. But 30.2 percent of blacks between the ages of 16 and 19 are unemployed, compared to 12.2 percent of white youths.

- The percentage of blacks below the poverty level was 28.4 in 1996, about the same as it has been every year since 1968. Meanwhile, the percentage of whites has fluctuated, from a high of 18.1 percent in 1959, to a low of 8.4 percent in 1973, and back up to 11.2 percent in 1996. The percentage of Hispanics below the poverty level (21.6 percent in 1973) has also fluctuated, but has recently been on the upswing and was 29.4 percent in 1996.

Such statistics speak the kind of stark truth no political rhetoric can capture because they reveal deep-rooted patterns of social and cultural discrimination that remain immune to any attempts at mere economic adjustments.

The nation's 34 million black people constitute 12.7 percent of the population. Of the 14 million blacks in the workforce, about 22 percent are in service occupations (almost double the percentage of whites), while 29 percent hold blue-collar jobs. Among the 48 percent who are white-collar workers, only 16.8 percent of black males were employed in managerial or professional specialty occupations, or just over half the rate for white males. As a result, many are leaving the corporate environment in favor of their own business; minority-owned businesses have risen by as much as 50 percent in recent years according to some reports.

The most important of the so-called "other" groups are the nearly 30 million people of Hispanic origin who constitute 11.1 percent of our official

INCOME OF INDIVIDUALS AND FAMILIES BY RACE AND HISPANIC ORIGIN, 1976–96

Category	1976			1996		
	White	Black	Hispanic	White	Black	Hispanic
Individuals						
Median income[1,2]						
Male	$ 26,248	$15,804	$18,622	$ 24,949	$16,491	$ 15,437
Female	9,525	8,976	8,873	12,961	11,772	9,484
Percentage below the poverty line	9.1%	31.1%	24.7%	11.2%	28.4%	29.4%
Families						
Median family income[2]	$ 41,040	$24,412	$27,098	$ 44,756	$26,522	$ 26,179
Mean Income[2] by Fifth and Top Five Percent[3]						
Lowest fifth	$ 13,828	$ 7,325	$ 8,653	$ 13,097	$ 5,651	$ 7,139
Second fifth	28,218	14,908	17,766	29,059	15,180	16,481
Third fifth	41,079	24,528	27,093	44,784	26,594	26,215
Fourth fifth	55,459	38,092	39,521	64,272	42,621	40,814
Highest fifth	93,031	64,184	66,286	129,773	84,627	87,309
Top 5 percent	136,355	87,415	94,177	225,126	135,719	150,775

[1]For year-round full-time workers over fifteen years old with income.
[2]Income levels in constant (1996) dollars.
[3]It appears that between the years 1974 and 1986, negative amounts were included in the aggregate. These data were revised to maintain comparability with the majority of years where negative amounts were treated as zeros.
SOURCE: U.S. Census Bureau, 1996, March Current Population Survey, and *Historical Income Tables.*

EMPLOYMENT STATUS OF THE POPULATION BY RACE AND HISPANIC ORIGIN, 1975–98
(numbers in thousands)

Year	Civilian Noninstitutional Population[1]	Total in Workforce	Percentage of Population	Number Employed	Employment/ Population Ratio[2]	Percentage of Unemployed
			White			
1975	134,790	82,831	61.5%	76,411	56.7%	7.8%
1980	146,122	93,600	64.1	87,715	60.0	6.3
1985	153,679	99,926	65.0	93,736	61.0	6.2
1990	160,415	107,177	66.8	102,087	63.6	4.7
1992	162,658	108,526	66.7	101,479	62.4	6.5
1994[3]	165,555	111,082	67.1	105,109	63.5	5.3
1996	167,760	112,502	67.1	107,048	63.8	4.8
1998[4]	170,915	115,314	67.5	110,715	64.8	4.0
			Black			
1975	15,751	9,263	58.8%	7,894	50.1%	14.8%
1980	17,824	10,865	61.0	9,313	52.2	14.3
1985	19,664	12,364	62.9	10,501	53.4	15.1
1990	21,300	13,493	63.3	11,966	56.2	11.3
1992	21,958	13,891	63.3	11,933	54.3	14.1
1994[3]	22,879	14,502	63.4	12,835	56.1	11.5
1996	23,454	14,956	63.8	13,397	57.1	10.4
1998[4]	24,227	15,881	65.6	14,388	59.4	9.4
			Hispanic[5]			
1975	NA	NA	NA	NA	NA	NA
1980	9,598	6,146	64.0%	5,527	57.6%	10.1%
1985	11,915	7,698	64.6	6,888	57.8	10.5
1990	14,297	9,576	67.0	8,808	61.6	8.0
1992	15,244	10,131	66.5	8,971	58.9	11.4
1994[3]	18,117	11,975	66.1	10,788	59.5	9.9
1996	18,977	12,532	66.0	11,345	59.8	9.5
1998[4]	20,797	14,133	68.0	13,158	63.3	6.9

[1] Age sixteen and over.

[2] Civilians employed as a percentage of the civilian noninstitutional population.

[3] Data for 1994 and later are not directly comparable with data for previous years because of a major redesign of the Current Population Survey questionnaire and collection methodology and the introduction of 1990 census-based population controls, adjusted for the estimated undercount.

[4] As of first quarter, 1998.

[5] Hispanics may be of any race.

SOURCE: Bureau of Labor Statistics, *Employment and Earnings* (monthly), January 1998.

population. Of these, 63 percent are of Mexican origin, 9 percent are of Puerto Rican origin, and 5 percent are of Cuban origin, so the vast majority of Hispanic Americans are from groups with established communities in this country. This may help to explain why median family incomes for people of Hispanic origin (who may be of any race) is higher than that for blacks. Of course, the incredible growth in the number of illegal aliens from Spanish-speaking countries (especially Mexico) means that income and population statistics regarding people of Hispanic origin are suspect at best.

Conservative estimates of the illegal alien population run as high as 6 million people living and working here on a regular basis, most of them providing cheap labor in the agricultural fields of California and Texas, the sweatshops of New York City, and the kitchens of hotels and restaurants around the country. Others work in individual households as housekeepers, maids, and gardeners, paid off the books so that their income is untaxed, and so their employers don't have to pay social security, unemployment and disability insurance, and payroll taxes. Because they have no legal rights, illegal aliens are usually paid less than the minimum wage, and, of course, they are never a threat as potential union members.

Of the nearly 13 million people of Hispanic origin in the workforce, only about 15 percent work in managerial and professional specialty occupations, while about 23 percent work as operators, fabricators, and laborers, and another 20 percent work in service occupations, which are usually low-paying. Nearly 14 percent of Hispanic people work in precision production, craft, or repair occupations.

THE NEW COLLEGE GRADUATE

Although it should be obvious to readers of this book that a college education is required for virtually every job that has long-term high earnings potential, it may come as a surprise that only about 25 percent of the American work-force has finished college. However, the percentage of college graduates is increasing, as is the market for their skills. The number of people graduating from four-year colleges and universities has increased from 935,000 in 1980 to 1,183,000 in 1997, according to the Department of Education. That number is expected to drop slightly around the turn of the millennium, then rise again, reaching almost 1.27 million by the year 2006.

While these numbers indicate an economy flooded with degree-holding job candidates, there is plenty of good news for today's new grads. College graduates are facing a much different employment picture from the one graduates of just a few years ago did. In early 1998, the national unemployment rate dipped to a twenty-four-year low, and hiring projections were strong in all fields. According to the National Association of Colleges and Employers

(NACE), nearly 70 percent of companies who participated in their annual survey said that they planned to hire more new college graduates in the spring of 1998 than they did the year before. By contrast, only 3 percent of participants stated that they would reduce their hiring levels.

Another positive trend for new graduates: Salaries are on the rise. Particularly in high growth fields like computer technology—where demand well exceeds the number of qualified candidates—salary levels are skyrocketing. Throughout other industries, earnings are rising—though not dramatically so—as a low inflation rate is keeping them steady.

It is important to realize that while unemployment is down, not all college graduates have taken jobs they consider to be ideal. Many new grads are employed with temporary agencies—either by choice, because they are exploring career options, or aren't yet ready to be tied to something permanent—or because they have not found a better option. In addition, many graduates accept jobs that don't require a college degree. This phenomenon is known as "educational underutilization" or "underemployment."

To be sure, many new graduates are being offered challenging jobs in growing fields that allow them to live up to their potential. Fields such as consulting, accounting, and computer-related services are among the fastest-growing and are snapping up the top students as quickly as possible—often making job offers early in the students' senior year. New graduates are also benefiting from corporate downsizing. Where more experienced, and more expensive employees have been let go, companies still have work that needs to be done and more often than not they choose to fill the gap with inexpensive, entry-level workers.

Over their lifetimes, college graduates continue to earn about 40 percent more than those without degrees, and the gap is widening. Median annual earnings for college graduates were about $35,500 in 1996, compared to $18,500 for high school graduates.

Aside from the high-tech arena, other fields that the National Association of Colleges and Employers named as particularly promising for new graduates included service-sector jobs such as merchandising and insurance. They noted that even manufacturing is making a strong comeback in the booming late 90s economy.

EMPLOYMENT GROWTH BY REQUIRED EDUCATION, 1992–2005

| Occupation Type | Employment | | Change, 1992–2005 | |
	Actual 1992	Projected 2005	Number	Percent
All jobs	121,099,000	147,482,000	26,383,000	21.8%
Jobs requiring a college degree	23,770,000	33,296,000	9,526,000	40.1
Executive, administrative, and managerial	6,905,000	9,276,000	2,371,000	34.3
Professional specialty	12,115,000	17,091,000	4,976,000	41.1
Technicians	1,169,000	1,806,000	637,000	54.5
Sales representatives and supervisors	2,198,000	3,060,000	862,000	39.2
All other	1,383,000	2,062,000	679,000	49.1
Jobs not requiring a college degree	97,329,000	114,186,000	16,857,000	17.3

SOURCE: Bureau of Labor Statistics, *Occupational Outlook Quarterly*, Summer 1994.

The following table puts the value of education in its starkest terms of dollars and cents. Over a lifetime, college graduates can expect to earn nearly twice what a mere high school graduate will earn, and a person with a professional degree like a doctor or lawyer can earn more than double the lifetime income of a college graduate.

AVERAGE ANNUAL EARNINGS[1] BY EDUCATIONAL ATTAINMENT AND SEX, 1996

Level of Education Completed	Men	Women
Less than 9th grade	$ 20,153	$15,150
9th to 12th grade (no diploma)	25,283	17,313
High school graduates	32,521	21,893
Some college, no degree	38,491	25,889
Associate degree	39,873	28,403
Bachelor's degree	52,354	36,555
Master's degree	70,859	44,471
Doctoral degree	86,436	62,169
Professional degree	112,873	90,711

[1] For year-round, full-time workers, ages eighteen and over.
SOURCE: U.S. Bureau of the Census.

BACHELOR'S DEGREES AWARDED BY SEX AND AS A PERCENTAGE OF THE
23-YEAR-OLD POPULATION, 1870–1997

Year	Total	Males	Females	As percentage of all 23-year-olds
1870	9,371	7,993	1,378	NA
1880	12,896	10,411	2,485	NA
1890	15,539	12,857	2,682	NA
1900	27,410	22,173	5,237	1.9%
1910	37,199	28,762	8,437	2.0
1920	48,622	31,980	16,642	2.6
1930	122,484	73,615	48,869	5.7
1940	186,500	109,546	76,954	8.1
1946[1]	136,174	58,664	77,510	5.6
1950	432,058	328,841	103,217	18.2
1955	285,841	182,839	103,002	15.1
1960	392,440	254,063	138,377	18.2
1965[2]	493,757	282,173	211,584	19.4
1970	792,317	451,097	341,220	21.8
1975	922,933	504,841	418,092	24.9
1980	929,417	473,611	455,806	21.8
1985	979,477	482,528	496,949	23.0
1990	1,049,657	491,488	558,169	28.2
1991	1,094,538	504,045	590,493	30.1
1992	1,136,553	520,811	615,742	30.6
1993	1,165,179	532,881	632,298	30.3
1994	1,169,275	532,422	636,853	31.6
1995	1,160,134	526,131	634,003	32.2
1996[3]	1,186,000	531,000	655,000	33.7
1997[3]	1,183,000	528,000	655,000	33.8

[1]Figures for 1945 not available.
[2]Data before 1965 include first professional degrees but do not include Alaska or Hawaii.
[3]Projected
SOURCE: U.S. Department of Education, *Digest of Education Statistics* and unpublished data.

Starting Salaries for New College Graduates

Over the last few years the strong demand for college graduates has led to rapidly increasing salaries. Of course those students who majored in information technology fields have led everyone else in the starting salary race. In 1997 the average offer for computer engineering graduates increased 5.8 percent to $39,722, according to the July issue of *Salary Survey,* conducted by the National Association of Colleges and Employers (NACE). The average offer to computer information sciences graduates is up 4.1 percent to $35,407, while those with degrees in computer science saw their average offer increase 3.9 percent to $36,597. Starting offers to electrical engineering graduates—also favorites of the computer industry—were also up 3.9 percent for an average of $39,513.

Because of the rebounding manufacturing sector, other types of engineering graduates also posted significant gains in their starting salary offers. Average offers to mechanical engineers increased 2.9 percent to $38,113; chemical engineers up 3.3 percent to $42,817; industrial engineers, up 4.8 percent to $38,027; and civil engineers rose 5.8 percent to $33,199.

Graduates in business disciplines also fared well, and many enjoyed markedly higher starting salary offers. Management information systems graduates in 1997 received salary offers 2.8 percent higher for an average of $34,778; accounting graduates saw their average offer increase 3.2 percent to $30,321; and marketing graduates earned a 4.1 percent increase for an average of $27,874. The average offer to economics and finance graduates rose 6.3 percent to $31,294, and business administration graduates received a 7.9 percent increase to an average $29,433.

Salary offers to humanities and social sciences graduates posted modest gains in starting salary offers over last year. The average offer to letters (English) graduates rose 2.0 percent to $23,533, while foreign language graduates saw their average offer up 1.8 percent to $25,608. Psychology graduates earned a 4.5 percent increase, averaging $23,315, but history graduates saw their average offer barely move, increasing just 0.2 percent to $24,688.

Further information on the July *Salary Survey* is available from NACE, 62 Highland Avenue, Bethlehem, PA 18017-9085 (http://www.jobweb.org/).

In 1998 the *Wall Street Journal* described the job market for new college graduates as "insane" and said it was the strongest market in over a decade. Not only did starting salaries rise, for the best, most sought-after students, the signing bonus and promise of a year-end bonus became a major part of the big companies' sales pitch.

Since almost 90 percent of surveyed companies said there was a shortage of qualified job candidates in 1998, the average number of job offers for men was 2.65 and 2.53 for women. Company recruiters said that the intensity level needed to hire M.B.A.s had now become part of the undergraduate recruiting scene, and many complained that they had not been able to meet their quotas. Some companies actually flew candidates to New York City for all-expenses-paid weekends.

How long this situation can last is anyone's guess, but with experienced workers almost fully employed companies have little choice but to recruit college grads. Consulting companies led the way with Andersen seeking

6,200 new grads, and Price Waterhouse Coopers more than 3,350. IBM said it would hire 3,000 new grads in 1998 (and went to Florida during spring break to launch its drive!). Dell Computer doubled its target number over 1997, while all the Wall Street brokerages each sought hundreds for their booming businesses.

WHEN SEEKING YOUR FIRST JOB
•
by Edward J. Dwyer, Jr.[1]

Many first-time job-seekers spend endless time agonizing over making the right choice. For those who have decided at age sixteen that medicine or law or carpentry is the profession they want to pursue, the choice is relatively easy when it comes time to start working. These people have had a clear-cut goal and have gone through the necessary preparation to achieve it. But most students don't feel strongly about any particular field, so the need to make a choice can trigger an excruciating personal debate. At times this uncertainty can even stop them from making any decision at all.

There is no need for the first job decision to be such a source of anxiety. There are a set of rational steps that a person can take when embarking on the process. There are also certain attitudes that one should bring into the process to inject a sense of reality and provide a framework for making the decision.

First of all we should say right up front that picking a first job does not constitute making a lifetime choice. Joseph L. Dionne, the president and CEO of McGraw-Hill, started his worklife as a high school teacher and coach, for example. Nick Buoniconti, who was the middle linebacker on the Miami Dolphins' Super Bowl championship teams, became a lawyer and player agent before he took over running the American Tobacco Company. Many a degreed lawyer has never practiced law. Conversely there are English majors who have found themselves in charge of technical operations. In fact one of the best market research consultants specializes in high-tech, using to the hilt his master's degree in library science. So when starting out you need not find the situation that you must fit for the rest of your working days. Nor will it necessarily be one for which your college education is particularly apropos.

It should be a situation that will help you build a career or profession, however. This means finding a job that will help you start building transportable skills. Also, you should go into your job search with the notion that you want to find something that makes sense for the next two years at least. This is the minimum amount of time in which you can become well-grounded and practiced in those skills. Then, too, it gives you time to build some concrete accomplishments. With this in mind then you should target a meaningful job in a good company in an attractive industry. So you will have to put some effort into doing your homework, but more about that later.

No matter what direction you may take, you will succeed and find satisfaction predominantly from hard work. So you should pick a functional field and an industry that strongly interest you. Since you will be putting a minimum of seven hours a day five days a week into the job you may as well spend the time performing activities that you find interesting and challenging. No one performs well over any length of time carrying out activities that they consider mere drudgery or routine. Those who get the promotions are those who bring enthusiasm and contribution to the job. While there is a certain level below which you may not be able to subsist, compensation should not be your most important criterion for judging the right situation. Survey after survey has shown that a vast majority of successful people who are happy with themselves and their jobs find the work itself to be their main source of satisfaction rather than their compensation. So you should try to find work that you feel is interesting and important.

Even though we have just dismissed compensation as the prime motive for job selection, we do want to make one point clear. You can garner from the pages of this book what the pay scales are by type of jobs and industries. One major implication that can be drawn here is that pay is not uniform by job category or across different size companies or different industries. You can get a reasonable idea of what you might expect as a new job-seeker given your background, the type of position you seek, and the industry in which you seek it. The key here is to have reasonable expectations. History majors with no work experience cannot command $30,000 in starting salary. So if you are a history major, set your sights accordingly, because there is nothing worse than going into the job market with an inflated sense of one's own value. It can only lead to dissatisfaction and make the search very long and painful.

---

[1]This article was written expressly for this book by Edward J. Dwyer, Jr., a highly successful management consultant and executive recruiter.

Getting Started

Now the homework part. The starting point for any job search is with yourself. You really have to know the kind of person you are and match your strong and weak points, likes and dislikes, knowledge and interests, etc., with the various opportunities that are in the job market. Standardized psychological tests are of limited value at this point. Such tests may help in directing you away from certain fields for which you would have little aptitude and interest, and generally toward ones in which you have both. But these tests won't help you decide specifically on banking versus brokerage or marketing versus sales. When trying to find your own focus as it relates to starting a career, there are a number of questions to ask yourself: "Who am I?" and "What would I like to do?" And "What do I want to get out of my career?" Your answers to these will tell you a lot about what you should aspire to be and not be. For instance, if you take rejection of your ideas and suggestions highly personally, you shouldn't look to a career in sales where even those most successful in selling the best products hear "yes" less than half the time. Or if retiring at age fifty is one of your goals, you had better be aiming at the fast track.

There is no set approach. You can make up your own questions to find your own personal profile or get suggestions from articles and books. A personal profile is simply a guide to help you take inventory. Rating each attribute on a scale of one to five is usually of benefit as well. Be as objective as possible; try to see yourself as others see you. Once you've taken this inventory you should look at the career fields you are considering versus the attribute areas and see how you match up. Since you may have little or no experience upon which to base judgments about career fields and their requirements, consult the media as well as your college placement office for help. And don't neglect to use any personal contacts you may have who are experienced in industries you may be interested in.

Targeting the Right Opportunities

Having taken inventory, you should then start doing research to find which industries, companies, and jobs will most likely provide the kinds of intellectual, psychic, social, and monetary rewards you seek. If you do not see yourself working as the product manager in charge of promoting the newest flavor in pudding pops, stay clear of marketing in food companies. You may see yourself as a salesman, but of what? You may be in a hurry to achieve that universal symbol of great success—six figures—so you want to find industries that have a reputation for allowing young people the opportunity to achieve that level quickly.

Most importantly, whatever your aspirations, aim for a situation that will allow you to start growing your skill and knowledge base in terms of gaining your career goals. If you are an engineer you may be tempted to go to work on a project that involves very lengthy and detailed work, such as designing and installing factory automation equipment for the furniture manufacturing industry. This is fine as far as it goes, but what might you be doing five years from now? You may want to become an expert in the detailed engineering work involved in installing such systems and you may see this aspect of the work as highly interesting and rewarding. On the other hand, you may see your first engineering job as a necessary stop on your career path to management responsibility. The attractiveness of a given job situation will depend on your longer range goals. In summary, certain companies and positions will fit you and your needs better than others. Finding the right ones will depend on how well you've prepared yourself.

Above all, approach the selection as a two-year decision. You should be ready to ask yourself and your prospective employers where you might be in two years. The picture you should have in your mind should have two dimensions: (1) the inventory of skills and experiences you will have acquired as well as the transferability of these; and (2) the level of responsibility you should have gained and the opportunity to achieve concrete results. (The most transferable assets of all are the latter.) See if this agrees with your own picture of where you want to be, and whether or not other recent graduates have achieved this at these companies.

Now ask the same question about the five-year timepoint. The key here is that your first job is not likely to be your last, so you want to assure yourself that the progress you make will not be lost if you move on. Still, you do not want to change companies too often even early in your career, so the two-year horizon provides some stability as you set sail on your shakedown run. Furthermore, you want to have a reasonable gauge of the progress you may have made should you decide not to move elsewhere.

A few words about selecting the appropriate industries and businesses to target: Given the current shakeout in American industry, job security is not what it used to be and probably won't be again. To say that the most promising opportunities are in growth industries is both obvious and oversimplified. To begin with, most large companies are portfolios of new and promising businesses, along with growing ones, mature ones, and declining ones. This is true even if the company concentrates in a highly attractive industry such as computers. Your choice of industry is important because industry knowledge is an important commodity that you can carry with you for the rest of your career to your own major benefit. So naturally you want to move into a business in an industry that has long-term potential. But don't be fooled; potential does not necessarily mean high-flying growth. Many high-flyers go out of business very quickly, and many old-line companies go on seemingly forever. Choose an industry that interests you and that has stability based on an extended future and on an environment where you can hone your skills.

The Interview Process

Naturally, before you get as far as weighing job offers, you must first go through an interview process, probably consisting of three or four separate sessions. The most important piece of advice to follow during the interview is to be yourself. The interviewer knows you are green. He or she is not looking for anyone to come in and bowl them over. The interviewers are looking for aptitudes, attitudes, social presence, and other intangibles that may indicate a bright and constructive future for you in their company. The appearance, courtesy, self-assurance, and intelligence you display in the process are more important than what you've done. So you don't want to fake it. The interviewers can easily spot insincerity and lack of candor. There is no surer way of not being invited back.

Remember also that the interview is a two-way street as far as information gathering goes. Don't be afraid to ask questions. You want to learn as much pertinent information about the company as they are learning about you. And you want to see if they're faking it. One problem about the interview process is that you are both trying to put on your best face, so often the less attractive side only surfaces after hiring. It is always best to get as much information as you feel you would need to make a decision, even down to visiting a potential work location and talking to people on the job if negotiations start to get serious.

Just remember that there is no certainty. This is not a science. Feelings may count more than anything else when you make your final decision. If in your gut the situation looks questionable, no amount of information will be enough to convince you otherwise, so don't take the job. Do not let lack of information or 100 percent assurance freeze you into indecisiveness. Take your best shot and then get to work.

Again, we want to remind you that choosing your first job is not a lifetime decision. Choosing an industry and general career path on which you can build for the rest of your working life will help you make the quickest progress toward your career goals since each successive move will build on already acquired strengths. So you should, by all means, take the time to prepare yourself by inventorying yourself and matching your strengths and interests with target industries, companies, and jobs.

Even so, your early career decision may come down to circumstance. If you can't find a situation that meets your requirements completely, you may be forced to settle for the best of the offers on the table. This decision will have the most effective long-term result if you make it on the basis of being a short-, not long-term decision.

Getting Off to a Good Start

There are three questions we can pose that address the issues you should be concerned with once you get the job:

- What does and what should one do in the first days, weeks, and months of a new job?
- How does one become an effective, accepted, and even respected member of the new organization?
- How long must the apprenticeship last?

In a series of sessions with graduating M.B.A. students, Bill Stack, a noted executive recruiter and president of William Stack Associates, posed these questions to his audience. His answers are equally appropriate for any level of graduate. What follows is based on the advice that Stack gave.

To begin with you should have a clear understanding of why you were hired. The principal reason you have received a job offer is your proven ability to learn. Your employer is prepared to teach you. This will be direct, practical, and immediate learning. The success with which you learn your new job will have immediate tangible results: pace of progress, money, position, and level of responsibility. At this stage the rewards are earned by the most effective learner.

Your attitude should be one of interest and of enthusiasm. Be cooperative, too. Strive to do every assignment well, going the extra, unasked-for yard. Be alert to the group's goals and the group discipline needed to achieve those goals. Ask for help from those who know the job, the procedures, the company. Ask pertinent questions, but don't ask unnecessary ones. A low verbal profile from the novice is highly desirable. Quiet self-reliance is a more highly prized quality than is challenging questioning. It is easy to cultivate hostility or at least irritation by needless questioning or challenging the system before demonstrating competence. Worse yet is the practice of picking others' brains and then regurgitating the words as one's own. Be deliberate rather than headstrong; be a problem solver, not a problem.

In the initial period you have one very strong and unique advantage. No one expects a great deal from you in the way of immediate productivity. In fact, most of your associates will assume that you won't be of much help for several months at least. If, through patient, quiet, and persistent effort you do achieve some modest success, the impact of this upon your fellow employees will have considerably more effect than at any other time in your career: In fact, you have all the cards in your hand to play a winning game right from the beginning.

The Fast Track

If you aspire to move into management and if you hope to win your way to top management responsibility, you are embarking on a very challenging, rigorous, interesting, and exciting career. It requires good business judgment, an eye for the big picture, tremendous physical stamina, the willingness to sacrifice one's personal satisfactions for the good of the organization, and a single-minded drive to succeed. So choosing the fast track really involves more than the simple wish to be judged as a success in the business world; it is the conscious choice of a lifestyle that is dominated by one's work, accompanied by the unceasing drive to do the best possible job and get to the top.

While progress in this quest demands superior performance at all times, realization of such high aspirations can be very elusive. The competition is tough and sometimes unethical. One's good standing can be very fragile in this heady atmosphere where big responsibilities may breed big egos. One mistake, and a promising career can be torpedoed very quickly. Advancement on the fast track also usually requires the active support and sponsorship of senior management. A minor disagreement on a particular course of action has caused the crash of more than one high-flyer because it bruised a higher-up's ego. So tact and the willingness to submerge one's individualism come into play. Furthermore, there is a large element of luck and serendipity involved. So one can spend all of his or her energy in producing superior results, pleasing the right people, and moving up the ladder, and still not realize the top rung.

Regardless of what your ultimate aspiration may be, you will enjoy your work more and realize greater satisfaction if you strive to do the best you can. Advancement comes most assuredly from such an approach. Taking a deep and active interest in your company's business produces a high degree of self-satisfaction, whether you are lucky enough to advance to the top or not. Furthermore, there is no more challenging time as the present for American business. There are few, if any, corporations whose markets are not being redefined or challenged by technology and competition. An explosion of new methodologies, new knowledge, new technologies, new products, and new markets are at work today. Just the heightened availability of information and computing power are forcing major changes. The new workers entering the business world today have a hidden advantage in that they better understand and feel more comfortable with this information base than any previous generation. This fact alone gives the work environment a much more positive perspective for the recent graduate. So you don't need to become president of the company or even come close to have an exciting and rewarding career. And you will probably be happier and more fulfilled if you approach your job with this in mind.

The People on the Job

As soon as you enter the business world you are in competition either explicitly or implicitly. Your work will be judged in relation to your associates, and your potential for advancement will be assessed accordingly. Assessment of job performance for the sake of bonuses and raises is normally done objectively, although the amount granted is usually based on relative performance. Assessment of potential and selection for advancement is essentially a subjective process, however. Though companies spend millions of dollars a year on assessment centers and the like to give the appearance of objectivity, this is mainly form rather than substance. The subjectivity in fact, can never be eliminated. So if you are tapped for advancement in any but a pure seniority system, it is because you have done your job better than some coworker with whom you were in competition. If you are working to get a better job, you can be certain that one or more other people are striving for the same thing. Hence, only your very best effort will get you there. .

Unfortunately the best person doesn't always win. Often in an organizational environment, ability, industry, intelligence, and good business sense, among other estimable qualities, don't carry the day. Other factors such as ultimate potential, strength in a particular functional area, such as marketing, or even physical appearance may be the deciding factors. In some cases it may be the relative power of the person who is advocating one candidacy over another—good old corporate politics. Business isn't always fair; the top candidate doesn't always win. The successful career person is the one who realizes this and continues undaunted. Complaints about lack of fairness will not win the appointment, but continued hard work usually does. He or she rests secure in the knowledge that sooner or later their ability will show and be rewarded.

This does not mean that everyone you meet in the business world is a shark looking for the first sign of blood. On the contrary, most of the people you meet will be dedicated, honest, friendly, and cooperative. You will meet all kinds of people with widely varying backgrounds, educational levels, and personal values. It is important for you to know that your success will depend to a great degree on your ability to relate to all of them equally well. Business is a team sport, and no matter how high you go you are still a member of the team and ever more dependent on it.

In fact one trait shared by nearly every successful manager is the ability to achieve optimum results from subordinates. Not just the good subordinates, but all subordinates. A good manager knows just how far to push each individual. Often the effective manager will ask a subordinate for, and get, more than the individual may have thought he could provide. It is this process of challenge and leadership in handling people that is perhaps the biggest key to success.

The Boss

What about your boss? Will he or she be noble, kind, and helpful? Probably not. In fact, you will probably find that the boss from whom you learn the most will be impatient and totally unreasonable in his demands on you. He will accept no excuses and won't ask for your opinion; he'll just tell you what to do. Lots of times this may not make much sense to you. While you may rightly wonder what you are doing in such a situation working for an autocrat whose instructions may not seem to be the best course, try to see it from the boss's point of view. Inherent in the boss-subordinate relationship is the fact that he or she is playing on a bigger field of operations than yours. If you look at the situation from this wider perspective, it should make more sense to you. As a result, your taking of direction should become more palatable, your execution more effective, and your progress toward your taking over your boss's job more rapid because you understand the bigger picture.

While bosses differ in style, what you have to insist on from any boss is that you be given the opportunity to learn and expand your competence. Get away as quickly as possible from the situation in which you are strictly a gofer. Actively seek to work for those who have the reputation for developing their subordinates. Don't be afraid to speak up in this regard. You are the first and most effective advocate for your career goals. No one else will take such good care of your future. Make sure you make your views known in a positive and constructive way. If the organization doesn't tolerate your taking an active role in your own career path, then maybe you should steer your career path elsewhere. Of course, the more effective you are in what you do and the more potential others see in you, the easier it is to make good things happen for yourself.

The finding of a "mentor" has been cited as a necessary ingredient for career advancement. Certainly this helps, but it doesn't normally come unmerited. Having a mentor means you have someone of influence higher up in the organization who is looking out for your career and advancement. While the selected person merited such treatment by working effectively, he or she must keep producing. It is not a situation you can force or fake your way into. It starts with finding the right kind of stimulating boss who will give you the opportunity to produce meaningful results and then it means going to work.

Peripheral Aspects

In the final analysis, only one person makes chief; every one else plays the role of Indian. For most of us our choice is relegated to what type of Indian we want to be. Ninety-nine percent of those who, at the start, say that their career goal is to run the company never make it. In many cases, those who never had it in mind as a goal make it instead. The point is that if you never get to whatever level you may have set as a goal for yourself, you are not a failure. It is important to put your career goals and accomplishments in perspective for your own peace of mind.

Too often overlooked are the positive peripheral aspects of a career in business. The deep and lasting associations established provide added dimensions to one's life. The constant challenge to one's wit and intelligence provides stimulation as well as opportunity for personal growth. The opportunity to make a positive contribution to the organization provides a source of great personal satisfaction.

THE JOB MARKET TODAY

Over the last five years, two workplace trends have significantly affected the working environment in which college graduates find themselves. The first is the ubiquitous penetration of the computer into every facet of American business operations. The second trend, which is partly driven by the first, is the increasing instability of work life in an American business landscape today, where layoffs have become a permanent part of business tactics. Both of these trends place further emphasis on the need for new, college-educated workers to choose jobs where they will learn transportable skills.

The Personal Computer Revolution

The personal computer revolution has made it possible to bring the productivity and quality-enhancing power of the computer to the administrative and managerial parts of a business. Over 90 percent of college graduates now use computers in their work, up from 43 percent in 1984. Also, those with a college degree were twice as likely to use computers at work as those with only high school diplomas. So the odds are high that you will encounter computers soon after you arrive at your first job.

This inevitable emergence of computing power has two implications for the new college graduate. The first is that the graduate who has a more than passing experience in the use of computers has a very desirable qualification that can yield an advantage in his or her job search. This does not mean that you must be able to program the computer or make the physical connections to the peripherals. It does mean that you ought to have an understanding of the computer as a work tool, including an appreciation for how spreadsheet, word processing, database, graphics, and other programs can be utilized to produce a more effective work result.

After you are employed, it means that you should place a premium on gaining an ability to use the large amounts of information and computing power available as a means to do a better job for yourself and your organization. This ability will come from mastering the basics through working with the computer and then applying the thinking processes and imagination gained from your educational experiences to get the most out of these basic computer skills in terms of output. Making the computer "sing songs" (i.e., do analyses that truly inform) that no one else can make "sing" is one of the surest roads to advancement in large business organizations today. However, if you are not a maestro at the computer keyboard, you will still need to master its more mundane uses. These skills, whether highly creative or boringly routine, are necessary and will be transportable.

Rising Job Instability

As I was growing up in the 1950s, I can remember the strident battles between the American car makers and the United Auto Workers or the steel manufacturers and their unionized workers over job security. In those days, the risk of losing one's job from the vagaries of an employer or the economy were almost universally a blue-collar concern. The vast majority of white-collar workers normally went to a job that was implicitly considered as lifetime employment. There seemed to be an unspoken social contract in effect. If the white-collar worker satisfactorily performed his job functions, the company would continue to employ him, barring some economic disaster. Conversely, if the company paid a fair wage and provided at least some minimum benefits, the worker would continue to provide his labor.

In the 1970s, that contract changed from the employee's viewpoint. With the vogue of career planning and the rise of headhunters to facilitate movement, white-collar workers began to look in an orchestrated way for career-advancing opportunities beyond their current employers. In the 1980s, employers turned the tables and began to lay off millions of "staff" workers who were considered not profit producing. Further along in the eighties, technological changes and regulatory changes produced employee terminations of earthquake proportions at formerly rock-solid employers like AT&T and IBM, as well as at many other U.S. companies. And, as the decade closed, foreign competition was placing increasing pressure on U.S. companies to become ever more productive. In response to all these changes and pressures, some perceptive people developed in the 1990s a solution that harnessed the growing power and decreasing costs of computing with a rethinking of the way the basic processes of a business are done to improve business productivity and profitability—an approach dubbed "reengineering." Under the banner of reengineering, American businesses today are continuing to lay off workers throughout their organizations in astoundingly high numbers.

At this point, the implicit expectations of lifetime employment have become moot. This places an even higher premium on using a criteria of "What will I learn that I can take with me?" as one of your highest criteria for targeting and choosing a first job opportunity. Remember that you will be employed at the discretion of your employer and, while you should avoid being paranoid, you are probably two or three times more likely to have that employment terminated involuntarily on short notice than you would have been in 1980.

Gaining intangible job rewards—such as industry knowledge and contacts or learning the basic skills of a fundamental process like sales—becomes even more important in today's workplace. For example, if a sales job is your target, you should find out who has the best training program within your chosen industry and focus on that company as your first choice. Once you are in that first job, you should dedicate yourself to learning everything that would be of value no matter where you are working. You will most likely also find that by learning and practicing these key skills, you will also be enhancing your chances for long-term advancement where you are currently working.

Some Final Advice

While the job selection process can be systematized to some degree, a good deal of intuition is also involved. When judging a company, trust the way you feel about its people and your chemistry with them. If you find the interviewer and the managers you subsequently meet attractive, compatible, and stimulating, trust the feeling. The odds are that you can prosper working in their environment.

The people for and with whom you work on your first job, as well as the potential for your career growth, are much more important than the salary, the title, or even the company. Your growth and success are primarily dependent on how well you exploit the potential and how effectively you work with those people.

In starting out you will probably be better served joining a large, well-established company. You will get better basic training and have more opportunity to grow at this stage.

Be sure to get the information you feel you need to make a good decision before accepting any offer. Always ask to talk to people of your own age group who have come into the company in the past few years. This is the best way to get a realistic look at what it's like to work there and how your career might progress. And remember: Make the best decision you can, but don't agonize over making the perfect decision. This is only your first job, not a lifetime choice.

Finally, you may wonder if trotting off to graduate business school immediately after graduation might make sense. In general, you will get far more out of business school by going after two or three years of work experience. This will allow you to assimilate the knowledge against a real world background, and you will know better whether you need this additional education.

THE NEW M.B.A.

Until the late 1970s, a master's degree in business administration provided the ticket to the fast track at many companies. But as that degree became more and more common in the 1980s, it became more of a necessity just to gain high visibility jobs in middle management. By 1990, there was such a glut of M.B.A.s that one in four business school graduates were without a job at graduation. Things began improving in the early 90s, and now another bull market for M.B.A.s is in full swing. In what some analysts are calling a "feeding frenzy," corporations are going after graduates from the top business schools with offers that can make heads spin.

This strong uptick in the M.B.A. market is attributable to several emerging changes in the U.S. economy in the mid-1990s. First, investment banks are seeing a resurgence in deal opportunities as the economy has improved. This has brought a strong source of M.B.A. jobs back into the market. Also, the cuts in corporate staff and middle management, as well as the unending list of companies being reengineered, have created a major growth market in consulting firms' recruiting. Finally, as companies reorganize responsibilities in flatter, more horizontal organizational structures, broader, more flexible managers are being sought to replace the old corporate managers who have been retired or let go. In the words of one corporate recruiting executive, "Hiring an M.B.A. is the least costly way we have to fill newly defined management positions after our organizational restructuring. We don't have to pay a recruiter, and we don't have to pay for relocation. And we get a more innovative and motivated employee as a result."

In the new corporate world, those who seem to get the best job offers are those whose undergraduate education and job experience encompass technical disciplines such as engineering and computers. Potential employers are prizing such cross-disciplinary managers more and more. With so much of current and future profit-performance improvement programs dependent upon applying computer technology to work process and service enhancement, such managers are seen as better able to smooth transitions and accomplish the changes needed. However, signing up these new managers is not quite as inexpensive as the recruiter above may lead one to believe.

While most of the 94,000 people who earned M.B.A.s in 1998 received offers of $60,000, for the graduates of America's best business schools, starting salaries were more commonly in the high five figures, with those from the top ten schools commanding a premium. In 1998, reports from Stanford, Harvard, Penn, and a few others revealed offers of $200,000 and more. It was not unusual for candidates to be lured by generous signing bonuses and even offers to repay student loans. Such offers were made most commonly by major consulting firms—whose business has grown by such incredible proportions in the past several years, they can't hire fast enough—and by investment firms, which have also profited immensely by the strengthening economy. As the table below shows, in a good year a starting salary in the low six figures can be easily achievable for those in the top of their class. Of course these students have invested a considerable amount to obtain their degrees, including $50,000 in tuition for two years as well as the wages lost during their time in school.

STARTING SALARIES OF M.B.A. GRADUATES, BY INSTITUTION

Rank/School	1997 Median Starting Salary
1. Harvard University	$82,000[1]
2. University of Pennsylvania (Wharton)	75,000[1]
3. Northwestern University (Kellogg)	75,000[1]
4. Columbia University	88,000
5. Stanford University	80,000
6. Massachusetts Institute of Technology (Sloan)	75,000
7. Dartmouth College (Tuck)	75,000
8. University of Chicago	75,000
9. University of California at Berkeley (Haas)	75,000
10. University of California at Los Angeles (Anderson)	75,000
11. New York University (Stern)	75,000

STARTING SALARIES OF M.B.A. GRADUATES, BY INSTITUTION

Rank/School	1997 Median Starting Salary
12. Duke University (Fuqua)	$71,600
13. University of Virginia (Darden)	71,000
14. University of Michigan	70,000
15. Carnegie Mellon University	70,000
16. Yale University	70,000
17. Cornell University (Johnson)	68,000
18. University of North Carolina, Chapel Hill (Kenan/Flagler)	68,000
19. University of Rochester (Simon)	66,000
20. University of Texas at Austin	65,000
21. Emory University (Goizueta)	65,000
22. Ohio State University (Fisher)	65,000
23. Indiana University at Bloomington	64,900
24. Vanderbilt University	64,000
25. Purdue University (Krannert)	61,900

[1]Estimate.
SOURCE: *U.S. News & World Report,* March 1998.

SALARIES OF EXECUTIVES AT CHARITABLE ORGANIZATIONS

Public scrutiny of executive salaries at charities dates back to the 1992 ouster of United Way of America president William F. Aramony, who was earning $463,000 a year in salary and benefits. The attention to the United Way's finances also revealed that directors in at least sixteen major cities earned over $100,000 a year. Executives at other charitable organizations found themselves defending their compensation to donors, the press, and even Congress, which debated legislation to limit the salaries of executives. But while the number of inquiries about the executives' pay has gone down since then, the pay levels have not. In fact, salaries have actually increased on the average, as boards of directors of charities with lower paid executives have felt a need to increase salaries to keep them on par with other organizations.

According to the *NonProfit Times,* the average nonprofit executive pay hike in 1996 was 4 percent, with the average national salary of a chief executive officer $84,936—$20,500 less than at an educational institution. Although salaries varied widely by type and size of organization, pay increases were less prevalent than improvements to benefits packages, giving employees more to lose if they leave their jobs.

According to a 1997 survey of 207 major charities by *The Chronicle of Philanthropy*, forty charities paid their CEOs at least $300,000, and eight paid their chief executives more than $500,000. The highest paid executive was John W. Rowe, president of Mount Sinai Medical Center in New York, who earned $1,056,636 in salary and benefits; the median salary was $199,206.

Oxford Health Plans had planned to pay its former chairman, Stephen F. Wiggins, $12.6 million in severance. But Governor George Pataki and the New York State Insurance Department pressured them to withhold the remaining $9 million from that package. Mr. Wiggins had already received $3.6 million in cash. The figures became public as the company was thinking of raising premiums by as much as 69 percent for individuals not covered under group plans. Wiggins had reportedly earned $30 million in stock options in 1997, and the founder of Oxford resigned when the struggling company began plans for major restructuring in management after failing to pay its doctors and hospitals.

Companies like Citizens Energy Corp., a nonprofit group formed by Representative Joseph Kennedy, have also continued stirring up controversy. The firm made tens of millions of dollars for friends and insiders, according to the *Wall Street Journal*. Company executives would not discuss actual figures, but William E. James, the group's former president of many years, claimed nothing inappropriate had taken place.

In addition, charities have begun to use for-profit subsidiaries in ways that can allow them to withhold yearly financial statements and tax returns, which nonprofit organizations must make available to whomever requests them. For example, Feed the Children delivered forty-three tons of food in 1996, but in trucks belonging to its for-profit subsidiary. And Minnesota Public Radio president William H. Kling made about $74,000 a year, which was reported to contributors, as required by law. But what it did not have to disclose was that Kling was also paid $380,000 yearly by an affiliated for-profit corporation. Shifting of costs and income between nonprofit and for-profit sides of an organization can make charities seem more efficient and allow for-profit companies more tax benefits, and without the usual disclosures, donors may not be aware of abuses taking place. Minnesota has become one of the few states forcing charities to disclose more subsidiary information, thanks to Matt Entenza, a Minnesota State Representative.

The following tables list the most recent compensation totals (including salary and quantifiable benefits) for leaders of some well-known charitable organizations. These figures are now a matter of public record since all groups seeking nonprofit status must report the salaries of their highest-paid employees to the federal government.

TOTAL COMPENSATION FOR LEADERS OF SELECTED CHARITIES, 1997

Organization (Location)	Chief Executives	Total Compensation
Arts and Culture		
John F. Kennedy Center for the Performing Arts	Lawrence J. Wilker, Managing Director	$248,299
(Washington, DC)	Mstislav Rostropovich, Music Director	355,365
Lincoln Center for the	Nathan Leventhal, President	355,533
Performing Arts	James Norton, Stagehand	201,994
(New York City)		
Metropolitan Opera Association	Joseph Volpe, General Manager	389,000
(New York City)	Marilyn Shapiro, Executive Director, External Affairs	304,000
Music Center of Los Angeles	Esther Wachtell, President[1]	200,000
County	Susan Pearce, VP	107,109
New York City Ballet	Arnold Goldberg, Orchestra Manager	156,000
	Gordon D. Boelzner, Music Director	122,000
Colleges and Universities		
Brigham Young University	Rex E. Lee, President	$138,386
(Provo, Utah)	Reed M. Izatt, Professor of Chemistry	133,335
Case Western Reserve	Agnar Pytte, President	268,631
University (Cleveland)	J. Blumer, Professer	288,076
Columbia University	Michael Sovern, President[1,2]	439,559
(New York City)	Eric Allen Rose, Assistant Professor of Surgery	1,386,873
Cornell University	Frank H. T. Rhodes, President	274,929
(Ithaca, NY)	Wayne Isom, Professor	1,780,013
Dartmouth College	James O. Freedman, President	303,673
(Hanover, NH)	Andrew G. Wallace, Medical School Dean	259,740
Duke University (Durham, NC)	Nannerl Overholser Keohane, President[1]	386,190
	Ralph Snyderman, Dean of Medical School	444,360
Georgetown University	Leo J. O'Donovan, President	220,807
(Washington, DC)	Robert B. Wallace, Professor and Chairman, Department of Surgery	700,498
Harvard University	Neil L. Rudenstine, President	241,645
(Cambridge, MA)	Daniel Tosteson, Dean of Medical School	312,934

TOTAL COMPENSATION FOR LEADERS OF SELECTED CHARITIES, 1997

Organization (Location)	Chief Executives	Total Compensation
Johns Hopkins University (Baltimore)	William C. Richardson, President[3]	$ 368,725
	John L. Cameron, Professor	555,299
Massachusetts Institute of Technology (Cambridge, MA)	Charles M. Vest, President	318,652
	R. J. Thome, Department Head	266,433
New York University (New York City)	L. Jay Oliva, President	332,377
	Saul Farber, Provost, Medical Center	346,345
Northwestern University (Evanston, IL)	Arnold R. Weber, President	354,928
	Artur Raviv, Professor of Finance	337,300
Princeton University (Princeton, NJ)	Harold T. Shapiro, President	295,494
	Randall A. Hack, President of Princeton University Investment Company	243,900
Stanford University (Palo Alto, CA)	Gerhard Casper, President	225,286
	John Niederhuber, Professor of Surgery	1,288,542
University of Chicago	Hannah H. Gray, President[1]	303,000
	Samuel Hellman, Dean of Medical School	597,717
University of Miami (Coral Gables, FL)	Edward T. Foote, President	310,981
	John Uribe, Associate Professor	586,866
University of Pennsylvania (Philadelphia)	Sheldon Hackney, President[1]	310,923
	Alan Wein, Professor, Urology	1,104,000
University of Southern California (Los Angeles)	Steven B. Sample, President	263,656
	Larry Dean Smith, Head Football Coach	726,448
Washington University (St. Louis)	William H. Danforth, Chancellor	144,896
	James L. Cox, Professor of Surgery	589,034
Yale University (New Haven, CT)	Benno C. Schmidt, Jr., President[1]	314,349
	John C. Baldwin, Professor of Cardiothoracic Surgery	502,996

Education Groups (Miscellaneous)

National Merit Scholarship Corporation (Evanston, IL)	M. Elizabeth Jacka, President	$170,625
	Marianne C. Roderick, Executive VP	109,669
Phillips Academy (Andover, MA)	Donald W. McNemar, Headmaster	167,001
	Neil Cullen, Chief Financial Officer	118,181

TOTAL COMPENSATION FOR LEADERS OF SELECTED CHARITIES, 1997

Organization (Location)	Chief Executives	Total Compensation
United Negro College Fund	William H. Gray, III, President	$ 175,000
(New York City)	Virgil E. Ecton, Senior Executive VP	126,000

Environmental and Animal Defense Groups

Organization (Location)	Chief Executives	Total Compensation
Ducks Unlimited (Memphis)	Matthew B. Connolly, Executive VP	$215,174
	Ed Puls, Former Chief Financial Officer	146,606
Environmental Defense Fund	Frederic Krupp, Executive Director	234,573
(New York)	Marcia Aronoff, Director of Programs	133,031
Greenpeace Fund	Steve D'Esposito, Executive Director[1]	49,281
(Washington, DC)	Venola Johnson, Treasurer	38,697
Humane Society of the United States (Washington, DC)	John A. Hoyt, Chief Executive Officer	172,442
	Paul G. Irwin, President	156,556
National Audubon Society	Peter A. A. Berle, President	197,137
(New York City)	Susan Martin, Senior VP	135,178
National Wildlife Federation	Jay D. Hair, President	275,329
(Washington, DC)	William H. Howard, Executive VP	156,922
National Resources Defense	John H. Adams, Executive Director	159,740
Council (New York City)	Tom Cochran, Senior Scientist	112,440
The Nature Conservancy	John C. Sawhill, President	202,118
(Arlington, VA)	W. William Weeks, Chief Operating Officer	142,372
North Shore Animal League	David J. Ganz, President	211,153
(Port Washington, NY)	Edward Hamilton, Veterinarian	108,595
Wilderness Society	Karin Sheldon, Acting President[1]	113,620
(Washington, DC)	Grant P. Thompson, Executive VP	111,625
World Wildlife Fund	Kathryn Fuller, President	201,650
(Washington, DC)	Paige MacDonald, Executive VP	174,400

Health Charities

Organization (Location)	Chief Executives	Total Compensation
American Cancer Society	John R. Seffrin, Executive VP	$253,537
(Atlanta)	Gerald P. Murphy, VP	205,220
American Heart Association	Dudley H. Hafner, Executive VP	311,064
(Dallas)	Rodman Starke, Senior VP	213,610
American Lung Association	John R. Garrison, Managing Director	225,898
(New York City)	Allen B. Rubin, Chief Operating Officer	138,260

TOTAL COMPENSATION FOR LEADERS OF SELECTED CHARITIES, 1997

Organization (Location)	Chief Executives	Total Compensation
Arthritis Foundation (Atlanta)	Don L. Riggin, President	$ 190,022
	Arthur I. Grayzel, Senior VP	174,016
Cystic Fibrosis Foundation (Bethesda, MD)	Robert K. Dresing, President[1]	322,351
	Robert J. Beall, Executive Medical VP	259,434
March of Dimes Birth Defects Foundation (White Plains, NY)	Jennifer Howse, President	161,443
	Vince A. Coughlin, VP	141,403
Muscular Dystrophy Association (Tucson, AZ)	Robert Ross, Executive Director	302,341
	Gerald Weinberg, Director, Field Organization	223,529
National Easter Seal Society (Chicago)	James E. Williams, Jr., President	195,000
	Donald E. Jackson, Executive VP	143,104
National Multiple Sclerosis Society (New York City)	Michael Dugan, President	183,592
	Thor Hanson, Senior Development Officer	248,454
Planned Parenthood Federation of America (New York City)	David J. Andrews, Acting President[1]	212,756
	Michael Policar, VP, Medical	171,557

Hospitals

ALSAC/St. Jude's Research Hospital (Memphis, TN)	Arthur W. Nienhuis, Director	$359,658
	Salwa Moustafa, Anesthesiologist	312,442
Baylor College of Medicine (Houston)	William T. Butler, President	451,052
	Bobby R. Alford, Executive VP	398,387
City of Hope (Los Angeles)	Sanford M. Shapero, President	374,639
	Karen M. Warren, Executive VP	279,513
Massachusetts General Hospital (Boston)	J. Robert Buchanan, Executive VP	572,251
	Robert Crowell, Surgeon	451,484
Mayo Foundation (Rochester, MN)	Robert R. Waller, President	454,905
	C. G. A. McGregor, Surgeon	449,448
Memorial Sloan-Kettering Cancer Center (New York City)	Paul A. Marks, President	1,145,000
	David A. Hidalgo, Chief Attending Surgeon	899,683
Mount Sinai Medical Center (New York City)	John W. Rowe, President	994,725
	Joel Kaplan, Senior VP, Clinical Affairs	1,205,689
Rush-Presbyterian-St. Luke's Medical Center (Chicago)	Leo M. Henikoff, President	441,757
	James W. Williams, Director of the University Transplant Program	692,650

TOTAL COMPENSATION FOR LEADERS OF SELECTED CHARITIES, 1997

Organization (Location)	Chief Executives	Total Compensation
Scripps Clinic and Research Foundation (La Jolla, CA)	Charles C. Edwards, President	$ 457,987
	Lauren W. Blagg, President, Scripps Memorial Hospitals	372,049
Shriners Hospital for Crippled Children (Tampa, FL)	Newton McCollough, Director of Medicine	271,449
	Colin Moseley, Chief of Staff	267,006

Human Service Groups

American Red Cross (Alexandria, VA)	Elizabeth H. Dole, President	$ 201,650
	J. Daniel Connor, Principal Officer, Southern California Region	342,901
Catholic Charities (Alexandria, VA)	Thomas J. Harvey, President	61,995
	Joe A. Heiney-Gonzalez, Deputy to President	58,360
Covenant House (New York City)	Sister Mary Rose McGeady, President	125,469
	James Harnett, Secretary[4]	133,281
Disabled American Veterans (Cincinnati)	Charles E. Joeckel, Jr., National Adjutant[1]	169,639
	Jesse Brown, Executive Director, Washington	113,796
Goodwill Industries International (Bethesda, MD)	David M. Cooney, President	198,153
	Stephen L. Snyderman, Management Information Systems Director	104,382
Habitat for Humanity (Americus, GA)	Millard Fuller, President	41,534
	David Rowe, Director, International Severance Pay	48,692
Hadassah, the Women's Zionist Organization of America (New York City)	Beth Wohlgelernter, Executive Director	106,000
	Alan Tigay, Executive Director, Magazine	86,806
Lions International Foundation (Oak Brook, IL)	Patricia F. O'Kelley, Division Manager	80,629
	Edward A. Lester, Manager, Donor Services	61,332
Rotary International (Evanston, IL)	Spencer Robinson, Jr., General Secretary	184,274
	James R. Fallen, Finance Officer	104,520

TOTAL COMPENSATION FOR LEADERS OF SELECTED CHARITIES, 1997

Organization (Location)	Chief Executives	Total Compensation
Salvation Army (Alexandria, VA)	Kenneth L. Hodder, National Commander	$ 48,233
	Jeffrey S. McDonald, Publications Manager	63,854
Second Harvest (Chicago)	Christine Vladimiroff, President	101,220
	Hilary Freeman, VP, Planning	77,582
Volunteers of America (Metairie, LA)	Clint Cheveallier, President	254,078
	Thomas J. Clark, VP	190,055
YMCA of the USA (Chicago)	David R. Mercer, Executive Director	230,630
	John E. Danielson, Associate Executive Director	176,913
YWCA of the USA (New York City)	Gwendolyn C. Baker, Executive Director	137,156
	Jane Towater, Associate Executive Director	108,513

International Relief and Development Groups

AmeriCares Foundation (Pittsburgh)	Robert Macauley, Chief Executive Officer	0
	Stephen M. Johnson, President	$165,076
CARE (Atlanta)	Philip Johnston, President	262,532
	William Novelli, Executive VP[5]	227,565
Catholic Relief Services (Baltimore)	Kenneth F. Hackett, Executive Director	110,000
	John A. Donnelly, Deputy Executive Director	95,000
Christian Children's Fund (Richmond, VA)	Paul F. McCleary, Executive Director	154,615
	Margaret McCullough, Deputy Executive Director	105,631
Compassion International (Colorado Springs)	Wallace H. Erickson, Chief Executive Officer	120,129
	Wesley Stafford, Executive VP	91,439
Larry Jones International Ministries/Feed the Children (Oklahoma City)	Larry Jones, President	123,361
	Frances Jones, Executive VP	90,747
MAP International (Brunswick, GA)	Larry E. Dixon, President	89,405
	Richard W. Wagner, Executive VP	100,859
Mennonite Central Committee (Akron, PA)	John A. Lapp, Executive Secretary	51,691
	Lynette Meck, U.S. Executive Secretary	47,743

TOTAL COMPENSATION FOR LEADERS OF SELECTED CHARITIES, 1997

Organization (Location)	Chief Executives	Total Compensation
Project Hope/People-to-People Health Foundation (Millwood, VA)	William B. Walsh, Jr., President	$ 174,901
	Robert Crane, Senior VP, Medical Operations	138,332
Save the Children (Westport, CT)	Charles MacCormack, President	178,586
	James Bausch, Former President	273,025
U.S. Committee for UNICEF (New York City)	Lawrence E. Bruce, Jr., President[1]	141,000
	Richard Gorman, Senior VP for Development and Public Affairs	165,000
World Vision (Monrovia, CA)	Robert Seiple, President	119,428
	John Jemelian, Senior VP for Finance and Administration	104,637

Jewish Federations

Greater Miami Jewish Federation	Jacob Solomon, Executive VP	$159,500
	Carol L. Effrat, Assistant Executive VP	115,000
Jewish Federation Council of Greater Los Angeles	Merve Lemmerman, Executive VP[1]	191,615
	Loren Basch, Director of Campaign[1]	148,729
Jewish Federation of Metropolitan Detroit	Robert P. Aronson, Executive VP	206,075
	Joseph Imberman, Endowment Director	104,974
United Jewish Appeal, National (New York City)	Brian J. Lurie, Executive VP	275,749
	Leon J. Twersky, Assistant Secretary	207,503
United Jewish Appeal— Federation of Jewish Philanthropies (New York)	Stephen D. Solender, Executive VP	308,696
	Adam Kahan, Chief Operating Officer	217,861

Museums and Libraries

American Museum of Natural History (New York City)	George D. Langdon, Jr., President	$ 274,335
	Myra Biblowit, Senior VP for Development	182,850
Art Institute of Chicago	James N. Wood, Director of the Museum	239,033
	Robert E. Mars, VP, Administrative Affairs	215,532
Carnegie Institute (Pittsburgh)	Robert C. Wilburn, President	166,950
	Andrew J. Hungerman, Assistant Treasurer	114,703
Los Angeles County Museum of Art	Michael Shapiro, Director	139,393
	Julie Johnston, Director of Development	96,073

TOTAL COMPENSATION FOR LEADERS OF SELECTED CHARITIES, 1997

Organization (Location)	Chief Executives	Total Compensation
Metropolitan Museum of Art (New York City)	Philippe de Montebello, Director	$ 204,564
	William H. Luers, President	189,730
Museum of Fine Arts (Boston)	Alan Shestack, Director	205,461
	Morton J. Golden, Deputy Director	186,247
Museum of Modern Art (New York City)	Richard E. Oldenburg, Director	194,064
	Sue B. Dorn, Deputy Director of Development and Public Affairs	161,282
New York Public Library	Timothy S. Healy, President	155,470
	John H. Masten, Executive VP	213,837
Smithsonian Institution (Washington, DC)	Robert McC. Adams, Secretary[6]	219,313
	Donald Moser, Editor	217,881
United States Holocaust Memorial Museum (Washington, DC)	Jeshajahu Weinberg, Museum Director	205,248
	Joseph Brodecki, Campaign Director[1]	174,119

Public Affairs Groups

Anti-Defamation League of B'nai B'rith (New York City)	Abraham H. Foxman, National Director	$209,728
	Sheldon Fleigelmann, Development Director	141,149
Carter Center (Atlanta)	John Hardman, Executive Director	118,990
Heritage Foundation (Washington, DC)	Edwin J. Feulner, President[7]	377,904
	Edwin Meese, Distinguished Scholar	226,864
Mothers Against Drunk Driving (Irving, TX)	Robert King, Executive Director	142,376
	Joseph King, Director, Marketing and Development	108,223
National Association for the Advancement of Colored People (New York City)	Benjamin Hooks, Executive Director[1] Wade Henderson, Washington Bureau Director	190,285 72,960
National Urban League (New York City)	John Jacob, President	195,427
	Frank Lomax III, Executive VP	139,135

Public Broadcasting

KCET Community Television of Southern California (Los Angeles)	William H. Kobin, President	$259,552
	Donald G. Youpa, Executive VP	182,147

TOTAL COMPENSATION FOR LEADERS OF SELECTED CHARITIES, 1997

Organization (Location)	Chief Executives	Total Compensation
KCTS Television (Seattle)	Burnill Clark, President	$ 175,952
	Walter Parsons, Senior VP	107,939
KQED (San Francisco)	Anthony S. Tiano, President	153,889
	Robert Johnston, Jr., Chief Financial Officer	114,972
Public Broadcasting Service (Alexandria, VA)	Bruce Christensen, President[1]	148,402
	Jennifer Lawson, Executive VP	118,400
Thirteen/WNET (New York City)	William F. Baker, President	215,719
	Lester M. Crystal, Executive Producer	358,838
WETA (Arlington, VA)	Sharon Rockefeller, President	175,683
	Neil B. Mahrer, Executive VP	208,789
WGBH Educational Foundation (Boston)	Henry P. Becton, President	185,412
	Norman Abram, Talent	234,250
WTTW/Chicago Educational Television Association	William J. MacCarter, President	168,067
	John Callaway, Senior Correspondent	166,859

Christian Groups

American Bible Society (New York City)	Eugene B. Habecker, President	$211,755
	Maria I. Martinez, VP for National Programs	128,863
Christian and Missionary Alliance (Colorado Springs)	David L. Rambo, President	80,404
	Duane A. Wheeland, VP	70,090
Focus on the Family (Colorado Springs)	Paul Nelson, Executive VP[8]	105,361
	Mike Trout, Senior VP[8]	117,917
Billy Graham Evangelistic Association (Minneapolis)	Billy Graham, Chief Executive Officer	95,746
	John R. Corts, Chief Operating Officer	124,108

United Way

United Way and Community Chest of Greater Cincinnati	Richard Aft, President	$204,460
	Pradip Patel, VP, Finance and Administration	108,357

TOTAL COMPENSATION FOR LEADERS OF SELECTED CHARITIES, 1997

Organization (Location)	Chief Executives	Total Compensation
United Way/Crusade of Mercy (Chicago)	Jack Prater, President[1] Frank Karr, Senior VP	$ 200,114 120,005
United Way for Southeastern Michigan (Detroit)	H. Clay Howell, President[1] Warren T. Burt, Jr., VP, Administration	203,262 148,830
United Way of Allegheny County (Pittsburgh)	William J. Meyer, President Robert J. Krasman, Treasurer	103,500 81,502
United Way of Central Indiana (Indianapolis)	Irvin S. Katz, President Dale F. DePoy, VP, Finance and Administration	103,500 81,502
United Way of Central Maryland (Baltimore)	Norman O. Taylor, President[9] James W. Brooks, Chief Financial Officer	195,171 87,813
United Way of Franklin County (Columbus, OH)	William L. Keller, President Keith Barsuhn, VP, Contributor Services	160,248 84,644
United Way of Greater Los Angeles	Herbert L. Carter, President Richard Sykes, Senior Vice President	205,694 135,456
United Way of Greater Rochester (Rochester, NY)	Joseph G. Calabrese, President William G. McCullough, Executive VP	146,825 89,603
United Way of Greater St. Louis	Martin B. Covitz, President[1] Stanley Wakeham, Senior VP, Campaign	206,430 142,248
United Way of King County (Seattle)	Roberta van der Voort, President[1] Rodney Wheeler, VP Resource Development	174,617 94,849
United Way of Massachusetts Bay (Boston)	Marian L. Heard, President Richard A. Millott, Senior VP	142,826 110,321
United Way of Metropolitan Atlanta	Mark L. O'Connell, President Brian Gallagher, Group VP	180,244 43,083
United Way of Metropolitan Dallas	Edward E. McDunn, President J. J. Guise, Vice Chairman, Board of Directors	165,600 130,625
United Way of New York City	Ralph Dickerson, Jr., President Lawrence Mandell, Executive VP	263,663 143,156
United Way of Southeastern Pennsylvania (Philadelphia)	Ted L. Moore, President Al J. Sassone, VP	203,192 139,301

TOTAL COMPENSATION FOR LEADERS OF SELECTED CHARITIES, 1997

Organization (Location)	Chief Executives	Total Compensation
United Way of the Bay Area (San Francisco)	Thomas Ruppaner, President	$ 184,981
	Frank Melcher, Executive VP	141,461
United Way of the Minneapolis Area (Minneapolis)	James C. Colville, President	195,567
	Terri D. Barreiro, Senior Director	99,780
United Way of the National Capital Area (Washington, DC)	Oral Suer, Executive VP	217,420
	Kenneth R. Unzicker, Corporate Affairs and Associate Campaign Director	167,665
United Way of the Texas Gulf Coast (Houston)	Judith B. Craven, President	140,000
	Mike Bisesi, Senior VP	83,506
United Way Services (Cleveland)	Jack C. Costello, President	209,560
	Gloria Pace King, Senior VP	123,050

Youth Groups

Big Brothers/Big Sisters of America (Philadelphia)	Thomas McKenna, National Executive Director	$108,010
	Dagmar McGill, Deputy National Executive Director	74,647
Boy Scouts of America (Irving, TX)	Ben H. Love, Chief Scout Executive[1]	287,217
	Joseph Anglim, Chief Financial Officer[1,10]	423,746
Boys and Girls Clubs of America (New York City)	Thomas G. Garth, National Director	207,738
	Joseph R. Burkart, Assistant National Director	152,025
Camp Fire Boys and Girls (Kansas City, MO)	K. Russell Weathers, Executive VP	148,179
	Emerson Goodwin, Director of Development and Communications	91,822
Father Flanagan's Boys Home (Boys Town, NB)	Rev. Valentine J. Peter, Executive VP	20,000
	Patrick Brookhouser, Director, Boys Town National Research Hospital	223,609
Girl Scouts of the USA (New York City)	Mary Rose Main, National Executive Director	212,088
	Florence Corsello, Controller	144,551
Junior Achievement (Colorado Springs)	Karl Flemke, President	202,146
	Ralph Schulz, Executive VP	148,174
Special Olympics International (Washington, DC)	Robert S. Shriver, III, President	150,000

TOTAL COMPENSATION FOR LEADERS OF SELECTED CHARITIES, 1997

Organization (Location)	Chief Executives	Total Compensation
Miscellaneous Philanthropy Organizations		
Independent Charities of America (San Francisco)	Patrick Maguire, President	$175,000
National Academy of Sciences (Washington, DC)	Frank Press, President[1]	317,580
	Robert M. White, President, National Academy of Engineering	291,628
Salk Institute for Biological Studies (San Diego)	Renato Dulbecco, President[1]	273,204
	Delbert E. Clanz, Executive VP	335,434
U.S. Olympic Committee (Colorado Springs)	Harvey W. Schiller, Executive Director	376,429
	John Krimsky, Jr., Deputy Secretary	282,977

NOTE: Compensation figures include benefits where applicable, but not expense allowances. [1]No longer holds position. [2]Includes $32,615 in supplemental pay in lieu of a waived pension contribution. [3]Includes $72,357 for housing. [4]Includes a one-time payment of $16,093. [5]Includes pay for unused vacation in the amounts of $30,538 for Mr. Johnston and $19,518 for Mr. Novelli. [6]The institution also provides Mr. Adams with use of a house it purchased in 1984 for $485,000. [7]Includes bonus of $159,100. [8]Includes relocation expenses of $10,150 for Mr. Nelson and $25,276 for Mr. Trout. [9]The institution also provided $70,241 in moving expenses, closing costs on a new house, sales commission on Mr. Taylor's previous house, and temporary housing in Baltimore. [10]Mr. Anglim, who retired in 1992 after forty years of employment, received an annual salary of $185,000 and an annuity of $352,502.
SOURCE: *Chronicle of Philanthropy,* 1997.

Where to Find Further Information

BOOKS

Whether you are young and just beginning to look for your first job or a bit older and returning to the workforce after an illness or staying home with the young children, the best way to start your search is with a visit to your local library. The same is true for the more than 10 million Americans who change occupations each year.

If you are like most people, you are puzzled or confused by the incredible assortment of jobs that exist in the United States, and the best way to overcome those feelings is by educating yourself about the job market. What jobs interest you? Are you qualified? What jobs are actually available?

The two most comprehensive books are the 1,000-page *Professional Careers Sourcebook* (Gale Research Publishing) and *The Occupational Outlook Handbook, 1998–99*, produced by the U.S. Department of Labor (this book can also be purchased at any U.S. government bookstore, or by calling the office of the Superintendent of Documents in Washington, 202–783–3238. It costs $38. Both books contain job descriptions, and the names and addresses of associations that can provide further information on career possibilities.

Other very useful general works include:

- *The Almanac of American Employers* (annual), Plunkett Publishing. Profiles and rankings of the nation's 500 most successful large corporations with 5,000 or more employees.
- *The Encyclopedia of Careers and Vocational Guidance* (new editions periodically), Ferguson Publishing, 4 volumes, 2800 pages. The first volume evaluates twenty-six industries with data on their histories, structures, career paths, and outlook; volumes 2–4 contain details about specific jobs.
- *The National Job Bank* (annual), Adams Media Publishers. Alphabetically arranged by state, this extensive (1,200 pages) directory encompasses more than 20,000 employer profiles with a great deal of pertinent information. Also available in separate volumes for each state.

609

ON-LINE JOB SOURCES

Once upon a time, searching for a new job was a long, tedious job that left you with ink-stained fingers and a living room littered with newspaper classified sections. Now, thanks to computers and the Internet, it's merely a long, tedious job that gives you carpal tunnel syndrome. Sifting through the vast amount of information on the Internet can consume an incredible amount of time, and many of the high-tech, do-it-all job sites lead to more distractions than job opportunities.

The first stop for a new on-line job-hunter is usually one of these all-in-one sites. There are hundreds of job and résumé clearinghouses on the Internet, most offering not only help-wanted ads from companies in every state, but also everything from career guidance to résumé-creation software, and a slew of other services. These Web sites—including current hot spots like **Monster Board** (http://www.monsterboard.com) and **Hotjobs** (www.hotjobs.com)—seem to offer every job-seeker's dream: Just e-mail them your résumé or fill out a few online forms and, bingo! You'll be miraculously matched up with the employer of your dreams without ever licking a stamp or picking up the phone.

The problem is, new sites like this spring up and collapse again every day, and thousands of other job-seekers are filling in the same forms, hoping to land a job the quick and easy way. Undoubtedly, some people meet this goal, but there are ways of using the Internet for a more directed job search, with a greater chance of success.

Career Counseling and General Job Information

If you find yourself looking aimlessly for a job, any job at all, there are some on-line services that can help to focus your search. Some are entire sites devoted to career information or advice; some are subsections of those giant résumé-posting sites. None of these services can fill all your research needs or replace talking to someone in a field that interests you, but they may be able to give you a *small* push in some direction.

First stop: the U.S. Government. The **Bureau of Labor Statistics** maintains an on-line version of the latest *Occupational Outlook Handbook* (http://stats.bls.gov/ocohome.htm), with a wealth of information to supplement what you've already found in this almanac. It's a typically drab government site, but for additional information on working conditions, training, salaries, and more, this is a great place to turn. The ability to search for jobs by keyword or by clusters of related occupations is a great time-saver, too. Another great government service is **America's Job Bank** (http://www.ajb.dni.us), which brings together the ubiquitous résumé–posting/job-listing services, an abundance of information on national job market trends, links to state labor departments, and well-annotated links to a wide variety of career-oriented Web sites.

On-line job-hunting has become a big business in its own right, and if you're so inclined, you can wade through a thousand glitzy, corporate-sponsored career information Web sites. **CareerMosaic** (http://www.career mosaic.com) is one well-publicized name in the world of on-line job-hunting; its career resource page includes a pretty good selection of general job-hunting tips, topical advice, interactive tools, and information on employers. The site is sponsored by *Fortune* Magazine, though, so there's a strong bias toward *Fortune* 500 companies. If your career goals don't fall within this field, you might want to seek advice elsewhere. **Kaplan Careers** (http://www.kaplan.com/career/) compiles some handy information, too, including sections devoted to different (sometimes off-the-wall) career types, but expect a lot of ads for Kaplan publications while you're there.

The **Career Resource Center** (http://www.careers.org/) is a great low-key alternative to sites like these, offering most of the same information with a less manic tone. Their "Career Gems" is an up-to-date listing of many of the better job-related Web sites, and the "Career References" section can point you to sites dealing with everything from basic job-search skills to state career resources to industry-specific information and contacts.

Some sites like these also include novelties like temperament tests or interactive career decision-making programs. These can be fun to take but ultimately are about as helpful as your daily horoscope—and they take a lot longer to complete. Richard Nelson Bolles maintains an on-line companion to his popular *What Color Is Your Parachute?* books, and devotes one section to these tests (http://www.tenspeedpress.com/parachute/counseling2.htm). Check here for a big list of them and some common-sense tips about acting on their results and predictions.

Regional Information

If your job search is prompted by a need or desire to relocate, you will *definitely* be able to simplify the process by going on-line. Some of the big Internet search engines (like Yahoo, Excite, or Snap!) offer state-specific pages that consolidate a variety of information about regional services and attractions. Do a search for "Alaska" on Yahoo, for example, and with a few quick clicks you can summon up a tidy compilation of links on travel, real estate, entertainment, employment data, and specific company Web sites within that state.

Remember those ink-stained fingers? That occupational hazard is disappearing because more and more newspapers and other periodicals are going on-line, and most of these offer a searchable classified section on their

Web site. This feature is an incredible blessing when you're looking for out-of-state jobs: If you're in Des Moines but you want to work in western Pennsylvania, how are you supposed to get your hands on the latest *Pittsburgh Post-Gazette*? Use your browser to go to http://www.postgazette.com, of course, and jump straight to the employment section of the classifieds—and while you're there, you can check out the apartment listings for a quick fix on rent and different areas of the city.

Before you start discussing salary with an out-of-state employer, you might want to make one more on-line stop. Many of those all-in-one job sites include cost-of-living calculators, so you see if that $30,000 a year job in Manhattan will let you maintain the lifestyle you've had for $20,000 in Cleveland. **Homefair** offers this service (plus international cost-of-living information) at http://www.homefair.com/calc/salcalc.html. And when it's time to hit the road for that big interview, you can create and print out directions from your front door to the company headquarters at **Mapquest** (http://www.mapquest.com).

Specific Employers

So now you know what you want to do, where you want to do it, and you've surfed your way around the Internet home of your "dream employer." Maybe you've really hit the jackpot: they've got online job listings, there's a vacancy for a job for which you're eminently qualified, and you've just emailed your resume to the human resources contact listed on the website. Time to take a break and wait for the job offer to roll in, right?

Don't log off yet. If it's not an entry-level job, there's a good chance that somebody at a lower position in the company is being considered for it; and even if it's an absolute bottom-of-the-ladder position, intended for new college graduates, current employees were probably turning in resumes for friends and relatives before the position was even vacated. File your resume with the human resources folks, by all means, but take extra time to track down some people in the department in which you'd be working. Even if the position is already filled, or even if you *don't* see any openings on the website, making yourself known to the right people can pay off: next time that position becomes available, your resume is already on top of the pile of candidates.

Depending on the size and technological state of the company, you might find nothing more than a front-desk phone number for the company—or you might find a searchable directory of email addresses for everyone from the CEO to an office assistant hired last week. If you dig up the email address for someone in the division you'd like to join, a few concise words about your qualifications and interest in the company will usually elicit a polite response. If that person consents, you might send a *simple, plain-text resume* in the body of an email message (unless they request something in a different format); if that particular person isn't currently hiring, they might be able to pass your data along to someone who is, and you can send along that professionally-typeset *curriculum vitae* when it's requested.

A final tip here: If possible, drop a quick line to someone in the company who already has the type of job you want, asking about their general job duties and satisfaction. The ease and informality of e-mail leads some people to be astonishingly honest in their correspondence, and you may learn something (about a boss from hell, imminent departmental restructuring, lousy food in the cafeteria) that lets you cross that particular company off your list. On the other hand, you might discover that your dream employer has finally come true—either way, Internet or no Internet, you'll still have to do some serious work to find the answer.

More Job-Hunting Sites

A search for "employment" or "job listings" on any major search engine will summon up an enormous list of sites that offer some combination of career information and job-listing services. For better or for worse, here is a very small sampling of sites to get you started:

Alta Vista Careers: careers.av.com

America's Employers: www.americasemployers.com/

Best Jobs in the USA: www.bestjobsusa.com/

CareerMosaic: www.careermosaic.com/

CareerNET: www.careernet.com/

Careerpath: www.careerpath.com

Career Resource Center: www.careers.org/

Getajob: www.getajob.com

HotJobs: www.hotjobs.com

JobSmart: jobsmart.org/tools/career/

Jobweb: www.jobweb.com

Monster Board: www.monster.com/

NationJob Online Jobs Database: www.nationjob.com/

US Careers: www.uscareers.com/

These two sites are directed specifically at first-time career hunters:

College Grad Job Hunter: www.collegegrad.com/

Entry-Level Job Seeker Assistant: members.aol.com/Dylander/jobhome. html

These sites focus on **federal jobs**—why they are (or aren't) desirable, which ones are available, what the qualifications are, and how you can improve your odds of getting one. For jobs and other data at the state level, try searching for "<state name> department of labor" on one of the major Internet search engines.

America's Job Bank: www.ajb.dni.us/

Federal Jobs Digest: www.jobsfed.com/

Federal Jobs.Net: federaljobs.net/

HRS Federal Jobs Search: www.hrsjobs.com/

Federal Job Source: www.dcjobsource.com/fed.html

State and City Information

You can search for more specific information on states and cities with any search engine, but these sites do a lot of the work for you, combining all kinds of state- and city-specific information into easily accessible pages:

Excite: www.excite.com/local/

Snap.com: local.snap.com

Yahoo: local.yahoo.com

Company Directories

To find a particular company's Web site, you can usually just type their name into any search engine. To locate businesses in a certain location, you can try the sites listed above. If you want to find a particular *kind* of company, though, or want statistics about a specific company that don't come from the organization itself, you have to pursue other options. To search by business field or category:

BizWeb: www.bizweb.com/

ComFind: www.comfind.com/

Excite: www.excite.com/guide/business/companies/

Yahoo: dir.yahoo.com/Business_and_Economy/Companies/

To search for company statistics:

EDGAR Database of Corporate Information: www.sec.gov/edgarhp. htm (for info on companies registered with the SEC)

GTE BigBook: www.bigbook.com (business profiles available for purchase)

STATE AND LOCAL INFORMATION

For help in locating state or local area information, you can contact the following:

State Occupational Information Coordinating Committee (SOICC). These committees may provide the information directly, or refer you to other sources. The addresses and telephone numbers of the directors of SOICC's are listed below.

State employment security agencies. These agencies develop detailed information about local labor markets, such as current and projected employment by occupation and industry, characteristics of the work force, and changes in state and local area economic activity. Addresses and telephone numbers of the directors of research and analysis in these agencies are listed below.

Most states have career information delivery systems (CIDS). Look for these systems in secondary schools, postsecondary institutions, libraries, job-training sites, vocational rehabilitation centers, and employment service offices. The public can use the systems' computers, printed material, microfiche, and toll-free hotlines to obtain information on occupations, educational opportunities, student financial aid, apprenticeships, and military careers. Ask counselors and SOICC's for specific locations.

Every state has education and training data that are organized by occupation or training program title, type of institution, and geographic areas. The database is compiled at the state level and includes more than 217,000 education and training programs offered by over 21,000 schools, colleges, and hospitals. If you are interested, contact individual state-specific data.

State occupational projections are also available on the Internet at: www.udesc.state.ut.us/almis/stateproj/

ALABAMA

Chief, Labor Market Information, Department of Industrial Relations, 649 Monroe St., Room 422, Montgomery, AL 36130. Phone: (334) 242-8859.

Executive Director, Alabama Occupational Information Coordinating Committee, Alabama Center for Commerce, Room 424, 401 Adams Ave., P.O. Box 5690, Montgomery, AL 36103-5690. Phone: (334) 242-2990.

ALASKA

Chief, Research and Analysis, Alaska Department of Labor, P.O. Box 25501, Juneau, AK 99802-5501. Phone: (907) 465-4500.

Executive Director, Alaska Occupational Information Coordinating Committee, Research and Analysis Section, P.O. Box 25501, Juneau, AK 99802-5501. Phone: (907) 465-4518.

ARIZONA

Research Administrator, Department of Economic Security, P.O. Box 6123, Site Code 733A, Phoenix, AZ 85005. Phone: (602) 542-3871.

Executive Director, Arizona State Occupational Information Coordinating Council, P.O. Box 6123, Site Code 897J, 1789 West Jefferson St., First Floor North, Phoenix, AZ 85005-6123. Phone: (602) 542-3871.

ARKANSAS

LMI Director, Employment Security Department, P.O. Box 2981, Little Rock, AR 72203. Phone: (501) 682-3159.

Executive Director, Occupational Information Coordinating Council/ Employment Security Division, Employment and Training Services, P.O. Box 2981, Little Rock, AR 72203-2981. Phone: (501) 682-3159.

CALIFORNIA

Chief, Labor Market Information Division, Employment Development Department, 7000 Franklin Blvd., Bldg. 1100, MIC 57, P.O. Box 826880, Sacramento, CA 94280-0001. Phone: (916) 262-2160.

Executive Director, California Occupational Information Coordinating Council, 1116 9th St. Lower Level, P.O. Box 944222, Sacramento, CA 94244-2220. Phone: (916) 323-6544.

COLORADO

Director, LMI, Colorado Department of Labor, 1515 Arapahoe Ave., Tower 2, Suite 400, Denver, CO 80202-2117. Phone: (303) 620-4977.

Director, Colorado Occupational Information Coordinating Council, 1515 Arapahoe Street, Tower Two, level 3, Suite 300, Denver, CO 80202. Phone: (303) 620-4981.

CONNECTICUT

Director of Research, Connecticut Labor Department, 200 Folly Brook Blvd., Wethersfield, CT 06109. Phone: (860) 566-2121.

Executive Director, Connecticut Occupational Information Coordinating Council, Connecticut Department of Labor, 200 Folly Brook Boulevard, Wethersfield CT 06109. Phone: (860) 566-7963.

DELAWARE

LMI Director, Department of Labor, 4425 N. Market Street, Wilmington, DE 19809-0965. Phone: (302) 761-8069.

Executive Director, Delaware OICC/Office of Occupational and Labor Market Information/DOL, University Office Plaza, P.O. Box 9965, Wilmington, DE 19809-0965. Phone: (302) 761-8050.

DISTRICT OF COLUMBIA

Chief of Labor Market Information, Department of Employment Services, 500 C St. NW., Room 201, Washington, DC 20001. Phone: (202) 724-7214.

Executive Director, District of Columbia Occupational Information Co-ordinating Council, 500 C St. NW, Suite 200, Washington, DC 20001-2187. Phone: (202) 724-7205.

FLORIDA

Chief, Bureau of LMI, Department of Labor and Employment Security, The Hartman Building, Suite 200, 2012 Capitol Circle SE, Tallahassee, FL 32399. Phone: (904) 488-6037.

Manager, Workplace Development Information Coordinating Committee, Bureau of Labor Market Information, Department of Labor and Employment Security, 2012 Capitol Circle SE, Hartman Bldg., Suite 200, Tallahassee, FL 32399-2151. Phone: (904) 488-1048.

GEORGIA

Director, Labor Information Systems, Department of Labor, 223 Courtland St. NE, Atlanta, GA 30303-1751. Phone: (404) 656-3177.

Executive Director, Georgia Occupational Information Coordinating Council, Department of Labor, 148 International Blvd., Sussex Place, Atlanta, GA 30303-1751. Phone: (404) 656-9639.

HAWAII

Chief, Research and Statistics Office, Department of Labor and Industrial Relations, 830 Punchbowl St., Rm 304, Honolulu, HI 96813. Phone: (808) 586-8999.

Executive Director, Hawaii State Occupational Information Coordinating Council, 830 Punchbowl St., Room 315, Honolulu, HI 96813-5080. Phone: (808) 586-8750.

IDAHO

Director, Research and Analysis, Department of Employment, 317 Main St., Boise, ID 83735-0001. Phone: (208) 334-6169.

Director, Idaho Occupational Information Coordinating Council, Len B. Jordan Bldg., Room 301, 650 West State St., P.O. Box 83720, Boise, ID 83720-0095. Phone: (208) 334-3705.

ILLINOIS

Economic Information and Analysis Manager, Department of Employment Security, 401 South State St., 2S, Chicago, IL 60605. Phone: (312) 793-2316.

Executive Director, Illinois Occupational Information Coordinating Council, 217 East Monroe, Suite 203, Springfield, IL 62706-1147. Phone: (217) 785-0789.

INDIANA

Deputy Commissioner for Field Support and Business Development, Department of Workforce Development, 10 North Senate Ave., Indianapolis, IN 46204-2277. Phone: (317) 233-5724.

Director, Indiana Occupational Information Coordinating Committee/Workforce Development/Technical Education, Indiana Government Center South, 10 North Senate Ave., Second Floor, Indianapolis, IN 46204-2277. Phone: (317) 233-5099.

IOWA

Bureau Chief, Research and Information Services, Department of Workforce Development, 1000 East Grand Ave., Des Moines, IA 50319. Phone: (515) 281-8181.

Executive Director, Iowa Occupational Information Coordinating Council, Iowa Workforce Development, 200 East Grand Ave., Des Moines, IA 50319. Phone: (515) 242-5032.

KANSAS

Chief, Labor Market Information Services, Department of Human Resources, 401 SW Topeka Avenue, Topeka, KS 66603-3182. Phone: (913) 296-5058.

Director, Kansas Occupational Information Coordinating Committee, 401 Topeka Ave., Topeka, KS 66603. Phone: (913) 296-3512.

KENTUCKY

Manager, LMI Branch, Department of Employment Services, 275 East Main St., Frankfort, KY 40621. Phone: (502) 564-7976.

Information Liaison/Manager, Kentucky Occupational Information Coordinating Council, 500 Mero Street, Room 2031, Frankfort, KY 40601. Phone: (502) 564-4258.

LOUISIANA

Director, Research and Statistics Division, Department of Employment and Training, P.O. Box 94094, Baton Rouge, LA 70804-9094. Phone: (504) 342-3141.

Director, Louisiana Occupational Information Coordinating Committee, P.O. Box 94094, Baton Rouge, LA 70804-9094. Phone: (504) 342-5149.

MAINE

Director, Labor Market Information Services, Department of Labor/BES, 20 Union St., Augusta, ME 04330. Phone: (207) 287-2271.

SOICC Director, Maine Occupational Information Coordinating Committee, State House Station 71, Augusta, ME 04333. Phone: (207) 624-6200.

MARYLAND

Director, Office of Labor Market Analysis and Information, Department of Labor, Licensing, and Regulations, 1100 North Eutaw St., Room 601, Baltimore, MD 21201. Phone: (410) 767-2250.

MASSACHUSETTS

LMI and Research Director, Division of Employment and Training, Hurley Building, 5th Floor, 19 Staniford St., Boston, MA 02114. Phone: (617) 626-6556.

Director, Massachusetts Occupational Information Coordinating Council/Division of Employment Security, Charles F. Hurley Bldg., 2nd Floor, Government Center, Boston, MA 02114. Phone: (617) 727-5718.

MICHIGAN

Deputy Director, Management and Financial Services, Employment Security Commission, 7310 Woodward Ave., Room 510, Detroit, MI 48202. Phone: (313) 876-5904.

Executive Coordinator, Michigan Occupational Information Coordinating Committee, Victor Office Center, 201 North Washington Square, 4th Floor, Lansing, MI 48913. Phone: (517) 373-0363.

MINNESOTA

Director, Research and Statistical Services, Department of Economic Security, 390 North Robert St., 5th Floor, St. Paul, MN 55101. Phone: (612) 296-6546.

Director, Minnesota Occupational Information Coordinating Council/Department of Economic Security, 390 North Robert Street, St. Paul, MN 55101. Phone: (612) 296-2072.

MISSISSIPPI

Chief, Labor Market Information Department, Employment Security Commission, P.O. Box 1699, 1520 West Charles St., Jackson, MS 39215-1699. Phone: (601) 961-7424.

SOICC Director, Mississippi State Occupational Information Coordinating Committee, 301 West Pearl St., Jackson, MS 39203-3089. Phone: (601) 949-2240.

MISSOURI

Chief, Research and Analysis, Division of Employment Security, 421 East Dunkin St., P.O. Box 59, Jefferson City, MO 65104-0059. Phone: (573) 751-3595.

Director, Missouri Occupational Information Coordinating Committee, 400 Dix Rd., Jefferson City, MO 65109. Phone: (573) 751-3800.

MONTANA

Chief, Research and Analysis, Department of Labor and Industry, P.O. Box 1728, Helena, MT 59624. Phone: (406) 444-2430.

SOICC Director, Montana Occupational Information Coordinating Committee, P.O. Box 1728, 1301 Lockey St., Second Floor, Helena, MT 59624-1728. Phone: (406) 444-2741.

NEBRASKA

LMI Administrator, Department of Labor, 550 South 16th St., P.O. Box 94600, Lincoln, NE 68509-4600. Phone: (402) 471-9964.

Administrator, Nebraska Occupational Information Coordinating Committee, P.O. Box 94600, State House Station., Lincoln, NE 68509-4600. Phone: (402) 471-9953.

NEVADA

Chief, Research and Analysis/LMI, Information, Development, and Processing Division, Employment Security Department, 500 East 3rd St., Carson City, NV 89713-0001. Phone: (702) 687-4550.

Manager, Nevada Occupational Information Coordinating Committee/ DETR, 500 East 3rd St., Carson City, NV 89713. Phone: (702) 687-4550.

NEW HAMPSHIRE

Director, Labor Market Information, Department of Employment Security, 32 South Main St., Concord, NH 03301. Phone: (603) 228-4123.

Director, New Hampshire Occupational Information Coordinating Committee, 64 Old Suncook Rd., Concord, NH 03301. Phone: (603) 228-3349.

NEW JERSEY

Staff Director, New Jersey Occupational Information Coordinating Committee, Labor Bldg., 5th Floor, CN057, Trenton, NJ 08625-0057. Phone: (609) 292-2682.

NEW MEXICO

Chief, Economic Research and Analysis Bureau, Department of Labor, 401 Broadway Blvd, NE, P.O. Box 1928, Albuquerque, NM 87103. Phone: (505) 841-8645.

SOICC Director, New Mexico Occupational Information Coordinating Committee, 401 Broadway NE, Tiwa Bldg., P.O. Box 1928, Albuquerque, NM 87103. Phone: (505) 841-8455.

NEW YORK

Director, Division of Research and Statistics, New York State Department of Labor, State Office Building Campus, Room 401, Albany, NY 12240. Phone: (518) 457-6369.

Executive Director, New York State Occupational Information Coordinating Committee/DOL, Research and Statistics Division, State Campus, Bldg. 12, Room 488, Albany, NY 12240. Phone: (518) 457-3806.

NORTH CAROLINA

Director, Labor Market Information, Employment Security Commission, P.O. Box 25903, Raleigh, NC 27611. Phone: (919) 733-2937.

Executive Director, North Carolina Occupational Information Coordinating Committee, 700 Wade Avenue, P.O. Box 25903, Raleigh, NC 27611. Phone: (919) 733-6700.

NORTH DAKOTA

Director, Research and Statistics, Job Service North Dakota, P.O. Box 5507, Bismarck, ND 58506-5507. Phone: (701) 328-2868.

Program Administrator, North Dakota State Occupational Information Coordinating Committee, 1720 Burnt Boat Dr., P.O. Box 5507, Bismarck, ND 58506–5507. Phone: (701) 328-9734.

OHIO

Administrator, Labor Market Information Division, Bureau of Employment Services, 78–80 Chestnut, 5th Floor, Columbus, OH 43215. Phone: (614) 752-9494.

Director, Ohio Occupational Information Coordinating Committee/ Division of LMI, Ohio Bureau of Employment Services, 145 South Front St., Columbus, OH 43215. Phone: (614) 466-1109.

OKLAHOMA

Director, Research Division, Employment Security Commission, 305 Will Rogers Memorial Office Bldg., Oklahoma City, OK 73105. Phone: (405) 557-7265.

Executive Director, Oklahoma Occupational Information Coordinating Council, Department of Voc/Tech Education, 1500 W. 7th Ave., Stillwater, OK 74074-4364. Phone: (405) 743-5198.

OREGON

Administrator for Research, Tax and Analysis, Oregon Employment Department, 875 Union St. NE, Salem, OR 97311. Phone: (503) 378-8656.

SOICC Director, Oregon Occupational Information Coordinating Committee, 875 Union St. NE, Salem, OR 97311-0101. Phone: (503) 378-5747.

PENNSYLVANIA

Director, Bureau of Research and Statistics, 300 Capitol Associates Building, 3rd Floor, 901 North Seventh St., Harrisburg, PA 17120-9969. Phone: (717) 787-3266.

Executive Director, Pennsylvania SOICC, Bureau of Research and Statistics, PA Department of Labor and Industry, 300 Capitol Associates Bldg., Harrisburg, PA 17120-0034. Phone: (717) 772-1330.

PUERTO RICO

Director, Research and Statistics Division, Department of Labor and Human Resources, 505 Munoz Rivera Ave., 20th Floor, Hato Rey, PR 00918. Phone: (809) 754-5385.

Executive Director, Puerto Rico Occupational Information Coordinating Committee, P.O. Box 366212, San Juan, PR 00936-6212. Phone: (787) 723-7110.

RHODE ISLAND

Labor Market Information Director, Department of Employment and Training, 101 Friendship St., Providence, RI 02903-3740. Phone: (401) 277-3730.

Director, Rhode Island Occupational Information Coordinating Committee, 101 Friendship St., Providence, RI 02903. Phone: (401) 272-0830.

SOUTH CAROLINA

Director, Labor Market Information, Employment Security Commission, P.O. Box 995, Columbia, SC 29202. Phone: (803) 737-2660.

Director, South Carolina Occupational Information Coordinating Committee, 1550 Gadsden St., P.O. Box 995, Columbia, SC 29202-0995. Phone: (803) 737-2733.

SOUTH DAKOTA

Director, Labor Information Center, Department of Labor, P.O. Box 4730, Aberdeen, SD 57402-4730. Phone: (605) 626-2314.

Director, South Dakota Occupational Information Coordinating Council, South Dakota Department of Labor, 420 South Roosevelt St., P.O. Box 4730, Aberdeen, SD 57402–4730. Phone: (605) 626-2314.

TENNESSEE

Director, Research and Statistics Division, Department of Employment Security, 500 James Robertson Pkwy., 11th Floor, Nashville, TN 37245-1000. Phone: (615) 741-2284.

Executive Director, Tennessee Occupational Information Coordinating Committee, 500 James Robertson Pkwy., 11th Floor, Volunteer Plaza, Nashville, TN 37245-1600. Phone: (615) 741-6451.

TEXAS

Director of Labor Market Information, Texas Workforce Commission, 101 East 15th St., Room 208T, Austin, TX 78778-0001. Phone: (512) 463-2616.

Director, Texas Occupational Information Coordinating Committee, Travis Bldg., Suite 205, 3520 Executive Center Dr., Austin, TX 78731. Phone: (512) 502-3750.

UTAH

Director, Labor Market Information, Department of Employment Security, 140 East 300 South, P.O. Box 45249, Salt Lake City, UT 84145-0249. Phone: (801) 536-7860.

Director, Utah Occupational Information Coordinating Committee, % Utah Department of Employment Security, P.O. Box 45249, 140 East 300 South, Salt Lake City, UT 84147. Phone: (801) 536-7806.

VERMONT

Director, Policy and Information, Department of Employment and Training, 5 Green Mountain Dr., P.O. Box 488, Montpelier, VT 05601-0488. Phone: (802) 828-4153.

Director, Vermont Occupational Information Coordinating Committee, 5 Green Mountain Dr., P.O. Box 488, Montpelier, VT 05601-0488. Phone: (802) 229-0311.

VIRGINIA

Director, Economic Information Services Division, VA Employment Commission, 703 East Main St., Richmond, VA 23219. Phone: (804) 786-7496.

Acting Executive Director, Virginia Occupational Information Coordinating Committee/Virginia Employment Commission, 703 East Main St., P.O. Box 1358, Richmond, VA 23211. Phone: (804) 786-7496.

WASHINGTON

Director, Labor Market and Economic Analysis, P.O. Box 9046, Olympia, WA 98507-9046. Phone: (360) 438-4804.

Executive Director, Washington Occupational Information Coordinating Committee, % Employment Security Department, P.O. Box 9046, Olympia, WA 98507-9046. Phone: (360) 438-4803.

WEST VIRGINIA

Assistant Director, Labor and Economic Research, JTP/ES Division, Bureau of Employment Programs, 112 California Ave., Charleston, WV 25305-0112. Phone: (304) 558-2660.

Executive Director, West Virginia Occupational Information Coordinating Committee, P.O. Box 487, Institute, WV 25112-0487. Phone: (304) 766-2687.

WISCONSIN

Director, Department of Workforce Development, Jobs, Employment, and Training Services Division, 201 East Washington Ave., P.O. Box 7946, Madison, WI 53707-7946. Phone: (608) 266-5843.

Coordinator, Wisconsin State Occupational Information Coordinating Council/Department of Workforce Development, DWE/BWI, 201 East Washington Ave., GEF-1, Room 221X, P.O. Box 7944, Madison, WI 53707-7944. Phone: (608) 267-9611.

WYOMING

Manager, Research and Planning, Department of Employment, P.O. Box 2760, Casper, WY 82602-2760. Phone: (307) 473-3801.

Acting Director, Wyoming Occupational Information Coordinating Council, Post Office Box 2760, 246 South Center St., 2nd Floor, Casper, WY 82602. Phone: (307) 473-3809.

Index